Schoenberg's Transformation of Musical Language

Arnold Schoenberg is widely regarded as one of the most significant and innovative composers of the twentieth century. It is commonly assumed that Schoenberg's music divides into three periods: tonal, atonal, and serial. It is also assumed that Schoenberg's atonal music made a revolutionary break with the past, particularly in terms of harmonic structure. This book challenges both these popular notions. Haimo argues that Schoenberg's "atonal" music does not constitute a distinct unified period. He demonstrates that much of the music commonly described as "atonal" did not make a complete break with prior practices, even in the harmonic realm, but instead transformed the past by a series of incremental changes. An important and influential contribution to the field, Haimo's findings help not only to reevaluate Schoenberg, but also to redate much of what has been defined as one of the most crucial turning points in music history.

ETHAN HAIMO is a theorist and composer, and is Professor of Music in the Department of Music, University of Notre Dame. He is the co-editor (with Paul Johnson) of *Stravinsky Retrospectives* (1987), and author of *Schoenberg's Serial Odyssey* (1990) and *Haydn's Symphonic Forms* (1995). As a composer, he has written orchestral, chamber, vocal, and solo compositions. His work has appeared in many books and journals, including *The Schoenberg Companion*, edited by Walter Bailey, the *Journal of Music Theory*, *Music Analysis*, and *Journal of the American Musicological Society*.

Music in the 20th Century

GENERAL EDITOR Arnold Whittall

This series offers a wide perspective on music and musical life in the twentieth century. Books included range from historical and biographical studies concentrating particularly on the context and circumstances in which composers were writing, to analytical and critical studies concerned with the nature of musical language and questions of compositional process. The importance given to context will also be reflected in studies dealing with, for example, the patronage, publishing, and promotion of new music, and in accounts of the musical life of particular countries.

Recent titles

The Music of Conlon Nancarrow
Kyle Gann

The Stravinsky Legacy
Jonathan Cross

Experimental Music: Cage and Beyond
Michael Nyman

The BBC and Ultra-Modern Music, 1922–1936
Jennifer Doctor

The Music of Harrison Birtwistle
Robert Adlington

Four Musical Minimalists: La Monte Young, Terry Riley, Steve Reich, Philip Glass
Keith Potter

Fauré and French Musical Aesthetics
Carlo Caballero

The Music of Toru Takemitsu
Peter Burt

The Music and Thought of Michael Tippett: Modern Times and Metaphysics
David Clarke

Serial Music, Serial Aesthetics: Compositional Theory in Post-War Europe
M. J. Grant

Britten's Musical Language
Philip Rupprecht

Music and Ideology in Cold War Europe
Mark Carroll

Polish Music since Szymanowski
Adrian Thomas

Edward Elgar, Modernist
J. P. E. Harper-Scott

The Music of Louis Andriessen
Yayoi Uno Everett

Schoenberg's Transformation of Musical Language
Ethan Haimo

Schoenberg's Transformation of Musical Language

Ethan Haimo

CAMBRIDGE UNIVERSITY PRESS
Cambridge, New York, Melbourne, Madrid, Cape Town, Singapore, São Paulo

Cambridge University Press
The Edinburgh Building, Cambridge CB2 2RU, UK

Published in the United States of America by Cambridge University Press, New York

www.cambridge.org
Information on this title: www.cambridge.org/9780521865425

© Ethan Haimo 2006

This publication is in copyright. Subject to statutory exception
and to the provisions of relevant collective licensing agreements,
no reproduction of any part may take place without
the written permission of Cambridge University Press.

First published 2006

Printed in the United Kingdom at the University Press, Cambridge

A catalogue record for this publication is available from the British Library

ISBN-13 978-0-521-86542-5 hardback
ISBN-10 0-521-86542-5 hardback

Cambridge University Press has no responsibility for
the persistence or accuracy of URLs for external or
third-party internet websites referred to in this publication,
and does not guarantee that any content on such
websites is, or will remain, accurate or appropriate.

Contents

	Preface	page ix
	Notes on the examples, cover art, and abbreviations	xi
1	"Atonality": a revisionist thesis	1
2	"Based on tradition": Four Songs, Op. 2, 1899	8
3	The principle of incremental innovation: *Verklärte Nacht*, 1899	23
4	Conservative song-cycle, progressive cantata: *Gurrelieder*, 1900–11	42
5	Programmatic music and its implications: *Pelleas und Melisande*, Op. 5, 1902–3	66
6	Consolidation: Six Songs, Op. 3, 1903–4	97
7	Abstract form, secret program: String Quartet, Op. 7, 1904–5	112
8	Referential centers? Lieder and fragments, Fall 1905	143
9	Absolute music and its consequences: Chamber Symphony, Op. 9, 1905–6	159
10	Crisis: *Friede auf Erden*, Op. 13, Ballades, Op. 12, and the reception of Schoenberg's music, August 1906 to July 1907	190
11	Motivic economy: String Quartet No. 2, Op. 10, movements one and two, March–December 1907	210
12	"Until then I lacked the strength and confidence": Two Songs, Op. 14, December 1907–March 1908	231
13	Beyond triads: the first layer of *Das Buch der hängenden Gärten*, Op. 15, March–April 1908	244
14	"On revient toujours?" Returning to Opp. 10 and 15, June 1908–February 1909	268
15	The analysis of Schoenberg's post-1908 music: Pieces for Piano, Op. 11, Nos. 1 and 2, February 1909	290
16	"Intoxicated by the enthusiasm": Five Orchestral Pieces, Op. 16; Piece for Piano, Op. 11, No. 3, May–August 1909	318
17	The birth (and death) of new music: August 1909 and beyond	346
	Notes	357
	Bibliography	412
	Index	423

Preface

In this book I discuss the extraordinary transformation in Schoenberg's musical language and thought during the period 1899–1909. To that end, I analyze many of the works from this period, sometimes in considerable detail. Where appropriate, I explore aspects of Schoenberg's biography and the reception history of his music. When necessary, I draw upon primary sources (Schoenberg's sketches, drafts, correspondence).

However, I do not provide (and had no intention of providing) comprehensive analyses of any of the works in question. Indeed I do not even discuss every single work from the period: some works (like the Six Orchestral Songs, Op. 8) are passed over almost entirely. Moreover, my analyses do not treat the works in question as autonomous entities, independent of their role in the evolution of Schoenberg's thought. Readers who are looking for comprehensive studies of Schoenberg's biography, reception history, sketches, and correspondence, or who are interested in analyses that treat the works as autonomous aesthetic objects should look elsewhere; there is a plethora of first-rate literature that does exactly that.

What this book does is to use the available evidence to answer one simple (but I daresay, crucially important) question: How did Schoenberg's compositional language get from what it was in 1899 to what it became by 1909 and what were the essential stages in this transformation? In short, this is a history of the evolution of (musical) ideas. It was this framework that guided my choices of what to discuss and what to leave unsaid, what to analyze and what to ignore. Although the temptation was strong to say everything possible about every work, I have tried to restrict my remarks only to those aspects of the compositions that reveal important stages in the evolution of Schoenberg's thought.

It is commonly assumed that Schoenberg's "atonal" music made a revolutionary break with the past, particularly in terms of its harmonic structure. The core argument of this book is that this assumption is wrong. There was no revolution in harmony that led to a complete sweeping away of all prior truths. Rather, there was an incremental path of evolution that began around 1899 and lasted until approximately July 1909. That evolutionary transformation is the topic of this book.

It is my honor and pleasure to have the opportunity to thank those who have helped bring this project to fruition. A grant from the National

Endowment for the Humanities was crucial in the early stages of writing this book. The Institute for Scholarship in the Liberal Arts at the University of Notre Dame generously provided grants to fund my research trips to Vienna where I was able to examine first-hand the extraordinary treasures of the Arnold Schönberg Center. I owe a big debt of gratitude to the extraordinary professional staff of the Arnold Schönberg Center – a wonderfully run research institute if ever there was one (and a credit to its director, Christian Meyer). I would like to single out Therese Muxeneder for particular thanks and praise: she consistently responded with alacrity and accuracy to my innumerable requests. Special thanks are also due to Lawrence Schoenberg, Nuria Schoenberg-Nono, and Ronald Schoenberg for their constant support and encouragement. Through his wonderfully perceptive criticisms and suggestions, my series editor, Arnold Whittall, has helped improve this book in more ways than I could possibly count. The warmest of thanks are due to Maria Stäblein (Illinois State University) who helped me decipher what I had been sure was completely undecipherable script in letters by Arnold Schoenberg, Mathilde Schoenberg, Anton Webern, Richard Strauss, and others. I would also like to thank Severine Neff (University of North Carolina, Chapel Hill), Joseph Auner (State University of New York Stony Brook), Paul Johnson, Peter Smith, and Susan Youens (all three, University of Notre Dame), Christopher Hailey (Franz Schreker Foundation), Stephan Weytjens (Catholic University of Leuven), Christian Martin Schmidt (Technische Universität, Berlin), Walter Frisch (Columbia University), Walter Bailey (Rice University), Sabine Feisst (Arizona State University), David Banga, and Michael Vidmar-McEwen (both graduate students, University of Notre Dame), all of whom at one point or another in the past decade answered questions, provided information that I needed for this book, and/or tried to steer me away from making foolish errors. Whatever errors and mistakes that remain are mine and mine alone (all the more so since I sometimes ignore the advice of others).

Finally, I want to thank my mother, Deborah Tepper Haimo (to whom this book is dedicated) for a lifetime of support and encouragement. Ph.D. in Mathematics, Harvard University (1964), Professor of Mathematics at the University of Missouri (now retired), President of the Mathematical Association of America (1992–3), Fellow of the Institute for Advanced Study at Princeton, Trustee Radcliffe College (1975–81), Member Harvard Board of Overseers (1990–5) and much more, she was a real trailblazer in academe (which, to put it mildly, did not welcome women with open arms in the 1950s) all the while raising five children. *Ad meah v'esrim, ima.*

Notes on the examples, cover art, and abbreviations

The examples from the Five Pieces, Op. 16 (original version) are copyright © 1922 by C.F. Peters. Reproduced by permission of Peters Edition Limited, London. All other musical examples are copyright © by Belmont Press/Universal Edition and are used by kind permission. The painting on the cover of this book is © 2005 Artists' Rights Society (ARS), New York/VBK, Vienna.

The texts of the musical examples (other than for Op. 16) are based on the ongoing complete critical edition of Schoenberg's compositions *Sämtliche Werke*, edd. Rufer, et al (Schott/Universal: Mainz, Vienna, 1966–). For obvious practical reasons, it was not possible to present all of the examples in full score. Therefore, many of the examples are reductions and I have not hesitated to make extensive simplifications (omission of articulations, dynamics, phrasing, doublings, and so forth) in the interests of clarity.

The following abbreviations are used for frequently cited items:

SI (Style and Idea): Arnold Schoenberg, *Style and Idea*, ed. Leonard Stein, trans. Robert Black (Berkeley and Los Angeles: University of California Press, 1975).

SW (Sämtliche Werke): Arnold Schoenberg, *Sämtliche Werke*, edd. Rufer, et al (Schott/Universal: Mainz, Vienna, 1966–).

HL (Harmonielehre): Arnold Schoenberg, *Theory of Harmony*, trans. Roy Carter (Berkeley and Los Angeles: University of California Press, 1978).

1 "Atonality": a revisionist thesis

> ... many people, instead of realizing its evolutionary element, called it a revolution.[1]
>
> In this period I renounced a tonal centre – a procedure incorrectly called "atonality".[2]

In 1939 a little-known author and poet, Ernest Vincent Wright, published a book entitled *Gadsby*.[3] If Wright's book were to be judged solely on its belletristic merits it would have slipped into obscurity long ago; rare is the book that is so utterly lacking in literary finesse.

> If Youth, throughout all history, had had a champion to stand up for it; to show a doubting world that a child can think; and, possibly, do it practically, you wouldn't constantly run across folks today who claim that "a child don't know anything." A child's brain starts functioning at birth; and has, amongst its many infant convolutions, thousands of dormant atoms, into which God has put a mystic possibility for noticing an adult's act, and figuring out its purport.[4]

The awkwardness of this passage is palpable. The odd turns of phrases, the stilted and pretentious vocabulary, the inexplicable use of an ungrammatical quotation, the rambling argument, and the generally inefficient use of language all combine to create a very inept impression. There is, however, a reason for this ineptitude and it is for that reason that Wright's book has not slipped into an otherwise well-deserved obscurity. As Wright proudly announced in the subtitle, his book was "*A Story of Over 50,000 Words Without Using the Letter 'E'.*"

Why would an author undertake such a task? Why would he want to exclude the use of the definite article, the past tense of weak verbs, all third-person pronouns, not to mention an estimated forty percent of English vocabulary? As Wright explains in the introduction, he did so "not through any attempt to attain literary merit," but "due to a somewhat balky nature, caused by hearing it so constantly claimed that 'it can't be done'."[5]

Mindful of, and presumably sobered by, this precedent, I nonetheless propose to talk about Schoenberg's compositions from 1899 to 1909 and (other than in this and the final chapter) to avoid entirely the use of the word "atonal". Unlike Wright's *Gadsby*, however, I believe the reasons for this restriction are anything but gratuitous. Without fear of hyperbole I would even venture to state that a proper understanding of the music in question is not possible unless we can start to free ourselves from the word "atonal".

To be sure, the case for using the word "atonal" cannot lightly be dismissed. It has come to be so widely accepted that it might appear to border on sheer contrariness to restrict its use. One might well be justified in wondering whether avoiding the word "atonal" would inevitably lead to awkward locutions like those that abound in Wright's novel. Finally, even if one argues that the literal meaning of "atonal" is inaccurate or misleading, the way in which the word has been used for more than a half-century should have established a contextual meaning that can be understood independently of its literal meaning.

All of these arguments in favor of the use of "atonal" might seem persuasive enough, but I believe that they are more than outweighed by the counter arguments. For one thing, Schoenberg himself came to dislike the term. From the 1920s on, he used it sparingly and reluctantly, often with scare quotes. He resisted the term because he argued that it was illogical:

> I find above all that the expression "atonal music", is most unfortunate – it is on a par with calling flying "the art of not falling", or swimming "the art of not drowning". Only in the language of publicity is it thought adequate to emphasize in this way a negative quality of whatever is being advertised.[6]

Schoenberg went on to state that:

> ... this expression is *wrong*: with tones only what is tonal, in keeping with the nature of tones, can be produced; there must at least be that connection of tones based on the tonal, which has to exist between any two tones if they are to form a progression that is at all logical and comprehensible; an opposite, "atonal" can no more exist among tones and tone-relationships than can an opposite "aspectral" or "acomplementary", among colours and progressions of colours.[7]

Schoenberg further claimed that the term was not chosen after a careful examination of the properties of the works in question. He stated that it originated as a term of scorn, coined by a journalist looking for a catchy phrase with which to pillory his music.

> Moreover the expression, atonal cannot be taken seriously as an expression, since that was not how it first came about; a journalist derived it by analogy from *amusisch*, as a means of overaggressive characterization – such, at least, was the context in which I first noticed it.[8]

Finally, if he were to choose a single term to describe this repertoire, Schoenberg felt that something other than "atonal" might better capture the sense of the music. Accordingly he suggested "polytonal" or "pantonal", terms that imply an expansion or evolution of past procedures, not their utter abrogation.[9]

A composer's view of his music is important; it deserves respect and attention. But it is not necessarily the final word. Even though Schoenberg both rejected the term "atonal" and provided us with some alternatives, his preferences need not be binding. We have the right to overrule Schoenberg's preferences if we can demonstrate that the term "atonal" really is the term that best characterizes the music in question.

I do not believe that such a case can be made. To the contrary, I think there are so many negative consequences that flow ineluctably from the use of the term "atonal" that we are far better off abjuring its use.

We can start by picking up where Schoenberg left off, with the recognition that atonality is a negative term. By its literal meaning, it seems to suggest that the one significant feature of an atonal composition is that it is not tonal. But precisely what does that mean? The closer one looks at this definition, the more dubious it becomes.

If atonality merely means that a composition lacks a tonic, then the definition is so broad as to be useless.[10] Many different kinds of compositions – from the twentieth century and before – lack an identifiable tonic. If compositions as diverse as Stravinsky's *Rite of Spring*, Lasso's *Prophetiae Sibyllarum*, and Schoenberg's *Erwartung*, Op. 17 are all "atonal", then this definition has little value: it offers no means of discriminating between dramatically different compositions whose pitch languages have almost nothing in common.[11]

One does little better by stating that it is the absence of a concluding triad that makes a composition "atonal". Here we have not only a negative definition but a highly reductive one as well. That Schoenberg's post-1908 compositions conclude with something other than a triad is not sufficient reason to group them together into a coherent period or to distinguish them from their immediate predecessors.

We might try to refine the definition by asserting that "atonal" does not just mean lacking a tonic or a concluding triad, but rather denotes music which lacks all of the important structural features of common-practice tonal music. According to this revised definition, anything that tonality is, atonality is not. If tonal music has a tonic, then atonal music must not. If tonal music employs a referential diatonic collection, then atonal music cannot. If tonal music differentiates between consonances and dissonances, with the former resolving to the latter, then atonal music will not make such differentiations. If tonal music employs triads and classifiable seventh chords and organizes these chords into coherent harmonic progressions, then atonal music must not.

On the face of it, this definition seems more logical, and one could argue that there are a number of twentieth-century compositions that do conform to this definition. None of those, however, is to be found among Schoenberg's pre-serial works (and perhaps not in the serial works either).[12] The problem is, when we actually look at Schoenberg's music from ca. 1909, we find that the revised definition is problematic precisely because it is inflexibly negative. Even in compositions where it is clear that there is no tonal center, where triads are not used as referential sonorities, and where the intervallic relationships are not in conformity with the traditional definitions of consonance and dissonance, there are still many features on the surface that bear a clear kinship with features we would find in Schoenberg's earlier compositions. Triads and various kinds of seventh chords do make appearances as chords, or as parts of chords, or as the components of linear successions. Various scale segments still appear on occasion. Melodic lines often outline patterns that are similar to those we find in previous works. There are also rhythmic/melodic formulas that sound suspiciously like patterns from earlier music. So too, most of the techniques of voice leading are indistinguishable from those of earlier repertoires. And the consonance-dissonance distinction lives on, albeit significantly transformed.

If we are to take our revised definition of atonality seriously, these elements pose a problem. The revised definition is founded on the assumption that atonality must mean the absence of anything tonal. Since many such apparent "anachronisms" appear in Schoenberg's post-1908 compositions, we are left with two options. Either we face up to the reality of the musical surface and entertain the possibility that these supposed anachronisms have structural significance (in which case the revised definition is useless), or we must deny, or at least downplay, the significance of these relics.

It is this latter attitude that underpins the analytical method most used for the explanation of the pitch structure of Schoenberg's post-1908 compositions. It is fair to say that since the 1970s, pitch-class set analysis has come to be the dominant analytical technique for this repertoire.[13] As it is typically practiced, pitch-class set analysis tends to downplay the significance of some of the prominent structural features of prior repertoires (triads, seventh chords, diatonic collections, and scalar segments) when they appear in Schoenberg's "atonal" music. For example, regarding the opening motive in the vocal line in Schoenberg's "Herzgewächse" Allen Forte has stated:

> Similarly, the opening "motive" of the voice, F-G-G♯-F♯-F♮, is not in itself a structural set, but a secondary formation, a nonset, the elements of which belong to other sets. In general, a given "melodic line" may not necessarily be a discrete structural component. This facet of Schoenberg's music has led to much misunderstanding and caused many blunders in the past, particularly

> where such secondary formations are "chromatic lines" (as in the case of the voice motive here), "whole-tone scales," or other familiar patterns. Schoenberg simply did not compose with these and other well-worn formulae, just as he did not compose with sets that properly belong to the vocabulary of tonal music – although, as will be evident in subsequent examples, such sets may be indirect results of the interaction of significant structural components.[14]

In this book I argue that it is mistaken to minimize the central role played by the many "well-worn formulae" that lie directly on the surface of Schoenberg's post-1908 music. The frequent presence in Schoenberg's post-1908 music of "familiar patterns" and "sets that properly belong to the vocabulary of tonal music" cannot be dismissed as merely coincidental to more important structural features.

The term "atonality" is also problematic because it encourages us to group all compositions defined as "atonal" into a single class. Implicit in such a grouping is the assumption that all of the works of the class share their most essential procedures and techniques.

This too is misleading. That all of Schoenberg's completed compositions between 1909 and 1920 lack triads as the concluding sonorities is not sufficient to support the thesis that they form a coherent period. Grouping all of these works into a single class promotes the mistaken notion that one aspect of the pitch language (the absence of concluding triads) is the only significant criterion for categorization. This is patently wrong. As we shall see in the last chapter of this book, there are far more meaningful and useful ways of dividing Schoenberg's works into periods than whether they do, or do not, conclude with triads. To assert the existence of an "atonal" period is to lump together works that are radically different from one another.

There is yet another conceptual problem prompted by the use of the term "atonal". Since Schoenberg's post-1908 compositions have come to be referred to as "atonal", it follows that the compositions before that point have been identified as "tonal". Admittedly, the term "tonal" does not have the drawback of being a negative term, but here too the reality of Schoenberg's compositions is rather more complicated than can be encapsulated in a convenient slogan. It is true that all of Schoenberg's pre-1909 compositions do conclude with triads. As such, there is a natural tendency to think of these compositions in terms of theoretical paradigms that we employed for the enormous body of compositions that are included in the "tonal" category. To do so, however, is to operate from assumptions that may not be valid. Schoenberg's pre-1909 compositions can no more be effectively described by a single slogan than can his post-1908 compositions.

Schoenberg's approach to tonality was a complicated and ever changing reality. As early as the songs of Opp. 2 and 3, his compositional approach included essential elements that are not readily compatible with the way tonality had been preached and practiced for more than two centuries in European classical music.[15] Over the course of the subsequent decade, those radical elements continually increased in significance. To refer to all of his pre-1909 compositions as "tonal" is to gloss over any recognition of this extraordinary transformation.

As indicated above, one of the negative consequences of the word "atonality" has been that its use has helped lead to a failure to admit that significant elements of the past persist in Schoenberg's "atonal" compositions. In embracing that reality we must not make a complementary error. That elements of his earlier pitch language persist after 1908 should not be taken to mean that Schoenberg's post-1908 compositions are merely modified tonal compositions. In particular, I firmly believe that key centers simply do not play any kind of a functional role in these works. Elements of Schoenberg's prior vocabulary and syntax remain in his post-1908 compositions; this does not mean these compositions merely present another way of expressing referential tonal centers.

There is a long tradition of writings about Schoenberg's post-1908 music that has made precisely that claim. For more than half a century, there has been a school of thought that has stubbornly resisted the notion that Schoenberg ever really did abandon referential tonal centers.

I am marginally more sympathetic to this line of thought than I am to the approach that obdurately refuses to recognize the significance of traditional harmonic elements in his "atonal" compositions. Faced with an arpeggiated triad in a line, or a dominant seventh chord as a simultaneity, or a chromatic scale segment within a melody, advocates of this approach have not consigned these elements to oblivion.

Although I am sympathetic to parts of their argument, I find their core conclusion is – ultimately – unsupportable. Invariably, advocates of this line of thought have insisted on hearing Schoenberg's compositions in terms of a referential tonic supported by modified versions of traditional harmonic progressions. Significant residues of past practice do persist in Schoenberg's post-1908 works, but not these residues. To claim that referential tonics are still applicable as late as 1909 is to ignore virtually every other important aspect of the pitch language. Those who persist in assigning tonal centers to works from this period are making a complementary error to those who downplay the existence of significant residues of past harmonic practice in those same works. Both approaches miss essential aspects of the music.

I should not like to leave the impression that everyone who has looked at Schoenberg's works from around 1908 has regarded them in the starkest of black and white terms as either "tonal" or "atonal". There have been some writers who have understood these works as a mixture of tonal and atonal elements. For example, David Lewin, in a much admired analysis of one of the songs from Schoenberg's Op. 15 remarked that "in general, now, I feel that tonality functions in this work mainly as one means of clarifying, enriching and qualifying a basically contextual ('atonal') structure."[16] And Reinhold Brinkmann in a similarly much admired analysis of Schoenberg's Op. 11, No. 1 frequently acknowledges the importance of tonal elements in what he otherwise sees as an atonal work.[17]

Seeing these works as a mixture of tonal and atonal elements is certainly an improvement over seeing them as one or the other, but I still find this an unsatisfactory solution because it assumes that Schoenberg's music is based on two different musical languages, tonal and atonal. As I propose to demonstrate, Schoenberg's pre- and post-1908 music cannot be divided into two separate, distinct, and different musical languages. Rather, all of Schoenberg's works from 1899–1909 are based on a single musical language. Although this language underwent significant changes, a basic core of techniques, procedures, and ideas remained in common.

In short, I believe we would do much better to dispense with simplifying slogans ("tonal" vs. "atonal") entirely. Trying to capture the complicated reality of Schoenberg's music with a pair of binary opposites is not just futile, it is deceptive. It impedes understanding.[18]

We come then, to the revisionist thesis promised in the title of this chapter (though the reader who has been following the argument to this point has probably already inferred what its essential outlines must be):

> From the beginning of his career Schoenberg subjected his pitch language to a relentless process of change. Step by step, Schoenberg continually modified or transformed many of the techniques that had characterized his music at the beginning of his career. From approximately 1899 to July 1909, one must understand the pitch-language of Schoenberg's works as comprising an ongoing extension and transformation of prior techniques, not a renunciation of them.[19]

In the course of the chapters to follow, we shall attempt to retrace the path of the transformation of Schoenberg's musical language during the decade 1899 to 1909. But this is not a story of pitch language alone. As we shall see, it is also a narrative about form, motive, aesthetics, and the idea of the modern.

2 "Based on tradition": Four Songs, Op. 2, 1899

> I venture to credit myself with having written truly new music which, being based on tradition, is destined to become tradition.[1]

Given the continuous, restless transformation of Schoenberg's compositional thought, any starting point we choose might appear to be at least somewhat arbitrary. Wherever we start, we are apt to feel slightly uncomfortable, as if we have entered without proper preparation into the middle of a complicated debate.

It cannot be helped: we have to begin somewhere and for the purposes of the present study there does not seem to be much point in going back to the juvenilia from the very beginning of Schoenberg's compositional career.[2] I propose instead to begin with Schoenberg's songs from 1899 (some of which appeared in the Four Songs, Op. 2). My criterion for choosing this as the starting point is my impression that with the 1899 songs Schoenberg first began to speak in his own distinctive voice.[3] To my ear, all of his pre-1899 compositions sound at least somewhat derivative, be they redolent of Wagner or Brahms or perhaps (as in the String Quartet in D, 1897) Dvořák.[4] With the songs from 1899, Schoenberg's music takes on a far more self-assured character and starts to sound – for want of a better term – Schoenbergian. At the same time, 1899 is also appropriate for a starting point because by that date Schoenberg had not yet advanced very far down the path that led to the transformation of so many of the important structural features of the pitch language he had inherited. Beginning in 1899 thus allows us to establish a clear base line for Schoenberg's compositional practice and thought.

Rather than survey all of the songs from 1899, I propose instead to focus on just one of them and to examine it in some detail. Not that such an approach is without its dangers. Given Schoenberg's constant striving for originality, the choice of but a single work carries with it the danger that aspects unique to that work might mistakenly be taken as normative or that important features that occur only in other works will be missed entirely. To avoid these pitfalls, I will cite similar passages from other, approximately contemporaneous works and, when necessary, will also direct our attention to important features in other songs if they are not included in the work under discussion.

"Based on tradition": Four Songs, Op. 2, 1899

Example 2.1

Without further ado, let us turn our attention to the first seven measures of "Schenk mir deinen goldenen Kamm (Jesus bettelt)", Op. 2, No. 2 (Ex. 2.1).[5]

A prominent feature of this passage is its only slightly elaborated homophonic texture. Excepting occasional passing-tone, appoggiatura, and suspension figures, Schoenberg presents a straightforward succession of chords whose surface rhythm is even sometimes (as in the piano part in the first measure) homorhythmic.[6]

Homophony is not the only texture that appears in Schoenberg's early songs, but it is extremely common. Many other passages in the songs reveal themselves to be little more than elaborated homophony. Therefore, it is fair to state that in his early songs, Schoenberg customarily (though not invariably) structured his music in terms of successions of chords.[7]

In the tradition from which Schoenberg's music sprang, chords were not arbitrary combinations of tones. Rather, the traditional rules of counterpoint dictate that all of the tones of a first species combination need to be consonant with one another.[8] It followed that seventh chords (and other chords with dissonances) did not appear as first-species combinations. In fifteenth and sixteenth-century choral music, this distinction was reflected in the part-writing: sevenths did not function as even locally stable tones. Rather, they were treated like (and were, in fact) dissonances (passing tones, neighbor tones, or suspensions).

Long before Schoenberg began to compose, the treatment of the seventh (and other chordal dissonances) had undergone a fundamental transformation. In both theory and practice, these dissonances had evolved into something much more than tones of figuration. Chordal dissonances had become integral components of chords, even to the point of appearing within first species combinations.

Quite early on, and particularly in instrumental music, the reality of the treatment of chordal dissonances was at odds with what theory said was supposed to happen. Composers increasingly treated the seventh and other chordal dissonances in ways that were dramatically different from their origins: chordal dissonances appeared without preparation; they failed to resolve properly or at all; they were themselves subjected to prolongation and elaboration by diminution; chords with dissonances even became temporary goals, the target of resolution of even more dissonant sonorities.[9]

By the time Schoenberg began composing, it was entirely normal to treat chordal dissonances such as the seventh as integral components of chords, locally stable, nearly indistinguishable from the remaining tones of the chord. Schoenberg took this stage in the development in the treatment of chords with dissonances as his starting point and promptly moved forward.

Schoenberg's chordal vocabulary differs from that of his predecessors primarily by its emphases. Like composers before him, Schoenberg's chordal vocabulary consists almost entirely of triads and seventh chords. What is striking about his arsenal of chords is the extraordinary pervasiveness of chords with chordal dissonances. Schoenberg's chords tend not to be completely consonant: root-position and first-inversion major and minor triads are relatively rare. Instead, there is usually an almost uninterrupted succession of seventh chords. In Ex. 2.1, after the first inversion C minor triad at the end of m. 1, every single chord from that point to the cadence on the downbeat of m. 6 (with but one exception) is some kind of a seventh chord. That this is typical of Schoenberg's language ca. 1899 can readily be confirmed by other works from this period. Schoenberg certainly was not the first composer to write progressions of chords in which one seventh chord followed another in immediate succession. Nevertheless, even though his penchant for writing successions of seventh chords rests on firm historical foundations, the very length of those progressions is striking and stretched at the limits of what previously was regarded as acceptable.

Pure triads are not only limited in number, they are also limited in location: they appear most often at the beginnings and endings of phrases. (Although this limitation is more marked in Op. 2, No. 2 than in other songs from 1899, it is an important tendency throughout this period.) Even when triads do occur within the body of a phrase, they tend to be shunted off to unobtrusive rhythmic locations (e.g. the first inversion G-flat triad at the end of m. 4). There are occasional exceptions: in Op. 2, No. 2, this is particularly evident in mm. 19–25, the beginning of the second stanza. Such exceptions aside, however, seventh chords tend to be the normative sonority within the body of phrases. It is also characteristic of his style that even though some chordal types (such as the half-diminished seventh) occur frequently, no one chordal type monopolizes the surface; rather there is a broad spectrum of different chords.

Schoenberg's arsenal of seventh chords also differs in its emphases from that of most previous composers. In earlier repertoires, the most common seventh chords were either diatonic (built on V, ii, IV, and vii) or were from a limited spectrum of chromatic chords (diminished sevenths, applied dominants, and augmented sixth chords). Other seventh chords, particularly ones with chromatic alterations (e.g. the half-augmented seventh), did occur, but relatively rarely.

Schoenberg stands these proportions on their head. Chromatic seventh chords have become far more common and prominent while diatonic seventh chords constitute a smaller percentage of the total than had been typical.[10] The half-diminished seventh chord appears fairly frequently.[11] Fully diminished seventh chords are somewhat less common; they do occur, but comparatively rarely.[12]

Other chromatically altered seventh chords occur somewhat more frequently than in the past.[13] For example, the chord on the downbeat of m. 16 includes the tones G-sharp E, F-sharp, C (marked 'Y' in Ex. 2.2). This might

Example 2.2

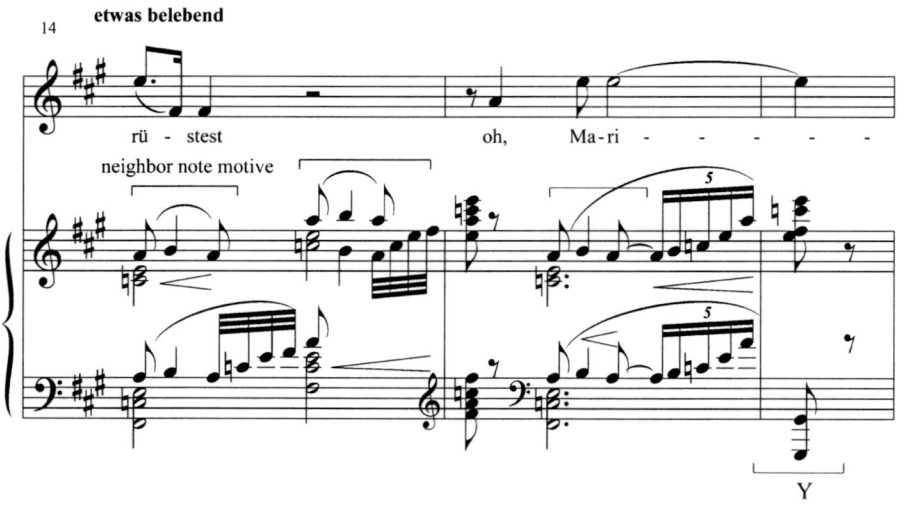

be understood as a G-sharp dominant seventh chord with a raised fifth (assuming enharmonic spelling), a chordal type that, though not common, did occur on occasion in earlier music.[14]

There is something else that is striking about the opening measures of this song: although chordal dissonances are virtually the norm, tones of figuration are relatively rare. In the seven measures of Ex. 2.1, there are only a few such tones: the C in the voice (and r.h.) at the end of m. 2 appears to be an upper neighbor; the G-flat in the l.h. on the third beat of m. 3 might be a suspension (although it can also be read as the ninth of the chord); in m. 4, the C in the right hand and the D in the left hand appear to be neighbor and passing tones, respectively.

The near absence of tones of figuration in these measures is not an invariable rule in the early songs: in other works from this period, the chordal background is elaborated by an array of passing tones, neighbors, and suspensions. Nevertheless, the almost complete absence of elaborative tones in some passages (like mm. 1–2) is indicative of an important component of Schoenberg's compositional thought: his interest in endowing all tones with structural significance. This is confirmed by two other prominent aspects of his compositional approach.

One was his tendency to create melodic/rhythmic patterns that could be understood as tones of figuration, but can equally well be understood as chord tones. For example, on the fourth beat of m. 2, the D-flat (l.h.) might appear to be a passing tone. So too, in m. 3, the E-flat and G-flat on the second beat suggest passing tones that are then rearticulated to become suspensions. Similarly, on the second beat of m. 4, the E (l.h.) and the octave Gs (r.h.) look like passing tones. In all of these cases another (equally persuasive) reading is possible: the putative non-chord tones change the quality of the chords by altering one of the degrees. Thus, for instance, in m. 2, the D-flat changes the minor seventh chord of the third beat into a half-diminished seventh chord on the fourth beat. So too, the E-flat, G-flat pair in m. 3 changes the dominant seventh chord of the downbeat into a half-diminished seventh chord. Finally, the E and then the octave Gs in m. 4 transform the minor seventh chord of the downbeat first into a half-diminished seventh chord (second beat) and then into a fully diminished seventh chord (second half of the second beat).

The other way Schoenberg invested apparent tones of figuration with structural significance was by assigning them prominent motivic roles: as a general rule, Schoenberg tends not to use tones of figuration unless they also have an autonomous identity as a motive.[15] In this song the most obvious of those is the neighbor note motive (a mild transformation of the figure in the piano in mm. 2–3) that comes to the fore beginning in m. 14 (see Ex. 2.2). Similar procedures can be found in other songs of this period.

Much like his chordal vocabulary, Schoenberg's harmonic progressions differ from those of his predecessors. Although there is no harmonic progression that is completely unprecedented, the sum total of progressions does create a language that differs in subtle, but important, ways from its predecessors.

What is most striking is the rarity of what had traditionally been the most common progressions, especially in the beginnings and middles of his phrases. Other than at cadences there is a virtually complete avoidance of chord progressions consisting of a dominant preparation chord followed by a V chord and continuing on to I. Instead, Schoenberg's harmonic progressions usually involve root motion by step or third. In the few cases (again, other than at cadences) where his progressions do involve a progression by fifth or fourth (as in mm. 2–4), the roots of the chords are not from the diatonic collection of the operative tonic.[16]

Instead, it is virtually a norm in the 1899 songs that adjacent chords do not have diatonic functions in a common key. For example, the first three chords of this song are an F-sharp minor triad, a C-sharp half-diminished seventh chord, and a first inversion C minor triad. The C-sharp half-diminished seventh chord has no diatonic function in F-sharp minor (or major) nor is there a diatonic collection in which both a C-sharp minor half-diminished seventh and a C minor triad can coexist. This has profound implications: if adjacent chords are incompatible with any single diatonic collection, then it follows that there will be a quick circulation of most or all of the twelve tones of the chromatic.[17] That is the case here: at the beginning of Op. 2, No. 2, eleven of the twelve tones appear by the downbeat of m. 2.[18] The only missing tone, B-flat, appears immediately afterward (m. 2, beat 3).

Although Schoenberg's harmonic progressions at the beginnings and middles of phrases are mostly unconventional, the harmonic progressions at the cadences tend to be somewhat more traditional.[19] Authentic and half cadences are still common means of effecting closure for phrases (although they are often disguised). In Ex. 2.1, the first phrase concludes in m. 6 with a clear authentic cadence while the much shorter second phrase modulates quickly up a half-step to G minor and concludes there with a half-cadence in m. 7. Prominent, and relatively traditional, cadences (half, authentic, and imperfect, respectively) also mark off at least three other significant phrase endings (mm. 19, 21, and 23).

Even though traditional cadences still appear in these songs, there is ample evidence that Schoenberg was also interested in disguising or finding substitutes for the standard cadential progressions. In mm. 24–5, there is a harmonic progression suggesting an imminent cadence in F-sharp minor: V^7/ii, ii, V. On the downbeat of m. 26, part of the expected F-sharp minor triad (the dyad, A F-sharp) does arrive. Almost immediately any sense of F-sharp is erased as the sonority is quickly transformed (see Ex. 2.3). The sense of closure, arrival, or stability is lost, causing this to function as an unusual deceptive cadence.

Example 2.3

Example 2.4

Schoenberg also formulated cadences with alternatives to the dominant. The most prominent of those is the final cadence of the song (see Ex. 2.4).

Schoenberg approaches the final chord, not through a traditional dominant or dominant seventh chord, but through a substitute: $V^{6/5}/V$. And this is not an unusual example: a number of other songs from this period also employ substitute chords as the preparation for the final triad, so much so, that non-traditional cadences of that sort are virtually the norm for the final cadence.[20]

This, in turn, has significant consequences for how we perceive tonal identity and harmonic function in these works. In prior repertoires, the normative use of the authentic cadence as the closing progression helped to create and foster harmonic norms and expectations. In Schoenberg's 1899 songs, the presence of a specific dominant chord (or any other chord) does not necessarily imply a specific harmonic function. It follows that our understanding of what constitutes harmonic closure is fashioned more by local context and emphasis than by norms of harmonic syntax.[21]

Even beyond the non-normative progressions found at some cadences, it is clear that Schoenberg was also interested in experimenting with other, even less traditional cadences. In "Schenk mir deinen goldenen Kamm", there is a particularly significant example (see Ex. 2.5).

At the beginning of m. 14, Schoenberg comes to what appears to be a kind of elided cadence. With the word "rüstest", we come to the end of the second of the two three-line segments that comprise the main body of the first stanza and the voice completes its phrase, followed by a rest. This has clear parallels (c.f. the rhythm, contour, and rhyme of the vocal line) to the prominent cadence at the beginning of m. 6 (refer back to Ex. 2.1). Thus the

Example 2.5

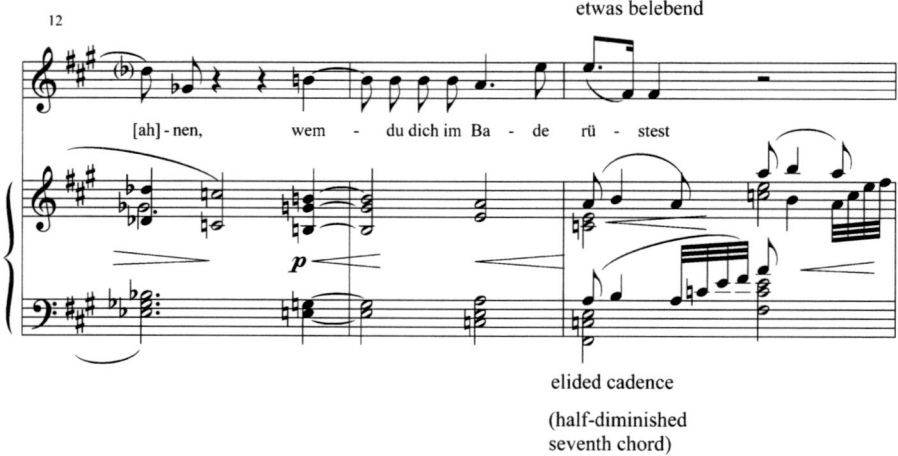

Example 2.6

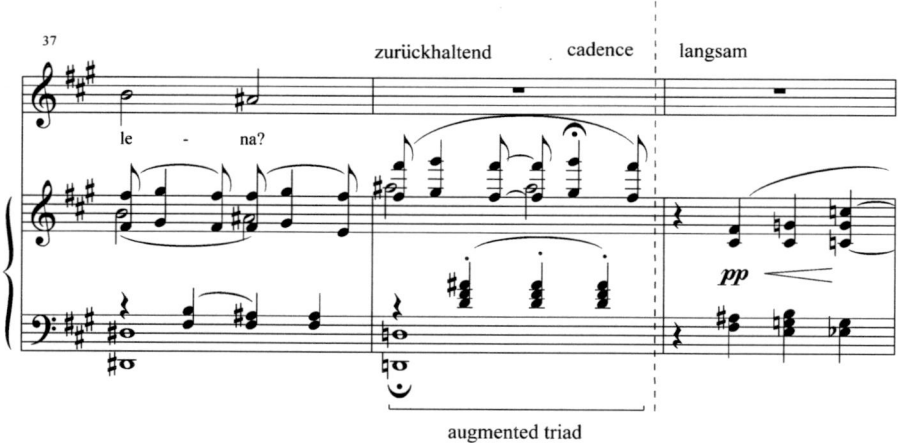

chord at the beginning of m. 14 marks both the end of one phrase and, by elision, the beginning of another. Significantly, the chord Schoenberg chooses for this purpose is not a simple triad; rather, it is a half-diminished seventh chord. By employing a dissonant chord at the cadence in m. 14, Schoenberg has posed a fundamental challenge to the idea that consonance (as traditionally defined) is necessary for a cadence.

The non-triadic cadence in m. 14 is not an isolated event. At the end of m. 38, the motion comes to a complete stop, followed by a rest at the beginning of m. 39 (see Ex. 2.6).

Given the cessation of motion in m. 38 followed by a rest and then by the return of the opening phrase in the following measure, it is perfectly reasonable to assume that there is a cadence at the close of m. 38. But the chord in question is not a major or minor triad or even a dominant seventh chord, as had been customary for almost all previous cadences. Instead, the closing sonority is an augmented triad. Like m. 14, here too we have a passage that suggests a cadence, but articulates the cadence with a rather non-traditional (and non-consonant) sonority.

The cadences in mm. 14 and 38 are exceptions: all other cadences in this song end on triads. As such, they play a central role in the establishment and confirmation of local key centers. In effect, the triads at cadences are often the only viable candidates for key centers for the simple reason that they are frequently the only triads in the phrase.

But the reason goes deeper than this. In music of the eighteenth and even the early nineteenth centuries, collection and key had been closely related. Generally speaking, when the identity of the diatonic collection is clear, the key is also clear, even in the absence of cadences.

In Schoenberg's music of 1899, such correspondences are largely inoperative. Because his collections are normally highly chromatic, collection and key are not synonymous.[22] Although there are occasional (and usually short) stretches which are limited to a particular diatonic collection (usually for text-painting or programmatic reasons), Schoenberg typically presents the complete chromatic collection (or a significant proportion thereof) within a given phrase. Therefore, it is frequently impossible to identify a tonal center in any given phrase in this song (or in most other songs from this period) based on the collection alone. To the extent that the establishment of a locally referential tonic is operative within the individual phrases of these songs, it would have to be by means other than collection.

Theoretically, it is possible to establish a tonal reference point solely through harmonic progressions. Even in a highly chromatic environment and lacking any cadence, one could still establish a referential tonal center if the harmonic progressions conformed to some of the basic paradigms of traditional harmony. But, as we have seen, in Schoenberg's 1899 songs, such paradigmatic progressions rarely exist except in connection with a cadence, and sometimes (as in the final cadence), not even there. In the present song – other than at the cadences enumerated above – none of the progressions conforms comfortably to any of the more traditional models of tonal music.[23] Therefore, only the cadential progressions serve effectively to establish or confirm tonal centers.

Since his non-cadential progressions do not normally function to establish unambiguous tonal centers, Schoenberg generally adopts one of several other procedures to establish a key at the beginning of a piece: he places a certain amount of agogic emphasis on the tonic triad by prolonging the tonic triad (as in the first measures of "Mannesbangen"); he begins with a short stretch of music with a diatonic or mostly diatonic collection (as in "Erhebung", Op. 2, No. 3 and "Waldsonne", Op. 2, No. 4); or, he simply makes the tonic triad the only root position triad in the general vicinity of the beginning of the piece (as in the present song and in "Erwartung", Op. 2, No. 1).

Because Schoenberg does not normally establish his key centers by their constituent collections or through their (non-cadential) harmonic progressions, modulation becomes a special challenge. Given the total, or nearly total, chromatic content of most phrases, the collection for every key is effectively equivalent to that of every other key. It follows that modulation cannot be suggested (as it can be in a purely diatonic environment) merely by introduction of a new tone, not present in the home collection.

The most obvious way Schoenberg addresses this problem is through cadences. Normally, we do not recognize that a new key has arrived because of a change in the operative collection or by a traditional harmonic progression. Rather, we know there has been a change of key simply by the appearance of a cadence. In the present song we know that there has been a modulation to G minor by m. 8, not because of any change in collection but because of the prominent half-cadence in G minor in m. 7, followed by the G minor triad at the beginning of m. 8. This has important implications: since the identity of a referential tonal center is often determined only by a cadence, the domain of influence of that referential center is highly limited.

Another procedure Schoenberg uses to imply modulation is the transposition of whole blocks of material. In this song, the first two measures (and the following downbeat) of the opening phrase are restated in almost completely literal transposition up one semitone beginning in m. 8 (see Ex. 2.7).

In this case, the transposition supports and confirms the modulation from F-sharp minor to G minor that had already been made clear by the cadence from the end of m. 7. That is not the case with another transposition from the end of this passage. Beginning on the last beat of m. 10 and continuing to the downbeat of m. 12, Schoenberg restates, in transposition, a portion of the opening phrase (from the last beat of m. 1 to the downbeat of m. 3). The interval of transposition (up three semitones), suggests that the opening F-sharp minor has modulated to A minor, a suggestion that is supported by the arrival of an A minor triad at the end of m. 13 (refer back to Ex. 2.5).

Example 2.7

In addition to cadences and the transposition of whole passages, Schoenberg sometimes also suggests keys by outlining or highlighting important scale degrees by linear motion, particularly in the bass.[24] This is particularly evident in the first phrase of this song, where there is a steady stepwise descent (migrating briefly from the bass to the tenor in mm. 2–3) from the opening F-sharp to A, a sixth lower in m. 5 (refer back to Ex. 2.1), the root and third of the tonic triad. (For a similar example, see the bass line in mm. 19–25.) In other passages, Schoenberg achieves similar results simply by circling around or resting on the tonic or the other tones of the tonic triad. An obvious example of this is the opening of Op. 2, No. 1, "Erwartung", with its famous five-note chord (see Ex. 2.8).[25]

Although Schoenberg's lines do occasionally outline central pitches through scalar patterns (as in Ex. 2.1) or highlight them by circling around them (as in Ex. 2.8), melodic patterns that clearly suggest a specific referential tonal center are relatively rare. Usually, Schoenberg's lines are highly

Example 2.8

ambiguous with regard to tonal outline or identity. Although scalar patterns are quite common in his songs, an important aspect of Schoenberg's style in these works is what might be termed "indeterminate scales": stepwise motions that resemble a scale, but which are not answerable to any specific diatonic collection.

This is a logical outgrowth of two other essential compositional features. As we have seen, Schoenberg tends both to restrict the use of non-chord tones and to construct his harmonic progressions so that adjacent chords cannot belong to a single diatonic collection. The indeterminate character of Schoenberg's scalar passages is a necessary consequence of these two characteristics. Since the melodic tones tend to be chord tones (and not elaborative tones), and since adjacent chords tend not to be from a single diatonic collection, it follows that the melody is going to be comprised of a chromatic cross-section of the chords forming the harmonic progressions. This cannot help but have the consequence that the resultant scalar lines cannot define a single diatonic collection.

If we turn our attention now to the motivic and thematic structure of Schoenberg's songs, we should notice that all of the songs from this period are fairly concise in their employment of thematic and motivic material. There is a fair degree of restatement, either at the original pitch level or in transposition, often with only minor alterations in pitch or rhythm. For example, virtually everything in mm. 7–13 is a transposition or repetition of material from the opening phrase (mm. 1–6). So too, the material of m. 26 (see Ex. 2.3, above) is restated at pitch and in transposition throughout mm. 27–33. And mm. 34–6 are slightly altered versions of mm. 14–17.

Finally, mm. 39–41 are a slightly altered version of mm. 1–2. Thus, well over half of the composition consists of literal, or transposed, versions of a very limited number of measures.

Although many passages are repetitions or transposed repetitions of prior passages, Schoenberg usually takes some steps to prevent stark equivalence. Frequently he does this by repeating (or transposing) only a part of a passage: breaking off early or starting late. As a result, Schoenberg rarely repeats or transposes passages in their entirety.

Another important component of the motivic concision of this song is Schoenberg's use of motives from the beginning of the song to create related ideas later in the work. As Walter Frisch has pointed out, a significant number of passages from later in the song are transformations of motives from the r.h. piano part in the first half of the opening phrase.[26] The opening four notes in the piano r.h. in mm. 1–2 (marked 'x' in Ex. 2.1, above) return a number of times in mildly transformed form in mm. 23–33. (See 'x' in m. 26, Ex. 2.3.) But the transformation of 'x' never goes beyond the stage it reaches in m. 26.[27] Therefore it would be an exaggeration to state that this song (or any of the songs of 1899) is an example of motivic organicism. Given the relatively limited scope of the motivic development in this song, one would also not be justified in stating that developing variation has already become a core component of Schoenberg's compositional approach. But clearly, the seeds of both are present.[28]

Such then are some of the prominent features of Schoenberg's compositional approach in his songs of 1899. From this we can see that although Schoenberg had already staked out a position at the very forefront of *fin de siècle* Viennese modernism, his music still retains powerful connections with the past. And that would prove to be a model for much of what was to come: in the coming decade, Schoenberg would continually push forward, all the while retaining roots deep in tradition.[29]

To close this chapter, I think it would be helpful to summarize those features of Schoenberg's 1899 pitch language that served as the point of departure for many of the most radical developments that were to follow.[30]

- Chords containing dissonances function as locally stable entities.
- Phrases (sometimes even including the cadence) can consist entirely, or nearly entirely, of seventh chords and other chords containing dissonances.
- Although a specific chordal type might be given emphasis, no one type of chord predominates in a work or even in an extended section.
- Adjacent chords are rarely answerable to a single diatonic collection.
- The circulation of the total chromatic is common within phrases.

- The diatonic collection rarely plays a referential role; when it is present, it frequently has a programmatic or a text-painting function.
- Tones of elaboration are rare; when they do occur they usually have a motivic function.
- Apparent tones of elaboration can often better be understood as effectuating quick changes in harmony.
- Harmonic progressions rarely conform to standard models (e.g. IV-V-I), except at cadences, and frequently not even there.
- Referential tonal centers are established most often by agogic or cadential emphasis on a triad, not by paradigmatic harmonic progressions.
- There is no necessary connection between chordal type (e.g. dominant seventh chord or diminished seventh chord) and harmonic function.
- Because of the constant circulation of the chromatic and the absence of paradigmatic harmonic progressions, it is often difficult or impossible to identify a referential center other than at a cadence.
- Some cadences come to rest on dissonant chords.
- Indeterminate scales are common.
- Modulation is effected, not by change in collection (which always tends toward the complete chromatic), but rather by the transposition of pre-existent blocks of material.
- A degree of motivic economy is normative; organic unity is not.

3 The principle of incremental innovation: *Verklärte Nacht*, 1899

> ... I knew I had the duty of developing my ideas for the sake of progress in music, whether I liked it or not.[1]

In 1899 Schoenberg was virtually unknown as a composer. Only four years before, he had been a clerk in a bank. His only composition teacher, Alexander Zemlinsky, was himself struggling for wider recognition and could exert only limited influence on his former student's behalf.[2] Schoenberg was not an accomplished performer. He had little standing and few connections in the Viennese musical establishment. As of 1899, none of his compositions had been published, and the only significant performance to his credit was the premiere in 1898 (by the Fitzner Quartet) of his String Quartet in D (1897).[3]

Because the Schoenberg of 1899 was so little known, there is no contemporaneous record of his opinions or beliefs on artistic matters. Unlike later, there was no devoted circle of students or followers hanging on his every word. His surviving correspondence from the period is limited. He kept no diary (or, if he did, it has not survived). He had written no essays and had completed no theoretical treatises.[4] In short, Schoenberg's minimal standing as a composer in 1899 is mirrored by an almost complete absence of contemporaneous documentary sources that could give any reliable clue as to his aesthetic and artistic beliefs at that time.[5] Therefore, here and in subsequent chapters, although I will make cautious use of Schoenberg's ex post facto writings about his early music, the emphasis will be primarily on a close analysis of the music.[6]

With the songs of 1899, Schoenberg had already staked out a position at the forefront of musical modernism. Yet, as we saw in the previous chapter, those songs did not make an abrupt break with the past. With *Verklärte Nacht* it should be clear that this balancing of the new with the traditional is a core component of Schoenberg's artistic identity. Throughout the decade 1899–1909, Schoenberg's compositional philosophy would rest on a fundamental principle: his commitment to the idea of incremental innovation.[7] In *Verklärte Nacht* and in many (though not all) subsequent works, Schoenberg actively, and with deliberate intent, devised at least one important aspect of the work's design that was innovatory.[8]

The most obvious innovation of *Verklärte Nacht* is that it is a programmatic work. Not that there was anything radical about programmatic compositions, per se, in 1899.⁹ What was novel about *Verklärte Nacht* was that it was a programmatic chamber work.¹⁰

At the end of the nineteenth century, chamber music was considered to be the last bastion of absolute music. Symphonic works were often (though by no means invariably) supplied with programs or programmatic titles. Solo keyboard works were frequently character pieces, often suggestive of programmatic ideas.¹¹ Among instrumental compositions, only chamber music remained doggedly resistant to the incorporation of programs, relying instead on traditional principles of abstract formal design. Schoenberg's decision to write a programmatic chamber work thus represents a conscious and deliberate attempt to contravene a well-recognized norm.

Just how conscious and how deliberate this attempt was can be inferred from some intriguing clues in the surviving documentary evidence. Among Schoenberg's papers is a rather substantial fragment (a particell of 255 measures; a full score of 135 measures) of a symphonic tone poem, *Frühlings Tod*, based on a poem by Nikolaus Lenau and dating from the year preceding *Verklärte Nacht*.¹² The scored version is for full (though by Schoenberg's later standards, a relatively small) orchestra.¹³ At the beginning of the particell, Schoenberg had initially written: "Frühlings Tod nach Lenau / für Streich Orchester". At some later point, he crossed out the word "Streich" and replaced it with "grosses".¹⁴ Thus it is clear that Schoenberg's first concept had been to write a programmatic composition for string orchestra.

That Schoenberg toyed with the idea of setting a tone poem for string orchestra is both an important harbinger of the innovations in the scoring of *Verklärte Nacht* as well as evidence of the incremental nature of his approach to innovation. With *Frühlings Tod*, Schoenberg was only thinking of a modest emendation in the norms of the genre, one that probably would have attracted little attention. A year later, with *Verklärte Nacht* Schoenberg had overcome his hesitations and had decided to make a more substantial, though still incremental, innovation.¹⁵ By writing a programmatic chamber work, Schoenberg consciously contravened some well-recognized norms of the time, and did so in a manner guaranteed to attract attention.

Sure enough, it did not go unnoticed. One newspaper reviewer wrote as follows about the premiere:

> The Rosé Quartet gave the last concert of its very successful season on Tuesday, March 18. After Hermann Grädener's formally correct quartet, a novelty by Arnold Schoenberg appeared quite unusual: a sextet after Richard Dehmel's poem "Die Verklärte Nacht". Since some of those present were so "uncivilized" as to be unfamiliar with the poem, this programmatic chamber music (God protect us in the future from this species) was

probably misunderstood by all listeners not in touch with the Secession. The general consensus was that this "transfigured night" was frightfully long, and that none of the many pizzicati, harmonics, mutes, etc. did anything to shed any light on it. Schoenberg certainly knows how to write for strings. Let's hope that he will soon use his gift on a work of pure chamber music.[16]

In a similar vein, another of the critics present noted that Schoenberg had "transferred the idea of composing after a poetic 'program' to the absolute type of music for the first time in this sextet". Given that he had serious reservations about program music in general, the critic felt that his review was "not the place to bring up anew the familiar but unresolved question of the validity of program music".[17] Another critic had similar concerns: "Program music ... appears to be about to encroach on chamber music. There is really no valid reason to oppose this expansion of its domain. If one can compose unclear orchestra music, one can just as well – or, just as poorly – create unclear chamber music."[18]

Generally speaking Schoenberg's innovations were not limited to a single dimension: in many compositions (and in particular, in the larger works), he would make innovations in several domains. Another innovative feature of *Verklärte Nacht* is its astonishing array of colors and sounds.

Once again, the contemporaneous newspaper critics recognized and commented on this innovation. The critic quoted at length above also remarked on the profusion of "pizzicati, harmonics, mutes, etc." So too, the second critic remarked that "the young composer has in any case proven one thing: unusual talent and a rare sense for sound". And for the third critic, the sonic surface was the most startling aspect of the composition.

> More remarkable than anything in this single uninterrupted sextet movement, which lasts for more than a half-hour in slow tempo, is the sound, which scarcely has an equal in the chamber music literature. In an older, worthwhile quartet by Schoenberg that Fitzner performed two [sic] years ago, the unusual charm of its colors attracted attention. The new sextet surpasses that work in this dimension in significant measure.[19]

Because pre-1900 chamber music had been the refuge of absolute music, composers did not normally attempt to exploit the coloristic resources of the string ensemble in string quartets, quintets, and sextets. Instead, the very homogeneity of the string family encouraged, and the aesthetic of absolute music suggested, an emphasis on formal structure and sophisticated thematic and harmonic relationships, not on coloristic effects.

Although there are many extraordinary sounds in *Verklärte Nacht*, one might be hard-pressed to make a convincing case that any specific sound is completely unprecedented in the chamber music literature. An exhaustive search of nineteenth-century chamber works would undoubtedly reveal that some earlier composers had used pizzicato in combination with arco, con sordino together with senza sordino, false harmonics in chordal combinations, extended passages of tremolo and so forth. But even if no one sound in *Verklärte Nacht* is unprecedented, the reviewer was very much on to something essential here: the sound of *Verklärte Nacht* "scarcely has an equal in the chamber music literature". Not because of any specific color combination but because of the unequalled variety of its sounds and the rapidity with which the different colors succeeded one another.

What made the instrumental sound of this work so innovatory was that Schoenberg did not treat any one type or limited group of types of sound production as normative. Instead, he alternated quickly and dramatically from color to color. There is hardly a group of phrases that does not have a color strikingly different from what came before it or from what follows it, or even, from almost everything else in the piece. It is that continuous succession of contrasts that constitutes the innovatory character of the sound of *Verklärte Nacht*.

Although the reviewers both noticed and commented on Schoenberg's innovations in genre and color, they did not mention its pitch language as breaking new ground. This is a telling omission, tacit confirmation of the incremental nature of Schoenberg's approach to innovation.

Nevertheless, notwithstanding the traditional nature of much of its pitch language, *Verklärte Nacht* does have its share of harmonic novelties, precisely as we should expect from a composer committed to the idea of incremental innovation. Although the critics at the premiere did not notice these innovations, others did: in 1910, writing in his *Harmonielehre*, Schoenberg reported that one chord in the work so aroused the ire of a concert society (the Vienna Tonkünstlerverein) that they refused to sponsor its premiere.[20]

> In my Sextet, *Verklärte Nacht* [measures 41–2] ... I wrote the inversion of a ninth chord ... without then knowing theoretically what I was doing – I was merely following my ear ... What's worse, I see now that it is none other than that particular inversion which the theorists condemned most resolutely of all ... Only now do I understand the objection, at that time beyond my comprehension, of that concert society which refused to perform my Sextet on account of this chord (its refusal was actually so explained). Naturally: inversions of ninth chords just don't exist; hence no performance, either, for how can one perform something that does not exist. And I had to wait a few years. To be sure, when it was then actually performed, nobody noticed anymore that a ninth chord occurs there in the fourth inversion. Today, of course, that sort of thing disturbs no man who is to be taken seriously.[21]

The principle of incremental innovation: *Verklärte Nacht*, 1899

Schoenberg's claim to the contrary, the ninth chord in fourth inversion might not have been the product of blind intuition.[22] Even within *Verklärte Nacht* there are a number of other prominent examples of ninth chords in inversion, and this suggests that Schoenberg was consciously interested in a thorough exploration of the use of these chords.[23] Furthermore, Schoenberg's systematic use of inversions of ninth chords was itself part of a larger trend: from this point forward we shall see clear evidence that Schoenberg consciously and deliberately sought to explore a broad array of new chordal types (including inverted ninths) and to find ways of incorporating them convincingly into his works. And finally, there are many aspects about the passage where the fourth-inversion ninth chord first appears that strongly suggest that Schoenberg placed that chord there with all due deliberation and with conscious intent. Chief among those is that the problematic chord is not buried in the middle of some nondescript phrase, but rather is carefully placed at a crucial moment in such a way as to demand attention. It is no wonder that the musicians of the Tonkünstlerverein both noticed the chord and were scandalized by it: Schoenberg virtually put a sign on it (see Ex. 3.1).

As we have already seen in the songs, clear cadences are relatively few and far between in Schoenberg's early music: in the 40 measures that preceded the passage in Ex. 3.1 there had been only one, somewhat heavily disguised and elided cadence (mm. 28–9). Therefore, the passage in Ex. 3.1 takes on added prominence as it creates expectations for a significant cadence, the first of any substance in the work.

Example 3.1

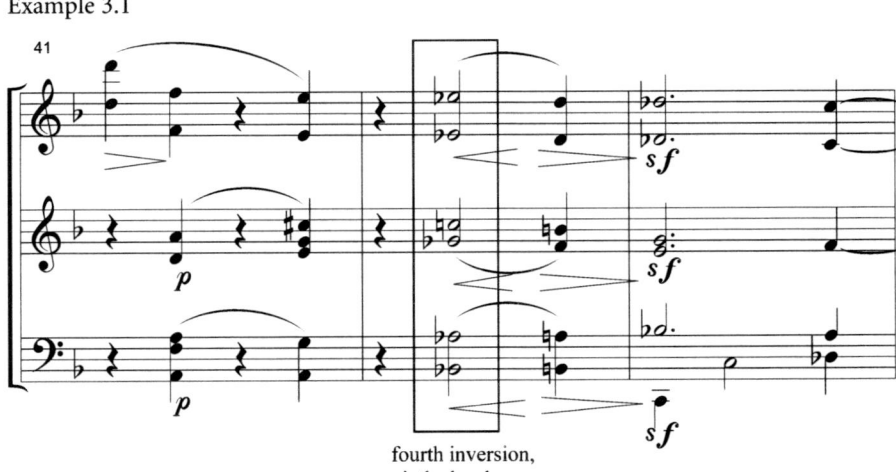

fourth inversion, ninth chord

At first, Schoenberg takes steps to intensify those expectations. At the beginning of m. 41, there is a sudden, dramatic, change in texture as the complicated ensemble of the previous measure (a highly elaborated diminished seventh chord on G-sharp) suddenly gives way to a bare octave on D in the upper register. As the volume descends precipitously from fortissimo to piano, and as the remaining instruments reenter, that octave D shows itself to be part of cadential 6/4 in D. After a grand pause on the third beat of the measure, Schoenberg continues on in almost textbook format to a root-position dominant seventh chord on A. One can scarcely imagine a clearer, more traditional cadential preparation, one that creates such clear expectations for the imminent arrival of a D minor triad. But instead of the expected D minor chord, Schoenberg proceeds directly to the famous ninth chord in fourth inversion. In effect, this is a kind of unorthodox deceptive cadence, one in which a chromatic substitute chord takes the place of the expected tonic triad.[24]

Although the fourth-inversion ninth chord in m. 42 (and in the parallel passage in m. 394) is the most prominent example of an inverted ninth chord, it is not the only such example. Intuitive or not, Schoenberg appears to be engaged in a systematic effort to find ways of incorporating these chords into his music. Three additional examples appear in Ex. 3.2.

There is another passage where (like the famous chord in Ex. 3.1) one could argue that an inversion of a ninth chord appears as a deceptive substitute for an expected triad (see Ex. 3.3). In m. 99, Schoenberg begins to set the stage for a powerful authentic cadence. After an applied vii^{o7}/V in

Example 3.2a

G dominant ninth
third inversion

Example 3.2b

B dominant ninth
third inversion

Example 3.2c

E dominant ninth
second inversion

m. 99, Schoenberg proceeds through an elaborated cadential 6/4 in mm. 100–101 and then on to an extended and elaborated dominant ninth in E in mm. 102–4. In a composition where dominants are both rare and heavily disguised – if not dispensed with entirely – this dominant chord is noteworthy, not only for its length, but for the extent and clarity of its preparation.

When the dominant finally resolves in m. 105, it does so to a sonority that is not a pure E triad. In addition to the E minor triad, there are two added tones, A-sharp and C-sharp. If we were to look at this sonority in

Example 3.3

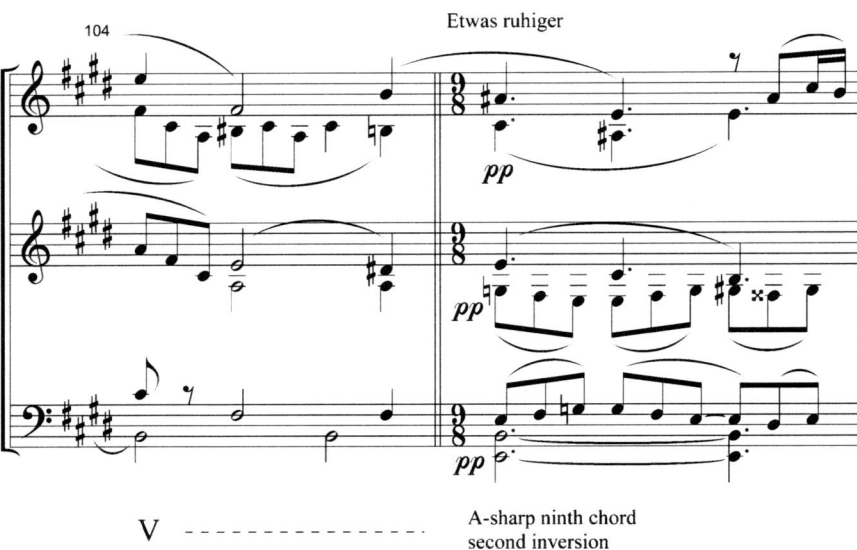

isolation, one could understand this as second inversion ninth chord with A-sharp as its root.

Given our post-Schenkerian world view, we do not normally think in these terms and do not normally look at sonorities in isolation. Faced with a complicated and dissonant sonority of this sort, we normally parse the surface into two hierarchically distinct categories: chord tone and non-chord tone. Our normal practice would simply be to dismiss the A-sharp and C-sharp as non-chord tones – somewhat unorthodox non-chord tones (they never really resolve, they simply drop out), but non-chord tones nevertheless.

But it is by no means clear that Schoenberg thought in those terms. Certainly in his later theoretical writings, Schoenberg questioned the very idea of non-chord tones.

> Before anything else, then, [let us affirm that] the non-harmonic tones do form chords (*Zusammenklänge*), hence are not non-harmonic; the musical phenomena they help to create are harmonies, as is everything that sounds simultaneously.[25]

A few pages later, Schoenberg is even more dogmatic:

> *There are no non-harmonic tones, for harmony means tones sounding together (Zusammenklang). Non-harmonic tones are merely those that the theorists could not fit into their system of harmony. And that [they could not] results from the arbitrary assumption of the theorists that the ear can attend only to the first five overtones.* [p. 318]

Example 3.4

As I cautioned above, we cannot assume that Schoenberg's 1910 comments are applicable to his 1899 music. But in this case, I believe Schoenberg has accurately described a core idea of his compositional approach in 1899. Given his tendency to think in terms of chords (Zusammenklänge) as the basic units of the syntax and his further tendency to search for ways of expanding the chordal vocabulary, it is reasonable to assume that Schoenberg may have thought of the sonority on the downbeat of m. 105 as a ninth chord in inversion, similar in function and character to its far more famous relative in m. 42.

There is other support for the idea that Schoenberg thought precisely in the terms indicated in the two quotations. In the songs of Op. 2, we saw that a prominent characteristic of Schoenberg's language in those works was the relative paucity of non-chord tones. Frequently, notes that had the appearance of non-chord tones (e.g. were off the beat and proceeded by step to a chord tone in the following sonority) could just as persuasively be regarded as chord tones: they effected a change of harmony, not merely an elaboration of one. Many passages in *Verklärte Nacht* confirm that this is a core component of Schoenberg's compositional thought. Consider the following passage (Ex. 3.4).

In the first measure of this passage, almost every one of the vertical sonorities created by the quickly moving contrapuntal lines produces a traditionally classifiable triad or seventh chord. The opening sonority (1) is a first inversion D minor triad. On the second sextuplet, with the move of the second violin's A to an A-sharp, the resultant chord (2) becomes a B-flat 6/4 triad (enharmonic equivalence of B-flat and A-sharp is assumed). With the continuation of the second violin line upward on the next sextuplet, the chord is transformed into a diminished triad on B in second inversion (3). Continuing on to the second eighth of the measure, the next changes in pitch produce a second inversion dominant seventh chord with a lowered fifth built on D (4). This succession of chord after chord in just the first eighth of the measure is not an isolated event (neither in this example nor in Op. 4 in general). With only a few exceptions, virtually every change of pitch in the counterpoint in this example produces a different, and readily identifiable, triad or seventh chord. This cannot be the result of accident or coincidence. The very complication and consistency of this procedure makes it certain that this resulted from Schoenberg's careful and conscious manipulation of the doublings and lines in order to produce a constantly changing succession of traditionally classifiable harmonies.

Another area of incremental innovation in *Verklärte Nacht* is Schoenberg's approach to cadences. In the songs of 1899, Schoenberg tended either to disguise authentic cadences or to avoid them altogether. He also devised a number of cadences with non-traditional harmonic progressions and experimented, if ever so tentatively, with non-triadic sonorities as the final chord of a cadence. *Verklärte Nacht* takes up these ideas and expands upon all of them.

Some traditional authentic cadences still do occur. At the same time there is a perceptible increase in cadences of a far less traditional sort. This is clear from the passage immediately following the famous fourth-inversion ninth chord (Ex. 3.5).

Example 3.5

The passage begins by returning to the schoolbook cadential preparation formula that had been so dramatically interrupted by the inverted ninth chord. Once again, there is an applied diminished seventh chord (vii^{o7}/V), followed by a cadential 6/4 and a root position dominant chord (m. 45), all in the strictest chorale style format. Like the earlier passage, here too (m. 46) the resolution is thwarted; Schoenberg replaces the expected tonic triad with a diminished seventh chord (vii^{o7}/IV), yet another new type of deceptive cadence.

Of even more significance is the other cadence in this passage, the one that occurs in m. 49 where the motion comes to a complete halt. Given its rhythmic character, it has the feel of a cadence. But the chord at this cadence is not a consonant sonority: it is instead an augmented triad. That alone would be innovative enough, but the chord does not remain complete. After the first beat, the two lower voices drop out, leaving a lone F-sharp in the first viola to complete the measure.

This ambiguous and enigmatic cadence is a logical extension of the experimentation with non-traditional cadences we saw in Op. 2. Schoenberg has chosen as the final chord of a phrase something that heretofore had been regarded as an unstable and ambiguous sonority, not a stable triad. What makes this so significant is that it is far from unique: there are other cadences in *Verklärte Nacht* that conclude on dissonant sonorities (e.g. mm. 132 and 269); there are also several other places that end on a single ambiguous tone (e.g. mm. 225–8).

It is not just the presence of unusual cadences that distinguishes *Verklärte Nacht* from its predecessors: one of the most striking features of *Verklärte Nacht* is the relative rarity of anything that could be characterized as a cadence of any sort, traditional or otherwise. Clear, unequivocal stopping points of any sort are few and far between, even ones that end on dissonant or ambiguous sonorities. Instead, Schoenberg frequently creates a fabric of considerable length in which a phrase will close at the very end of one measure while the next phrase will begin at the beginning of the following measure.

The extensive use of this technique meant that there are large stretches of music in which there are no cadences at all. In the more than fifty-measure passage from m. 50 (immediately following the enigmatic cadence on the transitory augmented triad in Ex. 3.5) up until the cadence on E in m. 105 (Ex. 3.3, above) there is not a single unambiguous cadence of any sort: authentic, half, deceptive, or unconventional.

The paucity of cadences ending on triads has significant consequences for the harmonic structure of the composition. Partly because of the absence of cadences, for significant stretches of the composition, no referential center is identifiable.[26] Schoenberg creates these tonally indeterminate regions by means similar to those he used in the songs of 1899: traditionally normative harmonic progressions (dominant preparation, dominant, tonic) are absent; seventh chords follow one another in interrupted succession; ambiguous chords (Schoenberg would later call them "vagrant" chords) predominate; adjacent chords do not belong to a common diatonic collection; there is a constant circulation of the total chromatic.[27]

The songs of 1899 also had stretches of music where no referential center came to the fore but given the comparatively diminutive dimensions of the songs, those regions never extended beyond a few measures. As a result, it was a relatively simple matter to establish recognizable referential centers in the songs: even the briefest arrival of a rhythmically emphasized triad was often sufficient, particularly given that the referential triad was frequently the only triad in the phrase. In a substantially larger work like *Verklärte Nacht*, strategies of this sort were insufficient: a single consonant root position triad would not have the power to establish itself as a referential tonic that could counterbalance the long stretches (sometimes extending beyond fifty measures) where no referential center was perceptible and where, sometimes, no triad was even present. Therefore, when Schoenberg wanted to establish a clear referential tonal center in *Verklärte Nacht*, he tended to employ far more explicit means than he had done in the smaller dimensions of his songs. For example, he restricts himself to a diatonic collection for an extended period (as in the ten opening measures of the composition). Or having arrived on a referential triad, he sits on it for an extended period (as in m. 105ff). Or he creates powerful authentic cadences with extensive preparation including a clear root position dominant (as in mm. 365–70).

As a result, *Verklärte Nacht* moves between two poles: regions – sometimes quite extended – lacking identifiable referential centers and other regions with clear referential centers. Thus, the work begins a section clearly in D and whose presence (at least to my ear) is perceptible at least up to m. 45. Soon after, Schoenberg moves into a region without identifiable referential centers. Other than a brief emphasis on B-flat in mm. 50–4, no referential center comes into focus until m. 105 where E is firmly established as a new point of reference (see Ex. 3.3, above). There then follows another long stretch without a clear diatonic region or an unambiguous tonal center. Other than a brief suggestion of D in mm. 181–5 (including a varied repetition of the passage containing the controversial fourth inversion ninth chord) and momentary emphases on other degrees shortly thereafter (e.g. B-flat minor in mm. 193–200), it is not until m. 229 that there is a solid emphasis on a new key, D major.

The principle of incremental innovation: *Verklärte Nacht*, 1899

The suspension of tonal definition for extended periods does not, however, create an undifferentiated flow. Rather, as he did in the songs of 1899, Schoenberg devised techniques to create motion, even in the absence of identifiable tonal centers. Just as he did in the songs of 1899, Schoenberg would often state a passage that lacked an identifiable tonal center and then restate it at some later point in transposition. For example, the tonally ambiguous two-measure phrase of mm. 75–6 returns in virtually literal form in mm. 83–4, transposed up three semitones (see Ex. 3.6a, mm. 75–6 and Ex. 3.6b, mm. 83–4). This technique enabled Schoenberg to create the impression of large-scale quasi-modulatory motion without the prior necessity of having established a key for the original phrase.

The sharply etched regions of clear tonal definition interspersed throughout the composition also play an essential role in the large-scale formal structure of the work. The striking contrast between the islands of tonal clarity and the intervening regions of tonal ambiguity and instability serves to highlight the most significant formal subdivisions of the work. By the very nature of their harmonically stable character, the diatonic regions function as important points of arrival and resolution, the central pillars of the formal design.

There is also a clear thematic structure: themes that appear in one part of the work return in equally clear and recognizable (though often varied) form elsewhere in the work. The multiple versions of the opening theme (mm. 202, 266, 370, and 401) are only the most obvious examples of this procedure.

Example 3.6a

Example 3.6b

The combination of regions with clear tonal definition and a reiterative thematic structure makes for a clearly apprehensible formal structure. But precisely what is that form? Over the years a number of commentators have proposed some intriguing answers to this question. Possibly following Egon Wellesz, Carl Dahlhaus has described the form as a kind of rondo.[28] By contrast, Wilhelm Pfannkuch suggested that sonata form was a more appropriate description, and saw *Verklärte Nacht* as a precursor of the large all-in-one forms that followed (*Pelleas und Melisande*, Op. 5, String Quartet, Op. 7, and Chamber Symphony, Op. 9).[29] And in a well-known article, Richard Swift made the novel suggestion that *Verklärte Nacht* is not one, but two sonata forms, preceded by an introduction, linked by a transition, and concluding with a coda.[30]

The multiplicity of different (and contradictory) formal models suggests something is amiss here. If the hunt for an appropriate absolute music formal model yields three different results for the same composition, then perhaps we are looking in the wrong place, in the realms of absolute music and not programmatic music.[31] Perhaps if we stop trying to force this work into an absolute music model and instead try to understand the form in terms of the program, we can be far more successful.[32]

Given the exceptional clarity of the large-scale tonal and thematic design of *Verklärte Nacht*, it is possible to make a very persuasive case for precise correlations between the ideas and actions represented in Dehmel's poem and Schoenberg's music: in true post-Wagnerian style, Schoenberg employs a succession of leitmotifs to illustrate the program.[33] The opening theme represents the couple walking together in the night ("Zwei Menschen gehn durch kahlen, kalten Hain"); the woman's confession and despairing outburst ("Ich trag ein Kind und nit von Dir") correspond to the themes beginning in m. 29; her admission of her longing for motherhood ("und hatte doch ein schwer Verlangen nach Lebensinhalt, nach Mutterglück") is reflected in the lyrical theme in E (mm. 105ff); the man's soothing response ("Das Kind, das Du empfangen hast, / sei Deiner Seele keine Last") matches up with the D major episode beginning in m. 229, and so forth.

Although it is possible to make a convincing case for specific connections between Dehmel's poem and Schoenberg's music, the form of *Verklärte Nacht* is considerably more sophisticated and subtle than the correlation of a succession of leitmotifs with the poem. Part of the reason for this is that Schoenberg chose a poem that describes ideas, attitudes, and moods more than it depicts actions, events, or natural phenomena. Therefore, Schoenberg was under little obligation to try to produce music that replicated sounds from the real world: there are no imitations of waves crashing, birds chirping, trains moving, or any of the myriad picturesque possibilities that composers have portrayed (and many critics have deplored) in music. Instead, Schoenberg attempted to portray the feelings and ideas of the protagonists of the poem in response to the crisis in their relationship. Chief among the ways he did so was through the manipulation of the contrast between diatonic stability and chromatic instability.

The central core of the plot of the poem might best be described as a love affair that is threatened with catastrophe but which is saved. In other words stability and happiness are at first threatened but after a crisis, finally restored and brought to a higher level. The islands of diatonic purity and clear tonal definition are the points which reflect the couple's love for one another or the happiness to which they aspire. These stable islands are threatened by harmonically unstable passages which depict the problems in the couple's relationship surface and threaten to destroy the stability represented by the diatonicism. Only at the end, after the transfiguration is complete are happiness and stability finally restored.

The form of *Verklärte Nacht* is thus most emphatically not merely a succession of themes that portray the ideas or actions of the poem. Nor are the areas of tonal stability and definition arbitrarily scattered through the work. Rather, the themes and the areas of tonal stability function together on a large scale to represent the poem in musical terms. Schoenberg exploited the distinctions between tonal stability and instability, and between diatonicism and chromaticism, as metaphors that parallel the distinctions between stability and instability, between happiness and despair, between conflict and resolution, in the relationships of the couple as described in Dehmel's poem.

The programmatic structure of *Verklärte Nacht* has a number of interesting consequences for the thematic and motivic structure. In order to illustrate the many different ideas and concepts of the story embodied in Dehmel's poem, Schoenberg needed a correspondingly extensive array of distinctive themes. As a result, *Verklärte Nacht* has a virtual parade of contrasting themes and motives.

At later stages of his stylistic development, Schoenberg – both as a composer and a theorist – became a well-known advocate of the idea of motivic economy and of thematic unity. The nonstop succession of distinctive themes in Op. 4 might lead one to conclude that *Verklärte Nacht* is the very antithesis of Schoenberg's later approach. That would be a mistake.

In the first place, as Walter Frisch has shown, there are clear motivic connections between some of the supposedly contrasting themes. This is clear from the themes that occur in mm. 34, 75, and 105 (see Ex. 3.7).[34] These themes are distinctive enough so as not to be confused with one another. At the same time, they share common motivic features (all three begin with a descending semitone followed by a tritone skip).

The thematic structure of *Verklärte Nacht* also relates to his later practice in that Schoenberg makes extensive use of the techniques of thematic transformation and development. It was part of Schoenberg's approach to the realization of the program that the various leitmotifs do not return in unaltered form. Rather, they are transformed, with the specific character of

Example 3.7

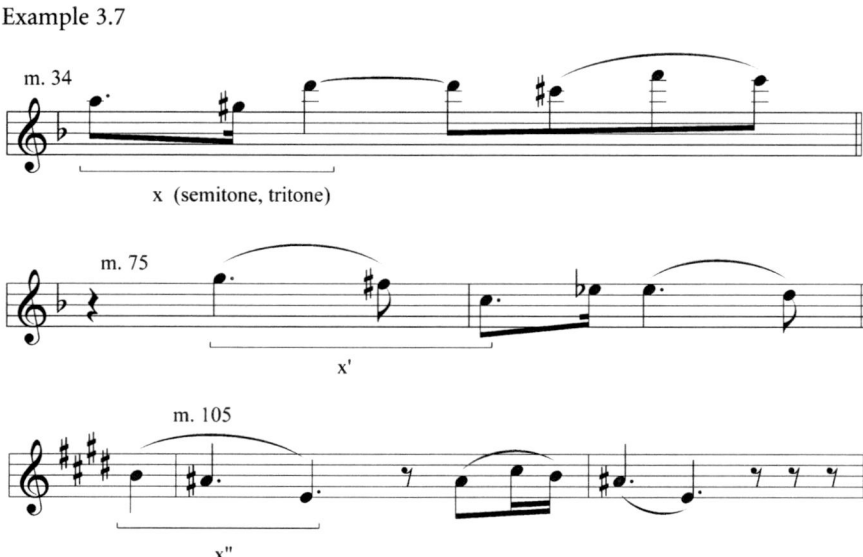

The principle of incremental innovation: *Verklärte Nacht*, 1899   39

those transformations reflecting the plot. This is clear from two instances of the "walking theme" (see Ex. 3.8a, mm. 3–6 and Ex. 3.8b, mm. 201–3).

The first appearance of the "walking theme" is characterized by a recurrent pedal tone in octaves on the tonic, a strict adherence to the D minor collection, a stepwise descent of the six-note melody through the D minor scale down to the tonic, and the outline of a minor sixth from the beginning to the end of the theme. Throughout, the dynamics are pianissimo. By contrast, in the second appearance of this leitmotif in mm. 201ff, there are no pedal tones, the collection of the accompaniment is highly chromatic, the theme has been shortened to five notes, the outline is now a tritone

Example 3.8a

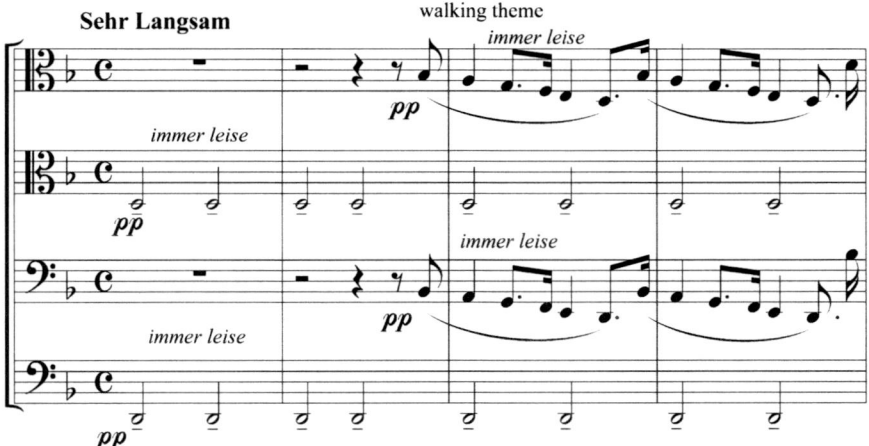

Example 3.8b

Example 3.9

(ending on A, the leading tone of B-flat minor), and the dynamics are fortissimo. And finally, unlike the earlier instance, the harmonic progressions do little or nothing to establish or support an identifiable referential center.

There is at least one additional way in which Schoenberg exploits the techniques of motivic transformation. A striking feature of *Verklärte Nacht* (and one that he later criticized) is its extensive use of repetition.[35] Schoenberg frequently states a phrase and then repeats the phrase immediately (sometimes in transposition). Sometimes he even creates nested complexes of repetitions. All told, a considerable proportion of the work consists of passages that are straightforward repetitions or transpositions of other passages.

But not all of these repetitions are literal. Instead, Schoenberg frequently varies the repetitions and does so in a manner that promotes a developmental process. Ex. 3.9 presents a characteristic instance.

The theme (marked 'x' in the example) appears in the first cello in m. 63, and is then repeated in octaves in m. 64. In mm. 65–6, however, the theme is transformed, as its most characteristic element (the quintuplet turn figure) is stripped away from the melodic line and moved into the accompaniment. What is left is only the descending chromatic line, now grouped into two-note phrases, extended through the final two measures of the phrase.[36]

These three techniques – the transformation of themes as per the program, motivic connections between apparently contrasting themes, and motivic development within phrases – show that motivic development and transformation are an important component of Schoenberg's language, even in a programmatic work like *Verklärte Nacht*. Paradoxical though it may seem, thematic prolixity and motivic integration are not polar opposites in Schoenberg's thought.

Verklärte Nacht demonstrates that the principle of incremental innovation was a core component of Schoenberg's compositional thought. In many dimensions – chordal vocabulary, harmonic progression, cadential structure, tonal definition, genre, and color – he made significant changes. But there was no sudden break with the past: the changes are best understood as extensions or modifications of prior practice, not as a rejection of the traditions from which his music sprang.

4 Conservative song-cycle, progressive cantata: *Gurrelieder*, 1900–11

> We must conclude that neither at the beginning nor at the end, nor in the middle is the key automatically present. On the contrary at every point firm measures of art are required to give the key unequivocal expression.[1]

Gurrelieder is a difficult composition to discuss and for a variety of reasons. One is simply its size: it is bigger, by far, than any of Schoenberg's previous compositions, perhaps bigger even than all of the pre-1900 works put together.[2] Another reason is its inordinately prolonged and complicated genesis. Schoenberg began work on *Gurrelieder* in the spring of 1900 and within a year had completed a draft of almost the entire composition. But he did not finish the orchestration until 1911 and the work was not premiered until 1913.

There is considerable doubt about the original plan of this work. For quite some time it was believed that Schoenberg initially conceived of *Gurrelieder* as a piano-accompanied song-cycle, a setting of the first nine poems of Jens Peter Jacobsen's *Gurresange* (in its German translation by Robert Franz Arnold). Only after abandoning the song-cycle did Schoenberg change his conception, transforming the work into the vocal-orchestral extravaganza we know today.[3] According to this version of events, Schoenberg embarked on the project because he intended to enter a composition contest for a song-cycle sponsored by the Tonkünstlerverein. Schoenberg either did not quite finish the work on time (according to Dika Newlin) or he decided that his song-cycle was unlikely to be awarded a prize by a conservative jury (according to Alexander Zemlinsky).[4] At that point Schoenberg abandoned the song-cycle and decided instead to set Jacobsen's entire epic as a massive work for soloists, choirs, and orchestra. Having made this decision, he transformed the original piano part from the first nine songs into an orchestral score, wrote an extensive introduction, transposed the second song to a new key, replaced the final cadences of some of the songs with transitions, and made numerous other changes and additions.

However, this may not be a completely accurate description of how *Gurrelieder* reached its final form. Ulrich Krämer has examined the manuscript evidence and has made a very strong argument that from the beginning, Schoenberg had both projects in mind – song-cycle and cantata.[5] Krämer marshals evidence that suggests that Schoenberg intended all along to write more than a mere cycle of nine piano-accompanied songs.

Nevertheless, it is clear that Schoenberg worked first primarily on the song-cycle and only later dropped that in favor of the vocal-orchestral project. This is important because there are some important distinctions between the never completed piano-accompanied song-cycle and the massive vocal-orchestral cantata we know today. Therefore, we shall begin by examining *Gurrelieder* in its version as a cycle of nine songs for piano and two solo voices. Only then will we turn our attention to the much expanded and, in many important respects, significantly modified vocal-orchestral version. (To distinguish between the two stages, I refer to the piano-vocal version as the "*Gurrelieder*-cycle" and to the work in its final form simply as "*Gurrelieder*".)

In keeping with the principle of incremental innovation, we might have expected Schoenberg to incorporate a number of novel features into the *Gurrelieder*-cycle. That is not the case; for reasons we will examine shortly, not only are there relatively few innovations in the *Gurrelieder*-cycle but also, those that exist are relatively subdued. Indeed, the most prominent innovation may be its scoring. Since the first nine poems of Jacobsen's *Gurresange* alternate between poems spoken in Waldemar's and Tove's voices, Schoenberg quite reasonably decided to set the work as a regular alternation of songs for tenor (Waldemar) and for soprano (Tove).

Although this is a perfectly logical response to the structure of Jacobsen's poetry, it was an innovation in 1900 to write a song-cycle for two alternating voices. All of the song-cycles that preceded this work and would have been known to Schoenberg or his likely audiences – Beethoven's *An die ferne Geliebte*, Schubert's *Die Winterreise* and *Die Schöne Müllerin*, and Schumann's *Frauenliebe und Leben* – were cycles for a single voice, not for an alternating pair of voices.

However, most other aspects of the work are scarcely innovatory at all. In particular, the pitch language does not appear to progress past that of *Verklärte Nacht*. To the contrary, there are many ways in which its harmonic structure is more conservative than its predecessor. We can see this in the very first song of the cycle, "Nun dämpft die Dämmrung".

In the first poem, Waldemar, king of Gurre, has paused momentarily while on the way to Gurre castle where he is to meet his lover, Tove. Looking about, he marvels at the serenity of the world at dusk. The poem is largely taken up with the various images ("dusk dampening", "clouds resting", "noiseless peace", "airy gates closing", "the sun dreaming") that Waldemar uses to describe the utter quiet around him.

Sensitive, as always, to the mood of the poem, Schoenberg sought to capture in musical terms something of the serenity of Waldemar's description. He did so by employing compositional techniques that, by comparison with his preceding works, seem rather conservative. We see this in the opening pair of vocal phrases and the piano's echo of that second phrase (see Ex. 4.1).

Both the first vocal phrase (a, mm. 1–4) and the second vocal phrase (b, mm. 5–8) last four bars each and end with clear half-cadences in E-flat.[6] Immediately following, in mm. 9–10, the piano restates the accompaniment of the second vocal phrase as a kind of echo (b'), yielding another half-cadence. In the very next passage, Schoenberg states additional, though varied, versions of both a (mm. 10–14) and b (mm. 14–17), yielding two more half-cadences. Thus, in a mere seventeen measures – the first seventeen measures of the song – Schoenberg has no fewer than five prominent half cadences. This profusion of clear cadences stands in sharp contrast to one of the most characteristic features of the compositional language of the songs of 1899 and of *Verklärte Nacht*.

Example 4.1

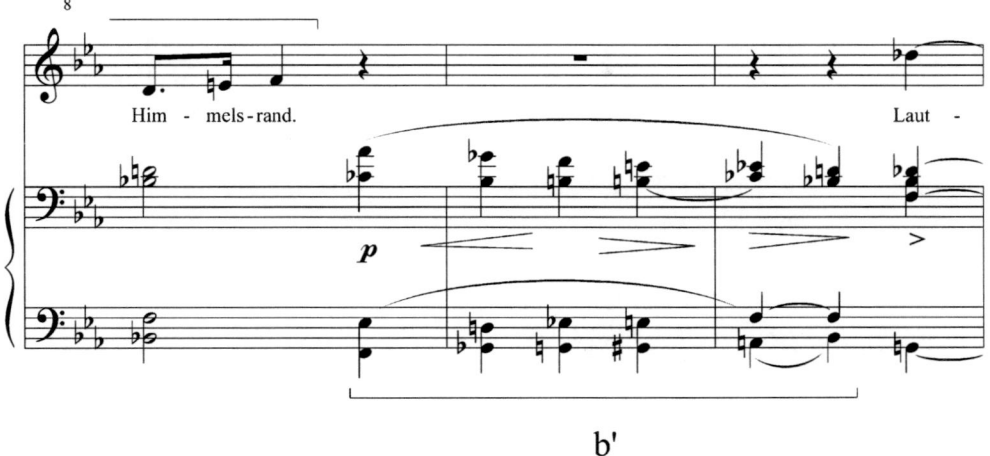

b'

It is not just the sheer number of cadences that is so surprising; it is their character as well. The cadences of the opening section of the first song are prepared by harmonic progressions that are considerably more traditional than was typical of Schoenberg's previous compositions. The first cadence is prepared by a Neapolitan sixth (enharmonically spelled), which leads to a cadential 6/4 and which, in turn, proceeds on to the dominant triad at the cadence. Correspondingly, the second vocal phrase (and therefore, the echo in the piano as well) moves from another Neapolitan sixth, through a French sixth (in the 6/5 inversion) and then finally on to the dominant. So too – again in sharp contrast with its predecessors – the chordal vocabulary of this song consists predominantly of triads, not seventh or ninth chords. As this song progresses, we find that this opening section is in no way exceptional. In contrast to the preceding compositions, triads are quite common and Schoenberg does not allow any extended stretch of music to pass without some kind of clearly articulated cadence.

Although the harmonic structure of the opening of this song is considerably less radical than was the norm in his preceding works, Schoenberg did not turn his back completely on progressive harmonic language. For example, the phrase (and thus the *Gurrelieder*-cycle as a whole) does not begin with a tonic triad or with any other diatonic chord from E-flat. Instead the opening sonority of the composition is a half-diminished seventh chord built on G, a chord that has no diatonic function in the key of E-flat.[7] Furthermore, in m. 2, Schoenberg proceeds on to an augmented triad built over A-flat, again, a chord without a diatonic function in E-flat. If one were to be presented with these two chords and only these two chords (the first two chords of the composition), there would be nothing that would suggest that the key center will be E-flat major. As a result of this chord choice, there is a quick circulation through the total chromatic: all twelve tones appear in the first phrase. Moreover, although triads do predominate, some more radical harmonies do appear. For example the last beat of m. 6 is the chord G E-flat B F, which might be regarded as a dominant seventh with raised fifth.[8] Finally, even though most of the cadences are considerably more traditional than those we encountered in previous works, some less than traditional harmonic progressions do occur at some cadences. For example, in mm. 68–9, Schoenberg prepares the E-flat triad (with added sixth) with a C-flat major triad (built on the minor sixth degree of the E-flat scale).[9]

Nevertheless, taken as a whole, the character of the pitch language of the opening section is decidedly more conservative than in the works of 1899. And the first section of the song is not an exception: if anything, the next major section of the song, mm. 18–31, is even more conservative. As in the first section of the song, here too there are clearly outlined cadences (mm. 23–4 and 31). So too, in both of the two phrases in this section the bass outlines a completely traditional harmonic skeleton, starting on the tonic and ending on the dominant. The solid foundation of the bass line is complemented by the persistent upper register octave pedal on the tonic that occurs on the second beat of each measure. This pedal lasts through most of the phrase, breaking away only at the move to the dominant at the phrase-ending half cadence.

The diatonic bass line, the upper register tonic pedal, the closing cadence, and the clear harmonic progression work together to produce an absolutely solid grounding in the key of E-flat. To be sure, as in the first section of the song, there are some slightly more progressive features: Schoenberg counterbalances the plainly diatonic tendencies of the second section with some mild chromaticism, mostly fairly straightforward chromatic substitution chords. In m. 20, instead of a simple, diatonic IV^7, Schoenberg borrows C-flat from the parallel minor. So too, the chord that connects the IV^7 with the II^7 in m. 22 is a half-diminished seventh chord (in 4/2 position) whose root is the raised fourth degree of the scale.

Another modestly progressive feature (one that will take on particular significance when Schoenberg transformed the *Gurrelieder*-cycle into the *Gurrelieder* cantata) is the character of the harmonic progressions in mm. 17–18 and mm. 23–4 (see Ex. 4.2).

Although there had been a profusion of clear cadences in the first seventeen measures, all of them had been half cadences. The tonic chord itself did not appear, not even within the body of the phrases. The harmonic progression of Ex. 4.2 is a particularly significant structural point, because it gives us the first clear suggestion of the tonic triad. Yet when

Example 4.2

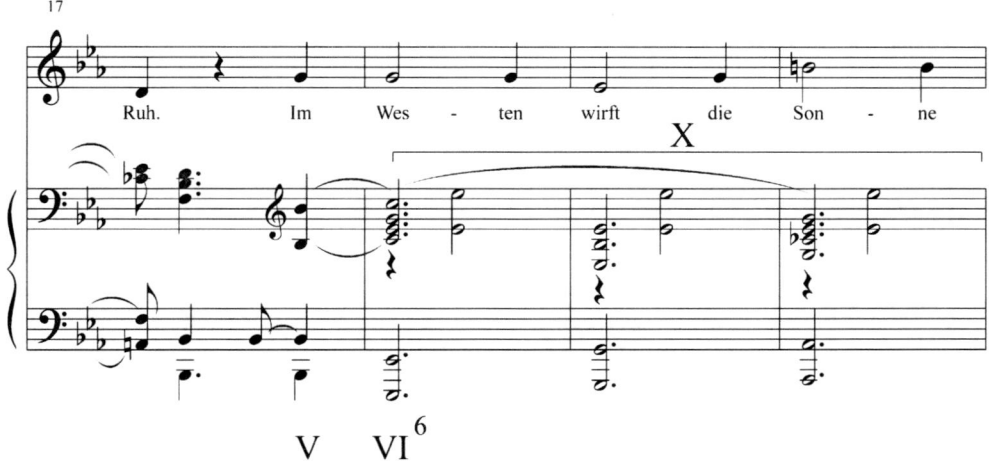

it finally arrives, it is not an E-flat major triad; instead, it is a substitute chord, VI^6.

Given that the C drops out in the next measure, all of our instincts are to dismiss C as a mere non-chord tone and to think of the chord simply as an E-flat major triad and not as a VI^6. Nevertheless, much like the cadence at m. 105 in *Verklärte Nacht* (see Ex. 3.3, previous chapter) Schoenberg has compromised the expected chord. This progression shows that even though the overall tenor of this song is significantly more conservative than its predecessors, there are still some glimmers of Schoenberg's interest in non-traditional harmonic features.

Because of the reiterative formal structure of the song (A B A' B' C B"), the character of the pitch language in the first two sections is not an exception, it is the norm.[10] Taken as a whole, therefore, the pitch language in the first song of the *Gurrelieder*-cycle is something of a surprise: in contrast to the immediately preceding works, Schoenberg has written a work that is significantly less radical.

The relatively conservative character of the pitch language of the first song might have been prompted, at least in part, by the imagery of its poem. As a general rule, in his early songs and programmatic compositions, Schoenberg tended to equate more peaceful poetic texts with clear tonal definition, diatonicism, and a triadic chordal vocabulary. By corollary, poems of a more unsettling character called forth tonal ambiguity, chromaticism, and a more dissonant chordal vocabulary. This tendency is clearly evident in the *Gurrelieder*-cycle: Waldemar's next poem (the third song of the cycle, "Ross! Mein Ross!") is anything but serene. Correspondingly, its pitch language is considerably less traditional than that of the first song.

Having paused to contemplate the peacefulness of the world about him at dusk in the first song, Waldemar now realizes that darkness is fast approaching, and that he and his horse are still quite some distance from Gurre castle ("bist noch in des Waldes Mitten"). Disturbed at the prospect of not reaching the castle or Tove that day, Waldemar spurs his horse forward ("Ross! Mein Ross! Was schleichst du so träg!"). Although the horse is galloping at a good pace ("es flieht der Weg hurtig unter der Hufe Tritten"), Waldemar is not satisfied, demanding that the horse go even faster ("Aber noch stärker mußt du eilen"). Thus, the first part of the poem depicts the almost desperate urgency with which Waldemar strives to outrace the quickly lengthening shadows and reach Gurre castle and Tove before dark.

Schoenberg matches his pitch language to this less-than-peaceful text. Gone are the recurring cadences, the traditional preparations of the dominant, the extended emphasis on a tonic pedal, and the many other tonic-defining features we observed in the first song. Instead, precisely like those sections of *Verklärte Nacht* that depicted the couple's conflict or unhappiness, so too in this song Schoenberg captures Waldemar's tension and urgency by the intense chromaticism within and between the phrases, by the avoidance of cadences, and by the lack of clearly defined tonal centers. Consider in this regard, the opening of the song (Ex. 4.3).

The song begins with a two-measure piano introduction whose second measure is a repetition of the first. Like other passages we have seen in Schoenberg's early works, the identity of the passage's tonal center is, at best, ambiguous. In familiar Schoenbergian style, the movement of the different voices yields a quick succession of different harmonies (a first-inversion dominant seventh on A, a first-inversion C-sharp minor triad, and so forth), without any of them establishing themselves as referential. These ambiguities are only intensified in the third measure where Schoenberg presents one of his favorite sonorities from this period: a first inversion half-diminished seventh chord, whose root is D-sharp. In more traditional contexts, a half-diminished seventh chord often functions as a substitute for the dominant. Since the eventual tonic of the song is E, the use of a D-sharp half-diminished seventh might lead one to wonder whether Schoenberg is about to banish the ambiguity of the first two measures and settle on E as a referential tonic. That is not what happens: in m. 4, Schoenberg rushes from a first-inversion F-sharp minor seventh chord on the first beat,[11] to a dominant seventh chord on D-sharp in the

Example 4.3

first half of the second beat, through a first inversion G-flat major triad, before concluding with a third inversion, dominant seventh chord on C.[12] Although Schoenberg has not used a particularly radical selection of chords in these measures (mainly dominant sevenths, half-diminished sevenths, and the like), their content and ordering are such that no tonal center is allowed to come to the fore. Schoenberg accomplishes this by means familiar to us from previous works: juxtaposing chords that do not belong to the same diatonic collection and by actively thwarting, or simply failing to follow up on, any key implications that are suggested. Thus, the first phrase concludes without ever having established a tonal center.

Schoenberg compounds the tonal uncertainty in the following passage, mm. 5–12. In mm. 5–7 he states a varied repetition of mm. 1–3 in transposition down a whole step. Schoenberg then follows this with a pair of measures, mm. 8–9, in which he presents varied versions of m. 3, outlining a D major triad in m. 8 and a half-diminished seventh chord on G-sharp (or dominant ninth chord on E) in m. 9. So too, although straightforward triads and dominant seventh chords are the chords of choice for the next passage (mm. 10–12), their succession (m. 11 is a transposition up a semitone of m. 10) is such that the impression emerges that the passage might settle on C-sharp as a tonal center and finally provide us with the tonal center we have been lacking. Nearly as quickly Schoenberg slips away, making it apparent that even this possible key center is not strongly enough established to take hold. The avoidance of a tonal center, the complex chromaticism, the truncated repetition of the first phrase and then the successive, altered transpositions of the third measure are in keeping with some of the more progressive tendencies in the pitch language of Schoenberg's early music.

As a result of these procedures no identifiable tonal center emerges in the first twelve measures of the song; however, this is not intended to be the permanent condition. Within three more measures, a tonic (E major) is firmly established.[13] How and why Schoenberg finally arrived on this tonal center merits careful attention.

The "how" is relatively simple and surprisingly traditional: in m. 14 Schoenberg settles on a root position dominant seventh chord of E major and then resolves immediately to a root position E major triad. Finally – after fourteen measures of instability – a clear tonal center has emerged and has been given at least some cadential and temporal emphasis.

The "why" seems equally clear: Schoenberg settled on a tonal center because of the nature of the poetic text, which changes its tone at precisely this point. True to his normal text-setting practice, the tonal instability of the opening of the song was motivated by the need to describe Waldemar's agitation and his fear that he would not reach Gurre castle by dark. The text associated with the arrival of the tonal center on E reflects a different vision:

Nun weicht der Wald, schon seh' ich dort die Burg die Tove mir umschließt,
indes im Rücken uns der Forst zu finstrem Wall zusammenfließt;
Now the forest is giving way; already I see over there the castle which holds Tove
While behind us the forest is flowing together into a dark wall.

As a result of his urgent importuning, Waldemar's horse has sped along at a fast pace, and they rapidly covered the ground that had separated them from Gurre castle. Now, finally, the forest has begun to thin out and the castle has come into view. As this is where the poem first specifically alludes to Waldemar's goal, Schoenberg makes this the first place in the song where a tonal center is established, and, as will eventually become clear, it is the tonal center with which the song shall conclude. This is entirely in keeping with what we have seen to be an essential textual-compositional strategy in

Schoenberg's early works: when the text (or program) alludes to conflicts, fear, unhappiness, or tension, Schoenberg sets this with tonally ambiguous or unstable passages; when a text alludes to happiness, joy, satisfaction, and resolution of conflict, Schoenberg sets this with tonally stable or plainly diatonic passages, often supported by clear (and traditional) cadences.

Although the arrival in E major in m. 15 seems solid at first, it quickly becomes apparent that it is not to be retained for long. After only a little more than four measures in this key a deceptive cadence (m. 19) prompts a quick return to the original tempo and motivic material of the song. Consequently, even though the E major triad returns one more time at the cadence point in m. 23, it has by then lost its tonic status and appears instead to be functioning as the dominant of A major in a half-cadence.

Once again it is the text that gives us clues as to the motivations for this quick deflection away from E major. Although Waldemar has caught sight of his goal – Gurre castle – he has not yet arrived there. He is still in the forest, and it is by no means certain that he can get to the castle before dark. Seeing this, he spurs his horse on to still greater efforts ("aber noch wilder jage du zu!") and this is reflected by a return to the tonally and rhythmically unstable material from the opening of the song (cf. mm. 20–2 and mm. 3 and 7–8). With his goal almost in reach but still needing an extraordinary effort to achieve it, Waldemar points to the quickly lengthening shadows and makes a series of vows:

Des Waldes Schatten dehnen	The forest shadows lengthen
über Flur sich weit und Moor!	across field and moor!
Eh' sie Gurres Grund erreichen,	Before they reach Gurre's ground
muß ich steh'n vor Toves Tor.	I must stand at Tove's door.
Eh' der Laut der jetzo klinget,	Before that sound which now rings out,
ruht, um nimmermehr zu tönen,	stops, never to sound again,
muß dein flinker Hufschlag, Renner,	your quick hoofbeat, Racer,
über Gurres Brücke dröhnen;	must clatter over Gurre's bridge.
eh' das welke Blatt, dort schwebt es,	Before the withered leaf, there it hovers,
mag herab zum Bache fallen,	might fall down into the stream,
muß in Gurres Hof dein Wiehern	your neighing must echo
fröhlich widerhallen.	joyfully in Gurre's courtyard.

The text divides logically into three four-line segments, each of which is centered on the word "ehe" (before): "Before they reach Gurre", "Before that sound ... ceases", "Before that withered leaf ... falls". Schoenberg divides the music for this section of the poem into three corresponding sections. For our purposes, it is the harmonic structure that is the most critical: throughout this part of the song the music moves quickly and restlessly from the suggestion of one key area to another, without ever firmly establishing any of them. The first section (mm. 24–30) suggests A major at its beginning, but quickly moves away, ending on the dominant seventh of E-flat. The next section (mm. 31–7) is an almost literal transposition of mm. 24–30, up a whole step, thereby giving glancing emphasis to B major at its beginning while ending on the dominant of F. The third section (mm. 38–45) is not a transposition of the two preceding sections, but it concentrates on some of the same motivic material. Tonally it too is highly unstable, suggesting B-flat minor briefly at its beginning but ending on the dominant of C in the middle of m. 45.

Therefore, this section of three phrases (mm. 24–45) has a dramatically unstable effect. The triads at the beginnings of phrases and the dominant seventh chords at the ends raise the possibility of establishing a key center, but every suggestion is contradicted. At the beginning of the phrases, Schoenberg accomplishes this by the sharp juxtaposition of triads or seventh chords from different diatonic collections (e.g. in mm. 24–5, A major, G-sharp major, E minor, C-sharp half-diminished, and F-sharp major). At the end of phrases, Schoenberg follows the prolonged dominant seventh chords not with their suggested tonics, but with a wrenching leap to a completely different region (e.g. the prolonged dominant seventh chord in mm. 29–30 is followed not by its suggested tonic, E-flat, but by a B major triad). The highly agitated rhythms and dynamics underscore the tonal instability and help create a highly charged atmosphere. By the end of this section, it might seem as if we are very far away from tonal definition and stability.

The remaining text of the poem suggests that a resolution is imminent. Because of his frantic urgings, the galloping horse has brought them near enough to the castle for Waldemar to know with certainty that he will be united with Tove that evening. Therefore he cries out:

Der Schatten dehnt sich,	The shadows lengthen,
Der Ton verklingt,	the sound fades away,
Nun falle, Blatt, magst untergehn:	fall now, leaf, you may perish:
Volmer hat Tove gesehn!	Volmer has seen Tove!

Schoenberg sets these last three lines first by employing sequential statements of truncated and elaborated versions of the passage that had first appeared in m. 24. This serves to intensify the tonal instability as chords from different diatonic collections follow one another in quick and accelerating succession.

But after a prolonged A-flat triad in mm. 50–1, Schoenberg finally provides the long-awaited resolution. The texture simplifies out to massive block chords which lead to a thunderous authentic cadence in E major on the last syllable of the phrase, "Volmer hat Tove gesehn!"[14] And this cadence is followed by a lengthy piano epilogue (mm. 54–65) that steadfastly reiterates and confirms the dominant-tonic progression in E major.

Finally – but only after much struggle – Waldemar has reached his goal. So too in Schoenberg's song – but only after much struggle – the tonic is finally reached.

The two songs we have examined from the *Gurrelieder*-cycle of 1900 may fairly be said to be representative of the range of harmonic language in the original version of the first nine songs: none is particularly more radical than "Roß, mein Roß!" and none is significantly more conservative than "Nun dämpft die Dämmrung". As such, this raises some puzzling questions about Schoenberg's stylistic evolution. If Schoenberg really was committed to the principle of incremental innovation, then we would have expected the *Gurrelieder*-cycle to be, on balance, slightly more radical than *Verklärte Nacht* and the songs of 1899. We would have expected there to be more experiments with new chords, more attempts to construct unusual cadences, and so forth. But taken as a whole, it appears that the pitch language of the *Gurrelieder*-cycle is noticeably more conservative than that of its predecessors.

Why is that so? Why would Schoenberg abandon, even if temporarily, what we thought was a fundamental principle of his compositional philosophy, the principle of incremental innovation? The answer starts to become clear once we compare the *Gurrelieder*-cycle with the *Gurrelieder* cantata. As we shall see shortly, in the vocal-orchestral version, Schoenberg does return to the path of incremental innovation. And this suggests that Schoenberg had two separate goals in mind for the two different versions of this project.

It is important for us to remember that the Schoenberg of the spring of 1900 was not yet recognized as the tremendously important and significant figure that we know today. Although he was clearly confident about his abilities and certain of his eventual recognition, he was still an unrecognized, struggling, and not very well connected twenty-five-year-old composer. It is entirely in keeping with that reality that he decided to write a song-cycle to submit to a contest. Like many another aspiring young musician today who is looking for a big break, Schoenberg evidently pinned high hopes on achieving recognition by winning a competition. (Since Zemlinsky was to be one of the judges, perhaps Schoenberg had some justification in entertaining hopes that he had a chance of winning.)

If we view the original nine-song piano-vocal cycle as a composition that was intended for a contest, some of its otherwise puzzling conservatism becomes understandable. Not that Schoenberg reverted to pure diatonicism or utterly conventional harmonic progressions, but there are no shockingly new chords in the *Gurrelieder*-cycle, certainly nothing like the prominent fourth-inversion ninth chord in *Verklärte Nacht* that so scandalized the Tonkünstlerverein. Nor are there many other striking harmonic novelties that would have attracted the ire of a conservative judging panel.[15] To the extent that it was possible for him to do so, he tried to write something that might not be too much of an affront to the conservative musicians whom he expected to dominate the jury.

At the same time, he constructed his composition so that when he turned it into a vocal-orchestral work, it would be capable of standing at the forefront of musical modernism. Thus, when he finished the song-cycle too late for the contest (Newlin's version) or realized (or was told) that even a conservative Schoenberg was too radical for the jury (Zemlinsky's version), Schoenberg simply abandoned the song-cycle, and turned his attention instead to the cantata. Once he no longer felt obliged to suppress his naturally innovatory inclinations in order to appeal to a conservative contest jury, Schoenberg could approach his project from a completely different direction: as an avenue for innovation.

To that end, the remaining poems from Jacobsen's *Gurresange* provided Schoenberg with everything he needed. The first nine poems formed a logical unit in that they told a self-contained love story and could easily be set as a cycle accompanied by piano. The remaining poems are another matter entirely. They bring in a host of other characters and unlike the first nine poems, the remaining texts are far more explicitly dramatic in character. Since they included some fairly powerful and striking images (dead warriors rising from their graves to go out on a night ride with Waldemar), Schoenberg clearly saw there were possibilities for correspondingly radical music and he seized the opportunity to transform his (relatively) conservative song-cycle into a far more progressive vocal-orchestral work. Every step he took in making this transformation offers support for this supposition.

The very scope of the forces needed was something of an innovation. Even today, the roster of musicians induces stupefaction: twenty-five winds (8 5 7 5), twenty-five brass (10 7 7 1), four (!) harps, celesta, enormous percussion section (including heavy chains), approximately eighty strings (ten stands each of violins 1 and 2; eight stands each of viola and cello), six soloists (in addition to Waldemar and Tove four more characters: the Wood Dove, a Peasant, a Jester, and a Narrator), three four-part male choirs, and one eight-part mixed choir.

One has to be struck with the very audacity of Schoenberg's vision. At the risk of belaboring a point, Schoenberg in 1900 was largely unknown and untested. As of that date, he had never even completed a work for orchestra, let alone one for an orchestra of this size. Not one of his compositions had yet been published and his catalogue included a grand total of two chamber works (one of which he had already disavowed) and somewhat more than a dozen songs. Yet he was so confident of his abilities, and so committed to the idea of innovation, that once he was freed of the constraints imposed by the contest, he threw caution to the winds and invested copious amounts of time and energy on a composition that lasts two hours and whose logistics are so daunting as to deter any but the most dedicated believers and advocates from even attempting to perform it.

Although there are some external innovations (e.g. the use of a kind of *Sprechstimme* for the narrator), it is in the internal structure of the music that Schoenberg's quest for incremental innovation can be seen most clearly. This is particularly evident in the many and significant additions and changes he made to the first nine songs.

It should be recalled that the piano-vocal song began without any preliminaries with the first measure of Waldemar's song "Nun dämpft die Dämmrung". Moreover, most of the songs concluded with a final cadence and a double bar.[16] This latter feature ensured that even the most tonally adventurous songs (such as "Roß, mein Roß") would ultimately settle upon and confirm a clear triadic center. What Schoenberg did in the revised version was to precede the first song with an extensive orchestral introduction and to replace the final cadences of each song with a transition that leads to the next without break.

This new adventurousness is evident in the newly written introduction. The harmonic effect of the introduction is substantially different (and much more innovative) than that of "Nun dämpft die Dämmrung" in spite of the fact that the motivic ideas of the song and introduction are extremely closely related to one another. (Most of the principal themes of the introduction are directly derived from ideas that appeared in "Nun dämpft die Dämmrung".)

The first (and principal) idea of the introduction is the striking, arpeggiated theme which appears for the first time in the third measure in the flute and piccolo. This idea (x) is restated almost constantly throughout the eighty-four measures of the introduction, both at its original pace and in augmentation (see Ex. 4.4).[17]

This is not a new theme. We should recognize it from "Nun dämpft die Dämmrung": it is a transformed statement of the uppermost line of the piano accompaniment from the beginning of the refrain in that song (Ex. 4.2,

Example 4.4

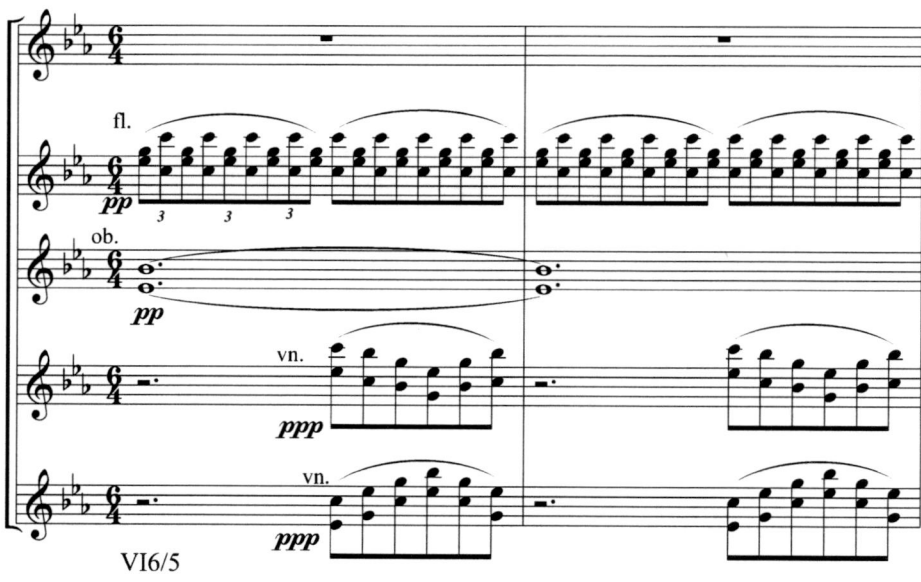

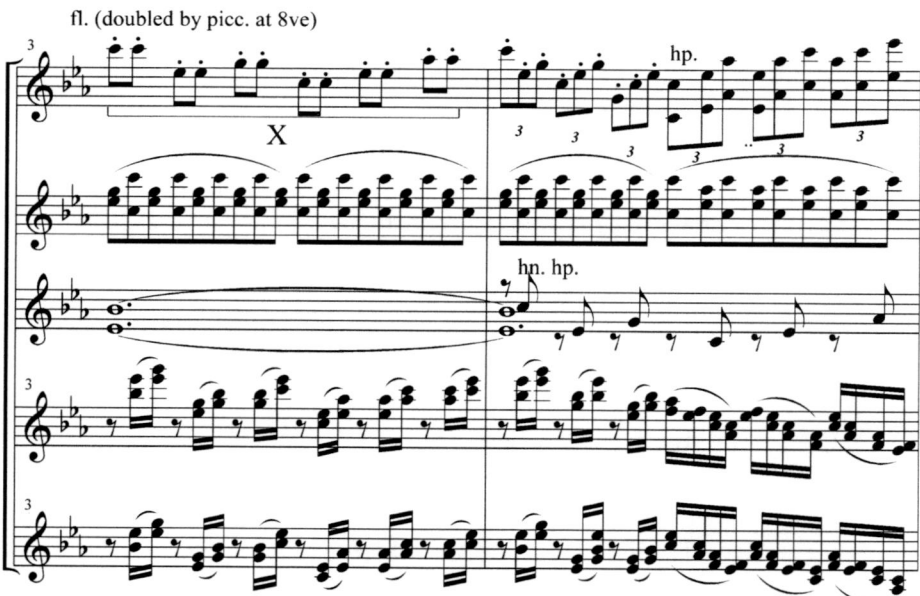

above). The texture, articulation, chordal support, and tempo have all changed, but it is still recognizable as a varied restatement of that idea.

This is not the only idea from the first song that is put to use in the introduction. Many of the remaining prominent motivic ideas from the introduction have clear origins in "Nun dämpft die Dämmrung".[18] For example, the thematic ideas that emerge after m. 27 of the introduction are slightly modified versions of material that appeared in mm. 1–17 of the first song of the *Gurrelieder*-cycle.

Significantly, it is not only motives that are transplanted from the first song. The introduction begins with a recurrent harmonic progression that focuses on, circles around, and stresses, none other than a first-inversion minor seventh chord on C (an E-flat triad with added sixth), a more dissonant and intense version of the sonority that appeared in place of the E-flat tonic triad at the first authentic cadence in the song. This chord is restated numerous times, remaining the central focus through m. 22, before moving to different regions.

Even though so much of the motivic and harmonic material from the introduction comes directly from the first song, the effect of this material is completely transformed in the introduction. The opening song of the piano-accompanied cycle moved quickly through several chromatic chords to a solid half-cadence in E-flat. Therefore, even though the tonic chord itself was not stated for quite some time, its identity was clearly established within a few seconds of the beginning of the song-cycle.

The newly written introduction is significantly different. Instead of a clear harmonic progression that quickly establishes E-flat as the tonic, Schoenberg begins with a far more equivocal progression, one that centers around the $VI^{6/5}$ a chord that is similar to the one that we first encountered in Ex. 4.2, but whose appearance here has been transformed and radicalized.

When the VI^6 chord appeared in the original song, it was only after there had already been five strongly articulated half-cadences in E-flat. Those recurrent half-cadences served to prepare the VI^6 and place it into a clear context where we understand it as a tonic substitute.

In the newly written introduction, the $VI^{6/5}$ chord has no such contextual support or clarification. Instead of being prepared by multiple dominant chords, the $VI^{6/5}$ chord is stated baldly as the first chord of the piece, without any preparation. Furthermore, the dominant chord is completely absent from the opening twenty-two measures, appearing for the first time only in m. 23. Even when the dominant does appear, it does not lead toward the $VI^{6/5}$ chord, but away from it, initiating the move to other regions. Finally, unlike the original song, where the chord was a simple triad in first inversion, the $VI^{6/5}$ is a dissonant chord and no clarifying tonic triad follows.

These are radical and radicalizing steps. They have brought Schoenberg to a point well beyond that which he had been willing to take when *Gurrelieder* was a contest piece destined to be judged by a conservative jury. Here, in the most unambiguous form, we have a dissonance-containing sonority usurping the structural function usually reserved solely for consonant triads.

In Schoenberg's previous works, there were many passages of significant tonal ambiguity, but those were normally preceded and followed by regions of clear tonal definition or by passages where the dissonant sonorities gave way to referential triads. In this orchestral introduction, the opening twenty-two measures are not immediately followed by a clearly defined tonal region. Nor does the dissonant sonority resolve to a pure tonic triad. Instead, Schoenberg quickly moves away from the opening region, without ever having stated the E-flat triad in a clear and unequivocal manner. And he never returns to it anywhere in the introduction. In mm. 36–8 Schoenberg does present some half-cadences in E-flat (using a progression derived from the first song). However, these half-cadences are not followed by an E-flat triad (not even by a VI$^{6/5}$), and immediately following Schoenberg moves decisively away from anything resembling E-flat.

The ending of the introduction also does nothing to clarify its tonal ambiguities. Instead of a clear final cadence, followed by a pause, the introduction leads directly into the first song, without any break at all. Since the first song began with a half-diminished seventh chord on G, Schoenberg makes this chord the final chord of the introduction. This means that the introduction never establishes a clear tonal center, neither at its beginning nor at its end.

The significance of the tonally obscure introduction is important in and of itself, but it is just one of the radicalizing steps that Schoenberg took in the second stage of *Gurrelieder*. In the original song-cycle, most of the songs had ended with clear cadences, followed by a break or a pause. But Schoenberg now excised the cadences, replacing them with written-out transitions. In a completely different composition, one with a more traditional tonal structure, that could have been a trivial difference, but in the context of this specific composition, it is crucial. Nothing could illustrate more plainly how Schoenberg went about transforming his relatively conservative song-cycle into a much more progressive new work, one that was at the forefront of his harmonic and tonal development. By excising the final cadences and writing transitions that connected the formerly distinct songs, Schoenberg went a long way toward blurring whatever tonal definition and clarity existed in the songs. Although some of the songs, like "Nun dämpft die Dämmrung", had numerous clear cadences within the body of the work itself, others did not. Although some songs remained centered around a single key area, others most emphatically did not. By excising their final cadences and creating a continuous flow, Schoenberg removed what, for some songs, was virtually the only unambiguous point of tonal confirmation.

Schoenberg made an equally significant change in the grand plan of the first part of the work. In the song-cycle, Schoenberg began with two songs in E-flat (both solidly confirmed by their final cadences). After moving to other keys in the third through eighth songs, Schoenberg returned to E-flat for the final song ("O wunderliche Tove"). Had Schoenberg limited himself to the original nine-song piano-vocal cycle, the result would have been a somewhat traditionally structured, tonally closed form, beginning and ending in E-flat, with the opening tonic receiving added emphasis by its appearance in both of the first two songs.

In the reconfigured orchestral version, Schoenberg broke away from those traditions. He lessened the emphasis on E-flat at the beginning, both by the tonally ambiguous introduction and by transposing the second song from E-flat to G-flat, thereby reducing the time spent in E-flat at the beginning of the work.

This is matched by what happens at the end of Part I. In the original song-cycle, the ninth song was in E-flat and closed with a definitive final cadence in that key, thereby closing out the cycle with the same key with which it had begun. In the new vocal-orchestral version, Schoenberg did not conclude with a clear cadence in E-flat at the end of the ninth song. Instead, the final cadence is excised and there is an extended orchestral interlude that draws upon themes from the first nine songs and leads to a newly written song, "Stimme der Waldtaube", which is in B-flat minor, not E-flat major. Thus, in its overall tonal plan, and in deliberate contrast to the piano-vocal cycle, Schoenberg carefully structured the revised version of the first section of *Gurrelieder* so that it is not framed by a common referential tonal center.

Taken as a whole, the evidence is unequivocal: in transforming the nine-song *Gurrelieder*-cycle into the opening section of the *Gurrelieder* cantata, Schoenberg deliberately and systematically radicalized the work. Freed from the practical constraints of trying to write a conservative contest composition, Schoenberg maneuvered himself back toward the forefront of musical modernism.

That Schoenberg was eager to return to his more characteristic role as a musical radical can also be seen in the character and content of Parts II and III, both of which were written after Schoenberg had decided to recast the piece. From the overall key plan on the largest scale, down to many details of local harmonic choices, the later parts of *Gurrelieder* show Schoenberg renewing his commitment to the principle of incremental innovation.

On the largest level, this is reflected by the key plan. Like the transformed version of the first part (but unlike the original *Gurrelieder*-cycle), the second and third parts are not framed by a single tonal center. Instead,

Part II (which is but a single song) is in B-flat minor (a continuation of the tonality of the end of Part I), while Part III begins in E-flat minor and ends in C major. In and of itself, a "progressive" tonal plan of this sort is not a particularly innovatory step: there are many examples in previous works by previous composers. But it is not merely the absence of an overall tonic that makes the tonal structure of Part III so adventurous. Rather, since the individual songs are not distinct entities marked off by tonic-defining cadences and separated by silence, the overall effect is to avoid clear tonic definition and confirmation for extraordinarily extended periods of time. At certain strategic locations, stretches of clear tonal stability or definition do occur (usually prompted by the text). But those moments of tonal stability are usually compromised or quickly contradicted by the continuation which moves on to other tonal regions without permitting a clear cadential close in the prior region. Furthermore, there are many prominent regions that lack any meaningful referential center.[19] Only toward the end of Part III does the composition come to rest upon and stress a single tonal region, supporting it with a significant cadence.

Several of the individual songs of Part III provide ample evidence of Schoenberg's renewed search for innovation. Waldemar's song, "Mit Toves Stimme" (Part III, mm. 312–54), embodies many of the progressive elements of Schoenberg's compositional thought that had been relatively subdued in the piano-vocal cycle.

In this song, Waldemar descends into despair over his separation from Tove. On the one hand, he perceives traces of Tove's presence all around him, embodied in nature: in the rustling noises of the forest ("Mit Toves Stimme flüstert der Wald"), in the reflections off the lake at Gurre castle ("mit Toves Augen schaut der See"), in the twinkling of the stars ("mit Toves Lächeln leuchten die Sterne"), and in the billowing clouds ("die Wolke schwillt wie des Busens Schnee"). On the other hand, Waldemar is heartbroken because he cannot get any closer to Tove than these inchoate manifestations of her essence. The song ends, not with any reuniting of their spirits, but with Waldemar plaintively and forlornly crying out for his beloved ("Das tote Herz, es schwillt, es dehnt sich, Tove, Tove, Waldemar sehnt sich nach dir!").

What is particularly striking about Schoenberg's setting of this poem is the extended tonal ambiguity of the song. Even by its end it is unclear what the principal, referential tonic was supposed to have been, or if it is even appropriate to suggest that there is a single, referential tonic for the song as a whole.

Based on the key signature (two flats) and the ending of the previous section (the ride of Waldemar's men, "Gegrüßt, o König"), we might have

Example 4.5

been inclined to expect G minor as the tonic, particularly since the last four measures of the transition from the previous song outlined an extended dominant seventh of G (see Ex. 4.5).

The opening phrase of "Mit Toves Stimme" is tantalizingly ambiguous in its tonal orientation. Instead of following up on and confirming the implications of the transition's closing dominant from G minor, the opening sonority of this song suggests instead the relative major, B-flat major. But no sooner have we adjusted our expectations to understand the passage as suggesting B-flat major than Schoenberg shifts the ground from under our feet: the phrase lurches from suggestions of G minor (the F natural is immediately inflected into an F-sharp) back to B-flat (by virtue of the dominant seventh on the downbeat of m. 314) and back again to G minor by means of the half-cadence that closes the phrase.

The force of the half-cadence in m. 315 might seem to have resolved the ambiguities and to have settled the matter in favor of G minor. And when the next phrase begins, its opening is transformed to conform to this apparent new bias in favor of G minor: Waldemar's first note is F-sharp instead of the F-natural in the corresponding spot in m. 312. So too, the opening B-flat major triad is absent and Schoenberg begins immediately on the augmented triad. Since this phrase is otherwise a literal repetition of the first phrase, it too comes to rest firmly on a half-cadence in G minor. Thus, unlike the first phrase, the second phrase has few ambiguities, and appears instead to confirm the centrality and stability of G minor.

G minor's victory is short-lived (see Ex. 4.6). Although the following phrase almost ends with an authentic cadence in G minor, that is the last point in the song where there is any hint of this key. In effect, as soon as

Example 4.6

G minor has triumphed over the opposition, it vanishes, never to return. It is quickly supplanted by a fairly strong cadential emphasis on the very triad with which it had been contending: Schoenberg arrives on a clear statement of B-flat major in m. 325 and repeats it in the parallel minor in the following measure.

The issue is not settled finally in favor of B-flat either. Just as quickly as he entered it, Schoenberg leaves B-flat, moving restlessly through suggestions of a number of different keys. Like G minor, B-flat has completed its role in this song and disappears for good: other than a fleeting emphasis on its dominant ninth in mm. 350–1, B-flat never returns as a key center.

"Roß, mein Roß!" also began with substantial tonal ambiguity, yet that song eventually settled down and established a clear referential key center. That does not happen here: unlike the original piano-vocal version of "Roß, mein Roß!" no lasting referential tonic is allowed to come to the fore in "Mit Toves Stimme", even at the end of the song. In "Roß, mein Roß!" Schoenberg first suggested that E major would be the tonic as early as mm. 14–15 and finally settled on it for good at the end of the song, confirming it with a series of powerful cadences. In "Mit Toves Stimme", Schoenberg moves fitfully from the suggestion of one key to another, never giving extended emphasis to any of them. At the end of the main body of this song, he does finally settle on the dominant of E-flat, and this is prolonged for a relatively long stretch of time. But unlike the piano-vocal version of "Roß, mein Roß!" of 1900 (though, of course, exactly like the orchestral-vocal version of 1901), this suggestion is never fully realized by means of the arrival of a root position E-flat triad. Instead, in m. 363, Schoenberg breaks away from the unrealized half-cadence in E-flat and moves on to the transition to the next song. Here too, no single key is permitted to come to the fore, and the transition ends, not with a half-cadence or with a dominant seventh chord, but with a tonally ambiguous tritone (m. 371 see Ex. 4.7). In short, there is ample evidence to support the notion that when Schoenberg returned to *Gurrelieder* after having abandoned the piano-accompanied song-cycle, he loosened the restraints and resumed his efforts to transform the musical language he had inherited.

Although the composition of the short score of *Gurrelieder* was essentially completed in 1901, Schoenberg did not finish the orchestration for another decade. Distracted as he was by other obligations and other compositions, it became difficult for him to return to this mammoth project. With each passing year, the pitch language of *Gurrelieder* became further and further removed from his current style. As such, *Gurrelieder* (like many of Schoenberg's larger works) teetered precariously at the edge of incompletion.

Example 4.7

When it was finally premiered (in 1913, to a tumultuous ovation of a sort that he would never again experience) Schoenberg had long ago left the sound and aesthetic of this work far behind. As such, *Gurrelieder* appeared to many (both Schoenberg's critics and his supporters) as a throwback to a distant past. And this has helped determine how *Gurrelieder* has been regarded ever since: as emblematic of the end of an era. This has obscured a far more complicated reality: in actuality *Gurrelieder* was both a modestly conservative song-cycle and a highly progressive cantata.

5 Programmatic music and its implications: *Pelleas und Melisande*, Op. 5, 1902–3

> ... the earlier symphonic poem, *Pelleas und Melisande* suggests a more rapid advance in the direction of extended tonality.[1]

Schoenberg began work on his next major composition, *Pelleas und Melisande*, Op. 5, in the summer of 1902, finishing it by February of the following year.[2] In many important respects this was a crucial, watershed work: it was Schoenberg's first completed orchestral composition;[3] it was – by far – his longest and most ambitious instrumental work to date; its pitch language and harmonic vocabulary were highly innovative; it confirmed the central importance of programmatic ideas in his musical thought.[4]

Curiously, *Pelleas und Melisande* has been one of the least studied and least discussed of all of Schoenberg's major works. Some writers and critics have been less than enthusiastic about the artistic success of this composition, and perhaps this is the reason why it has received less attention than works of comparable importance. However, the relative neglect of *Pelleas und Melisande* may not be due to an objective estimation of its supposed artistic shortcomings. Its comparative obscurity is probably attributable more to the major change in musical taste and fashion that followed closely on its completion. Just about the time Schoenberg completed *Pelleas und Melisande*, programmatic music began a precipitous fall from favor in artistic and academic circles, both in Vienna and elsewhere. Increasingly, programmatic music was seen to be aesthetically and intellectually inferior to absolute music. The victory of absolute music has been so total that for much of the twentieth century it was difficult for anyone to take programmatic compositions seriously. This, more than anything else, may be the reason why *Pelleas und Melisande* has been shunted to the sidelines. Overcoming these powerful prejudices is thus a prerequisite for a proper understanding, not only of this work as an independent aesthetic object, but also of central aspects of Schoenberg's compositional language at a crucial stage in his stylistic development.

The circumstances surrounding the origins of *Pelleas und Melisande* reflect Schoenberg's difficult, and frequently embittering, struggle for artistic recognition and financial security. At the same time, this period also marks Schoenberg's first real success in attracting powerful supporters.

In 1901 Schoenberg had married Mathilde Zemlinsky, the sister of his friend and onetime teacher. By the middle of 1901, she was pregnant with their first child (Trudi, born 8 January 1902). Although he was already in his late twenties, Schoenberg had not yet been successful in obtaining the kind of professional position that would allow him to support a family. Up to this point, his principal sources of income seem to have been from the orchestration of other composers' operettas and from serving as a copyist.[5] This suggests that it was probably mostly financial exigency that motivated Schoenberg to take a position as the conductor and director of music of the newly opened Überbrettl literary café in Berlin (the "Bunte Theater"), beginning in December 1901.[6] Although the literary cafe was coming into prominence as a venue for relatively artistic popular endeavors, and although Schoenberg did try his hand at writing a few cabaret compositions (the so-called "Brettellieder"), this position cannot have been the fulfillment of his professional goals.[7] In any event, the seriousness of Schoenberg's interest in this type of employment became a moot point since the Überbrettl café promptly ran into financial difficulties. Because of this, his six-month contract was not renewed and his brief career as a cabaret musician came to an abrupt end. Thus, by July 1902, Schoenberg was living in a city where he was even more unknown than he was in Vienna and was without a reliable source of income.

It was just shortly before the termination of his work at the Bunte Theater that Schoenberg met Richard Strauss.[8] Ten years Schoenberg's senior and already well established in the musical world, Strauss was in a position to help Schoenberg, both financially and artistically. After Schoenberg showed Strauss copies of *Verklärte Nacht* and the as yet unfinished *Gurrelieder*, Strauss recognized he was dealing with a composer of immense talent and potential. To his credit, he seems to have gone out of his way to help the younger, and quite penurious, composer.[9] He directed whatever work he could to Schoenberg, including the copying of parts for one of his own compositions.[10] He was also instrumental in obtaining two scholarships for Schoenberg from the Liszt Foundation.[11] If that were not enough, he interceded on Schoenberg's behalf to try to help him obtain a teaching position at the Stern Conservatory.[12]

In one of their meetings in 1902, Strauss apparently suggested to Schoenberg that Maurice Maeterlinck's recently published play, *Pelléas et Mélisande* (1893), would be an attractive subject for a musical composition.[13] At first, Schoenberg considered turning the play into an opera but his plan for an opera seems to have gotten no further than a brief synopsis of the themes planned for an orchestral introduction. Instead, he decided to turn Maeterlinck's play into a symphonic poem. Many years later, Schoenberg stated that he regretted not having set Maeterlinck's play as an opera, but he denied that the reason he abandoned the operatic project was that he became aware of Debussy's opera, which had received its premiere in Paris on 30 April 1902. Yet Schoenberg never gave any other explanation for why it was that he did not set Maeterlinck's play as an opera. The lack of direct documentary evidence does not allow any firm conclusions here, but we can infer what Schoenberg's motivations might have been from related biographical and documentary facts.

On 18 March 1902, approximately a month before his first encounter with Strauss, Schoenberg had his most significant professional accomplishment to date. Almost two and a half years after it had been completed, *Verklärte Nacht* was finally premiered in Vienna. This was also a breakthrough for Schoenberg because it was performed by a very prestigious ensemble: the Rosé Quartet (augmented with two players from the Vienna Philharmonic). Given the Rosé Quartet's renown, it is not surprising that the concert attracted considerable attention: there were thirteen extended reviews of the concert in Vienna's newspapers and in all of those reviews Schoenberg's work was the centerpiece of the discussion.

The publicity occasioned by the performance of *Verklärte Nacht* has to have made Schoenberg realize just how thin his catalogue was in the spring of 1902. If anyone had been impressed by *Verklärte Nacht* and would have asked Schoenberg if he had any other works that they might consider for performance, all he could supply was a few songs.

It was precisely at this time that Schoenberg was introduced to Strauss who, in addition to being a composer, was also a successful and active conductor. Only a few years earlier (1898) Strauss had been appointed conductor of the Berlin Court Opera. He also regularly conducted orchestral concerts in Berlin and throughout Europe.

Although Schoenberg may have started out with the idea that writing an opera on Maeterlinck's play would be an attractive idea from a purely artistic perspective, he must have had second thoughts when he considered this in the light of his tenuous professional situation. To work on an opera would take at least a year or more of his time (this with *Gurrelieder* still sitting unfinished on his desk) and Schoenberg must have realized the immense practical obstacles that he would face in trying to arrange a performance of a new opera once it was finished. On the other hand, if he were to write a purely orchestral composition, in relatively short order he could add to his catalogue a work that would be more likely to find a performance.[14]

It is obvious not only that Schoenberg was thinking along these lines, but also that he was hoping that his new work would be performed by Strauss himself. This can be inferred from a letter Strauss wrote to Schoenberg on 19 July 1902, only a few weeks after Schoenberg had begun work on the symphonic poem. Strauss wrote: "Your score of *Pelléas and Mélisande*, which I look forward to with interest, I would have to receive at the latest by the beginning of September in Berlin, if it will be possible for me to consider it."[15] Clearly Schoenberg had expressed his hopes that Strauss would consider performing his new work on one of the orchestral concerts he was to conduct during the coming season. The evidence of this letter, in conjunction with the details of his biography during this period, and the regret he expressed in 1950 at not having set Maeterlinck's play as an opera, build a plausible circumstantial case that the reason Schoenberg abandoned the idea of an opera was, at least in part, a practical one.

If so, then it must have come as a bitter disappointment to Schoenberg that in his letter Strauss asked for the work so soon ("at the latest by the beginning of September"). Schoenberg had begun composing the symphonic poem only a few weeks before Strauss' letter. It must have been clear to him how unlikely it was that he could complete it in the six more weeks mentioned by Strauss. (He did not finish the orchestration of the score until February 1903, long after the deadline Strauss had set, and Strauss never did conduct *Pelleas und Melisande*.)[16]

In *Pelleas und Melisande*, as in the later layer of *Gurrelieder*, Schoenberg renewed his commitment to the principle of incremental innovation, making this composition the focus of many advances in compositional language. Some of the most obvious innovations of this work are orchestrational. Taking advantage of the powerful situations and images described in Maeterlinck's play, Schoenberg went out of his way to produce sound combinations that were as novel as they were striking. To take but two examples, the scene where Melisande lets her hair down to Pelleas who is standing below her balcony (mm. 244ff) and the scene where Golaud and Pelleas are wandering in the catacombs under the castle (mm. 283ff), are portrayed with inimitable combinations of orchestral color. Schoenberg also seems quite consciously to have looked for novel techniques of producing sound. The most prominent of those was his use of trombone glissandi, the execution of which he described in detail in a note to the score. Whether or not Schoenberg actually can be credited with the invention of this technique (as he himself claimed), its use is tangible evidence of his constant and restless search for innovations in multiple dimensions of the musical fabric.[17]

Although the orchestrational innovations of *Pelleas und Melisande* are important, nowhere is the innovatory character more significant than in the pitch language. The chordal vocabulary, dissonance treatment, and harmonic progressions of *Pelleas und Melisande* all take significant steps forward.

Although *Pelleas und Melisande* is less straightforwardly chordal than most of Schoenberg's previous works, the chord remains a fundamental unit of musical structure and much of the work can be understood in terms of clearly demarcated successions of chords. A comparison of the chords used in this work with those of previous works quickly reveals the extent to which *Pelleas und Melisande* has advanced past the harmonic vocabulary of its predecessors.

Up through *Gurrelieder*, the most common chords Schoenberg used in his compositions were triads and seventh chords, with seventh chords gradually monopolizing more and more of the surface. Characteristically, Schoenberg did not use one chordal type to the exclusion of others. Instead (as we saw in the 1899 songs), his chordal vocabulary is characterized by a profusion of different types.[18]

The chordal vocabulary of *Pelleas und Melisande* does not dramatically alter this picture: sevenths remain the standard chordal unit and a broad variety of different chordal types are used. Triads are mostly limited to cadences, to the more peaceful situations suggested by the program, or to rhythmically subsidiary locations. Ninths are also a component of the harmonic vocabulary, but as before, occur less frequently than seventh chords.

These similarities are tempered by some significant differences. For one thing, the relative proportions of the different chordal types undergo a noticeable shift. Schoenberg tends more and more to favor the use of seventh chords that have augmented or diminished fifths between the root and fifth or between the third and seventh. One of those, the half-diminished seventh chord (mmM), had already been a frequent component of Schoenberg's chordal vocabulary.[19] It remains so, while other, similar, chordal types (MdM, MMd, MMm, mmm) appear more and more frequently. Ninth chords appear more often than previously, and do so in all four inversions (including the fourth inversion) and with multiple alternations of the degrees. Furthermore, more and more often, the ninth is placed in the middle of the fabric, instead of being paired with the seventh and situated in the soprano.

It follows that the relative increase in the use of these chordal types comes with a corresponding decline in the predominance of the remaining seventh chord types and, of course, of triads. This does not mean that the more diatonic or traditionally common chordal types are abruptly abolished; but there is an unmistakable decline in their relative frequency.

At the same time, Schoenberg introduced new chordal types into his vocabulary, and placed some of them in prominent locations where they were guaranteed to attract attention. Some of these are straightforward

Example 5.1

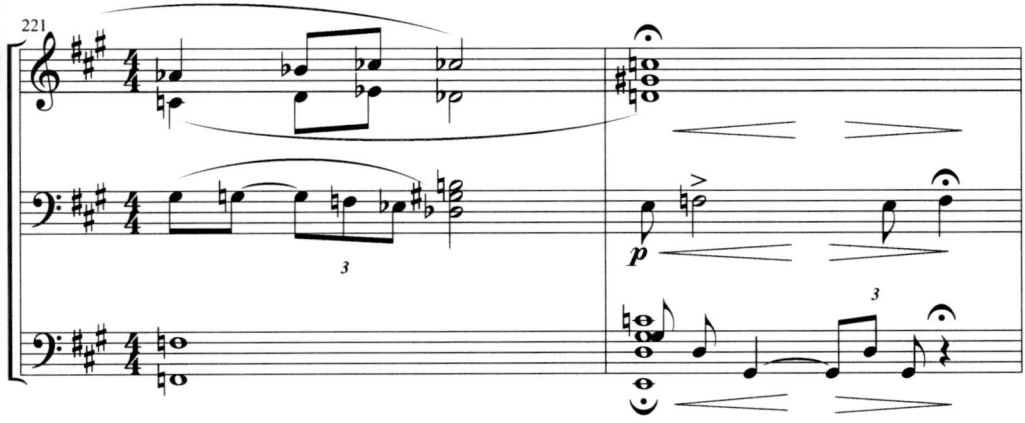

extensions or combinations of prior types. A good example of this is the chord that occurs at the cadence at m. 222 (see Ex. 5.1).

This chord includes five tones: E G-sharp C D and F. It might best be understood as a dominant seventh chord on E with a raised fifth (B-sharp, enharmonically spelled as C) and a minor ninth.[20] Schoenberg has added a minor ninth to an altered dominant seventh chord and has separated the ninth from its traditional pairing with the seventh, placing it in an inner voice within the chord. No single one of these features is novel: dominant seventh chords with raised fifths were well known variants; dominant ninth chords had been in use for more than two centuries; the placement of the ninth in an inner voice was not the most common position, but there are precedents as early as the eighteenth century. By combining all of these features in one chord, Schoenberg has stretched the traditional principles of chord formation to their very limits.

Schoenberg also created other chords that pushed even further past those limits. The most famous of those are the chord of fourths that appears in mm. 85–6, just before the first statement of Pelleas' theme (see Ex. 5.2), and the whole tone hexachord (partitioned by register into two augmented triads) that occurs in mm. 291–2 as part of the depiction of the eerie scene where Pelleas and Golaud wander together in the vaults below the castle (see Ex. 5.3).[21]

Much of the fame of these two chords results from the attention Schoenberg gave them in his *Harmonielehre*.[22] Since they appear so few times in the composition one might be excused for wondering whether they really are that significant, particularly since the discussion in *Harmonielehre* seems motivated more by Schoenberg's desire to demonstrate that he did

Example 5.2

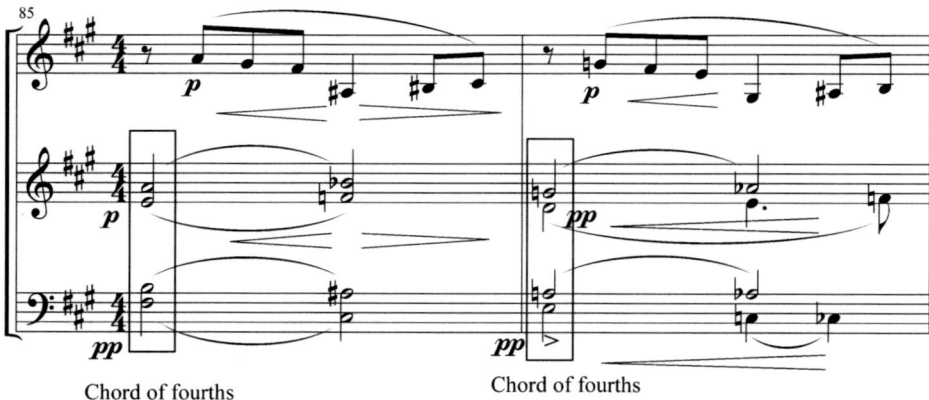

Example 5.3

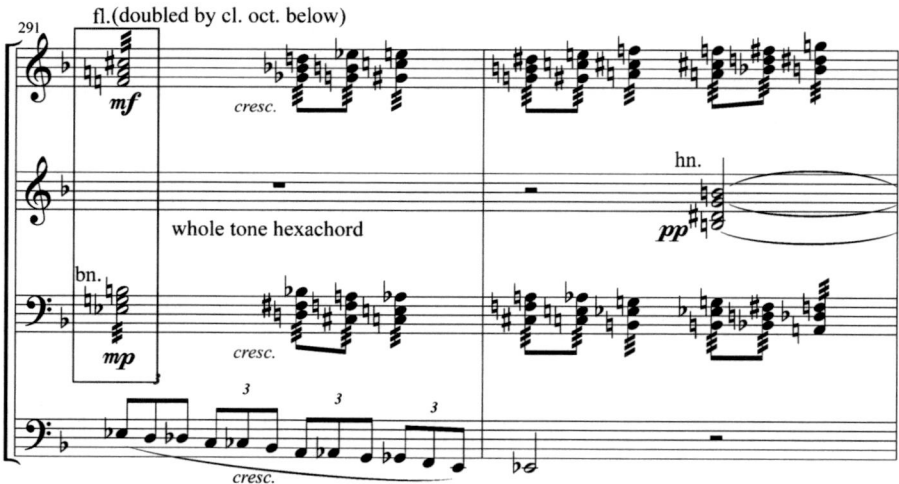

not copy the chords from other composers than to describe their compositional significance within *Pelleas und Melisande*.[23]

Although these chords only make limited appearances in this work, they are very important as representatives of a general class of new chordal types. It is that general class that begins to take on a significant role, somewhat tentatively in *Pelleas und Melisande*, but increasingly so in the works that followed. It is characteristic of the evolutionary character of Schoenberg's thought that although some chords are "new", they are usually extensions or modifications of traditional ideas of chord formation. The chord of fourths from Ex. 5.2 exemplifies this complicated duality in a number of important ways.

The triad had been the basis of harmonic vocabulary for several hundred years because it is the maximal collection of different pitch classes that can be combined such that every pitch of the sonority can be consonant with every other pitch in the sonority (thereby satisfying the laws of first species counterpoint for every possible combination of voices). With the chord of fourths, the situation would seem to be dramatically different. With one exception, the tones of the four-note fourth chord are not consonant with one another. It would seem as if this sonority is completely incompatible with the notion of chord as preached and practiced for several hundred years: it is not a consonant sonority, not even a consonant sonority with a single added dissonance. It is a dramatically dissonant sonority with multiple dissonance relationships and with no clear indication as to which tone needs to resolve.

Nevertheless, this chord can be understood as an extension of prior concepts of chord formation. There are at least two ways in which this is so.

The first is simply that there were historical precedents: the chord of fourths had already appeared in numerous guises in prior music.[24] Chief among those was the situation in which the third of the dominant seventh chord was delayed by a suspension: the sonority that occurs at the point of the suspension is a chord of fourths (see Ex. 5.4).

Given traditional theoretical perspectives, the four tones of that chord would not be considered of equal standing: the suspension would clearly be understood as subsidiary to the remaining notes of the sonority. For prior generations of composers (and most theorists), the "chord of fourths" was not considered an entity unto itself.

It appears to be a fundamental characteristic of Schoenberg's compositional thought that he took a completely different stance: "*There are no non-harmonic tones, for harmony means tones sounding together.*" Given this attitude, Schoenberg could employ chords of fourths and firmly believe that he was building on tradition, not breaking with it.

Example 5.4

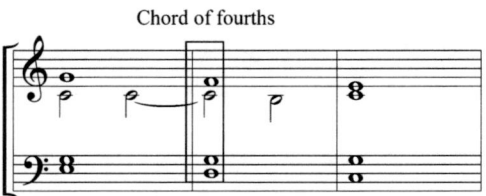

Chord of fourths

A second way in which the chord of fourths can be understood as a modification of prior ideas is through a kind of analogy. In the nineteenth century, new chords were sometimes derived by a process in which composers took chords that were accepted and understood in one guise, and, by analogy, tried them out in a related guise. Some good examples of this are the "root position Neapolitan sixth chord", the "diminished third chord", and the fourth-inversion ninth chord which were derived by analogy from the Neapolitan sixth, augmented sixth, and root position ninth chords respectively. In this spirit, the chord of fourths might be understood as an analogy to the chord of thirds. Just as a traditional seventh chord could be understood to be derived from the repeated superposition of diatonic thirds over a root ("tertian" harmony), so too, a chord of fourths might be seen as an analogy that substitutes another diatonic interval (perfect fourths) for the diatonic thirds ("quartal" harmony).[25]

For Schoenberg's predecessors, the dissonant character of the fourth itself as well as the multiple dissonances present in a chord formed from fourths would have made it impossible for them to accept quartal harmony as analogous to tertian harmony. Given Schoenberg's notion of chordal dissonance, it was quite possible for him to think in precisely those terms.

The other famous chord of *Pelleas und Melisande* – the whole tone hexachord of Ex. 5.3 – reflects this balance between innovation and tradition. The innovative aspects of this chord are not hard to recognize: a six-tone chord that includes a whole tone collection was hardly standard fare at the turn of the century, at least in German music. If one uses traditional measures, the whole tone hexachord, like the chord of fourths, includes a rather substantial level of dissonance. At the same time, the disposition of the tones of the whole tone hexachord reflects Schoenberg's attempt to ground this new sonority within historical traditions. The tones of the hexachord are not randomly distributed in musical space; rather the hexachord is clearly divided, instrumentally and registrally, into two distinct augmented triads.

The registral division of the whole tone hexachord into two augmented triads is a specific manifestation of an important general principle, one that will be central to the development of Schoenberg's harmonic vocabulary for the next decade: the principle of "localized consonance". At this stage, Schoenberg's new chords cannot be consonant to the point that every element of the chord will be consonant with every other element; only major and minor triads (and then, only in root position and first inversion) can fulfill that requirement, and consonant triads are fast disappearing from his lexicon. But this does not mean that any level or type of dissonance is acceptable within a chord. Instead, Schoenberg tends to construct new

Programmatic music and its implications

sonorities so that traditional sonorities (triads, seventh chords) are localized within a segment or a portion of the harmony.[26] The division of the whole tone hexachord into two augmented triads is a prototypical example of this kind of localized consonance.[27]

The idea of localized consonance as a criterion for chord formation is a logical – almost predictable – step given Schoenberg's treatment of seventh chords in the compositions leading up to this point. Within the seventh chord there was also a kind of localized consonance: the root together with the third and fifth and the seventh together with the third and fifth. It was but a small step to chords like the triadically partitioned whole tone hexachord in *Pelleas und Melisande*.

Although the chord of fourths and the partitioned whole tone hexachord themselves play only a limited role in this composition, the larger class to which they belong (extensions of the traditional chordal vocabulary) has begun to take on a noticeable role, somewhat tentatively in this work, but increasingly so in the works that follow. By way of illustration of the range of Schoenberg's expanded and expanding harmonic vocabulary, Ex. 5.5 shows three such chords that appear in various locations in the composition and in various contexts, from highly exposed, to unobtrusively woven into the fabric.

The first chord (Ex. 5.5a, m. 273) includes the tones D-flat, F, A-flat, and E-flat, a combination with multiple dissonances.[28] Although it is not a commonly recognized or traditional chordal type, it clearly relies on the principle of localized consonance (the embedded D-flat triad) and could be understood as a first-inversion D-flat ninth chord with an omitted seventh.

At the beginning of the second chord of the example (Ex. 5.5b, m. 322) there is a complicated sonority that includes the tones B E D-sharp F-double sharp A-sharp. In the second half of this measure, a second

Example 5.5

m. 273, 1st beat   m. 322   m. 451

(examples have been simplified)

sonority is created when the A-sharp moves by step to a B-sharp while the remaining tones are held in common.

The structure of the two sonorities in this measure is similar to that of the whole tone hexachord of Ex. 5.3 which was best understood as a larger entity composed of two augmented triads. So too, these complicated simultaneities can best be understood as triads (E minor versus D-sharp major in the first half of the measure; E minor versus B-sharp minor in the second half) partitioned by register. Therefore, the principle of localized consonance is operative here as well.

The last chord in Ex. 5.5 appears at two transpositional levels in m. 451 (Ex. 5.5c). In its first appearance, it includes the pitch classes F, B-flat, D-flat, F-flat, and A-flat. Given the instrumental assignments and the articulation, this sonority divides into two component elements: a half-diminished seventh chord in the horns pitted against an F in the lower brass. At the same time, the F in the lower brass might be understood as an alternative fifth degree for the chord: it fits together with the B-flat, D-flat, and A-flat to form a minor seventh chord. Either explanation fits well with the principle of localized consonance. At the end of this measure the same chord appears in transposition.

Crucial though the expansion of the chordal vocabulary is for the continuing radicalization of his harmony, it is only a part of what makes the compositional language of *Pelleas und Melisande* so innovatory. Of at least equal significance is the evolution of his treatment of non-chord tones.

We have already seen in the early songs that Schoenberg often constructed the surface as a straightforward succession of chords. *Pelleas und Melisande* was conceived from the start as an orchestral work and in keeping with the character of orchestral writing of the period, *Pelleas und Melisande* has considerably more elaboration with the diminutions giving at least the appearance of traditional non-chord types: passing tones, neighbor tones, suspensions, and so forth. Be that as it may, the hierarchical distinction implied by the traditional categories of non-chord tones is becoming less and less useful as a theoretical construct for Schoenberg's music.

Part of this is due to Schoenberg's continued tendency to organize the surface so that contrapuntal motion produces a succession of traditionally classifiable harmonies, precisely as we saw in earlier works. There is a profusion of such instances in *Pelleas und Melisande*; m. 255 provides a typical example (see Ex. 5.6).

In this passage, there are four contrapuntal lines (with one of the inner lines sometimes splitting into a fifth line). The four beats of the measure are regularly divided into eighths, with an inner voice breaking into

Example 5.6

sixteenth-note motion in the last beat. With each change of an eighth, a different, traditionally classifiable, harmony results: the first vertical sonority is a root-position dominant-seventh chord on B; on the second eighth of the beat the two lower voices remain in position, with the two upper voices (A and F-sharp) moving by step (to B and G, respectively) producing an augmented triad; at the beginning of the second beat, the harmony becomes a third-inversion dominant-seventh chord on C (B-flat enharmonically spelled as A-sharp); this is followed, on the second half of the beat, by a root position A-sharp minor triad. So it goes for the rest of the measure, with various seventh chords and triads appearing with each eighth note attack. Only toward the end of the example, when the surface attack rhythm breaks into sixteenth notes, are simultaneities produced that are not traditionally classifiable harmonies (including a modified chord of fourths – A D G C F-sharp – on the last sixteenth of beat 3).

One of the many consequences of this procedure is that it is impossible to understand the passage as the elaboration of a single, referential harmony, or even as a progression of several such harmonies. There are no criteria that might justify elevating any one of the simultaneities to a superior hierarchical level over the others: the rate of harmonic motion is so quick that no one chord is given particularly more emphasis than any of the others. The chord progressions also do nothing to establish any one of the harmonies as referential: although there are two places in this example where the counterpoint yields consonant triads, those sonorities are shunted off into weak rhythmic positions and are not prepared by their dominants (or by credible dominant substitutes), thereby preventing them from achieving hierarchical priority over any other sonority.

Taken in isolation, the melodic-rhythmic patterns of this passage are not dramatically different from those of prior repertoires. The chromatic lines, the appoggiatura figures in the descant, the outline of an E-triad in the first solo cello are all familiar enough. It is the way in which Schoenberg has combined them that has such radical implications. By making every change in the counterpoint produce a classifiable sonority, Schoenberg has posed a significant challenge to the concept of hierarchy. Instead of these common figures elaborating referential harmonies, they produce a succession of different harmonies, none of which can be said to be hierarchically prior to any of the others.

Toward the end of the excerpt, where the attack rhythm breaks into sixteenth notes, there are several places where the surface rhythmic-melodic patterns bear a strong familial resemblance to traditional tones of elaboration and where the harmonies that result are not traditional triads or seventh chords: on the last sixteenth of the third beat, the G-natural looks very much like a passing tone; at the beginning of the fourth beat, the C that is tied over from the previous beat looks like a suspension, even resolving downward by step; by the same token, the A-sharp sixteenth note on the final eighth of the measure looks as if it might be an accented lower neighbor.

Although these three tones have the surface melodic-rhythmic characteristics of traditional tones of elaboration, the continuing evolution of Schoenberg's pitch language has brought us to the point that we should no longer be completely confident about the value of invoking the notion of non-chord tones to explain the function of these notes. Admittedly the G at the end of the third beat looks much like a passing tone. But in what sense is it a passing tone? In prior contexts, we would have made this assignment, not just because of the stepwise, chromatic motion and the off-beat placement within the line in which it appears, but also, because it would have been foreign to the operative harmony which means that it would be dissonant with at least one of the chord tones of that harmony. Since chords with dissonances are now virtually the rule and since it is no longer always clear which tone is the dissonance and which the consonance, there are no criteria that would permit us to assign the G to a lower hierarchical level than a chord tone. Furthermore, although the chord that results with the arrival of the G (A D G C F-sharp) is not a traditionally classifiable harmony, it is almost identical to the famous chord of fourths that Schoenberg uses elsewhere in this very composition. Therefore, we can hardly dismiss this as an incidental simultaneity, a chance result of the counterpoint, subsidiary in some sense to the "real" chords.

A similar situation obtains with the putative suspension on the fourth beat of the measure. The C is tied over from the previous off-beat and resolves downward by step – precisely the rhythmic-melodic pattern one expects from a suspension. The intervallic succession formed with the bass is one of the most traditional of suspension formulas: 4–3. This could suggest that we should think of the suspended C as an elaborative tone which is subsidiary to the B which is a structural tone.

Once again, the situation is not so simple. When the C moves to the B, the overall result is not a move from a sonority with dissonance to one without, but from one dissonant sonority to another. The C-B does form a 4-3 with the bass and that is a move to less dissonance, but the C also had formed a perfect fifth with the F. When the suspension figure moves down to B, it creates a diminished fifth with the F – in other words, a move to more dissonance, not a resolution to less dissonance. Furthermore, it is not the case that there is a move from an unclassified harmony (at the point of suspension) to a classifiable harmony (at the point of resolution). The motion of the suspension to its "resolution" yields two seventh chords: an F minor seventh chord in first inversion on the beat which becomes a half-diminished seventh chord when the C moves to B.

This leaves only one remaining possible non-chord tone: the A-sharp on the last eighth of the measure. On the face of it, this one seems more promising than the previous two: not only does it have the melodic-rhythmic profile of a lower neighbor, but also, when it resolves to the B, the result is a completely consonant sonority (a first-inversion, E major triad). Surely here we could argue that we have all of the conditions necessary for a hierarchical ranking: the A-sharp can be understood as clearly subsidiary to the B to which it resolves and can be seen as different in function from the remaining chord tones of the E major triad against which it is contrapuntally juxtaposed. Perhaps we should not be overly hasty in writing the obituary of non-chord tones in Schoenberg's music?

Given the evolutionary character of Schoenberg's language, it should have been expected that some passages or parts of passages might reflect traditional procedures or notions more than others. The occasional appearance of an unequivocally clear non-chord tone might simply be ascribed to the fact that at any given point in time, any language (musical or otherwise) is bound to be something of a composite, rather than a rigorously logical edifice of syntactical purity. Thus, one might argue that the existence of this neighbor note (and others like it elsewhere in *Pelleas und Melisande*) suggests that it is still useful to think of some tones as having an elaborative function in his music. That said, the expansion of Schoenberg's chordal vocabulary is making it difficult to establish consistent criteria that would permit us to distinguish between chord tones and non-chord tones, even when a tone has the melodic-rhythmic characteristics of traditional non-chord tones.

Schoenberg is also undermining the status of non-chord tones from another direction. He frequently introduces tones that we might feel ought to be non-chord tones in that they form a sharp dissonant relationship with a clearly articulated triad or seventh chord. When we try to classify these dissonances we find that they do not conform comfortably to any of the traditional categories (passing tone, neighbor, and so forth). We can see this clearly in one of the striking occurrences of the "fate" motive (see Ex. 5.7).

In this passage, the "fate" motive (A G-sharp F C-sharp) unfolds against a sustained D minor triad.[29] On the downbeat of m. 75, the resultant sonority includes the notes D F A and G-sharp. Our (historically conditioned) inclination would be to assume that the D minor triad is the operative sonority, and that the G-sharp is a tone of elaboration. Yet, the G-sharp does not conform to any of the traditional types of dissonance: it does not have the rhythmic-melodic profile of a neighbor, passing tone, or suspension, or any of their common variants. At the very end of the measure, the G-sharp moves down to an F, "resolving" not by whole- or half-step, but by a skip.

Example 5.7

Programmatic music and its implications

This is no isolated example: there are many places in *Pelleas und Melisande* where Schoenberg devises passages which contain notes that might be thought to be foreign to a given sonority, but lack any of the requisite melodic-rhythmic characteristics of traditional non-chord tones. By detaching dissonance relationships from their moorings in traditional contrapuntal patterns, Schoenberg goes a long way to obliterating the concept of resolution, which, in turn, helps throw into question the possibility of rigidly separate categories for dissonance and consonance.

The two previous examples have shown that the concept of non-chord tones is being challenged on several fronts. One final example is useful at this point, not so much because it demonstrates procedures absent from the previous examples, but because it illustrates the increasing practical impossibility of determining which tones of a complicated texture might reasonably be adjudged to be elaborative and which might be considered to be structural (see Ex. 5.8).

In this example, Golaud's leitmotif is juxtaposed opposite one of Melisande's principal leitmotifs. The contrapuntal juxtaposition of these lines creates a succession of problematic intervallic relationships. The overall effect is to make it difficult to determine which tones might be considered to be structural and which to be elaborative.

The first measure begins with an F major triad which lasts for the first two beats. On the fourth beat of the measure, there is a G minor seventh chord in third inversion. While these two fixed points seem clear enough, what can we make of the third beat? Shouldn't we understand the B as a passing tone?

Example 5.8

Given that the B-natural left a prominent chord tone (C) by step and continues on by step to another prominent chord tone (B-flat), our first inclination would be to assume that the B-natural is a chromatic passing tone. If that is so, then what do we do with the D in Golaud's theme? If we assume that the operative harmony is an F major triad, then the D is an unclassified dissonance, apparently arbitrarily approached and left. On the other hand, why should we assume that it is the D that is the dissonance? Couldn't we just as logically regard it as the root of a D minor seventh chord in first inversion? Wouldn't that be entirely in keeping with the normative character of Schoenberg's harmonic vocabulary, where the contrapuntal motion produces a succession of triads and seventh chords?

If we grant that the D should be thought of as a chord tone, then perhaps we have to rethink our judgment regarding the B as well. If the arrival of the D making a D minor seventh chord is justifiable here, then why not a half-diminished, minor ninth chord (B D F A C) in second inversion? According to this scenario, B would be a chord tone – the root of the chord, no less – and could not be dismissed as a passing tone. If we accept this as possible, then why not regard B as structural right from the start? Isn't the sonority so created (F A B C – a major triad with an added lowered fifth) strikingly similar to that created by the combination of the "fate" motive with the D minor triad (D F G-sharp A – a minor triad with an added lowered fifth)?

The conundrums found in the next measure are even more intricate, but I shall refrain from describing them in blow-by-blow detail because the point should already be clear. Increasingly, the concept of hierarchical distinctions is inoperative because it is becoming harder and harder to determine what the referential sonority might be.

An important contributor to the difficulties in making hierarchical distinctions between tones is the character of Schoenberg's rhythm. In more traditional contexts, rhythm had played a crucial role in clarifying which tones were stable and which were elaborative. More so than in any previous piece, Schoenberg employs rhythmic patterns in *Pelleas und Melisande* that make it very difficult to establish hierarchical rankings between tones.

Perhaps the most prominent marker of this interrelationship is Schoenberg's increasing use of a fabric of four or more clearly delineated lines, none of which moves in lockstep with any other. This has the effect of producing a quickly moving attack rhythm. In more traditional contexts, a fast attack rhythm would usually merely be a surface elaboration of a simpler harmony. In Schoenberg's music of this period, that is not always (or even most often) the case: instead of elaborating a slower moving harmony, the changes of pitch within the individual lines frequently produce equally quickly moving changes of harmony. This is particularly so in that many of the individual simultaneities that result from the movement of the lines comprise traditionally classifiable chords (as we have seen in our examples). So too, Schoenberg's increasing use of 4:3 and 3:2 (and other more complicated) proportions between lines must be understood as an important component of this trend in that relationships of this sort can markedly accelerate the number of simultaneities vying for attention within a limited temporal span.

From the preceding discussion and examples, it should be clear that by 1903, the very notion of non-chord tones has come into question in Schoenberg's music. Increasingly, it is becoming difficult to make unambiguous, hierarchical distinctions between notes.[30]

A similar transformation is taking place on a much larger scale: longer and longer stretches of music are constructed in which it is difficult or impossible to identify a referential tonic around which the passage might be said to center. Even when a key center is established, it is often highly transitory or tenuous, grounded not in extended harmonic progressions or clearly articulated diatonic collections, but in the local and evanescent emphasis of a chord, a melodic line, or a pedal tone. Correspondingly, there are relatively few places in the work where there are prominent, clear cadences (let alone traditional authentic cadences).[31] Although these trends have precedents in Schoenberg's earlier works, *Pelleas und Melisande* takes them to a new level.

The broad scope of this work (a single, uninterrupted movement of more than forty minutes) contributes to this transformation. *Pelleas und Melisande* is approximately twice as long as *Verklärte Nacht*. Although there were many passages in *Verklärte Nacht* that lacked identifiable tonal centers, those passages were typically framed by other passages – some quite extended – that were unambiguously clear in their definition of a tonal center. In *Verklärte Nacht* one was rarely more than a minute or so away from a sharply etched arrival on an emphasized or extended triad that functioned as a referential tonal center.

In the intervening three and a half years much has changed. Passages with clearly etched tonal centers have become fewer in number, less extended in duration, and more widely separated from one another. This transforms the pitch landscape: it makes it difficult to hear those sections that lack unambiguous tonal centers as being dependent upon the brief and relatively rare sections with clear tonal definition. The balance has been shifted so far that most of the places where a local tonic is established sound more like local points of emphasis or color, rather than like enduring pillars around which other events are structured and to which they relate.

Example 5.9

We can hear this right from the beginning of the composition, where Schoenberg assiduously avoids the establishment of a tonal center for the first forty-three measures of the work. This lasts more than four minutes in most performances, longer than many of Schoenberg's early songs in their entirety (see Ex. 5.9).

The work begins with Melisande's first leitmotif, a short melodic figure ('a') with a slightly elaborated, chordal accompaniment, the entire complex of which is immediately repeated in transposition up three semitones. This is followed by another statement of 'a' at its original pitch level, which is not completed, being interrupted shortly before its close by a statement of the "fate" motive ('b'). Here, in concentrated form, are some of the most characteristic features of Schoenberg's pitch organization in the absence of referential tonal centers.

The first two notes in the principal melody (A, B-flat) are accompanied by an augmented triad built over F-sharp in the bass. It would be difficult to imagine a more ambiguous, and less tonic-defining, opening for a composition. Those ambiguities are only compounded on the last eighth of the upbeat to the first measure as Schoenberg slides the three tones of the augmented triad down a half step, while moving the principal melody in contrary motion up a half step, yielding the simultaneity F A C-sharp B, another chord with an embedded augmented triad. This sonority is fleeting, as the moving bassoon line promptly transforms the chord (on the final sixteenth of the upbeat) into a half-diminished seventh chord on B (in second inversion). At the beginning of the first complete measure, the moving bassoon line continues to move over the sustained chordal accompaniment, creating a quick succession of different simultaneities. By the end of the phrase, a half-diminished seventh chord on B (in root position) emerges as the closing sonority of the phrase.

Having just spent considerable time discussing the problematic status of hierarchical pitch relationships in this work, the difficulties and contradictions we would face in attempting to separate the notes of this phrase into the categories of chord tones and elaborative tones (and to do so with any degree of logical consistency) should be obvious enough. For the sake of argument, let us assume for a moment that such difficulties do not exist, and that the passage can logically be reduced to a simpler harmony. With those stipulations in mind, one possible reduction would yield a passage consisting of an augmented triad on F-sharp followed by an arpeggiated half-diminished seventh chord on B.

Even when it is reduced in this (questionable) manner, the succession of chords still does not yield a clear and unambiguous tonal center. The opening chord is an augmented triad, a sonority that by its symmetrical nature discourages attempts to focus on a single tonal center. In more traditional contexts, the strictly symmetrical quality of the chord was often tempered by treating one of the tones of the chord as a chromatic elaboration. Therefore, the augmented triad usually appeared as part of a chromatically altered V-I (or applied dominant) progression, in which the fifth degree of a dominant (or applied dominant) chord was raised and would continue on by chromatic step upwards to the third of the following chord. If the opening chord of *Pelleas und Melisande* were to have that implication, then we would expect it to be followed by a consonant triad built on one of the three following roots: B, E-flat, or G, but no such progression can credibly be read into this passage.[32] Instead, the augmented triad is followed by another, almost as ambiguous, sonority, a half-diminished seventh chord.

The succession of chords in this example is paradigmatic of Schoenberg's non-tonic-defining harmonic progressions at this stage in his development. In those passages where he does not wish to project a referential tonic, Schoenberg tends to use chords (usually seventh chords or ninth chords) with symmetrical subsets (augmented or diminished triads, whole tone scale segments, and diminished seventh chords). Because of those symmetrical components, these chords can equally logically imply two or more different key areas. He then studiously avoids approaching this chord from, or continuing on to, any other chord that would confirm any of those key areas. On the other hand, when Schoenberg does use a chord that has traditional diatonic functions (as does the half-diminished seventh chord) or common chromatic function (such as an augmented sixth chord), he tends to surround that chord with sonorities that (because of their pitch content) cannot easily be reconciled with whatever key or keys that would be implied by that chord. Therefore, since a half-diminished seventh chord on B is potentially a diatonic chord in A minor (ii^7) or C major (vii^7), Schoenberg avoids surrounding that chord with any other chords that might easily be understood as components of either of those two keys.

However, we must also remember that – for the sake of argument – we have arbitrarily stripped this passage of its allegedly "elaborative" tones. When these are added back, the difficulties in identifying an unambiguous tonal center become even more acute. Since it is often difficult to tell which tone is structural and which is elaborative, it becomes correspondingly difficult to identify what the referential harmony might be (or even whether there is one) at any given point. This compounds the difficulties in identifying a referential tonal center, and highlights just how closely the difficulties in distinguishing hierarchical relationships on the small scale are related to the difficulties in distinguishing hierarchical relationships on the larger one.

Nonetheless, a case can be made that the passage is not completely free of all references to, or hints of, a referential triad – however attenuated such relationships may be. Recognizing those hints allows us to understand how this (non-tonic-defining) opening is a logical outgrowth of essential aspects of Schoenberg's earlier pitch language.

Since the work begins with a key signature of one flat, there are two keys that this could suggest: D minor and F major. A case can be made for both of these in the first two phrases.

If we look again at the first sonority of the work, we can see that a D major triad is embedded in it. Seen from this perspective, the opening sonority would be a D major triad (in first inversion) with an added sixth (B-flat). By the same token, the remaining sonorities of the first phrase can also be seen to include an embedded triad: a D minor triad with an added sixth (B-natural).[33] A voice exchange (F B) prolongs this sonority in the outermost voices.

From this perspective, we might understand the opening phrase to begin with a D major triad with an added minor sixth and to proceed to a D minor triad with an added major sixth. Since the second phrase of the work is three semitones higher than the first phrase, it follows that the second phrase is based on an F major triad with an added minor sixth (C-sharp = D-flat) that proceeds to an F minor triad with an added major sixth. Looked at in this way, the opening key signature might actually have some meaning: although they are heavily disguised, both D minor/major and F major/minor can be seen in this passage.

If it is useful to think of the opening as a traditional harmony with an added dissonance (another instance of the principle of localized consonance), then the harmonic structure of the opening of *Pelleas und Melisande* should not come as a surprise or be seen as constituting a dramatic break with prior modes of Schoenberg's harmonic thought. The orchestral introduction to *Gurrelieder* also began with the extended presentation of a sonority that might be understood as a triad with an added tone. Seen as such, the opening of *Pelleas und Melisande* is an extension of previous ideas.

However, the very difficulties we faced in even recognizing the embedded triadic content of these measures should suggest that this evolution has some radical implications. A comparison of the first phrases of *Pelleas und Melisande* with the opening of the orchestral introduction to *Gurrelieder* reveals just how far forward Schoenberg had moved in the few months that separate the two passages.

In the *Gurrelieder* passage, it was possible to focus on the embedded E-flat major triad as a coherent component of the wider sonority without undue difficulty: the lowest sounding note of the sonority was the E-flat; the harmonic rhythm was extremely slow, giving a listener ample opportunity to concentrate on the E-flat triad as a coherent subcomponent of the larger sonority. The sonority was mostly uncomplicated by additional elaborative tones and certainly not by chromatic tones, also making it easier to isolate the E-flat triad as a significant subset of the total sonority. The embedded D and F triads in the opening phrases of *Pelleas und Melisande* share none of those mitigating factors. In the opening sonority, the elements of the D major triad are distributed in such a way that it is difficult to group them together as a coherent entity: the fifth of the chord is split off from the rest of the triad and placed in the melody; on the other hand, the B-flat (which is not part of the D-triad) is grouped together with the D and F-sharp orchestrationally and rhythmically, making an augmented triad into the most prominent and rhythmically coherent surface feature of the sonority; the root of the D-triad is placed, not in the bass, but buried in an inner voice; the contrapuntal elaboration of the surface makes identification of any referential sonority difficult because of the challenges of distinguishing between chord tones and elaborative tones; the overall collection is hardly diatonic.

The procedures employed in the first phrase (and described above) are typical of those Schoenberg uses throughout the work to avoid clear tonal centers within his phrases. Moreover, it is important to recognize that Schoenberg does not construct longer stretches of music that lack tonal centers simply by expanding his phrases. Instead, Schoenberg builds longer stretches by taking the short, tonally ambiguous, phrases and subjecting them to various transformations: frequently, the phrases are restated in transposition (often in toto and without alteration); also common are straightforward, untransposed, repetitions of a given phrase; and more and more often, Schoenberg also employs varied repetitions (both at the original pitch level and in transposition). Finally, it is common for whole groups of such related phrases to themselves be subjected to repetition or transposition.

The repetition and transposition of tonally ambiguous phrases has significant consequences for the way in which we can hear and understand pitch relationships in the work. Although many phrases may lack identifiable tonal centers, this does not mean that we have been set adrift in a featureless chromatic sea. The use of repetitions and transposed repetitions creates a structural dynamic in which it is possible to hear the phrases that are so related in relative terms. In the opening measures of *Pelleas und Melisande*, we may not be able to determine if there is a tonal center for the first phrase, but we can easily apprehend a very basic kind of pitch dynamic in the first few measures: reference, departure, and return. The opening phrase ('a' and its accompaniment) presents the pitch material and thereby establishes our point of reference. By presenting a transposed form of 'a' and its accompaniment, the second phrase articulates a readily audible departure from that original, referential level. By restating the original (if slightly abbreviated) form of the 'a' in m. 3, Schoenberg creates a sense of return.

The notions of reference, departure, and return are, of course, some of the most basic concepts of pitch manipulation in prior repertoires. That Schoenberg would make use of an analogous idea in passages that lack readily identifiable tonal centers shows the obvious derivation of fundamental aspects of his evolving language from its historical antecedents. Although there are clear genealogical connections, there are also some crucial differences, and these are differences that are to have profound implications for Schoenberg's subsequent works. In a more traditional context, we would be able to recognize the referential region (the opening key), the departure (to whatever secondary keys), and the return (to the original key), purely through the harmonic progressions and the content of the collections; we do not need a motivic framework to recognize modulation. In the absence of identifiable key centers, the recognition of large-scale harmonic motion is dependent, virtually entirely, on motivic relationships. Given the intense chromaticism typical of most phrases, transposition does not necessarily yield distinct collections: the difference between permutational and combinational systems.[34] Thus, one of the

Example 5.10

(canonic voices only; other parts omitted)

most important notions in Schoenberg's evolving thought is the idea that large scale harmonic motion is closely tied to motivic relationships.

Another prominent feature of *Pelleas und Melisande* that counteracts the establishment of clear tonal centers is Schoenberg's increasing interest in symmetrical relationships. In the discussion of Schoenberg's chordal vocabulary, we have already seen that chords with symmetrical subsets are beginning to take on central importance. On a larger scale, we can also see Schoenberg's growing interest in transpositions that yield symmetrical relationships.

Toward the beginning of the work, when Melisande is wandering alone in the forest, there is an extended passage in which her leitmotif is stated a number of times in transposition. Since the interval of transposition is two semitones, the repeated transpositions outline a whole tone scale (see Ex. 5.10).[35]

Although there are many passages that lack an identifiable tonal center, and although passages of that sort are far more numerous and extended than in prior works, there are passages where a local referential tonal center comes to the fore. As in prior works, Schoenberg uses a fairly broad spectrum of techniques to establish tonal centers: from relatively traditional procedures (V-I progressions, stretches of pure diatonicism, and so forth) to considerably less conventional procedures (of the sort we have examined in previous chapters). Whether or not a local tonic is initially established by a non-dominant preparation chord or by an elaborated V-I progression, Schoenberg's tonal centers (other than those established by pedal tones) tend to be relatively short-lived and tend not to be confirmed by closing cadences or other emphases in the same key. For instance, the first clearly expressed tonal center in the composition, the F major statement of Golaud's theme (mm. 44ff), does not remain in that key even for a complete four-bar phrase. The first phrase of the theme closes on a dominant seventh chord in G, and the second phrase of the thematic statement starts (in m. 48) as if it is to be in G minor. To compound the lack of tonal stability, the second phrase does not remain in G, but follows the first phrase in transposition, thereby ending on the dominant of A (at the end of m. 51). This key lasts somewhat longer than its immediate predecessors (as is reflected by the change in key signature in m. 55), but, like its predecessors, is relatively weakly articulated, lacking any strong cadential confirmation of the key. Thus, within only a few measures, three different keys have been suggested (F, G, A), and none of them is particularly stable.

Taken together with the non-traditional harmonic progressions and the intense chromaticism, the lack of closure makes it very difficult for those key areas that are suggested to have much, if any, organizing power outside of their immediate domains. As those immediate domains tend to be very short and often separated by lengthy regions of suspended tonality, *Pelleas und Melisande* takes a significant step away from the idea of tonal centers as the organizing framework for the pitch structure of a composition. It is not that tonal centers are completely absent; rather, their organizing power is dramatically diminished. Compared with Schoenberg's previous instrumental composition (*Verklärte Nacht*), the difference is striking. In *Verklärte Nacht* identifiable tonal centers last for considerable stretches of time, are sometimes characterized by pure diatonicism, and their constituent phrases often begin and conclude in the same key. *Pelleas und Melisande* chips away at all of these.

The harmonic vocabulary and structure may be the most progressive features of this work, but in other important realms as well, *Pelleas und Melisande* contributes significantly toward the continuing evolution of Schoenberg's language. One of the most significant such areas is the extraordinarily sophisticated treatment of the technique of motivic transformation.

As in *Verklärte Nacht*, Schoenberg's approach to the program was not pictorial or imitative. Instead, he brought Maeterlinck's drama to life by devising a limited number of basic themes, each of which represents a certain character, a particular aspect of a character's personality, or an idea. In its basic outlines, Schoenberg realizes the drama by how the themes are ordered and combined. As such, Schoenberg is acting as a loyal disciple of Wagner, and his themes are clearly functioning as leitmotifs. Schoenberg followed Wagner in another respect: in Wagner's operas the leitmotifs are not etched in stone. He frequently made the motivic transformation of the

Programmatic music and its implications

Example 5.11

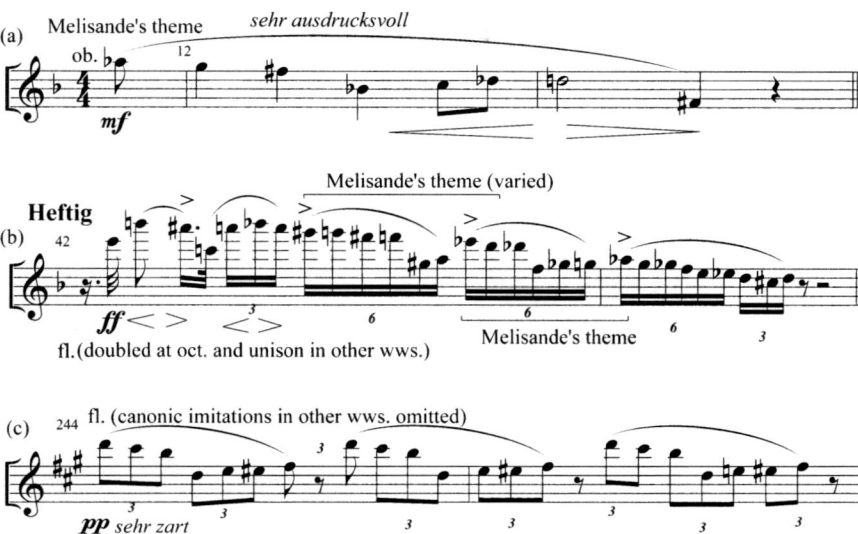

principal motives an important part of the dramatic characterization and development: as the dramatic situations and experiences of the protagonists change, this is reflected in corresponding transformations of the motivic material. In *Die Meistersinger*, a slow moving and stately version of the Meistersinger's theme is associated with Hans Sachs, but that leitmotif appears in sprightly diminution to represent his disciples. So too, in the Ring cycle, the perfect fourths of Fafner and Fasolt become augmented fourths when Fafner is transformed into a dragon.

As in *Verklärte Nacht*, Schoenberg makes the idea of the transformation of leitmotifs an essential aspect of his treatment of the dramatic action. In its first appearance (when Melisande is first seen wandering in the forest), her theme is slow and uncertain, highly chromatic and indeterminate in tonal center (Ex. 5.11a). When Golaud appears on the scene and tries to woo Melisande, she reacts in fright and shock, trying to flee. Correspondingly, the rhythmic character of her theme is completely transformed (5.11b). And when she is standing on the balcony of the castle, combing out her hair and then letting it tumble onto Pelleas below, her theme is transformed yet again, this time more diatonic in pitch content and with gentler rhythms and orchestration (Ex. 5.11c).

Although the idea of motivic transformations being motivated by the dramatic action is not new with Schoenberg, aspects of his treatment of the idea do have significant repercussions for his future development, particularly in that he took an appreciable step beyond Wagner.

Although Wagner's leitmotifs were altered in response to, or in conjunction with, the dramatic action, most of the time those changes were relatively circumscribed (frequently, limited to a single dimension, such as a diminution or augmentation). As a result, even after their transformation, Wagner's leitmotifs usually remain easily recognizable, not just by experts, but by relatively unsophisticated listeners as well. Not so with Schoenberg. The changes he makes in his leitmotifs are often so far-reaching (for example, compare Exx. 5.11a and 5.11b) that considerable mental effort and ability is required to identify them. For professional theorists or musicologists, such relationships are not challenging, but they are at the limit of or beyond the abilities of many amateur listeners. These challenges to musical comprehension are frequently compounded when (as is often the case) several different transformed motives are combined in complex contrapuntal combinations.

The implications of the technique of programmatically inspired motivic transformation for Schoenberg's future development are many and far-reaching and are not limited to programmatic compositions. By sharpening and refining his skills at using a limited core of motivic ideas to portray different dramatic events, Schoenberg made great strides toward developing the compositional techniques that would eventually allow him to construct large abstract compositions from a very limited stockpile of motivic ideas.

Schoenberg's manipulation of the motives in *Pelleas und Melisande* with respect to the programmatic context has another important dimension. In *Verklärte Nacht*, Schoenberg made motivic connections between otherwise distinct leitmotifs. In *Pelleas und Melisande*, Schoenberg continues with this idea: although the basic motives of the work are clearly differentiated from one another, there are connections between many of them. Most notable is the relationship of Melisande's first theme to themes of both Pelleas and Golaud, a connection that itself has programmatic overtones.[36]

In terms of its large-scale structure, *Pelleas und Melisande* lies on the cusp of a significant change in Schoenberg's approach toward form. *Pelleas und Melisande* is Schoenberg's last avowedly programmatic composition. Since Schoenberg's abandonment of programmatic forms came so early in his career, it has been easy to downplay or overlook the importance of this aspect of Schoenberg's thought. This is particularly the case since *Pelleas und Melisande* was written at just that point in history when programmatic music began a precipitous decline in prestige and popularity – a decline from which it has never really recovered. It is reflective of that change in attitudes that, although Schoenberg had been a committed advocate of programmatic music up through 1903, he quickly bent with the prevailing winds and became – at least in public – a committed advocate of absolute music. All of these factors have had significant impact on how we have understood (and valued) *Pelleas und Melisande*.

Nothing could be better illustrative of the sea change in aesthetic attitudes than Schoenberg's later relationship to his own programmatic music. Schoenberg did write another programmatic work after *Pelleas und Melisande*, the String Quartet, Op. 7.[37] Yet Schoenberg effectively hid this fact for almost forty years, acknowledging (and then, only with obvious reluctance) its programmatic character when asked by a student in 1940.[38]

One of the most telling bits of evidence of the extent and character of the change in Schoenberg's public attitudes toward programmatic music is Alban Berg's analysis of *Pelleas und Melisande*.[39] Although Berg is the author of record for the analysis, there is evidence to indicate that Schoenberg directed, or at the very least, strongly influenced, Berg's analysis.[40]

Given his servile relationship with his former teacher (which is amply – and sometimes excruciatingly – documented by their correspondence), it is inconceivable that Berg would have published an analysis that differed in any essential respect from what Schoenberg would have wanted.[41] It is likely that Berg sought out very precise instructions and suggestions from Schoenberg before he began writing his analysis, and just as likely that he submitted his work to Schoenberg for approval before he sent it off to Universal Edition for publication. Aside from the clear hints in the correspondence that this is exactly what happened, there is also some implicit evidence for this hypothesis in Berg's analysis itself. Schoenberg did not set all of Maeterlinck's play: he excised entire scenes and characters. How was Berg to know which scenes and characters had been cut unless Schoenberg told him? In his analysis, Berg assigns names to the various leitmotifs. He calls the second of those the "fate" motif. It cannot be coincidental that in his original verbal sketch for the orchestral introduction to the projected opera, Schoenberg had mentioned a "fate" motive. It is beyond coincidence that Berg assigned precisely this name to this leitmotif. Why not the "tragic" leitmotif? Or something else? It has to be that Berg got the name for this motif directly from Schoenberg.

That Schoenberg sat down with Berg and gave him the basic outlines of the analysis would be of little importance were it not for the content of that analysis. Although Berg dutifully acknowledges the programmatic basis of the composition, he opens his analysis with a forceful statement of principle. He asserts: "It is never purely descriptive; the symphonic form of absolute music is always maintained."[42] He goes on to describe the work as having an abstract musical design: a symphony with multiple, but uninterrupted, movements. According to this analysis, the work begins with a slow introduction, proceeds on to an allegro first movement (beginning m. 44), a scherzo (beginning m. 161), a slow movement (beginning m. 329), and a recapitulatory finale (beginning m. 561).

Given the nature of their relationship and the implicit evidence that Berg consulted Schoenberg on this analysis, it is highly unlikely that Berg would have claimed the existence of an absolute musical structure for *Pelleas und Melisande* without having had obtained prior approval from Schoenberg. Or, to put this more bluntly: can one possibly imagine the browbeaten, fawning, servile character that Berg was forced to be in Schoenberg's presence would have dared to print an analysis of *Pelleas und Melisande* that contradicted the wishes of his mentor?

This whole line of argument could be dismissed as irrelevant if Berg could have arrived at this analytical result independently of Schoenberg. If the composition parses cleanly and convincingly into an abstract multi-movement symphonic design, then undoubtedly Berg could have seen and described that design even without Schoenberg's prompting.

The problem with this suggestion is that the analysis of *Pelleas und Melisande* as an abstract symphonic design is – to put it delicately – farcical. Everything is wrong about it: the "exposition" and "recapitulation" begin in keys other than the tonic; the "scherzo" and "slow movement" are preceded and followed by huge stretches of music that have nothing to do with the "scherzo" or "slow movement".[43] If the "scherzo" begins at m. 161 and the "slow movement" not until m. 329, then precisely where in the formal structure does Golaud's "theme of suspicion" (m. 223) fit? Or the scene with Melisande combing her hair in the castle window (m. 244)? Or Golaud's interruption (m. 255)? Or Golaud and Pelleas in the castle's catacombs (m. 283)? Must all of these be dismissed as "transitions"? What raises the sections that are identified as structural pillars to their positions of privilege? Is there anything about them that is more important than the sections that are not so privileged? Other than the return of Melisande's first theme, there is very little that is recapitulatory about the "recapitulation" (nor is it, by any means, the sole site of recapitulatory activity). Not to mention that new leitmotifs are introduced in the "recapitulation", including a very important theme that appears at its beginning (m. 461, English horn). In short, we can analyze *Pelleas und Melisande* as an abstract symphonic design only if we are willing to ignore its tonal structure (such as it is) and consign huge stretches of the composition to formal irrelevance. Alban Berg was far too smart and perceptive to have come up with an analysis this inept on his own. He had to have had help from someone who had an aesthetic axe to grind. Only Schoenberg fits that bill.

The date (1920) of Berg's analysis is suggestive. By 1920, the debate about the relative merits of absolute music and programmatic music was over. Although the programmatic idea had enjoyed a renewed period of popularity among some composers toward the end of the nineteenth century, this renewed interest had also led to a wave of bitter criticism, particularly by Eduard Hanslick and his supporters.[44] As Sandra McColl has documented, by the turn of the century – just at the time Schoenberg was writing his early programmatic compositions – Hanslick's arguments were beginning to prevail.[45] In this environment, programmatic music was increasingly regarded and portrayed as inferior to absolute music. More and more, it was treated with condescension and dismissed as a simplistic, superficial, naive (or merely misguided), principle of formal organization.[46]

Schoenberg's response to this critical revolution was telling. He could brush off criticism of his compositions as being too radical; he might well have regarded such criticism as a badge of honor. He could admit that his music was too complex for easy comprehension; for him, that was also probably a compliment. But he could not accept his music being considered simplistic, superficial, or naive. Nor could he stomach the idea that his music would be seen as embracing outdated principles. In this context, it is interesting to note that – as Walter Bailey has documented – the criticisms of *Verklärte Nacht* at its premiere were directed, not at its harmonic innovations, but at its programmatic basis.[47] Therefore, shortly after he finished *Pelleas und Melisande*, Schoenberg bent with the prevailing winds, abandoned his public allegiance to programmatic composition, and became, to all appearances, a committed advocate of absolute music and its principles.

But what was he to do about those works he had already written and for which it was impossible to hide the programmatic basis? Although Schoenberg occasionally disparaged some of his early compositions in his later writings, other evidence (such as his arrangement of *Verklärte Nacht* for string orchestra in 1917 and his conducting of *Pelleas und Melisande* in Amsterdam in November 1912) demonstrates that he remained very proud of these works and was eager to keep them on the concert stage.

It is in this context that we must read Berg's (*recte* Schoenberg's) analysis of *Pelleas und Melisande*. In the milieu of progressive musical circles in 1920, Schoenberg knew that he could not get a sympathetic hearing for a programmatic work. His response was to adapt an old work for the new aesthetic climate by dressing it up in fashionable (but ill-fitting) clothes.[48]

All of this would be an irrelevant bit of *Rezeptiongeschichte* were it not for the fact that Schoenberg's (ex post facto) insistence on viewing *Pelleas und Melisande* as having an abstract structure has helped determine how we have heard this work. Unfortunately, that has helped ensure that we would misunderstand this work, both as an autonomous work of art as well as an important stage in Schoenberg's stylistic and compositional development. To hear *Pelleas und Melisande* as an abstract musical design is to condemn it to aesthetic failure. Alas, Schoenberg's ex post facto embarrassment at having once been a writer of programmatic compositions has made it very difficult to hear this work as it must be heard – not as a flawed work of abstract structure, but as a sophisticated work of programmatic structure.[49] To hear *Pelleas und Melisande* as it should be heard may require modern listeners to jettison deeply ingrained prejudices about programmatic music.[50]

Fair enough: jettison away.

6 Consolidation: Six Songs, Op. 3, 1903–4

> ... it seems to me that I have moved in many roundabout ways, sometimes advancing slowly, sometimes speedily, sometimes even falling back several steps.[1]

In the late summer of 1903, Schoenberg moved back to Vienna. His stay in Berlin had lasted less than two years and had brought mixed results. His inability to find suitable employment and Richard Strauss' failure to commit to a performance of *Pelleas und Melisande* must have been the biggest disappointments. On the other hand, there were some successes. Chief among those were the first two performances of *Verklärte Nacht* (the premiere in Vienna, 18 March 1902 and a performance in Berlin on 30 October 1902). Far more than any of his previous performances, these helped establish Schoenberg's reputation as a promising new figure in the world of contemporary music. Also of significance was his success in obtaining a publishing contract: toward the end of his stay in Berlin he signed a contract with Dreililienverlag for the publication of twelve songs and *Verklärte Nacht*.[2] At long last Schoenberg was a published composer whose works were beginning to be performed by significant ensembles on important concert series.

Encouraging though these accomplishments may have been, they were still not enough to procure suitable employment for the young composer. Upon his return to Vienna he was obliged to support himself with the humdrum activities of copying and arranging.[3] Orchestrating other composers' operettas and copying their scores and parts might not have been the most elevating work, but it kept Schoenberg financially solvent and left him with at least some time to compose. Curiously, he did very little composing between the completion of *Pelleas und Melisande* (28 February 1903) and the beginning of his next major composition, the String Quartet, Op. 7 (begun around July 1904). During this sixteen-month period, Schoenberg seems to have completed only eight songs (Op. 3, Nos. 1, 2, and 5; Op. 6, Nos. 1, 4, and 5; Op. 8, Nos. 1 and 2) and started, but did not finish, a few others ("Deinem Blick", "Wie kommt es", "Darthulas Grabgesang"). By comparison with the preceding three years (during which he wrote *Verklärte Nacht*, *Gurrelieder*, and *Pelleas und Melisande*) this marks a significant downturn in the breadth and scope of his compositional activity.

There are a number of fallow spots of this sort scattered throughout Schoenberg's career, and some of them seem to have played an important role in his development. Given the usual continuous evolution of his compositional thought, an occasional slackening of the pace gave him the opportunity to make his newest ideas a thoroughly integrated part of his musical language. That appears to be the case with the period between *Pelleas und Melisande* and the String Quartet, Op. 7. None of the eight songs from this period makes a dramatic leap forward in the development of his pitch language. Nor are there other arresting novelties (of instrumentation, genre, and so forth) as there had been in the preceding works (and would be in many of the works to come). But these songs do consolidate the gains made thus far and serve as preparation for the big changes that were to follow. In this chapter, we shall examine two representative songs: "Wie Georg von Frundsberg von sich selber sang" (Op. 3, No. 1) and "Geübtes Herz" (Op. 3, No. 5).

"Wie Georg von Frundsberg von sich selber sang" (Op. 3, No. 1)

Schoenberg's first contract with the Berlin-based music publisher, Dreililienverlag, resulted in that firm's printing of three collections of songs, Opp. 1, 2, and 3, as well as *Verklärte Nacht*. Given that the continuous pace of his development had carried him well past the pitch language of his early songs (many of which antedated *Verklärte Nacht*), it is reasonable to suppose that Schoenberg would have wanted some newer, more up-to-date works to include in the forthcoming collections. That is precisely what happened: three of the songs that eventually appeared in Op. 3 were composed during the period between the completion of *Pelleas und Melisande* and the beginning of his work on the String Quartet, Op. 7. One of those newer works, "Wie Georg von Frundsberg von sich selber sang", was written in March 1903 (immediately after finishing *Pelleas und Melisande*) and was placed in the position of honor as the first song of the Op. 3 set.[4]

In contrast to his previous tendency to focus on the works of a single poet (Dehmel in 1899 and Jacobsen in 1900–1), Schoenberg now went through a period where his poetic interests were more eclectic. His sources from this period ranged from Petrarch and Goethe to Gottfried Keller, Hermann Conradi, Julius Hart, and others. For the text of the present song, Schoenberg chose a poem from the collection, *Des Knaben Wunderhorn*.

The form is in a moderately traditional ABA' and its three principal sections (mm. 4–14, mm. 15–26, and mm. 27–39) correspond to the three stanzas of the poem.[5] That said, the formal subdivisions are rather subtly articulated. The end of the first stanza (m. 14) is marked only by a slight pause in the harmonic motion: Schoenberg stands on a B-flat half-diminished seventh chord in the piano for the better part of two measures. (Other than the final tonic chord of the song, this is the longest span of time devoted to a single harmony in the work.) He then begins the middle section by bringing the voice back in with some mildly contrasting material. The boundary between the second and third stanzas is much more sharply delineated. Upon finishing the second stanza, the voice drops out. After a three-measure, quasi-sequential, transition in the piano, there is a clear return of the voice's opening material at the original pitch level.

The tripartite division of the song is also supported by the large-scale harmonic structure, again, more subtly than overtly. Schoenberg does not set the middle section off by having it articulate a tonal center that is in clear contrast to that of the two outer sections. In these outer sections, there are several points where the tonal center of D-flat major comes clearly into focus. On the other hand, there is no clearly defined tonal center anywhere in the B section. The overall harmonic structure is not a contrast between different, and clearly defined, tonal regions, but rather a contrast between the two outer sections with clear tonal centers, and a middle section in which no tonal center ever comes to the fore.

Reflecting his usual concern for providing an appropriate setting of the text, the ABA' form also fits well with the most obvious surface reading of the poem: the embittered knight describes his own stalwart character and devotion to his lord in the somewhat triadic and relatively diatonic setting of the first stanza; he uses slightly contrasting material (more chromatic and dissonant) in the middle section to describe those who connive for success at court, and returns to a modified (but now more dissonant) version of the opening material to describe his despair at the lack of thanks he has received.

As is typical of Schoenberg's songs, the A' section is not a literal repetition of the A section. But there are parallels: the first five measures of the A' section, mm. 27–31, rework mm. 9–13 from the A section. So too, the passage from the end of m. 37 to the beginning of m. 39 is a varied restatement of mm. 9–10 (which, in turn, is based on mm. 4–5). Other than these two passages, the remainder of the A' section is better understood as loosely based upon, rather than as a varied repetition of, the A section.

One of the most notable features of Schoenberg's songs from this period is the intensity of the motivic organization and the corresponding centrality of the various techniques of developing variation.[6] In contrast to the programmatic instrumental works (which tended toward motivic

Example 6.1

prolixity), Schoenberg builds each of the songs from a carefully limited arsenal of basic motives that are then subjected to a succession of developmental transformations.[7] Op. 3, No. 1 is a prototypical example of this approach.

In the opening piano phrase (see Ex. 6.1), three basic motivic ideas appear: a four-note, stepwise moving line (x), a turn figure (y), and a step-skip descending figure (z). Although all three of these appear in several different guises over the course of the song, it is the first that is the most pervasive and undergoes the most thoroughgoing development. The opening piano phrase begins with the simultaneous statement of two inversionally related instances of the x-motive: a descending version in the uppermost line and an ascending version in the bass. The differences between these two versions are based on more than their contour; their orderings of whole (w) and half (h) steps are also different. The upper line has the intervallic succession of w-h-h (descending), while the lower line has the succession of w-h-w (ascending). Over the course of the song, the x-motive appears with at least five more of the eight possible combinations of whole and half steps: h-w-h and h-h-h (m. 4), w-h-w (mm. 5–6), h-h-h

Example 6.2

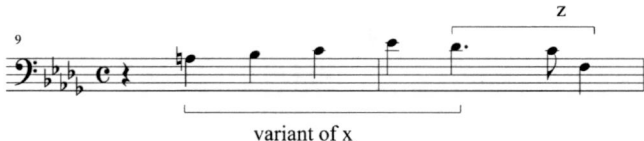

variant of x

(m. 8), and, with a different rhythmic profile, w-h-h (m. 18, bass). This last example demonstrates another important aspect: in addition to appearing with a variety of intervallic successions and directions, the x-motive is also subjected to a broad range of other transforming variations. We see this in the continuation of the topmost line in m. 2. After the decoration of the D-flat with a turn figure, the x-motive can be seen to continue one more step to C, thereby becoming a five-note figure: F, E-flat, E-double-flat, D-flat, C.

The somewhat disguised extended form of the x-motive is immediately repeated in simple form in the next measure. The bass line is a straightforward derivative of the x-motive, but it has been extended from four notes to six, with an intervallic succession of h-w-h-h-h. At the same time, the uppermost line is also an elaborated version of the descending x-motive (w-h-h), one that stops on the second note and repeats it three times (the last two times in syncopation) before continuing and completing its descent to the D-flat. (The multiple versions of the x-motive also show the continuing importance of indeterminate scales as an important feature of Schoenberg's music.)

The x-motive undergoes a number of other transformations. Another of the variants appears in the melodic line in mm. 9–10 (see Ex. 6.2). In place of the simple ascending stepwise motion in earlier versions of the x-motive, Schoenberg has delayed the arrival of the final note of the motive by skipping past it to its upper neighbor and then dropping back by step. This particular variant appears a number of times and itself leads to further variations of the basic motive (e.g. voice line m. 18).

The apparently new motive in the vocal line at the beginning of the B section (m. 15) demonstrates additional ways in which the x-motive develops (see Ex. 6.3). On close examination, this apparently contrasting idea shows itself not to be completely new, but rather, a derivative of the x-motive. It is an instance of the descending h-h-h version of the motive, with the last two notes of the motive displaced up an octave. Almost immediately Schoenberg takes steps to clarify just how the seemingly contrasting idea is related to the opening motive. In mm. 17–18, in the piano left hand, the new motive is repeated. When the leap is made to the higher register, the last two notes of the motive (C-flat and B-flat) are stated

Example 6.3

with octave doubling. This yields a clear statement of the original single-register version of the x-motive in the lowermost register. If that were not clear enough, Schoenberg follows this up with another statement of the x-motive, this time entirely in octaves. Schoenberg has taken the original motive, made a fairly far-reaching transformation of it – one that might not be immediately recognized as such – and then follows up by clarifying the relationship. This procedure – leaping several steps ahead in a musical argument such that the connections are not immediately apparent, and then coming back to fill in the missing stages – is a central strategy of Schoenberg's compositional technique.[8] So too, Schoenberg's practice of transforming a scalar line by displacing one or more of its tones by an octave will gradually become one of the central features of his compositional practice.

Although the x-motive is the most prevalent motive in this song, the y- and z-motives also occur frequently and are also subjected to extensive developmental transformations. Taken together, the three motives so completely saturate the composition that it is difficult to find a measure that does not include at least one instance of one of them.

It is also important to recognize that the three motives function, not as distinct and disjunct entities, but as related elements in a larger whole. Part of this is due to the simple fact that there are some obvious intervallic relationships between the different motives: the y-motive begins with a three-note stepwise ascending figure – almost a retrograde (or inversion) of the beginning of the x-motive; the z-motive starts on D-flat and ends on F – the exact reverse of the first statement of the x-motive. Over the course of the song, the various developmental transformations and extensions of the motives yield further connections.

As a whole, the chordal vocabulary of this song is similar to that of *Pelleas und Melisande* – much as one would expect for a composer who was consolidating his gains. There is a pervasive use of all possible seventh chords (especially those with symmetrical subsets), occasional use of ninth chords (sometimes in inversion), sparing use of more radical chords, and careful limitation of triads to a few locations. Although traditional chords (e.g. dominant sevenths and augmented sixths) do appear, Schoenberg has effectively completed the separation of chord type from standardized harmonic functions. In more traditional contexts, specific chord types played clearly defined roles: we normally expect a dominant seventh to continue to a triad whose root is a fifth lower; we expect the tones of the augmented sixth to resolve outward to an octave that is either the dominant or the tonic. In the syntax of this and other songs from this period, however, a chordal type does not prompt specific harmonic progressions. For example, in the opening two measures (refer back to Ex. 6.1) there are four dominant seventh chords in a row, yet not a single one resolves to its tonic.

A difference between these songs and the preceding instrumental works is the higher proportion of cadences, primarily a result of Schoenberg's tendency to set the individual lines of poetry to clearly formed phrases. In general, Schoenberg avoids the most traditional types of cadences, particularly the authentic cadence. Instead, he uses a variety of less traditional cadences, although some of these retain connections with the past. The final cadence (similar versions of which also occur in mm. 4–5, 9–10, 27–8, 38–9, 40–1) is a comparatively close relative of the authentic cadence: Schoenberg approaches the final tonic from a second-inversion dominant seventh with lowered fifth – an augmented sixth chord (see Ex. 6.4a). Other cadences are considerably less traditional: in mm. 7–8 Schoenberg approaches the tonic chord from a minor seventh chord built on the sixth degree (see Ex. 6.5, below). Some stopping points cannot be classified in traditional terms at all, as they close on dissonant sonorities. Most notable of those is the long pause on the half-diminished seventh chord (mm. 14–15) that delineates the boundary between the A and B sections (Ex. 6.4b).

Example 6.4a

altered V   I
(2nd inv. dom. 7th
with lowered 5th)

Example 6.4b

cadence on half diminished 7th

The character of the cadences is a specific manifestation of Schoenberg's general tendency to have a mix of traditional and radical harmonic progressions. With the exception of a brief diatonic passage in mm. 5–7 (and more on that in a moment), the pitch environment is highly chromatic. This is expressed in two ways. Most simply, Schoenberg makes frequent use of chords whose tones are not limited to a single diatonic collection (e.g. MdM, MMm). Or, when the chords employed are compatible with a diatonic collection (e.g. Mmm, mmM), Schoenberg normally juxtaposes that chord with another chord that cannot be reconciled with the same diatonic collection. For example, in mm. 1–2 (see Ex. 6.1, above), the last chord of m. 1 is a root position dominant seventh chord built on F-flat, a chord which is part of the diatonic collection of B-double-flat major.

Example 6.5

Yet the two chords around it (dominant seventh chords built on A-flat and G-flat, respectively) answer to two other diatonic collections. This promotes the quick circulation of the total chromatic: the first phrase (mm. 1–2) omits only G.

These features are also reflected in the character of the root motion. In more traditional repertoires, the standard harmonic progression was that of root motion by perfect fifth (e.g. V–I, I–IV, ii–V, and so forth). Another common progression involved root motion by diatonic step to or from an important structural degree (e.g. IV–V, V–vi, I–ii). In this song, the first of these types is almost completely absent. Instead, there is a high prevalence of root motion by ascending and descending thirds (major and minor) or by tritones. Stepwise root motion also exists, but it bears little resemblance to the stepwise progressions of more traditional repertoires because when root motion by step does occur, the two chords are almost never answerable to the same diatonic collection.

There is one interesting exception to the otherwise pervasive chromaticism of this song. From the beginning of m. 5 until the downbeat of m. 8, there is a diatonic respite: with the exception of the G-natural in m. 7, every tone in this passage is a member of the D-flat major diatonic collection (see Ex. 6.5).

The motivation for Schoenberg's choice of a diatonic collection here is probably tied to the text. The virtually unadorned diatonic collection, coupled with the otherwise rare use of consonant triads, gives this passage a simple and ingenuous flavor that accords well with the poem's description at that point of a knight who is not capable of the kinds of intrigue that are necessary for advancement at court.[9]

As in prior works, the establishment of a tonal center most often results simply from a clear statement of a consonant triad in root position. Given that the surface consists almost entirely of successions of dissonant chords, the relatively few consonant triads that do occur attain referential status almost by default. In this song virtually the only root position triads that occur at all are D-flat major triads.[10] When these triads occur they are almost always given at least some degree of rhythmic emphasis, often supported by some kind of a cadence. Since virtually no other consonant triads appear in root position anywhere else in the song, and no other triad is given rhythmic or cadential reinforcement, D-flat is the only tonal center that is established in the song.

Although D-flat major is given referential emphasis in a number of places in this song, those passages in which D-flat is established are isolated, and separated from one another by other passages for which no referential tonal center could be said to be present. Schoenberg achieves the suspension of tonal centers by the exact inverse of the procedures he uses to establish tonal centers: he avoids any emphasis on root position triads and avoids any focus on a single diatonic collection. D-flat is established in the first section of the song but disappears after m. 10. From that point until the return of the opening ideas (at the beginning of the A' section) in m. 27, no other tonal center comes into focus. (If one were to begin playing this work at m. 12 and were to stop in m. 26, it is highly unlikely that a listener would be able to identify a referential tonic for this passage.) The reasons for this are familiar from similar passages in prior works: the continuous circulation of the total (or near-total) chromatic, the almost complete absence of simple triads, the failure of chords to continue on to their traditional resolutions, and the lack of stable cadences.

"Geübtes Herz" (Op. 3, No. 5)

Our second example will be "Geübtes Herz", Op. 3, No. 5, a work that followed fairly close on the heels of Op. 3, No. 1.[11] For his text, Schoenberg chose a poem by Gottfried Keller; its twelve lines divide into three stanzas.

Like Op. 3, No. 1, "Geübtes Herz" both reflects and transcends the formal structure of the poem. On the one hand, there appears to be a fairly clear correlation between the poem's form and that of the music: the three stanzas of the poem correspond to the three most obvious subdivisions of the song (mm. 1–15, mm. 16–24, mm. 24–41). Schoenberg differentiates these sections by tempo (the middle section is "etwas bewegter"), by texture (the voice drops out at the close of the first and second stanzas), by motives (those of the middle section appear – at least at first – to contrast with those of the outer sections), and by tonality (the outer sections define B major, the middle section does not). The thematic correspondences between the first and third sections (cf mm. 6–8 and 31–3) suggest an ABA' form.

On the other hand, because of Schoenberg's artful use of the techniques of variation and transformation, much of the motivic material from the B section is comprised of transformations of motives from the A section.

The formal structures of the two songs we have examined have some essential common features, and these are shared by other songs from this period. As a general rule, Schoenberg constructs his songs around a relatively simple and traditional formal framework, usually a tripartite song form. Invariably, the A' section is only loosely based on the A section, more a transformation than a repetition. The B section normally offers only a partial contrast to the two outer sections as the contrasting ideas of the B section frequently turn out to be transformations of motives from the A section.

Having analyzed the motivic structure of Op. 3, No. 1 in considerable detail, it is not necessary to repeat that exercise for the present work, particularly since the procedures involved are so similar. Suffice it to say that, much like Op. 3, No. 1, "Geübtes Herz" uses a carefully limited arsenal of basic motives that appear at the beginning of the song and that are subjected to wide ranging transformations over the course of the work. Virtually every phrase of the piano part (and to a lesser extent, the vocal part) can be understood in relationship to at least one of the basic motives in the composition (most prominently, the three-note figure in the right hand in m. 2).

As a general rule, Schoenberg tends to use a more explicitly chordal texture in his songs than in his instrumental works. To a limited degree, that is also true of the present work. "Geübtes Herz", however, is never as starkly chordal as are some of the other songs: there are no stretches of homorhythmic texture comparable to that of the first measures of Op. 3, No. 1. It follows that there are comparatively more tones of diminution in this song. Nevertheless, what we find in "Geübtes Herz" should confirm what we discovered in the prior instrumental works. Although many of the tones of diminution have the appearance of traditional non-chord tones, it is often difficult to sustain a logical and clear-cut distinction between chord tones and non-chord tones. Ex. 6.6 illustrates.

In the first half of m. 4, we might be inclined to assume that the B in the piano is a suspension resolving to the A-sharp, in which case the governing harmony is an MdM seventh chord built on E and stated in third inversion. (The sustained A-sharp in the voice would strengthen this assumption.) But the A-sharp might just as logically be seen to act as the non-chord tone, resolving to G-sharp, in which case the stable notes in the sonority would be E, G-sharp, and D. That might imply that the B was a chord tone after all (part of a dominant seventh chord on E). Similarly, in the second half of the

Example 6.6

measure, the A-sharp in the piano r.h. appears to function as a neighbor to the G-sharp. If that were the case, then the governing sonority would be a G-sharp mMM seventh chord in second inversion. But the G-sharp could just as easily be understood as a passing tone. According to that interpretation, then the governing sonority would be a B MMm seventh chord in first inversion. There is not sufficient information to decide between the possibilities.

This example (and it is only one of many possible such examples) confirms that the concept of non-chord tones is becoming increasingly problematic in Schoenberg's music. It is becoming more and more difficult to assign differing hierarchical functions with any hope of logical consistency.

Although "Geübtes Herz" has more tones of diminution than does "Wie Georg von Frundsberg von sich selber sang", the chordal vocabulary is virtually identical. Like its predecessor, "Geübtes Herz" also has a predominance of seventh chords (particularly those with symmetrical subsets), a smattering of ninth chords, and it also reserves triads for a limited range of functions.

Its treatment of cadences is also similar, the one difference being that there are fewer obvious stopping points than in Op. 3, No. 1. In "Geübtes Herz", the only really unmistakable cadences occur in the final phrase: there is a fairly clear authentic cadence in m. 38 that is followed immediately by a kind of plagal extension in mm. 40–1 (the penultimate chord is a first inversion dominant seventh chord on the lowered second scale degree). Although the cadence at m. 38 is the only unambiguous authentic cadence, there are several other places (mm. 5–6, 8–9, 12–13, and 30–1) with V–I progressions, although most are rather heavily disguised. A few other less traditional cadential types also occur: in mm. 14–15 the A section simply peters out on a heavily elaborated first inversion C major triad (Ex. 6.7a);

Consolidation: Six Songs, Op. 3, 1903–4

Example 6.7

(a)
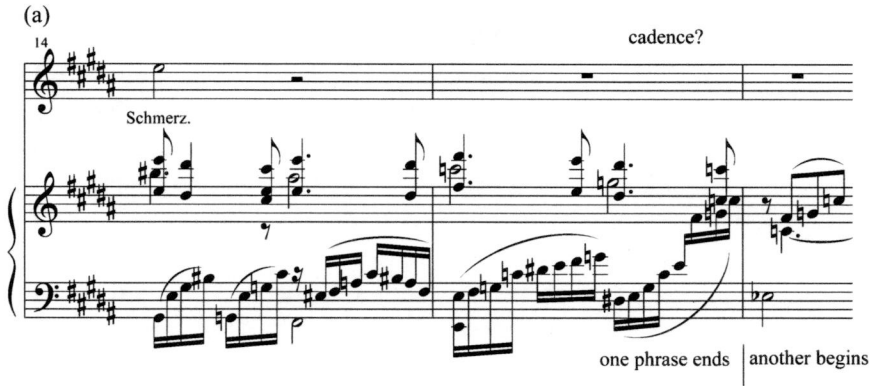

(b)
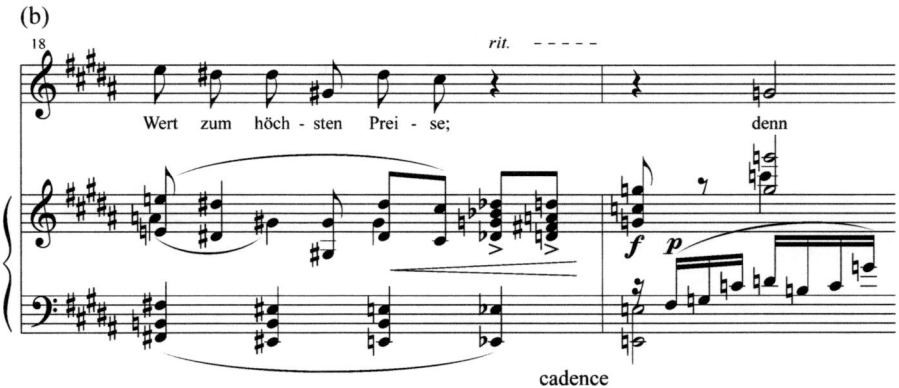

(c)

in mm. 18–19 one phrase ends and another begins by using a rather unorthodox harmonic progression (Ex. 6.7b); in mm. 24–6 the B section ends, not with a consonant chord, but with an augmented triad (Ex. 6.7c).

Also similar to Op. 3, No. 1 are the procedures Schoenberg uses to establish referential tonal centers. Like the previous song this is usually accomplished simply by the placement of a consonant triad in a prominent rhythmic position. Unlike the previous song, Schoenberg touches upon two tonal centers other than the one that opens and closes the work. As we saw in Ex. 6.7a, the A section closes in m. 15 with a rather veiled elaboration of a first inversion C major triad. In the B section that follows there are two places with slight emphasis on C major or minor sonorities: mm. 16, 19. Since these are virtually the only points in the B section where there is a clear triad that is also rhythmically emphasized, the sense of C as a local tonic arises almost by default. There are also slight emphases on G-sharp that emerge over the course of the first eight measures (and that return in comparable locations in the A' section). The opening piano phrase begins with a B major triad, but closes in m. 3 with a G-sharp minor triad (see Ex. 6.8). Given the few instances where triads appear at all, let alone with rhythmic emphasis, the emphasis on the G-sharp minor triad could suggest a struggle with B for primacy. That competition continues in the first vocal phrase (mm. 4–8). Not only does another root position G-sharp minor triad appear in a rhythmically emphasized location (the downbeat of m. 5), but also it is prepared by a chord that can be understood as an altered dominant (m. 4). Furthermore, in mm. 5–8, the prevailing chromatic collection thins slightly, almost to a diatonic collection (and one that is closer to G-sharp minor than to B major because of the E-sharps and F-double-sharps).

Example 6.8

Schoenberg has created a passage in which two different triads aspire to tonic status at the same time. Ultimately, one of them wins out, but before that happens, there is a period where it is unclear which one it will be.[12]

The period between *Pelleas und Melisande* and the String Quartet in D minor, Op. 7 is distinguished neither by striking innovation nor by prolific production. In describing his development, Schoenberg noted that sometimes he advanced slowly, other times speedily. Clearly, the songs of 1903–4 represent one of the slower periods. But this was only a temporary lull: in the year that followed, having consolidated his gains, Schoenberg resumed his forward momentum with a vengeance.

7 Abstract form, secret program: String Quartet, Op. 7, 1904–5

> ... the harmonies produced by those independently moving parts changed so fast and were so advanced that the ear could not follow their meaning.[1]

On 31 May 1902, Alexander Rosé, business manager and brother of the violinist Arnold Rosé, wrote to Schoenberg telling him of the strong reactions, pro and con, to the recent premiere of *Verklärte Nacht*. He went on to say how much his brother admired and valued Schoenberg's talent, so much so that the Rosé Quartet was exploring the possibility of a second performance of the sextet in Vienna in 1903. Then, in what was probably a response to a request by Schoenberg, Rosé stated that it was not possible for the quartet to perform *Verklärte Nacht* on its upcoming summer tour (which was to take them as far afield as Russia). That this decision was motivated by practical considerations was made clear by the closing sentences of the letter. He asked, "Have you nothing new, a nice quartet? Something that one can take on tour?"[2] Rosé was letting Schoenberg know that if he did have, or could soon write, a string quartet, it was not only guaranteed a performance in Vienna, but also on tour throughout Europe. This was a professional opportunity the likes of which Schoenberg had never had.

Rosé wrote Schoenberg again on 18 October 1902, breaking the bad news that the additional performance of *Verklärte Nacht* was not going to happen, again due to practical considerations. Once more he inquired about a string quartet, reminding Schoenberg that if he had one available his brother would be eager to perform it, even that year.[3]

Schoenberg did have a quartet, the String Quartet in D (1897), a work that he had written under Zemlinsky's loose guidance and instruction. The prospect of having a work performed throughout Europe by one of the leading chamber ensembles of the day must have been enticing, particularly for a composer who was as little known as Schoenberg was in 1902. However, he had the good sense to recognize that his 1897 quartet was not even close to being on a par with his more recent works and that it would not further his reputation to have it resurrected. To be able to take advantage of the opportunity that Rosé had raised, he would have to write a new quartet.

Schoenberg was unable to do so immediately. At the time of Rosé's October 1902 letter he was still in the throes of *Pelleas und Melisande* and even though he had just missed the deadline Strauss had set, he undoubtedly continued to nurture hopes that Strauss would perform the work upon its completion. With that in mind, he was not about to abandon his half-written tone poem to begin a string quartet. Moreover, in the late summer of 1903, came the disruptions of his move from Berlin back to Vienna. This was also the period when he felt it necessary to write some new songs and revise others for his forthcoming first publications.

In spite of all of these hurdles, sometime in 1903–4 Schoenberg did find the time to embark on a new string quartet and by the summer of 1904 had made some real progress on this composition, now known as the String Quartet Fragment (1903–4).[4] However, this progress turned out to be illusory: by July 1904 he had stopped work. Sometime between July and November 1904, he discarded most of what he had written and radically changed his conception of the work, eventually producing the composition that we know of as the String Quartet, Op. 7.

Because it was never completed, the String Quartet Fragment (1903–4) has received relatively little attention.[5] That is unfortunate because it is an interesting fragment that provides some important information about the evolution of Schoenberg's compositional thought.

The String Quartet Fragment (1903–4) consists of eighty measures of a fugue (clearly intended to be the first movement), a 26-measure draft/sketch of what appears to be the beginning of a scherzo movement, and a few other drafts and sketches (to which I shall return shortly).[6] Every indication is that Schoenberg conceived of this project as an abstract instrumental work, his first extended foray into absolute music since the String Quartet in D (1897).[7]

With its fugal opening, Schoenberg continues to stretch the envelope of traditional pitch language (see Ex. 7.1). One of the innovatory features of *Pelleas und Melisande* was its extended avoidance of an opening referential triad. The String Quartet Fragment approaches this problem in a similar manner and expands upon it.

Although the key signature suggests F major or D minor, only the latter seems even remotely possible and even then, it is limited to the first four notes (B-flat A C-sharp D, a melodic figure that is compatible with D minor). After that brief hint, any sense of D minor as a referential center is quickly lost in the prevailing chromaticism (all twelve tones appear by m. 6), not to mention the absence of any chords, progressions, or melodic figures that might support D minor.[8]

The remainder of the fugal exposition also provides no meaningful support for D minor. After the opening statement of the fugue subject (in the viola beginning on B-flat), the remaining three voices enter on E-flat (vn. 2, m. 5), B-flat again (vn. 1, m. 8), and F (vc. m. 12), hardly a

Example 7.1

Langsam ($\bar{\bar{\smash{d}}}$)

transpositional plan that breathes D minor. Since the fugal answers are all real, they transpose the uncertainty and chromaticism of the opening statement to two new transpositional levels. If that were not enough, Schoenberg employs a double exposition, with the second exposition (beginning at m. 20) restating the original entries in retrograde order.[9] When Schoenberg returns to the original pitch level of the fugal statement (mm. 24–5 and 31–3), there is even less support for D minor than there was in the opening because the harmonies created by the counterpoint tend to contradict any D minor implications of the four-note figure.

The nearly total lack of a hint of a referential center in the double fugal exposition is radical enough, but this is not the end of the story. As the movement proceeds, no triad gets extended emphasis, not at the beginning of phrases, not within phrases, not at the end of phrases, and not even at the end of major sections. As late as m. 80, the point where the movement breaks off, there has not been a single clear cadence that ended on a clearly articulated triad. The harmonic structure of the opening of *Pelleas und Melisande* had already posed a challenge to tonal definition; with the String Quartet Fragment it appears that Schoenberg was about to take a significant step beyond even that.

And then he flinched.

On 13 July 1904, Schoenberg wrote to Oskar Posa, bringing him up to date about his current work:

> I am not working all that much. I have begun a new orchestral song (the 4th). I believe it will be very good ... My quartet is resting. Perhaps I'll come back to it.[10]

In discussions of this letter, it has been assumed that the string quartet to which Schoenberg is referring as "resting" is the String Quartet, Op. 7.[11] Admittedly, there is some evidence to support this viewpoint: on pages 4–8 and 15–17 of Schoenberg's Sketchbook I, there are sketches and drafts for passages that are part of the first section of Op. 7, and these passages clearly antedate Schoenberg's letter to Posa (see Table 7.1).

But why should we assume that the quartet to which Schoenberg referred was Op. 7? As of 13 July 1904, Schoenberg had written considerably more of

Table 7.1. *Chronology, Sketchbook I and collated manuscripts*[12]

Date	Page (in Sketchbook I)	Contents/Remarks
7 March 1904	—	Score of "Natur", Op. 8, No. 1, completed
March 1904	1	Sketches for String Quartet Fragment (1903–4)
	2–4	Sketches for Op. 8, No. 2
	4–8	Sketches for Op. 7
	5	Sketches for String Quartet Fragment
	7	Sketches for String Quartet Fragment
	9–12	Sketches for String Quartet Fragment
9 April 1904	—	First draft of Op. 8, No. 2, completed
	13–14	Sketches for Op. 8, No. 4
	15–17	Drafts and sketches for Op. 7
	18–20	Draft for Op. 8, No. 4
25 May 1904	—	Op. 8, No. 2 draft (orchestral version) completed
3 July 1904	—	Score of Op. 8, No. 4, completed
	20–1	Sketches for Op. 8, No. 5
13 July 1904	—	Letter to Posa: Op. 8, No. 5 begun; quartet "resting"

the String Quartet Fragment than he had of Op. 7. By the time of the letter to Posa, Schoenberg had written 80 measures of a fugue, 26 measures of a scherzo movement, and a considerable number of additional sketches. As of that same date, he had only written about 30 measures from the opening section of Op. 7. Might it not be at least as likely that when Schoenberg was referring to his quartet as "resting", he was talking about the String Quartet Fragment and not the String Quartet Op. 7?

Yet even this explanation has its inconsistencies. If we assume that there were two quartets (the Fragment and Op. 7) and also assume that the entries in Sketchbook I occur in approximately chronological order, then the contents of pages 1–17 are very odd. It appears that Schoenberg was writing two quartets and bounced back and forth from one to the other without rhyme or reason. On pp. 1, 5, and 7 it is the Fragment; on pp. 4–8 it is Op. 7 (pp. 5 and 7 include both works); on pages 9–12 Schoenberg zigs over to the Fragment but on pages 15–17 he zags back to Op. 7. This makes little sense; it seems scarcely credible that he would work on two different quartets at the same time. There is a much simpler explanation: before 13 July 1904 there was only one string quartet and all of the sketches up to p. 17 in Sketchbook I belong to that quartet.[13] In other words, some of the passages that were later incorporated into Op. 7 were originally part of the work we now think of as the Fragment.[14]

It is likely that something like the following scenario took place: sometime in 1903 after returning to Vienna from Berlin, Schoenberg began to work on a string quartet. The evidence suggests that he planned a multi-movement non-programmatic composition with the movements structured according to traditional abstract designs (fugue, scherzo). He made substantial progress on the first movement, a fugue. He also began to sketch out parts of two other movements: a scherzo and a movement in D minor. Although the fugue was clearly intended as the first movement (shades of Beethoven's Op. 131) there is no evidence to show where Schoenberg intended to place the other two movements. In the fugue, he made yet another step forward in his harmonic language by suppressing even the initial tonic reference for an extended period.

Sometime before 13 July 1904, Schoenberg evidently became dissatisfied with what he had written and he decided to break off work. His letter to Posa shows his ambivalent feelings about the work: he tells Posa that the quartet is resting and that *perhaps* he will come back to it ("Vielleicht komme ich aber doch noch dazu"); it is not a given that he will return, only perhaps.

Between July and November 1904 Schoenberg did come back to the quartet project. When he did so he abandoned most of what he had already written (the fugal and scherzo movements) and started afresh. Virtually the only thing that remained intact was the material he had written for the non-fugal D minor movement.[15] This is the material that had appeared on pp. 4–8 and 15–17 of Sketchbook I. We know it as part of the opening of the first movement of the String Quartet, Op. 7 (mm. 1–12, 38–49, 50–4, 48–50 of the *Erste Niederschrift*).[16]

Thus the evidence suggests that the String Quartet Fragment (1903–4) and the String Quartet, Op. 7, are not two distinct, completely separate, entities. It is more likely that they represent two different stages of the same project. As we examine the final result – the String Quartet, Op. 7 – we shall have the opportunity to compare the two stages and to try to understand the significance of the differences.

Even when he resumed writing, the new work did not flow smoothly from his pen: Schoenberg found it necessary to sketch and revise passage after passage. As a result, he did not complete his new quartet until September 1905. True to its promise (if somewhat belatedly) the Rosé Quartet premiered the work in the Bösendorfersaal of Vienna on 5 February 1907.[17] The critical storm that this premiere sparked was of unprecedented intensity and marks the point where Schoenberg became a famous (or, for many, an infamous) figure.

As was so often the case, Schoenberg – with all due deliberation and intent – guaranteed there would be controversy by staking out a position at the extreme forefront of musical modernism. The pitch language of his preceding compositions had already been at least as radical as that of any other composer writing at the turn of the century. The String Quartet, Op. 7 represents an appreciable step even beyond that. One of the things that made that step even harder for audiences and critics to take was the formal plan of the new work. Instead of couching his harmonic innovations in a relatively short composition, or at least, one divided into clearly distinct movements, Schoenberg constructed the work as an uninterrupted whole. Although the work is subdivided into sections that correspond (if somewhat loosely) to traditional movements, there are no complete, formal breaks between those movements. In any event, recognition of the components of the form is complicated in that the quartet is cyclic, with the themes from the first section recurring throughout the work.[18] To compound the challenges he posed for his listeners, the unremitting intensity of the quartet's expression and the density of its musical information are prolonged for approximately forty-five minutes. Unprepared as many listeners may have been for Schoenberg's harmonic innovations in any form, many more were incapable of listening patiently to those innovations for the better part of an hour without interruption or pause. It is little wonder that the reactions of some of those at the premiere were so strident, with one member of the audience even making a point of leaving by the emergency exit in the middle of the performance.[19]

The ferocity of the reactions to this quartet might suggest that Schoenberg made some kind of dramatic break with the past in this work but that is not the case. Although there are a number of innovations and changes, there is nothing that constitutes an unusually large leap forward or an abrupt change of direction.

That said, there is one dimension where Schoenberg might appear to have made a rather sudden break with his own practice: the form. Between 1898 and 1904, Schoenberg wrote no absolute music: every composition he completed during this period was based on a text. With the String Quartet, Op. 7 (and for the first time since his quartet of 1897), Schoenberg wrote a composition based, at least to some extent, on abstract formal models. From this point forward, he would never again complete an avowedly programmatic composition. Thus Op. 7 might seem to mark the point of a significant change in compositional direction and philosophy.

To a certain extent that is true, but the contrast is considerably less sudden and total than it might appear. For one thing, the String Quartet, Op. 7 is not a pure instance of absolute music: it is also based on a secret program.[20] In any event, as Walter Bailey has carefully documented, Schoenberg never completely abandoned the programmatic idea; to varying degrees, many of Schoenberg's subsequent works are a mixture of programmatic and absolute elements.[21] Still further, the String Quartet Fragment (1903–4) shows that while Schoenberg's first impulse had been to try to write a completely abstract work, he found himself unable to sustain this break with his past.[22] For all of these reasons, the structure of Op. 7 does not constitute as dramatic a divergence from Schoenberg's prior approach to form as one might have expected.

One reason why one might assume that the programmatic and abstract principles would be incompatible can be seen in their differing approaches to the issues of thematic repetition. In programmatic compositions, the choice and placement of themes is determined to a significant degree by the text (or, perhaps more precisely, by the composer's interpretation of that text). If the program refers to the same idea in different places, then the composer has a very strong motivation to reflect that repetition of ideas by a corresponding repetition of thematic material (e.g. the several appearances of the "walking" leitmotif in *Verklärte Nacht*). By corollary, when an idea is completely absent from a section of the text, the composer is unlikely to have justification for using the leitmotif that denotes that idea in the corresponding section of music.[23]

It follows that when the programmatic text introduces a completely new concept, then the composer is normally obliged to represent that new concept with a correspondingly new thematic idea. As a result, the total number of themes can (and frequently must) proliferate to the extent that the text demands. It also follows that completely new themes can be introduced very late in the composition (e.g. the "transfiguration" leitmotif in *Verklärte Nacht*).

In absolute music (and, in particular, in absolute music based on traditional formal models such as sonata form) the choice and placement of themes is determined by formal principles that are far more schematic. Moreover, the aesthetic of late nineteenth and early twentieth-century absolute music tended to regard thematic economy as a necessary condition of artistic worth. These two factors motivate approaches to the employment of themes in abstract forms that can differ dramatically from those of programmatic music.

In absolute music based on traditional formal models, thematic recurrence is not determined by the content of a text, but by the structure of the specific formal model employed. Most traditional formal types tend to limit the principal themes to a relatively small number, most of which are introduced early in the course of the piece. There are also limitations on where new themes can be introduced. To introduce a completely new theme at the end of the recapitulation in a sonata form, for example, would be to challenge one of the most widely accepted axioms of traditional formal logic.

Given that the patterns of thematic repetition for absolute and programmatic music can differ so markedly, it is particularly noteworthy that the thematic structure of this quartet is, relatively speaking, concise. All four movements are based, at least in part, on those traditional formal models (sonata form, scherzo and trio, tripartite song form, rondo) that rely heavily on the principle of thematic recurrence. Unlike his previous programmatic compositions in which completely new thematic ideas were introduced even very late in the work, here, the initial part of a movement or section provides all of the motivic material to be used in that part of the work. Since there are cyclic aspects to this work, this is true not only for the individual movements, but to some extent, for the work as a whole. The principal theme of the second movement is actually a transformation of an idea from the first movement. So too, the theme of the finale is a transformation of the principal theme of the slow movement. Furthermore, thematic ideas from the opening movement return constantly throughout the work. As a result, this sprawling work is based on a relatively limited number of distinct thematic and motivic ideas, most of which are introduced in the first part of the composition.

Example 7.2

(a) Etwas weniger bewegt

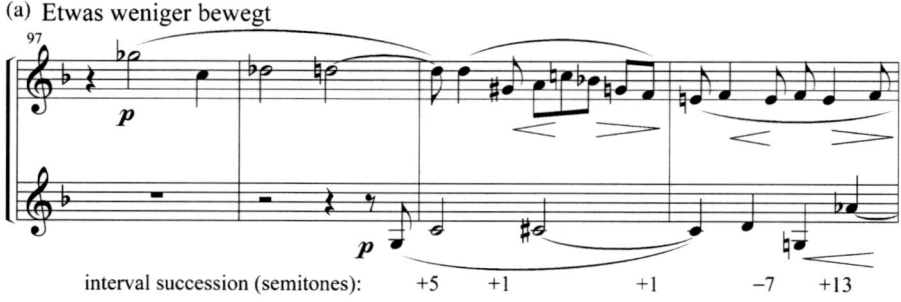

(b) interval succession (semitones):   +5   +2   +2   −7   +12

Kräftig (nicht zu rasch)

Moreover, as in his previous programmatic compositions, there are motivic relationships between apparently different leitmotifs, and this is another one of the ways in which Schoenberg effects a reconciliation of the absolute and programmatic principles. We see this in a comparison of the theme of the fughetto from the exposition of the first movement (Ex. 7.2a) and the principal theme of the second movement (Ex. 7.2b).

The difference in character of the two passages could hardly be sharper. The fughetto theme is relatively slow, in 4/4, piano, legato, and occurs in a polyphonic texture. The scherzo version is fast, in a heavily syncopated 3/4 meter, *forte*, non-legato, and is the uppermost voice of a homophonic texture. Furthermore, the intervallic succession of the two themes is not the same. The first five notes of the scherzo theme yield the succession (in semitones) +5 +2 +2 −7 +12; the corresponding segment of the transition's theme is: +5 +1 +1 −7 +13.[24]

Notwithstanding these differences, there is no question but that the two passages are close relatives of one another. That Schoenberg took pains to make the principal theme of the second movement a transformation of an important theme of the exposition of the first movement is tangible evidence of his growing interest in making a limited number of themes function as the basis of an entire composition.

The transition from the programmatic to the abstract approach was also facilitated by Schoenberg's adaptation of another technique that had been important in his prior compositions. In this quartet (and in most of his subsequent abstract compositions) there is a synthesis of the technique of thematic transformation with the use of the varied reprise. As we saw in the songs between *Pelleas und Melisande* and Op. 7, Schoenberg customarily built his song forms around a very simple formal premise: usually, ABA'. That simplicity was often only apparent, as the A' section was rarely, if ever, a literal repetition of the A section.

Although Schoenberg made use of those large, abstract, traditional formal types (sonata form, scherzo/trio, song form, and rondo), all of which rely heavily on the principle of the reprise, he does not treat the reprises of his abstract forms literally. As in his songs, the reprise structures of his abstract forms are far-reaching transformations of the original material. In this quartet, the return of material is never an occasion for unvaried restatement; rather, it is an opportunity for continued development and transformation.[25]

Another reason why Schoenberg's move to abstract forms did not constitute as abrupt a *volte face* as one could have expected has to do with the character of his programmatic texts. It is important to remember that Schoenberg's choice of texts for Opp. 4 and 5 was entirely his own. The nature and structure of the texts he did choose can provide useful information about his compositional aims.

Based on the nature of his settings of the texts for Opp. 4 and 5, it seems reasonable to infer that Schoenberg's choice of text was heavily influenced by the possibilities he saw for thematic recurrence. He was clearly interested in texts that included either the explicit restatement of ideas or their implicit recall. In Dehmel's *Verklärte Nacht*, the various statements of the "walking" leitmotif are either explicitly called for by the poem, or are easily read into the text. Similarly, in *Pelleas und Melisande*, the frequent statements and combinations of the leitmotifs for Pelleas, Golaud, and Melisande were made possible by the multiple appearances and interactions of those characters in the play.[26] Even though his two previous programmatic compositions were not organized according to traditional formal models, the very nature of the texts that Schoenberg chose made it inevitable that the compositions would be saturated with the kinds of recurrences that are also characteristic of traditional forms. In this quartet, Schoenberg took this process one step further by writing his own text, thereby ensuring not only the recurrence of themes, but also the possibility of organizing those themes into traditional formal patterns. For all of these reasons, Schoenberg's turn to absolute music was not as abrupt as one might have thought.

Nevertheless, there was nothing inevitable about Schoenberg's adoption of the principles of absolute music. Given the totality of his commitment to conjoining music with words in the period 1898–1904, Schoenberg's (partial) turn to absolute music in 1904–5 is somewhat surprising.

In the absence of any direct testimony by Schoenberg about this issue, one can only guess at the motivations that prompted him to take this step. There are, however, enough clues in his writings, his biography, and in the cultural context in which he worked to make some reasonable inferences about the reasons for this change in direction.

As we have discussed earlier, the Viennese critics did not pillory Schoenberg after the first performance of *Verklärte Nacht* because they thought his music was inept, amateurish, or ineffective. Nor did they criticize (or, in most cases, even mention) his harmonic innovations. To the extent that they did criticize him, it was because of their antipathy to the very idea of programmatic music itself and because of their displeasure at his having extended the principle to the genre of chamber music.[27]

I am convinced that the growing hostility to the programmatic idea was one of the reasons why Schoenberg began to move away from a public embrace of the programmatic idea beginning with Op. 7. We must remember that the premiere of *Verklärte Nacht* marked a major turning point in Schoenberg's professional career. Up to that point, he had had very few performances of any sort and never a performance by an ensemble that was as renowned as the Rosé Quartet. In some important respects, the premiere of *Verklärte Nacht* was Schoenberg's "major league" debut, an event that could well determine how seriously he was to be taken as a composer in one of the most important musical centers in Europe. Like any young and untested composer, he must have been looking forward with great expectation, not so much to the performance itself (which he could not attend because he was in Berlin), but to the reactions from other musicians and critics. Having received some positive reviews for his String Quartet in D (1897), Schoenberg was undoubtedly hoping to receive even greater critical acclaim for the infinitely more accomplished *Verklärte Nacht*.

When the reviews finally came, they were mixed. On the one hand, there was clear recognition by the critics of Schoenberg's compositional talent and abilities, but this was tempered by their strongly negative reaction to the programmatic idea in general and their annoyance at Schoenberg's extension of that idea to chamber music in particular. Several phrases from the reviews must have been particularly frustrating for the young composer. One critic stated: "Schoenberg certainly knows how to write for strings. Let's hope that he will soon use his gift on a work of pure chamber music." Another critic, after having complained at length about the programmatic idea remarked: "The young composer has proven one thing: unusual talent and rare sense for sound. One anxiously awaits his further development." A third critic began by reminding his readers that many questioned whether the programmatic idea has any validity. He continued: "Arnold Schoenberg ... has confronted us with this new-old subject. Whether the young, talented artist shall succeed in his own way in contributing something to its clarification, no one can know."[28]

If there is one constant thread that runs through Schoenberg's biography, it is his hypersensitivity to criticism. He appears to have been one of those people who are constitutionally incapable of accepting criticism with anything approaching equanimity. Given this character trait, it is highly likely that Schoenberg was profoundly affected by the (partially) negative critical reaction to *Verklärte Nacht*. In his view, he had written a masterpiece (and history has proved him right) and had every right to expect appropriate recognition. Instead, the critics carped at him, not for the quality of his compositional skills, but for his adherence to a particular compositional philosophy.

It would appear that Schoenberg's turn away from avowedly programmatic structures was not only a response to inner compositional needs, but also a reaction to the barbs of the critics. In later life, Schoenberg would try to adopt a public pose of utter indifference to, or total disdain of, critics. A studied dismissal of the critical establishment became an important component of the persona he wished to project to the public. But that persona was never anything but a pose: throughout his life he was profoundly troubled and bewildered by criticisms of his music.[29]

Seen from this perspective, some of Schoenberg's motivations become more understandable. We might have assumed that his turn toward abstract designs reflected a positive compositional decision based on the inner necessities or implications of the musical material. There is undoubtedly at least some truth to that assumption, but it is also probable that he adopted abstract formal principles at least partially as a means of covering his tracks and hiding from the critical and intellectual establishment an important – nay, essential – part of the structure of his work.

What Schoenberg said when the secret was finally disclosed is highly revealing. In 1940, in a class at UCLA, Leonard Stein asked Schoenberg whether the form of Op. 7 was based on a "definite program". Schoenberg reluctantly responded: "Oh yes, very definite, but private!" Schoenberg then chided Stein for even raising the subject, stating, "One does not tell such things any more!"[30] Even forty years after the fact, Schoenberg was anxious to hide his programmatic past.

Schoenberg's remark also casts light on some of his earlier actions with respect to Opp. 4 and 5. One particularly telling fact is Schoenberg's apparently purposeful suppression of the program for the first performance of *Pelleas und Melisande*.[31] When the tone poem was finally premiered (26 January 1905), no synopsis of the plot was printed in the concert program, effectively forcing the audience to approach it as a work of absolute music.[32] By that point, Schoenberg was eager to distance himself from the public acknowledgment of his commitment to the programmatic idea.

The accumulated evidence suggests that in 1904, Schoenberg was still committed to the programmatic idea as a compositional principle and still relied on a program to structure his instrumental works – his failure to complete the String Quartet Fragment as an abstract work is strong evidence for this supposition. At the same time, the evidence also shows that he was dismayed about the critical reaction to his devotion to programmatic music. Therefore, he tried to have it both ways: on the one hand he wanted to continue writing programmatic music; on the other hand, he felt it was necessary to hide the programmatic basis of his work from public view.

This presented Schoenberg with a dilemma. He obviously knew that he could not simply write a programmatic quartet and then call it an abstract composition. If he wanted to write a programmatic composition and to be able to hide that reality from the public, he needed a good cover: the work was going to have to have at least some credibility as an abstract structure. A central irony of this work is that in order to hide some of his deeply felt compositional beliefs, he was obliged to begin cultivating an approach to form that had not been a significant component of his compositional thought before this point. This could not help but have repercussions for his subsequent development.

Given this background, it should be clear that an analysis of the form of Op. 7 must account for both absolute and programmatic strands, separately and in their interaction. We will begin with a consideration of the program.[33]

I. 1) a) revolt, defiance; b) longing; c) rapture.
    2) a) dejection; despair; fear of being engulfed; unaccustomed feelings of love, desire to be wholly *absorbed* in.
    b) comfort, relief (she and he)

       c) new breaking out: dejection, despair; and
       d) transition to
   3) battle of all the motives with the decision to begin a new life (I. Development Section)
[blank line here]
       c) mild argument
II. 1) "feeling new life"
       a) aggressive vigor, fantasy development, verve.
       b) new love: tenderness, devotion, rapture, understanding, extreme sensual intoxication (repeat part of II 1. a)
   2) disappointment (hangover), (brief).
   3) a) return to dejected moods, despair, transition to
       b) the return of the first mood, I. 1.a   (II. Dev. Section)
       c) transition to gentler tones
III. 1) a) increasing longing for the loved ones left behind, transition to despair over the pain it has caused them.
       b) falling asleep. A *dream image* shows the ones left behind, each mourning in his own way for the one who is far away, thinking of him, hoping for his return.
       c) transition to the decision to return home; increasing longing for peace and rest.
       d) homecoming; joyful reception, quiet joy and the arrival of rest and harmony.

On the largest scale, it is apparent that the program for this composition has a number of important similarities with that of *Verklärte Nacht*. Like the earlier work, the story that is sketched out here also depicts first a crisis and then, eventually, the happy resolution in the relationship of a couple. Like Op. 4, so too this work (also in D) depicts the transition from stormy struggle to peaceful resolution with the traditional use of minor for the struggle and major for the resolution.

Schoenberg divided the program into three main sections. The first describes the ups and (mainly) downs of what appears to be a rather stormy relationship. The second section is an attempt (ultimately unsuccessful) to start afresh. The third section, after beginning in near despair, describes the eventual coming to terms between the lovers, ending with a state of peace and harmony.

In terms of the correlation of the program to the composition, it is clear that the first section of Schoenberg's program corresponds to the opening movement (up to rehearsal E, mm. 1–398), the second section corresponds to the scherzo movement (up to rehearsal K, mm. 399–951),[34] and the final section corresponds to the final two movements.

Although the correlation between the larger divisions of the form and the program is fairly clear, it is somewhat more difficult to assign the subheadings to specific musical passages. There are several reasons why this is so. The first is simply that Schoenberg's program is not particularly detailed. He seems to have used it as a rough outline for his composition, perhaps more an *aide-mémoire* than a detailed blueprint. In any event, there is at least one point where the program is clearly incomplete: in the third section of the first movement, there is a subheading "milde Auseinandersetzung" (mild argument) that is labeled 'c,' but which is not preceded by an 'a' or 'b'. Space was left for those two sections, but never filled in.[35] It is also possible that the program underwent changes during the course of the compositional process, and these changes were never reflected in the outline. Since neither Schoenberg nor members of his circle wrote a guide to the program for this work (as Berg did for Op. 5), it is not possible to know for sure what, if any, changes were made. Finally, it is also possible that the program does not represent a comprehensive chronological listing of all of the details of what happens in the music. Some of the subheadings within the outline might simply be a list of all of the ideas that would be portrayed within a large section, but not necessarily their exact order. This argument gains credibility given that even within sections themes frequently appear, disappear, and then return.

Although it is not possible to be certain about many aspects of the correlation between the program and the music, the broad outlines of the correlation of the story and the music are clear, and that is more than enough for us to understand some of the essential aspects of how the program and the absolute structure interact. And it should not escape our attention that there are some important differences between this treatment and that of his two previous programmatic compositions.

In Op. 7, Schoenberg does not seem to be using his themes as leitmotifs that represent specific characters or ideas. It appears that he depicts the program principally by the general character of the music: its dynamics, tempo, and type of harmony. It is the stormy, agitated surface of the beginning of the work that suggests the "Auflehnung" (revolt) of the program, not so much the specific group of themes that are used. We see this because those same themes return in a number of places in the composition, but do not always convey a sense of "Auflehnung". This is, perhaps, clearest at the very end of the composition, where a version of the opening theme returns. In its first appearance (m. 1) this theme and its accompaniment had been highly agitated and unsettled, an appropriate

Example 7.3
(a)

Nicht zu rasch.

(b)

Breit, ruhig, doch nicht all zu langsam

depiction of "Auflehnung" (Ex. 7.3a). At the end of the composition, however, the theme is substantially slower and gentler; the harmonic motion has become slower; the accompaniment is far calmer (Ex. 7.3b). In other words, it is the quiet presentation that is the essence of the depiction of the final line of the program, "stille Freude und Einkehr von Ruhe und Harmonie" (quiet joy and the arrival of rest and harmony), not the specific themes employed.

It seems unlikely that it would be coincidental that there is such a change in Schoenberg's approach to the realization of a program in the very composition in which Schoenberg first attempted to synthesize the programmatic and abstract ideas. Schoenberg's use of leitmotifs in *Verklärte Nacht* and *Pelleas und Melisande* was sophisticated, subtle, and highly effective at interpreting the literary models upon which the two works were based. But Schoenberg may have concluded that it would not be possible to write a composition with any pretense of traditional abstract structure while continuing to treat his leitmotifs precisely as he had done up to this point. The patterns of thematic repetition in programmatic texts are not readily compatible with those of abstract formal designs: narrative stories do not usually fall into sonata or rondo forms. Moreover, his interest in thematic integration (as reflected by using transformed versions of the same theme in different movements) is awkward to reconcile with leitmotifs. Schoenberg may have begun to use abstract designs, at least in part, to disguise the programmatic basis of his music, but the very use of those designs could not help but transform the character of his programmatic music.

Although the use of abstract forms transformed the character of Schoenberg's programmatic music, this was not a one-way street. Just as much as it was difficult for Schoenberg to reconcile his prior approach to leitmotifs with traditional abstract forms, so too, it was difficult to write traditional abstract forms while relating a narrative; again, narrative stories do not usually fall into sonata or rondo forms. It follows that the programmatic character of the work guaranteed that those forms would be anything but textbook versions of traditional forms. This can be seen clearly in the structure of the first movement.

Schoenberg organized the first movement as a kind of sonata form. It begins with a rather extensive exposition that presents a number of important thematic ideas and eventually leads into a development section which employs many of the most typical development-section strategies of late nineteenth-century development sections: themes and motives are brought back, combined, broken apart, and subjected to sequence.[36]

One of the fundamental formal problems of this movement is identifying where the recapitulation begins. From a thematic viewpoint this is not all that difficult: the opening theme returns at m. 301 with much of the character that it had had in the opening measures. And from this point forward (up to the beginning of the scherzo movement at m. 399), most of the principal thematic ideas from the exposition return in approximately the same order they had in the opening of the movement.

The problem is that there is no corresponding harmonic return: the recapitulation (if that is what it really is) begins with the opening theme restated in C-sharp minor, not D minor. The remainder of the "recapitulation" neither transposes the exposition at a single transpositional level, nor does it ever bring the movement back to D minor in any form. The result is a very unusual type of sonata form, one whose themes are stated and restated in approximate conformity with the thematic plan of the traditional model, but one that lacks the harmonic structure characteristic of tonal forms.

The incomplete tonal structure of the recapitulation is, at least in part, a consequence of the synthesis of a traditional formal model with the program. Schoenberg's program depicts a crisis in the relationship of two lovers. The disparate feelings of the protagonists are laid out in the exposition. The incompatibility of those feelings creates a crisis that reaches its zenith in the development section (Kampf aller Motive). By the end of the movement, there still has been no solution. Instead, the man makes the decision to begin his life afresh (Entschluß neues Leben zu beginnen), presumably by breaking off the troubled relationship with his lover and leaving. Since Schoenberg usually used the return to the tonic to suggest the resolution of conflict, it would have been inappropriate, on programmatic grounds, to close the first movement with a return to the original tonic. A return of that sort would have implied a type of resolution in the couple's relationship that was not implied by the program until the very end of the work. Therefore, the recapitulation of the first movement remains tonally open, never returning to the opening key.[37]

The second and third movements are organized along very similar lines. Both are loosely based on traditional formal types: the second movement as a scherzo and trio, the third movement as a song form. Like the first movement, these movements do not come close to conforming to textbook models of traditional forms. In both cases, the reprises are drastically reduced and lack any return to the initial tonal centers. This lack of closure may also be a consequence of the demands of the program and the desire to create a single overall form.

In the second movement, the scherzo (beginning at m. 399 in G-flat major) continues on to a trio (beginning at m. 532). In a more traditionally oriented form, the trio would normally be followed by a return to the scherzo, restated in its original key. Beginning at m. 706, Schoenberg does bring back a version of the scherzo's theme, but it has been heavily transformed and there is no clear return to G-flat major as a tonal center. Still further, this reprise is seriously abbreviated and lacks anything like a clear cadential closure in any key.[38] Instead, the reprise gives way to a complicated (and extended) section that functions as both another development section and as a recapitulation of themes from the first movement.

Like the first movement, much of the motivation for this formally incomplete and tonally open section can be traced to the program. The

Neues Leben (new life) was not successful: it provided no resolution to the crisis in the protagonist's life. He was no less unhappy in his new situation separated from his original love. Instead, it led to Enttäuschung (disappointment) and a return to the despair of the first movement. This implies that it would not have been possible for Schoenberg to have a literal reprise of the A section of the Scherzo, one that closed on the same confident note with which the movement had begun.

The third movement follows this pattern exactly. It suggests a traditional formal type (three-part song form), but it also attenuates the repetition of the A' section and avoids any clear sense of closure. Like the previous two movements, the demands of the program helped determine the specific shape of the form. The despair of the separation determines the initial mood of the third movement, but the movement does not end on that note and this means there cannot be a tonally closed reprise of the A section.

The program also suggests how the composition must end. After a dream that brings an image of his loved ones before him (slow movement), the wayward lover makes the decision to return home. He has a strong desire for peace and tranquility, for a resolution of their conflict. He returns and is accepted back (final movement). Finally, everything is transformed into peace and harmony. In harmonic terms, Schoenberg represents this by the only solid tonal closure in the composition, the cadence in D major. In formal terms, the principal theme of the final movement brings back and transforms the principal theme of the third movement. The final movement gives way to a coda in which the principal themes from earlier in the work are brought back and transformed. This is particularly the case with the opening theme, which, in its initial appearance, had been aggressive and unstable. At the end of the composition, this theme has become gentle and stable, allowing the work to close with a feeling of resolution and finality.[39]

The most obvious conclusion that can be drawn from this survey of the form of Op. 7 is that the work cannot be understood if either of its two principal formal components is examined in isolation. Seen solely as an instance of abstract formal structure, it is a perplexing composition, one in which prominent aspects of the form seem to have no rational motivation. Seen solely as a programmatic composition, the work is equally perplexing, for it would lead one to miss entirely the essential role of the abstract forms in the overall design. Only when both components are given appropriate weight can we appreciate this quartet on its own terms as an independent and autonomous work of art, and understand its pivotal role in the evolution of Schoenberg's formal thought.

Over the course of the evolution of Schoenberg's compositional language, changes in one dimension of the compositional fabric are rarely isolated events, lacking significant consequences in other dimensions. Among other things, his turn to absolute music seems to have prompted Schoenberg to begin cultivating the art of counterpoint, as if the two ideas were paired in his thought (a pairing that was even more explicit in the String Quartet Fragment). Counterpoint is not incompatible with programmatic music (or with any texted music for that matter), but there can hardly be anything more emblematic of abstract compositional craft than the learned devices of strict counterpoint. Given Schoenberg's newfound interest in presenting himself to the world as a proponent of absolute music, it is hardly surprising that he would adopt some of the most obvious manifestations of abstract musical craftsmanship.

This is not to say that Schoenberg's pre-Op. 7 compositions were devoid of contrapuntal devices: the augmentations and diminutions in the introduction and the canonic imitations toward the end of *Gurrelieder* as well as the fugal treatment of one of Melisande's leitmotifs are obvious examples. Nevertheless, passages of this sort are relatively rare before 1905. That changes, and does so in a significant way, with the String Quartet, Op. 7. From this point forward, Schoenberg regularly includes passages written in a strict polyphonic style, and frequently incorporates elements of traditional contrapuntal art into his compositions.

Most obvious are passages like the extended quasi-canon from the exposition of the first movement (which is clearly related to the opening of the String Quartet Fragment). Although this idea had been adumbrated by the fugal passage in Op. 5, it is now given a far lengthier and more complex role, accounting for a significant proportion of the exposition of the first movement and returning (in modified form) elsewhere in the movement. Schoenberg bases his canonic passage on a twenty-eight note theme that appears in complete form for the first time in the second violin. This complete statement is anticipated in the first violin by an incomplete statement (at the tritone transposition), one that begins with the seventh note of the theme and continues on to the end (for the first four measures of this passage, mm. 97–100, see Ex. 7.2a. above; for the next four measures, mm. 101–4, see Ex. 7.4).[40]

The use of strict imitative writing is one of the most obvious manifestations of Schoenberg's new interest in counterpoint. Another particularly striking aspect – all the more so in that there is relatively little precedent for it in his previous compositions – is the frequent use of learned contrapuntal devices.[41] Over the course of the work, the various themes are subjected to many of the traditional contrapuntal transformations: inversion, augmentation, diminution, and invertible counterpoint at the octave, a remarkable contrast with his earlier works where such features were relatively rare.

Example 7.4

In the opening measures of the quartet (Ex. 7.3a), there are three motivic strands, a principal theme in the violin stated opposite important subsidiary themes in the viola and cello. This thematic complex returns in mm. 30ff, transposed up a half-step. When it returns, the registral distribution of the three strands is altered: the principal melody now appears in the bottom voice, a conscious use of the technique of invertible counterpoint at the octave. Similarly, at m. 79, the principal theme returns in the cello, transposed to the dominant. This time it appears in augmentation, another of the traditional contrapuntal devices. So too, in m. 389 the fughetto theme appears in the cello, thereby initiating another section of imitative entries. This time the imitation in the violins is by inversion. Finally, consider the passage in mm. 313–20 (Ex. 7.5). In this passage, the basic motive (marked M) appears in diminution and, at the end of the excerpt, in inversion.

These examples represent only a small sampling of the instances of traditional contrapuntal devices that appear in this work. In contrast to the limited appearances of such techniques in his previous works, contrapuntal transformations now become pervasive.[42]

This has important implications. Just as his turn to absolute music seems to have prompted Schoenberg to begin incorporating more explicitly polyphonic writing into his language, so too, the resultant emphasis on textures composed of independent lines had significant consequences for other aspects of that language.

The most significant of those was the intensification of something that – in a different context – had already become an important component of his compositional technique. We have seen that Schoenberg often organized the surface so that the moving voices combined with the remaining voices

Example 7.5

to create quick-moving successions of harmonies, usually a string of seventh chords. The use of a polyphonic fabric with complex rhythmic interactions between the lines takes this procedure to a new level of intensity. Consider, for example, even a relatively uncomplicated passage from the exposition of the first movement in which only three of the instruments are playing (see Ex. 7.6).

Since the three lines are moving independently of one another, the overall attack rhythm is extremely quick, with at least one of the voices moving to a new pitch at every eighth. In only four beats (at a fairly quick

Example 7.6

[Musical score excerpt, measure 14, four staves in 4/4 time, marked *p* throughout, with beat positions labeled "1 2 3 4 5 6 7 8"]

1: D-flat F dyad
2: B-flat minor triad
3: G diminished 6/3
etc.

tempo), eight different vertical combinations result (and are so marked in the example).

In prior repertoires, we would normally understand polyphonic passages with rhythmic profiles like this to have a simpler harmonic rhythm; we would think of some tones as being elaborative, others as structural. However, as we have seen even in Schoenberg's less explicitly polyphonic music, it had proved increasingly difficult to reduce complicated surfaces to simpler background harmonies with any hope of certainty or logical consistency. That is even truer of passages like the one under discussion.

A first inversion, diminished triad occurs on the second beat of the first measure of the example. The G in the viola moves immediately to an A and this is followed promptly in the second violin where the D-flat moves down to a C. In the span of a single quarter note, there are three different simultaneities. Given historical precedents, we might be strongly tempted to try to reduce this fast-moving succession to one that is simpler and slower moving.

But how? And by invoking what criteria? Is there any basis for arguing that any one of these three sonorities is more stable than the other two? Or that some of the tones are elaborative while the others are structural?

If we were to argue that the first inversion, diminished triad on G is the referential sonority, then we would have to understand the A in the viola as a passing tone and the C in the second violin as an incomplete neighbor, a kind of backwards escape tone. Well and good, but couldn't we just as logically argue that the trichord with which the beat concludes (B-flat, A, C) is the referential sonority? If we understand this as a root-position ninth chord on B-flat (minus third and fifth), then we would have to understand the G in the viola as the non-chord tone and the D-flat in the second violin as the incomplete neighbor, an almost exact mirror image of our previous reading. On what basis could we choose between the two readings? On what grounds could we claim that one is more stable than the other? Are not both equally common as chords in Schoenberg's music of this period?

Things hardly improve when we continue on to the second half of the measure. In quick succession we hear four different trichords, only one of which (a G-flat minor triad in first inversion) is entirely consonant. If that triad were the referential goal, then the G and A in the viola (third beat) would have to be regarded as passing tones. Yet that G-flat minor triad seems very weakly articulated, scarcely capable of being the referential center of the second half of the measure. Couldn't an equally strong case be made that it is the diminished triad immediately preceding that is referential? And according to either scenario how can one possibly interpret the final eighth of the measure?

We have already encountered many passages with precisely these kinds of ambiguities in Schoenberg's music. What is novel is not so much the concept, but the texture in which it occurs.

The newly adopted texture simultaneously permits and encourages the continued headlong evolution of Schoenberg's harmonic vocabulary. Increasingly, the conjunction of the different lines produces ever less traditional harmonic combinations. In this respect, the passage we have been examining is a relatively mild version of what we find elsewhere in the quartet because at least a fair number of the simultaneities that occur in these measures are relatively traditional harmonies. The opening major third suggests an incomplete triad, the simultaneity on the second beat is a first inversion diminished triad, and at the end of the second beat, the resultant trichord (B-flat, A, C) might be understood as an incomplete ninth chord. But harmonies in many other passages in the quartet are not even close to being this tame. One passage from the fughetto can stand for many (refer back to Ex. 7.4, above).

In earlier repertoires, the laws of counterpoint dictated that the conjunction of three or four different polyphonic lines would result in the frequent occurrence of major and minor triads or some of the most common types of seventh chords. In the passage in Ex. 7.4, consonant triads and traditional seventh chords are few and far between. This is not to say they are entirely absent: for example, a D-flat major, root position triad (enharmonically respelled) occurs at the end of m. 102 and a first inversion

D major triad on the second half of the second beat of m. 103. Most often, these chords are given no more prominence than any other sonority: by and large they are given neither agogic nor metric emphasis.

Rather than triads or common seventh chords, more and more we see new types of simultaneities. Of course, even in prior repertoires, one can find all kinds of unusual sonorities if one arbitrarily isolates a simultaneity in the middle of a complex contrapuntal passage. In earlier repertoires, unorthodox trichordal combinations of the sort that appear on the downbeat of m. 103 would invariably be clarified in some manner by the surrounding context. That is, it would become clear what tone was dissonant and the dissonant element in the sonority would normally resolve fairly quickly and directly, leading to a stable, consonant triad. What makes the passages from Op. 7 so innovatory is that there are no such resolutions. Unorthodox sonorities like the trichord on the downbeat of m. 103 proceed, not to consonant sonorities, but rather, to other, equally unorthodox trichords. In the passage under discussion, the F-sharp, F, A-flat trichord becomes F-sharp, A, A-flat on the second beat of the measure. This particular trichord is just as dissonant and just as resistant to traditional classification as the previous sonority. Although this second trichord does continue on to a first-inversion D major triad, that chord is very weakly articulated and very brief, yielding promptly to a new dissonant trichord, G, A, E-flat, on the third beat of the measure.

A striking characteristic of this music is that the quick pace of the attack rhythm brings about an almost equally quick harmonic rhythm. Over the course of m. 103, there are the following intervallic combinations (reading from the bass up): d8/d3; m3/d3; m6/m3; M9/m6; M9/d8; M9/d7; A5/d5; A5/d4.[43] As can be seen from this list, one of the obvious consequences of the pace of change is that no single vertical sonority gains prominence as a referential sonority. The pace of change is so quick that as soon as a chord is formed it is transformed into another chord, preventing any one chord from achieving rhythmic stability. The overwhelming prominence of trichords that are not triads and the organization of those trichords into successions that do not lead to, or are not anchored by, referential triads or traditional seventh chords is a significant step forward in the continuing radicalization of Schoenberg's harmonic vocabulary.

Even though the vertical sonorities that result from the conjunction of the different lines are often non-triadic, this does not mean that Schoenberg has sundered all connections with prior procedures. The relationships between specific pairs of voices often conform surprisingly well to some very traditional concepts of counterpoint, particularly in their placement of traditionally consonant intervals in prominent rhythmic positions.

If we isolate the second violin and viola parts and examine the relationships between them, what we find is that the intervallic relationships are not quite as radical as we might have expected, given the less than traditional simultaneities produced by the three voices. Measure 103 begins with a stable minor third between the second violin and viola. When the viola skips up to an A-natural on the second beat, this does create a fairly sharp dissonance. Because of its rhythmic profile, the A-flat in the second violin would undoubtedly be treated as a suspension in more traditional repertoires and would resolve downward by step to an imperfect consonance. In the present case, the violin part does move (to D) and does move to a consonance, but it does so by leap, not by step: a variant on the traditional idea (and one that we have seen Schoenberg use in prior works).

A succession of dissonances follows on the third beats, but the measure closes with a resolution to a major third (enharmonically spelled). In the remainder of the excerpt, many of the intervals formed in these two voices fit fairly comfortably into relatively traditional contrapuntal relationships. The faster moving values tend to create traditionally dissonant intervals, while traditionally consonant intervals tend to be either in metrically strong positions or are given agogic emphasis.

This is about as radical a passage as one can find in the quartet: in most other passages the pairings of the voices produce contrapuntal combinations that are even less of a challenge to traditional norms. To illustrate this, we can turn back to a passage we had been discussing earlier (Ex. 7.6, above). If we focus on and isolate any one of the three possible combinations of two voices, we find dissonance-consonance relationships that often appear to be rather tame, almost as if they are written in accord with traditional laws of species counterpoint. We see this clearly when we examine the bottom pairing, the viola and cello. In the first measure of the example, the A in the second beat in the viola looks like a traditional passing tone. Similarly, the B on the third beat and the D-flat on the fourth beat resemble passing and neighbor tones respectively. The only even slightly problematic relationship is created on the last eighth of the measure when the cello moves to B-flat, but even this looks like an incomplete neighbor. Similar situations result when we examine the other pairings. Taken in isolation, the intervallic relationships of each of the pairings seem to be compatible with traditional contrapuntal notions of dissonance treatment.

One of the reasons for this has to do with the character of Schoenberg's lines. As has been the case since the earliest of his compositions we have examined, stepwise motion predominates (frequently producing indeterminate scales). In the faster moving lines, skips are almost always followed or preceded by steps. Even where several skips occur in succession, either there is an arpeggiation within a chord or the second is a reverse skip which returns the line to a point stepwise removed from the first note of the passage.

The predominance of stepwise motion in the faster moving lines is what makes it possible for the different pairings of voices to conform so cleanly to traditional patterns of contrapuntal treatment. It is a property of the chromatic collection that any dissonant interval can be changed to a consonant interval if one of the two tones is held while the other moves by whole- or half-step. Any dissonant interval formed between two voices can be transformed into a consonant interval if the faster moving line moves by step. This is often what happens in the discrete pairings of voices.

I have purposely chosen a passage of three voices to illustrate the point. The predominance of stepwise motion in the lines (particularly the faster moving lines), when taken together with the property described above, means that Schoenberg's two-voice contrapuntal pairings produce combinations that might not have incensed even relatively conservative observers of the time.

But, of course, the fabric is not always limited to two voices. Although the individual pairings might be compatible with traditional notions of species counterpoint, the simultaneities created by multiple voices are often anything but traditional. Classifiable triads and seventh chords do occur, of course, but so do vertical sonorities that cannot be readily classified in traditional terms. And this serves to highlight a crucial conceptual connection with Schoenberg's earlier music. We have already seen that Schoenberg's novel chords in *Pelleas und Melisande* and elsewhere relied heavily on the principle of localized consonance. When building new chords, Schoenberg took pains to construct them in a manner that segments of those chords (usually isolated by register or orchestration) had subsets formed from traditional triads or closely related harmonies. The procedures Schoenberg employed for the organization of his counterpoint are virtually identical. The simultaneities that result from the combination of all of the voices are often anything but traditional, but the contrapuntal relationships between pairs of voices are frequently relatively traditional in their treatment of dissonance.

Schoenberg's adaptation of the idea of localized consonance to contrapuntal technique is evident not only when the voices in a passage are rhythmically independent from one another, but also, when two of the voices fall into a 1:1 relationship and are then pitted against other voices. Consider the second violin and viola in Ex. 7.5 (above) where the two lines move in complete lockstep. The intervals that Schoenberg chooses for this pairing are none other than parallel thirds, making the intervallic relationships completely unobjectionable by traditional measures. But this combination does not occur in isolation; it is juxtaposed with two other voices creating a host of radical four-note simultaneities.

A necessary consequence of the growing importance of these types of contrapuntal passages is the continued decline of the simple triad as a prominent entity on the musical surface. The continuous use of polyphonic surfaces encourages and intensifies this trend. More and more often, there are extended passages that are not only completely devoid of triads, they are even sparsely populated with traditional seventh chords.

The near total absence of triads means that cadences are few and far between, reserved primarily for the largest formal units. It further follows that longer and longer stretches of the musical surface are not tied to identifiable key centers. Unambiguously defined key centers come into focus only at a relatively few important points of formal articulation, with their organizing force not extending particularly far in either direction.

As in prior works, the relative infrequency of clearly defined tonal centers prompts Schoenberg to use the technique of transposition to create a sense of large scale motion. In Op. 7 this tends to be more the transposition of themes or motives than (as in Opp. 4 and 5) whole blocks of material. A typical example is the transposed (and augmented) statement of the principal theme that occurs in the cello beginning in m. 79 (Ex. 7.7).

Had this been the only instance of the principal theme that was ever presented, it is not at all certain that it would have established a clear and unambiguous tonal center. The absence of a clear diatonic collection and the almost complete lack of anything resembling an A triad (excepting only the fleeting appearance on the second sixteenth of m. 79) make it unlikely that this statement would have been sufficient to establish A as a key center. Although we may not be able to identify the key center of mm. 79ff, we can recognize that we have moved away from the original pitch level of the work because the opening of the work was clearly in D and here there is a clear transposition of that opening theme.

There are other passages where it is not possible to identify a tonal center for the original statement but it still is possible to infer large-scale motion. An obvious instance of this occurs very near the beginning of the composition. The highly chromatic passage that appears in mm. 8–10 does not focus around any referential triad or tonic pitch (see Ex. 7.8). The sequential alternation between perfect fourths and major thirds in the cello line works counter to the establishment of a referential diatonic collection. The succession of augmented seventh chords is incompatible with any single tonal center. In spite of our inability to identify a tonal center for this

Example 7.7

passage, we can easily recognize that the passage that follows in mm. 10–12 (the beginning of which appears at the end of the example) is a transposition up four semitones. It follows that we can recognize the distance traveled from the first to the second, even though neither has an identifiable key center.

Although there are occasional pairs of transposed passages like those seen in Ex. 7.8, Schoenberg uses the technique of literal repetition (or transposed literal repetition) far more sparingly than in prior works. In Op. 7, varied repetitions are the norm and literal repetitions the exception.

Schoenberg's growing reluctance to restate phrases in literal form should be seen as a manifestation of his increasing belief that repetitions should be varied, and that the changes made should embody or reflect the developmental process. As we have already seen in our discussion of form, this is a

Example 7.8

central component of Schoenberg's thought on the largest level of structure: Schoenberg's reprises are varied, often extensively, and frequently function to synthesize prior strands of development.

Non-literal repetition is also embodied on the small scale, in the formation of Schoenberg's themes. The opening theme of this quartet is a model instance of these procedures (see Ex. 7.9).

This theme is a particularly elegant illustration of the technique of developing variation in which a very few basic motives are combined to produce a rather extended theme. Already a factor in prior works, developing variation starts to become more and more central to Schoenberg's compositional approach, spreading out through the work to involve a greater proportion of the thematic material. This is manifested both in the formation of individual themes from a limited arsenal of motivic kernels (as in Ex. 7.9), and in the production of further thematic ideas by a continuous process of developmental change. For example, the theme that occurs in the second violin in mm. 14–17 (see Ex. 7.6, above) is a reformulation of the very same motivic elements that Schoenberg had used in the opening theme.

This does not mean that the technique of developing variation has been extended to permeate the entirety of the composition, accounting for all themes. It does not seem possible to claim with credibility that any of the principal contrasting themes that occur later in the quartet should be understood to be derivatives of the opening theme. To take an obvious

Example 7.9

1. See m. 6 for identical rhythm.
2. See mm. 2, 3, 4, 5, 6 for this rhythm.
3. See end of this measure, beginning of next for same pitch succession, but different contour.
4. See next measure for varied ending (E instead of F).
5. See m. 4 for an interval expansion version of this figure.

example, the theme of the fughetto (see Ex. 7.4 above) is as different as a theme can be from the opening theme. If anything, Schoenberg seems to have gone to some lengths to make this theme different from those that had preceded it and there does not seem to be a convincing path of development that connects it with its antecedents. This may be due, in part, to the programmatic nature of the composition, with its need for distinct themes. Even though all of the thematic material is not derived from a single source, there is no question that this work is the most motivically concise of Schoenberg's instrumental works to date. And it cannot be entirely coincidental that there is a noticeable increase in the importance and centrality of motivic concision and of developing variation in a composition that is as beholden to the principles of absolute music as it is to the principles of programmatic music.

In some important ways, Schoenberg's String Quartet, Op. 7 represents both an end and a beginning. As Schoenberg's last narrative programmatic composition, it has many important features that will not play a significant role in subsequent compositions. As his first extended attempt to confront the challenges of absolute music, it represents the germination of ideas that will take on increasing importance in works to come.

8 Referential centers? Lieder and fragments, Fall 1905

> Very soon it became doubtful whether such a root still remained the centre to which every harmony and harmonic succession must be referred.[1]

For a brief period after the completion of the String Quartet, Op. 7, Schoenberg turned his attention back to the writing of lieder. During the fall of 1905, he completed five songs: "Alles", Op. 6, No. 2 (6 September), "Der Wanderer", Op. 6, No. 8 (15 October), "Am Wegrand", Op. 6, No. 6 (18 October), "Lockung", Op. 6, No. 7 (26 October), and "Mädchenlied", Op. 6, No. 3 (28 October).[2] The pitch language of this group of songs is noticeably more radical than that of the songs that were written between *Pelleas und Melisande* and the String Quartet, Op. 7, only a year or so previously.

The five songs of this group vary considerably in compositional character, technique, and structure. In this chapter, I examine selected aspects of each, paying particular attention to those features that touch upon some of the central themes we have been following.[3]

During this same period, Schoenberg also started a number of other works which were never finished. Chief among these is a chamber piece, *Ein Stelldichein* (begun 21 October 1905). This was clearly intended to be a major project and Schoenberg made considerable progress on it, but at some point he broke off work, never to return. This is one of the more intriguing of the many fragments in Schoenberg's legacy, and merits close attention.

"Alles", Op. 6, No. 2

Alone among the five songs from this period, "Alles" returns to Schoenberg's favorite poet from his early period, Richard Dehmel. Like most of Schoenberg's songs, the formal structure is relatively simple: a two-part, varied reprise form (A, mm. 1–24, A', mm. 25–36) with piano postlude (mm. 36–41). As is usual, the A' section is a highly varied transformation of the A section. Also like many other compositions from this period, Schoenberg's use of the various techniques of motivic transformation and developing variation is subtle, effective, and pervasive. Particularly noteworthy is the way in which themes appear and reappear, each time with a different intervallic succession. The five-note theme (x) that appears for

Example 8.1

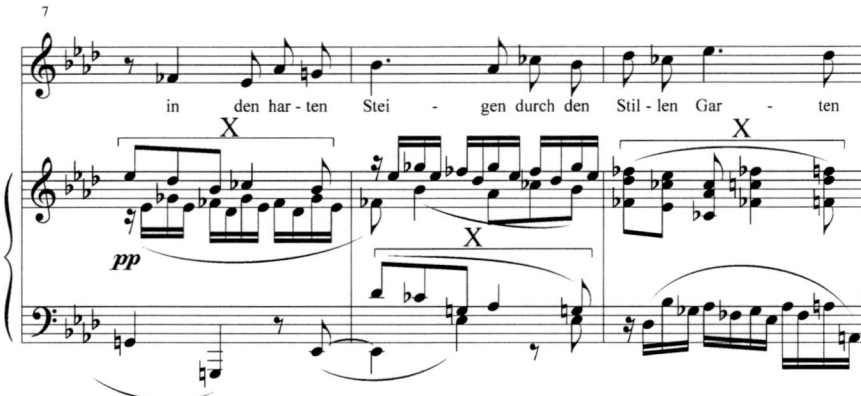

the first time in the topmost line in the piano in m. 7 reappears many times over the course of the song, but in a variety of transformations. After its initial statement in m. 7, further statements of x appear in mm. 8–13, each time with a different intervallic succession (see Ex. 8.1).

For the most part (and unlike most of Schoenberg's previous songs), the texture of this work is polyphonic. This, in turn, permitted Schoenberg to incorporate some of the contrapuntal devices and techniques (e.g. invertible counterpoint: cf mm. 2 and 6) that had appeared in such profusion in the String Quartet, Op. 7. This does not signify a permanent change in Schoenberg's propensity to distinguish between genres and as a general rule his songs will continue to be more homophonic than his instrumental works. But the presence of polyphonic texture within a song is a clear indication of the increasing importance of counterpoint and contrapuntal techniques for Schoenberg's compositional thought regardless of genre.

By far, the most striking aspect of this song – one with obvious significance for Schoenberg's development – is the way in which the tonic is projected over the course of the composition. Or, perhaps it would be more accurate to say the way in which the tonic is *not* projected over the course of the composition.[4] Up until the final cadence, there is not a single clear instance of the tonic triad and even the final cadence is less than traditional, so much so that the final A-flat triad sounds like a surprise, almost an afterthought (see Ex. 8.2). Although a somewhat disguised dominant had surfaced in the first beat of m. 40, it quickly dissolves and the penultimate sonority might best be understood as an incomplete first-inversion dominant-seventh chord on A. Even at the final cadence, the supposed tonic is not strongly articulated: it is simply stated, not confirmed by supportive harmonic progressions.

Example 8.2

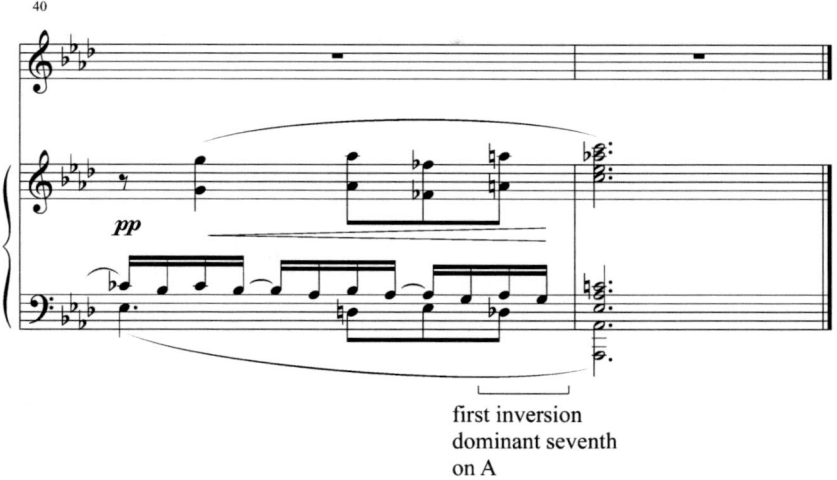

first inversion
dominant seventh
on A

Example 8.3

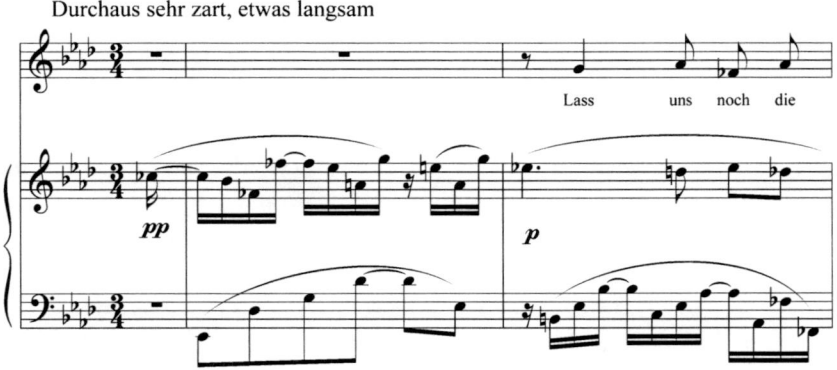

One might argue that there are a number of earlier points where it is possible for a diligent analyst to identify A-flat as a potential referential center (for example, the dominant-tonic progressions in mm. 1–2, 5–6, 10–11, 25, and 34–5). But those statements are so veiled that for many listeners (even for highly trained listeners, even after multiple hearings) there is little sense that A-flat is firmly established.

The opening two measures provide a good example of how A-flat major is so weakly projected until the very end of the composition (see Ex. 8.3).

On the one hand, there is a clear arpeggiation of the dominant seventh of A-flat in the bass in m. 1. In m. 2, the bass line continues, first with further arpeggiation of the dominant (if one ignores, for the moment, the B-natural) and then with an equally clear arpeggiation of the tonic triad. If the bass line could have been heard in isolation, there might have been some strong support for A-flat as a referential tonic, right from the beginning.

The problem is that this line is not heard in isolation and that the clear arpeggiations in the left hand are not supported by what happens in the right hand. In prior repertoires, one might have tried to reconcile the two lines by attempting to distinguish between chord tones and non-chord tones. If we try to analyze the passage in that manner, we can make some headway, at least at first. The opening C-flat could be understood as a suspension, resolving to the chord tone B-flat. So too, the F-flat might be understood as resolving to the chord tone E-flat. And in m. 2, the D natural in the r.h. could be understood as a lower neighbor.

Alas, the remaining tones in the r.h. cannot be so easily explained. How do we view the A naturals (during the third and fourth beats)? They seem to have no obvious contrapuntal function or obvious point of resolution. Does this mean we should see them as chord tones, perhaps helping to form an altered dominant seventh chord – with a lowered fifth – a moderately common chord type in Schoenberg's early works? And how do we understand the E-natural in the third beat? As an enharmonic equivalent to F-flat – in other words, as a reappearance of the minor ninth, once again resolving to E-flat (on the downbeat of m. 2)? And is there any explanation for the B-natural in the left hand in m. 2? As a displaced incomplete neighbor to the following B-flat a diminished octave higher? Or as an incomplete neighbor of the C in the l.h. in the second beat?

Even if we accept all of these explanations for the "non-chord" tones (and some of these seem more than a bit dubious), this would still fail to capture the overall sense of the passage. There are so many of these tones and they occur in such quick succession that it is difficult to distinguish between supposed chord tones and supposed tones of elaboration. Because of the relatively slow tempo and the contrapuntal texture, the "non-chord" tones create sonorities along the way that have as much claim to stability and cogency as the putative dominant and tonic. For instance, in m. 1, on the second eighth note, the D-flat in the bass and the F-flat in the right hand create a consonant interval, suggesting perhaps, a D-flat minor triad. Similarly, from the fourth to the fifth eighths of the measure, the intersection of the "chord" and "non-chord" tones produces an incomplete dominant seventh chord on A (assuming enharmonic equivalence of C-sharp for D-flat). This is followed immediately (on the last eighth of the measure) by a second-inversion seventh chord on A (missing its third, but perhaps the D-flat's influence persists?). Long before the dominant seventh has completed its arpeggiation, other local sonorities have come to the forefront of our attention, making it difficult to isolate the dominant and tonic chords as independent entities.

There is nothing completely new about this approach. As we have seen in prior works, Schoenberg had long organized the surface of his compositions in such a manner that the motion of the different voices produced fast moving successions of harmonies. The difference here is that this procedure is applied even to the hints of the tonic and dominant chords at the beginning of the composition and this makes it very difficult to establish a tonic. Since there is no place – other than the final cadence – where there is an unambiguously stated tonic chord, the tonic is less clearly articulated in this work than in any previous song. The final cadence does create a sense of motion to less dissonance and this does impart a sense of closure, but it is far from certain that this particular triad was the inevitable, irresistible, and only possible focus of that resolution.

In the 1922 edition of *Harmonielehre*, Schoenberg defines tonality as:

> ... a formal possibility that emerges from the nature of the tonal material, a possibility of attaining a certain completeness or closure (*Geschlossenheit*) by means of a certain uniformity. To realize this possibility it is necessary to use in the course of a piece only those sounds (*Klänge*) and successions of sounds, and these only in a suitable arrangement, whose relations to the fundamental tone of the key, to the tonic of the piece, can be grasped without difficulty.[5]

To my ear, at least, this composition does not meet Schoenberg's definition of tonality. It seems clear to me that the "sounds (*Klänge*) and successions of sounds" of this song are not used in a "suitable arrangement, whose relations to the fundamental tone of the key, to the tonic of the piece, can be grasped without difficulty." I venture to say that if one were to remove the final triad from this piece, and take a poll of competent listeners asking what the final chord would be, I doubt very much whether there would be much, if any, uniformity in their answers. (Given the presence of a dominant seventh chord on A as the penultimate chord, I suspect a common guess would be D, not A-flat.) And if a "referential tonic" cannot be grasped at all (let alone "without difficulty"), then in what sense is it referential?[6] Seen from this perspective, I would argue that "Alles" is without a meaningful referential tonic.

As such, "Alles" brings to the smaller dimensions of the song the lack of "completeness or closure (*Geschlossenheit*)" that had already begun to be a distinguishing feature of Schoenberg's larger instrumental compositions (and which we will examine in more detail in the coming chapter). Beginning with "Alles", we see that the lack of an easily graspable referential center is no longer only a feature of sprawling instrumental works, but has become a feature even of relatively short songs.

"Der Wanderer", Op. 6, No. 8[7]

In many important ways, "Der Wanderer" contrasts sharply with the previous work. "Alles" was relatively short and compact; "Der Wanderer" is one of the longest of Schoenberg's songs. "Alles" sets a work by one of Schoenberg's favorite poets (Dehmel); "Der Wanderer" is Schoenberg's only setting of a poem by Nietzsche. "Alles" is typical of Schoenberg's song forms, in that it is a simple form with a tightly controlled motivic structure; "Der Wanderer" is an unusual (at least for Schoenberg) form (ABCA'), in which the B and C sections do not have evident motivic relationships either with each other or with the surrounding A sections. "Alles" is primarily polyphonic; "Der Wanderer" returns to the more typical melody-with-chordal-accompaniment texture of Schoenberg's songs. In spite of these differences, there are also some important areas of common concern.

Even though the texture of "Der Wanderer" is more homophonic than its immediate predecessor, Schoenberg employs imitation (mm. 13–16) and makes use of the technique of invertible counterpoint (cf mm. 1 and 71), further evidence of the growing importance of contrapuntal procedures and traditional devices for Schoenberg's compositional technique. Also like its predecessor, "Der Wanderer" retains the rhythmic structure of motives and themes while constantly changing their intervallic successions (e.g. mm. 1–7, piano r.h.).

Most significantly, just as "Alles" avoids clear statements of a referential tonic, "Der Wanderer" elaborates on a similar theme. This is evident from the very beginning of the song, where the opening figure in the piano creates an interesting ambiguity (see Ex. 8.4). Although Schoenberg's initial adherence to the diatonic collection of the key signature, and his

Example 8.4

placement of a downbeat G after an upbeat octave on D might seem to suggest a tonal center of G minor – with the G even being approached by its dominant – other aspects of the passage make that definition something less than certain. Instead of confirming G, the passage continually seems to drift toward D. The emphasized octave Ds in the l.h., the rhythmic flow of the r.h. figure toward its final D, the placement of D as the lowest sounding tone in each phrase all combine to compromise the stability of G. Rather than projecting a stable root position, tonic chord, the passage appears to suggest a 6/4 chord.

By intimating what the tonal center could be, but failing to confirm it, Schoenberg reveals yet another approach to constructing passages without clear tonal centers. Moreover, his interest in this problem is not limited to the beginning of the song. Even after its equivocal initial statements, G minor never receives much emphasis. Other than a brief cadence-like arrival on a unison G in m. 21, the presumed tonic disappears completely from view until its reemergence toward the end of the song (m. 70).

In the intervening passages (that is, most of the song) there are long stretches without clear referential tonics, including most of the B section. In his own analysis (written many years after the fact), Schoenberg identifies several key areas (he calls them "regions") in the C section of the song. He sees this section beginning in D, moving to B-flat, F (first major, then minor) and back to B-flat, where the section ends.[8] Most of the key areas Schoenberg identifies are very weakly articulated, with the suggested tonic either never stated in complete form or appearing together with prominent tones of dissonance.

Although most of Schoenberg's previous works included stretches (some quite lengthy) that lacked referential tonal centers, at some point he had proceeded to a fairly clearly emphasized arrival on a triad. Even in those cases where the tonal uncertainty was prolonged throughout the song – as we have just seen with "Alles" – Schoenberg normally settles on a stable triad to conclude the work. "Der Wanderer" marks a significant milestone in that it fails to provide a stable triad as the final sonority (see Ex. 8.5).

Instead of concluding with a clear, root position, G minor triad, Schoenberg concludes with a 6/4 position. As at the beginning of the song, the energy of the principal motive (in the l.h. in augmentation) is directed toward the final D, not toward the preceding G. As a result, the final sonority is a G minor triad in second inversion. Schoenberg had already used second inversion triads as cadential sonorities in the middle of a work. Here he extends the idea to the final cadence as well. Schoenberg was probably aware that there were historical precedents for ending a work with an apparent 6/4: "Eusebius" from Schumann's *Carnaval*, Op. 9 is an

Example 8.5

obvious example. The innovation of Schoenberg's contribution is not its use of a second inversion triad as a cadential goal; rather, it is the use of that chord as the only real point of cadential closure anywhere in the composition. Although "Eusebius" closes with an E-flat triad in second inversion, E-flat had never been in doubt as the referential center of that work and had appeared in more stable manifestations elsewhere in the work (e.g. a solid authentic cadence in m. 24). In "Der Wanderer", Schoenberg undermines the stability of G minor at every opportunity, including the final cadence.

"Am Wegrand", Op. 6, No. 6

Schoenberg completed his next song, "Am Wegrand", only three days after "Der Wanderer". As with its immediate predecessor, this song is Schoenberg's unique setting of a poet, in this case, a poem by John Henry Mackay.

Here too Schoenberg constructs subtle and sophisticated formal structures from rather simple premises. The work divides into two principal sections (mm. 3–16 and 22–36) that are preceded and followed by short sections for piano solo. The second section (mm. 22–36) simultaneously restates earlier material and combines it with new material. For example, at mm. 22ff, the bass line is a restatement of the vocal line from mm. 3ff, while a new theme is added in the vocal line.[9] In m. 27, Schoenberg transposes this whole complex to G and redistributes its material, thereby showing his continuing interest in compositional devices such as invertible counterpoint.

This song reflects some of Schoenberg's central preoccupations from this period. Versions of the motives that first appear in the piano part in m. 1

Example 8.6

continue through much of the composition, but with constantly changing intervallic successions. So too, "Am Wegrand" reflects Schoenberg's continuing quest to expand his harmonic vocabulary. A number of radical chords appear (even beyond the now common instances of chords of fourths as in mm. 12 and 18). Particularly prominent is the five-tone chord that appears in mm. 20–1 (see Ex. 8.6) and that has the crucial function as the preparation for the (altered) reprise. Like many of Schoenberg's other radical chords, this one also can be understood to include traditional elements and to rely on the notion of localized consonance. It is possible to understand this chord as having two layers: the bottom three tones of the chord (B D F) form a diminished triad, while a minor third, B-flat D-flat, appears in the upper register.

Also striking is the extended emphasis on whole tone structures, particularly in the altered reprise.[10] Beginning in m. 23, chords and lines outline clear sonorities based on segments of the whole tone scale. Most prominent, is the extended whole tone scale in the voice and top layer of the piano r.h. in mm. 33–5 (see Ex. 8.7).

In contrast to the two previous songs, there is a clear and unequivocal confirmation of a referential tonal center at the beginning of the work: the constant reiteration of a pedal tone in the first seven measures unequivocally establishes D as the opening referential center.

Nonetheless, the clarity of tonal definition in "Am Wegrand" is not that much greater than the two preceding songs. Other than the places where pedal tones are used to establish a referential center, there are very few other points where there is any real sense of referential stability. With the

Example 8.7

exception of infrequent arrivals on stable triads (e.g. D-flat, m. 10, E-flat, m. 15) the texture is comprised of a succession of chords that imply no specific key, or if they do (as with the dominant seventh chords in m. 24), the implied triads never appear. Other than through pedal points – a rather blunt tool – referential centricity in this work is weakly and infrequently articulated. As such, this work is concerned (though in a different manner) with the same issues Schoenberg faced in the prior two songs.

"Lockung", Op. 6, No. 7

Continuing his brisk pace of composition, Schoenberg turned first to a new chamber work, *Ein Stelldichein*. However, he did not stop writing lieder, and he completed his next song, "Lockung", only eight days after finishing "Am Wegrand". The text he chose was a rather curious poem by Kurt Aram (once again, Schoenberg's unique setting of a poet) that depicts a cat who is trying to catch a mouse by tricking it into believing there is no danger (undoubtedly a metaphor for sexual seduction).[11]

This song is relatively well known because on two separate occasions Schoenberg wrote about it, describing it as exemplifying important aspects of his progressive harmonic practice. In *Harmonielehre* (published 1911), Schoenberg cited "Lockung" as an example of "schwebende Tonalität": "Two pregnant examples of fluctuating tonality [schwebende Tonalität] from my own compositions are: *Orchesterlied*, Op. 8, No. 5, 'Voll jener Süsse', which wavers principally between *Db* and *B* major; and Op. 6, No. 7 (*Lied*), 'Lockung', which expresses an *Eb*-major tonality without once in the course of the piece giving an *Eb*-major triad in such a way that one could regard it as a pure tonic. The one time it does appear, it has a tendency, at least, toward the subdominant."[12] Many years later (in the 1940s) in *Structural Functions of Harmony*, Schoenberg returned to this song, again mentioning its schwebende Tonalität (which here is translated as "suspended tonality"). This time, Schoenberg provides harmonic analyses of a number of passages from the song, and remarks that "many parts of the song must be analysed in **sm**"[13] (i.e. in the submediant minor: C minor).

Given the significant differences in the tonal structure of the two works he cites, it is not entirely clear precisely what Schoenberg meant by schwebende Tonalität. Nevertheless, his analytical description does capture an important element of the harmonic structure of this song. Through much of the song, the supposed tonic, E-flat, is not perceptible (although sometimes a version of its dominant is).[14] Up until the ending of the song, a more likely candidate for tonic status would be C minor, as Schoenberg intimated in his analysis in *Structural Functions*. The ambiguity is not entirely dispelled by the final measures: the concluding E-flat tonic is a simple octave, not supported by the remaining notes of the triad. Still further, it is approached, not from a dominant chord, but simply by descending half-step motion from the lowered second degree.

For these reasons, Schoenberg's summary conclusion – that the song "expresses an E♭-major tonality" – is an interesting and problematic analytical assertion. What does it mean to claim that a single octave at the end of a work takes on referential status for the whole work, particularly when it was neither predicted nor implied in any meaningful sense beforehand? In what sense does this tonic achieve referential status and what does that referentiality imply? In what way is the prior material (the entire song) integrated with this "tonic"? Perhaps this assertion lays itself open to the most obvious reductio ad absurdum: if one simply writes anything – anything at all – and then slaps on a triad at the end, is it a referential center for the whole work?

For our purposes, however, it is probably not necessary to judge whether or not Schoenberg's (ex post facto) analytical explanations are conceptually (or perceptually) sound (or for that matter, are in accord with his own definition of tonality). What is important is that in the fall of 1905 Schoenberg's compositional language has developed to the point that he has written a composition of sixty-five measures and withheld any clear definition of a referential tonic until the last measure. Whether or not its arrival endows the whole song with a referential center may be debatable; what is not debatable is that this is another realization of a concept that has been a central focus of the songs from this period.

Example 8.8

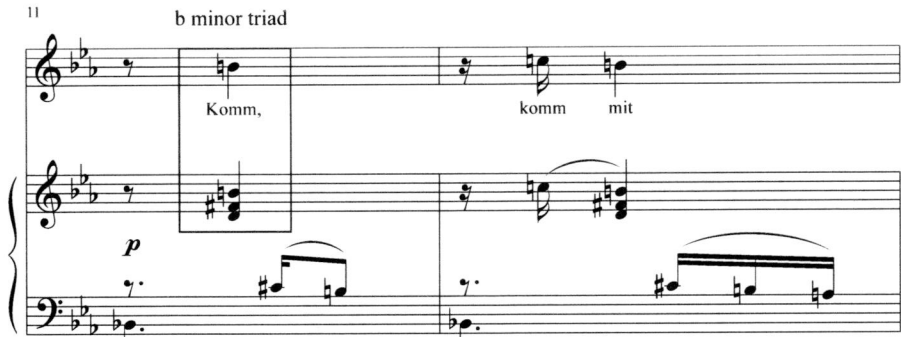

The harmonic vocabulary that Schoenberg uses in this song also reflects incremental steps forward. It is instructive to compare the harmonic vocabulary of this composition with that of the songs from Schoenberg's most recent period of lieder writing, in 1903–4: in a little less than two years, there has been an appreciable change in Schoenberg's repertoire of chords. Although there are still occasional triads and seventh chords, more and more of the chords do not readily fall into traditional categories. Consider, in this regard, the chord that occurs in mm. 11–12 (see Ex. 8.8).

In his analysis in *Structural Functions*, Schoenberg calls this a dominant chord, not even putting a slash through the V to indicate that it is an altered chord.[15] But this is no ordinary dominant. The core elements of the chord (those that appear to have the most stability) are the four tones: B-flat, D F-sharp and B-natural. By identifying this as a dominant chord, Schoenberg implies that this is a chord built on B-flat, with a raised fifth, missing seventh, and (enharmonically spelled) minor ninth. (I would suggest that it is also possible to understand this chord as another instance of Schoenberg's penchant to employ the principle of localized consonance in building his chords: there is a consonant, and registrally compact, subset, a B minor triad that is pitted opposite a registrally distinct B-flat.)

"Mädchenlied", Op. 6, No. 3

Like the other songs from this period, "Mädchenlied" was written quickly (it was completed only two days after "Lockung"), and is another of Schoenberg's unique settings of a poet (Paul Remer). Also like the other songs from this period, the basic formal plan is rather simple. Schoenberg employs a modified bar form (AA'B) in which the B section, though contrasting in tempo, retains numerous explicit thematic and motivic connections with the preceding A sections. (Because of those motivic connections it could also be viewed as a kind of variation form, AA'A"). In the rather droll text, the young girl first describes how angry her mother would be if she knew how ardently her lover kissed her (the A section). Next, the girl describes how violently angry her brother would be if he knew how ardently her lover kissed her (the A' section). Then in the last section of the text, the girl describes how jealous her sister would be if she knew how ardently her lover kissed her (the B section).

In contrast to its immediate predecessor, a referential tonic appears in unambiguous form, right at the beginning of the work. Because of the formal plan, that tonic is never absent for very long, returning in equally clear form at the beginning of the A' and the end of the B sections. Therefore, this work avoids most of the issues of tonal ambiguity that characterized other works from this period.

"Mädchenlied" more than compensates for the relative conservatism of its overall tonal structure with some of the most radical harmonic vocabulary seen up to this point in Schoenberg's compositions. In addition to the now typical use of almost every possible type of seventh and ninth chord in every possible inversion, Schoenberg also makes extensive use of other less-than-traditional chords such as whole tone pentachords (e.g. m. 11 and m. 24). He also introduces some sonorities that are very difficult to classify in traditional terms. For example, the progression in mm. 13–14 has two types of harmony (see Ex. 8.9).

The passage begins sequentially, in which the pattern on the first beat of m. 13 is transposed two times, each time up three semitones. But what is being transposed? Because of the arpeggio-like structure in the l.h. as well as the doubling and skips, the F and B-flat seem to have unquestioned status as chord tones. But what about the other tones? The D and D-flat seem to coexist and there seems to be no mechanism for determining whether the A-flat, G, and E are, or are not, individually or in total, chord or non-chord tones.

Equally innovatory is the sonority that begins on the last beat of m. 13 and lasts until the end of m. 14 (marked X). This too cannot be reduced to a single traditional chord. Instead, this seems to be another instance of Schoenberg's use of the idea of localized consonance, with two registrally distinct strands, an F-flat minor seventh chord (in the l.h.) and an A-flat/E-flat fifth in the r.h.

Ein Stelldichein

A striking feature of Schoenberg's oeuvre is the large number of compositions that he started, but never completed. There seem to be three fairly

Example 8.9

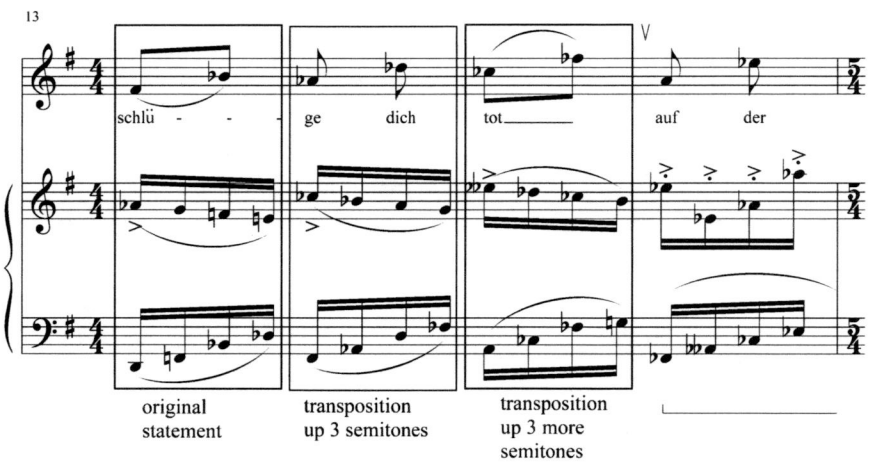

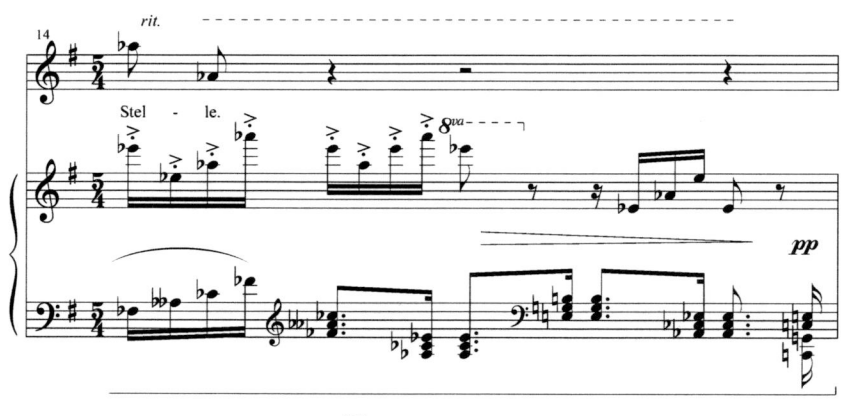

distinct categories of incomplete compositions. One is made up of very large works on which Schoenberg had made considerable progress but was interrupted for some reason. After the interruption, Schoenberg found it difficult to pick up the thread and complete the work. *Jakobsleiter* (interrupted by Schoenberg's military service in World War I) and *Moses und Aron* (interrupted by Schoenberg's emigration from Nazi Germany) are the most prominent members of this category. At least three other major works (*Gurrelieder*, Variations for Orchestra, Op. 31, and the Second Chamber Symphony, Op. 38) very nearly fell into this category.

Another category includes works that are best understood as early drafts for compositions that were eventually completed. Typically, these works have no obvious motivic or thematic connections with the completed works that follow them (and thus are not, literally speaking, first drafts), but the instrumentation, character, or chronology make it clear that the works are related in a general way. The programmatic string sextet fragment, *Toter Winkel*, can be understood as a kind of first draft for what evolved into *Verklärte Nacht*; the fugal string quartet fragment of 1904 is very probably an early stage of what became the String Quartet, Op. 7; the Passacaglia for Orchestra is a preliminary version of what became the Variations for Orchestra, Op. 31.[16]

A third category of incomplete works is made up of relatively short compositions (such as songs) that Schoenberg started, worked on for a brief period and then abandoned. There are a number of those works in the period between the String Quartet, Op. 7 and the beginning of the Chamber Symphony, Op. 9. During this period Schoenberg started, but did not complete, eight songs for voice with piano accompaniment: "O wär mein Herz", "Was thust, was denkst du", "Ich weiß nicht", "O süße Blick", "Die Poesie", "Lied eines Sünders", "Apostatenmarsch", and "Die Kürze".

Ein Stelldichein does not fit comfortably into any of these three categories. Schoenberg wrote a rough draft of a slow section (Sehr langsam) of ninety measures, and then more than forty measures of a fast section (Sehr rasch, heftig). As such, this fragment is too big to fit into the category of works Schoenberg barely began and in which he quickly lost interest. Nor does it fit into the category of shorter fragments that served as rough first drafts for other works. As far as is known, there was no external event that functioned to interrupt his work. For reasons we may never know, Schoenberg simply stopped working on this composition and instead began work on the Chamber Symphony, Op. 9.

Ein Stelldichein does provide us with some interesting evidence regarding Schoenberg's evolving attitudes toward programmatic music. In some important respects *Ein Stelldichein* is different from Schoenberg's previous programmatic compositions. Schoenberg's three completed programmatic works (*Verklärte Nacht*, *Pelleas und Melisande*, and String Quartet, Op. 7) are all based on texts that tell a clear story. This allowed Schoenberg to employ a broad array of leitmotifs to describe the action (e.g. the "walking" leitmotif in *Verklärte Nacht*), or portray a character (Golaud's leitmotif in *Pelleas und Melisande*), or depict a specific mood (neues Leben fühlend of Op. 7). By contrast, the poem Schoenberg used for *Ein Stelldichein* (Dehmel) is rather subtle and elliptical, lacking a clear narrative storyline.

It is probably not happenstance that the motivic structure of this fragment contrasts with Schoenberg's other completed programmatic works. To varying degrees all of the completed programmatic compositions are motivically and thematically garrulous. By contrast, *Ein Stelldichein* is very sparing in its use of themes. Not only does the opening slow section work with a very few basic themes, but also, the fast section begins with a transformation of one of those themes (cf piano, mm. 1–2 and 92ff).

For all of these reasons, *Ein Stelldichein* occupies an interesting niche in Schoenberg's development: it is programmatic, but different from any of his prior programmatic works. It is a chamber composition, but one for a mixed ensemble (perhaps in that sense it prefigures the Chamber Symphony). It is (relatively speaking) tightly controlled in terms of motivic structure, something that has not been a feature of Schoenberg's instrumental compositions before this point. Were it not for its title and associated poem, one might not have guessed that there was anything programmatic about it. It appears that the program has been reduced to providing a general mood or atmosphere, lacking significant control over the formal structure or the choice or the placement of themes. As such, *Ein Stelldichein* plays an important role in the transition toward how Schoenberg would treat the programmatic idea for the rest of his career. As Walter Bailey has shown, programmatic elements remain in Schoenberg's works up to the end, but never again as narrative stories that direct the formal and thematic structure of the work. Instead, like *Ein Stelldichein*, programmatic elements are a component, usually a subsidiary one, in an environment where the emphasis was tilted decisively in the direction of absolute music.

For all of their diversity, the songs and fragments of the period between the String Quartet, Op. 7 and the Chamber Symphony, Op. 9, share some important common threads: an interest in experimenting with weakening or deferring the establishment of a referential tonic and the continued radicalization of the harmonic vocabulary. With *Ein Stelldichein* Schoenberg also continued his slow transition toward absolute music. These important tendencies merge in Schoenberg's next major work, the Chamber Symphony, Op. 9, and to that pivotal composition we can now turn.

9 Absolute music and its consequences: Chamber Symphony, Op. 9, 1905–6

> ... to an ever increasing extent the tonic could merely be proved, intellectually, to be in command while it steadily became harder to hear.[1]

Toward the end of 1905, Schoenberg made a few sketches for a new orchestral work.[2] As Jan Maegaard has shown, one of its themes bears a strong resemblance to a theme from the scherzo section of the Chamber Symphony, Op. 9. This suggests that the fragment is the first stage of work on what became the Chamber Symphony.[3] In line with his restless search for innovation, Schoenberg quickly dropped plans for a conventional orchestral ensemble, writing instead a symphony for a chamber ensemble of fifteen soloists.[4]

There may have been practical motivations for not writing an orchestral work at this point in his career. In 1905 Schoenberg had two other compositions with orchestra on his desk, neither of which had been performed, and, as it turned out, neither of which would be until far in the future. *Gurrelieder* was not premiered until 23 February 1913 and the Six Songs with Orchestra, Op. 8 would not be performed (and even then, only songs 1, 2, and 5) until 29 January 1914.[5]

Although Schoenberg cannot have been happy with the number of performances he had received by late 1905, there was one really bright spot in his career. From the moment that the Rosé Quartet had seen the score for *Verklärte Nacht*, its members had become his advocates. Not only had they given the work its premiere in March 1902, but also, they performed the work two more times (19 February 1904 and 1 March 1904).[6] If that were not enough, sight unseen they had asked Schoenberg to send them a quartet and had promised it multiple performances. This – as we have seen – prompted Schoenberg to write what became the String Quartet, Op. 7. Given the devotion of this ensemble, Schoenberg must have calculated that while a work for orchestra might remain unperformed for an indefinite period, a work with a string quartet at its core might appear in concert more quickly. That is exactly what happened: in February 1907, the Rosé Quartet premiered the Chamber Symphony, Op. 9 in an extraordinary week in which they also gave the first performance of the String Quartet, Op. 7.

By writing a symphony for a chamber ensemble, Schoenberg, with obvious conscious intent, challenged some basic conventions relating to genre (as, in different ways, he had already done with *Verklärte Nacht* and *Gurrelieder*).[7] The novel instrumentation of the Chamber Symphony (eight winds, two horns, five strings) also made it possible for Schoenberg to exploit a new type of sound, one that would remain a central feature of his orchestrational palette even when he returned to more traditional scoring in 1909. In his prior orchestral works a characteristic aspect of Schoenberg's approach to orchestration had been to make extensive use of mixed doublings. That is, a line in one instrumental family (e.g. strings) would be doubled at the unison or octave by instruments from one or both of the other major families (e.g. winds and brass) with the specific instruments chosen a function of the range of the doubled line. (See, for example, the opening measures of *Pelleas und Melisande*.) In the Chamber Symphony, this type of doubling continues, but in addition, there is a new kind of sound, one in which the families are not mixed, but rather, in which each of the different lines of the polyphony are assigned their own solo instrument. This "broken consort" sound, so characteristic of the sound of twentieth-century music, has its first extended exposure in this composition and would be characteristic of the sound of Schoenberg's orchestral works from this point forward.[8]

Although the innovations in instrumentation and genre are both important, the most significant change of this new work is its form: for the first time since his apprenticeship with Zemlinsky, Schoenberg wrote an instrumental composition that had no program, not even a secret one.[9] This was a crucial step as the turn to absolute music would transform Schoenberg's music in a multitude of consequential ways.

Like the String Quartet, Op. 7, the Chamber Symphony, Op. 9 is an all-in-one composition, a single, uninterrupted movement with individual sections that correspond to the traditional movements of a symphony.[10] Like Op. 7, the various themes and motives are not confined to specific movements, giving the work a cyclic character. But unlike Op. 7, the themes of the finale of Op. 9 are mostly near-literal repetitions of themes from earlier in the work, not (as in Op. 7) thoroughgoing transformations. It appears then, that an immediate consequence of Schoenberg's decision to abandon a narrative program is the tightening of the motivic structure and a resultant significant step toward the eventual ideal of motivic economy.

But it is important not to overstate the case. Schoenberg did not change overnight from a composer who used a plethora of different themes, as prompted by a program, to a composer who would construct a major, multimovement work from a single basic motive or group of motives. By later standards, the Chamber Symphony is still rather garrulous in its use of a variety of different, contrasting, thematic, and motivic ideas. The abandonment of the programmatic idea was one of the factors that permitted Schoenberg to proceed down the path of development toward motivic economy, but it is inaccurate to claim that the notion of organic structure is immediately present once Schoenberg abandoned narrative programs.

In later years, Schoenberg tried to claim that not only did the thematic design of the Chamber Symphony exhibit aspects of organic structure, but also, that that structure was the result of a "subconsciously received gift from the Supreme Commander".[11] Schoenberg's comments about his own works are often of great use, but in this case we should not be unduly influenced by Schoenberg's attempt to influence the interpretation of his work. The Chamber Symphony – Schoenberg's ex post facto suggestions to the contrary – is not a work characterized by motivic organicism. Rather, it is exactly what we should expect from a composer who has only just abandoned programmatic structure: a work with a wonderful variety of distinctive themes that fit together into a whole because – in true late romantic style – they complement one another.[12] That the number of these themes is fewer than in his earlier programmatic compositions points the way to what Schoenberg would eventually regard as a compositional ideal, but this was not an ideal that he had yet attained (nor, at this time, saw as an ideal).

Schoenberg's abandonment of the programmatic idea had significant consequences for other aspects of his compositional thought. Obviously enough, one of those was the issue of abstract form.

It is interesting that, from the perspective of its formal structure, Schoenberg's first non-programmatic instrumental work represents something of a dead end: Op. 9 is the last instance of an all-in-one structure in Schoenberg's early compositions. Schoenberg would not return to this type of work until the Piano Concerto, Op. 42, written nearly forty years later.[13] Thus, immediately after writing the Chamber Symphony, Op. 9, Schoenberg abandoned large, multi-component single movements in favor of works with separate (and considerably more concise) movements.

To a significant extent, the trend toward concision is already evident within the Chamber Symphony. This is most obvious when it is compared with Schoenberg's previous instrumental work, the String Quartet, Op. 7. In contrast to the quartet, the Chamber Symphony is considerably more compact, approximately half the duration in most performances.

This is an extraordinary development, and one whose significance has not been adequately recognized. What we see is that as soon as Schoenberg abandons a narrative program, his compositions immediately become significantly shorter.

The Chamber Symphony, Op. 9 represents Schoenberg's first foray (at least in a mature composition) into the world of purely abstract formal structure. Because the programmatic and abstract ideas are often portrayed as polar opposites, one might be inclined to assume that the abandonment of programmatic organization prompted a significant change in the nature and character of the form. To some extent that is true, but in keeping with the evolutionary character of his thought, Schoenberg had prepared the way for abstract organization of Op. 9 by the hybrid structure of Op. 7. The formal structures of Op. 9, though smaller and more compact, have similarities with those of Op. 7. At the same time, there are some important differences that were prompted by the lack of a programmatic narrative.

As in Op. 7, in the Chamber Symphony, Op. 9, Schoenberg builds the macrostructure from several smaller movements. Four principal movements form the core of the symphony: an opening movement, a scherzo, a slow movement, and a finale. In between the scherzo and the slow movement is an extended development section, in which Schoenberg works with the themes introduced in the opening two movements. In the finale, no completely new themes are introduced; instead, this section combines and reworks the themes and motives of the other movements.

In Op. 7, the basis of Schoenberg's approach to form was the principle of varied reprise, a principle that was particularly suited to mediation between the programmatic and abstract approaches (and had clear connections to the formal procedures in Schoenberg's songs). In Op. 9, we can see that this is a bedrock principle of Schoenberg's approach to form, even in the absence of a program. All three of the core movements employ versions of highly abbreviated and heavily varied reprises.

The form of the first movement is, perhaps, the most difficult to decipher. It has prompted two competing interpretations, sonata and double sonata form, both of which have their merits, but neither of which seems to work perfectly.[14] At the risk of further muddying the waters, I would like to suggest a third alternative: the movement has some of the characteristics of a rondo. This yields the structure seen in Table 9.1.

Table 9.1.

Refrain 1 (A)	mm. 10–31
Couplet 1 (B)	mm. 32–56
Refrain 2 (A')	mm. 57–67
Couplet 2/Development (C)	mm. 68–135
Refrain 3 (A")	mm. 136–47
Coda/transition	mm. 148–59

The return of the principal theme at its original pitch level in mm. 57ff and 136ff creates the basic skeleton of the rondo. As is characteristic of Schoenberg's treatment of repetitions, neither return is literal. The A' section restates only a measure or so of the principal theme of the refrain and reduces the secondary theme of the refrain (mm. 16–31) to a short reference (mm. 62–4). The A'' section restates even less, merely presenting a measure or so of the principal theme before subjecting it to development.

The structure of the first movement illustrates some essential aspects of Schoenberg's approach to large-scale abstract form. On the one hand, in order to achieve coherence, Schoenberg restates thematic material. On the other hand, when material returns it does so in either highly varied or abbreviated form.

In addition, Schoenberg starts to develop something new, a synthesizing reprise. This is particularly evident in the scherzo. In a bow to tradition, the scherzo is, at least nominally, a three-part form, with a trio (mm. 200–48) sandwiched between the scherzo (mm. 160–99) and its varied reprise (mm. 249–79). The actual form of this movement defies such casual simplifications because the final section cannot reasonably be characterized as a varied restatement of just the scherzo. Rather, the themes from both the scherzo and the trio appear in the final section of the movement and from its first measure. The only time the principal theme of the scherzo returns at its original pitch level (and then only its first few measures), it is pitted opposite the trio's theme (mm. 249ff) – hardly the stuff of which reprises are usually made.

For these reasons, it is better to think of the third section of the scherzo, not as a reprise of the opening section, but rather as a synthesis of the first two sections. Schoenberg creates a kind of dialectical structure: an initial group of ideas in the scherzo, an opposing set of ideas in the trio, and then a synthesis of the two.[15]

The slow movement is built on similar lines. It begins with a section that has three prominent statements of a slow lyric theme (mm. 383ff, 391ff, and 405ff) that are separated by short episodes. After this opening section concludes, there is a brief return of the opening fourths motto, an idea that, up to now, had only been used to mark off the major divisions of the form. This time it functions as a kind of feint as the slow movement resumes with a section that gives every appearance of being the B section of an ABA' form.[16] A new theme makes its appearance (viola, m. 415), the tempo picks up slightly, the texture thickens, and the dynamics increase.

But like so many of his ABA' forms, the supposedly new theme is not completely new at all. Instead, it incorporates a version of the slow movement's principal theme, a relationship Schoenberg makes explicit toward the end of this section. There is no return to the A section beyond this brief transformation of the B theme into the A theme. For all intents and purposes, there is no reprise; much like the scherzo, the reprise is replaced by a synthesis.

It is a further indication of just how central this approach has become for Schoenberg's thought, that a similar process takes place on the largest scale: the last movement also functions as a synthesizing reprise. The finale has no new themes of its own; instead it recalls themes from both the first and third movements (curiously, though, not the scherzo). Although themes return, this is no reprise in any traditional sense of the word. Instead, themes and motives from the first and third movements are brought back and stated in various kinds of combinations. This is clear right from the beginning of the finale (mm. 435–7). A prominent theme from the first movement (the first theme of Couplet 2, see m. 68, viola) returns, appearing in octaves in the violins. In counterpoint opposite this idea is a version of the theme from the B section of the slow movement (see Ex. 9.1).

The abandonment of the programmatic idea exerted a considerable influence on yet other areas of Schoenberg's evolving thought. In his programmatic compositions, Schoenberg exploited some well-recognized stylistic conventions (less charitably, one can call them clichés) to support and underscore his interpretation of the program. In that spirit, minor was used to depict sadness and despair, tonal uncertainty portrayed conflict, and pure diatonicism represented stability.

Example 9.1

The identification of specific pitch patterns with specific dramatic situations created a problem for Schoenberg's compositional development. In order to continue to be able to develop his harmonic language, he needed to continue experimenting with new and ever more radical harmonic combinations and to extend their presence to all corners of the composition. If he relied on the traditional programmatic associations of dissonant combinations with instability and conflict, then he would have been forced to limit those kinds of harmonies to specific moments of the dramatic action. He would not have been able to make radical, non-traditional harmonies function as referential or normative. The abandonment of the programmatic idea freed him from these restrictions.

The impact was immediate. Although the radicalization of Schoenberg's harmonic vocabulary and language had been a continuous process, the final abandonment of the programmatic idea prompted a quantum leap forward. The Chamber Symphony, Op. 9 thus stands at a crucial juncture in Schoenberg's development, one in which, for the first time, non-traditional harmonic elements take on a central role in all aspects of the structure of the work and are not limited to specific dramatic situations.

This is obvious from the opening measures of the composition. The work begins with a six-note chord of fourths that unfolds over the first two measures (see Ex. 9.2).

Although Schoenberg had employed chords of fourths in his previous compositions, its role in the Chamber Symphony differs from its

Example 9.2

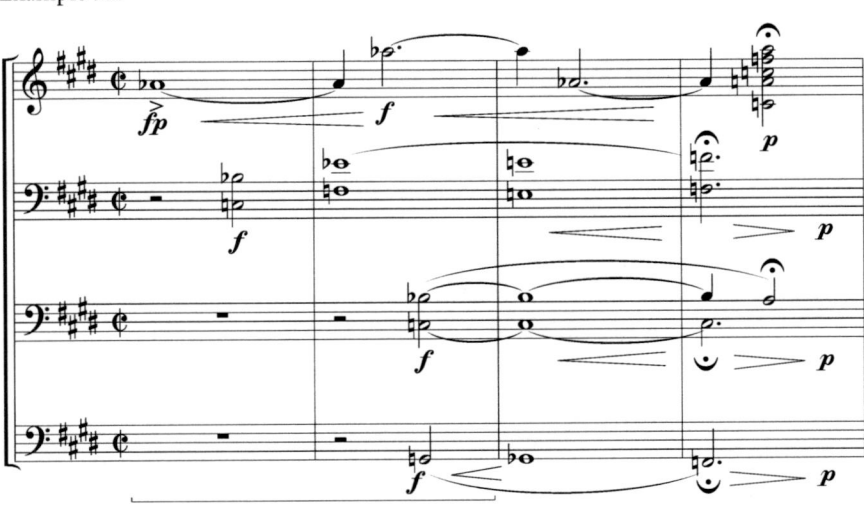

chord of fourths

predecessors in a number of important ways. In the first place, its use is not restricted in function, prominence, or location. In *Pelleas und Melisande*, Schoenberg used a chord of fourths, but it was limited to one passage, was employed to portray a specific aspect in the drama, and was not given undue prominence. Rather, the unusual and unfamiliar character of the chord helped determine what kind of role it could (or could not) play in the drama.

In the Chamber Symphony, having freed himself from the conventions of programmatic music, radical sonorities like the chord of fourths start to come into their own. The chord of fourths is highlighted as an independent element, appearing as the very first chord of the composition and returning at every important formal juncture; it is the crucial marker for the beginnings of the major sections of the work. The chord of fourths functions not as an illustrative programmatic tool, but as a principal theme, subject to repetition, development, and elaboration.

Partly due to the new opportunities made possible by the abandonment of the programmatic idea, and partly due to Schoenberg's continuing restless search for new ways of manipulating his material, the Chamber Symphony, Op. 9 pushes considerably beyond what had previously been considered the outer limits of pitch organization. This is evident at every level of structure, from the overall organization down to the level of detail.

The Chamber Symphony begins and ends with a key signature of four sharps, thereby suggesting a key of E major. This should prompt us to ask what this means. In what sense is this piece in E major? To what extent does the E major triad exert referential control over the composition?

To place this in context, it is instructive to compare the Chamber Symphony with Schoenberg's three previous large-scale instrumental works, *Verklärte Nacht*, *Pelleas und Melisande*, and the String Quartet, Op. 7. There is a clear evolution in the degree to which a triad is treated as having referential status.

In *Verklärte Nacht*, D (first minor, then major) exerted a palpable control over large sections of the composition. The composition began with an extended emphasis on D as a pedal point, supported by the diatonic collection of D minor and by frequent root position D minor chords. D returned as a referential tonic in several other locations, most notably the D major section of the man's response, and the extended D major section with which the work concludes. Thus, the work begins in D, it ends in D, and has a central point of emphasis in D.

Being in a key in *Verklärte Nacht* was a process that involved much more than the isolated appearance of a tone or a chord. In the places where D was the tonic, it was supported by a number of other factors. These included extended rhythmic emphasis of the tonic chord, preparatory dominants, drawn-out pedal tones, lengthy adherence to the tonic's diatonic collection, and themes that were compatible with the tonic.

The tonic areas of *Verklärte Nacht* did not extend to all corners of the composition; there were extended stretches without identifiable referential centers. But the emphases on D at the beginning, middle, and the end were so strong and so well supported that there could be no question as to the identity of the overall tonic. For that reason, one should be entirely comfortable in claiming that D is referential for the entire composition. We can still hear regions outside of the tonic (and the extended sections where no tonic of any sort is perceptible) in terms of the overall tonic: they are subordinate to, and can be heard in relationship to, D.

Schoenberg's next extended instrumental composition, *Pelleas und Melisande*, changes this dynamic in a number of significant ways. Although this composition concludes with the extended emphasis on a triad (D minor), that triad is not nearly so readily perceived in the opening of the composition. One could argue that the first clearly identifiable tonal center of the composition is not D minor, but F major. At the beginning of the work there is little or nothing to indicate that D minor will be the key of the composition as a whole; we do not really know what the overall tonic will be until the end of the work. As a result, there are real questions as to the extent that the tonic functions in this piece. In what sense does D minor govern the entire composition?

The String Quartet, Op. 7 presents a similar picture. Although the overall tonic of the composition (D minor), is clearly stated at the outset and returns (in the major) at the end of the work, there are significant limitations of its scope and stability. Chief among those is the sheer size of the many passages where there is no recognizable referential center. Even where there is a referential center, it is of relatively short duration, yielding only a few brief moments of referential clarity. Therefore, in the String Quartet, Op. 7 it is not clear that it means much to state that D is referential on a global scale.

The Chamber Symphony represents a significant additional step down this path of development. One could argue that there is a sense in which E major achieves some status as the overall key of the composition because of the strongly emphasized E major triads at the end. Much like *Pelleas und Melisande*, there is no similar referential clarity at the beginning of the composition. It is clear that Schoenberg purposely attenuated the degree to which E major functions as the controlling sonority at the beginning of the symphony.

By beginning the composition with a phrase that closes far away from the tonic (on an F major triad in m. 4), Schoenberg has, with due deliberation, prevented E major from achieving referential status at the beginning of the work. Instead of E major, we hear either F major (if we hear the chord at the cadence as a tonic) or B-flat major (if we hear it as a dominant).[17] In either case, there is nothing that points us ineluctably in the direction of E major.

The Chamber Symphony does place some emphasis on E major in the passages that follow the slow introduction, but E major is presented in a strikingly ambiguous and tentative manner, one that seriously undermines its standing as a referential sonority (see Ex. 9.3).

Example 9.3

After the cadence on F in m. 4, Schoenberg states the chord of fourths as a theme in the horn. The collection of the horn's theme (D G C F B-flat E-flat) is a subset of the diatonic collection of B-flat major.[18] As a result, it is possible, at least for a moment, to hear the opening line as a continuation of the implications of B-flat major (if F is understood as a dominant).

Schoenberg very quickly erases any sense of B-flat major (or any other key) in mm. 6–7 by the use of a descending whole tone sequence of augmented triads in the lower voices, stated opposite a sustained G B D-sharp augmented triad in the winds and horns. Schoenberg only begins to bring a key into focus by stating a diminished seventh chord (D-sharp F-sharp A C) on the downbeat of m. 8, a chord than can suggest a turn toward E major. Rather than a direct move to E, Schoenberg sustains the diminished seventh chord into the second beat while introducing a new figure in the lower strings. This figure – the head motive of the principal theme – arpeggiates down from A to D and then up an octave.

After adding these tones (D and A) to the diminished seventh chord, Schoenberg proceeds to a resolution on a first inversion E major chord on the second beat of m. 8. Could this be the referential E major sonority implied by the key signature and the one that corresponds to the E major chords that appear at the end of the symphony?

Perhaps it is. But a number of factors combine to weaken the organizing power of this sonority, maybe not totally, but more than enough to call its referential status into question. The added tones (D and A) in the lower strings hardly serve to reinforce the sense that the diminished seventh chord acts as a dominant of E. The placement of the tones encourages us to hear this as a different chord entirely: as a root position dominant ninth chord on D. Given the symmetrical quality of the diminished seventh chord, there is no way to know which of four possible tonics it might imply without additional clarifying factors. The addition of the D and A might seem to settle the question: this implies that the tonic is G, not E. The sense that E major might not be our goal is intensified by the fact that the D natural is the lowest sounding note of this sonority and that it contradicts (or at least challenges) D-sharp, the leading tone of E.

As we have seen in preceding works Schoenberg has been exhaustive in his search for chords to replace the traditional dominant seventh or ninth chord. Couldn't this be another example of that? Couldn't we understand this ninth chord on the lowered seventh degree as yet another replacement for the traditional dominant?

But even if we accept this sonority as some new kind of dominant replacement, the resolution to the first inversion E major triad is anything but satisfactory and does almost nothing to support the status of E major as a referential sonority. The ninth chord does not lead immediately to an E major triad. Instead, the C of the ninth chord is held over for an additional eighth note, only moving down to the B after the beat.

One might argue that this should not faze us, that there is an explanation for the C: it is a suspension – it has the proper rhythmic structure – and it is thus explained as a tone of elaboration, hierarchically subservient to the B to which it resolves.

But before we casually dismiss the C as merely a tone of elaboration, we should remember that for quite some time, the distinction between chord and non-chord tone has been difficult to maintain in Schoenberg's music particularly since the sonorities produced by "non chord tones" are indistinguishable from sonorities Schoenberg elsewhere treats as distinct, locally stable harmonic entities.

In m. 8, immediately after the compromised arrival on E, Schoenberg repeats the progression without further clarifying the status of E. Therefore there is very little sense of E major as a stable, referential sonority. It occurs for only a fleeting moment, in first inversion, off the beat, prepared by the dominant of a different chord, and has to struggle with an augmented triad for attention, hardly the recipe for a strong, unequivocal, stable tonic.[19]

What follows is stronger – but only marginally – as support for E. The principal theme begins to unfold in the cello, using the already introduced head motive as its jumping off point. Several E major triads arrive in quick succession (see Ex. 9.4).

In m. 10, the first inversion E major triad lands on the downbeat, and lasts for a full beat. Similarly, in m. 11, the E major triad lasts for two complete beats. And this time, the E major triad is even in root position. Shouldn't this finally be enough to allay our doubts about E as the point of reference?

But even here, E major does not really establish itself as a rock of referential stability. The single most prominent factor that functions to weaken the stability of E major is the character of the theme.

In some (though by no means all) of Schoenberg's earlier themes, it is fairly obvious just from the theme itself what key must be used to support that theme. Given only the opening first violin line of the String Quartet, Op. 7, for example, one could scarcely imagine that any other key than D minor could be operative.

Can we make any such claim about the principal theme of the Chamber Symphony? At almost the very beginning of the theme are D naturals, hardly the first tones one thinks of when trying to establish E major. After leaping up from the D to G-sharp, the top part of this line continues on in a

Example 9.4

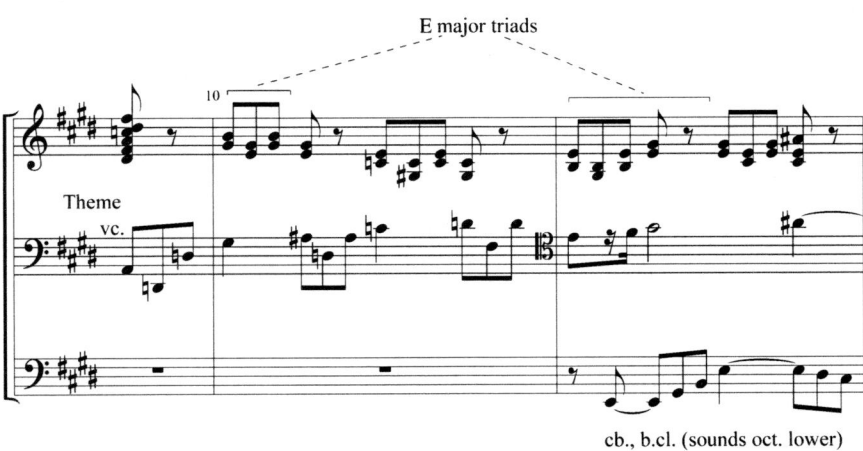

whole tone scale, ascending from the G-sharp on the downbeat of m. 10 all the way to the C-natural in m. 12.

E does get a bit more support beginning at m. 16, where it is sustained as a kind of pedal tone in the bass for five measures. Nonetheless, a pure E major triad appears over this pedal tone only for the briefest of moments (m. 19, third beat), hidden within the phrase and immediately abandoned (see Ex. 9.5).

This is followed by an extended passage (mm. 21–31), where there is no hint of E at all and where no triad of any sort seems to come to the fore until m. 32. When a triad finally does surface, it is not E major, but F minor. At the beginning of m. 32 a contrasting theme enters, prepared by its dominant, no less. (This theme is discussed below. See Ex. 9.8.)

In short, if a perceptive first-time listener were asked at m. 33 what seemed to be the key of the composition, his or her conclusion would likely

Example 9.5

be that it was in F major/minor. Up to that point in the composition, there is considerably more support for F than for E.

As the work progresses, E does occasionally get some support, but that support is either equivocal or is balanced by equally strong support for other regions. The further we proceed into the body of the movement, the less we should be inclined to accept any key area as referential: the competing claims are just too strong. At m. 68, there is another arrival on E, this time supported by a moderately traditional authentic cadence, but this is not enough to counteract the centripetal forces that have been pulling us in many other directions. The sense of E minor lasts but for a measure or so, and by this point in the composition we cannot be swayed by so little.

To summarize: the overall tonic of the composition can be considered referential only in retrospect, once the composition concludes. E major (or minor) is not clearly established at the beginning of the composition and scarcely rises above competing candidates (notably F). Furthermore, E is articulated only weakly and intermittently. Even when it is articulated, its domain is highly limited, and is scarcely felt when not actually present. Finally, the first movement neither begins in E major nor ends there.

In and of itself, this is not entirely new in Schoenberg's instrumental compositions. There had been a somewhat similar procedure in *Pelleas und Melisande*, where what turned out to be the overall tonic was, at best, only dimly recognizable at the beginning of the work. The Chamber Symphony goes at least one step beyond that, picking up from where Schoenberg had left off with works like "Lockung", but now doing so on a grand scale.

The limited role of the overall tonic is only part of a larger picture: many (though not all) of the subsidiary keys are also very weakly articulated. The techniques Schoenberg uses to attenuate the force of the subsidiary keys are similar to those for the principal tonic: he avoids traditional supportive harmonic progressions, standard cadences, diatonic collections, extended emphasis on the local tonic triad, and themes that suggest a particular key. Subsidiary keys are established in a process that sometimes consists of little more than a single triad that appears suddenly and disappears quickly from the scene.

For instance, the key of the slow movement is established in a manner that is rather tenuous (see Ex. 9.6). The clearest moment of emphasis on G actually happens before the movement begins: the transition from the previous section comes to a strong and solid close on a root position G major triad (m. 381). This confirms the implications of the key signature (one sharp) to which Schoenberg had turned a few measures previously (m. 378).

As the slow movement proceeds, there are a few further emphases that provide support for the initial G, but typically they are weakened or compromised in some fashion. Although the closing chord of the first phrase is the dominant ninth of G (m. 382), this does not continue to a G triad. Instead, Schoenberg thwarts expectations for a resolution to the tonic by having the bass jump down to B while the upper voices are still sounding. So too, even though the first group of phrases concludes with a kind of authentic cadence (m. 385), both the dominant and the tonic are so heavily elaborated, that the resolution to, and emphasis on, G is compromised.

Very little else about the movement contributes to the reinforcement or support of G as a key center. This is evident in the character of the principal theme. By itself, there is hardly anything that would suggest G major. Perhaps its initial note (G, m. 382) and its final note (D, m. 386) hint at a possible identity, but this seems a rather exiguous basis for a key, particularly since the collection of tones used in the melody in mm. 381–6 is the total chromatic.

Weakly articulated though the key of the slow movement may be, it is one of the most stable and clearly articulated of all of the subsidiary keys in this work. A case in point is the second movement, the scherzo. Its key signature (three flats), would imply that E-flat major or C minor is the operative key, but there is not a single unambiguous statement of a root position triad built on either of these tones anywhere in the opening section of this movement. If either E-flat major or C minor really does function as the referential tonic, then it achieves this status without actually appearing in the music.

Example 9.6

This raises an interesting question. What does it mean for a work to be in a key if the tonic triad of that key does not appear?

Historically, there are precedents for a work in which a tonic is implied, but not explicitly stated. The work of this type that undoubtedly had the most direct influence on Schoenberg was Wagner's Prelude to *Tristan* where the opening implies A minor, even though no A minor triad appears.

Example 9.7

C minor 6/4
with added A-flat

In the first section of the scherzo of Schoenberg's Chamber Symphony, the closest we ever get to a clear tonic statement is the second inversion C minor chord that punctuates the opening of the movement. In traditional terms, a 6/4 chord would scarcely merit consideration as a referential sonority and this chord is further compromised by the sustained A-flat in the oboe and contrabass (see Ex. 9.7).

In this respect Schoenberg goes considerably beyond Wagner. Not only is the tonic absent, but virtually every other appurtenance of C minor is absent as well. The collection of tones used throughout the opening scherzo is closer to the total chromatic than the C minor collection; there is not a single identifiable cadence of any sort, let alone one in C minor; not only is the tonic absent, but also, there is no clear statement of the dominant or any of its traditional substitutes; the principal melodies (e.g. the oboe line in mm. 160–70) have no identifiable characteristics that suggest C minor.

What then constituted the rationale for Schoenberg's choice of key signature? If we look at the example (Ex. 9.7), we find that there are two ways in which Schoenberg hints at C minor. The first is simply that the initial version of one of the prominent motives uses a particular grouping of tones that we normally associate with C minor. Consider the four-note counter motive, B C B E-flat that appears at the beginning of the scherzo (marked x in the example). In more traditional repertoires, the diminished fourth is customarily found only between the leading tone and the third degree of the scale in minor. This figure, with its leap from B to E-flat could imply C minor. The half-step motion suggests that the lower of the two tones (in this case, B) functions as a leading tone, again implying C minor.

Finally, throughout much of the scherzo, G functions as a pedal tone. In the first three measures of the movement (mm. 160–2) and then for a significant chunk of the first section of the scherzo (mm. 170–8), Schoenberg places a strongly emphasized G in the bass. Not until the middle of the trio do a few root position C minor triads finally appear (mm. 209 and 211). But even when the scherzo returns (m. 249), there are no C minor triads.

Is this enough? Do these factors really combine successfully to suggest C minor?

If being in a key can mean as little as providing emphasis to a tone that has historically served as the dominant to another tone and making occasional use of a characteristic figure of a key, then I suspect that any composition of Schoenberg might be judged as being in a key. But to my ear, the scherzo is not in C minor, nor in any other key.

The lack of clear tonal definition in the Chamber Symphony is also due, in large part, to its radical chordal vocabulary. The chord of fourths with which the Chamber Symphony opens is only the best known of the many less-than-traditional chords that Schoenberg employs in this work. Schoenberg continues the process of incremental evolution, a process that yields a vocabulary marginally different from its immediate predecessor but considerably removed from that of the compositions of only a few years earlier. In the following section, I shall attempt to provide a picture of the chordal vocabulary of the Chamber Symphony by starting with some generalizations and then moving on to specific examples.

There are still some traditional chords in this composition, but their proportion is noticeably smaller than was the case even in the String Quartet, Op. 7. Simple triads have continued to dwindle: there are lengthy stretches (e.g. the scherzo) where hardly a single uncompromised triad appears. Those triads that do occur are usually limited in their placement: they tend to occur at the ends of phrases or the beginnings of phrases, rarely within the body of a phrase itself, or if they do they are disguised. They tend to appear in those phrases that are at the beginning of significant formal divisions. Still further, they tend to appear more in the first movement than in later movements.

Another indication of the changing role of the triad is the frequent appearance of 6/4 positions of the triad, particularly at phrase endings. It seems that Schoenberg is using second inversions in place of simple triads.[20] Beginning at m. 113, there are three phrases, all of which come to cadential stops, not on root position or first inversion triads, but on second inversion A major triads (mm. 113, 116, 119). Even when root position triads do occur they tend to last only for a moment, as if Schoenberg could not wait to leave them. Other than at major divisions of the form (e.g. m. 4, the end of the slow introduction), those triads that do appear usually are left immediately after they are struck. A final indication that Schoenberg was feeling somewhat uncomfortable with the use of pure triads is the heavy elaboration that is applied to many of those triads that do occur, elaboration that is so extensive that it often threatens to make the perception of the triad nearly impossible. None of this is entirely new: there has been a steady decline in the role of the triad from Op. 2 onward. But Schoenberg's treatment of the triad in Op. 9 takes this to a new level.

It is unlikely that Schoenberg ever consciously adopted a staged plan for the disappearance of triads in his music. It is more likely that triads gradually disappeared because Schoenberg intuitively felt that their presence was inappropriate. It is likely that Schoenberg felt that unadorned, temporally extended, root position triads could not readily be integrated into the fabric because they were so much less dissonant than everything else that surrounded them.

As such, Schoenberg seems to have taken as axiomatic one of the basic assumptions that underlies much of the music that preceded his, something that might be called the "law of fullest sonority". Generally speaking, composers did not permit sudden drops in sonority from sonorities with imperfect consonances or dissonances, to sonorities with pure consonances (fifths, octaves, and unisons) except at phrase endings.

Schoenberg understood the "law of fullest sonority". In his own counterpoint textbook, *Preliminary Exercises in Counterpoint*, Schoenberg states (with respect to counterpoint in two voices) that "incidental meetings of the voices must produce harmonies, and because of this the one voice added to a CF should as often as possible produce a third, or a sixth, or a fifth rather than a prime or an octave. Prime and octave should be reserved for the beginning, to express the tonality unequivocally, and for the end, to confirm it."[21] Similarly, in his instructions for counterpoint in three voices he states:

> It is always advantageous, though not necessary, to use full triads. A fluent and correct voice leading and treatment of dissonances, however, is more important. It may thus happen occasionally that all three voices meet in primes or octaves. Although this is not entirely wrong, it had better be reserved for beginnings and endings. As a general rule, however, either at least one consonant interval or a dissonance in the form of a *conventionalized formula* should be added to a prime or an octave.[22]

Because Schoenberg's chordal vocabulary had developed to the point that seventh chords (or even more dissonant sonorities such as the chord of fourths) were the norm, it brought the simple triad to approximately the same position that the unison and octave had been in Renaissance counterpoint, or the open fifth had been in Classical and Romantic harmony: a sonority that, by contrast with the rest of the texture, was too thin to be integrated smoothly into the prevailing fabric. Schoenberg's steady reduction of the triad's presence might best be understood, not as evidence of a conscious master plan to abandon the triad as a basic element of sonority, but rather as the inevitable result of his continuing adherence to the "law of fullest sonority" in light of his increasing use of chords with multiple dissonances.

Although triads are now rare, seventh chords remain a common unit of harmonic structure. However, there have been some significant changes in the role and scope of the seventh chord. In the first place, the relative proportion of different chord types has continued to change. Dominant seventh chords and diminished seventh chords have become less common though both still appear on occasion. Minor and major sevenths make less frequent appearances than they did in Schoenberg's early songs. Instead, the emphasis is placed on seventh chords such as the half-diminished, dominant seventh chords with raised or lowered fifths (MMd and MdM, respectively), and half-augmented sevenths (MMm and mMM). The common factor that unites most of Schoenberg's preferred seventh chords is the presence of symmetrical subsets (the 036 trichord embedded in the half-diminished seventh, the 048 trichord embedded in the half-augmented sevenths, the 048 and 024 trichords embedded in the dominant seventh with raised fifth). And, of course, Schoenberg continues to employ many ninth chords, including all possible inversions.

At the same time, the Chamber Symphony marks a significant turning point in that the balance of its repertoire of chords starts to shift noticeably away from even those seventh chords (such as the half-augmented) that are the least traditional. Schoenberg increasingly turns to sonorities that are not easily classifiable in terms of straightforward seventh or ninth chords. The most obvious of those is the six-tone chord of fourths with which the composition begins. But this is only one representative of the newer, more radical, chordal vocabulary. In addition, Schoenberg makes more and more use of four- or five-tone sonorities in which a triad or seventh chord forms a subset of the chord: the principle of localized consonance at work. Although this type of sonority has already appeared in Schoenberg's earlier works, it has changed from being a relatively isolated phenomenon to something far more pervasive.

As for how his chords are combined into progressions, Schoenberg mostly continues with the procedures he used in his preceding compositions. In many cases, it is no longer possible to make an unambiguous identification of the root of a chord. In those places where the chords are most traditional and where roots are identifiable, chord progressions with root motion by fifth are relatively rare, usually reserved for those (very few) moments where Schoenberg wants a clear authentic cadence. Instead, most root motion (when a root can be identified) is by step or third.

Given Schoenberg's preference for symmetrical subsets in his chords, many of those chords are not compatible with any single diatonic scale. In those instances where a chord is diatonic, Schoenberg tends to counteract those diatonic implications relatively quickly. Typically, the tones of a given sonority are not compatible with the diatonic collection of more than one or two adjacent chords. This helps promote as normative a situation in which most, or all, of the twelve chromatic tones circulate, often within a very short span.

Although elaborated homophony remains an important component of Schoenberg's vocabulary, contrapuntal passages have at least as much prominence in this work as they did in Op. 7. Making meaningful or useful generalizations about the language of Schoenberg's contrapuntal passages is at least as difficult as making generalizations about his chordal vocabulary and progressions, but several observations are nonetheless possible, particularly because they reveal some essential commonalities with his harmonic practice. One is that Schoenberg typically avoids situations in which the motion of the different voices of the counterpoint within a phrase results in a clear triad, particularly on an accented beat. The second is that Schoenberg usually takes pains to ensure that pairs of voices work smoothly together with respect to dissonance treatment – hence the numerous passages of parallel thirds – a further application of the principle of localized consonance in contrapuntal textures.

Such then is the overall picture of Schoenberg's pitch language in the Chamber Symphony. In the interests of documenting and confirming these generalizations, we turn now to analyses of several representative examples. Let us begin with one of the seemingly least radical passages in the Chamber Symphony, the place in the first movement where Schoenberg first presents his contrasting F minor theme (see Ex. 9.8).

Schoenberg prepares the F minor triad in m. 32 with a relatively clear dominant chord on C, thus highlighting the arrival of the new theme and its key area with a dominant-tonic progression. On the one hand, this has some rather obvious traditional aspects and demonstrates that even at this late date, Schoenberg still regarded dominant-tonic progressions as particularly appropriate for marking off significant points of arrival. On the other hand, Schoenberg's purposeful weakening of the cadence is a sign of a growing discomfort with this progression and presages its coming disappearance from his music.

Example 9.8

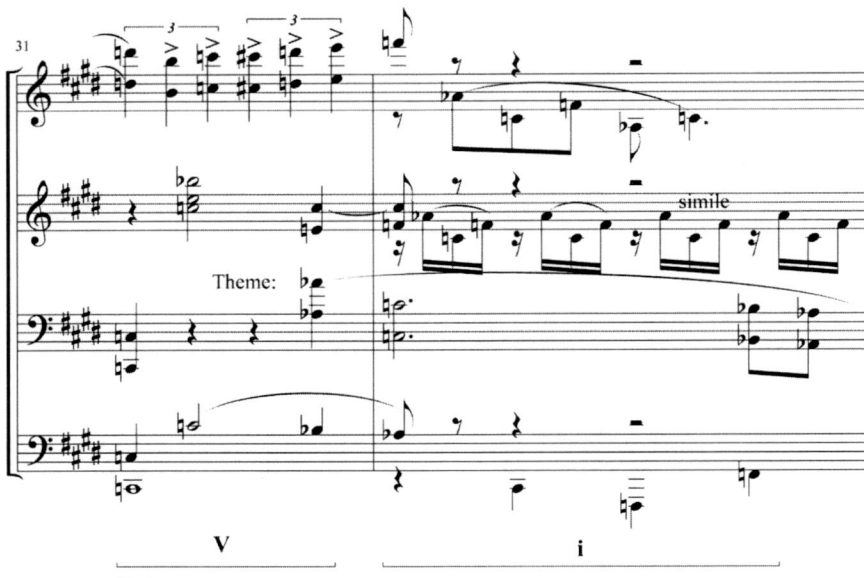

One of the means by which Schoenberg weakens the progression is his placing of a gap in the bass, separating the dominant and tonic chords from one another.[23] At the same time, the A-flat in m. 31 (viola, cello, English horn, the first note of the new theme) completes the dominant chord, not with its diatonic fifth but with a raised fifth. In addition, the uppermost line (violins) seems to suggest an added ninth (D, downbeat of m. 31), which first seems to disappear, then returns, and ultimately moves upward to the

Absolute music and its consequences: Chamber Symphony

Example 9.8 (cont.)

leading tone E. When the F minor tonic chord does appear (m. 32), it is initially only in second inversion (C in the bass), with the root of the chord arriving in the bass only on the third quarter of the measure.

Although the F minor chord, as defined and prepared by its dominant, can be understood to act as a local referential tonic beginning at m. 32, like virtually all of the referential tonics of this composition, it is very weak and short lived. Almost immediately, Schoenberg takes steps to counteract its strength and stability. He does so by using a deceptively simple succession of chords: a series of root position triads that are presented in a relatively slow harmonic rhythm. He first moves to a D-flat major triad (m. 33) possibly suggesting the progression i-VI in F minor. But instead of continuing with anything that might be compatible with F minor, in m. 34 Schoenberg skips the bass to F-sharp. He then mimics the preceding progression in an accelerated, quasi-sequential transposition up a semitone: an F-sharp minor triad proceeds to an inverted D major triad. Within the twinkling of an eye, Schoenberg has erased the referential status of F minor.

The D major chord serves as the springboard for the next stage of the progression. In m. 35, Schoenberg hints for a few moments that D major will act as a local point of reference: on the third beat of the measure, an A major triad (V of D) emerges ever so briefly from its surroundings. Note well its immediate preparation: the traditional A major triad comes after a rather less than traditional chord that includes five tones: A D F B-flat and E-flat. A trichordal subset of this sonority is none other than a three-tone chord of fourths. Thus, even in a phrase otherwise dominated by simple triads, Schoenberg incorporates a version of his opening sonority, and interleaves it into the voice leading as the preparation for a local dominant.

Having arrived on the dominant of D in the middle of m. 35, Schoenberg slows the pace of the melody, thereby establishing this point as the end of a four-bar phrase. He even suggests a half cadence – not on the dominant of the original key of the phrase, but rather on the dominant of its sixth degree.

Just as quickly, the following phrase changes the harmonic focus. The first chord of the phrase (end of m. 35) is the dominant seventh of F-sharp, but this is not followed by anything resembling an F-sharp triad. Instead, in the texture that is his trademark, the pace of the harmonic rhythm is positively vertiginous, with every change of tone in the different voices creating a new harmony. Beginning on the downbeat of m. 36, Schoenberg rushes through an D diminished triad (first eighth: D E-sharp G-sharp) which mutates instantly into a non-traditional tetrachord (B D E-sharp F-sharp – note the B minor triad subset), and then on to a D major triad which quickly becomes a dominant ninth chord. In a more traditional repertoire, this chord might suggest a turn toward G but that is not the goal of the following progression. Instead, we hear a diminished seventh chord over C (m. 36, third quarter). Although the next two chords (A, half-diminished seventh, m. 36, beat four, first eighth and C minor seventh, m. 36, beat four, second eighth) are both theoretically compatible with G minor (II^7 and IV^7 respectively), moving to them has prevented the resolution of the dominant ninth on D. In any event, G as an even remotely possible referential center is quickly erased and Schoenberg starts to suggest D: the appearance of an augmented sixth chord on the second beat of m. 37 strengthens that sense of D, as does its surprisingly traditional resolution to the cadential 6/4 of D minor on the third beat.

Just as G minor had disappeared with barely a trace, so too, even this hint of D minor is short lived. By the beginning of m. 38, it is gone: Schoenberg rushes through three ambiguous harmonies: a half-augmented seventh on F (beat one), a French sixth on A (beat two), a different French sixth (beat three), and the final chord of the phrase: a less than traditional combination of the previous French sixth with an A-flat. This acts as the preparation for the varied restatement of the theme, beginning, once again, in F minor.

Although most of its progressions are – to say the least – unorthodox, this is one of the most traditional passages in the Chamber Symphony. With the exception of a few sonorities, every chord is a triad, seventh, or ninth chord. In several places in the phrase, the harmonic successions even coalesce to suggest tonal centers, albeit for very brief spans of time.

The harmonic vocabulary and syntax of many other passages are considerably less traditional. Consider the passage that follows shortly after the excerpt we have just examined, a passage that leads to the return of the opening theme at its original pitch level (see Ex. 9.9).

In the first measure of this excerpt (and this is mirrored by the similar passage in mm. 48–9) there is a rapid succession of sonorities, none of which lasts for more than the briefest of moments. Our experience with

Example 9.9

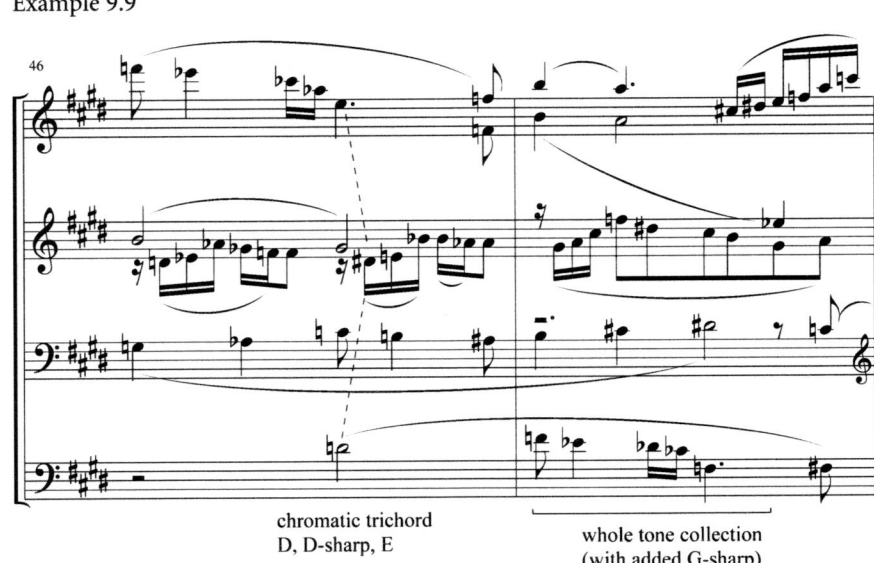

Example 9.9 (cont.)

similar passages suggests that there is no logical way that this can be reduced to a simpler harmonic background by the segregation of the surface into chord- and non-chord tones.

The very first sonority we hear in the first eighth of m. 46 is a root position dominant seventh chord built on G. This chord does not proceed to any kind of C chord; instead, while holding two common tones (G and B) the motion of voices in the counterpoint quickly transforms the sonority into an A-flat, third-inversion, half-augmented, seventh chord (mMM). On the second beat of the measure, the A-flat seventh chord continues, but only for one sixteenth, and now in root position with its seventh lowered (mMm). When the G-flat descends by half-step on the second sixteenth of the second beat (with the remaining three tones being held common), the chord morphs into a first inversion, half-diminished seventh chord on F, and then with the descent of the E-flat to C-flat it morphs again into a first-inversion, diminished triad on F.

This should all be quite familiar from our previous analyses: Schoenberg creates a dynamic musical surface in which the motion of the different voices creates a quickly moving succession of seventh and ninth chords, none of which lasts long enough to establish itself even as a locally stable sonority. Although some of the individual chords (such as the dominant seventh on G) are compatible with some diatonic collection, pairs of adjacent chords are not, thereby precluding the establishment of a referential center.

Up to the middle of m. 46 it is possible to describe all of the simultaneities of this passage, no matter how brief their span, as traditionally classifiable chords such as dominant and half-augmented sevenths. The sonorities that occur in the second half of this measure are considerably less traditional. The third beat begins with a four-tone sonority (C D G-sharp E) that might be identified as a second inversion, dominant seventh chord on E with a raised fifth. On the second sixteenth of the beat, Schoenberg adds a D-sharp to the mix. The addition of the D-sharp brings to the forefront a new kind of sonority that is becoming an increasingly important component of Schoenberg's vocabulary. When the D-sharp is added to the remaining tones, it creates a trichordal subset that is the chromatic trichord (012).

Up to this point in his career, with only occasional exceptions (e.g. chords of fourths) Schoenberg tended to form his chords from four or five tones that can be reduced to stacked thirds (i.e. seventh and ninth chords). Usually the component thirds are major or minor, but Schoenberg also uses diminished thirds between the third and fifth (as in the French sixth) or between the fifth and seventh (as in the dominant seventh with raised fifth).

Forming chords in this manner makes possible a wide variety of sonorities, but there are some combinations that do not readily occur. Chief among those is the chromatic trichord (012). Although, theoretically, it can result from a combination of the root of the ninth chord with a major seventh and a minor ninth, sonorities of this sort were relatively rare before the Chamber Symphony. One of the important features of this work is its increasing use of segments (like the 012) that had not been typical of chords built from stacked thirds.

One could argue that I am making too much of this moment: the sonority I have just described lasts but for a duration of a single sixteenth note, and that at a very quick tempo. This is true, but it misses the point. Schoenberg's harmonic rhythm frequently changes at precisely this frenetic pace, so we cannot deny the significance of this harmony without denying the importance of virtually every other harmony he uses. And in any event, even if we dismiss this sonority as too evanescent to be of significance, the fact remains that another 012 surfaces in the following measure (on the fourth beat) and elsewhere in this work. Moreover, in subsequent compositions chords with 012 trichordal subsets start to appear with ever greater frequency and with considerably more rhythmic emphasis.

The principal harmony of the following measure (m. 47) provides still further evidence of the evolution of Schoenberg's harmonic vocabulary. With the exception of the G-sharp on the second sixteenth of the first beat, the first three beats are comprised of the whole tone collection. Although whole tone segments can result from chords built from stacked thirds (e.g. the dominant seventh with a raised fifth) and have occurred as an occasional component of Schoenberg's chordal repertoire, what occurs here is a significant metamorphosis of prior ideas. For most of this measure, it is not so much that there is a discrete chord at work; it is the whole tone collection that is prolonged.

The whole tone collection appears more frequently, and in more prominent positions in the Chamber Symphony than in any other of Schoenberg's previous compositions. Although the extent of emphasis on this collection is unusual, aspects of its use highlight essential principles that are typical of Schoenberg's harmonic language from this period.

The most obvious of those is that Schoenberg never presents the whole tone collection (or the larger sub-segments thereof) in such a manner that it constitutes a discrete, closed, phrase or section consisting only of the whole tone elements. Schoenberg's practice is to treat whole tone segments as a subset of a larger collection that includes at least one element from outside of the whole tone collection. For instance, in m. 47, even though the whole tone collection monopolizes most of the measure, a G-sharp appears within the first beat, and other elements outside the whole tone collection appear in the fourth beat. Similarly, in mm. 50–2, the whole tone scale is prominent, but other elements are added at the beginning and the end, thereby framing the whole tone collection with elements foreign to it.

Schoenberg's reluctance to treat the whole tone scale as a discrete, self-contained harmonic entity is significant, because it is further evidence of an important aspect of his harmonic language. In a variety of different contexts, we see that the idea of symmetry plays a significant role in Schoenberg's harmonic language. Whether it is the 012 trichord that we have just examined, or his frequent use of symmetrical trichords (024, 036, 048) within his seventh chords, symmetrical elements make frequent appearances. The whole tone scale (and many of its subsets) is more evidence of Schoenberg's interest in symmetry.

But it is a defining aspect of Schoenberg's treatment of symmetry that he is rarely interested in symmetry that is stark and total. He almost always treats symmetrical collections or elements as subsets of larger collections.[24] The symmetrical elements may be prominent and may even saturate the surface (as they do mm. 47 and 50–2) but such segments are rarely allowed to stand completely alone.

The previous examples would have been considered radical in the hands of almost any other composer, but they are not Schoenberg's most innovatory passages in this composition. Many other passages in the Chamber Symphony have even fewer traditional elements and even fewer connections with traditional compositional techniques. Let us turn to a passage from the beginning of the work's principal development section (see Ex. 9.10).

The first beat of our example presents the trichord E A B, which we might think of as a chord of fourths, but one in which (unlike the first chord of the piece) the component elements are not arranged in register by fourths. In any event, this sonority does not remain for very long: the beginning of the second beat outlines an A major triad in some of the instruments (in vn. 1, va., hrn., bsn., and cl.) while, simultaneously, the oboe and English horn arpeggiate an E–B dyad. If we insist on trying to ascribe sonorities to traditional paradigms then we might wish to think of the second beat as a ninth chord on A, but missing its seventh (A C-sharp E B). But this does not work very well: on the second half of the beat, vln. 2 and va. jump up a tritone to add an E-flat to the mix. Even if we dismiss this as some kind of elaborative tone this does not address the fact that the E–B in the oboe and English horn acts more like an independent sonority (one that outlines the principal theme) than the fifth and ninth of an A chord.

Example 9.10

The harmonies that are created in the second half of the measure are only scarcely more traditional than those of the first. Perhaps there is a B-flat minor triad on the third beat, but it lasts only for a moment as the bass quickly jumps in with a D-natural, yielding a major-minor tetrachord (0347). Similarly, the fourth beat does give us one somewhat traditional chord, a seventh chord, C E-flat G B-flat (= A-sharp), but it lasts only for a quick eighth before being transformed into another less than traditional sonority.

I will spare the reader a similar blow-by-blow account of the remaining two measures of the example, but, as can readily be confirmed, the situation is no different from the measure we have examined. That is, although the motion of the counterpoint occasionally does come together to produce some triad or seventh chord, just as often the counterpoint produces simultaneities that are not understandable as triads or seventh chords. And nothing in the rhythmic structure clarifies which of these types are normative: i.e. no more emphasis (agogic or metric) is given to the traditional harmonies than to the less-than-traditional. Nor is it really possible to simplify the surface by assigning some notes status as elaborative tones. Any attempt to do so is arbitrary because it is no longer possible to determine which might be the chord tone and which might be the tone of elaboration.

This demonstrates that as of 1905–6 there are already passages in Schoenberg's music – and some are quite extended – in which traditional triads and seventh chords hardly exist, let alone play a central role. But there are some important limitations on the placement and function of passages of this sort. For one thing, passages like this are mostly limited to development sections. Passages that consist mostly of non-triadic harmonies do not occur where themes are first presented nor at the ends of major sections.

Radical though the harmonic vocabulary of this passage may be, Schoenberg has retained some important syntactic links with the past. Even though the total pitch-class content is highly chromatic (eleven of the twelve tones in the first measure of our example, ten of the twelve in the second) the chromaticism is not always evenly spread across the surface. Some of the individual lines or pairings of lines produce diatonic, or very nearly diatonic, segments. At the beginning of the first measure of our example, the first beat and a half include only tones from the D major collection; the bass line from the end of m. 303 through the first beat of m. 305 yields a segment of the E-flat minor scale; the oboe's restatement of part of the principal theme outlines an open fifth (EB) that suggests an E triad.

Another important link to the past is Schoenberg's continued fealty to the principle of localized consonance. This is evident in the pairing of vln. 1 with the clarinet and bassoon in mm. 304–5. These two lines move mostly in note against note counterpoint, and from the second eighth of m. 304 forward, the intervals between the two lines are limited to thirds (frequently spelled as augmented seconds). Other pairs of lines, particularly ones that are also rhythmically paired, also tend to place traditionally consonant intervals at significant points of intersection. This can be seen in the interaction between vln. 2 and the bass line in mm. 304–5. In both measures the initial interval between the lines is a perfect fifth. In m. 304 the final note of the vln. 2 line forms an octave with the bass; in m. 304 although the comparable interval is dissonant (a minor seventh), the bass line moves up by step for its last note of the measure, thereby producing a consonant sixth with vln. 2.

The transformation of Schoenberg's pitch language in the decade 1899–1909 did not proceed at a regular pace. In some works he surged forward; in others he retreated. The Chamber Symphony is most decidedly more an instance of the former than the latter. With it the nature of his pitch language had shifted so far away from what his contemporaries could absorb that when this work was first performed it prompted a near riot. That stormy reception may have helped contribute to one of the most serious artistic crises Schoenberg ever faced. It is to this crisis we now turn.

10 Crisis: *Friede auf Erden*, Op. 13, Ballades, Op. 12, and the reception of Schoenberg's music, August 1906 to July 1907

... a new art is not to be measured by the laws of the old.[1]

With the completion of the Chamber Symphony, Op. 9, we enter into one of the most unsettled periods of Schoenberg's life, a period that saw dramatic changes in his compositional approach, professional standing, and personal relationships. Beginning in the late summer of 1906, many aspects of Schoenberg's life began to unravel. It is not overly dramatic to speak of this period as a time of crisis – compositionally, professionally, and personally.

The manuscript record provides some clear hints of this crisis. From 1899 through 1904 Schoenberg had followed fairly clear patterns of compositional activity. After deciding on a project, he would generally work consistently on that project and that project alone, until it was complete.[2] Once he began working, he usually proceeded quite rapidly: several weeks for *Verklärte Nacht*, approximately one year for *Gurrelieder* (exclusive of the orchestration), about eight months for *Pelleas und Melisande*.

After *Pelleas und Melisande*, there was a significant change in Schoenberg's compositional work habits. In contrast to its predecessors, the String Quartet, Op. 7, did not proceed quickly: it took him approximately a year and a half to complete, more than twice the time required for *Pelleas und Melisande*. And for the first time in his career, Schoenberg was unable to work on a project without interruption. Again and again he stopped work on the quartet to take up other projects. Some of those (the canons) may have been technical studies that were related to the quartet. But that does not explain his work on the songs Op. 6, No. 5, Op. 8, No. 4, Op. 8, No. 5, Op. 8, No. 6, Op. 6, No. 8, and Op. 8, No. 3, all of which were written in the middle of his work on Op. 7.[3]

A similar situation obtains for the Chamber Symphony, Op. 9. Because there is no beginning date in the manuscript, it is not known precisely how long it took Schoenberg to write this work: it may have been as many as nine or ten months (October 1905 to July 1906) or as few as four (April–July 1906). In any event, here too Schoenberg found it hard to devote himself exclusively to a single project: he interrupted his work on the Chamber Symphony at least five times (for four songs and one piano piece, none of which was completed).[4]

Schoenberg's lack of focus in Opp. 7 and 9, however, is trivial when compared to the situation that developed after the completion of Op. 9. We can recognize how dramatically his working methods had changed when we study the sketchbook (Sketchbook III) he used during this period.[5] The picture that emerges for the years 1906–8 is a composer in a creative crisis.

Schoenberg completed the draft of the Chamber Symphony, Op. 9 on 16 July 1906 and the fair copy nine days later (25 July 1906). In Sketchbook III, the last entry for Op. 9 is on p. 31. On the very next page, dated 1 August 1906, Schoenberg sketched out the first three measures of what would become the Chamber Symphony No. 2.[6] But Schoenberg immediately interrupted his work on the barely nascent Chamber Symphony and on the next page of Sketchbook III (p. 33) we find a fragmentary sketch for a song, "Besuch". The text is a poem by Dehmel, marking a return to the poet whose works were so extraordinarily influential in Schoenberg's early development.

Schoenberg immediately lost interest in that song and on pp. 33–4 of the sketchbook (p. 33 is dated 14 August 1906), he returned to the Chamber Symphony No. 2, and began to work out the beginning. Just as quickly he dropped that piece and tried to start three different songs, "Über unsre Liebe", "Greif aus", and "Am Himmelsthor" (pp. 35–7). For one of these proposed projects Schoenberg turned again to Dehmel ("Über unsre Liebe"), while the other two attempts were to poetry of Conrad Meyer. To no avail: neither Schoenberg's one-time favorite poet nor a new poet provided sufficient impetus to complete any of these songs.

Then, once again, it was back to the Chamber Symphony No. 2 (pp. 38–9). This time Schoenberg managed to get a little further: to the equivalent of mm. 53–8 (through the end of the A section and the beginning of the B section).

Yet again Schoenberg abandoned the Chamber Symphony No. 2 and tried once more to produce a song. Again he turned to Dehmel and tried to use his one-time most reliable poetic source to stimulate his inspiration. Curiously, he went back to a poem, "Aus schwerer Stunde", he had tried to set before (in 1899) but had been unable to complete.

This time he almost succeeded. He managed to sketch out much of the song in Sketchbook III (pp. 40–1) and even began to write out a fair copy in ink on a separate piece of paper (archive number U87). But he just could not go the last mile: at m. 16 of the fair copy, he breaks off, never to return.

Then, a surprise: immediately following the sketches of "Aus schwerer Stunde", Schoenberg turns in another direction entirely. On pp. 42–5 there are sketches for an opera, *Und Pippa tanzt!* based on a play by Gerhart Hauptmann. For a time it looked as if this project would take off: in addition to the material in Sketchbook III, there are sketches and drafts in separate manuscripts. In the sketchbook Schoenberg worked out several themes for the characters of Hauptmann's play. On the separate sheets, he wrote the instrumental introduction and the beginning recitative, a stretch of more than 60 measures.

Since Schoenberg never completed this opera it has largely been ignored, but if we look at the situation from the vantage point of late 1906/early 1907, Schoenberg had devoted more effort to this opera than any of the other projects from this period and this suggests that it was the most important fragment between July 1906 and March 1907.

Nevertheless, this too was dropped, and it is followed in quick succession (pp. 45, 46, and 47) with three more fragments, a string quintet, a choral work with instrumental accompaniment ("Des Friedens Ende"), and yet another song ("Patrouillentritt"), none of which amounted to very much.[7]

Then, two more attempts, one of which – finally – succeeded. On p. 47 of Sketchbook III, Schoenberg began a work for chorus. Although he interrupted it for another (futile) song project ("Wenn schlanke Lilien", p. 48), this time he returned and completed the choral composition: it is the work we know as *Friede auf Erden*, Op. 13.

Even this is not the end of the story. After completing *Friede auf Erden*, things still did not settle down and Schoenberg continued to jump from project to project. On the same day he completed the fair copy of *Friede auf Erden* (9 March 1907), Schoenberg returned to Sketchbook III and on p. 57 made some sketches for what would become the String Quartet, No. 2, Op. 10.[8] Almost immediately, he dropped this idea and turned instead to writing songs. In quick succession, he started three songs, "Der verlorene Haufen", "Jane Grey", and "Jeduch". By the end of April 1907 Schoenberg did finish the first two of these, and they were published as the Two Ballades, Op. 12 (as Op. 12, No. 2 and Op. 12, No. 1 respectively.).

There are few periods in Schoenberg's career that have as little to show for themselves as do the nine months between the completion of the fair copy of the Chamber Symphony, Op. 9 and the composition of the Ballades, Op. 12. During this period, Schoenberg started more than a dozen projects, yet was able to complete only three relatively short works: two songs and a composition for chorus. Throughout, we see an apparently paralyzing indecision as to his compositional direction: is he going to write songs, abstract works, or an opera?

Taken in isolation, Schoenberg's inability to concentrate on a single composition, his failure to complete most of the projects he started, and his difficulty in deciding upon a compositional direction, need not be proof of a compositional crisis: there could be perfectly benign explanations for the apparently unsettled nature of his compositional habits during this period. But Schoenberg's compositional indecisiveness did not happen in isolation.

Although its full implications would not be evident until the summer of 1908, a major contribution to Schoenberg's artistic and personal crisis occurred sometime in 1906 when the young painter Richard Gerstl became a part of Schoenberg's circle. At about the same time Schoenberg began to paint (it is likely that he got some advice from Gerstl but it is not clear if he had formal lessons). It soon became clear that painting was no dilettantish whimsy on Schoenberg's part. A mere four years later (10 October 1910), he put on a one-man show of his art works, exhibiting forty-seven water colors and oils at Hugo Heller's Art Gallery and Bookshop in Vienna. Thus, at the very same time that he was jumping from one compositional project to the next, he was also opening up a whole new region of artistic expression, one that he clearly took very seriously, and one that has to have taken a significant amount of his time.

Schoenberg's sudden infatuation with art is also important because Gerstl's relationship with the Schoenberg family evolved into something more than a casual friendship. Two years later (summer 1908) Schoenberg discovered that his wife Mathilde and Gerstl were carrying on an affair, a revelation that led to a series of crises culminating first with Mathilde's abandonment of the family and later, with Gerstl's suicide. Although the explosive events of the affair and suicide lie outside the time frame of this chapter, it is unlikely that the crisis arose in a vacuum. It is more likely that marital difficulties were lurking beneath the surface even before 1908. If so, this may also have contributed to the overall crisis Schoenberg faced beginning in July 1906.

There was yet another source for Schoenberg's apparent malaise: the stormy reception of his music. During a period from the end of January to the beginning of February 1907, there were three highly publicized performances of Schoenberg's compositions in Vienna. The first, on 26 January 1907, was an all-Schoenberg song program (Liederabend) presented under the auspices of the Ansorge Society in the Ehrbar-Saal.[9] This was followed on 5 February 1907 with the premiere of the String Quartet, Op. 7, performed by the Rosé Quartet. Only three days after that (8 February), the Rosé Quartet teamed up with wind players from the Court Opera for the premiere of the Chamber Symphony, Op. 9. These three performances and the critical firestorm that followed transformed Schoenberg's position in European musical life.

Schoenberg's public career as a composer effectively began in the 1897–8 season with a performance on 20 March 1898 of the String Quartet in D major by the Fitzner Quartet.[10] Although this event did not receive an enormous degree of publicity, the quartet was relatively well received and it was clearly a positive first step for the young composer.[11] With the possible exception of one or two performances of some of his songs (in 1898 and 1900), there is no record of further public performances of Schoenberg's works for nearly four years.[12] In effect, after a promising beginning, Schoenberg virtually dropped from sight (literally as well as figuratively: his move to Berlin and his brief career as a cabaret musician came during this period).

It was the premiere of *Verklärte Nacht* by the augmented Rosé Quartet in March 1902 that marked Schoenberg's effective debut as a composer. The emergence of this work had at least four significant consequences. First, the premiere attracted considerable attention, much of it quite positive.[13] Second, from the moment they saw this work, the Rosé Quartet – one of the most celebrated chamber ensembles in Europe – became Schoenberg's champion. Third, other important musicians – Strauss and Mahler being the most notable – began to lend Schoenberg support after having become acquainted with this work. Finally, the success of the premiere and the support of important musicians led to additional performances: most immediately in October 1902 (by Waldemar Meyer's Quartet in Berlin) and then again by Rosé in Vienna in 1904.[14] The overall effect was to create the impression among an influential circle, that Schoenberg was a highly promising and immensely talented young composer, one who merited close attention.

Nevertheless, the growing recognition that Schoenberg was a composer worth watching did not immediately translate itself into many performances.[15] It also appears that the radical character of his musical language was beginning to stir up some opposition. Perhaps this is why it proved so difficult for Schoenberg to secure a performance of *Pelleas und Melisande*. That work had been complete since February of 1903, but it took nearly two years to arrange a premiere, and then only when Schoenberg conducted the work in a concert of a society he helped found.

When *Pelleas und Melisande* was finally premiered (25 January 1905) it did not pass quietly. This time there was a strong reaction by the critics, mostly negative. At the same time, it is clear that Schoenberg had begun to attract an enthusiastic core of supporters. All of this had significant consequences. In the first place, it confirmed the growing impression that Schoenberg was an extraordinarily talented, radical young composer, one whose pitch language was highly innovative. In addition, it was also becoming clear that Schoenberg's music was prompting strong reactions, pro and con, making any concert of his music a potential event.

This, then, was the extent of Schoenberg's public reputation before January/February 1907: a growing circle of devoted supporters, an increasingly vocal group of opponents, and the recognition by Vienna's many music critics that there was hot copy out there, just waiting for an opportunity.

That opportunity came with the three concerts of late January and early February 1907. This succession of performances provided the fuel that sparked an extraordinary explosion. In the weeks following the three performances there was an unprecedented flood of critical reactions to Schoenberg's music.

From Zemlinsky's letters to Schoenberg after the premiere of *Verklärte Nacht*, we can infer that Schoenberg was very interested in the reviews of his works and hoped for positive reactions and public acclaim.[16] A sign of his yen for public recognition is the fact that before these concerts Schoenberg – still on the borders of penury – subscribed to the newspaper clipping service, the Observer, contracting with them to receive copies of the expected reviews of the three concerts.

For many of us it can be a shock to realize how many newspapers there were in Vienna at the beginning of the twentieth century. In addition to several mass-circulation dailies, there were newspapers of virtually every political stripe: liberal, progressive, social democratic, official, Christian social, Catholic Conservative, German nationalist, and anti-Semitic. Although some of these newspapers had relatively low circulation (a few thousand), many of them maintained an active schedule of concert reviews.[17] In addition to the Viennese newspapers, critics for papers in other cities (Berlin, Prague, Graz, Leipzig, Mannheim) also wrote reviews of Viennese concerts. There was also a highly active speciality press, with several music weeklies providing news and reviews. All of these periodicals had their reviews clipped by the Observer. In the days and weeks that followed the three performances, a veritable flood of reviews (more than fifty) poured into Schoenberg's hands.[18]

It was not merely the extent of attention that made the reaction to Schoenberg's music so significant. Perhaps as proof of the old adage that there is no such thing as bad publicity, the critics' condemnation and rejection of his music coupled with the violence and fury of their language helped make Schoenberg famous and the aftermath of these concerts a crucial turning point in the history of music. From this point forward, virtually everything that Schoenberg did happened on center stage.

This is, of course, a well-known story. For many it is even a comforting narrative (The Parable of the Misunderstood Artist), one that has allowed – maybe even encouraged – subsequent composers to proceed with even more radical steps, disregarding the reactions of contemporary critics or audiences in the firm belief that history would eventually prove them right.[19]

It is not my purpose, however, to engage in the popular sport of ridiculing the critics of Schoenberg's music. Yes, some of those critics clearly were philistines and yes, some of them had personal or professional grudges against Schoenberg or his supporters (principally Mahler). What is important is not so much what the critics thought and wrote about Schoenberg's music. What is important is Schoenberg's reaction to their reviews. I am interested, in short, in a kind of secondary reception history: how the reactions of the audiences or critics influenced Schoenberg's subsequent compositional development. I do this from the belief that Schoenberg – contrary to his brave attempts to deny it – was profoundly influenced by negative reactions to his music.

Of course, if we know anything about the history of the reception of Schoenberg's music, it is that it went from bad to worse, from hostile to enraged, from incomprehension to utter rejection. We also know that to the extent his works were accepted at all, it was only years after their first performances.[20]

Although some of this is true, a systematic reading of the reviews of the 1907 concerts suggests that the reality was somewhat more complex. To demonstrate, let me begin with a review of the lieder concert that appeared in the 7 February issue (1907, No. 6) of the *Musikalische Wochenblatt/ Neue Zeitschrift für Musik*.[21] This was a respected weekly music magazine (published in Leipzig) that was directed at professional musicians and serious amateurs throughout the German-speaking world.[22]

The review is by the magazine's contributing editor in Vienna, Theodor Helm (1843–1920). Helm, it should be stressed, was no musically illiterate newspaper hack. Rather, he was a highly educated professional (with a doctorate), one who taught music history and aesthetics at Horak's Conservatory.[23]

There are several things that are particularly notable about Helm's review. In the first place, although he is clearly disturbed by the music, Helm's language and vocabulary are relatively temperate. Although (two years after the fact) he could not resist getting in another swipe at *Pelleas und Melisande* ("nur noch in grauenvollem Andenken"), he acknowledges Schoenberg's talent ("ein echtes Talent") and admits that the typical Schoenberg song was interesting and expressive ("in ihrer Art interessant, ausdrucksvoll"). Furthermore, he stresses that although he is no hidebound reactionary, he simply cannot follow Schoenberg's radical harmonies, dissonance treatment, harmonic progressions, and vocal lines ("doch auch eine in die Nerven schneidende Musik, bei welcher der Berichterstatter, obwohl gewiss nicht rücksichtlich gesinnt, unmöglich mehr überall mitgehen kann"). Clearly, for Helm, the problem with Schoenberg's music was its pitch language.

At the same time one of the most interesting revelations of this review is the unexpected light it sheds on the early reception history of Schoenberg's works. As Helm's review shows, there was considerable public support for Schoenberg's works. Helm points out that the concert was a public success ("äusseren Erfolg"). Not only did the audience demand the repetition of several of the songs ("einige Lieder mussten wiederholt werden"), but also, at the end of the concert, the composer was called to stand for thunderous applause ("zuletzt wurde der Komponist stürmisch gerufen").[24]

Helm tells us of this partly because he is a responsible, sober, and informed critic, one who was writing for a respected professional journal. He felt that it was his obligation to tell his readers that the works had been well received. But he was clearly troubled by this reaction; in his professional opinion, the songs were highly problematic. Yet the audience was responding enthusiastically, even demanding encores. How could this be?

Helm's explanation for this phenomenon is that Schoenberg's circle of admirers was there in full force ("die engere Verehrergemeinde Schönberg's – zu welcher, wie es scheint, auch Direktor Mahler gehört – vollzählig eingefunden"). He implies that there was something unrepresentative, maybe even illegitimate about the audience's reaction.[25] He suggests that if Schoenberg's works had appeared in a venue that was not packed with his claque, the reception would be far less enthusiastic.[26] By singling out Mahler by name as one of the supporters, Helm also appears to imply that Schoenberg was being given an unwarranted advantage by being placed under the protection of such an important figure.

The image of a Schoenberg premiere as a resounding public success with the audience clamoring for encores is – to put it mildly – not exactly the image history has bequeathed to us. Could Helm have been mistaken?

Apparently not; very similar descriptions occur in other reviews, and not just for the lieder concert.[27] This is not to say that all of the reviews described the audience reaction as uniformly positive: to the contrary, many of the other reviews place far more emphasis on the boisterously negative reactions that also seemed to have been a part of the response to all three of these concerts. It is clear that there was some rather aggressive hissing, booing, and whistling at the conclusion of the performances. It also seems indisputable that some of the audience voted with their feet and left the hall during the performance. Some of the reviewers go so far as to claim that Schoenberg's supporters were in the minority and that his opponents were in the majority. But time and again, the reviews mention that there was a solid, enthusiastic, core of supporters. Helm is not alone in leaving the impression that Schoenberg's supporters were the majority and not only for the lieder concert. For example, in a review that appeared on 10 February 1907 in the newspaper *Vaterland* the reviewer (Richard von Kralik) notes that a considerable portion of the audience responded with enthusiasism to Schoenberg's String Quartet, Op. 7 ("eine große Zahl begeisterter Anhänger, die dem Quartett eine enthusiastische Aufnahme bereiteten"), a reaction that von Kralik did not share.[28] From all of this, we must conclude that – contrary to conventional wisdom – Schoenberg's works actually were received with widespread enthusiasm by a considerable proportion of the audiences in attendance at the premieres.

But even if our impression of what the audiences' reactions had been is faulty, one cannot deny the fact that the critics rejected Schoenberg's music and did so with vitriol almost unmatched in the annals of criticism, so much so that to this very day a word association test using the phrase "musical invective" would frequently elicit "Schoenberg" as a response.

In its broadest outlines, this is exactly what happened. Almost all of the critics did respond with fury, scorn, abuse, disbelief, and outrage to Schoenberg's works. They pilloried the music using incendiary expressions such as "eine Parodie auf die moderne Tonkunst" (Richard Wallaschek). But this too is not the entire story. Although the overwhelming majority of the reviews were negative, that verdict was not unanimous. One of the reviews was even extraordinarily enthusiastic – of the "hats off, gentlemen, a genius" variety. This was the review by Dr. Wilhelm von Wymetal that appeared in the *Neue Badische Landes-Zeitung* in Mannheim on 6 February 1907.

Beginning with the opening line ("Es ist ein Name erklungen: Arnold Schönberg") and continuing throughout the review, von Wymetal lauds Schoenberg, comparing him favorably with the leading figures of music ("Der Name Schönberg wird weithin klingen, wie heute die Namen Strauß und Mahler"). Von Wymetal acknowledges that there was criticism ("Die zünftige Kritik sagt, das sei keine Musik"), but dismisses their opinion by citing Mahler's approval of Schoenberg's works ("Gustav Mahler, der Konzertsaal und Theater sonst scheu meidet, sitzt erregt da und klatscht lebhaft nach jedem Lied"). Von Wymetal closes with an unprecedented encomium: "Zum Abschied: Es ist ein Nam' erklungen: Arnold Schönberg. Hic Rhodus, hic – propheta![29] Schönberg ist Schönberg, und ich will an dieser Stelle, wo er noch nie genannt wurde, sein Prophet sein. Merkt Euch den Namen! Denn es kann sein, daß er klingen wird bis ans Ende der Tage!"

Although there are no other reviews of this sort, there was an extraordinarily thoughtful review by Dr. Elsa Bienenfeld that appeared on 12 February 1907 in the *Neues Wiener Journal*, an independent, mass-circulation daily.[30] She argues that the job of the critic is not to offer up subjective opinions, but to educate the readers as to the intentions and goals of the artist, thereby allowing them to make informed judgments. She asserts that Schoenberg's fundamental goal is unity and that in the String

Quartet, Op. 7 and the Chamber Symphony, Op. 9, he reworks traditional forms in furtherance of that goal. Throughout, the tone of her review is high-minded and serious, utterly devoid of inflammatory language or simplistic value judgments. Instead, she accords Schoenberg's music extraordinary respect, treating it as high-minded and important art that must be taken seriously.[31]

The von Wymetal and Bienenfeld reviews are, of course, exceptions. Most of the remaining reviews are ferociously negative and angrily abusive. In them, several common themes emerge. The reviewers bitterly criticize Schoenberg for the (in their view, intolerable) length of the works, particularly given the uninterrupted flow of both Opp. 7 and 9. They also direct their ire at Schoenberg's pitch language: more and more we hear complaints about the "cacophony" of his works. We also find frequent suggestions that Schoenberg is perpetrating a fraud.

From the preceding, we can see that Schoenberg heard decidedly mixed messages in the aftermath of the three concerts. On the one hand, it is clear that a significant percentage of the audiences responded highly favorably to the new works. There were also a few – very few – positive reactions in the press. Admittedly, the positive reactions, both in the concert hall and in the press, came almost exclusively from Schoenberg's circle of friends and admirers: it is clear that Schoenberg had filled the halls with his supporters.[32] Yet one need not regard the presence of supporters (as many of the critics surely did) as illegitimate or as of no value. Quite the contrary. That Schoenberg had a highly devoted following whose numbers were enough to fill concert halls and to demand curtain calls and encores should be interpreted as evidence of his success, not of his failure. On the other hand, there is no denying the existence of considerable opposition to his music and that this opposition occasioned highly contentious scenes. Moreover, there is no question but that the overall verdict in the press was overwhelmingly negative.

For our purposes the crucial question is what Schoenberg's reaction was to all of this, how it affected him and his future compositional development. Unfortunately, he left almost no record of his reactions although there are some clear statements in his correspondence with Arnold Rosé that he dreaded the onslaught.[33] I believe it is likely that the powerful reactions, pro and con, had some kind of effect on Schoenberg, and in particular on his compositional development. But can we isolate and identify what that response was?

It is clear that Schoenberg had already been in some kind of compositional crisis, even before the three controversial concerts. As we have seen, for a fairly extended period (August 1906 to March 1907) he had been unable to complete any of the many projects he had begun. In the immediate aftermath of the concerts, Schoenberg quickly finished three compositions (*Friede auf Erden*, "Jane Grey", and "Der verlorene Haufen"). Could this not suggest that Schoenberg's reaction to the controversy was a renewed resolve? That it sparked a confident defiance in response to the opinions of his opponents?

That might be the proper interpretation of this evidence. But there is one other fact that could put Schoenberg's completion of these works into a rather different light: all three of the compositions may have been written as entries for contests.[34] If this is true, then Arnold Schoenberg – the composer of *Verklärte Nacht, Gurrelieder, Pelleas und Melisande*, the String Quartet, Op. 7, and the Chamber Symphony, Op. 9 – broke his silence with works that were intended for competitions. This has the feel, not of confident defiance or renewed resolve, but of an almost pathetic hunger for acceptance and validation.

If that was Schoenberg's goal, it was not realized. Need it be said that his entries were unsuccessful? And to add insult to injury, can it have helped Schoenberg's ego that the winners of the ballade competition (Hans Hermann, Heinrich Eckl, and Gustav Lazarus) were hardly distinguished figures?[35]

Thus Schoenberg's finally breaking out of his writer's block does not help us to determine what effect – if any – the critical onslaught had on Schoenberg. But could there be something in the music itself? Is it possible that the critical reaction prompted Schoenberg to make changes in his compositional approach?

In at least one of the post-concert compositions, it appears that Schoenberg deliberately restrained his more radical tendencies. Although *Friede auf Erden*, Op. 13 is not exactly an easy-listening composition, its pitch language is considerably less radical than that of its immediate predecessor, the Chamber Symphony, Op. 9. A comparison of these two works is highly revealing. In Op. 9, pure triads were a rare species; in Op. 13, they are common. In Op. 9, diatonic passages were virtually absent; Op. 13 begins with five-and-a-half measures of pure diatonicism. In Op. 9, the form was recondite, complicated, and subtle; in Op. 13, the formal divisions are clear and straightforward. In Op. 9, radical chords (like the chord of fourths) were frequent and prominent; in Op. 13, although some non-traditional chords appear, they are neither frequent nor prominent.

This is not to say that Schoenberg suddenly ceased being Schoenberg and began writing a knock-off of the *Blue Danube Waltz*. There are many highly sophisticated subtleties in Op. 13 – the imitation at the tritone in the first phrase, for example. But *Friede auf Erden* has the feel of a work that strives for a somewhat wider acceptance, not of a work that demands acceptance on its own terms without compromise.

If it was Schoenberg's intention to reach out to a wider audience, it was at least partially successful. Although the work did not win any prize (if it was submitted to a competition), every indication is that its premiere was a real success. On 10 December 1911, the day following the premiere, Franz Schreker wrote Schoenberg: "Your work had an undoubted success – I was called back three times. No hissing or anything like that."[36]

At the premieres of Opp. 7 and 9 there had also been considerable audience support for Schoenberg (though most of that came from Schoenberg's circle). As Schreker's letter indicates, what made Op. 13 different was that there was little or none of the obstreperous opposition that marred the audiences' otherwise positive reception in 1907. So too, the critical establishment responded much more favorably than they had for the premieres of Opp. 7 and 9. This is not to say that the praise was anything like unanimous: there were still reviews that were highly critical. What criticism there was did not – could scarcely have begun to – equal the ferocity of the responses in 1907.

There may be another explanation for the (relatively) restrained pitch language of *Friede auf Erden* – an eminently practical reason. Schoenberg originally intended the work to be a cappella. As he had been moderately active as a choral conductor, he knew full well the practical limitations of that ensemble. He knew he would have to tone down the chromaticism, the dissonance treatment, and the skips used within the individual lines. And he seems to have tried to do just that: by comparison with Op. 9, Op. 13 is rather tame.

Even with these restraints the work was (and still is) far beyond the capacities of many otherwise proficient choirs. The work proved to be so difficult in rehearsals that the plan for a performance in 1908 had to be abandoned. The work was successfully premiered only after Schoenberg added instrumental parts that doubled the vocal lines.

This suggests that at least some of the restraint in the pitch language of *Friede auf Erden* was due to practical reasons (and was not a direct response to the critical onslaught). This is given added credence since the next two pieces, the Ballades, Op. 12, return to a more chromatic harmonic language.

That said there is something vaguely hesitant about Schoenberg's pitch language in the Ballades and in most of the compositions and fragments written in the period covered by this chapter. Although *Friede auf Erden* is perhaps the most obvious in this respect, the pitch language of much of what Schoenberg wrote in the period from August 1906 to July 1907 is less

Example 10.1

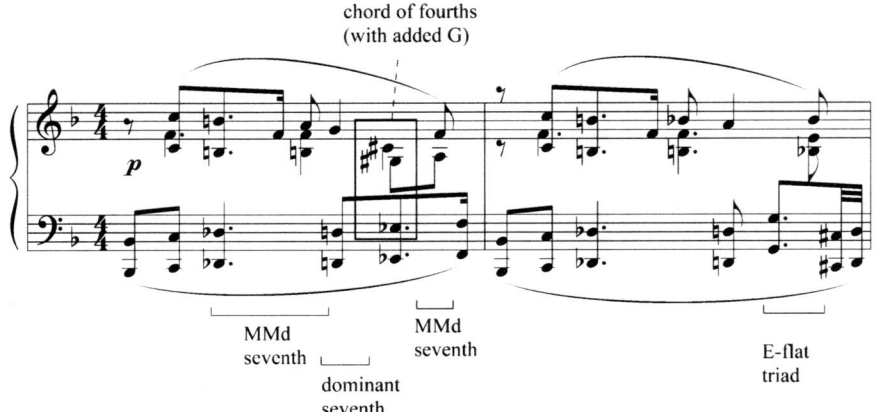

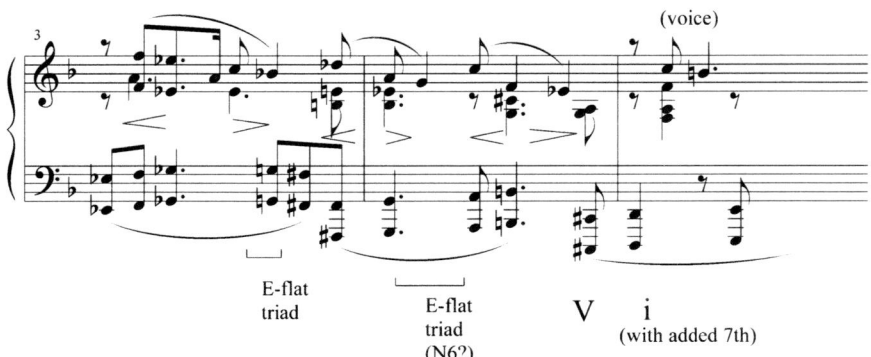

obviously radical than that of Op. 9. We can see this in the opening five measures of "Jane Grey" (see Ex. 10.1).[37]

Although Schoenberg does exhaust the total chromatic fairly quickly, and although the opening four measures are filled with an array of vagrant and chromatic seventh chords, there are a surprising number of pure triads (mostly E-flat major) and diatonic seventh chords in these measures. Less traditional chords (like chords of fourths) do not play anything close to the prominent role they did in Op. 9, although there are a few instances here as well (e.g. m. 1, beat 4). As a whole, the harmonic syntax is more restrained: Schoenberg settles on a referential triad in m. 5, prepared by an almost conventional dominant seventh (with a lowered fifth), which itself can be heard as having been prepared by the Neapolitan (the E-flat triads in mm. 2–4). Notwithstanding occasional progressive features (e.g. Schoenberg adds a seventh to the referential triad), the overall syntax is – at least by contrast with much of Op. 9 – comparatively traditional.

Example 10.2

"Jane Grey" is not an aberration. The other ballade, "Der verlorene Haufen", presents a similar picture (see Ex. 10.2). After beginning with a straightforward sequence, it settles on a referential triad (D minor) fairly quickly (toward the end of m. 5), makes comparatively liberal use of triads and diatonic seventh chords, gives less prominence to aggressively radical harmonies, and, in general, tones things down – not as much as *Friede auf Erden*, but recognizably more than the Chamber Symphony, Op. 9.

It does seem that the Ballades and *Friede auf Erden* are less radical than Op. 9, but then, so is almost everything that Schoenberg wrote during this period, even the pieces that were begun before the stormily controversial concerts. The opening measures of the Chamber Symphony No. 2 demonstrate this (see Ex. 10.3).

Example 10.3

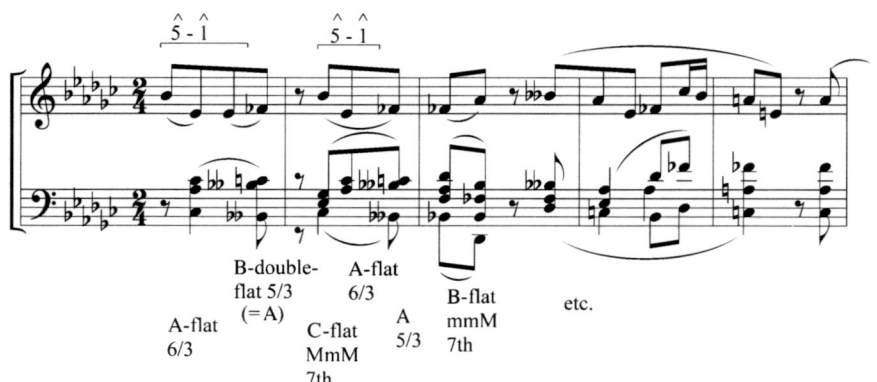

The chronology clearly indicates that Schoenberg composed these measures (which set the tone for much of the first movement) well before the brouhaha occasioned by the three concerts in 1907. Yet, they are neither a continuation nor an intensification of the more radical tendencies of Schoenberg's pitch language. Comparatively conservative features abound.

A clear referential center (E-flat minor) is confirmed by a solid, highly traditional cadence at m. 11, with a root position dominant seventh chord leading directly to a metrically stressed tonic triad. Although no E-flat minor triad appears before m. 11, the tonic triad is adumbrated by the several reiterations of the descending fifth, B-flat to E-flat in the primary melodic voice.

The chordal vocabulary is also comparatively restrained. The very first chord is an A-flat minor triad in first inversion and it proceeds immediately to a B-double-flat minor, root position triad. Not until the third chord of the piece is there a chordal dissonance (the B-flat of the C-flat major seventh chord in m. 2) and this promptly gives way to A-flat minor and A minor triads. This is significantly more triadic than most of Schoenberg's recent works.

Example 10.4

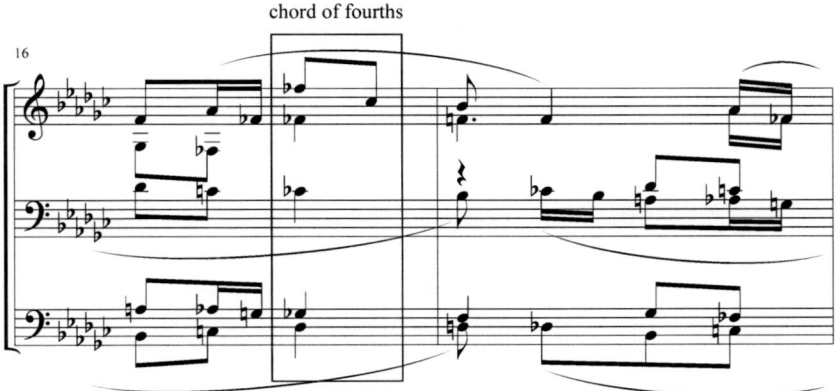

Although it is considerably more triadic than its immediate predecessor, this should not be read to mean that the layer of the Chamber Symphony No. 2 that Schoenberg wrote before the three concerts is utterly devoid of all traces of the more modernist chordal vocabulary. We can see this in mm. 16–17 of the 1907/8 draft (see Ex. 10.4).

At the end of m. 16 Schoenberg presents a clear chord of fourths, the very chord whose prominent presence in the Chamber Symphony, Op. 9 made such a notable contribution to that work's radical character. Its use here shows Schoenberg's continued commitment to expanding his chordal vocabulary well beyond traditional chord types.

But there are some crucial differences between how chords of this sort are used in the two Chamber Symphonies. In Op. 9, chords like the chord of fourths were often placed in the most prominent of locations, aggressively demanding the listeners' attention. As a result, more than one of the critics at the premiere pointed to the chord of fourths as evidence of what they saw as Schoenberg's excessive radicalism. By contrast, in the Chamber Symphony No. 2, the chord of fourths is, if not hidden, then given much less prominence. It has become more a seamless part of the fabric than a sharply emphasized novelty. As such, it is a kind of return to the status this chord had in *Pelleas und Melisande*. Thus even when Schoenberg used some of the more radical harmonies, it was in a context that attenuated their prominence.

The relatively tame pitch language of the Chamber Symphony No. 2 suggests that the controversial concerts of January and February of 1907 could not have been the proximate cause of Schoenberg's temporary retreat from the advanced position he had staked out in the Chamber Symphony, Op. 9. The evidence shows that the pullback began even before those concerts took place.

But this too may be an oversimplification. Even during the period of supposed retrenchment, there were occasional flashes of radicalism that are as advanced as anything in Schoenberg's music up through Op. 9. One of the most intriguing of these is the never completed song, "Aus schwerer Stunde".

The pitch language of this fragment is extremely radical, particularly when it is compared with almost everything else that Schoenberg wrote in the yearlong period covered by this chapter. In many ways, its pitch language is at a level of innovation that would not be equaled until the Two Songs, Op. 14 and the later layers of the String Quartet No. 2, Op. 10 (see Ex. 10.5).

In virtually every respect, the pitch language of this fragment stakes out a position even beyond what Schoenberg had dared to do in the Chamber Symphony, Op. 9. The key signature (five flats) suggests that Schoenberg intended an overall tonic of either B-flat minor or D-flat major. Yet neither of these two triads nor their dominants appears in clearly explicit form anywhere in the fragment. True, on the last eighth of the upbeat to m. 1, Schoenberg passes through a fleeting D-flat triad. So too, on the third beat of m. 1, when the voice and l.h. piano drop out, what remains is a B-flat minor triad. But neither of these is readily apprehensible as a discrete triad, let alone strongly enough emphasized to achieve a referential status.

In any event, the absence of a recognizable tonal center in this fragment was virtually inevitable because its chordal vocabulary is so radical. There are almost no pure triads at all (the emphasized C minor triad on the downbeat of m. 8 is a rare exception). Common diatonic seventh chords (dominant seventh, minor seventh, major seventh) are almost as rare and even when they do occur (e.g. the minor seventh chord on the second beat of m. 7), they are typically shunted off to metrically inconspicuous locations. A few years earlier, Schoenberg's favorite chords had been seventh chords with symmetrical trichordal subsets (such as mmM, MMm, and MMd) or ninth chords in inversion (frequently with the ninth in a voice other than the soprano). Chords of those types still appear (e.g. m. 1, downbeat, m. 3, downbeat, m. 7, beat 3), but not with anything like their prior frequency. Instead, there is a plethora of chords that cannot readily be assigned to traditional categories: for example, the chord that emerges on the second beat of m. 1 (C G D-flat F A), or the chord on the last beat of m. 1 (G B-flat D-flat A-flat), or the third beat of m. 2 (E-flat G D-flat F). In place of traditional chords, Schoenberg makes ever more frequent use of chords based on the principle of localized consonance. Although the chord on the third beat of m. 2 may not conform to any traditional chordal type (unless one wishes to understand it as a ninth chord omitting its fifth), the

Example 10.5

two voices in the piano r.h. are part of a succession of parallel thirds that continues to the end of m. 3.

The radicalism of the pitch language of "Aus schwerer Stunde" highlights the complicated nature of Schoenberg's stylistic development, particularly during this year of crisis. This song is placed chronologically in the same period as the beginning of Schoenberg's work on the first layer of the Chamber Symphony No. 2. This means that at virtually one and the same time we find Schoenberg employing a vocabulary rich in triads and one virtually without traditional chords, a syntax that includes a prominent dominant-to-tonic cadence and a syntax that is utterly devoid of traditional progressions, a fabric in which a tonic is readily identifiable and one in which there is scarcely a triad, let alone a tonic. Within the larger context of the period covered by this chapter, the radical pitch language of "Aus schwerer Stunde" reinforces the impression that Schoenberg was in a compositional quandary, unsure of his eventual direction.

Because of the complicated path of Schoenberg's development in the period covered by this chapter, it is difficult to make the case that the stormy reception of his music had an unambiguous effect on the development of his chordal vocabulary and pitch language. There is, however, one aspect of his stylistic development in which it appears that Schoenberg did respond to the criticism of his music in an unequivocal manner.

One theme that surfaced again and again in the reviews of Opp. 7 and 9 was the critics' angry rejection of the all-in-one form, particularly when, as in Op. 7, this led to a composition that lasted nearly an hour without a significant break. (Similar criticisms had been leveled against *Pelleas und Melisande* two years earlier.) Perhaps it is coincidental, but it seems significant that in the aftermath of the controversial concerts, Schoenberg abandoned the all-in-one form. Not until nearly forty years later (the Piano Concerto, Op. 42), would Schoenberg again write an instrumental composition whose single movement was a conflation of several traditional movements.

Schoenberg also seems to have reacted to the critics' complaints, not only by dividing his instrumental compositions into separate movements, but also by reconfirming his commitment to shortening the length of his movements. Although the process of reducing the size of his instrumental works had already begun with the Chamber Symphony No. 1, Op. 9 (as a result of the abandonment of narrative programs), the aftermath of the three concerts seems to have prompted Schoenberg to reaffirm his commitment to writing shorter instrumental movements. The first movement of the String Quartet No. 2, Op. 10 is only 233 measures long and the second movement (in a very quick tempo), only 275 measures. In a typical performance, these last about seven minutes each, approximately half the size of the movements within the String Quartet, Op. 7.[38]

The total picture that emerges from the period from August 1906 to July 1907 is complex and, in some ways, contradictory. This is a period in which Schoenberg started more than a dozen projects but finished very few of them, a period in which he wrote some highly radical music but also some far less radical music, a period in which he became a famous composer but also one in which he started a second career as a painter. Central to this period was the polarized reaction to his music, occasioned by the three concerts. Schoenberg emerged from these concerts as a famous and an infamous figure, as the object of adulation and as the object of outraged opprobrium, as the savior of music and as the destroyer of music. It is indicative of how deeply this affected Schoenberg that in the years to come he would remember mostly the negative. When he looked back on his public career, he recalled the venom, the catcalls, the whistles, and the outraged reviews. He did not give equal weight to the fact that his works had also elicited adulation.

Although it is not possible to point to a series of unequivocal changes that we can identify as a direct result of his reaction to the reception of his music, I am convinced that the violently polarized reaction to his music reinforced and intensified the paralyzing compositional crisis that had begun after the completion of the Chamber Symphony No. 1, Op. 9. With Op. 9, Schoenberg had finally cut loose from programmatic principles. He had taken traditional harmonic vocabulary and syntax to previously unknown realms and had begun to develop a new vocabulary of harmonies. But after Op. 9 it is clear he was unsure of where to go next. As a fundamental part of his makeup he believed that he had to go forward: history demanded it. But where? Schoenberg's inability to complete compositions, his exploration of painting as a new avenue of artistic expression, his contradictory radical/conservative harmonic tendencies, his whiplash-inducing changes from lieder to chamber works to opera and back again, and his submission of his compositions to competitions, all combine to paint a picture of a composer who was unsure of his direction, a sentiment that the violently divided reactions to his music can only have intensified.

11 Motivic economy: String Quartet No. 2, Op. 10, movements one and two, March–December 1907

> ... repetition in music, especially when linked with variation, shows that *different things* can arise from *one* thing.[1]

The String Quartet No. 2, Op. 10 may well be the most heterogeneous of all of Schoenberg's compositions.[2] No other of his compositions has four movements of such strikingly different character. No other of his compositions begins as an instrumental work and ends as a vocal work.[3] No other of his compositions has movements both with, and without, key signatures. No other of his compositions juxtaposes the tune of a farcical folksong in one movement and a setting of a deadly serious poem in the next. Although Schoenberg took several steps to unify the cycle (using motives from the first two movements as the basis for the principal ideas of the third movement and returning to an F-sharp triad at the end of the finale), the fact remains that the two halves of the work reflect two distinct stages of his compositional development.

Given the extended and complicated genesis of the quartet, a degree of diversity was probably inevitable. Some of the first sketches are dated 9 March 1907, the same day Schoenberg completed *Friede auf Erden*, Op. 13, and only a short time after the three controversial concerts in Vienna.[4] No sooner had Schoenberg made a few sketches for this new quartet than he dropped it to write the Ballades, Op. 12. Upon completing those songs, he returned to the quartet. For much of the summer and early fall of 1907 Schoenberg bounced back and forth between it and the Chamber Symphony No. 2, finishing the first movement of Op. 10 (1 September 1907), almost finishing the first movement of the Chamber Symphony No. 2, and writing substantial chunks of the second movements of both works.

Schoenberg was unable to finish the quartet (or for that matter, any of the movements of the Chamber Symphony No. 2) in 1907. Instead he turned in another direction entirely, back to songs, completing "Ich darf nicht dankend" (Op. 14, No. 1) on 17 December 1907 and "In diesen Wintertagen" (Op. 14, No. 2) on 2 February 1908. These were followed by the first phase of work on *Das Buch der hängenden Gärten*, Op. 15: in March and April 1908, Schoenberg completed (at the very least), songs III, IV, V, VII, and VIII.[5] Only after these interruptions did Schoenberg go back and complete the String Quartet No. 2. He finished the third movement on 11 July 1908, the second movement on 27 July 1908, and the final

Motivic economy 211

movement at about the same time. (The Chamber Symphony No. 2 remained incomplete for more than thirty years.)[6]

It is clear that Schoenberg's conception of Op. 10 changed over the course of its composition. In the first stage of work, there is no evidence that Schoenberg had intended the quartet to be anything other than a purely instrumental work.[7] By the summer of 1908, he had made the decision to add a voice to the ensemble for the last two movements.[8]

Therefore, Schoenberg's work on the String Quartet, Op. 10 divides into two distinct phases. In this chapter we shall limit our attention to the first phase, a period when Schoenberg appears to have intended to write an abstract instrumental work.

One of the most notable features of the first phase of the String Quartet No. 2, Op. 10 is its motivic economy. In the first movement Schoenberg restricts himself to a highly limited arsenal of motives and takes pains to relate even those to one another.[9]

From the very first measure, Schoenberg demonstrates his interest in this idea. The work begins with the principal melody in the first violin ('x') in a phrase that extends for five measures (see Ex. 11.1). This is a classic example of how to build an extended phrase from the varied repetition and transformation of a carefully limited number of basic elements.

The first measure presents a four-note figure ('a') which is made up of two smaller cells: a stepwise descent from A through G-sharp to F-sharp ('b'), and then a skip up to C-sharp ('c'). Rhythmically prominent is the dotted eighth – sixteenth figure ('d'), in the middle of the measure.

Measure 2 begins by restating 'a', but in accelerated form, compressed into two beats instead of the three of m.1. The dotted figure ('d'), remains in the middle of the measure, but given the acceleration of 'a', 'd' is now associated with 'c' instead of with 'b'. After completing the accelerated statement of 'a', Schoenberg adds a new note, B, on the last beat of m. 2, thereby extending 'a' into a five-note figure. The repetition of 'a' in m. 2

Example 11.1

creates a new motivic figure ('e'), that cuts across the boundary of mm. 1–2, outlining a descent from C-sharp, through A and G-sharp to F-sharp. Motive 'e' is not entirely new; it can also be understood as a permutation (or rotation) of the elements of 'a'.

In m. 3, Schoenberg takes the recently created 'e' and restates it, but with an interesting transformation. Just as the initial version of 'a' was compressed and accelerated in m. 2, so too 'e' is compressed and accelerated in m. 3, moving from its high point to its low point in only one beat instead of the two beats of mm. 1–2. Schoenberg omits the G-sharp and changes the final F-sharp to F-natural, thereby expanding the range of 'e' to an augmented fifth. He changes the position of the dotted rhythm ('d') yet again, moving it to the beginning of the measure.

Having stated the principal idea and restated it in transformed form, Schoenberg now moves to close off the phrase: the melody continues downward with a mixture of half- and whole-steps (an indeterminate scale segment) that is a varied and expanded version of 'b'. It pauses (augmentation of 'd') first on C-sharp, an octave down from its high point in mm. 1–3. But just as the second statement of 'a' (m. 2) was expanded when C-sharp moved down to B, so too here, 'b' is extended by a final move to B-sharp. In the process, the phrase expands from four measures to five.

Schoenberg employs identical procedures to form the next important idea, 'y', the thirteen-measure theme that appears in the viola in mm. 12–24 (see Ex. 11.2). Like 'x', this melody is also the result of the varied repetition of a rigorously limited arsenal of basic motives.

Example 11.2

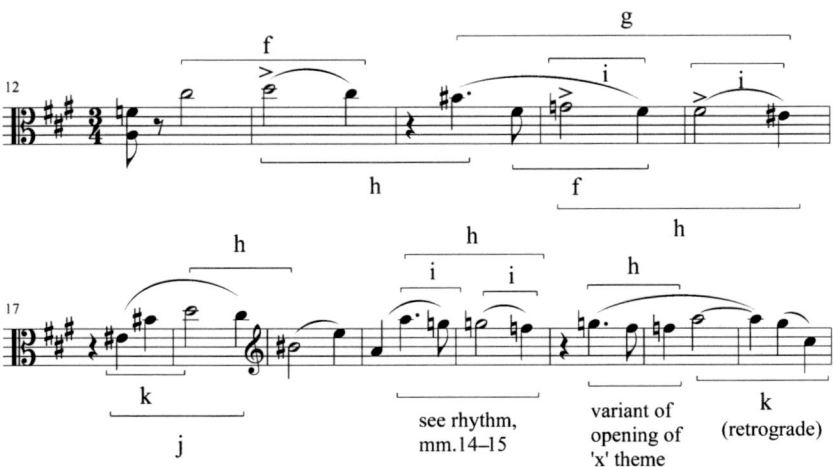

Motivic economy

The theme begins with a neighbor figure, 'f'. A somewhat longer and more involved figure follows ('g'), one that might at first give the impression of being contrasting material. But 'g' is not completely new. Embedded in 'g' is a transposed repetition of 'f'. The joint between 'f' and 'g' creates a descending chromatic line D C-sharp B-sharp, 'h', which returns immediately as the descent from G to E-sharp in mm. 15–16. Because of the repeated F-sharp, 'h' in mm. 15–16 divides into two rhythmically parallel units ('i') G/F-sharp and F-sharp/E-sharp, the second a transposition of the first. A continuation of the transpositional pattern would yield a third instance of 'i' beginning on E-sharp. Although there is no complete third statement of the sequence, the following measure (m. 17) begins with the expected E-sharp.

The next segment of the melody ('j', mm. 17–19) is a conflation and combination of important features from the first two phrases. It begins with an upward leap from E-sharp to B-sharp, the two pitches that had been the boundary pitches of 'g', thereby acting as a retrograde summary. This is followed by an ascent to D and then a chromatic descent through C-sharp to B-sharp, a nearly literal restatement of 'h'. The rest of this theme follows similar patterns: motives are restated, recombined, transposed, and transformed, yielding a melodic line that is at once diverse and unified. Toward the end of the melody (m. 22) there is even a subtle reminder of 'x'.

Schoenberg also takes concrete steps to relate the different themes of the movement to one another. We have already seen aspects of this in 'y' where some of the components of 'x' return in varied form.[10] A far more explicit instance emerges when we compare 'y' with another one of the important themes that Schoenberg uses in the movement, the melody ('z') that appears in the first violin in mm. 43–51 (see Ex. 11.3).

Like its predecessors 'z' unfolds as a result of the sophisticated application of the techniques of developing variation. Significantly, 'z' is not an independent theme; rather, it is clearly derived from, and related to, the two other principal themes, 'x' and 'y' – most closely to 'y', but to 'x' as well.

Example 11.3

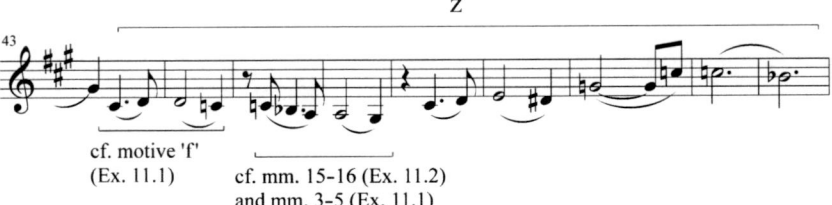

cf. motive 'f'
(Ex. 11.1)   cf. mm. 15-16 (Ex. 11.2)
and mm. 3-5 (Ex. 11.1)

The connections between 'z' and 'y' are unmistakable, right from the outset.[11] Both begin on a C-sharp on the second beat of the measure and step up to D, which is prolonged for the first two beats of the following measure. In 'y' (Ex. 11.2), the move from C-sharp to D had been without adornment; in 'z' the downbeat D is preceded (end of m. 43) by an anticipation. This rhythmic variation only broadens and intensifies the interconnections: the resultant rhythm of mm. 43–4 (a dotted quarter and eighth leading to a downbeat half-note) had been prominent in 'x' (mm. 4–5) and in 'y' (mm. 14–15, 20–1, and with a further variation, mm. 22–3).

The next phrase of 'z' (mm. 45–6) also shows clear connections with both 'x' and 'y'. The more obvious of the relationships is with 'y', as the figure in mm. 45–6 is a clear variation of mm. 15–16. But there are also palpable connections with 'x', particularly mm. 3–5, with its stepwise descent.

There are precedents for motivic relationships between apparently different themes in Schoenberg's instrumental compositions: we encountered instances of this idea as early as *Verklärte Nacht*. What is so significant about the first movement of the String Quartet No. 2 is the pervasiveness of this idea. It goes even beyond motivic relationships between the three principal themes of the movement 'x', 'y', and 'z' creating a network of motivic connections that, at one time or another, binds every significant theme or motive in the movement to every other theme or motive by a chain of transformations. Let us follow just one of those paths of development: the many different patterns that spring from the middle-voice counterpoint to 'y' (see Ex. 11.4).

Motive 'q' begins life as a relatively nondescript accompanimental figure, a stream of five eighth notes that begins after the downbeat. With its twists and turns, this seemingly commonplace figure seems designed more to fill out the texture and to provide a constant rhythmic impetus than to attract attention as a significant motivic entity.

Almost imperceptibly, this anonymity is stripped away as Schoenberg starts to transform 'q' into patterns that resemble important motivic and thematic ideas that have already appeared. For example, in m. 21, 'q' is transformed into a variant of the opening theme of the composition (see Ex. 11.5).

Example 11.4

Motivic economy 215

An important further stage of the development of 'q' occurs in m. 33, with the return of the 'x' theme. This time, 'x' (now in vln. 2) does not return with its original accompaniment; instead, various versions of 'q', including those that appeared in mm. 19–24, now act as the accompaniment to 'x' (see Ex. 11.6). Thus 'q', originally the counterpoint to 'y' now takes on a new role as the counterpoint to 'x'. It is all the more interesting, then, that when 'z' (which, as we have seen, is a close relative of 'y') enters in m. 43, 'q' is, at first, absent. But toward the end of the first statement of 'z' and throughout its restatement, 'q' returns with a vengeance in the two inner parts (see Ex. 11.7).

Example 11.5

Example 11.6

Example 11.7

By using 'q' as the counterpoint to the restatement of 'z' Schoenberg has effectively closed the circle: 'q' now has functioned as a counterpoint to all three of the main themes of the exposition. Yet even this is not the end of its development.

Up to this point, 'q' had functioned only as a subsidiary voice, never as the principal voice. Beginning in m. 58 (toward the end of the restatement of 'z') that changes. A new variant of 'q' appears, first in violin 1 and then in all of the other instruments. As can be seen, the version of 'q' that emerges in m. 58 is no mere accompanimental figure (see Ex. 11.8). This version of 'q' takes center stage in m. 58, is repeated in imitation at the octave in m. 60, then later in inversion, at other transpositions, and in stretto.

Motivic economy

Example 11.8

Moreover, this thematic version of 'q' has a small, but highly significant variation. In terms of contour and intervallic succession, it most closely resembles the version that had appeared in m. 50 (cf. vln. 1, m. 58, with vln. 2, m. 50), but its rhythm in m. 58 is unlike that of any previous instance of 'q'. Up to this point, 'q' had always appeared as a steady stream of eighth notes. In m. 58, Schoenberg changes 'q' so that it has a dotted rhythm for the last beat of the measure. By making this change, Schoenberg has forged a clear bond with the opening theme of the composition ('x'), and the rhythmic motive ('d'), that had been so prominent a component of that theme. Schoenberg reinforces the connection with 'x' by stating a version of that theme in augmentation in the cello in mm. 63–6.

By m. 65, 'q' has already made an extended journey. It began life as the unobtrusive accompaniment to the second of the three principal themes ('y'), became the accompaniment for the two other principal themes ('x' and 'z') and then stepped forward as a theme in its own right – albeit one that reveals essential connections with the opening principal theme. And this is hardly the end of the saga; over the course of the rest of the movement, 'q' continues to appear, is subjected to even more transformations, and forges still more relationships with other motivic ideas in the movement. As a result, 'q' pervades the work.

The 'q' motive is far from unique in this respect: all of the important motivic ideas of the first movement have a similar function. As a consequence, every single prominent (and virtually every not-so-prominent) motivic idea in the movement can be understood as a statement, transformation, or combination, of a carefully limited number of basic thematic or motivic ideas.

Thus an extraordinary network of motivic relationships binds the movement into an integrated whole. Using a limited number of basic elements, Schoenberg forms his principal themes by a flexible process of developing variation. He limits the number of those themes, thereby making much of the movement accountable directly to those themes and only those themes. Yet the principal themes are not distinct entities; there is a multiplicity of motivic connections between them. Still further, Schoenberg does not treat any of his motivic ideas or themes as immutable. Instead, there is a constant process of development, in which the various ideas are transformed, varied, and combined, thereby revealing further relationships.

No single one of these procedures is unprecedented in Schoenberg's works. But never before had Schoenberg employed these techniques on such a grand scale and in such a systematic manner. Some of the songs are based on a highly limited number of motives. But none of those songs comes close to the size of the first movement of Op. 10. Schoenberg had begun to limit the number of his principal themes in the String Quartet No. 1 and the Chamber Symphony No. 1. But neither of those works has anything like the degree of thematic economy we see here. There are motivic connections between some of the leitmotifs of *Verklärte Nacht* or *Pelleas und Melisande*. But never before had those connections been so exhaustive. And many of Schoenberg's prior works employed the procedures of motivic transformation and development to create new ideas and to relate them to one another. But never before had those procedures penetrated so deeply into every corner of a movement, nor had they been so comprehensive in their influence, nor had they been so multi-dimensional in their impact.

The motivic unity characteristic of the first movement of Op. 10 is an important byproduct of Schoenberg's abandonment of programmatic music. During the first phase of Op. 10, Schoenberg's emerging commitment to absolute music also brought about other important changes in formal structure and in particular, a renewed interest in traditional forms (such as sonata form).

The Chamber Symphony, Op. 9 had also been an abstract composition (the first since the Quartet in D of 1897) and also structured its forms (however loosely) around traditional models. Nevertheless, Op. 9 still retained some of the most prominent external characteristics of Schoenberg's programmatic works. Like those compositions, it was cast as a single long movement, played without a break and with a plethora of motives and themes. Like the programmatic compositions, its different themes were of strikingly different character and tone.

The first two movements of the String Quartet No. 2 (and the 1907 phase of the Chamber Symphony No. 2) thus mark an important change in direction. By writing self-contained movements with very tightly controlled motivic and thematic structure, Schoenberg finally seems to have made a decisive break with his programmatic past – not just with the underlying philosophy, but with the details of the macrostructure as well.

There is an interesting twist to this change: when Schoenberg finally cut the tie with programmatic music, his immediate impulse was to employ traditional formal models. However, this turn to traditional formal models was both short-lived and highly limited: it was limited to four movements (only one of which was completed at the time) from two compositions (Opp. 10 and 38) written over a period of approximately six months in 1907.[12]

Moreover, there is some circumstantial evidence to suggest that Schoenberg very quickly become uncomfortable with this new direction: he was incapable of completing the String Quartet, Op. 10 or the Chamber Symphony No. 2 as purely abstract compositions. As long as Op. 10 was intended to be a purely instrumental work, Schoenberg simply could not make much progress: in the fifteen months between March 1907 and June 1908, Schoenberg was only able to write the first movement and some of the second movement. By contrast, once he decided to turn it into a vocal work, progress was immediate: in approximately four months (June to September 1908), Schoenberg completed the second movement and wrote the third and fourth movements. In (roughly) quantitative terms, after turning the quartet into a vocal work Schoenberg wrote a little less than twice the music in a little more than a quarter of the time.

In the case of the Chamber Symphony No. 2, the situation was even more extreme. Schoenberg was unable to finish any of its movements in 1907. After writing most (but not all) of the first movement and some of the second movement, Schoenberg stopped work. Two fitful attempts (in 1911 and 1916) to finish the work did not succeed, and the composition remained a fragment until 1939, six years after his emigration to the United States.[13] Interestingly, as he did with the String Quartet, Op. 10, Schoenberg attempted to break the impasse by abandoning the purely abstract plan of the work. At some point (perhaps as late as 1916), Schoenberg considered changing the Chamber Symphony No. 2 into a melodrama based on a spoken text. In Sketchbook III there is a page of text that bears the heading: "Text zur II. Kammersymphonie. (Melodram) Titel: 'Wendepunkt' Orchesterwerk v AS". Although nothing seems to have come of this proposed reformulation of the work, it is another indication of Schoenberg's difficulty in completing abstract works with traditional forms at that stage in his development.

Because the first movement of the String Quartet, Op. 10 was the only movement actually completed during the period covered by this chapter, we are necessarily constrained in making claims about the formal structure of the other movements. It may well be that the final form of those movements does not reflect Schoenberg's original intentions. This may not be a serious problem for the first movement of the Chamber Symphony No. 2, which got very close to the end before Schoenberg stopped work, but it is particularly acute for the second movement of the Chamber Symphony No. 2 (whose composition sprawled over three decades) and for the second movement of the String Quartet No. 2, where only a bit less than half of the movement was finished at this stage. Because the first movement of Op. 10 was the only movement actually completed at this stage, we shall focus our attentions on it.

The first movement of the String Quartet, Op. 10 is probably the clearest example of traditional sonata form in any of Schoenberg's compositions, at least until the twelve-tone works. There is a clear exposition that presents the principal thematic and motivic material of the movement, an equally clear development section that subjects that material to relatively traditional kinds of development, a recapitulation that restates some of the principal ideas of the exposition, and a coda that brings the movement to a close.

That said there are many subtleties and complications to this form. The most obvious of those is the difficulty in finding the precise location of the principal sections. In his analysis of this movement (based in part on a suggestion by Schoenberg), Walter Frisch argues that the recapitulation begins in m. 146.[14] There is strong evidence in support of this view: the general pause at the end of m. 145, the return to the opening theme immediately following in m. 146, and the reprise (though in retrograde) of the succession of triads (F major to F-sharp minor) that had appeared in the opening measures. By contrast, Arnold Whittall sees the recapitulation beginning at m. 159, with a return to the tonic. Whittall describes Schoenberg's placement of the recapitulation as at m. 146 as "a curious suggestion in view of the strong *ritardando* leading to the return of the tonic key in bar 159."[15]

The existence of a disagreement over so basic an issue as the placement of the beginning of a recapitulation is revealing, particularly when the principals to the disagreement are so distinguished. But it is not a matter of either of the two sides being in error. The existence of the conflicting interpretations highlights an important ambiguity about the form of this movement.[16] That, in turn, is indicative of an important aspect of Schoenberg's formal thought, one whose influence can be felt well beyond the narrow confines of this period. Frisch is right. There is a sense of return at m. 146, with restatements (though in transposition) of the opening theme. This point does initiate a passage in which an F major triad that leads, in m. 159, to an F-sharp minor triad, a clear reversal of the opening progressions of the movement. But Whittall is right too. The F-sharp minor triad, the triad of the opening measure, does not reappear until m. 159. Furthermore, the point chosen by Frisch as the beginning of the recapitulation falls in the middle of a *ritardando* that began well before m. 146 and ends only with m. 159. And unlike m. 146, m. 159 initiates a passage that includes the literal repetition (at its original pitch level) of one of the themes of the exposition. Ambiguities of this sort, where no clear-cut boundary exists between different sections, will remain one of Schoenberg's favorite formal strategies, even after he had turned away from traditional forms.

Another important feature of the form of the first movement of Op. 10 (and one with ample roots in his past) is Schoenberg's avoidance of literal reprises: very little in the recapitulation is restated without significant alteration and transformation. Perhaps the closest Schoenberg comes to a literal repetition is the restatement of the 'y' theme. Even here, the principal and subsidiary voices are switched in registers (allowing Schoenberg to continue his interest in exploiting learned devices such as invertible counterpoint at the octave). But even passages like this are relatively unusual; the norm is to restate material in far less literal form, often involving extensive transformations. Neither the 'x,' nor the 'z' themes ever appear in their original form at their original pitch level in the recapitulation.

The harmonic language from the period March–December 1907 is characterized by some of the same ambivalence that we saw in the works and fragments from Schoenberg's crisis of 1906. At times, the language is – by Schoenberg's standards if almost nobody else's – mildly conservative. At other times, some of his most radical tendencies come to the fore.

The first movement begins and ends with clear statements of F-sharp minor triads. Scattered throughout the movement, a few other equally prominent and equally clear triads make appearances, often at important points of articulation: the beginnings and endings of sections, phrases, and themes. This might seem to be a slight step backward from the pitch language of the Chamber Symphony, Op. 9.

In spite of their more frequent appearance, Schoenberg's treatment of triads in the first movement often has a curiously tentative quality to it, as if he were slightly uncomfortable with the triad's traditional role as a stable entity. There are even a number of places in the movement where triads appear to impart, not stability, but instability. In his perceptive analysis of the first movement, Walter Frisch has pointed out that Schoenberg's "bold stroke here ... is to reverse the expected associations of tonality/consonance with stability, and of atonality/dissonance with instability." Frisch points out that the opening 'x' theme is highly unstable, notwithstanding its clear triadic opening. He further notes that the theme "refuses to hold to its F♯-minor point of origin, but begins right away to wander tonally and in m. 11 literally falls apart on F major (one can certainly not speak of any cadence or close on F)."[17]

I think this is exactly right: notwithstanding its triadic content, the 'x' theme is highly unstable. The result is a complicated set of contradictory impulses: although triads sometimes appear in passages that are unstable (as in the opening phrases), in other places they retain their traditional role as a point of resolution.

The contradictory tendencies exemplified in Schoenberg's treatment of triads, is reflected in a larger sense by the heterogeneous nature of the harmonic vocabulary and its syntax. In addition to prominent, unadorned triads, diatonic seventh chords still appear, mixed together with chromatic seventh chords, ninth chords in inversions, chords of fourths (or fifths), and more radical sonorities. As with the triads, so with the other sonorities, there seems to be little correlation between the degree of traditional dissonance and functional stability. Some passages that are highly dissonant (in traditional terms) appear to be stable – even more than other passages (like the opening) that have clear triads. In order to see how this works, let us turn to a detailed examination of two different passages from the first movement.

We begin with the passage that includes the first statement of the 'y' theme (see Ex. 11.9). As Frisch notes (in the analysis cited above), the

Motivic economy

Example 11.9

'y' theme seems to possess all of the stability that was lacking in the 'x' theme. "It unfolds at a constant tempo, which Schoenberg marks significantly as the *Hauptzeitmaß*, or principal tempo, almost as if what preceded is to be taken as *Vorspiel*. The smooth linearity of its bass line and the regularity of the melodic structure ... gives the theme a stability or solidity."[18]

The stability that Frisch describes is not a product of the presence of clearly articulated triads placed in prominent locations: there are no clearly articulated triads at all in this passage. Although triads and other more traditional sonorities do not appear as obvious surface elements, they are not completely absent but instead are woven into the fabric. To take just a few examples: on the very last eighth of m. 12, there is a third-inversion, dominant seventh chord; on the first beat of m. 13, a root position B minor triad makes a brief appearance; on the second beat of m. 17 a second-inversion, dominant seventh chord appears; on the last eighth of m. 17 there is an evanescent, first-inversion, E-sharp minor triad.

But these triads are not functioning in traditional terms: they are no more stable than the other, traditionally more dissonant, sonorities in the passage. The context makes it clear that they are not locally referential consonances to which the remaining sonorities are subordinated. Nor do they have traditional functional implications: the dominant seventh chord at the end of m. 12 does not follow a traditional dominant preparation chord nor does it function as a preparation for a tonic chord or for any recognizable tonic substitute. The triads and seventh chords that do exist seem to function no differently than do the many less-than-traditional sonorities that surround them.

One of the means Schoenberg uses to accomplish this end is familiar: the near-speed-of-light of his harmonic rhythm. No sonority, triadic or otherwise, lasts long enough, or is presented in clear enough form, to take on any kind of referential status. As always, there is a succession of sonorities – triadic and not, traditional and not – that proceeds at such a pace that it is not possible to isolate any of them as having primacy. In the first measure of the excerpt, there is an augmented triad on the first eighth, a C-sharp D-sharp A trichord on the second, a first-inversion A major triad on the third, a return to the C-sharp D-sharp A trichord on the fourth, a C-sharp minor triad on the fifth, and a C-sharp dominant seventh chord on the last. None of these sonorities seems to function at a higher hierarchical level than any other.

We have seen this kind of harmonic rhythm from the very first songs we examined. It has long been impossible to simplify the surface and to understand passages in a hierarchical manner such that some tones or sonorities function as referential while others are elaborative. However,

Motivic economy

there is a subtle shift here. In Schoenberg's earlier works (up until Op. 9), he tended to anchor passages of this sort (as opposed to developmental passages) around triadic points of reference. That was particularly so if the phrase involved was – as here – a principal theme being stated for the first time. Here (like most of the themes from Op. 9) those points of reference are absent. Instead, the theme proceeds from beginning to end without ever establishing any triadic points of reference.

The passage we have just examined may not have any clear triadic reference points, but it does have a residual triadic presence embedded within the fabric. Other passages in the quartet are devoid of even that residual presence. Good examples of that are provided by the three measures that lead to the (Schoenberg/Frisch) recapitulation (see Ex. 11.10).

Over the course of these three measures, the polyphonic lines never combine to create a pure triad, not even for the most fleeting of moments. In and of itself that is not completely unusual: we have already seen many examples in his previous works where pure triads are absent, some even for extraordinarily extended periods of time (some, far longer than here). But in previous works, in most of the cases where there are no triads, at least there were seventh chords.

In Ex. 11.10, there are a few seventh chords, but very few. A diminished seventh chord on D surfaces briefly on beat three of the first measure of the excerpt. So too, on the downbeat of the second measure, a second inversion minor seventh chord on B-flat makes a brief appearance. Perhaps a bit

Example 11.10

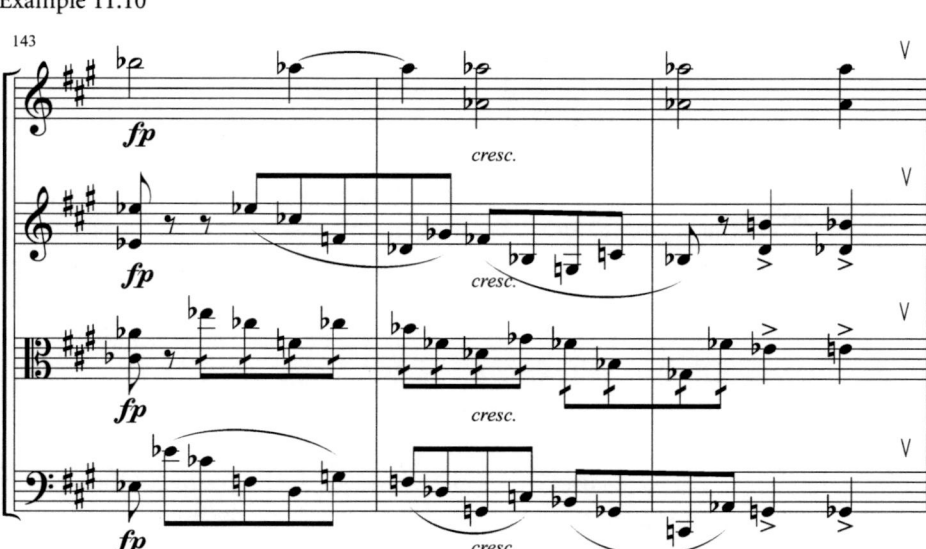

more debatably, one might isolate a minor dominant ninth chord on G (with a missing fifth) on the last eighth of m. 143. But that is all: two, or maybe three, brief sonorities in three measures. Not only have pure triads disappeared, but seventh chords have very nearly disappeared as well.

Although there are no triads and hardly any traditional seventh chords this does not mean that there are no ties to the past. Instead, we should understand that Schoenberg is continuing to employ the principle of localized consonance, and this leads to the construction of sonorities that include triadic structures as subsets of larger sonorities.

For example, we might describe the chord that appears at the very beginning of the example as a confluence of two layers, one of which is a second-inversion, A-flat minor triad. Similarly, at the end of the example, the last two chords are pentachords both of which have seventh chord subcomponents: the chord on the second beat has a first-inversion, half-augmented, seventh chord (MMm) on E-flat in the lower three parts, while the last chord of the measure includes a root position dominant seventh on G-flat, again in the lower three parts. It should also be noted, that these chords continue an important trend in Schoenberg's works to have sonorities that are either symmetrical (as is the pentachord on beat two), or that have a symmetrical subset (as does the pentachord on beat three).

Schoenberg's ambivalent treatment of triads and his increasing willingness to construct passages (even apparently stable passages) entirely from non-traditional chords should renew a familiar question: to what extent does F-sharp minor serve as a referential center in this movement? It is my (obviously subjective) impression that in some senses, the tonal definition is slightly stronger than in the Chamber Symphony, Op. 9. By contrast with that work, we have a fairly clear triad at the beginning of the work and the same triad at the end.

Nevertheless, I am not sure that F-sharp minor functions in a meaningful way as the referential center for the entire movement. Granted, F-sharp minor triads do appear at the beginning of the movement, at its end, and at the beginning of the recapitulation (as defined by Whittall). But the statements of F-sharp have little real organizing power: with one exception, I cannot feel their influence outside of their immediate vicinity. The exception: toward the end of the movement (m. 202) Schoenberg lands on an F-sharp in the cello, and holds it for more than nine measures. Over this pedal tone, Schoenberg builds a variety of harmonies, making a point of returning, again and again, to F-sharp minor (or major) triads (mm. 202, 204, 206, and 211).

Unlike its previous appearances (at the beginning of the work and at the beginning of the recapitulation) this time F-sharp does seem to have some referential status and some influence beyond its immediate vicinity. After the pedal drops out (in m. 211), Schoenberg keeps cycling back to various statements of F-sharp: in mm. 218–20 (another pedal), 226, 227, and 231–3. Because of these recurrences and because of the amount of time spent on F-sharp, I can hear F-sharp as being present, in at least some sense, throughout this passage, even in places (e.g. m. 213) where it is not explicitly present.

Is this enough to ground the work in the key of F-sharp? Ultimately, the answer to this is more a subjective judgment than a scientific conclusion. To my ear, F-sharp has only limited organizing power for the movement as a whole. In spite of its presence at the two ends of the movement, I find that its influence has been reduced to the point that it is difficult to hear other passages in terms of – that is, hierarchically subservient to – F-sharp.

In the 1907 phase of work Schoenberg seems to have written only about half of the second movement: there are drafts for most of what became mm. 1–176. Curiously, the apparent order of composition does not reflect the order in the completed movement: there is very little correlation between the order in which a segment was composed and where it fits in the eventual scheme of the second movement[19]

It is difficult to know with certainty whether Schoenberg worked on the different passages knowing from the start where they would fit into the movement or whether he wrote various separate fragments and only later stitched them together into a whole. Although we might prefer to believe that it would be the former, it may well have been the latter and there is some evidence that suggests that the "various thematic units ... were continuously reshuffled and recombined, almost like pieces of a puzzle, until the final form was reached."[20] Therefore, it is probably best if we refrain from any comments about the overall harmonic structure and form, since we cannot know for certain whether the final version reflects Schoenberg's intentions, circa 1907.

Although we are somewhat limited in what we can say about the second movement during its 1907 phase, there is enough evidence to address an important problem – the meaning or intent of the quotation of "O du lieber Augustin". In the completed version of the movement, this popular Viennese folksong appears, seemingly out of the blue, beginning in m. 165 (see Ex. 11.11).[21]

This quotation has prompted several different interpretations, the most popular of which seems to be that it is "self-referential commentary on the disintegration of the musical language".[22] Arnold Whittall puts it rather starkly, suggesting that the quotation "lends support to the probability, hinted at by Schoenberg himself, that he was experiencing a particularly severe psychological crisis at the time. He might conceivably have felt at

Example 11.11

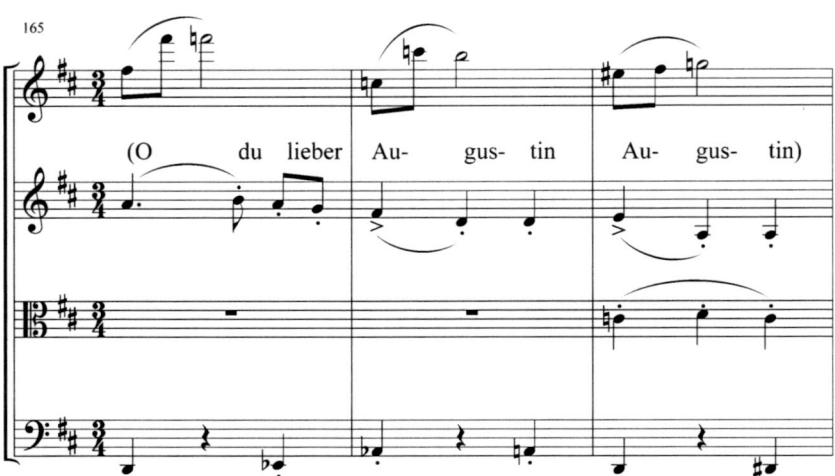

times that if 'all was lost' as far as tonality was concerned then he was also lost as a composer."[23] Another reading hypothesizes that the quotation also refers to the breakdown of his marriage (due to the Gerstl affair): "One does not need much imagination to think of the words of the text of the song "alles ist hin" (all is lost). This may have meant for Schoenberg not only the breaking up of a domestic situation but also a musical surrender."[24]

I do not believe that any of these interpretations can be squared with the facts.[25] The idea that Schoenberg ever felt that "all was lost" as far as tonality is concerned is highly problematic. I believe that it seriously misrepresents Schoenberg's attitudes regarding his transformation of pitch language. The evidence is overwhelming that he thought he was extending and expanding harmonic vocabulary and syntax as part of a historically inevitable process. He felt he was an agent of forward moving development, not a catalyst for disintegration and thus viewed what he was doing in positive, not negative terms. Similarly, the suggestion that the quotation was a reference to his marriage is almost certainly in conflict with the chronology. Although, he was probably aware his marriage was in trouble before the summer of 1908, and may even have suspected a relationship between Mathilde and Gerstl, there was no open break until late that summer when Mathilde abandoned the family.[26] Does it really make sense that Schoenberg would say "alles ist hin" about his marriage before the catastrophe?

Another drawback for this explanation of the meaning of the quotation is its failure to explain the use of the folksong as a whole, as opposed to one line from it. If the line "alles ist hin" is read out of context, it might well suggest defeat or despair. (Hence the interpretations that see the movement as part of a crisis, marital or compositional.) However, despair is emphatically not the general tenor of this folksong.

"O du lieber Augustin" is a folksong that is based on the mishaps that befell a bagpiper named Augustin. According to one version of the story Augustin got too tipsy one night at his favorite tavern and passed out in the street. This happened while Vienna was suffering from a bout of the plague, and when there was a municipal patrol whose job it was to go out at night to collect the corpses of plague victims. The patrol came across Augustin lying in the street, took him for dead and dumped him, stripped of his possessions, into a mass grave for plague victims. Fortunately for Augustin, he was able to rouse himself before being buried alive. The words "alles ist hin" reflect Augustin's befuddlement upon waking up minus his possessions.

One of the (innumerable) variants of the text appears below. (I should stress that there is no official version; this is, after all, a folksong.)[27] The tone of the song is droll, maybe a little mischievous, having a bit of fun at Augustin's expense – typical graveyard humor.

> O du lieber Augustin,
> 's Geld is hin, 's Madl is hin;
> o du lieber Augustin,
> alles is hin.
>
> Wollt noch vom Geld nix sagn,
> hätt i nur 's Madl beim Krag'n!
> o du lieber Augustin,
> alles is hin.
>
> O du lieber Augustin,
> 's Geld is hin, 's Madl is hin;
> o du lieber Augustin,
> alles is hin.
>
> Geld is weg, 's Madl is weg,
> Augustin liegt im Dreck!
> o du lieber Augustin,
> alles is hin.

That character is in line with what Schoenberg did in the second movement. After a rather earnest scherzo in mm. 1–164, the bottom suddenly falls out in m. 165. Clearly, this was meant as a gentle joke, and the folksong with its amusing connotations was part of the joke. In Schoenberg's words:

> A scherzo is the kind of music which should provoke gaiety. And so I could have understood a kind of smile when ... I combined my themes in a tragicomic manner with a popular Viennese song, the words of which may be translated as follows: "Alas, poor boy, everything is lost."[28]

After the little joke, in a masterful series of strokes, he transforms the Augustin theme back into some of the other – considerably more earnest – themes of the movement. Much like Beethoven, he was capable of turning gentle humor to serious ends, but only after he had a bit of a laugh.

"All is lost"? His marriage? His compositional direction? Hardly. Schoenberg may have been unsure of his exact compositional direction in 1907, but the second movement of Op. 10 is not evidence of despair. What is wrong with us? Can't anyone take a joke anymore?

In some respects, the music from the summer of 1907 represents a continuation of the compositional crisis that had plagued Schoenberg ever since the completion of the Chamber Symphony, Op. 9: his turn to traditional forms was both brief and inconclusive, he was unable to finish any of the projects he had started, and his harmonic language was slightly less radical than had been the case a year earlier. But this was no dead end – far from it. The application of the idea of motivic economy to a large, abstract composition laid the foundation for central aspects of his future development.

12 "Until then I lacked the strength and confidence": Two Songs, Op. 14, December 1907–March 1908

> Furthermore, it became doubtful whether a tonic appearing at the beginning, at the end, or at any other point really had constructive meaning.[1]

Toward the middle of 1907, Schoenberg seemed to be making real progress on two sizeable instrumental compositions, the String Quartet, Op. 10 and the Chamber Symphony No. 2. By December 1907, however, he had stopped work on both of these projects and changed directions yet again, turning back to vocal music, the Two Songs, Op. 14, which he completed on 2 February 1908.[2]

Although there were occasional zigs and zags, the evolution of Schoenberg's pitch language had followed a fairly consistent course: a steady decline in triads, diatonic seventh chords, diatonic collections, traditional harmonic progressions, standard cadences, and dissonance resolution, paralleled by a corresponding rise in the use of chromatic seventh chords, vagrant chords, radical new harmonies (most of which were extensions of traditional chords), and the constant circulation of the total chromatic. After completing the Chamber Symphony, Op. 9, however, Schoenberg's forward development stalled. As we have seen, he completed relatively few compositions in the immediate aftermath of Op. 9 and the pitch language of most of what he wrote was (with occasional exceptions) less radical than that of Op. 9.

The Two Songs, Op. 14 mark the beginning of Schoenberg's breaking out of his crisis and his return to a more radical direction.[3] However, there is something oddly tentative about the pitch language of these two works. At times (particularly in Op. 14, No. 1) the chordal vocabulary and syntax is as radical as anything Schoenberg had ever written. On the other hand – and to my ear, incongruously – the two songs also incorporate some comparatively conservative features. Collectively, the songs give the impression that Schoenberg wanted to push even further forward, but lacked "sufficient strength and sureness" to do so. We shall return to this topic below.

"Ich darf nicht dankend", Op. 14, No. 1

"Ich darf nicht dankend" is Schoenberg's first setting of a poem by Stefan George (1868–1933).[4] Just as Richard Dehmel had been the principal poet of his early songs, so too, George's works dominate Schoenberg's vocal compositions in 1907–8. In addition to "Ich darf nicht dankend", Schoenberg used poems by George for the last two movements of the String Quartet No. 2 ("Litanei" and "Entrückung"), for the fifteen songs of *Das Buch der hängenden Gärten*, Op. 15, and for two other songs that he started, but never completed ("Friedensabend" and "Der Jünger").[5]

On the large scale, the song divides into two distinct sections (A: mm. 1–15; A': mm. 15–30) that correspond to the two stanzas of George's poem. Similarly, at the level of detail, Schoenberg constructs a clearly articulated musical phrase for each of the eight lines of George's poem. That clear phrase structure highlights some of the more radical features of the pitch language of this work (see Ex. 12.1).

In prior repertoires, phrases were normally shaped by harmonic progressions that led to a relatively stable chord, usually a triad. By December,

Example 12.1

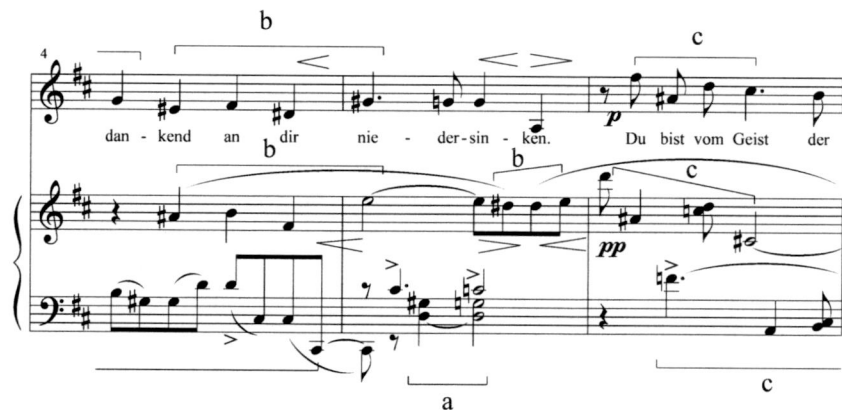

1907, however, Schoenberg was well past the point where stable root position triads are normative at the ends of his phrases. In this song, the only root position triad that appears at the end of any phrase is the B minor triad that occurs at the very end of the song. Nevertheless, although Schoenberg does not use traditional harmonic progressions and chords for his cadences, he continues to treat the end of a phrase as a point where the harmonic tension is lowered, creating a state of relative repose.

The opening piano phrase comes to a close on the second beat of m. 3. At least some of the ending character of this point is a product of non-harmonic means: the slowing of the attack rhythm on the fourth quarter of m. 2 and the change of texture with the entry of the voice in m. 3. In addition, the chordal vocabulary also contributes to the creation of a sense of relative closure.

Given the otherwise high level of dissonance in the phrase (up to this point, there has not been a single triad or diatonic seventh chord) it might have been too abrupt a contrast to bring this phrase to a close on a sustained consonant triad. Instead, Schoenberg returns to one of his favorite techniques from the Chamber Symphony, Op. 9, ending the phrase with a D major triad in second inversion, thereby retaining a level of dissonance, even while providing at least some sense of resolution. He also weakens the force of the closing sonority by having the elements of the chord arrive piecemeal and by overlapping the piano's closing phrase with the voice's entry.

For the cadence at the end of the first vocal phrase (m. 5), Schoenberg employs even less traditional techniques. Once again, an array of non-pitch parameters reinforce and underscore the sense of closure: the voice completes its statement of the first line of the poem, it drops down to its lowest point and pauses for a rest, the piano's harmonic rhythm slows down, and a completely new motive ('c') follows in m. 6. Instead of a triad at the cadence point, Schoenberg employs a chord of fourths in the piano l.h. as the core of the closing harmony, over which both the piano r.h. and vocal line add additional tones. Once again, Schoenberg attenuates the close by elision techniques.

The next phrase ending is at the downbeat of m. 8, and is also supported and clarified by an array of non-pitch factors. This time, Schoenberg returns to another second inversion triad (F-sharp minor) as the chord of closure. As with the cadence to the first phrase, Schoenberg is reluctant to dwell even on a dissonant triadic sonority: here too, the notes of the chord enter piecemeal, and he allows the chord to congeal only the briefest of moments (an eighth note), before proceeding with the next phrase.

The next cadence (m. 11, downbeat) does end on a consonant sonority (a first inversion D minor triad), but it hardly functions as a stable point of arrival. In the first place, it is not preceded by anything that can easily be understood as a dominant chord (the preceding sonority including a chord of fourths in the r.h. piano plus additional tones in the voice and piano l.h.). Thus the triad's arrival is sudden and (given the otherwise near-total lack of triads in the work), unexpected. Its departure is equally precipitous. Schoenberg treats the triad almost as if it is an embarrassment, giving it as little emphasis as possible and leaving it immediately.

As a general rule Schoenberg gradates the strength of his phrase-endings, reserving the strongest ones to mark off the largest formal divisions. All of the cadences discussed so far have been subsidiary cadences. Much stronger are the cadences that mark off the endings of the two major sections of the composition. On the downbeat of m. 16, there is a clearly emphasized and strongly articulated cadence that comes at the end of the first principal section of the song (see Ex. 12.2). Correspondingly, there is an unequivocal cadence at the end of the composition.

Example 12.2

Example 12.3

Although the cadence at m. 16 is clearly emphasized by rhythmic means (more so than its predecessors in mm. 3, 5, 8, and 11), even here Schoenberg apparently felt that it was not appropriate to employ a consonant triad at this point. He appears to have calculated that a consonant triad (root position or first inversion) would create too strong a sense of closure, something that might not be appropriate at this point in the song. Instead – as he did elsewhere (e.g. m. 8) – he uses a second inversion triad. This allows for a relative reduction in the level of harmonic tension, without the sense of finality that might have been imparted by the arrival of a root position, or even first inversion, triad.

Schoenberg reserves the use of a root position triad for the closing chord of the composition (see Ex. 12.3). After stating a version of the opening progression of the composition, he closes the song by stating a root position B minor triad.

Throughout this book I have purposefully avoided making critical evaluations of Schoenberg's compositions – that has not been the point of this study. To be sure, the reader would be correct to assume that, as a general rule, I am highly enamored of Schoenberg's music. Nevertheless, the reader would also be correct to assume that my love is not blind – there is an occasional work that I do not think is entirely successful. For the most part, however, such judgments are irrelevant. This is not a book of criticism; it is a book about the transformation of musical ideas.

It is for precisely that reason that I raise the issue of the effectiveness of the closing cadence of Op. 14, No. 1. To my ear, the final chord sounds wrong, out of place, foreign to the remainder of the composition.[6] In the rest of the song, triads of any sort have been rare – root position triads almost nonexistent. Even when triads occur, they are heavily disguised (e.g. the B major triad on the last eighth of m. 3) or immediately abandoned (e.g. the B minor triad on the third quarter of m. 4). They most emphatically do not occur for extended periods of time in strongly exposed locations as the end of significant phrases. By using a clear, unadorned, strongly emphasized, root position triad as the final chord of the composition, Schoenberg seems to be contradicting the harmonic norms of the rest of the song. To my ear, it would have been far more logical and consistent for Schoenberg simply to have concluded with the A-D-G trichord (as in m. 1). As it stands, the ending seems slightly risible (and I have heard more than one listener react to it with a surprised chuckle).

I am not in the habit of blithely suggesting "improvements" for Schoenberg's works – the very idea strikes me (should strike anyone) as impertinent. However, I feel justified in questioning the consistency of the final cadence because the record suggests that Schoenberg himself was troubled by the jarring contrast between the pure consonance of the final triad and the comparative dissonance of everything else.

We know this partially because in his next works, Schoenberg did make the leap and did end his compositions with non-triadic sonorities. With the Two Songs, Op. 14, he did not yet have the courage – yes, I believe that word is apposite – to take what was an awesome historical step: to end a composition with something other than a triad. With the Two Songs, Op. 14, standing on the bank of the Rubicon, Schoenberg could not cross.

This is not mere speculation based solely on my (subjective) reaction to what seems to be an inconsistent chord choice. There are clear indications in Schoenberg's own (almost contemporaneous) words that he had lacked the courage to take this step in this composition. In 1910, on the program for the premiere of *Das Buch der hängenden Gärten*, Op. 15, Schoenberg wrote:

> With the George songs I have for the first time succeeded in approaching an ideal of expression and form that has been in my mind for years. Until then I lacked the strength and confidence to make it a reality. But now that I have set out along this path once and for all, I am conscious of having broken through every restriction of a bygone aesthetic; and though the goal toward which I am striving appears to me a certain one, I nonetheless already feel the resistance I shall have to overcome; I feel how hotly even the least of temperaments will rise in revolt, and suspect that even those who have so far believed in me will want to acknowledge the necessity of this development.[7]

One of the reasons the final cadence sounds so odd is the extraordinary consistency of the harmonic vocabulary of the rest of the song. It seems clear that Schoenberg went to great lengths to make the opening harmonic progression into a kind of referential norm.

The song begins with a harmonic progression that is comprised of two trichords, A D-sharp G-sharp, and A D G (refer back to Ex. 12.1).[8] This progression ('a') permeates the composition, appearing in a variety of ways. Schoenberg restates 'a' in transposition in m. 5 (l.h.) to close the first vocal phrase. And this is just the beginning. In m. 9, immediately after having presented all of the principal motives of the composition, Schoenberg begins to extend the domain of 'a', having it appear in the middle of phrases, not just at their boundaries. He makes it function as a harmonic motive, subjecting it to some of the developmental procedures he applies to other motives. In m. 9 (piano, r.h.), 'a' occurs in transposition and is immediately restated in sequence. Instead of being used to mark the end of the phrase, this version of 'a' acts as preparation for the first inversion D major triad on the downbeat of m. 11. Other versions of 'a' occur frequently throughout the remainder of the composition: mm. 12, 13, 14, 15, 16–17, 19, 24 (three times), 25, 27 (twice), and – in my opinion, regrettably – only an incomplete version in the final measure, m. 30.[9]

One of the prominent characteristics of his use of the 'a' motive is Schoenberg's care to keep it intact. Although he does subject its constituent elements to some slight rhythmic manipulations (e.g. the arpeggiation in m. 19, piano, l.h.), the 'a' motive is readily recognizable in all of its appearances. This is an important reason why it is able to function as a referential harmonic norm. Other than at its first appearance, it does not appear alone: it always sounds together with at least one other motive, frequently a version of 'b' or 'd'. This, in turn, has important consequences for the harmonic structure.

Although 'a' has a tendency to appear in counterpoint to 'b' or 'd', there is no standard pattern to those combinations. In order to make the comparison clear, we shall refer to the bottom tone of the 'a' motive as

'0' (zero) and measure the number of semitones (mod. 12) to the first two tones of 'b'. Thus, in m. 1, where A is the lowest tone of 'a', the E-sharp and F-sharp with which 'b' begins are, respectively, 8 and 9 semitones distant. But in m. 5 where D is 0, the D-sharp and E of 'b' are 1 and 2 semitones higher. By the same token, in m. 12, where E-flat is 0, the G and A-flat of 'b' are 4 and 5 semitones distant.

It is not only the varying transpositional levels that prevent the formation of common harmonic structures. The 'b' motive does not always appear in the same place (rhythmically) with respect to 'a'. For example, in m. 9 (l.h.), the 'b' motive begins immediately after the first chord of 'a,' instead of waiting until after the second chord, as was the case in mm. 1, 5, and 12. (Even if it had begun in the same place as the other instances, its first two tones would be 2 and 3 semitones distant – different from all of the other instances.)

Similarly, common harmonic structures are not possible from the combinations of 'a' and 'b' because the 'b' motive does not always have the same succession of intervals. For instance, in m. 13, after the repetition of its first tone (D-sharp) 'b' ascends four semitones to G. This is unlike the other instances we have examined, all of which had an ascending semitone in this location.

By using an invariant core idea ('a') to which various additions are appended, Schoenberg creates a group of related harmonies. And it should not escape our attention that the core element of this group of harmonies is a symmetrical, trichordal subset. Thus, the group of harmonies that dominates this composition is a logical continuation of Schoenberg's practice in forming chromatic chords (such as the half-diminished and half-augmented seventh chords) in which there is a symmetrical trichordal subset.

This method of constructing harmonies is also significant in that it can be seen as a logical extension of another idea that is increasingly important to Schoenberg's compositional thought. From the beginning of his career, various kinds of motivic integration have been a component of Schoenberg's compositional technique: forging motivic relationships between different themes, subjecting themes to various kinds of transformations, and constructing themes by a flexible process of developing variation. The common denominator of these procedures is controlled change: holding some elements fixed while changing others. Schoenberg's harmonic practice in Op. 14, No. 1 – his holding of the 'a' motive fixed and adding varying elements to it – is an extension of this motivic idea to the harmonic realm.

"Ich darf nicht dankend" also employs developmental techniques in other, more familiar, ways. Over the course of the song, Schoenberg limits himself to a handful of themes and motives: the opening chords of m. 1 ('a'), the answering idea in the l.h. ('b'), a mildly contrasting idea in m. 6 ('c'), and a lyric idea that first surfaces in the piano in mm. 11–12 ('d' in the l.h. upper voice). These four ideas pervade the song, accounting for virtually all of its motivic material. As always, the various motives appear in a wide range of guises.

For example, the 'b' motive completely saturates the first phrase: other than the transposed restatement of the 'a' theme in m. 5, virtually everything else in the first phrase is part of some version of this motive. Not one of the other statements of 'b' in the first phrase is exactly like the initial statement. Some of them involve far-reaching transformations. In its original manifestation the 'b' motive appears as a succession of eighth notes, each of which is repeated, weak to strong. Its intervallic succession (exclusive of the repetitions) is $+1 -5 +13 -13$ (in semitones). In m. 2, the piano r.h. answers with another, related version, even beginning with the same two pitch classes: E-sharp and F-sharp. However, this version of 'b' is in augmentation and strips away the repetitions. Still further, although the first two pitch classes of the restatement are the same as the original statement, everything after that is different: its intervallic succession is $+1 -3 +4 -1$.

So it goes in the rest of this phrase: each of the remaining statements of 'b' in the first phrase retains enough features of its predecessors to be recognizable, but not one of the versions is identical, either to the first statement or to one another. And the treatment of this motive in this phrase is the norm: over the course of the rest of the song, all of the other principal motivic ideas undergo similar developmental processes.

Some of the transformations of the 'b' motive have additional significance because Schoenberg uses them to break down the distinctions between the different motives. In the right hand in m. 5, at the end of the first phrase, Schoenberg states the beginning of another version of the 'b' motive: the three eighth notes. Because of its rhythmic placement, this acts as a lead-in to the 'c' motive that first appears in m. 6. When the 'c' motive first appears, we have no reason to think of it as a new entity. Only after it appears several times (subjected to various transformations) do we begin to understand it as a separate idea.

Similarly, after the initial statement of the 'd' motive beginning in m. 11 ("tenor" voice, l.h.) and its immediate, transposed, restatement in imitation (r.h., m. 11) Schoenberg begins the piano interlude with passages composed of the 'a', 'b', and 'd' motives. In the left hand at the end of m. 12, the piano begins with what appears to be another version of 'b'. In m. 13, this merges seamlessly into a version of 'd' (while in counterpoint to 'a'). An identical procedure occurs in mm. 13–14 where the "alto" voice takes up the 'b' theme that becomes the 'd' theme, while accompanied by the 'a' theme. (Note here that Schoenberg has kept the transpositional relationships largely intact, while employing invertible counterpoint at the octave.)

As a result of all of these processes, "Ich darf nicht dankend" is a tightly organized composition, one in which a carefully limited arsenal of basic motivic and harmonic ideas join together in a flexible process of developmental transformation that pervades the work – that is, everything but its last chord.

"In diesen Wintertagen", Op. 14, No. 2

Schoenberg completed "Ich darf nicht dankend" by 17 December 1907 but he did not complete the next song, "In diesen Wintertagen", until almost two months later (2 February 1908) – this from a composer who was capable of writing a song in a matter of hours. In many important respects, "In diesen Wintertagen" is a mirror image of "Ich darf nicht dankend": where its predecessor was radical, this song is conservative and vice versa.[10]

"In diesen Wintertagen" is Schoenberg's only setting of a poem by Karl Henckel.[11] On the largest scale, the formal divisions of Schoenberg's song correspond to the three strophes of Henckel's poem. After a brief piano introduction (mm. 1–4), the first section of the song (mm. 5–21) is a setting of the first strophe of the poem. A brief piano interlude (mm. 21–3) leads directly into a setting of the second strophe in a section (mm. 24–32) that contrasts in texture though not in motive with the first section. After another piano interlude (mm. 33–8), Schoenberg sets the final strophe in a section (mm. 39–60) that functions – in now typically Schoenbergian fashion – as a synthesis, incorporating aspects of the textures of both of the first two sections of the song. A moderately extended piano solo (mm. 60–71) serves as a coda.

As was the case in the previous song, so too here, Schoenberg is sensitive to the division of the poem into verses: with only a few exceptions (in the middle section) he sets each line of the poetic text with a clearly articulated musical phrase. Like its predecessor, Schoenberg uses an array of non-pitch related elements to highlight the beginnings and endings of those phrases, the rests in the vocal part being only the most obvious. And, again like the previous song, Schoenberg reinforces the non-pitch parameters with harmonic progressions that lead to points of relative repose. But unlike its predecessor, Schoenberg does not wait until the final cadence of the composition to conclude a phrase with a clear, root position triad. Indeed, some of the phrase-ending harmonic progressions of this song are considerably more traditional than anything in Op. 14, No. 1. The

Example 12.4

piano introduction and its concluding cadence at the beginning of m. 5 provide a good illustration (see Ex. 12.4).

Although Schoenberg takes some steps to blunt its impact, the identity of this cadence is not open to question: it is a clear authentic cadence in C major. For a composer who had just completed a song in which even a single root position triad sounded out of place, this is a striking contrast. Although C major does not immediately leap out as the referential center of this phrase, it quickly becomes apparent that C major is a perfectly logical point of reference for this phrase. As a result – in contrast to Op. 14, No. 1 – the cadence does not seem out of place, does not appear to be a foreign object grafted onto an unwilling host.

The cadence in C major seems convincing because Schoenberg prepares it in a variety of meaningful ways, chiefly by according the diatonic collection of C major a privileged status. For one thing, the first two chords immediately exhaust the diatonic collection of C, employing all seven of its tones and no others. For another, when tones foreign to the C major collection do occur in the rest of the phrase, Schoenberg treats them in a manner that makes clear they play a subsidiary role: each of those chromatic tones proceeds by half-step to a tone from the diatonic collection of C. As a result, Schoenberg clearly has created a situation in which non-diatonic tones are hierarchically subservient to the diatonic tones.

The contrast with the preceding song could not be greater. In that work, there was no clear indication that B minor would serve as a referential triad until its appearance as the last chord of the song. Nothing about the choice of chords, progressions, or collection in that song pointed unequivocally toward B minor as an inevitable goal. As a result, it is rather debatable whether any aspect of the concept "referential" really applies. The triad is "there", but there seems to be no meaningful sense in which other events refer to it. Here, C major takes on a referential function from the very first phrase of the work, confirmed by a relatively strong authentic cadence. We hear C major not just as another chord, but one with a privileged hierarchical status. Other chords, other tones, refer to it, are understood in terms of it, and are subservient to it.

The establishment of C major as a chord of reference in the first phrase has some important consequences. Unlike most of Schoenberg's preceding works, the domain of the referential center is not limited to a narrow stretch of music surrounding the triad (or, as in the previous song, just the triad itself). Rather, its influence is rather more extensive. One of the reasons for this is that Schoenberg never really permits any other referential centers to challenge C major. Although there are a few other triads in the work, even triads prepared by their dominants (e.g. B-flat, m. 6), Schoenberg gives no other triad the kinds of harmonic, rhythmic, and cadential emphases he gives to C. The cadence on C at the end of the piano introduction is not the only such cadence in the work: an almost identical cadence occurs in the first phrase of the third section (m. 42). And in a number of places, the various elements (particularly the uppermost and lowermost voices) of mm. 1–5 return at their original pitch level (e.g. mm. 10–14, 21–3, 51–4, 60–1). Thus, even though these passages do not confirm C major with a cadence, the recurrence of this material at its original pitch level implies C major, in much the way that in more traditional repertoires progressions ending on a chord other than the tonic can, nevertheless, define a tonic.

Seen from this perspective, "In diesen Wintertagen" might appear to suggest a conservative turn in Schoenberg's thought, almost as he made an abrupt artistic volte-face beginning with the final chord of Op. 14, No. 1. As is so often the case the reality is not so simple. The final cadence of the composition makes this clear (see Ex. 12.5).

In contrast to the clear, almost surprisingly traditional, cadences on C that had occurred in mm. 5 and 42, the final cadence of the composition is far from traditional. For one thing, no dominant chord prepares the final sonorities. Furthermore, the elements of the final sonority emerge only gradually: the G on the downbeat of m. 69, the octave Cs in the bass on the next beat, and the E natural in the alto immediately after. These are all of the elements of the C major triad but they are not the only components of the final sonority. Instead, the final tone of the chord – the final tone struck in the song – is an A. This song concludes, not with a pure, root position, C major triad, but with a chord that includes all of the elements of a C major triad plus an A.[12] It is as if this work is a photographic negative of the preceding song: whereas "Ich darf nicht dankend" ended on a clear

Example 12.5

triad, even though there had been no preparation for that chord, "In diesen Wintertagen" does not conclude with a clear triad, even though there had been significant preparation for it.

It is important to note that the final tone of the chord, the A, does not emerge out of nowhere. Rather, it is part of a statement of a version of one of the most important motives of the composition, the opening melody in the voice (mm. 5–6). By returning to this motive and stating at the end of the composition, Schoenberg has made the specific nature of the final chord a contextual matter: the content of that chord is dictated by the motivic context of this composition as much as it is by traditional syntax of earlier music. This will prove to be an important concept in Schoenberg's music.

The inner contradictions of these two songs suggest that Schoenberg was at a turning point in his development. As of Op. 14 he may have lacked the confidence to take the next logical step ("gebrach es mir dahin in Kraft und Sicherheit"), but that would change, and soon.

13 Beyond triads: the first layer of *Das Buch der hängenden Gärten*, Op. 15, March–April 1908

> But now that I have set out along this path once and for all, I am conscious of having broken through every restriction of a bygone aesthetic.[1]

After completing the Two Songs, Op. 14, Schoenberg did not return to either of the two large instrumental compositions (Opp. 10 and 38) that lay, unfinished, on his desk. Instead, he continued to write songs, turning once again to the poetry of Stefan George. The resultant project, *Das Buch der hängenden Gärten*, Op. 15, would occupy his attention, off and on, from approximately March 1908 until March 1909.[2]

Scholars of Schoenberg's music are particularly fortunate in that much of his manuscript legacy has survived and is readily available for study. The sheer scope of what is available is extraordinary: sketches, drafts, and fair copies of many of his compositions, as well as drafts of many never-completed works. It is also fortunate that Schoenberg was keenly aware of his position in history and this led him to date many of his manuscripts. As a result, we know an enormous amount about the chronology of Schoenberg's works.

Yet even in a legacy that is as well preserved as Schoenberg's, there are occasional lacunae. One of most disappointing of those relates to Op. 15: only seven of its fifteen songs are dated (see Table 13.1). Thus, at an important point in his career, the record is tantalizingly incomplete.[3]

Drafts of the songs of Op. 15 appear in a number of separate manuscripts, only four of which have dates: SH 10 (*Sammelhandschrift* 10), SH 14, SH 22, and SH23. SH 10 has the most comprehensive chronology: Schoenberg entered dates for all four of its songs (Nos. 3, 4, 5, 8). The remaining manuscripts are less well documented. SH 14 (which includes a draft of No. 7, a sketch of No. 6, and the fragment "Friedensabend") has a date only for the draft of No. 7. In SH 22 (which includes a draft of No. 13, and sketches for Nos. 14 and 15), only No. 13 has a date. SH 23 (which includes a sketch of No. 14 and a draft of No. 15) has a date only for No. 15. The manuscripts with the drafts of songs 1, 2, 9, 10, 11, 12 have no dates at all.

The simplest explanation of the available evidence is that Schoenberg worked on Op. 15 in three stages: the first in March/April 1908, the second around September 1908, and the last in February 1909. However, this impression may be deceptive: since we have no idea how the eight undated songs fit into the chronology, some or all of them could have preceded the

Table 13.1.

Song	Date	Manuscript
Op. 15, No. 4, "Da meine Lippen"	15 March 1908	SH 10
Op. 15, No. 5, "Saget mir"	25 March 1908	SH 10
Op. 15, No. 3, "Als Neuling trat ich"	29 March 1908	SH 10
Op. 15, No. 8, "Wenn ich heut nicht deinen Leib"	13 April 1908	SH 10
Op. 15, No. 7, "Angst und Hoffen"	28 April 1908	SH 14
Op. 15, No. 13, "Du lehnest wider eine Silberweide"	27 September 1908	SH 22
Op. 15, No. 15, "Wir bevölkerten"	28 February 1909	SH 23

first stage, or served as a bridge between the second and third stages, or followed what appears to be the last stage. The point is, we simply don't know. Therefore, in this chapter, we will consider only the five songs (Nos. 4, 5, 3, 8, and 7) that we are certain Schoenberg wrote between March and April of 1908.[4]

"Da meine Lippen", Op. 15, No. 4

For a brief period (late 1907 to early 1909), Schoenberg's interest in the poetry of Stefan George developed into an abiding passion, comparable to his immersion in Dehmel's poetry around 1899. In many respects the two poets could not be more different. George was one of the leaders of the revolt against realism in German literature; Dehmel had deep ties to the nineteenth-century German Romantic poetic tradition. George's poetry displays the influence of Greek classical forms, the Parnassians, and the French symbolists; there was not a trace of French influence in Dehmel's poems. George's poems, intended for an intellectual aristocracy, are often esoteric and remote; Dehmel's tend toward passionate overstatement.

Since George did not subdivide the poems from *Das Buch der hängenden Gärten* into stanzas, Schoenberg could not rely on his usual expedient of having the large formal regions of the song conform to the poem's strophes. Instead, he divides the song into two large sections (mm. 1–12 and mm. 13–26), corresponding to the two complete sentences in George's poem (lines 1–3 and 4–7).

Although the song divides clearly into two distinct sections, separated by a brief piano interlude, and although the second section is a (highly) varied repetition of the first, simple letter designations (A A') can scarcely begin to capture the richness and subtlety of the song's formal relationships. Rather, that formal subtlety is a direct outgrowth of the increasingly central role of developing variation and associated techniques in Schoenberg's compositional practice.

The song begins with a descending, indeterminate scalar motive (a1) in the voice (doubled by the piano), supported by a spare, chordal, accompaniment (see Ex. 13.1). Although many variants of this motive appear, accounting for a significant proportion of the song's material, it is not just Schoenberg's now normative penchant for motivic economy that is so significant here. Rather, Schoenberg is beginning to take the technique of

Example 13.1

developing variation to a new level. We can see this clearly when we follow the evolution of the motives of this song.

In its initial manifestation, the opening motive is a straightforward scalar descent through four tones, G-sharp G F E. Therefore, we can readily understand the next four notes (A G-sharp G F) as a varied restatement (a2), beginning on A (suggesting a transposition), but with an altered intervallic succession (−1 −1 −2 instead of −1 −2 −1). At the same time, there is an additional layer of subtlety here: there is significant overlap between the pitch content of a1 and a2 in that they share three pitches, G-sharp, G, and F. Thus, another way of understanding a2 is as a restatement of the first three notes of a1 (G-sharp, G, and F) with a prefix (A).

A number of new motives emerge from the juncture of a1 and a2. (There are many possible ways of slicing the surface; we will single out as significant motives only those that recur.) One of these is a five-note idea (b1) that includes all of a1 and the first note of a2. This immediately reveals itself as important by its recurrence: the last five notes of the first measure constitute another, overlapping, instance of this motive (b2) with a different succession of intervals. Another motive that results from the intersection of a1 and a2 is c1, a four-note motive that includes the last two notes of a1 and the first two of a2. This too shows itself to be important when the first phrase closes with an inversion of this motive: c2 (F G D-sharp E-sharp). Rounding out the picture of the first phrase, one should note that the bass line (E E-sharp F-sharp G-sharp) is a3, a version that retains (in inversion) the intervallic succession of a2, but with the same two boundary pitches (E and G-sharp) as a1.

The second phrase (mm. 3–6) continues this process: the motives of the first phrase are repeated but transformed. In m. 3 the vocal line has many similarities to b2: its contour and rhythm are identical although its intervallic succession is changed (−2 −1 −2 +2 instead of −1 −1 −2 +2). We might identify this statement as b3. Embedded within b3 is a further statement of 'a' (a4), one that begins with the same note (G-sharp) as a1. Moreover, b3 is not hermetically sealed by the bar-line. Instead, its rhythmic energy continues on to F-sharp on the downbeat of m. 4, expanding b3 into a six-note motive. In the next measure, it becomes apparent that the last five notes of b3 can be viewed as a new motive (d1) since this is restated in imitation in the lowest line of the piano part. This leads directly into a similar though varied statement in the 'alto' line (piano, r.h.) in m. 5, which itself leads into another variant in the bass line in m. 6. Simultaneously, in mm. 4–6 in the voice, there is yet another transformation of 'b' (b4), this one with new rhythmic patterns, and in particular, the dotted rhythm.

Example 13.2

Beginning in the second half of m. 6, a new motive appears ('e'), first in the piano and then, almost immediately, in imitation in the voice (see Ex. 13.2). In many respects, this motive contrasts with what had come before. Where the 'a', 'b', 'c', and 'd' motives moved mostly in eighth notes, mostly by step, this new motive moves only by leaps and mostly in quarter notes.

The contrast is not as stark as it might seem. With respect to the rhythm, the overall picture has not really changed. In mm. 1–6, the principal lines mostly moved in eighth notes while the accompaniment mostly moved in quarter notes. In the phrase beginning in m. 6 there is effectively a reversal of roles: the accompaniment moves in eighth notes while the principal line moves mostly in quarter notes – a kind of invertible counterpoint of rhythm. When the principal line breaks out of its strict limitation to quarter notes, it does so with dotted rhythms, exactly the rhythmic pattern of motive b4 (mm. 4–5). There are some clear pitch connections as well: the first three pitch classes of the motive 'e' (A-flat E G), are identical to three of the first four pitch classes of a1. The most striking difference is the expansion in register, an idea that takes on considerable importance over the course of the song (e.g. mm. 8–14, piano, l.h.). As the vocal line continues, it descends from the high point G through E to C-sharp. This adds two tones to the vocal line (E and C-sharp) that had already played an important role in the cadence in mm. 5–6. Thus, the contrasting melody in mm. 7–9 is actually a reformulation of central pitches of the first two phrases. In addition, the connections with the preceding phrases are not limited to the (somewhat recondite) motivic processes that produced the vocal line: the running eighth-note line in the piano's l.h. in mm. 6–8 fortifies the connections with the previous phrases by continuing the process of development and transformation of the motives that had been prominent in the piano in mm. 1–5.

Having demonstrated that the apparently contrasting ideas of mm. 6ff emerge as transformations of prior material, it should not be necessary to continue with a note-by-note analysis of the rest of the song. The essential point should be already clear: continuing and intensifying prior trends, Schoenberg has made motivic integration a central compositional technique, one whose influence extends to every corner of the composition. Motivic relationships are not just important: they have become a sine qua non of the compositional structure.

Schoenberg's application of developing variation and similar techniques in Op. 15 No. 4 (and other pieces from this period) is not a completely open-ended process, one in which new patterns emerge from the beginning to the end of the piece without pause. After approximately the midpoint of the composition Schoenberg tends more to recycle readily recognizable versions of earlier patterns than to create new ones. This is not to say that the developmental process comes to an abrupt end. But from approximately the middle of the composition, both the pace and the breadth of that process become more circumscribed. For example, the second section of this song begins with familiar material in both the voice and piano (see Ex. 13.3).

The vocal line in these measures is a version of the vocal line from the beginning of the composition, but it is far from being a literal repetition. It is a sophisticated mixture of repetition, transposition, and transformation. In some ways, it acts as if it is a transposition down a semitone from the original (the G-sharp G F of the first measure becomes G F-sharp E in m. 13: marked x in the example). It also retains key pitches of the melody in their original locations (the successions E A and F G D-sharp of mm. 1–2 are retained in mm. 13–14: marked y and z, respectively, in the example), thereby suggesting a varied restatement, a concept that is reinforced by the use of rhythmic diminution.

Example 13.3

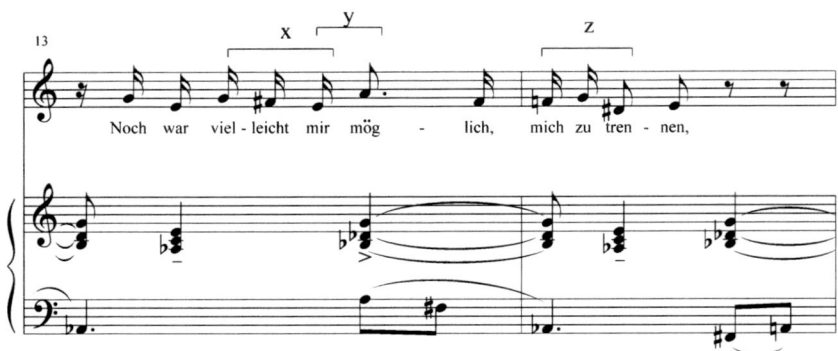

Example 13.4

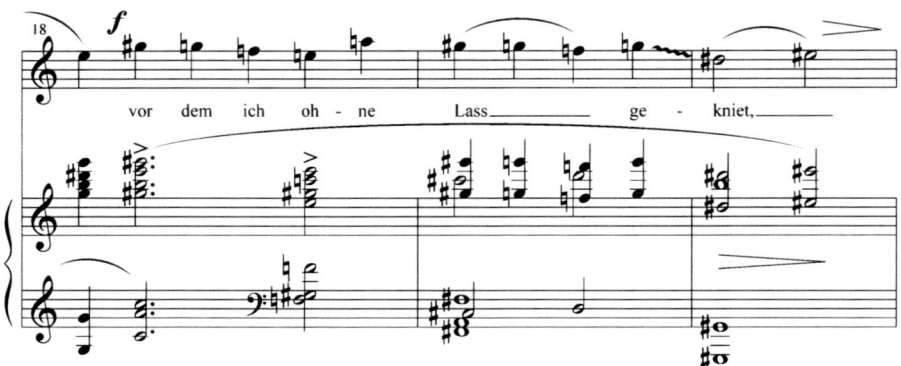

At the same time, the piano accompaniment is a straightforward continuation of the material from the preceding measures (mm. 11–12). The chords in the right hand and the melody in the left hand in mm. 13–14 are exactly the same as those in mm. 11–12. Thus, the passage in mm. 13–14 is a synthesis of prior events, combining a variant of the melody of mm. 1–2 with the piano part from mm. 11–12.

After the mid-point of the composition, the pace of development is slower and its range more circumscribed. As Schoenberg draws closer to the end of the song, he increasingly turns to variants that are readily recognizable as restatements – sometimes nearly literal restatements – of prior material. For example, at m. 18 Schoenberg reaches the climactic point of the song, and marks it with an explicit return to the opening melody (see Ex. 13.4).

Although stated in augmentation and an octave higher than in its original appearance, nothing else about the melody is changed: its pitch succession is absolutely the same as at the beginning of the work. Even though the specific harmonies in the accompaniment in mm. 18–20 are not identical to those of mm. 1–2, Schoenberg uses the same closing figure: F-sharp to G-sharp. The overall effect is to create a strong sense of return, beginning at m. 18.

Therefore, Schoenberg has devised a clear plan for the motivic structure of this song, and it is one that we will encounter frequently in other works from this period. He begins with a simple motivic idea, gradually, but relentlessly, transforms it, eventually creating material that is quite distant from its origins. After approximately the midpoint of the work, Schoenberg stops creating new ideas but returns to prior patterns, using material that may be highly varied, but is still recognizable as a variant of past ideas. Finally, Schoenberg returns to passages that are clearly recognizable as repetitions or near-repetitions of prior events. This final step is an important part of his strategies for closure.

The technique of suggesting impending closure at the end of a work by returning to familiar material from the beginning of the work is particularly important because of the changes that have occurred in Schoenberg's pitch language. Here, in this song, for the first time, Schoenberg uses as his final sonority something that is neither a consonant triad, nor a triad with an added sixth (as he had done in Op. 14, No. 2). In so doing, he has – finally – broken away from the association of triadic consonance with closure. In Schoenberg's previous works there is ample reason to question whether the closing triad has referential organizing force for the entire movement, but there is no question but that it does signal closure by closing with a consonant sonority, often the only time in a work where a consonant sonority is given both agogic emphasis and metric stress.

The abandonment of the triad as the agent of closure poses important challenges and has significant consequences: the lack of a recognized formula to mark the end of a work impels Schoenberg to search for a logical replacement. Significantly, he does not do so by devising some kind of regular substitute chord of closure: the specific chord Schoenberg uses to conclude this song (to which we shall return shortly) does not become a norm. Instead of a specific chord, Schoenberg creates the sense of closure by motivic means, by returning to only slightly altered versions of prior material. He first provides a clear restatement of the opening vocal line (mm. 18–20) and then, in mm. 21–5, an equally clear restatement of the piano part from mm. 9–11. By coming back to readily recognizable passages, stated in the same order as they were in their original appearances, Schoenberg has created an obvious, if simple, mechanism for signaling the impending end of the work. But this is not really new in his works: this is

Example 13.5

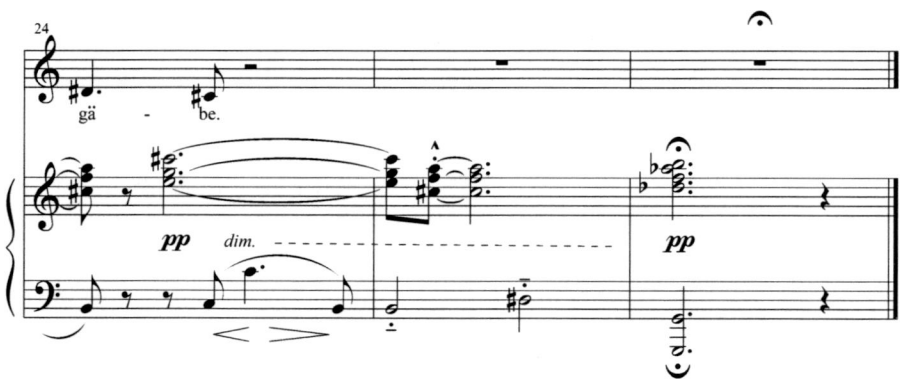

none other than a version of the reference-departure-return dynamic we saw as early as *Pelleas und Melisande*, where Schoenberg creates a sense of motion and return even in the absence of a referential tonal center.

In the present case, Schoenberg doesn't simply stop in m. 25 when he completes the parallels with mm. 9–11. Instead, he continues on for one more measure (see Ex. 13.5). This is really an extraordinary moment: encapsulated in this closing figure is a summary of the evolution of Schoenberg's harmonic language.

There are many important links to tradition here. For one, this figure has the rhythmic feel of a traditional cadence: the bass slows and then all motion comes to a halt in m. 26 with a chord. Although the final chord is neither a simple root position triad nor an obvious derivative of a triad, it is not that far removed from its historical antecedents. One can understand it as either a less-than-standard ninth chord on G (MdMm) or perhaps a D-flat dominant seventh chord over a G. Still further, the closing interval in the bass (from D-sharp to G) is familiar to us as a common bass interval for Schoenberg's cadences; it was one of the most popular of his choices for alternative cadences in his previous music. We can understand this cadential figure as a logical continuation of processes that have been under way since the first works we have examined. Schoenberg began this process by devising substitutes for the authentic cadence. He gingerly experimented with cadences that employed chords other than root position triads. At first he limited those to locations within the body of the work, and did not place them as the final chord of the composition. Gradually, even that limitation began to recede. He used a 6/4 chord as the final chord in "Der Wanderer", Op. 6, No. 8. Then he used a triad with an added sixth in Op. 14, No. 2. Now, finally, he uses a sonority that, although it retains some aspects of traditional chord construction (and

Beyond triads: the first layer of *Das Buch der hängenden Gärten*

thus provides a degree of resolution), is appreciably removed from a simple triad.

Although the specific chord found at the final cadence does not appear anywhere else in the song, its general type is not unusual at all. It is a sonority with which we are quite familiar, one that makes use of the principle of localized consonance. What is novel is not the chord type per se, but Schoenberg's placement of it at the end of the song. We can define this chord type rather precisely: it is a chord of n elements (where n is >/= to 4) where a subset, n−1, forms a triad or common seventh chord and where the remaining element forms an interval of a semitone with at least one of the other elements. In the case of the final chord of the song, n = 5, and the n−1 subset is a dominant seventh on D-flat. The remaining element (G) forms the interval of a semitone with the A-flat. We shall refer to this type of sonority as an "added-semitone chord".[5]

Instances of added-semitone chords pervade the composition. For example, in the first phrase of the song (refer back to Ex. 13.1), there are four in quick succession. On the fourth quarter of m. 1 there is an F-sharp minor triad in the piano opposite a G-sharp in the voice (and upper line of the piano). When the vocal line moves to G, it creates another instance. Similarly, the last quarter of m. 1 has two overlapping added-semitone tetrachords: first a D major triad with an added F in the vocal line; then a G pitted against that same triad.

If we broaden the definition of this type slightly to include incomplete triads and seventh chords as the locally consonant component of the chord, we see even more sonorities that fit into a family of similar types. For example, the very first sonority of the song pits an A-E dyad (an incomplete triad) in the piano against a G-sharp (a semitone away from A) in the voice (and upper line of the piano). Similarly, the chord that begins on the second eighth of m. 3 juxtaposes D C A in the accompaniment (an incomplete seventh chord) opposite G-sharp (a semitone away from the A) in the voice. Seen from this perspective, a significant proportion of the sonorities in the composition belong to one type: chords built from (complete and incomplete) triads and common seventh chords with an additional tone that is a semitone away from one of the other chord tones.

Although chords based on the principle of localized consonance constitute the largest single component of the chordal vocabulary of this song, other types occur. Most notably, there are still a few triads and they are not all hidden away in a rhythmically weakened corner. For example, on the downbeat of m. 2 there is a root position G-sharp minor triad, on the downbeat of m. 4, a first inversion D major triad, and on the downbeat of m. 6, a second inversion C major triad. Nevertheless, although a few triads do appear, Schoenberg does not treat them as stable entities.[6] Even when he lands on a root position triad on the downbeat (as he does in m. 2), he does not permit closure. Instead, as in m. 2, the rhythmic energy of the phrase continues on, leading the phrase to conclude with a dissonant sonority – a reversal of traditional syntax (and a continuation of a trend we observed in the first layer of the String Quartet No. 2).

Thus, although Op. 15, No. 4 may be the first composition that ends with something other than a triad (or a triad with an added tone as in Op. 14, No. 2), it is the logical continuation of trends we have been following for quite some time. In the earliest works we examined, Schoenberg did treat specific triads as referential, both on the large scale (the overall tonic) and on the more local scale (the referential tonic of a phrase or section). However, even in the earliest works, passages with identifiable referential tonics alternated with other passages (sometimes quite extended) where it was not possible to identify a referential triad. In subsequent works there was a steady reversal of proportions: passages with identifiable referential centers became fewer and shorter, while passages without identifiable referential centers became more frequent and much longer. At the same time, Schoenberg systematically challenged most of the other norms of key definition: traditional cadences were either abolished or compromised in some way, compositions did not necessarily begin with the establishment of the tonal center with which the piece would end, the link between collection and key was severed, the association between chordal type and harmonic function was erased, and harmonic progressions did not define a specific tonic. This led to a point where when Schoenberg did state a triad at the end of Op. 14, No. 1, it seemed out of place. Ending Op. 15, No. 4 with a sonority other than a triad is the next logical step, perhaps the only logical step Schoenberg could have taken, given the progressive transformation of his language.

Although there is no tonic tone or triad, not all of the twelve tones are treated completely equally: Schoenberg endows certain tones with a significance that raises them above the rest. In this song, a strong case can be made that G-sharp, E, and G-natural function as comparatively stable tones. They achieve this status because they appear most often as the beginning, ending, or boundary tones of important motives or phrases.[7]

In the first phrase of the song (see Ex. 13.1, above) the opening motif in the melody ('a') begins on G-sharp and descends to E. This is followed by a varied repetition (as was discussed in detail above), in which the G-sharp (on a relatively stressed point in the measure) is prefaced by A and continues on to close on E-sharp. In the bass line, there is the opposite, an ascent from the opening E to a G-sharp at the end of the phrase. Since the bass begins with E and the melody with G-sharp, these two tones form the registral boundaries of the first sonority.

The next vocal phrase, mm. 3–6 continues by using G-sharp (m. 3) and E (m. 6) as its beginning and ending tones. This is followed immediately with a juxtaposition of E and G-sharp (= A-flat), both in the piano part (m. 6) and its canonic imitation in the next vocal phrase (beginning m. 7).

As the song continues, G-sharp (A-flat) and E, continue to play central roles: A-flat functions as a kind of pedal tone or appears on the downbeat in every measure from m. 11 to m. 16; the reprise of the opening motive begins with G-sharp (m. 18); there is a return to the G-sharp in the bass in m. 20.

Schoenberg eventually moves away from an exclusive reliance on G-sharp and E. Instead, he gradually brings G-natural into play as an important tone. It too takes on some of the functions that, at least initially, had been discharged by G-sharp and E. G acts as the beginning of phrases (mm. 6, 13, 15), as the high point of prominent motives (mm. 7, 8), as end point of the top line in the piano interlude (mm. 11–13), and as the bass tone for the final cadence.

What we see, therefore, appears to be an informal substitute for some of the structural functions once held by the triad. Schoenberg had come to the point where he no longer wanted the triad to function as a point of stability and closure, probably because of concerns over sonority. At the same time Schoenberg seems to have felt the need for something with analogous function. This composition is not in 'G-sharp' or 'G' or 'E'. To make such a claim would be to strip the idea of being in a key of any real meaning. But those three tones do have priority over the other nine tones. In a largely intuitive manner, Schoenberg has devised a technique for establishing contextual tones of reference in the absence of triads.[8] And it should not be overlooked that this use of specific tones as points of reference is intimately tied to the highly compact motivic structure. In a tangible manner, the motivic structure has become the central organizing force in Schoenberg's compositions.

"Saget mir", Op. 15, No. 5

As far as is known (given the limitations of the chronology), the next song Schoenberg composed is "Saget mir", Op. 15, No. 5, which he completed on 25 March 1908, only ten days after Op. 15, No. 4.[9] Given their close temporal proximity, it is not surprising that "Saget mir" shares many important compositional features with its immediate predecessor. Just as "Da meine Lippen" used tones of contextual reference, so too, "Saget mir" does something very similar: D frequently acts as a kind of contextual point of reference. Again and again, phrases end, begin, or place some important emphasis on D. This is clearest in (though not limited to) the vocal line where D (or C-double sharp) serves as the beginning or ending (sometimes both) of phrases in mm. 2, 4, 9, and 15.

In terms of its harmonic vocabulary, this song is also similar to its predecessor. Added-semitone chords predominate, interrupted by only the occasional seventh chord (usually ones that are symmetrical or have symmetrical subsets).[10] For example, the opening tetrachord in the piano is an added-semitone chord: a diminished triad (F-sharp A C) with an additional tone (G) that is a semitone away from F-sharp. The second chord is a dominant seventh with a lowered fifth (MdM), a symmetrical seventh chord (see Ex. 13.6).

There is one important sense in which the harmonic vocabulary of this song differs from its predecessor: unlike the previous song, no pure triads appear anywhere in this song, even in metrically weak positions. Although we are prevented by the gaps in chronology from saying this with utter

Example 13.6

certainty, this may be the first work of Schoenberg's to abjure completely the use of triads.

In the earlier works we examined, we noted that Schoenberg had a tendency to make a distinction between the texture of his songs and that of his instrumental compositions, with the accompaniments of the songs tending to be homophonic while the instrumental works tended to be more polyphonic. Although Schoenberg's pitch language had evolved far away from that of the earliest works, it is a measure of just how tied he was to traditional modes of thought, that the accompaniments of his songs still tend to be more homophonic, even (as is this song) very nearly homorhythmic. And this observation can help us recognize some other traditional elements in Schoenberg's approach.

For example, even though there is not a single pure triad in this song, the voice leading and harmonic syntax is surprisingly familiar. Consider in this regard the voice leading and harmonic connections between the chords in the first phrase (Ex. 13.6). Almost as if it were directly drawn from some theory textbook (Schoenberg's own *Harmonielehre* comes to mind), the principal melody is lodged in the soprano, the inner voices move predominantly by step (or hold common tones), and the bass is noticeably more disjunct. Parallel fifths are absent.

Other aspects of the syntax are tantalizingly familiar: altered – but not unrecognizably so – versions of harmonic progressions from earlier works still occur. We can see this most clearly if we examine the relationships between the embedded triads or seventh chords of the sonorities. For example, the opening chord is an added-semitone tetrachord, whose triadic subset is an embedded diminished triad on F-sharp. In prior repertoires, a diminished triad on F-sharp would have tended to resolve to some kind of G chord. In this song there are no triads, but the following chord can be understood to be a seventh chord (MdM) built on G.

There should be no misunderstanding: I am not claiming that this opening pair of chords implies that Schoenberg has established G (or C). That simply is not the case: one cannot blithely ignore the effect of either the added tones within the chords themselves or the surrounding context. What I am trying to demonstrate is that even in this non-triadic environment, one in which radical chords occur, one in which there is no implied triadic reference point, there is still an essential core of traditional structure.

We should remember that even in Schoenberg's earlier works (except for the places where he wished to establish a local referential center) he customarily built his phrases so that, at the most, there would be two or occasionally three chords which owe allegiance to a single key. Invariably, Schoenberg would then immediately contradict that implication by proceeding to other chords that are not readily reconciled with that key. In the present case, the embedded harmonies of the chords of m. 2 fulfill a similar function. In m. 2, the first chord (an added-semitone tetrachord) has an embedded E major triad, while the final simultaneity of m. 2 (a mMM seventh chord on B) has an embedded B minor triad. Neither of these trichords have diatonic function in G (or C), but they do provide the tones necessary for chromatic completion. Thus, the progressions of the embedded harmonies of mm. 1–2 follow syntactical patterns that are similar to those that characterized Schoenberg's harmonic progressions in prior works.[11]

Like its immediate predecessor (and like most of the songs of Op. 15), "Saget mir" displays an extraordinarily intense level of motivic organization but unlike its predecessor, this motivic organization does not manifest itself in the form of a fluid and nearly continuous process of developing variation. This is not to say that the techniques of developing variation are completely absent. Instead, Schoenberg places considerable emphasis on a somewhat different type of approach, one in which the motivic ideas are not so much altered and transformed in a continuous process, but are repeated, often with only small (though frequently significant) alterations, in a variety of different combinations and at different levels of transposition. For example, the phrase in mm. 13–15 is a multi-layered combination of a number of prior passages (see Ex. 13.7).

The vocal line is almost exactly a transposition up a semitone of the vocal line in the opening two measures (see Ex. 13.6, above) but with three significant changes. The first is that Schoenberg begins his transposed repetition by starting from the second note of the original, omitting the first. This creates an interesting subtlety: since the second note of the original melody is a semitone below the first, when Schoenberg omits the first note

Example 13.7

and transposes the remainder up a semitone in m. 13, the beginning tone of the vocal line is F-sharp, the very tone with which the vocal line began in m. 1. This helps create a feeling of reprise.

Another important change Schoenberg makes in the melody further strengthens the direct connections with the original statement and thus reinforces the feeling of reprise. Had the vocal line in mm. 13–15 been an exact transposition of mm. 1–2, it would have ended on an E-flat. But as can be seen in the example, Schoenberg continues on past the E-flat in mm. 14–15 and closes the vocal phrase on D. By continuing on to this extra tone, Schoenberg has closed with the same tone as the first phrase (and in the process, has further emphasized D as a contextual tone of reference).

There is one more significant change. In m. 14, Schoenberg adds an extra tone, the E-natural, which one might be tempted to dismiss as a kind of chromatic passing tone. This tone should not be so lightly overlooked: by adding this tone, Schoenberg has made another direct pitch connection back to the original version of the vocal line, where E preceded the closing D. The addition of E and D, neither of which is part of the literal transposition, reinforces the connections with the original version. Thus Schoenberg creates connections in two dimensions: on the one hand, the vocal line in mm. 13–15 is a transposition of mm. 1–2; on the other hand, it is a varied restatement of those same measures at the original pitch level.

So far we have discussed only the vocal line of mm. 13–15, but there is much of interest in the piano part which is also a conflation and combination of (only slightly altered) prior events. Consider the right hand part in mm. 13–15. Measure 13 is an exact restatement of the r.h. in m. 7, which is itself a restatement (up an octave) of the r.h. in m. 5. Similarly, the continuation from m. 13 is a restatement of the continuation from m. 5, but there is a crucial difference: although the passage in the r.h. in m. 13 is a restatement (at the original pitch level) of the passage from m. 5, the continuation in m. 14 is a restatement of the equivalent of m. 6, not at the original pitch level, but rather in transposition. Thus, the r.h. in mm. 13–14 restates mm. 5–6, but at two different levels of transposition.

It is possible to describe other, similar, connections in this song, but I trust that the essential point is clear: in contrast to the preceding work, this song relies more on the restatement and recombination of only slightly altered blocks of material, rather than a continuous, flexible process of developing variation. This is not a matter of one approach supplanting the other; rather, these two approaches to motivic organization will coexist in Schoenberg's works until his turn to radical athematicism.

The use of this type of motivic organization has interesting consequences for the form. Since the motivic development never really leads us far away

Example 13.8

from the original motives, there is never any real reprise. Therefore, unlike the previous song, Schoenberg cannot use the process of return to suggest impending closure. Instead, he effects closure by taking a harmonic progression that occurred earlier in the song (in mm. 3–4), and by restating three slightly different versions of that progression in quick succession (see Ex. 13.8).

Since there are no other threefold repetitions in the song, the very fact of the multiple statements suggests a winding down. At the same time, the progression Schoenberg uses has some obvious antecedents. By dropping the bass a fifth, Schoenberg clearly hints at a dominant-to-tonic progression, a sense that is intensified by the presence of other elements of the dominant chord on D and the tonic chord on G.[12]

I hasten – yet again – to caution that while the presence of these traditional elements helps create a feeling of closure, they are not anywhere near enough to establish G as a referential tonic. The presence of so many other elements that do not belong to D major or G major triads neutralizes any sense of G as a referential tonic or of D and G major triads as functional harmonic entities. Therefore, Schoenberg has done here what he did not do in Op. 14, No. 1: he has chosen a final sonority that is not out of step with the prevailing sonority in the rest of the song.

"Als Neuling trat ich", Op. 15, No. 3

The next song, "Als Neuling trat ich", was completed on 29 March 1908 (only four days after "Saget mir") and thus, not surprisingly, shares many of the features of its immediate predecessors. For this reason, it will not be necessary to go into quite the same degree of analytical detail as we did with the two previous songs. Rather, the presence of common features gives

Beyond triads: the first layer of *Das Buch der hängenden Gärten*

Example 13.9

us the opportunity to concentrate on identifying some of the more important trends in Schoenberg's compositional language during this period.

Most obviously, the chordal vocabulary of this song is strikingly similar to that of its two predecessors. Other than the occasional, isolated triad (e.g. m. 17, beat three), the typical chord is one with an embedded triad or seventh chord – usually an added-semitone type – or another non-traditional chord (such as the chord of fourths: see m. 1, beat four). However, there is an important difference in the way in which Schoenberg handles the chordal vocabulary of this song as compared to the previous two songs. Instead of the homophonic (sometimes even homorhythmic) structure of the previous two songs, this work is far more polyphonic. As a result, Schoenberg rarely settles on clear, easily apprehensible, rhythmically isolated, chordal sonorities. The surface is often far more slippery, with motion in one or more voices typically preventing the focus on a single sonority (see Ex. 13.9).

This is a familiar texture in Schoenberg's compositions, one in which a quick harmonic rhythm results from the motion of the individual voices, thereby producing a fast-moving succession of different harmonies. In contrast to Schoenberg's earlier works where that succession was mostly made up of seventh chords, here the harmonies tend to be added semitone chords. For instance, in the first measure, the opening sonority pits an incomplete seventh chord (A E-flat G) in the r.h. opposite a D in the l.h. This is supplanted quickly by another added-semitone sonority (D A D-flat F). In turn, this is transformed into a similar sonority (an augmented triad on D-flat plus G). The techniques (and pace) of voice leading are similar to those of earlier works; the principal difference is the identity of the component sonorities of the fast-moving successions.

There is another very important aspect to this passage, again, reflecting the evolutionary character of Schoenberg's thought. We have seen in earlier polyphonic works that Schoenberg had a tendency to pair voices together rhythmically. When he did so, he typically invoked the principle of localized consonance by having the voices move in parallel thirds or sixths. That very same principle is clearly in force throughout this song. Accordingly, the upper two voices of the piano often appear in rhythmic coordination, and when they do so, they are often, as in the opening measure, in parallel thirds.

At several points in the song (e.g. m. 10), Schoenberg even expands the use of parallel motion to include parallel fifths. This may not be the first time Schoenberg has transgressed that hoary part-writing rule in his compositions, but it is one of the most explicit. The relatively late date of his willingness to use parallel fifths in an obvious manner is one of the clearest possible indications of the powerful hold of tradition on this, the most radical of composers.

Before leaving this song, it is worth noting that in terms of its motivic techniques, "Als Neuling trat ich" falls neatly between the approaches offered by the previous two songs. The vocal line, in particular, unfolds by a flexible process of developing variation, quickly and steadily generating new patterns. In that sense it follows the same path of motivic development that we saw in Op. 15, No. 4. On the other hand, the piano part is far more constrained in its motivic development. It restricts itself to a very few basic motivic ideas, constantly restating varied (though not identical) versions of those motives. In this sense, it resembles Op. 15, No. 5. Taken together, this suggests that Schoenberg is not wedded to a single technique of motivic construction. Rather, he has a range of possible means of realizing the basic principle of motivic economy.

"Wenn ich heut nicht deinen Leib", Op. 15, No. 8

Schoenberg completed the next song, "Wenn ich heut nicht deinen Leib", Op. 15, No. 8, on 13 April 1908, approximately two weeks after "Als Neuling trat ich".[13] Because it shares so many features with its predecessors, we need not dwell on those, but can concentrate instead on one interesting aspect of its harmonic structure.

In this song, a surprisingly large percentage of the harmonies belong to a single family of related chords in which the 048 trichord (the augmented triad) appears alone, or as part of added-semitone tetrachords. The opening two measures (see Ex. 13.10) are typical. In these two measures three of the four possible augmented triads appear, either as simultaneities or in arpeggiated form.

Because of its intervallic content, the augmented triad is unique among the four triadic types (major, minor, diminished, and augmented) in that

Example 13.10

Example 13.11

there are only four distinct transpositions (in terms of pitch-class content). It seems clear that Schoenberg recognized this property and used it as a compositional resource in this work. By m. 2, three of the four possible augmented triads have appeared. In mm. 3–5, the augmented triads that occur duplicate those that already appeared in mm. 1–2.

In mm. 6–7, the l.h. breaks into octaves and shorter phrases while the tempo broadens. This creates the impression of mild contrast with what came before (see Ex. 13.11).

It is at this very point that Schoenberg finally introduces the one transposition of the 048 trichord that was absent from the first five measures ('a' in Ex. 13.11). At the beginning of m. 6, the C A-flat E trichord unfolds in the left hand. Thus Schoenberg highlights the mild contrast in texture and motive with the one augmented triad that has not yet appeared.

I believe this is evidence of a new mode of compositional thought, one that will eventually become a central feature of his compositional strategies. From this point forward, we can find numerous examples in which it is clear that Schoenberg determined specific details of the course of development by exploiting specific properties (usually intervallic properties) of his material.

There are some hints of this idea in Schoenberg's prior works: the specific levels of transposition chosen for the canonic imitation of Melisande's theme beginning at m. 22 of *Pelleas und Melisande* may be an early manifestation of this kind of idea.[14] Although there may have been isolated precursors to the treatment of the principal motive of Op. 15, No. 8, they were just that – isolated. What we see in this song (and will find with increasing frequency in works to come, particularly the twelve-tone works) is something that had not been a significant part of Schoenberg's earlier works: a mode of musical thought in which specific aspects of the compositional structure follow from the specific intervallic and pitch-class content of the thematic material.

"Angst und Hoffen", Op. 15, No. 7

"Angst und Hoffen", Op. 15, No. 7 (completed 28 April 1908), is the last song that can definitively be assigned to the spring of 1908.[15] Given that only six weeks elapsed from the first to the last of the five dated songs from this period, it is not surprising that "Angst und Hoffen" shares so many prominent features with its predecessors: indeterminate scale segments, localized consonance (e.g. the frequent passages in parallel thirds), tightly controlled motivic organization, closure effected by contextual means (here, the recall of the opening harmonic progression at its original pitch level), the absence of referential triads, the presence of contextual tones of reference and relative stability (E-flat and D are the most prominent), added-semitone sonorities, and the constant circulation of the total chromatic (most phrases include all, or nearly all of the twelve tones). At the same time, there are some significant features that were not present in any of the other songs and these innovations point to the emergence of some important changes in the nature and character of Schoenberg's compositional thought.

One obvious innovation is the restriction of the piano part to the right hand alone. Whether or not Schoenberg is the first composer who ever wrote an accompaniment for a single hand, the decision to limit the accompaniment to the right hand helps to create an inimitable sound for this song: high tessitura, narrow compass, thin texture.

Beyond triads: the first layer of *Das Buch der hängenden Gärten*

This song is also of importance because we can see in it indications of a new kind of approach to harmonic structure. Three excerpts (which account for a significant percentage of the song) illustrate (see Ex. 13.12).

As can be seen in these excerpts, two chord types predominate: the augmented triad (x) and a trichord consisting of stacked fourths, one of

Example 13.12a

Example 13.12b

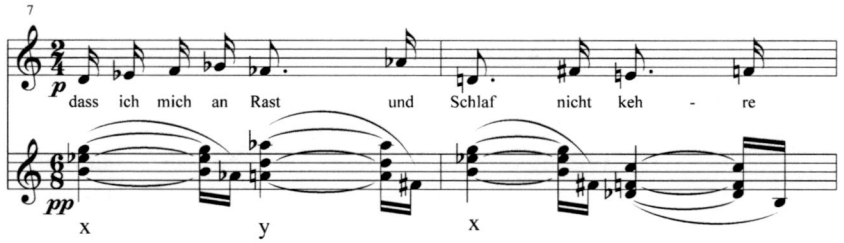

Example 13.12c

final cadence: statements of x and y at original pitch level (c.f. m. 1)

which is perfect, and the other, augmented (y). I would like to focus on the second of these. There are aspects of Schoenberg's treatment of this chord that point in a new direction. Chief among those is the way in which Schoenberg manipulates this chord using techniques similar to developing variation.

"Developing variation" may not be the correct term: although Schoenberg's use of this term (and, alas, many others) was never completely systematic, he did seem to reserve it to describe how a melody worked, not chords. But if we think of developing variation as a specific manifestation of a general concept – a developmental process that produces new patterns via carefully controlled change – then what happens in this song is closely related to developing variation.

Consider the progression in m. 1 (Ex. 13.12a): Schoenberg moves from the opening augmented triad (x) to the altered chord of fourths (y) in such a manner that the uppermost voice moves by half step (D to E-flat, m. 1). Since the B-flat of the first chord is held as a common tone, this means that the second chord has the augmented fourth on the bottom and the perfect fourth on top.

Compare this with the next instance of a version of this progression, in m. 3. Once again, the progression is made up of two chords, an augmented triad (x) that leads to an altered chord of fourths (y). This time the upper voice does not move upward by semitone; instead it descends by semitone. As a result, the altered chord of fourths does not have the perfect fourth on top: it is at the bottom. In m. 7 (Ex. 13.12b), we encounter yet another version of this progression: once again the uppermost voice ascends by semitone. This does not yield a transposition of m. 1 because the altered chord of fourths places the perfect fourth at the bottom. Thus, what we see is a series of carefully controlled transformations of the original progression. All three instances retain some important common features, but they present that common material in several different ways.

In turn, the developmental treatment of the opening progression plays an important role in the large-scale form. After the statement of the opening progression in m. 1, all of the subsequent instances of that progression in mm. 3–17 are versions of the varied forms described above and do not appear in their original form. In mm. 18–19 – the last two measures of the composition – Schoenberg returns to the original version of the progression and at its original level of transposition (Ex. 13.12c). This creates an unmistakable sense of return and fosters a clear feeling of closure. Thus we have a familiar three-phased formal dynamic here: starting from an initial statement (reference); moving through logical transformations of the opening pattern (departure); retrieving stability and promoting closure by the restatement of the opening material in its original distribution (return).

Although the origins of the two basic chords of this song may have deep roots in tradition, the use of procedures akin to developing variation to vary the progression and to shape the form points in directions leading away from traditional modes of compositional thought. This is, perhaps, the key to understanding all of the songs from this period: a unique synthesis of tradition and innovation.

14 "On revient toujours"? Returning to Opp. 10 and 15, June 1908–February 1909

> Yet the overwhelming multitude of dissonances cannot be counterbalanced any longer by occasional returns to such tonal triads as represent a key.[1]

Whenever possible, the Schoenberg family left Vienna in the summer months for a vacation where the family could relax and Schoenberg could compose. In early June 1908, Mathilde Schoenberg, the couple's two children (Trudi, aged 6 and Georg, aged 2), and Mathilde's mother, traveled ahead to Gmunden on the Traunsee to make arrangements for their annual summer retreat, leaving Schoenberg behind in Vienna to finish his teaching obligations. Unfortunately, this would prove to be a holiday like no other, for it was during this period that the simmering crisis in Schoenberg's marriage finally broke out into the open.

Even before the summer, Schoenberg may have been aware that his wife was involved in some way with their friend, the painter Richard Gerstl. At the very least we know that at the same time the family was in the process of moving to Gmunden for their summer vacation, Schoenberg and his wife were in the midst of a marital crisis. During the three-week period that Schoenberg was in Vienna and his wife was in Gmunden, they communicated through the mail, and Mathilde's half of the correspondence has survived. The picture that emerges is of a marriage that was in trouble.

It got worse. Shortly after Schoenberg arrived in Gmunden around 28 June 1908, Gerstl also appeared on the scene. To further complicate the situation, Mathilde's mother (Carla Semo von Zemlinszky) and brother (Alexander Zemlinsky) were present, as were a number of Schoenberg's students, thus ensuring that the troubled couple would have little or no privacy to work out their problems.[2] The results were, perhaps, predictable, and by the end of August the crisis boiled over to the point that Mathilde left her husband and children and ran off to live with Gerstl. At this point, some of Schoenberg's students (including Anton Webern) intervened and convinced her to return to her family. Several months later, disconsolate at the abandonment and distraught at being cut out of Schoenberg's circle, Gerstl committed suicide.

Given the enduring power of the belief in a necessary connection between the private life of a composer and the content of his works, it is not surprising that the tragic events of 1908 have been grist for the mill. There seems to be widespread agreement that the final movements of

Op. 10 are inextricably bound up with Schoenberg's reactions to the crisis in his personal life prompted by the Gerstl/Mathilde affair. According to this reading, Schoenberg's marital crisis could not have been compartmentalized as merely a personal tragedy; it had to have been an artistic watershed as well. As a result, many writers trace a clear line of influence from the tragedy to Schoenberg's works. Many see in the marital crisis the catalyst for the final abandonment of tonality.[3] Others see a somewhat more complicated line of influence. Bryan Simms suggests that Schoenberg's return to Op. 10 represents a "stylistic retrenchment". That is, having already crossed the frontiers into "complete atonality" in the first layer of Op. 15, Schoenberg's return to a "late tonal" language in Op. 10 has to be understood as a step backward.[4]

By definition, a step backward is a step in a negative direction. Therefore, if there was a step backward, then there had to be an appropriate (negative) cause. Clearly the proximate cause has to be the marital crisis. If this is true, then Schoenberg's decision to make the quartet a vocal work and his choice of texts for the final two movements confirms the hypothesis that the form and content of the quartet was shaped by the Gerstl/Mathilde affair.

Respectfully, I must demur. There are serious problems with the argument that a direct link exists between the 1908 crisis in Schoenberg's personal life and the direction of his artistic development. Even granting that there was a "stylistic retrenchment" in the last two movements (and I will take issue with that in a moment), and even accepting (and I don't) the proposition that a composer's choice of texts is necessarily autobiographical in nature, the chronology of Schoenberg's compositions does not support the existence of a causal connection between the marital crisis and the alleged retrenchment.

What we do know is that Schoenberg arrived in Gmunden on approximately 28 June 1908, after a three-week period of separation in which he and Mathilde had exchanged frequent letters. Although it is clear that there were real problems with their marriage, the correspondence of June 1908 suggests that the situation was not yet hopeless. For example, on 24 June 1908, only a few days before his arrival in Gmunden, Mathilde wrote Schoenberg the following letter:

> My dear, dear Arnold,
>   You are so dear and good and I am tremendously happy about everything you have written me. I also love you so very much and cannot live without you – Now you are coming in 3 days. The time is going by so terribly slowly. If it were only Thursday. I don't dare hope that you might come earlier. However, should that be, write me immediately saying when I can expect you. I speak about you constantly with the children so they will not be at all shy.

> The little one perhaps for a few minutes but certainly no longer ... Many, many kisses, my dearest, good Herzerl from your
> Mathilde[5]

Reading between the lines of the letters from this period, it is obvious that there were problems with the marriage. Nonetheless, it also seems obvious that as of late June 1908, Schoenberg did not yet have reason to believe that "alles ist hin".[6]

The crisis was not far off. Gerstl showed up in Gmunden shortly after Schoenberg's arrival and by late August this did lead to an explosion. But even if he suspected that his wife was involved in an affair, it was probably only toward the end of the summer that Schoenberg realized just how serious the situation was. His remarkable success at composing (he completed the third movement of Op. 10 in less than a week and the fourth movement seems to have followed quickly behind) suggests that he was not completely aware of the seriousness of the situation until late August.

We know that within a few days of his arrival, Schoenberg had sent word to his student, Karl Horwitz, who had remained behind in Vienna, asking him to send copies of the two George poems that were to serve as the textual basis for the two final movements of Op. 10. It is certain that the poems arrived by 5 July 1908, because on that date Schoenberg wrote Horwitz, thanking him for sending the poems. We also know that Schoenberg got right to work and wrote very quickly because he completed the draft of the third movement of Op. 10 on 11 July 1908 – only six days later.

The correspondence with Horwitz is crucial because it helps to confirm that Schoenberg did not make the decision to set the George poems after arriving in Gmunden. It suggests that Schoenberg had already done preparatory work on the third movement even before he came to Gmunden. If so, then the hypothesis that his choice of the George poems had anything to do with the breakup of his marriage falls apart.

Schoenberg's request to Horwitz to send him two specific poems could only mean that Schoenberg already knew the poems in question (but not by memory) and had already decided to use them in his composition. He did not ask Horwitz to send him the whole book so he could rummage through it, looking for appropriate material; he asked him to copy out and send him two specific poems. Thus it is likely that even before he arrived in Gmunden – that is well before the marital crisis careened toward its tragic climax – Schoenberg had already decided to transform the quartet into a work with voice and had already chosen two specific poems of George for that purpose.

Schoenberg was able to tell Horwitz precisely what poems to copy and where to find them because the page numbers and the opening line or two of the texts for both poems were already written down in Sketchbook III (and this suggests that Schoenberg had not left Sketchbook III behind). On page 105 of Sketchbook III, there is a series of brief sketches that outline some of the ideas Schoenberg was thinking of using for what would become the fourth and final movement of Op. 10. The first of those is a brief five-measure sketch on staves 2–4 of p. 105 in Sketchbook III. In the final version of the quartet, the excerpt on p. 105 appears, little changed, as mm. 21–5 of the fourth movement where it is the opening phrase of the vocal line.

In the left-hand margin Schoenberg identified this as the third movement of the string quartet and wrote out the poetic source: "Stefan George (123. 7 Ring)", a reference to the page number where the poem Entrückung appears in *Der siebente Ring*.[7]

On the same page of Sketchbook III, Schoenberg jotted down several other ideas he was thinking of using. On staves 6–9 of p. 105 is a phrase that sets a few words from the beginning of the fourth stanza of George's poem. In the final version of Schoenberg's quartet, this passage appears, with some changes, as mm. 51–61. The remaining sketches on p. 105 of Sketchbook III (labeled S30, S31, S32, S33, S34 in *SW*) are versions of various other passages intended for the fourth movement, including an early version of the opening measures.

Unfortunately, Schoenberg failed to date these sketches. Thus, although it is likely that the sketches for the fourth movement antedated his arrival in Gmunden in late June 1908, we do not know exactly when. All we know is that these sketches were written between 17 December 1907 and 28 June 1908. Nonetheless, this is enough for us to know that they originated from a period that was before Schoenberg knew his marriage was collapsing.[8]

Although it is not possible to state with certainty where exactly the sketches fall in this period, what we do know is enough to throw serious doubt on the idea that Schoenberg's personal troubles had anything to do with the decision to resume work on Op. 10 and to turn it into a vocal work. Rather, there is another scenario that fits much better with the available evidence.

When Schoenberg returned to Vienna from Berlin in 1903, he was obliged to support his family with hack-work (copying scores, orchestrating operettas, and making arrangements for piano). Gradually, Schoenberg began to develop a reputation as a gifted teacher of harmony, counterpoint, and composition, and the focus of his energies shifted toward pedagogy. Alban Berg, Anton Webern, Egon Wellesz, Karl Horwitz, Elsa Bienenfeld, Zdzislaw Jachimecki, Heinrich Jalowetz, Viktor Krüger, Robert Neumann, O. de Ivanov, Wilma von Webenau, Rudolf Weirich, and Erwin Stein, are among the students who are known to have worked with Schoenberg by 1908.[9] Working with Schoenberg was typically an intense experience and one that was highly time consuming, both for the pupil and the teacher.[10] As a result, beginning around 1904 or 1905 there is a perceptible change in Schoenberg's rhythm of composition. More and more, Schoenberg tended to concentrate his compositional activities in the summer months when he and his family were vacationing in such places as Rottach-Egern (1906), Gmunden (1907, 1908), and Steinakirchen (1909).

During the rest of the year Schoenberg did not abandon composition entirely, but the ever-increasing burden of his teaching responsibilities made it difficult for him to get the necessary momentum to work on larger compositions during that time of year. Thus we see an emerging pattern of Schoenberg using the summer vacation for extended work on larger compositions while during the academic year he sketched ideas for those larger compositions or wrote smaller compositions like songs.[11]

This seems to be exactly what had happened with the String Quartet, Op. 10. The first sketches for Op. 10 are dated 9 March 1907. As Christian Martin Schmidt points out, these include sketches of all of the principal themes of the first movement (which, of course, are widely separated from one another in the final version of the work).[12] There is no evidence that Schoenberg began to weave these ideas together into a continuous draft of the first movement at that time. Instead, Schoenberg put the quartet aside and concentrated on shorter compositions (Op. 12, Nos. 1 and 2, which were completed in April 1907). Only after his teaching obligations diminished, did Schoenberg return to the quartet: during the summer of 1907, he completed the first movement, made significant progress with the second movement, and (possibly) sketched out the opening of an instrumental slow movement. During that same summer, Schoenberg also worked on the other big project from this period, the Chamber Symphony No. 2.

The following academic year, this cycle repeated. Schoenberg may have tried to keep the quartet going for some time after his return (the paucity of dated sketches makes it hard to tell exactly when he broke off work). By December he had clearly given up and once again his focus had shifted to shorter compositions. From December 1907 to June 1908 we know that – at the very least – Schoenberg worked on a number of shorter compositions: Op. 14, Nos. 1 and 2; Op. 15, Nos. 4, 3, 5, 7, 8. There is no evidence that Schoenberg was able to continue working on the draft of the String Quartet, Op. 10 after December 1907.

Instead, Schoenberg did approximately what he had done the previous year. Knowing that he would not have enough time for extended, uninterrupted, work until late June, he wrote out isolated sketches for important ideas of the quartet so that he would have them ready for the summer when he could work them out into a continuity draft. On pages 105–8 of Sketchbook III (that is, after December 1907), there are a series of isolated concept sketches (i.e. not a continuity draft), some of which would be incorporated into the eventual drafts of the third and fourth movements.

Thus, there is no evidence to support the theory that it was Schoenberg's marital crisis that prompted him first to stop writing the quartet, then to turn back to it, transforming it into a vocal work that used triads as final sonorities. He did not put the work aside for personal reasons; he put it aside for practical reasons, and many a composer at many a university today can empathize with those reasons. His return to triads (after the non-triadic songs of Op. 15) does not represent a "retrenchment" any more than his resumption of Chamber Symphony No. 2, Op. 38 in the 1930s was a "retrenchment". Rather, Schoenberg did what most composers do when they resume a work: to the extent that it is possible, they try to complete it in the manner in which it had begun. Since the first two movements made use of triads as points of arrival or resolution, Schoenberg obviously did not feel it was possible completely to discard those premises in the remaining movements, even though the intervening songs of Op. 15 had done just that. Schoenberg's employment of a slightly more traditional harmonic vocabulary is a result of internal compositional demands and not a response to the crisis in his marriage. In any event (as we shall see shortly), there are important ways in which the later layer of Op. 10 constitutes a push forward, not a step backward.

As we saw in chapter 11, all available evidence suggests that in the first stages of his work on Op. 10, Schoenberg was contemplating the most traditional work he had written in a decade. It appears that he was intending to write a completely instrumental work, possibly with the standard four movements. This was a work in which the first movement followed fairly closely the traditional model of sonata form and had no known programmatic features. Not since his String Quartet in D (1897) – the product of his apprenticeship under Zemlinsky – had Schoenberg written anything remotely as traditional as this.

Ultimately, Schoenberg's core personality and beliefs had to reassert themselves. For all of his love and respect of the music of the past, he was no Miniver Cheevy.[13] By disposition he was an innovator, the most radical of the radicals, the leader of the avant-garde, not an epigone. After returning from his summer holiday in 1907, Schoenberg put the nascent String Quartet, Op. 10 aside – as practical necessities dictated – and concentrated on smaller compositions. It was in this period that Schoenberg finally summoned up the courage to come to grips with the hesitations that had dogged him ever since the completion of the Chamber Symphony, Op. 9 in 1906. One manifestation of this came with his harmonic language: step by step in the works of Opp. 14 and 15, he pushed forward past what anyone might previously have thought had to be the outer limits of harmonic organization.

This created something of a problem for Schoenberg. Sitting on his desk were two large, unfinished compositions: the String Quartet, Op. 10 and the Chamber Symphony No. 2. In terms of their traditional formal structure and pitch language, these two works represented trends that Schoenberg had just abandoned. This pitted Schoenberg the ambitious young composer against Schoenberg the radical. Schoenberg, the ambitious young composer, needed compositions to add to his still thin catalogue and did not want to abandon works on which he had already spent considerable time. He has to have been anxious to exploit a situation that every aspiring composer dreams of: the likelihood that one of the premiere ensembles of the day (the Rosé Quartet) would perform virtually any chamber work for strings that he might write.

Schoenberg, the radical composer has to have had a different perspective. Having turned back to a decidedly radical direction during the intervening winter, Schoenberg has to have looked back at his unfinished works with mixed feelings. On the one hand, he just couldn't abandon them – he had written too much simply to consign them to oblivion. On the other hand, his most recent music had made these two fragments look like detours from the main line of his development.

Although this may be why the Chamber Symphony No. 2 remained unfinished for nearly three decades, Schoenberg did manage to find a way to salvage the String Quartet, Op. 10. Sometime after December 1907 and before July 1908, he made a series of decisions that transformed this quartet from a mildly traditional work into one that was more in tune with his renewed commitment to radicalism, yet without creating a totality that was unworkably heterogeneous. When we retrace the sequence of sketches that he made after 17 December 1907, we can see this transformation unfold.

In its early phases, Op. 10 was entirely instrumental and there is no hint that Schoenberg contemplated anything other than a rather traditional multi-movement structure. A first movement in sonata form, a scherzo as the second movement, and a sketch for what may have been meant as an instrumental slow movement all contribute to this picture. Nevertheless, it is clear that in 1907 Schoenberg's thoughts about the quartet's overall structure were not far advanced. In addition to only the barest outlines of a slow movement (and it is by no means certain that the sketch on p. 96 of

Sketchbook III was meant for a slow third movement of the quartet), there are no identifiable sketches at all for a finale in the 1907 layer of Op. 10.

During the academic year 1907–8, Schoenberg rethought his compositional direction and, waving away his former hesitancy, returned to his position at the forefront of the avant-garde. The first hint of that transformation is the brief sketch that appears on p. 105 of Sketchbook III. In the final version of the quartet, the movement of which this sketch is a part would become part of the fourth, and final, movement, not, as Schoenberg first indicated, the third movement.

Regardless of where the movement eventually was placed, the innovative nature of the idea cannot be denied. Just as much as *Verklärte Nacht* (and secretly, the String Quartet, Op. 7) challenged the association of chamber music with absolute music, so too, by the simple expedient of adding a vocal part to the ensemble, Schoenberg contradicted some of the core assumptions of the genre.[14]

String quartets, of course, were the prototypical genre of chamber music – and that meant absolute music. On the other hand, German lieder tended to be either with piano accompaniment (sometimes with an obbligato instrumental part) or with orchestra, but typically not with an ensemble like a string quartet. By adding the vocal part to the string quartet, Schoenberg found a way to challenge both norms at one and the same time.[15] That alone suggests that the resumption of work on Op. 10 was not a retrenchment, but rather, a resumption of Schoenberg's drive for innovation, a tangible sign of his breaking out of his crisis of confidence or direction and resuming his position as a leader of the avant-garde. As we shall see shortly, many other aspects of the movement confirm this interpretation.

Schoenberg's labeling of the sketch on p. 105 of Sketchbook III as "III. Satz" (third movement) has prompted much speculation about Schoenberg's overall plan for the quartet, particularly given his eventual decision to make "Entrückung", the fourth, not the third, movement. Evidence of this change in plans follows on p. 108 of Sketchbook III (that is, only three pages after the sketches for "Entrückung") where Schoenberg made a number of preparatory sketches for a setting of George's poem "Litanei". Although the sketches for "Litanei" follow the sketches for "Entrückung" (and thus probably were written later), in the final version of the quartet, "Litanei" is the third, not the fourth movement.

The usual explanation for this state of affairs is that Schoenberg first intended "Entrückung" to be the third movement and "Litanei" to be the final movement but, at some point, changed his mind and reversed their order, thus yielding the version of the quartet we now know.

And what is the reason that has been given for this change of order? Why, the crisis in his marriage, of course. According to this interpretation, Schoenberg first placed "Litanei" at the end, tangible evidence of the despair and dejection that afflicted him because of his crumbling marriage. Only later did he change his mind, placing "Entrückung" last, indicative of "a more optimistic, life-affirming (really art-affirming) position, signified in part by the ordering "Litanei"-"Entrückung".[16]

This too is unlikely: there is little credible evidence to support the theory that Schoenberg ever contemplated an "Entrückung"-"Litanei" ordering.

The simple fact is we do not know precisely when Schoenberg wrote the initial sketches for "Entrückung" or "Litanei". We only know that they were most likely written sometime between 17 December 1907 and 28 June 1908. Since we do not know when exactly it was that Schoenberg became aware of the Gerstl/Mathilde affair, we cannot know whether the sketches preceded or followed his becoming aware of the affair.[17] In short, the assumptions that the ordering of the movements was changed and that the change in order was a result of emotional conflict are unsubstantiated. The available evidence can far more logically support a significantly different scenario.

Some time after 17 December 1907 Schoenberg wrote out some preparatory sketches for a setting of Stefan George's poem "Entrückung" and marked these as intended for the third movement of the string quartet. Given the nature of these sketches (the thematic ideas for the principal sections) it is reasonable to assume that Schoenberg wrote them sometime during the academic year, in preparation for, and anticipation of, his summer vacation where he would have the time to devote to full-time composition.[18]

There is no reason to assume that these sketches were intended as the third movement of a four-movement cycle. A simpler explanation might simply be that Schoenberg was planning for "Entrückung" to be the third and final movement of a three-movement cycle. The final version of the quartet (a four-movement work) may have blinded us to the possibility that Schoenberg might originally have had a different (that is a three-movement) plan in mind. It is also possible that he did intend "Entrückung" as the third of four movements but was planning on adding an instrumental movement to follow it. Indeed, the very next page of Sketchbook III includes a discarded sketch that could have been an early idea for an instrumental fourth movement.

There is one bit of evidence that has been advanced in support of the idea that "Litanei" was originally intended to be the last movement. As has frequently been pointed out, "Litanei" begins with clear quotations from the first two movements, thereby imparting a cyclic character to the work.

Given the traditional placement of the cyclic return in the finale, some have argued that the presence of cyclic elements in "Litanei" indicate that it was originally intended to be the finale.[19]

This conclusion is also based on unsupported assumptions. It is significant that "Litanei" is not fully cyclic: although it quotes themes from the first two movements, it does not quote from "Entrückung". Had "Entrückung" ever really been intended to precede "Litanei", then wouldn't we expect a cyclic summary of themes to include its themes as well? But, of course, they do not. "Litanei" does summarize – exactly as we should expect – the themes from the two preceding movements, but it does not quote anything from "Entrückung" because "Litanei" never was intended to be the last movement.

Although one cannot say with utter certainty, there is another scenario that better fits the available evidence. Sometime after returning from his summer vacation in 1907, Schoenberg decided to transform Op. 10 into a vocal work. In that spirit, he wrote out sketches of the principal themes for "Entrückung", intending to use this as the third movement of his quartet with either no other movement or an instrumental movement following.

At some point thereafter, Schoenberg must have looked at the overall plan of this three-movement quartet and hesitated. If he proceeded with this plan he would have three distinct and separate movements, one traditional, one rambunctiously ironic, and one wildly radical vocal movement with its otherworldly poetry (and music to match). Schoenberg has to have felt that this proposed quartet would not hang together as an integrated whole.

Faced with this dilemma, Schoenberg hunted around for a solution. It appears that his first thoughts were to write something that would start to connect the disparate elements and draw them together. On p. 106 of Sketchbook III – that is, immediately after the sketches for "Entrückung" – Schoenberg made a sketch (S35) for a passage that appears to have been intended as a means of reconciling the disparate material of the quartet.[20]

Schoenberg gave no indication as to where he was thinking of placing this sketch.[21] Perhaps it was intended as part of a separate movement, perhaps not. Regardless of where Schoenberg intended to place this passage, the sketch is important because it gives the first indication that after having decided to add a vocal movement to his quartet, Schoenberg was looking for a way to integrate the disparate material of the different movements.

This is followed by another sketch (S36) that makes it crystal clear that Schoenberg did intend the previous sketch to recall the theme of the first movement. In sketch S36, the connections with the principal themes of the first and second movements are unmistakable. Equally obvious are the connections with sketch S35: the transposition of the first movement's theme is identical in both sketches.

Significantly, S36 shows that Schoenberg has decided upon another George poem, "Litanei". In the margin, before the first measure of the sketch, Schoenberg wrote the number 148: the page number in George's book *Der siebente Ring*, where "Litanei" appears.

Taken in its entirety, the evidence suggests that after having decided to radicalize his quartet by concluding with a setting of George's poem, "Entrückung", Schoenberg realized that the resultant three-movement cycle might simply be too diverse to hold together as a coherent whole. Therefore, he rethought the overall plan of the quartet, deciding to insert an additional movement – a setting of another George poem – before the "Entrückung" movement. He addressed the problem of coherence by having the new third movement use the principal themes of the preceding two movements. This had the effect of making a smooth transition from the two instrumental movements to the two vocal movements.

It would appear, then, that the available evidence strongly suggests that "Litanei" was never intended as anything but the third movement. But even if I am wrong, and even if Schoenberg had originally intended "Litanei" to be the final movement, there is one more piece of evidence that should prove that the decision to switch the order of the movements took place before Schoenberg arrived in Gmunden (that is, before the collapse of his marriage, before Mathilde's flight, before Gerstl's suicide).

When Karl Horwitz fulfilled Schoenberg's request to send the two poems that had been left behind, he did so by copying them by hand. It is highly significant that the two poems appear on this sheet with "Litanei" first and "Entrückung" second – this, in spite of the fact that "Litanei" (p. 148) occurs after "Entrückung" (p. 122) in George's book. It is unlikely that Horwitz would have put them in this order unless it reflects the order in which Schoenberg had requested the poems. If so, this supports the notion that Schoenberg's decision to place "Litanei" third and "Entrückung" fourth was made before Schoenberg left for his summer vacation, and thus well before the Gerstl/Mathilde crisis reached its peak.

Without question, Schoenberg's marital crisis was a terrible tragedy, one that embittered or destroyed three lives. But it was a personal tragedy, not an agent of artistic change. Schoenberg chose to return to the quartet because he had the time to, not because he was turning his back on modernism. He decided upon the order of the movements for internal, musical, reasons, not because he despaired over the breakup of his marriage. He resumed using triads because the coherence of the composition depended on it, not because his personal problems sent him seeking solace in bygone harmonies.

After receiving the copies of the George poems from Horwitz, Schoenberg seems to have gotten right to work, determined to make full use of his precious vacation time. Having already decided on a four-movement work, he turned his attention first to the third movement, "Litanei". Only six days after receiving the copy of the poems (11 July 1908), the third movement was complete.

Although the third movement's addition of a vocal part of the string quartet reflects Schoenberg's return toward more radical directions, the formal structure of the movement might be seen to represent some considerably more traditional tendencies. Following Schoenberg's own suggestion, it has been customary to describe the third movement as a set of five variations with a coda – a rather traditional formal type. But there are some interesting complications and subtleties to Schoenberg's use of this formal type and they should throw into question the assumption that his use of the variations format reflects traditional tendencies. We can bring this into focus merely by asking a disarmingly simple question. What kind of variations are these?

The answer is that they fit no traditional mold. Schoenberg does not use the constant bass, chaconne, or passacaglia techniques. It should be equally clear that these are not melodic outline or strophic variations in which decorated versions of a theme return in their entirety in each strophe. Moreover, what is perhaps the most striking characteristic of this set of variations is that they make absolutely no use of the techniques of diminution or decoration.

Instead of using traditional variation techniques, Schoenberg forms the first five strophes of the poem into distinct mini-sections, in which some or all of the four motivic ideas from the first and second movements undergo a succession of transformations and developments, and where new material is sometimes added to the mix (e.g. the motive in the voice in m. 13).[22] We can best understand these procedures and their significance by looking closely at the theme (see Ex. 14.1) and then at one of the variations.

The theme of the movement is a compilation and combination of four prominent motives taken from the first two movements. It begins with a version of the opening theme of the first movement, transposed to E-flat minor and given a significantly different rhythmic profile ('a'). In counterpoint to this theme are two statements, at two different transpositions (one beginning on B-flat, the other on G-flat) of the neighbor figure first heard in m. 12 of the first movement ('b'). This is followed (mm. 2–4) by a version of one of the prominent themes of the second movement ('c'), also

Example 14.1

transposed to fit into this movement. Finally, the theme of the movement concludes with a version of one of the important secondary themes of the first movement ('d'), transposed here so as to begin and end on B-flat, the dominant scale degree of E-flat minor. Like the first motive, so too this last one has a significantly different rhythmic shape than it did in the first movement: the only thing that has really been retained is the intervallic succession. The four motives taken from the first two movements serve as the basis of the variations that follow. The procedures in the second variation are typical (see Ex. 14.2).

This variation begins by restating the first three motives of the theme ('a', 'b', and 'c') at their original pitch level. In keeping with Schoenberg's

Example 14.2

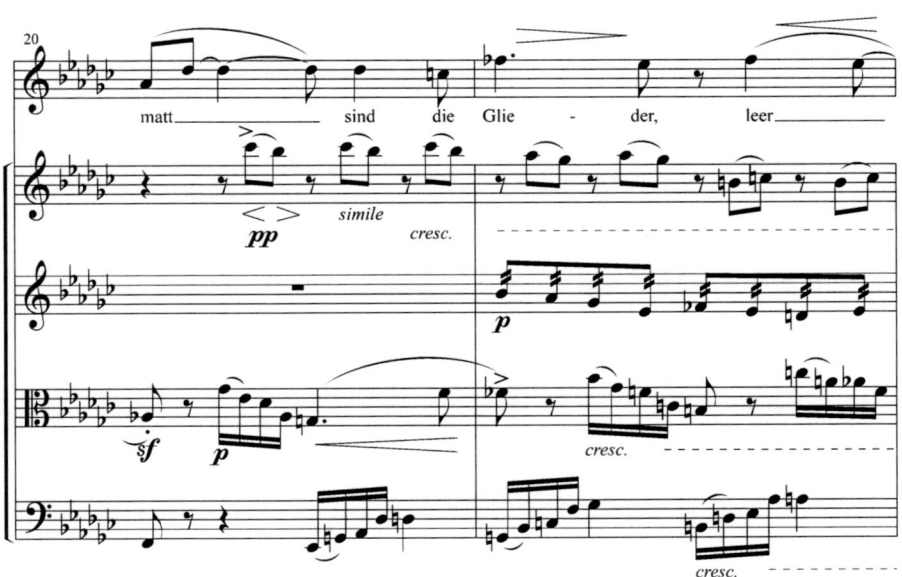

post-Op. 7 interest in traditional compositional devices, the relationships are transformed by invertible counterpoint at the octave. Other than a few minor changes (e.g. the repetitions applied to 'b' in the viola), the first three motives remain largely unchanged. Thus, at first, the variation is rather limited in scope.

Example 14.2 (cont.)

What follows is less a formal variation than it is a kind of mini-development section. It begins in m. 19, while the 'c' motive is still unfolding in the cello. In the viola (in imitative response to the statement of 'c' in the cello) is another statement of 'c', but this time in inversion. Or to be more precise, it is a truncated and inexact inverted imitation. A comparison of the intervallic succession shows just how approximate this imitation is. The original statement of 'c' (mm. 18–20, cello) has the intervallic succession (in semitones) $+3 +2 +5 +2 +4 - 8 +4 -10$; by contrast, this imitative answer has the succession $-4 -2 -5 +1 +8 -1$. This is followed, in mm. 20–3, by a profusion of other, transformed versions of motive 'c' in the two lower instruments, leading to a climactic intensification in m. 23.

The other instruments participate equally in this process, also taking elements of the first three motives and also subjecting them to developmental transformations. The first violin concentrates mostly on motive 'b', the second violin elaborates on material from the vocal line (from m. 13) and then on motive 'c'. The variation concludes by returning to the last motive of the theme ('d') which appears in a loose diminution in mm. 24–5. Taken as a whole, this variation begins and ends with relatively literal statements of the four basic motives, in between which is a section where those themes are subjected to extensive development.

One of the stages of that development merits particular attention. In m. 23 in the first violin there is a version of motive 'b' and in mm. 24–5 in the voice there is a variant of motive 'a'. What is significant about these two statements is the way in which they employ register as an element of variation. Reduced to its essence, the first violin part in m. 23 is nothing more than a neighbor figure (motive 'b'). But that figure plays out over four octaves. Similarly, the vocal line in mm. 24–5 (beginning on the G-flat) is a version of the opening theme of this movement (and thus, of course, of the first movement as well). Instead of appearing in one octave, the stepwise movement from G-flat to F is expanded to a ninth. This technique is not completely new – examples can be found in earlier compositions – but it is about to take on an increasingly central role in Schoenberg's compositional technique.

The techniques Schoenberg uses in the third movement yield a constant process of variation in which the four motives undergo an extensive range of transformations. The quasi-strophic formal structure means that we never venture terribly far away from the original manifestations of the four basic motives: even late in the movement, the four basic motives still appear in readily recognizable form and at their original levels of transposition.

Because of the clear triadic outline of its opening theme and the strophic character of its form, E-flat minor triads (either vertically or horizontally) are a frequent feature of the third movement. It follows that the E-flat minor triad can be understood to have considerably more referential force than triads have had in many of Schoenberg's other works from the period preceding this movement. This is not to say that the movement returns to a purely triadic vocabulary or to an entirely traditional harmonic syntax. Nor is it to say that the E-flat triads are omnipresent. But no other triadic sonority gets anything like the recurring emphases given to E-flat minor and as a result, E-flat minor is never far from our consciousness.

Not so for the final movement. Although it ends clearly with an extended F-sharp major triad, and although other F-sharp triads occasionally take on some degree of structural significance elsewhere in the movement, one would be hard pressed to understand F-sharp (or any other triad) as having referential status for the entire movement. For much of the movement, no referential triadic center of any sort is in evidence. This is reflected in Schoenberg's decision (in contradistinction to the previous movements) to assign no key signature to the movement.

Following Erwin Stein, it has been customary to describe the fourth movement as a kind of sonata form. According to this analysis, there is an introduction (mm. 1–21), an exposition (mm. 21–66) with two contrasting themes (beginning m. 21 and 51, respectively), a development section (mm. 67–99), a reprise (mm. 100–19), and a coda (mm. 120–56).[23] Inasmuch as the subdivisions of the proposed sonata form correspond fairly closely to the principal changes of theme, tempo, and texture of the quartet, this is a credible analysis if we recognize that the "recapitulation" is anything but a literal restatement of the exposition and is followed by a rather substantial coda in which developmental and recapitulatory processes continue.

The justifiably celebrated introduction sets the stage for the movement by creating an inimitable sound world, one that captures the otherworldly feeling of George's poem. It succeeds in creating this mood, not only because of the mysteriously ascending lines, the ***ppp*** dynamics and the

Example 14.3

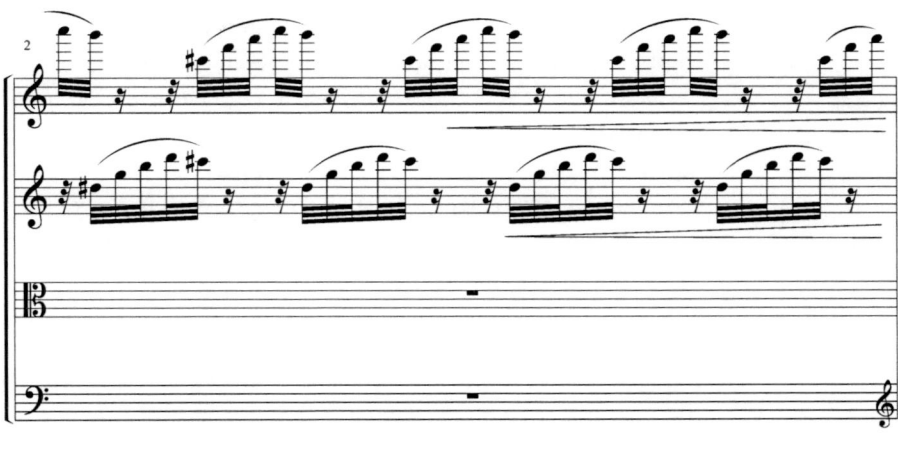

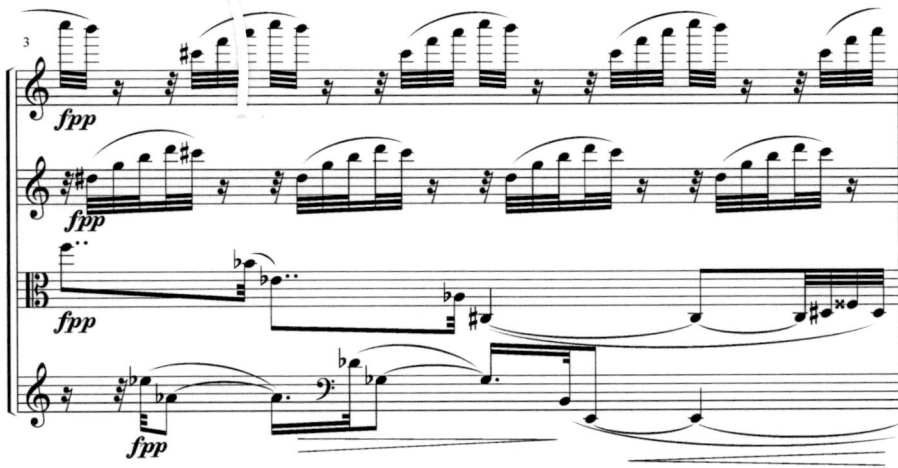

muting, but because there is no identifiable tonal center or consonant triads. Nevertheless, there are still tangible connections to traditional vocabulary and syntax (see Ex. 14.3).

The movement begins with an eight-note figure ('A') in the cello that then appears successively in transpositions up perfect fifths in the remaining three instruments, one after another. In what is by now typical of Schoenberg's construction of themes, the 'A' theme is itself the result of a flexible process of developing variation: a four-note motive, 'a1' (G-sharp B G F-sharp) is followed by a transposed variant, 'a2' (A-sharp D F E), in which the overall contour and final interval remain fixed while the other two intervals are altered in size.

Although 'A' suggests no tonal center nor clearly outlines any consonant triads, there are clear connections with Schoenberg's past. As we have seen in detail, one of the important identifying characteristics of Schoenberg's earlier works was the way in which the surface would be comprised of a quickly moving succession of seventh chords (usually, seventh chords with symmetrical trichordal subsets), in which motion in one of the voices of the counterpoint would produce a quick change in harmony to a related type. 'A' embodies exactly that kind of procedure.

The first three notes are an arpeggiation of an incomplete seventh chord (root, third, seventh, no fifth) built over G-sharp. But this seventh chord is changed into a different chord when, with characteristic voice leading, the motion in the (implied) top voice, G to F-sharp, changes the quality of that seventh chord, suggesting the incomplete seventh chord G-sharp B F-sharp. The last half of 'A' has a virtually identical procedure: there is another arpeggiated seventh chord (this one complete): F-sharp A-sharp D F, after which the motion in the (implied) top voice, F to E, yields a different seventh chord: F-sharp A-sharp D (= C-double-sharp) E. As has been typical of Schoenberg's chords for some time, embedded within these last two seventh chords is the symmetrical 048 trichord, F-sharp A-sharp D. Thus, although the movement begins with multiple statements of a motivic idea that has no identifiable referential tonal center and no apparent triadic basis, the harmonic structure and voice leading of that motive is a direct continuation of procedures Schoenberg had been using for a decade.

Immediately after its first statement, Schoenberg repeats 'A' three times in succession in an ascending sequence with the perfect fifth as the interval of transposition. Schoenberg follows up in m. 3 by turning the perfect-fifths sequence into a thematic idea in the viola and cello. This is not just an isolated event: versions of this idea will appear in a number of different contexts over the course of the movement (e.g. m. 6).

Although there is no referential triadic center anywhere in the introduction, not all tones are treated equally. Instead, Schoenberg makes use of a technique that he had developed in the first songs of Op. 15 whereby one tone is set apart and given more emphasis than others in the vicinity. In m. 3, the descending succession of perfect fifths leads downward to where it stops, on E in the cello. Although that E is held only into the next measure, this is the first tone in the movement that has been isolated and given any real weight. The impression that this tone has an important role is confirmed only three measures later (m. 7) where that E returns in the cello and where it remains for much of the remainder of the instrumental introduction.

The picture that is emerging is not terribly different from what we saw in the songs of Op. 15. Schoenberg does not use simple triads or diatonic seventh chords, but the chords he does use are clear descendents of those harmonies. The harmonic progressions are hardly traditional, but the voice leading is virtually identical to that of earlier works. There is no identifiable referential triad, but one tone (E) is given special emphasis and attention.

Given its consistent avoidance of pure triads, the instrumental introduction is one of the least traditional sounding passages in the entire movement. Yet even where straightforward triads and other traditional features do make occasional appearances, the harmonic vocabulary and syntax is far from a retrenchment. Consider, in this respect, Schoenberg's setting of the first vocal phrase (see Ex. 14.4).

The traditional aspects of this phrase are offset by many other, considerably less traditional, features. For example, the vocal line is completely diatonic: the only tones that appear are the seven tones of the F major diatonic collection. Taken in isolation, this might be seen as a somewhat conservative feature. However, nothing else in the phrase points in the direction of F major (or D minor). In the first place, the B-flat is withheld until the last note of the melody, thereby inhibiting the unequivocal identification of the collection until the phrase is over. Furthermore, as is typical of Schoenberg's works in this period, the phrase as a whole exhausts the chromatic. In any event, the opening skip in the vocal line (from D to G) is far more characteristic of G minor than F major. Moreover, other than the C minor triad in m. 23, none of the accompanying chords has recognizable function in F major. Finally, there is a prominent

Example 14.4

Example 14.4 (cont.)

countersubject in the first violin, and it is another example of one of Schoenberg's indeterminate scales – a predominantly stepwise descent with no recognizable diatonic identity at all, let alone F major.

The chordal vocabulary displays a similar mixture of elements. On the one hand, there are a few clear triads in this phrase. On the downbeat of m. 22 there is a first inversion E-flat major triad; on the downbeat of the following measure, there is a root position C minor triad; finally, the phrase concludes with a second inversion F-sharp minor triad. Only the last of these acts particularly stable, and it is a 6/4 chord – yet another case where Schoenberg uses the dissonant second inversion as a cadential sonority.

In between the triads Schoenberg employs a number of non-triadic sonorities, types that should be quite familiar to us from previous works. The phrase begins with an A D G-sharp trichord: the altered chord of fourths with one of the fourths augmented (the chord that is so prominent in Op. 14, No. 1).[24] In the second half of m. 22, an A G C F tetrachord appears and this too might be understood as a version of the chord of fourths (but missing a D between the A and G). At the end of m. 23 is another version of the altered chord of fourths (here with the upper fourth spelled as a diminished fifth) trichord: G C G-flat. Still further, there is a straightforward augmented triad on the downbeat of m. 24 that is followed, in the second half of the measure, by an added-semitone tetrachord – one with an augmented triad as a subset. Finally, the second to last chord of the phrase has the tones A D G B – another added-dissonance chord, this one with a major triad as the n-1 subset.

Although the last two movements of Op. 10 end with triads and the songs of Op. 15 do not, it makes little sense to describe the two works as having significant differences in their pitch language. Our survey of the harmonic language and chordal vocabulary of these works has demonstrated that they are virtually identical in these two dimensions. Other than the use or non-use of triads as closing sonorities almost everything else is identical: both use the same types of chords (added-semitone tetrachords, chords of fourths, seventh chords with symmetrical subsets, augmented triads and – very rarely – triads) in approximately the same proportion; both tend to exhaust the chromatic within phrases; both make extensive use of indeterminate scales; both use octave transfer to project melodies in several registers; both have similar kinds of harmonic progressions; both employ the same type of harmonic rhythm and voice leading; both make use of the principle of localized consonance; both have a tightly organized motivic structure; both employ developing variation.

After his return to Vienna from his disastrous holiday and after Mathilde's return to the family, Schoenberg eventually was able to resume composing. Once again, given his heavy teaching schedule, he concentrated on smaller works. On 27 September 1908, Schoenberg completed another of the songs from *Das Buch der hängenden Gärten*: number 13. Because of the dearth of dated manuscripts, we simply do not know whether this was the only song Schoenberg worked on during this period. But it is enough for us to recognize that when Schoenberg returned to work on this song cycle, he picked up from where he left off: the language of this song is indistinguishable from that of those written before the interruption. There is the same vocabulary of chords, the same concentrated motivic work, the same use of localized consonance, and the same employment of indeterminate scales. Just as Op. 10 had turned back to the use of triads so as to maintain some consistency for the composition as a whole, so too in Op. 15, No. 13, Schoenberg avoids triads as final sonorities – not because of the influence of his private life on his compositions, but because of his desire for unity and because he wanted the later movements to fit together with the earlier movements. In that sense, one can say "On revient toujours".[25]

15 The analysis of Schoenberg's post-1908 music: Pieces for Piano, Op. 11, Nos. 1 and 2, February 1909

> Most critics of this new style failed to investigate how far the ancient "eternal" laws of musical aesthetics were observed, spurned, or merely adjusted to changed circumstances.[1]

If the traumatic events of the late summer and fall of 1908 (Mathilde's affair and Gerstl's suicide) were not enough to destroy his equanimity, on 21 December 1908, the Rosé Quartet and soprano Marie Gutheil-Schoder premiered Schoenberg's String Quartet No. 2, Op. 10. This performance ended in a near riot with unprecedented disorder in the concert hall followed by a torrent of abusive reviews in the press. Given all of this turmoil, it is hardly surprising that Schoenberg found it virtually impossible to compose: during the four-month period from October 1908 through January 1909, there is no evidence that he completed a single composition.[2] Eventually, Schoenberg did regain his composure and was able to resume writing. In a sudden burst of activity, he quickly wrote four short compositions: the song "Am Strande" (completed 8 February 1909), the Piano Pieces Op. 11, Nos. 1 and 2 (completed 19 and 22 February 1909, respectively), and finally, the last song of *Das Buch der hängenden Gärten*, "Wir bevölkerten", Op. 15, No. 15 (completed 28 February 1909).

The two songs need not detain us for long. "Am Strande" has received a fair amount of attention because of some doubts that have been raised about its date of composition (1908 or 1909?), about the uncertain authorship of its text (Rilke?), and about Schoenberg's intentions regarding its possible inclusion as part of Op. 14.[3] Although it is an attractive, tightly organized work, it does not mark any particularly significant change in Schoenberg's compositional language or style and, therefore, in the interests of brevity, we can bypass it.[4] Similarly, "Wir bevölkerten", the last song of the Op. 15, fits comfortably with the other works of the cycle (as we should expect).

Instead of vocal music, Schoenberg turned his attention in a different direction, to piano music. This is a significant step: although he had made a few isolated attempts to write piano music, he had not completed any work for solo piano since 1894, more than a decade before.[5]

Some have suggested that Schoenberg had been reluctant to write piano music because he was not himself a pianist and had no particular affinity for the instrument.[6] This is possible, but I have my doubts: a lack of confidence in his abilities never seems to have been an enduring part of Schoenberg's personality. Indeed, in his correspondence with Busoni, Schoenberg proudly claimed of these pieces that they "laid the foundations for a modern piano style".[7] Given that Busoni was one of the most celebrated pianists of his day, these are hardly the sentiments of someone who was diffident about his ability to write for the instrument.[8] It is more likely that Schoenberg's relative lack of interest in piano music before 1909 was part of a larger trend: the decidedly subsidiary role that abstract instrumental music of any sort had played in his output.

Although abstract instrumental music did not comprise a significant component of Schoenberg's compositional activities before 1909, it is clear that there is a gradual pattern of his moving in that direction. His first instrumental works were unabashedly programmatic (Opp. 4 and 5). The next instrumental work (Op. 7) was allegedly abstract, but secretly programmatic and followed directly on a failed attempt at an abstract work, the String Quartet Fragment, 1903–4. A purely instrumental work followed (Op. 9), one with no known program, but one whose formal structure retained essential features of the programmatic works. With his next works, the Second Chamber Symphony and the String Quartet No. 2, Op. 10, it appeared at first that Schoenberg had finally broken away from his programmatic past and solidified his commitment to absolute music, even to the point of employing traditional forms. However, he was unable to sustain this step and had to backtrack: he added a vocal part to the String Quartet No. 2, Op. 10 and considered turning the Second Chamber Symphony into a programmatic work. Thus the Piano Pieces, Op. 11 represent a crucial stage in his compositional evolution: once again Schoenberg had tried his hand at abstract instrumental music, but this time he succeeded. And from this point forward, abstract instrumental works would comprise an essential (though never exclusive) part of his compositional output.

Schoenberg's turn to absolute music has also been important because of the increasingly privileged status of absolute music in twentieth-century aesthetics. As the century wore on, programmatic music fell further and further from favor while abstract music (and in particular, abstract music characterized by motivic unity) came to be prized as the optimum vehicle for artistic worth. Because of the transformation in aesthetic attitudes and because of their extraordinary motivic concision, the first two pieces of Op. 11 (and especially, Op. 11, No. 1) have become virtual icons of absolute music. Reprinted in popular anthologies and virtually obligatory material for any course on twentieth-century analysis, Op. 11, No. 1 has come to be seen as the epitome of what absolute music ought to be in the twentieth century.

Precisely because of that iconic status, there has been a considerable amount of interest in developing analytical tools that can explain the structure of this music. But just what are the most appropriate tools for this purpose and how should they be employed?

It is fair to say that for many, the answer to this question has been clear. A new theory, pitch-class set analysis, has been developed to explain the structure of this music and to serve as the basis for analysis.[9] Although there has been some criticism, there seems to have emerged a wide consensus that some version of this method is the most appropriate technique for the analysis of atonal music in general and Schoenberg's post-1908 music in particular.[10]

Pitch-class set analysis is primarily the product of Allen Forte and a devoted cadre of subsequent theorists whose work has been inspired by Forte's seminal ideas. In a series of highly influential articles and books, Forte and his supporters have argued that atonal pitch-class sets are the essential determinants of the structure of many twentieth-century works. Devotees of this analytical method believe that Schoenberg's post-1908 music is "atonal" and that (as Forte has argued) in Schoenberg's atonal compositions every note, without exception, is a member of at least one significant pitch-class set.

Pitch-class theory itself is beyond reproach: there can be no question but that it is well formed, consistent, and logical. For the music of some composers, particularly those who consciously compose with pitch-class sets (e.g. Robert Morris) it can be an indispensable analytical tool. But is pitch-class set analysis an appropriate tool for the understanding of the structure and organization of Schoenberg's works?

I have argued elsewhere that pitch-class set analysis – as preached and practiced by Allen Forte and many of his followers – is not an acceptable tool for the understanding of Schoenberg's works.[11] If we accept Forte's claim that every single note must be a member of at least one significant pitch-class set, then one or the other of two complementary flaws emerge, either one of which is fatal. If one identifies as significant analytical objects only those groups of notes that comprise coherent units on the musical surface, then there does not seem to be any rhyme or reason to the appearance of pitch-class sets. Instead of a carefully limited group of referential sets, there is an unmanageable proliferation of sets, one that displays all the hallmarks of random distribution. On the other hand, if one tries to limit the number of sets and to mark for attention only those groups of notes that produce a desired group of pitch-class sets, then one is forced into making completely arbitrary analytical decisions about what notes to include (or to exclude) as the components of those analytical objects.[12] One is obliged to draw amorphous and irrational shapes ("shmoon" as one wag, somewhat uncharitably, has called them) on the score in an attempt to include (or to avoid including) some pitches.[13] One can only decide which should be the members of the favored group of pitch-class sets by making unwarranted claims about Schoenberg's intentions. For all of these reasons, Forte's approach – including the modified linear approach he employed in his analysis of *Das Buch der hängenden Gärten* – must be rejected as of little or no use for Schoenberg's music.[14]

However, might not a somewhat less uncompromising version of pitch-class set analysis still be useful? Perhaps a version that does not insist that every single note must be a member of at least one significant pitch-class set? Or perhaps a version that concentrated on smaller sets such as trichords and tetrachords instead of the pentachords, hexachords, and heptachords favored by Forte? Wouldn't such a modified version allow us to avoid the two complementary flaws cited above? If pitch-class set analysis were used in this manner, it might yield results like those illustrated in an analysis of the first phrase of Op. 11, No. 1 (see Ex. 15.1).[15]

As can be seen in the example, two pitch-class sets make a significant number of appearances in these phrases: trichord 014 (Forte pc set 3–3) and tetrachord 0148 (Forte p-c set 4–19). In just the first phrase alone, the 014 trichord appears no fewer than four times while overlapping statements of 0148 saturate m. 3. Since these same pitch-class sets make numerous other appearances elsewhere in the piece, many would assert that this proves that pitch-class set analysis is a very useful technique for the explanation of the structure of this work (and others like it). Many would also argue that the presence of certain pitch-class sets as obvious surface entities in some places gives us the justification to regard as analytically significant other, considerably less explicit, instances of those same pitch-class sets. For example, one might not be inclined to consider as significant the 014 trichord that results from the intersection of the last two notes of

Example 15.1

the melody with the top note of the accompanying chord (F D-flat E) but the presence of so many other 014 trichords has led many analysts to feel justified in extracting this trichord as well. Therefore, because of the precision of its analytical observations and its ability to explain Schoenberg's music in terms that are entirely independent from tonal theory, pitch-class set analysis appears to have been accepted with a good deal of enthusiasm, even by some who might not accept Forte's broader claims.

Although I acknowledge its ability to identify and describe certain types of relationships with great precision, I have doubts about the value of limited pitch-class set analysis as the sole, or even the principal, analytical tool for Schoenberg's music. Limited pitch-class set analysis founders on many of the same grounds as does the more comprehensive version advocated by Forte. In some ways it is less successful. Forte's method at least accounts for every single note, working from the assumption that "Every pitch belongs to at least one significant set; there are no 'independent details' . . . Every detail, no matter how minute, is an integral part of the complete musical conception."[16] By contrast, limited pitch-class set analysis fails the test of comprehensiveness. It identifies some notes and figures as significant, but consigns many others to irrelevance, even when those figures constitute prominent events on the musical surface.

For example, in mm. 1–3, the most obvious division of the musical surface is into a melody accompanied by two chords. As we have seen, according to a limited pitch-class set analysis of this composition, 014 and 0148 are supposed to be significant sets. Therefore, we might pounce on the second chord (B-flat A D-flat) with a cry of "Eureka": it is a 014 trichord.

But what about the other chord (in m. 2)? Should we just ignore it because it is "merely" a 016 trichord (which we have not identified as a significant set)? Can we do this? Is this a legitimate method of analysis? We have two absolutely clear trichords that could not be more similar (in terms of rhythm, meter, duration, and function within the phrase). Yet we completely ignore one of them while we exalt the other to a privileged status.

Proponents of this method would undoubtedly argue that they are justified in exalting the 014 to a privileged status while consigning the 016 trichord to near-oblivion for the simple reason that the 014 trichord occurs more often. That is true: over the course of this movement one can find more clear and obvious instances of 014 trichords than one can find of 016 trichords.

But there is something highly suspect about this logic. If it were the case that 014 trichords were omnipresent (comparable, say, to the triad in tonal music), then, perhaps, one might be justified in raising the 014 to a privileged status. That is not the case; although there are a number of prominent occurrences of the 014 trichord, with the exception of one or two passages (notably, mm. 1–3 and 34–8), they do not come close to monopolizing the musical surface. Only a small minority of the clear trichords that do occur on the surface of the composition are 014 trichords. Thus it appears we are declaring a small minority of the work's chords to be important and most of the rest of the work to be irrelevant.

One might argue that the way to fix this problem is by expanding the arsenal of pitch-class sets we identify as important. Instead of dismissing the 016 as irrelevant, we might also include it as a significant set. Like the 014 trichord we could point to a number of places in the work where clear 016 trichords occur as prominent entities on the musical surface (e.g. the final chord in the r.h. in the last measure of the piece). Admittedly, there might not be quite as many 016s as there are 014s, but there are enough of them to constitute a significant class.

But aren't we now on the proverbial slippery slope? If we admit the 016 to our exclusive club of significant trichords, then why stop there? Why not the 024? It too occurs on occasion as a prominent chord (e.g. m. 8) and as a prominent linear succession (e.g. bass line, mm. 2–4). Or what about the 026 trichord? It is the final trichord of the accompaniment at the close of the first large section of the composition (m. 11) and occurs in a number of other locations. In no time at all, we will have raced all the way down the slippery slope, gathering up all twelve of the possible trichords along the way. (The results would be no different for tetrachords, pentachords, or hexachords.) In the end we would have more a pile of statistics than an analysis.

I am not suggesting that there never can be any value whatever in identifying pitch-class set equivalencies in a composition. With respect to the pitch-class sets identified in Ex. 15.1, I am not claiming that there is no possibility of a relationship between the chord in m. 3 and the first three notes in the melody in mm. 1–2. Where there are several obvious and coherent musical entities that are equivalent pitch-class sets, as is the case here, one may well be justified in *proposing* a connection between them (based on shared intervallic properties). One is not justified in assuming that one has, ipso facto, proved much of anything simply by asserting that two entities are the same pitch-class set (any more than one has proved anything about a tonal composition merely by claiming that a chord in, say, m. 3 is related to a chord in m. 100 simply because they are both triads). Nor is one justified in assuming that one has explained anything essential about a work by piling up massive lists of such instances. In other words, circling two pitch-class sets does not give one the justification to say "QED" because virtually nothing has been demonstrated. Perhaps a significant analytical observation could be demonstrated, but simply asserting equivalence is not enough.[17]

One of the reasons for this is the highly abstract nature of pitch-class set relationships. In our example, we have identified the first three melodic tones as being "equivalent" to the chord in m. 3, but when we say two groupings of tones are "equivalent" what we mean is that they can be reduced to the same normal order, a highly refined abstraction. It is possible that the actual appearance of the tones might so thoroughly disguise the equivalence as to make it virtually irrelevant.[18] To an extent, that is the case with this instance. In our example, it is true that the three pitch-classes of the opening melody (B G-sharp G) have been transposed up two semitones to yield the collection D-flat B-flat A, but this is not a transposition in the traditional sense of the word. Rather, it is a transposition only in the most abstract of senses: a transposition of pitch-classes (the addition, mod.12, of a constant to pitch-class numbers), and thus is a transposition that may or may not preserve order or contour. As a result, in their actual compositional realization, these equivalency relationships can be attenuated. One cannot claim that there is no possibility of a significant analytical relationship; that would be a significant overstatement. At the same time one is not justified in assuming, a priori, that the relationship is, of necessity, analytically significant.[19]

Another problem with pitch-class set analysis is that, by its very nature, it tends to stress one kind of equivalency (pitch-class set equivalence) at the expense of other relationships, even fairly strong motivic relationships. As we shall see in more detail shortly, in mm. 9–11, Schoenberg restates the principal melody from mm. 1–3 in a much-altered form. The motivic connections between the two passages are unmistakable. Yet from a pitch-class set analysis point of view there are few significant intersections between the pitch-class sets of these two melodic events (the first is hexachord 013457; the second hexachord 023468). This is not to say that pc-set analysis is incapable of addressing relationships between non-equivalent pc-sets. On the contrary, Forte and others have developed and employed extraordinarily sophisticated tools (e.g. z-relationships, inclusion and similarity relationships) to measure degrees of relatedness between non-equivalent pitch-class sets. Nevertheless, even though tools are available to clarify degrees of relatedness of non-equivalent sets, pc-set analysis is clearly most comfortable with the identification of equivalencies, hence the proliferation of "shmoon" in most pc-set analyses.

From the preceding, it should be clear that – at the very most, and then only if we recognize its limitations – we might use pitch-class set analysis as a tool to identify some potential motivic relationships. As such, it can have some value, particularly in identifying certain kinds of motivic connections. At the same time, we must not delude ourselves into believing that it can identify all possible motivic relationships. On the contrary, it tends to identify equivalence only in a very narrow sense of the word.

Rather than rely heavily on pitch-class set analysis, I prefer to emphasize the placement of this composition within the historical context from which it arose. That context included Schoenberg's relentless transformation and expansion of the language he had inherited. As we have seen, by 1909 that transformation was extensive: pure triads had all but disappeared, referential tonics had vanished, and dissonances did not resolve. Extensive though it was, Schoenberg's transformation of the language he had inherited was not total. Our analyses of Op. 11, No. 1 and similar works ought to reflect that reality.

Therefore, I propose to look in considerable analytical detail at Op. 11, No. 1 and to do so from a perspective that reflects both this music's origins in the past as well as its transformation of prior modes of musical thought.[20]

In his first attempts to compensate for the abandonment of programmatic structure, Schoenberg organized his music around traditional formal types: sonata, rondo, and song form. Ultimately, Schoenberg's turn to traditional forms proved to be a dead end: he found it very difficult to complete abstract works with traditional forms and as a result compositions like Opp. 10 and 38 teetered precariously at the edge of incompletion.

With Op. 11, Schoenberg begins a very successful period of writing abstract compositions. It cannot be happenstance that his breaking out of this stalemate coincides with the point where traditional formal types cease to appear in his abstract instrumental compositions: from this point forward (until the evolution of the twelve-tone method), traditional formal types vanish. This is not to say that those works are formless. On the contrary, particularly on the level of the phrase, it is usually quite clear how the surface divides into coherent musical units.[21] Nevertheless, it is a striking characteristic of the formal structure of this music that although it is easy to recognize contrasts and distinctions from phrase to phrase, those phrases do not readily coalesce into larger formal sections, united by shared characteristics.[22]

A contributing factor to the lack of clearly defined large-scale divisions is the intensity of the motivic structure. Continuing the trend we have been following in Schoenberg's music, Op. 11, No. 1 strives toward a type of motivic unity in which a few basic motivic ideas serve as the source for the entire work. It is no overstatement to assert that the predominant organizing principle of this work is its motivic structure.

Although the first movement of the String Quartet No. 2, Op. 10 had demonstrated Schoenberg's ability to construct an entire abstract movement from a limited arsenal of motives, in Op. 10, the motivic structure was not completely autonomous, but rather, functioned in tandem with sonata form. Even in the Op. 15 songs there were residual ties to traditional formal ideas in that the songs were settings of poems that often suggested traditional AA' or ABA' forms. In Op. 11, No. 1, the motivic processes achieve functional autonomy and become the guiding structural principle of the composition.[23] Instead of following a traditional formal design, the work's form evolves from the motivic structure as a succession of dialectical arguments, a continuous process of opposition and reconciliation.

Op. 11, No. 1 begins with a principal melodic line in mm. 1–3 ('A') that can be divided into two halves (see Ex. 15.2). The first half is the three-note motive, B, G-sharp, G. This three-note figure is properly treated as a distinct analytical object because the melody pauses on the G, breaking the previous consistency of durational values, and because the chord in the accompaniment interrupts the melody at this point. Let us designate the general motive type which this represents as 'a' and the specific appearance as a1. Very simply, 'a', at least in its original manifestation, might be thought of as a three-note motive which begins by descending through a small skip (three semitones) and continues in the same direction with a smaller interval (one semitone).

If we accept the notion that the opening three notes form a basic motive, then we should also recognize that the remainder of the principal melody in mm. 2–3 constitutes a varied repetition: a2. Beginning from A, the melody descends four semitones to F, repeats the F and then descends a semitone to E. The contour and final interval remain the same, while the opening

Example 15.2

interval (major third) expands the corresponding interval (minor third) from a1, and a new element, the repetition of the middle tone is added.[24]

As we have defined it, 'a' is sufficiently vague a description (essentially only a contour) and the potential operands so numerous that it would be possible to claim that any trichord that descends (or ascends) from the first note to the third, with the first interval larger (or smaller) than the final is an instance (or an inversion) of 'a'. If so, the claim of relationship between a1 and a2 might appear to be trivial. It is not; significantly, the changes from a1 to a2 are very nearly the minimum possible. The opening interval of the trichord, which had been three semitones in a1 is expanded by the minimum possible distance to four semitones. The closing interval, a descending semitone, is held fixed. This careful limitation on the pace of the transformations enhances the significance of the connections between the motives.

The statement of a1 in mm. 1–2 and its modified repetition, a2 in mm. 2–3 constitute only the most obvious motivic layer: there is also a secondary layer of motivic relationships that emerges at the joint between the two discrete statements of 'a'. Let us designate this general motivic type as 'b', and the specific three-note figure G-sharp, G, A, as b1. A general description of 'b' is a three-note motive that begins by descending through a small interval (in its first instance, one semitone), then reverses direction with a larger interval (two semitones). Again, this is little more than a generalized contour description.

Taken by itself, it might seem capricious to isolate 'b' as a distinct motivic entity. After all, this figure is extracted from the middle of the phrase, and there are no rhythmic, phrasing, or other features that seem to isolate it as a distinct, apprehensible, unit. What justifies the consideration of 'b' as a significant motive is not its initial appearance, which is moderately veiled, but the many different ways in which this motive returns. Instances of 'b' saturate the first few measures, involving almost every note. The next statement is immediate and overlapping: G, A, F (b2) is a modified, inverted, repetition of b1. Just as the opening interval of a1 is expanded to form a2, so too here, b2 follows from b1 by the process of interval expansion. At the same time, the alto voice in mm. 2–4 unfolds two overlapping statements of 'b': B, D-flat, C (b3); then C, B-flat, B (b4). The bass voice in mm. 2–4 presents another version of this idea, with a further expansion of the component intervals (b5). So too, the continuation of the top line in m. 4 yields yet another statement of 'b', overlapping the end of the first phrase and the second (b6), F, E, G.

Because of the extreme abstraction of these basic motivic types ('a' and 'b'), one might be justifiably skeptical of the significance of some of the motivic relationships detailed in the previous paragraph. For example, given the two-note figure F and E (at the end of the phrase that closes in m. 3), *any* subsequent note would create an instance of 'a', 'b', or (the soon-to-be described) 'c'. For example, if the two-note melody in m. 5 had descended by skip downward from E, rather than ascending (as it does) from E to G, we could also have described it as a version of 'a'. Similarly, had it ascended to any note from that E, it would still have been a version of 'b'. So too, if it stepped downward from the E by semitone, this would be an instance of 'c' (described below).

Although 'a', 'b', and 'c' are sufficiently abstract that essentially any trichord could be identified as one of these three types, it does not follow that all such identifications are trivial. Rather, the specific realization of these trichordal types is what endows them with contextual significance. For example, the instance of 'b' that overlaps the first and second phrases (F, E, G) might not be adjudged as particularly significant since any final note from F-sharp upward would yield some version of 'b'. But note the carefully controlled process that has led to this particular instance. The first statement (G-sharp, G, A) presents 'b' in the most compact representation possible (as do b3 and b4). The next, overlapping, statement of 'b' (b2: G, A, F) while holding in common two of the pitches from 'b', inverts its contour and expands both of the component intervals (1, 2 becomes 2, 4). In an environment of limited changes, b2 is a modestly ambitious step away from b1. Thus, it is important to understand that b6 plays the role of filling in the gap created by b2. Whereas b2 expanded both component intervals and expanded the second interval by more than the minimum, b6 returns to, and smoothes over, this relatively significant abruption. It returns to the original contour of b2, returns to the same opening interval (one semitone), and neatly splits the difference between their closing intervals (3 instead of 2 or 4). By repeating the E at the beginning of m. 4, b6 takes on the repeated note motive that had been part of b2 and a2. In a unique way, therefore, b6 synthesizes numerous prior strands of the development. This is a representative small-scale example of an approach that is taking on increasing importance for Schoenberg's compositional thought: leaps forward in the developmental process are explained or smoothed over by following events that fill in the gaps.

The thrice-stated five-note motive in the tenor voice (mm. 4–5, 6, 8) constitutes a new and apparently contrasting motivic idea ('B').[25] Although one must not ignore its differences with prior material, it is not entirely new in that it conflates several previous events (see Ex. 15.3).

Embedded within the linear succession are two overlapping, inverted statements of 'a': D, F-sharp, A (a3) and F-sharp, A, A-sharp (a4). The first

Example 15.3

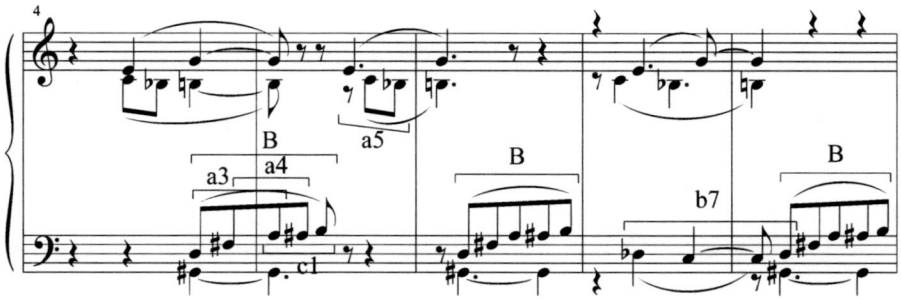

of these involves the most expanded version of 'a' we have yet encountered (+4, +3). Had it been stated directly after a1 (−3, −1), it might have been difficult to hear any plausible connection with that trichord other than (inverted) contour – a slender basis for a relationship. However, since there has been an orderly process of intervallic expansion, it is possible to hear a3 as a logical continuation of a process that began in mm. 1–2.

The closing trichord in the left-hand motive of mm. 4–5 introduces a new motivic type. Schoenberg takes the chromatic trichord (which had appeared in b1, b3, and b4) and restates it as an ascending chromatic scalar segment. I designate this reordering as 'c' and this specific instance as c1. Just as the opening melody in mm. 1–3 (A) combines 'a' and 'b,' so too, this five-note motive (B) combines 'a' and 'c'.

The polyphonic complex that appears first in mm. 4–5 is repeated twice more in mm. 5–8. Each time the complex is subjected to a number of variations, and these make a significant contribution to the continuing process of developmental variation.

At the end of m. 5, the opening duo between the top two voices is altered so that instead of starting together with the alto voice, the top voice begins first. This has the effect of producing a composite line E, C, B-flat, yet another version of 'a' (a5). There has been an orderly progression that has led us to this point. The motive 'a' first appears (a1) with the intervallic succession of −3, −1. In mm. 2–3 (a2) this becomes −4, −1. Finally, in the composite line in m. 5 (a5), it becomes −4, −2, an ordering that is to take on particular significance in the varied restatement of the principal melody in mm. 9–10. In the third statement of the polyphonic complex in m. 7, Schoenberg adds a prefix to the five-note motive in the tenor yielding yet another linear statement of 'b' (D-flat, C, D: b7).

In mm. 9–11, there is a varied restatement of the principal theme (A2, see Ex. 15.4). In the most simplistic of terms, we can hear this as a pitch/interval variation of mm. 1–3, since the rhythms and much of the basic

Example 15.4

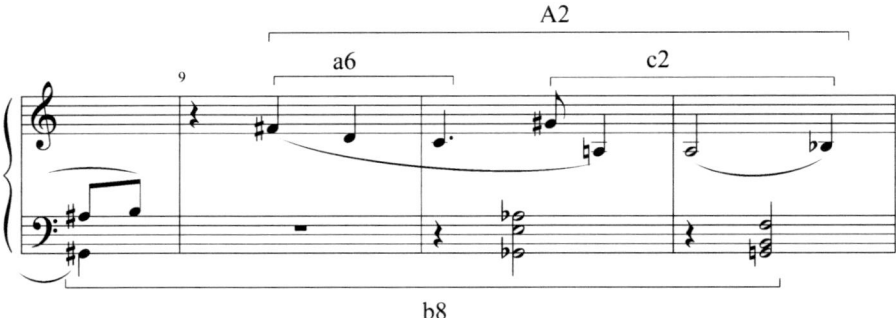

contour of mm. 1–3 have remained fixed. At the same time, the pitch choices reveal further stages in the ongoing development (and transformation) of the basic motives.

The opening trichord in mm. 9–10 presents the succession F-sharp, D, C – yet another statement of 'a' (a6). This has the same intervallic succession (−4, −2) that occurred in the composite line in the varied, second statement of the polyphonic complex at the end of m. 5 (a5). Thus, the first trichord in m. 9 combines the contour and rhythms of mm. 1–2 with the intervallic succession of m. 5.

This is also true for the second half of A2; once again the rhythms remain the same while the pitch succession changes. But this time there is a prominent disruption of contour, as the G-sharp in m. 10 seems oddly out of register. This too can be seen as a developmental synthesis of prior events.

The new pitch succession is, of course, none other than a version of 'c' (c2), the chromatic scalar segment derived from 'b'. At the same time, the dramatic dislocation in register recalls the registral placement of G-sharp as the lowest note of the three statements of the polyphonic complex in mm. 4–8. As in the first half of this phrase, so too here the specific content combines several different lines of development from earlier in the work. Also of significance, yet another version of 'b' (b8) unfolds slowly in the lowest voice in mm. 8–10 (G-sharp, G-flat, G), this time yielding the chromatic trichord.

In its totality, the varied restatement of the principal theme in mm. 9–11 conflates and combines all of the principal strands of the development from the previous measures. The changes made in the opening motives lead to other motivic ideas that vary dramatically in intervallic order, registral distribution, and rhythmic profile. And this is not the end of the process of development: the new patterns seen in mm. 9–11 are themselves transformed and in turn prompt subsequent lines of development.

Example 15.5

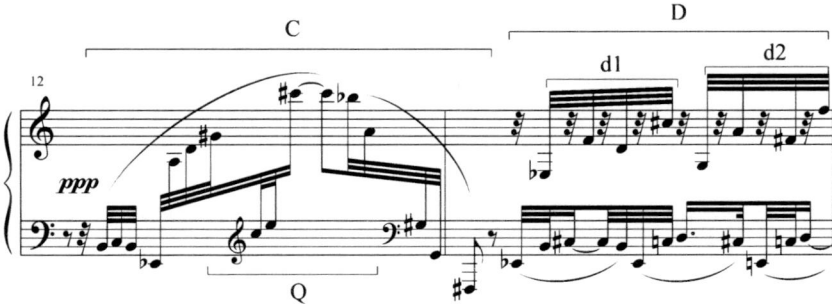

This brings us to m. 12, one of the most famous measures of music in all of Schoenberg's output and, arguably, in the twentieth century as well. In a sudden eruptive burst, everything changes. So much so that mm. 12–13 appear to be unlike anything we have heard so far in the composition (see Ex. 15.5).

This initiates a powerful dialectic. The work begins with eleven measures that are relatively homogeneous and that form a compact three-part form. The passage that follows (mm. 12–13) contrasts with the opening eleven measures in just about every meaningful way. However, Schoenberg does not allow this unmediated contrast to stand. As the work progresses, Schoenberg alters, develops, and eventually combines these contrasting ideas in a process that leads to the reconciliation of what had initially appeared to be incompatible ideas.

Measures 12 and 13 divide neatly into two distinct phrases. In the first of those ('C'), the texture has thinned out to one line, the dynamics have gone down to triple piano, the motion has increased to 32nd notes (the fastest previous rhythmic value was the eighth note), and the registral space has expanded in both directions. In addition, Schoenberg makes use of the one pitch class that had not appeared in the first eleven measures: E-flat, the lowest note in the piece to that point. Rhythmically, this first phrase divides clearly into two distinct, if asymmetrical, sub-phrases, the first pausing on the highest note thus far (C-sharp) while the second rockets downward to the lowest note thus far (F-sharp).

In the second phrase ('D', m. 13) we return to a multi-voice texture in which the lower voices all gradually (if irregularly) creep up by chromatic half-steps while the r.h. presents a new motivic idea ('d', a broken chord) which is immediately restated in transposition up four semitones. Here too, E-flat plays a prominent role, serving as the starting tone for both the left and right hand components of 'D'.

Example 15.6

In mm. 14–18, immediately after having stated the contrasting material, Schoenberg starts the process of returning to familiar material (see Ex. 15.6). At first, Schoenberg states a new motive ('e') a partially arpeggiated F A C-sharp E tetrachord, coloring the sound with an innovative piano harmonic.[26]

In between two statements of motive 'e' (in mm. 14 and 16) is a figure in the uppermost register.[27] When we hear this idea in m. 15, it might not immediately be apparent what its origins are. But by m. 17, it has become clear that there has been a process of return to a version of the 'A' theme and that the G-sharp/G (x) and F-sharp/D (y) figures were designed to recall moments in the first 11 measures where these pairs of pitch-classes had been associated with one another, i.e. m. 1–2 (G-sharp G) and m. 9 (F-sharp D).[28]

By making a gradual return to a version of the 'A' theme (one that is nearly, but not quite) identical to the version of mm. 9–10, Schoenberg has accomplished an important developmental step. With the return to a readily recognizable version of the opening material immediately after the presentation of the contrasting material, Schoenberg has outlined the approximate limits of the musical dialogue. Correspondingly, from this point forward the techniques of motivic development and transformation,

Example 15.7

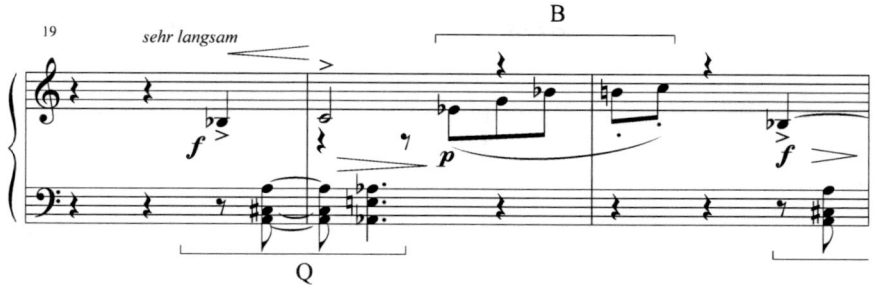

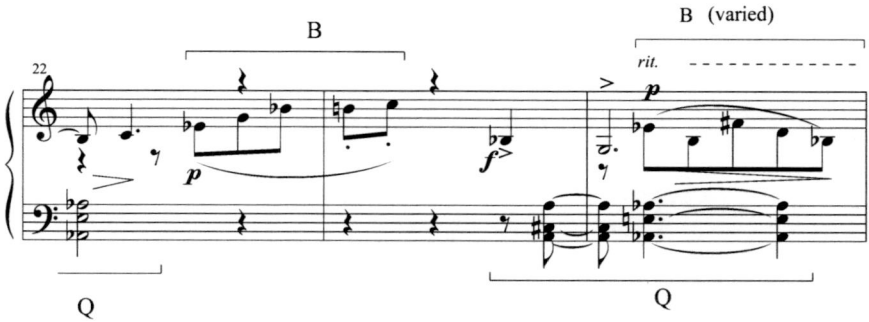

flexible though they may be, do not result in an endless succession of new motivic or thematic ideas. From m. 15 forward, almost everything can be recognized as a varied repetition or transformation of the ideas that surfaced in the opening fourteen measures of the composition.

Although the remainder of the work (with a few exceptions, e.g. mm. 40–1) holds fairly closely to the motivic and thematic ideas presented in the first 14 measures, Schoenberg does more than present a succession of varied versions of the ideas we have heard earlier in the composition. As the composition unfolds, Schoenberg starts to make associations between what had initially seemed to be irreconcilable motivic and thematic ideas, thereby resolving the tensions created by the seemingly incompatible material. We can see this process at work in the next section, mm. 19–24 (see Ex. 15.7).

The most obvious connection with prior events is the restatement, in transposition (up a semitone plus an octave), of theme 'B', the tenor line from mm. 4–8. It returns unaltered in interval succession and durational pattern. It even retains the threefold repetition (with variations) that had characterized the appearances of 'B' in the earlier passage: first statement, m. 20–1, second statement mm. 22–3; third statement m. 24. Also like the earlier passage, the first two statements are only slight variants of one another, while the third statement constitutes a more thoroughgoing transformation.

When the 'B' theme returns in mm. 20–4, it does so stripped of its original supporting voices. In mm. 4–8 'B' had appeared accompanied by, and in counterpoint to, a three-voice polyphonic complex. In mm. 19–24 that accompaniment/counterpoint does not return. In its place is something rather different: an accented two-note figure in the right hand, accompanied in syncopation by two chords (Q).

Although clearly quite different from the accompaniment/counterpoint in the earlier passage, there are a few points of intersection between 'Q' in mm. 19–24 and the accompanying voices in mm. 4–8. Most notable are some recurring pitch associations: in mm. 4–8 the alto voice had always begun with a C B-flat figure; in mm. 20–4, the first two statements of 'Q' begin with accented statements of this figure in retrograde. So too, just as G-sharp had functioned as the lowest sounding note in mm. 4–8, all three versions of 'Q' close on the very same G-sharp (enharmonically spelled as A-flat).

While these pitch associations (and of course the transposed restatements of 'B') do point to mm. 4–8 as an important source for mm. 19–24, the motivic origins of mm. 19–24 are not limited to mm. 4–8. 'C' is also an important source for mm. 19–24.

One of the most obvious of those connections is a straightforward and extensive pitch association. The pitch-class content of 'Q' is none other than a de-arpeggiation of an extended segment of 'C'. In m. 12, the six-note segment that starts with the seventh note of 'C' is G-sharp C E C-sharp B-flat A ('Q' in Ex. 15.5). In mm. 19–20 (and again in mm. 21–2), Schoenberg restates the content of 'Q' in reverse order and states them as (slightly broken) chords.

Another important connection between mm. 19–24 and m. 12 results from the transposition Schoenberg chooses for 'B'. By transposing 'B' up a semitone, the version of 'B' that occurs in mm. 19–24 has as its first and lowest note E-flat. As we have seen, E-flat was the only tone excluded from mm. 1–11 but was a highly prominent tone in m. 12 (both in 'C' and 'D').

The third statement of 'B' and its accompaniment 'Q' in mm. 23–4 differs markedly from their two immediate antecedents. The specific content of this variant has its origins, not in one, but in multiple prior passages. This is clearest with respect to its pitch-class content: the variant of 'B' in m. 24 has the pitch-class succession E-flat B F-sharp D B-flat. No prior passage had this precise collection of tones; this pentachord appears to unite prominent pitch-class associations from the two different transpositional levels of the 'B' theme. By changing 'Q' so that the second note of its top voice is G (and not C), Schoenberg outlines an augmented triad (G E-flat B, m. 24), and that specific augmented triad had been an important pitch-class subset in the two transposed statements of 'B' in mm. 20–1 and 22–3. By continuing to a completely different augmented triad (F-sharp D B-flat), Schoenberg points back to the three original statements of 'B' in mm. 4–8, where that trichord had been a subset.

Thus we see that the motivic material of mm. 19–24 is rooted equally strongly in mm. 4–8 and mm. 12–13. This illustrates a crucial aspect of the formal process: Schoenberg works toward a reconciliation of what had originally been two profoundly contrasting ideas. At their inception the ideas of mm. 4–8 and 12 had seemed mutually incompatible and apparently irreconcilable. That incompatibility created a formal tension – how could these contrasting elements coexist in the same piece? By drawing on motives from one and pitch-collections from the other, Schoenberg is revealing to us that common ground can be found.

It would be possible to continue from this point and demonstrate in detail how each subsequent passage in this piece reworks, transforms, and (frequently) combines or synthesizes its antecedents, all the while retaining clear thematic or motivic connections with the material presented in the first fourteen measures of the composition. I trust that this is unnecessary and that the developmental processes and techniques that I have described in detail for the first third of Op. 11, No. 1 are clear enough so that any interested reader could continue the analysis of the thematic/motivic structure to the end of the piece without my aid.

Before turning to the harmonic structure of this composition, however, it is necessary to comment briefly about one other important aspect of the thematic structure: the return of the opening themes (A and B) in m. 53 and part of theme C in m. 64, all at their original pitch levels. These returns are in keeping with what we have seen to be an important feature of Schoenberg's approach to form. We noted as early as *Pelleas und Melisande* that Schoenberg developed a method for imparting a sense of motion and return, even in the absence of referential tonal centers: the technique of statement, departure, and return. We also saw in the songs of Op. 15, that Schoenberg returned to that technique as a tool to effect formal closure in the absence of concluding triads. An identical process is at work in Op. 11, No. 1. The initial appearances of the A, B and C themes (mm. 1–3, 4–8, and 12, respectively) constitute the "statements"; the varied and transposed versions of A, B, and C in the middle of the composition are the "departures"; the return of A, B, and C at their original pitch levels in mm. 54–64 are the "return", thereby establishing closure.

The preceding analysis of the motivic structure of this work reveals a culmination of one important strand of Schoenberg's compositional thought: the drive toward organic motivic unity.[29] But does that unity extend to the harmonic dimension?

There has long been a powerful impetus to start the analysis of the harmonic structure of this work with a search for harmonies that are in some way equivalent to the pitch structures formed by the linear motives (all the more so given Schoenberg's later assertion that musical space is a unit).[30] If we do make such a search on that basis, we find that there are a number of prominent instances in this composition where the harmonies are straightforward verticalizations of collections of pitch-classes that appear elsewhere in linear form. For example, the opening three notes of the principal melody in mm. 1–2 are B G-sharp G (see Ex. 15.2, above). These same three pitch-classes form the sustained chord in the accompaniment in mm. 4–5 (see Ex. 15.3, above). Similarly, as we saw earlier, the pitch-class content of the two broken chords in mm. 19–20 (and again in mm. 21–2) is none other than a de-arpeggiation of a central segment of the line from m. 12 (see Q in Exx. 15.5 and 15.7). Still further is the famous passage in mm. 34ff where the principal melody unfolds simultaneously in three voices with the transpositions for those voices chosen so as to create a succession of 014 trichords, the very same trichord that makes up the opening three notes of the principal melody (see Ex. 15.8).

Perhaps equally famous is the last bar of the composition where the final simultaneity, E-flat A D G-sharp, is a de-arpeggiation of a prominent segment from m. 12: the tetrachord that began on the famous, not previously heard, E-flat (see Ex. 15.9 and compare with Ex. 15.5, above).

Although this is not an exhaustive listing of all of the harmonies in this piece that are equivalent (in terms of pitch-class sets or pitch-class content) to linear segments from elsewhere in the piece, the examples cited do

Example 15.8

Example 15.9

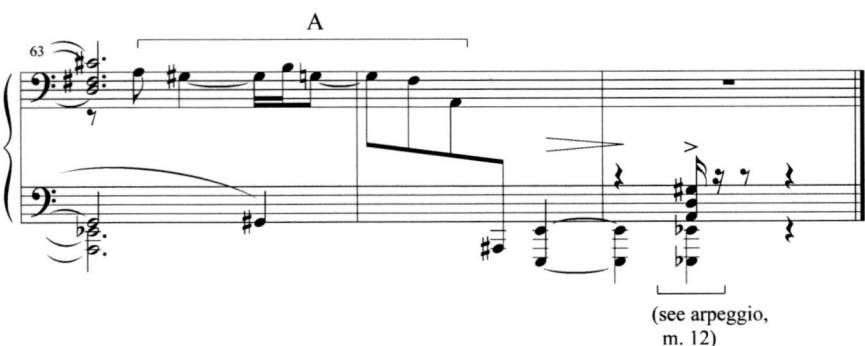

(see arpeggio, m. 12)

constitute a significant proportion of such instances, and thus enough examples have been cited to make two essential points. The first is that there are some significant one-to-one associations between the horizontal and vertical dimensions in this work. Without question an important aspect of the design is the explicit association between some linear segments and some harmonies.[31]

However, although some connections of this sort exist, it is not possible to say that those connections are anything close to pervasive. It is by no means possible to claim that all of the harmonies in this work are verticalizations of linear events. And that raises some interesting analytical questions.

Consider, for instance, the very first chord we hear, the trichord in the accompaniment in m. 2: B-flat F B (see Ex. 15.2, above). Given the undeniable connections between linear segments and chords elsewhere in this composition (as illustrated above), it might be natural for us to wonder whether this specific trichord (B-flat F B) or, at the very least, its general type (the 016 trichord) would occur elsewhere in the composition in prominent locations.

If those are our expectations, then we are destined to be disappointed. The specific trichord (B-flat F B) never occurs as any kind of coherent segment anywhere else in the composition: its first appearance (in m. 2) is also its last. And although a number of trichords of the same type (016) can be found, I am highly dubious that any one of them falls into a particularly strong relationship with the chord from m. 2.

Advocates of pitch-class set analysis, limited or otherwise, might argue that this last assertion is unsupportable. Their counterargument might go as follows: the chord in m. 2 is a 016 trichord; other explicit 016 trichords appear elsewhere in the piece; most analytical claims start from the identification of identities; ergo, there is an irrefutable basis for claiming an analytical connection between the chord in m. 2 and other passages in the composition.

This may be so, but as I argued in the opening section of this chapter, given the degree of abstraction in pitch-class sets, the identification of equivalencies does not, ipso facto, prove anything. We should approach any claims of analytical significance with respect to pitch-class set equivalency with a certain dose of skepticism. When we look at those 016 trichords that follow the 016 chord in m. 2, that skepticism should be intensified, not allayed.

After m. 2, the first time any 016 trichord occurs as anything approaching a distinct analytical object is in m. 12, the famous contrasting passage (see Ex. 15.5, above). In quick succession there are two overlapping 016 trichords. The first begins with the previously unused E-flat and includes the notes E-flat A D; the second trichord overlaps immediately: A D G-sharp.

Although these may be equivalent pitch-class sets, virtually nothing about the appearances of the 016 trichords in m. 12 recalls anything of the appearance of the equivalent trichord from m. 2. The pitch-class content, the registral distribution, and the texture are so different as to raise serious questions about any claim of relatedness.

Now we should be perfectly clear here. I am not stating that the two passages have no possible basis for a relationship. They do; one cannot deny the presence of equivalent pitch-class sets. The question is not whether a theoretical basis for an analytical relationship exists; the question is whether any other aspects of the musical surface support that relationship. The answer to that question is clearly a resounding "no". Moreover, the example I have used is in no way unusual: no subsequent 016 trichord relates any more convincingly to the accompanimental trichord of m. 2 than do the ones we have examined. Still further, the accompanimental trichord in m. 2 is far from the only sonority in the composition that seems to have no obvious connection with other events.

So where does that leave us? If we are wedded to pitch-class set analysis, we should be very troubled by what appears to be arbitrary or inconsistent procedures. On the one hand, some of the chords are clear de-arpeggiations of linear passages – of this there can be no doubt. On the other hand, many other harmonies cannot be explained in this manner.

But if we regard the chord in m. 2 and others like it in terms of its connection with Schoenberg's past procedures, then they are not problems at all. Rather, they are precisely what we should have expected to see in Schoenberg's music at this point and they should be understood (and appreciated) as such.

If we see the trichord in m. 2, not as separate from the principal melodic line, but as creating a harmony together with that melody (as has been the assumption in all Western music up to this point in history), then we should immediately recognize a clear kinship with chords Schoenberg has been using in other works from this period. This is an instance of an added-semitone harmony: a dominant ninth chord on G with an additional tone (G-flat), that falls into a semitone relationship with at least one of the other chord tones (in this case, two: G and F).

This chord is hardly exceptional. Added-semitone chords and other chords that contain traditionally dissonant intervals (particularly non-diatonic seventh chords, chords of fourths, and augmented triads) dominate the surface of this work, just as they have in all of Schoenberg's recent compositions. Perhaps the only real difference is the ongoing change in the relative proportions: a continued rise in the percentage of added-semitone sonorities and similar chords; a continued decline in the percentage of straightforward diatonic chords, including a near-total (but not total) eclipse of consonant triads.

Seen in this light, the other chord of the first phrase (in m. 3, see Ex. 15.2, above) is, not a different type, unrelated to the chord in m. 2, but a member of exactly the same family. If we take the entire sonority (melody and accompaniment) and not just the accompaniment, the resultant sonority at the point of attack (second beat of m. 3) is B-flat A D-flat F, another added-semitone tetrachord (an augmented triad on F with B-flat forming a semitone relationship with the A).

If we see the passage in m. 3 in the context of the evolution of Schoenberg's harmonic language, we should recognize many significant points of intersection with what has been characteristic of his pitch language. For example, after the harmony is formed on the second beat of m. 3, the principal line continues on to an E. In so doing, it creates a new harmony: B-flat, A D-flat and E. This too is an added-semitone tetrachord (an A major triad with the fourth tone, B-flat, forming a semitone relationship with A). This situates this passage as a logical extension of Schoenberg's treatment of harmonic and contrapuntal material from earlier in his career.

From virtually the first composition we examined, we saw that a characteristic feature of Schoenberg's language was a fabric in which there was a very quick-moving harmonic rhythm. Most often that rhythm was created not by changing all of the elements of a chord simultaneously, but by holding most of the chord tones fixed while one voice moved. In Schoenberg's earlier works, the motion in one voice would normally produce a fast-moving succession of seventh chords. Frequently, melodic segments in the moving voices might resemble traditional tones of elaboration (neighbor, passing tone, or suspension), but they did not function that way since, very early on, Schoenberg had effectively erased the distinction between chord tones and tones of elaboration.

What we see in m. 3 is a passage that is the clear continuation of that earlier practice. On the first beat of m. 2, Schoenberg states an F in the principal melody. On the second beat, while the F is held, Schoenberg adds a trichord that, together with the melodic tone, creates an added-semitone tetrachord. The F in the principal line takes on the rhythmic and melodic shape of a suspension, but as in Schoenberg's earlier music, this suspension figure does not act entirely like a traditional suspension. There is no resolution to a completely consonant sonority. As befits a cadence, Schoenberg closes the phrase with a slight reduction in dissonance (a major triad plus added semitone instead of an augmented triad plus added semitone). At the same time, there is something else, something that is pure Schoenberg: the motion from one chromatic harmony (an added-semitone chord) to a different, but related chromatic harmony (another added-semitone chord). The vocabulary may have changed dramatically in the decade since 1899, but many basic elements of the syntax remain.

If we understand Schoenberg's harmonic language in this work in these terms, we should also be able to see significant analytical relationships between chords that, in pitch-class set terms, may not be particularly closely related. For example, earlier we discussed the difficulties of finding any meaningful explanation for the 016 trichord in m. 2. If, instead of thinking of this as an isolated trichord, we see it (together with the melody tones) as forming two overlapping added-semitone tetrachords, then there are some obvious connections with other harmonies. The two tetrachords of m. 2 are highly similar to the two added-semitone tetrachords of m. 11 (G B F A and G B F B-flat). And this is highly suggestive from a formal/harmonic point of view: the opening and closing harmonies of the first eleven measures are based on similar added-semitone tetrachords that share multiple common tones (G B F).

When seen from this perspective, we discover an essential truth: the harmonic language of Op. 11, No. 1 does not constitute a complete break with the music of the past. Undeniably the differences in harmonic language between Op. 2 and Op. 11 are startling. But Schoenberg did not make that journey by one abrupt leap; he did so by a succession of transformative steps.

It is not only the harmony in Op. 11, No. 1 that retains identifiable connections with Schoenberg's prior practice. One prominent feature we noted in many of Schoenberg's previous works was the use of indeterminate scalar segments: lines that look like part of a scale (steps and half steps moving in a given direction), but are segments of no diatonic scale. In prior works Schoenberg also made extensive use of chromatic scale segments – one specific type of indeterminate scale.

It is a clear mark of the incremental nature of Schoenberg's evolution that even after the abandonment of referential tonal centers and even after the nearly total abandonment of triads, indeterminate scale segments, and particularly chromatic segments, remain a prominent feature. In Op. 11, No. 1, perhaps the most notable of those is the passage that occurs in mm. 34–8 (refer back to Ex. 15.8).

In the right hand is the restatement of 'A' with its broken 014 trichords supporting each note of the melody. The left hand is something else entirely. Beginning with the G in m. 35, there is a steady chromatic ascent up from G, ending on the D in m. 36. In the next phrase (mm. 37–8) Schoenberg does almost the same thing: this time ascending from C to A-flat.

This chromatic scale does not unfold in a single register. Rather, as he has done in prior works (although never as systematically as here), Schoenberg states the chromatic scale by alternating between a lower and upper register. This has the obvious consequence of creating two other indeterminate scale segments: whole tone scale segments in the different registers.

Looking at this passage from this perspective does more than simply highlight the clear connections of this passage to Schoenberg's prior stylistic practice. The disjunct scalar passage also plays an essential role in the dialectic process we saw to be central to the work's formal structure.

A striking aspect of the varied repetition of 'A' in mm. 9–11 (A2, Ex. 15.4, above) was the seeming misplacement of the G-sharp. Given that A2 began by following the contour of A1, up until we arrive on the G-sharp it had been possible to understand A2 as an interval-expansion variation of A1: B G-sharp in A1 (three semitone descent) had been answered by F-sharp D in A2 (four semitone descent) and the G-sharp G in A1 (one semitone descent) had been answered by D C in A2 (two semitone descent).

The G-sharp rather forcefully breaks that pattern. It almost sounds out of place, as if it is in the wrong register. This seems to be confirmed by what follows: the next two notes in the theme, A B-flat, return to the lower register, leaving G-sharp exposed at the upper extreme of the melody's register. With these last three notes, in effect what we have is another instance of a chromatic scale segment stated in multiple registers: G-sharp A B-flat. Following another octave displacement downward, this chromatic scale continues past the B-flat to the B and C in m. 12.

This extension of the chromatic line is somewhat veiled, given that it crosses over the phrase boundaries. We might not have accorded it too much significance had there been no further consequences. But there are. In m. 12, in the famous contrasting idea, the latent implications come into full force (Ex. 15.5, above). After reaching the highpoint on C-sharp, there is a straightforward chromatic scalar segment: B-flat A G-sharp G F-sharp – straightforward except that this five-tone chromatic scalar segment ranges over five octaves. When another version of this idea resurfaces in mm. 34–8, it does so as accompaniment to the triple statement of the A theme, thereby providing a clear example of Schoenberg's process of dialectical synthesis.

The use of indeterminate scalar segments is only one of many significant stylistic features that are clear holdovers from the earlier stages of Schoenberg's development. At the same time that the chromatic line unfolds in multiple registers in mm. 34–8 (Ex. 15.8), there is an important link with past practice in the right hand: the top two voices proceed in parallel major thirds.

This is none other than an example of the technique of localized consonance, a technique that has long been a central feature of Schoenberg's compositions. By Op. 11, No. 1, key centers are gone, consonant triads are gone (or thoroughly hidden), dissonances do not resolve to completely consonant sonorities, traditional harmonic progressions are absent, and diatonic collections have vanished. Extensive though these changes are, important residues of past practice remain: Schoenberg's continued use of parallel thirds is clear evidence of that.

This has significant implications for how we analyze this work. If we start from the premise that the parallel major thirds are meant to imply localized consonance (and therefore, relative stability), we will treat the passage in a significantly different manner than if we start from the premise that these are intervals made up of four semitones and part of a succession of 014 trichords.[32] Suffice it to say that the evidence amassed over the course of this book strongly suggests that the former would be more in line with the historical evolution of his style.

Another prominent feature of this work, one that ties it clearly to its immediate predecessors, is Schoenberg's tendency to establish local tones of referential emphasis.[33] In Op. 15, although there were no referential triads, Schoenberg gave some tones and sonorities more emphasis than others, returning to them at the beginnings or endings of phrases, or giving them agogic or metric emphasis. That is also a prominent aspect of the pitch language in Op. 11, No. 1.

In the first few phrases (mm. 1–11 see Exx. 15.2, 15.3, and 15.4, above), Schoenberg gives E, G, and B a degree of emphasis not matched by any other tones in the first eleven measures. B is the opening note in m. 1, the closing note in the tenor voice in mm. 5, 6, and 8, a component of the phrase-ending chord in m. 11, and the opening note of the contrasting idea in m. 12. G appears on the first downbeat (m. 2), is the ending tone in the soprano in the three mini-phrases in mm. 4–8, and is the bass note in the chord that brings the section to a close (m. 11). Finally, E is the goal tone of the first phrase (m. 3) and is extended through the threefold repetition in mm. 4, 5, and 7.

As was the case with Op. 15, Schoenberg uses a variety of techniques to give specific pitches emphasis: repetition, high point, low point, beginning of a phrase, ending of a phrase, durational or metrical emphasis, and accent. In part because of the ad hoc character of these techniques and Schoenberg's avoidance of their heavy-handed application, the emphases that he creates tend to be subtle. Notwithstanding the subtle nature of the emphases and in spite of the ad hoc method of their establishment, I do believe that the existence of local tones of referential emphasis is clear enough that different observers looking at the same passage should come to similar, even identical, conclusions as to what the most prominent notes would be.

Although specific pitches do receive local emphasis in this and other compositions, I think it would be (has been) a serious mistake to jump to the conclusion that there is a kind of tonality at work here.[34] That E receives agogic, repetition, metric, and phrase-ending emphasis must not prompt us to claim that this piece is 'in E' (or 'on E') or anything of the sort. To make such a claim is, I believe, to go beyond – far, far, beyond – what the music supports.

In compositions of any significant size in the eighteenth and nineteenth centuries, the initial referential tonal center was always displaced, if temporarily, by other (subsidiary) referential tonal centers. In Op. 11, No. 1 there is a similar process at work. Schoenberg moves from a region in mm. 1–11 with its emphases on E, G, and B, to a new area where completely different emphases appear. Beginning in m. 12, E-flat starts to come into focus as the contextually established tone of reference: when it first appears (m. 12) it is the lowest note thus far; E-flat is the first note in the new phrases beginning in m. 13 in both the right and left hands; E-flat (D-sharp) is the concluding note of those phrases in m. 14 and is given a strong *sf* accent; E-flat is the initial tone of a succession of phrases in mm. 20, 22, 24, and 25.

I am most emphatically not claiming that the piece has modulated to E-flat or is in E-flat or anything of the sort. I am merely arguing that by virtue of the emphases given to it – and comparable emphases are not given to any other tone – E-flat takes on a hierarchically superior status in comparison with the remaining pitch material. As such, this is analogous (but far from identical) to the idea of motion to a subsidiary key area in tonal music.

It is clear that Schoenberg has ideas for how to treat the interaction between the different, contextually established, referential tones, in a manner that is particularly apposite for his compositional language. As we discussed at length earlier, a central feature of the motivic structure of this work is its dialectical approach to the material. In some important ways, the differing contextual emphases contribute to that process.

In the first eleven measures, the principal tones of emphasis are E, G, and B. These are supplanted beginning in m. 12 by E-flat which is given an extended period of attention. In other words, in terms of its pitch hierarchies, as was the case with the motives, there is a dialectical opposition of material. Only at the end of the composition is there a synthesis. The final phrase of the composition joins these emphases together into a new structure (refer back to Ex. 15.9, above).

Beginning in the middle of m. 62, there is another version of the 'A' theme, this one with some significant permutations of order. This statement of A places the B as the highest tone and gives added agogic emphasis to the G, which is tied over into m. 63. The melody then makes a precipitous descent down to a much-extended E. In other words, all three principal tones of the opening eleven measures are put on prominent display here.

The return of these elements functions as more than just a reprise; rather this is part of the process of synthesis. Immediately following the E, the bass (in octaves for emphasis) steps down to E-flat supported, evanescently, with a chordal statement made up of three of the notes from the contrasting idea of m. 12. Thus, Schoenberg has created a synthesis of the contrasting emphases of the composition.[35]

Op. 11, No. 2 followed close on the heels of Op. 11, No. 1: Schoenberg began work on the second piece only three days after completing the first. As one might expect for two works that are so close in chronology, they share many significant features. Curiously though, they have had remarkably different reception histories. Op. 11, No. 1 has been the focus of many analyses and has been virtually a fixture in almost all discussions, theoretical or analytical, of Schoenberg's "free atonality". It has been a constant in one of the most widely used anthologies for analysis in the United States (Burkhart's *Anthology for Musical Analysis*), appearing in edition after edition. By contrast, Op. 11, No. 2 has received substantially less attention: there are significantly fewer published analyses, not only of the whole work but also, of excerpts from it.[36]

Perhaps some of the difference in attention can be ascribed to the fact that Op. 11, No. 2 is a bit more motivically diffuse than its more favored predecessor. Furthermore, there is no trichord or tetrachord in Op. 11, No. 2 that occurs with anything like the frequency of the 014 or the 0148 in the earlier piece. Finally, the connection with earlier pitch language is rather more explicit on the surface in Op. 11, No. 2: triads and other traditional elements are much less disguised in this work than they are in Op. 11, No. 1. All of these have combined to make a work that is a little less typical of what we have come to expect from Schoenberg from this period.

Having already subjected Op. 11, No. 1 to an extended and detailed analysis, I have no intention of trying my readers' patience by doing the same thing for Op. 11, No. 2. However, my decision to concentrate on Op. 11, No. 1 is not based on the belief that Op. 11, No. 2 is any less authentic an example of Schoenberg's pitch language from this period. On the contrary, the presence of so many traditional elements on the very surface of the work bolsters my claim that Schoenberg's pitch language in Op. 11, Nos. 1 and 2 represents not a break with, but rather an expansion and transformation of, the past.

16 "Intoxicated by the enthusiasm": Five Orchestral Pieces, Op. 16; Piece for Piano, Op. 11, No. 3, May–August 1909

> May I venture to say that, in my belief, even works of my third period, as, for example ... the *Five Orchestral Pieces*, Op. 16 ... are relatively easy to understand today.[1]

We come now to one of the most perplexing and mysterious junctures in Schoenberg's compositional career. In the span of only a few short days, a central aspect of Schoenberg's compositional language underwent a radical transformation, perhaps the most dramatic, abrupt, and far-reaching transformation of his entire career. Before this point Schoenberg's music had changed constantly and relentlessly, but always gradually. Not here. With little warning and with minimal precedent, Schoenberg went from writing intensely motivic music to writing music in which there were no repeated themes, no recurrent motives, and a complete avoidance of learned devices. This is an aesthetic transformation unlike anything else in his career. Is it really possible that the composer of Op. 16, No. 1 is the same as the composer of Op. 16, No. 5? Or that the composer of Op. 11, No. 1 is the same as Op. 11, No. 3? Or that these works were written in so brief a period?

Many years later (1949), Schoenberg recalled this stage of his career and even he acknowledged that particularly radical changes occurred during this period:

> Intoxicated by the enthusiasm of having freed music from the shackles of tonality, I had thought to find further liberty of expression. In fact, I myself and my pupils Anton von Webern and Alban Berg and even Alois Hába believed that now music could renounce motivic features and remain coherent and comprehensible nevertheless.[2]

Intoxicated? It would seem so. Comprehensible and coherent? Perhaps – but if so, this is a type of comprehensibility and coherence heretofore unknown in his works. In this chapter, we retrace Schoenberg's steps during this extraordinary transformation.

Over the years, Schoenberg's catalogue of compositions had gradually expanded to the point where it included a fairly wide variety of works that could be performed in a number of different venues. When Schoenberg began to compose the Five Orchestral Pieces, Op. 16 in 1909, he had available more than a dozen piano-accompanied songs, a programmatic string sextet, two string quartets (one with voice), a tone poem for orchestra, a chamber symphony, several pieces for solo piano, a composition for chorus, and a set of songs for voice with orchestra. As a result, he had a good chance of being able to provide a fairly broad spectrum of performers with compositions if they expressed interest in his works (unlike 1902 where he did not have a quartet he felt he could send the Rosé Quartet after their successful premiere of *Verklärte Nacht*).

Partly as a result of his expanding catalogue, by 1909 Schoenberg's public career as a composer was beginning to take off. Not only were there a growing number of performances of his works by a variety of distinguished performers, but also, for good or ill, his compositions were attracting an enormous amount of attention. It is fair to state that by 1909, Schoenberg was already a famous figure.

Notwithstanding this fame, Schoenberg was clearly frustrated with the difficulties he faced in getting his works performed. In May 1909 he was nearing 35 years of age – Mozart's age at his death. Although Schoenberg had written two works with orchestra (*Pelleas und Melisande*, Op. 5 and Six Songs, Op. 8), as of 1909 he had been able to arrange only a single performance of *Pelleas und Melisande*. Even that performance came to pass only through a (subsequently defunct) composers' society (one that he had co-founded), and at that, only when he himself had conducted. In other words, by 1909, seven years after having completed *Pelleas und Melisande*, the supposedly famous Arnold Schoenberg had not been able to find a single orchestra (established or otherwise) or a single conductor (ditto) who was willing to perform a single one of his works with orchestra, not even the Vienna Philharmonic, his hometown orchestra (a fact that would embitter him permanently against Vienna and its celebrated orchestra).

So what does a frustrated composer who has not been able to get his works performed do? Then – as now – an ambitious composer might try to use his or her connections. That is exactly what Schoenberg seems to have done. Given the fragmentary state of his correspondence from this period, we do not know how many colleagues Schoenberg wrote to with requests to consider his works for performances. The evidence that does exist suggests that Schoenberg tried very hard – sadly, mostly in vain – to convince various musicians to take on his works.[3]

One of those was Richard Strauss. From the time of his first period in Berlin (1902–3), Schoenberg had entertained hopes that Strauss would conduct his compositions. Despite repeated requests, however, Strauss would not to commit to performing Schoenberg's works. Strauss was very proper, very polite. He even addressed his letters to "Arnold Schönberg, Komponist" and he was clearly hesitant to reject Schoenberg's works out of hand.

In his desire to be polite, Strauss inadvertently may have prompted Schoenberg to embark on the project that became the Five Orchestral Pieces, Op. 16. In a letter dated 20 May 1908 Strauss, once again, rejected *Pelleas und Melisande*, telling Schoenberg that the programs for the winter of 1908/1909 were already finished and published. In effect, Strauss implied that he would not have programmed *Pelleas und Melisande*, even had he received the score earlier. (He could have scheduled it for the 1909/1910 season or for any subsequent season had he been interested.) Instead, Strauss went on to suggest another possibility: "However, I would be pleased if towards autumn you will send me a few (not too long) pieces to have a look at and would be very happy if I could find something among them which I could serve to the Berlin Opera House public, which unfortunately is madly conservative, without too great a risk."[4]

As of May 1908, Schoenberg had nothing of that sort to send. His catalogue had certainly expanded, but at that time it included no short orchestral works. (Nor did it then – or perhaps ever – include anything likely to find favor with a "madly conservative" public.) Strauss' letter also arrived at a very awkward time, making it highly unlikely that Schoenberg would be able to dash off a set of new orchestral works and get them to Strauss "towards autumn". In May 1908, Schoenberg had three major works on his desk in various stages of incompletion (four if one counts *Gurrelieder*): Opp. 10, 15, and 38. And (whether he was yet aware of its extent) he was on the brink of a catastrophic marital crisis. Therefore, there was no reasonable chance that he could immediately respond to Strauss' suggestion.

A year later, he could. The String Quartet No. 2, Op. 10 and *Das Buch der hängenden Gärten*, Op. 15 were now completed. The Chamber Symphony No. 2 was not, but Schoenberg had effectively abandoned the work, at least for the near term. And though terrible scars clearly remained, the marital crisis had abated.

Later in his career, it was common for Schoenberg to decide to write a particular composition because of a commission: for example, *Pierrot Lunaire*, the Fourth String Quartet, the String Trio, and the Prelude to the Genesis Suite. However, even as late as 1909, Schoenberg had not once been commissioned to write a composition. Instead, he seems to have begun specific compositions for one of three reasons: 1) he hoped to submit the composition to a competition (the *Gurrelieder* song-cycle, the Two Ballades, Op. 12, and possibly *Friede auf Erden*, Op. 13); 2) a performer had mentioned that they might be interested in performing a work for an ensemble for which Schoenberg had no works available, thereby stimulating Schoenberg to try to fill the breach (*Pelleas und Melisande*, String Quartet, Op. 7; possibly also the Chamber Symphony, Op. 9 and the

String Quartet No. 2, Op. 10); 3) Schoenberg simply decided to write a work but apparently had no specific performer or performance in mind (*Verklärte Nacht*, Six Orchestral Songs, Op. 8, most of the lieder).

Schoenberg's lack of success in finding performances of his two other works with orchestra has to have been something of a deterrent to his beginning yet another such work (or, for that matter, to completing *Gurrelieder*). Why would Schoenberg devote time and effort to a project that had no prospects for public performance? All of this suggests that it very well may have been Strauss' remark that prompted Schoenberg to embark on the project of Five Orchestral Pieces, Op. 16. Schoenberg clearly hoped that he might leapfrog past the hurdles in his path by having a major new work performed by one of the best-known conductors of the day, in Germany's capital city.

If those were Schoenberg's hopes, he was destined to be disappointed, and cruelly so. After he completed the first four of the five pieces, he sent a copy to Strauss, hoping to receive a commitment for a performance. In his letter, Schoenberg beseeched Strauss for help:

> So it comes about that I, now 35 years old, have only had one single orchestral performance!! You are the best person to understand what this means and you can see from this how thankful I would be if you were able to perform the pieces. You are also the person who could best risk taking somebody like myself under his protection. People in Europe believe in you, and even if you made a mistake it would not be taken too badly. Perhaps you can decide in my favour this time.[5]

On 2 September 1909, Strauss returned the score. His accompanying letter was not encouraging.

> Dear Herr Schoenberg!
> It is very painful for me to have to return your score without a promise of a performance. You know that I am glad to help and even have courage. But in terms of content and sound, your pieces are such daring experiments that for the present I dare not perform them before the more-than-conservative Berlin public. If you would take some well meant advice from me, then have a sympathetic conductor, perhaps Löwe or Nedbal, conduct the pieces in a couple of rehearsals, or even rent a good orchestra yourself for the same purpose in order to try out the pieces, for I fear that you will find no conductor who would, without further ado, take on the pieces for performance. Should you, as I heartily hope, find a publisher for the pieces, then I myself would try to ask a Berlin orchestra to play the works in a couple of rehearsals; unfortunately I cannot promise more than that at this time.
> With kind regards,
> Yours truly,
> Dr. Richard Strauss[6]

Even today (nearly a century after their composition) there are more than a few conductors who would hesitate before placing the Five Orchestral Pieces, Op. 16 on a concert program (and one has to wonder how many of them would agree with Schoenberg's assessment ca. 1948 that the pieces "are relatively easy to understand today"). Nevertheless, although the transformations in his musical language were already so extensive that they made even an erstwhile radical like Strauss flinch, the first four pieces retain many ties to the past. When we examine those compositions, we see both the clear connections with what came before as well as the chasm that separates them from what follows.

Op. 16, No. 1

In the Piano Pieces, Op. 11, Nos. 1 and 2, Schoenberg began to develop an approach to form that did not rely either on narrative programs or on traditional formal types. Op. 16 continues this trend; while they are anything but formless, the pieces are not based on traditional formal models. Rather, Schoenberg continues to work out forms that are tied closely to the motivic structure.

On its largest scale, Op. 16, No. 1 divides into two, asymmetrical sections, mm. 1–25 and mm. 26–128. The first section is expository in character, presenting virtually all of the motivic ideas that are to appear in the rest of the piece.[7] The second section is unified around a simple idea: an omnipresent trichord (D A C-sharp) that runs without pause, over which Schoenberg layers a succession of ostinati, punctuated by statements of versions of the themes and motives presented in the expository section.

In the first twenty-five measures Schoenberg presents an extended succession of contrasting thematic/motivic ideas (A, B, C, etc., see Ex. 16.1). Each of these ideas lasts for – at most – a few measures, and is quickly supplanted. Schoenberg differentiates these ideas from one another by register, texture, instrumentation, rhythm, intervallic succession, and harmonic structure. Usually, the different ideas are also separated from one another by rests (mm. 3–4, 6–7, 9–10, 19–20). Even where there are no separating rests (mm. 15, 22, 24), significant changes in other dimensions (register, motive, instrumentation) make the subdivisions clear.

Were a first-time listener to pause after hearing only the first twenty-five measures, he or she might be excused for wondering if this is to be a work of almost chaotic diversity. But Schoenberg has no intention of slipping into motivic anarchy. No less than in his preceding works, the motivic structure of Op. 16, No. 1 is tightly controlled: after m. 25 there are no new motivic ideas. Instead, the motives from the opening measures return constantly

Example 16.1

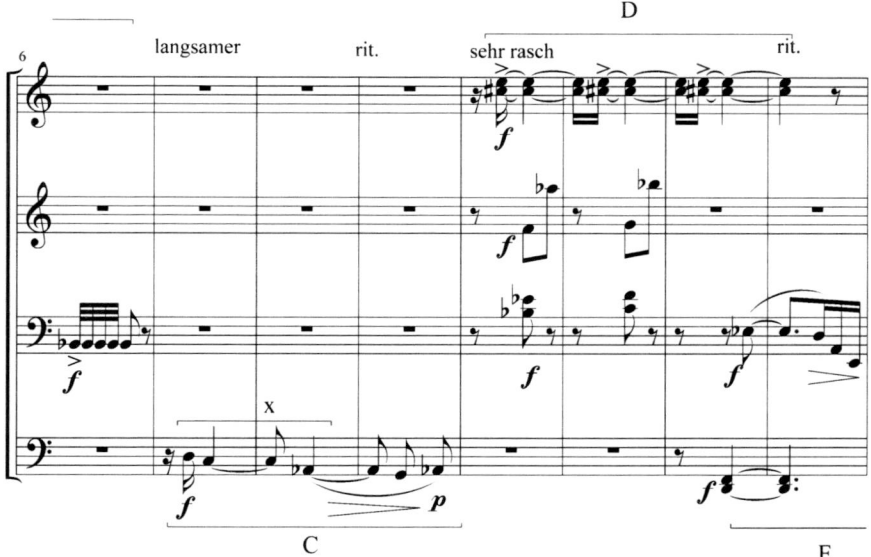

throughout the remainder of the work, usually in only slightly transformed versions. For example, in mm. 36–8, shortly after one of the ostinati has begun, Schoenberg brings back a version of the opening phrase (see Ex. 16.2).

This is far from an exact repetition; the uppermost line (oboes, clarinets) does retain the intervallic succession (in transposition) of the cello line

Example 16.1 (cont.)

in mm. 1–3 but much else has changed. Notwithstanding the many differences with the beginning phrase, no even slightly competent listener could miss the direct connection between mm. 1–3 and mm. 36–8.

As the work progresses, Schoenberg does vary and transform his motives, creating material whose relationship with earlier events might not be as obvious as in the passage we have just examined. In mm. 54–6, for instance, a brief passage in quarter notes occurs in the trumpets, doubled by xylophone, celesta, flute, and piccolo. In the trombones there is a line in longer values (see Ex. 16.3).

Example 16.2

Example 16.3

This is not really a new idea. Schoenberg has taken the first four notes of the principal line from mm. 1–3 (A), retained its contour, varied the intervallic succession (+1 +4 −1 becomes +2 +4 −1 in Trumpet I and +2 +3 −1 in Trombone III), and then presented the material in counterpoint (retaining the parallel fifths in the inner voices as well).

Furthermore, although the opening twenty-five measures may initially give the impression of motivic diversity, a closer examination reveals an intense process of motivic transformation within the opening section itself, right from the first measure. In the first phrase (mm. 1–3, refer back to Ex. 16.1), the principal line 'A' can be understood as consisting of a three-note motive (x1: E F A) with the intervallic succession +1 +4 that is followed immediately by an exact transposition of that motive (x2) up four semitones (G-sharp A C-sharp).[8] Inverted variants of this same motive appear simultaneously in the clarinets: in Clarinet I, the intervallic succession is −1 −3 (x3) and then −2 −1 (x5) while in Clarinet II it is −1 −3 (x4) followed by −1 −1 (x6).[9] Additional versions of x are embedded in many of the various themes and motives in the first twenty-five measures.[10]

There is a third strand in the polyphony of mm. 1–3, the running line of sixteenth notes in the contrabass clarinet and contrabassoon. We can understand this passage in two ways, both of which highlight the intensity of the motivic relationships in Op. 16, No. 1. This passage includes three variants of a descending motive ('y'), the last of which is abbreviated. Although the intervallic succession is different each time (y1: −1 −6 −2 −1 −4; y2: −2 −2 −1 −6 −1; y3: −1 −5 −2) there are obvious commonalities between the three statements. At the same time, it is possible to see embeddings of versions of 'x' within 'y'.

In m. 5, there is another four-note descending figure ('z') that, though not identical to any prior statement of 'y', has some important similarities. Similarly, the contrabass line in the third phrase ('C') has some similarities with the principal line of the first phrase ('A'), particularly the intervallic succession of the first four notes (−2 −4 −1) and the rhythm (like A it begins with an upbeat sixteenth followed by a more extended note).[11]

The point should be clear: Op. 16, No. 1 reflects Schoenberg's interest in constructing an abstract design in which there is a tightly interlocking web of motivic and thematic relationships. The movement restricts itself to an arsenal of ideas that are presented in the expository opening. Over the course of the movement, those ideas undergo a process of transformation and alternation. Within and between the apparently different motives are a network of transformational and developing variational relationships that bind the whole together as a coherent unit.

Related to the intensity of the motivic process is Schoenberg's extensive use of a sophisticated battery of traditional compositional devices and techniques. There is canonic imitation at the octave with diminution (m. 5), simultaneous statements of diminutions and augmentations (mm. 79ff), and stretto entries at the octave (mm. 87ff).

In other important dimensions, Op. 16, No. 1 also shows itself to be a logical continuation of its immediate predecessors. Like the preceding works, there are almost no pure triads or other diatonic chords on the surface. It follows that there is no referential tonic, no operative key. The chordal vocabulary and the melodic lines contain the same repertoire of chords present in other compositions from this period. The opening line in mm. 1–3 unfolds an augmented triad in the longer values (and the shorter as well). So too, Schoenberg still has a tendency to employ the principle of localized consonance as is evident from the frequent use of stable thirds or fifths between voices and the frequent embedding of triads or seventh chords as discrete segments within more complex sonorities. And although Schoenberg would soon claim that octaves should be avoided, they still occur.

All told, this piece is a logical follow-up to Op. 11, Nos. 1 and 2. There is no break with the past, but rather there is the continuing extension and transformation of material. No intoxication here.

Op. 16, No. 2

Schoenberg did not date many pages in either the working manuscript or the fair copy of Op. 16, but from the pages he did date, it appears that he wrote the five pieces in order and in relatively quick succession. He completed the first piece on 23 May 1909, finished its fair copy on 9 June 1909, and completed the fair copy of the second piece only six days later (15 June 1909). Given the close temporal proximity of the first two pieces, it is not surprising that they share so many common features.

Like the first piece, the form of the second does not conform to any traditional models, but like its immediate predecessor, it is anything but formless. On the largest scale, the movement divides neatly into a clear tripartite structure (mm. 1–22; 23–76; mm. 77–92).[12] The various themes and motives of the opening section (itself a tripartite form: mm. 1–9; 10–17; 18–22) give way to a significantly different arsenal of themes and motives in the second section. This contrast of ideas prompts Schoenberg, once again, to employ a kind of dialectic form. The final section of the piece is a reconciliation of what came before in that it includes both material from the opening section (thus contributing to the sense of closure) as well as from the contrasting middle section. In the final section of the work, Schoenberg first restates a version of the opening theme at the original pitch level (mm. 77–9; cf. mm. 1–3), then a version of the ostinato from the middle section (mm. 79–85; cf. mm. 47–55) over which he places a version of another of the themes from the opening section (mm. 81–5; cf. mm. 10ff).

Example 16.4

In many other dimensions, the first two movements show their close kinship. Like all of his prior abstract instrumental works, Schoenberg holds closely to a narrow range of thematic and motivic ideas, all of which are subjected to various transformations as the movement progresses. Not only are there a limited number of motives, but also, the motives themselves result from the application of the techniques of developing variation. For example, in the opening measures, the principal line (cello I) is structured so that its last two notes, G E (a2), are a transposition down a semitone of its first two notes, G-sharp F (a1), a relationship that is reinforced by the transposition of the supportive harmony (h1 and h2, see Ex. 16.4).

Like its immediate predecessors, the harmonic vocabulary of Op. 16, No. 2 does not include prominently exposed triads or diatonic seventh chords. Instead, it has the typical collection of chromatic chordal types from this period: added-semitone tetrachords and pentachords, chords of fourths (often with one of the component fourths augmented), as well as dense chords built by stacked thirds that include six or more tones. As has been typical for quite some time in Schoenberg's works, there is little or no intersection between the pitch-class content of adjacent chords. Therefore, there is a continuous circulation of the twelve tones of the chromatic. Also like its predecessor, Op. 16, No. 2 relies heavily on traditional contrapuntal devices: canonic imitations, fugal passages, and statements in inversion or augmentation. There are no referential triads (and effectively no isolated triads of any sort), but Schoenberg does not treat all tones alike. Much like his practice in Opp. 11 and 15, he gives emphasis to specific tones by using them comparatively more often as starting tones, ending tones, high points, low points, or by giving them agogic or dynamic emphasis. In the very first phrase, G-sharp and F function as both the beginning and ending tones. In the second phrase (mm. 4–8), F and A have a similar function. Schoenberg also continues to use octaves both as an essential interval between contrapuntal voices as well as reinforcement through orchestrational doubling at the registral extremes. Finally, as in the previous work (and similar to Op. 11, No. 2), ostinatos play a prominent role. No intoxication here, either.

Op. 16, No. 3

During the summer of 1909, it appears that Schoenberg had settled into a fairly stable compositional language, one that included a number of common features: intensive motivic relationships, the frequent use of imitation and other traditional compositional devices, a continuous circulation of the total chromatic, a highly chromatic chordal vocabulary (added-semitone tetrachords, pentachords, chords of fourths, and altered seventh and ninth chords), relatively simple (though not traditional) forms, the frequent use of ostinati, and the assignment of referential emphasis to a limited group of tones. Op. 16, No. 3, completed only days after the second piece (the fair copy is dated 1 July 1909), has many of these same features.

Like its two predecessors, it employs a fairly simple form, a ternary (mm. 1–11, 12–31, and 32–44) whose three sections are closely related. So too, the pitch language is highly chromatic with a steady circulation of all twelve tones. For example, even though the pace of harmonic rhythm in the first section (mm. 1–11) is extremely slow, and even though the musical surface is limited almost entirely to a succession of unadorned pentachords, Schoenberg still employs all twelve tones over the course of these measures. The chordal vocabulary is also similar to that of the first two pieces: added-semitone tetrachords, modified chords of fourths, and non-functional seventh and ninth chords, particularly ones with symmetrical subsets (e.g. the opening chord can be understood as a ninth chord in first inversion with a symmetrical trichordal subset). Though not in any key, Schoenberg treats the opening chord (C G-sharp B E A) as a kind of referential touchstone, returning to it at critical points in the form: as the first chord of the third section (m. 32) and as the closing chord of the piece.

However, the most prominent technical feature of the third piece is its extensive use of canons. In the first two pieces of Op. 16 there had been fairly widespread use of canonic imitation and other learned musical devices, but in neither of those pieces were those features the central

Example 16.5

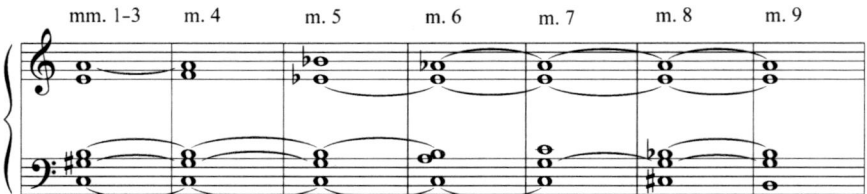

agent of the musical design. In Op. 16, No. 3, canons are the principal organizing feature of the work.[13] Schoenberg has shown his fealty to the great traditions of the past by devising highly sophisticated (though deceptively simple) canons (see Ex. 16.5).

In this example, I have reduced the score to its barest essentials, showing the pitch succession of the chain of five-voiced chords that extends through the first eleven measures. As such, the intervallic properties of the canon are easily identified. The work begins with a pentachord (C G-sharp B E A) whose five voices proceed according to a strict formula: each voice ascends a semitone and then descends two semitones. The resultant canon is simple, even simplistic. By itself, it might not appear to be a particularly sophisticated idea, but there is also an elegant rhythmic dimension to this canon. Schoenberg devises a systematic pattern for the ordering of the entries of voices. The alto is the first voice to move. As can be seen in the example, it begins by ascending a semitone in m. 4 (E to F) and then moves down a whole tone in the next measure (F to E-flat). The soprano follows. It begins its semitone ascent in m. 5, the ending point of the alto's three-note formula. Like the alto, the soprano also completes its pattern immediately, moving down a whole tone on the downbeat of the next measure (m. 6). The remaining three voices follow suit, thereby creating a kind of daisy chain: the end of the pattern in one voice is always the beginning of the next. When all five voices have completed their three-note pattern, the resultant chord (B G B-flat E-flat A-flat, m. 9) is a transposition down a semitone of the original chord.

A closely related canon governs the final section of the piece.[14] In m. 32, Schoenberg returns to the opening chord of the composition and initiates an inversion of the original canon: this time each voice descends a semitone and then ascends a whole tone. Correspondingly, when all five voices have completed their patterns, the resultant chord (C-sharp A C F B-flat, m. 38) is a semitone above its opening position. This canon utilizes the very same daisy chain pattern we saw in the opening canon: the end of the pattern in one voice is the jumping-off point for the next one.

Although the use of canons and other features (enumerated above) tie the third piece both to its two immediate predecessors as well as to a larger historical tradition, Op. 16, No. 3 hardly gives the impression that it was a conservative work. To a considerable degree that is due to its inimitable orchestration.

Within the span of each of the sustained, slow-moving chords, the instrumentation creates a constantly mutating palette of orchestral colors and timbres.[15] In *Harmonielehre*, Schoenberg coined the term "Klangfarbenmelodie" (tone color melody) to describe melodic progressions defined not by pitch but by timbre. Schoenberg drew an analogy between "pitch-melodies" where changes in pitch constitute the melody (the traditional definition of melody) and "timbre-melodies" where changes in timbre constitute the melody (a far less traditional definition). There has been considerable disagreement as to whether Op. 16, No. 3 is a realization of Schoenberg's idea of Klangfarbenmelodie, and it is by no means certain that Schoenberg was referring specifically (or only) to procedures employed in Op. 16, No. 3 when he used this term.[16] It is also possible that Schoenberg was referring to something else entirely, even harmonic progressions.[17]

Whether this passage does or does not constitute an instance of Klangfarbenmelodie, there can be no question that the sound world of Op. 16 startled contemporaneous listeners. Richard Strauss – an orchestral innovator if ever there was one – specifically mentioned the sonic qualities of Op. 16 when he returned the score stating that it was far too daring an experiment for him to consider programming in Berlin.

Innovative though its orchestration may be, this piece as a whole makes no abrupt break with the past. Everything else about the composition suggests a continued commitment to the evolution of tradition, not a break with it. Still no intoxication.

Op. 16, No. 4

In virtually all of its essential stylistic and compositional features, Op. 16, No. 4 strongly resembles its immediate predecessors. Like the preceding three pieces, the form of Op. 16, No. 4 is both relatively simple yet conforms to no classical model. The first section of the piece (approximately mm. 1–20 – there is no hard and fast division) presents a succession of apparently contrasting motivic ideas. The remainder of the work restates, combines, and transforms these ideas. Roughly speaking, then, one can thus speak of an expository opening and a developmental and synthesizing continuation.[18] Like the preceding pieces, the motivic structure of this piece is tightly organized. Like Op. 16, No. 1, the first impression is that there is great motivic diversity and contrast. But Schoenberg very quickly pulls in the reins, and there is virtually nothing after the first twenty measures or so that cannot be understood as a direct descendant of one of the motivic ideas from the expository section. Like the earlier movements, there are close motivic relationships between what at first appear to be contrasting thematic/motivic ideas. Also like its predecessors, its motivic ideas are subjected to a broad range of transformative procedures: intervals are widened and narrowed, motives are extended and shortened, contour is reversed, and rhythms are altered. Ideas that may not have seemed related at the beginning become related by the end of the piece.[19] We also see Schoenberg making ample use of traditional compositional devices: imitation, transposition, inversion, retrograde, and more. The harmonic vocabulary and syntax are also in line with that of the preceding pieces: chromatic seventh and ninth chords, chords of fourths (sometimes with at least one augmented fourth), added-semitone tetrachords and pentachords, and related sonorities.[20] As in his previous pieces, he tends to form adjacent chords from mutually exclusive pitch-class collections. Ergo (again like its predecessors), there is a constant circulation of the twelve tones.

Need I go on? In virtually every significant dimension, Op. 16, No. 4 shows an extraordinarily close familial resemblance to the other compositions of this period. Sobriety reigns.

Op. 11, No. 3

Schoenberg's next two pieces, Op. 11, No. 3 and Op. 16, No. 5 belong to a different artistic world. With no warning whatever, Schoenberg suddenly abandoned techniques that – up to this point – we had had every reason to believe were core aspects of his compositional approach. Nowhere else in his career is there as sudden and as striking a shift in compositional language as occurs after Schoenberg completed Op. 16, No. 4.

Although the chronology is not complete, enough information exists to give us a fairly clear idea of when this transformation took place (see Table 16.1). From his correspondence with Richard Strauss it is apparent that as late as July 1909, Schoenberg still had not decided precisely how many pieces were to be included in the Orchestral Pieces, Op. 16. In a letter of 14 July 1909, Schoenberg told Strauss that he had "written 3, a fourth one can be added in a few days at most and perhaps two or three more will come to life afterwards."[21] Schoenberg's estimate of when the fourth piece would be completed was exactly right: he finished the draft of Op. 16, No. 4 on

"Intoxicated by the enthusiasm": Five Orchestral Pieces

Table 16.1.

Date	
14 July 1909	Letter to Strauss; Schoenberg states that three pieces of Op. 16 are done and several more will follow.
17 July 1909	Schoenberg completes draft of Op. 16, No. 4.
18 July 1909	Schoenberg finishes the fair copy of Op. 16, No. 4.
28 July 1909	Schoenberg writes to Strauss and includes a copy of Op. 16, Nos. 1–4; tells Strauss a fifth and final piece is planned.
7 August 1909	Draft of Op. 11, No. 3 is completed.
11 August 1909	Fair copy of Op. 16, No. 5 is completed.

17 July 1909 and completed the fair copy the very next day, 18 July 1909. Ten days later, it appears that Schoenberg had finally decided upon a definitive overall plan for Op. 16. On 28 July 1909 he sent Strauss a copy of the first four pieces of Op. 16, and stated that a fifth and final piece was in the works. The exact point at which Schoenberg actually began writing Op. 16, No. 5 is unknown: he did not enter a date at the beginning of that piece. It is possible – even likely – that Schoenberg's next step was to turn briefly away from writing orchestral pieces to write another piece for piano. We do not know exactly when he began Op. 11, No. 3, but we do know that he completed it on 7 August 1909, three weeks to the day after completing the draft of Op. 16, No. 4 and a little more than a week after sending Strauss the first four pieces of Op. 16. At some point, Schoenberg turned back to Op. 16 and wrote the fifth piece. There is no date of completion on the draft of Op. 16, No. 5 itself, but Schoenberg did date the fair copy 11 August 1909, only four days after completing Op. 11, No. 3. Since we do not know exactly when he began Op. 11, No. 3 or Op. 16, No. 5, we have no way of knowing whether, or how, these two pieces overlapped.

Whether or not Op. 11, No. 3 precedes, follows, or overlaps with Op. 16, No. 5, the evidence suggests that the two works were written in close chronological proximity to one another. Since both of these works are equally representative of the extraordinary change in Schoenberg's music that took place so suddenly in August 1909, for practical reasons alone (the more manageable dimensions of the score), we will turn our attention to Op. 11, No. 3.

In our discussion of many of the works we have examined in this book, we have included a consideration of the work's form. If we try to do the same for Op. 11, No. 3, we quickly confront a succession of irresolvable problems. It is not just that the form of this piece is unconventional: each in their own way, the forms of almost all of Schoenberg's abstract works from this period are unconventional. The issue is even more basic. Simply put, there is no motivic basis for relating the various sections of the work to another. Consider the opening measures of the piece (Ex. 16.6).

The piece begins with a vigorous and densely polyphonic passage (mm. 1–2) in which the bass line, in octaves, and the alto line (beginning C-sharp D-sharp) take on leading roles. By m. 3, however, the original texture has changed. At the end of m. 2, the right hand launches into a new format and rhythm: a single line in thirty-second notes that includes a

Example 16.6

literal repetition (marked 'y'). The bass line also changes its character, though a little later than the right hand. In the first two measures the left hand had concentrated almost exclusively on a single rhythmic motive (marked 'x'); there are four instances of this motive in the first two measures. After completing the last of those (end of m. 2 to the downbeat of m. 3), the left hand turns mostly to block chords. Therefore, we have a solid basis for identifying two fairly distinct (though slightly overlapping) phrases: an opening phrase that closes on the downbeat of m. 3 (in the l.h.) and a subsequent phrase that begins on the upbeat to m. 3 (in the r.h.).

What happens in the first three measures is by no means exceptional: over the course of the rest of the piece we can similarly distinguish phrases from one another by contrasts in texture, rhythm, motive, register, dynamics, and articulation. That we are able to parse the surface of this piece into phrases is clear evidence both of the consistency of the content of the individual phrases as well as the clarity of the contrast between adjacent phrases.[22] The first phrase is a distinct entity not only because it concentrates on a limited group of motives, but also because those motives are distinctly different from those of the phrases on either side.

Well and good. Analyses of form often begin with the identification of a work's constituent phrases. But can we go beyond this first stage? At first it appears that we can: the first two phrases clearly function as part of a larger two-phrase entity. The overlap between the beginning of the second phrase in the r.h. and the conclusion of the first phrase in the l.h. ties the two phrases together. Although in most respects the first two phrases are contrasting, they do share a number of common elements. The chords in the middle stave in m. 1 ('p') have some clear similarities with the chords in the middle stave of m. 3 ('q'): they both have two trichords, both share a common rhythm, and both have a voice exchange in their outer voices. So too, the second trichord ('a') of the 'q' motive is identical to a trichord that

Example 16.7

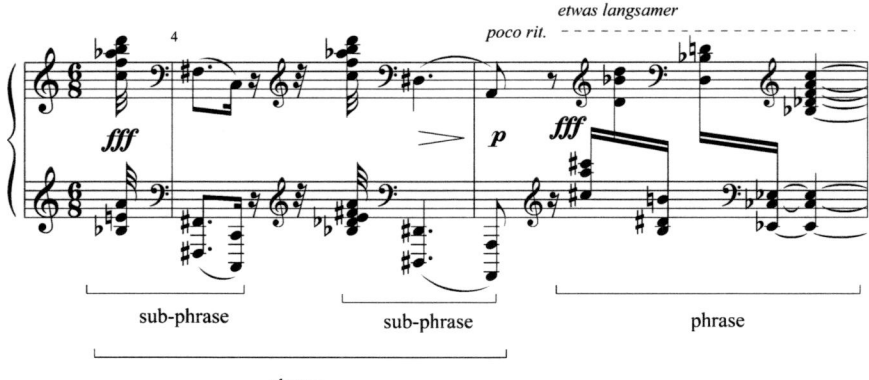

has already appeared twice: in m. 1 (third eighth, r.h.) and in m. 2 (fifth eighth note, middle stave).

We find similar relationships in the next section of the work (see Ex. 16.7). Much like the beginning three measures, we can readily parse the surface into phrases: this time there are four short, but clearly distinct mini-phrases (mm. 3–5, 5–6, 6–7, 7), the first of which itself subdivides into two sub-phrases. Each of the four has enough internal consistency to be considered a distinct and coherent entity. Each one also contrasts with the phrases on either side so as to be considered as separate from them, an impression that is reinforced by the rests and the changes in tempo.

Although the four phrases can clearly be distinguished from one another, a case can also be made that they join together to form a larger section. All of them have an overall contour that descends markedly from the highpoint which (with one exception) is always at the beginning of the phrase. All of them have a simple texture with one active part. With the exception of the first pair, all of the phrases feature regular rhythms. Therefore, there is a solid basis on which to consider mm. 4–7 a coherent unit. In turn, that means that the first seven measures of the work fall into two clear, and mutually contrasting, sections: mm. 1–3 and mm. 4–7.

In several of the earlier pieces of Op. 16 (notably 1 and 4) Schoenberg also had begun by presenting a succession of contrasting musical ideas. Sometimes the succession of new ideas was so long as to give an initial (but short lived) appearance of motivic anarchy. In those works, however, the introduction of new ideas had a clear limit: after approximately a quarter of the work had elapsed, no new material appears; instead, all prominent material from that point forward can be understood as a restatement, variation, or transformation of material from the beginning of the piece.

What sets Op. 11, No. 3 so totally apart from its predecessors is its lack of any return to prior material. Instead of placing a limit on the expository section, Schoenberg continues on to more phrases or groups of phrases that introduce still more new ideas. The opening ideas do not give way temporarily to other ideas; they give way permanently to those ideas, which – in turn – have their own fleeting moment on center stage only to disappear forever.

Nothing like this had ever occurred in Schoenberg's music. Although there had been a wide variety of approaches to theme and motive in Schoenberg's previous works, every single piece before Op. 11, No. 3 (including the programmatic works) treated motivic return (or at least varied return) as a sine qua non of musical structure. Although organicism was not present from the beginning of his career, Schoenberg had never done anything remotely like what he does in Op. 11, No. 3 or in the compositions that were to follow over the course of the next few years. By any measure, his sudden abandonment of the principle of motivic return is as surprising as it is unprecedented.

Only eight years later (1917) Schoenberg would write that the "artistic exploitation of *coherence* aims at *comprehensibility*" and that "coherence is based on repetition".[23] He made it clear that coherence, comprehensibility, and repetition were indispensable components of musical thought. The compositions after 1917 and before August 1909 are consistent with that aesthetic stance. Clearly, however, Op. 11, No. 3 and the other works that follow do not subscribe to those core aesthetic principles.

Something else of great import is also missing from Op. 11, No. 3 and the pieces to follow. At the beginning of his career, Schoenberg had showed very little interest in absolute music. Rather, he cultivated two types of genres with word/tone relationships: vocal music (primarily songs) and programmatic music. Beginning with the String Quartet, Op. 7, Schoenberg turned his attention increasingly to absolute music. When he did so – and even in a hybrid work like Op. 7 – there was a clear emphasis on the traditional techniques of compositional artifice: canons, inversions, imitation, augmentation, diminution, and invertible counterpoint at the octave. From that point forward, learned techniques were always present in Schoenberg's abstract works. So much so that it is fair to state that in the first two pieces of Op. 11 and the first four pieces of Op. 16, traditional compositional devices played absolutely central roles in the structure of the respective works. In Op. 11, No. 3, however, those devices vanish, utterly and completely, not only between phrases (as would necessarily be the case given the lack of thematic/motivic return) but even within phrases.

The contrast is stunning. In a matter of days and with no apparent transition Schoenberg has gone from writing motivically concise compositions that were filled with traditional compositional devices, to works in which these features were completely absent. Never – before or since – did two adjacent works of Schoenberg demonstrate such a stark contrast in compositional approach.

This is not to say that there are no areas of stylistic common ground between Op. 11, No. 3 and its immediate predecessors. In terms of its chord vocabulary (the typical array of non-functional sevenths and ninths, added-semitone tetrachords and pentachords, and chords of fourths), its intense chromaticism (adjacent sonorities generally have no or few tones in common, leading to the circulation of all, or nearly all, the twelve tones within phrases), its continued use of the principle of localized consonance (e.g. parallel thirds, as in m. 1, r.h.), its use of indeterminate scales (e.g. m. 21), its avoidance of simple triads (and thus referential tonal centers), its use of octaves, and many other features, Op. 11, No. 3 is an obvious and direct descendant of its predecessors.

In short, in almost every way Op. 11, No. 3 appears to be exactly what we should have expected from a composer who for at least a decade had treated the principle of incremental innovation as a byword. With two exceptions, everything conforms neatly to the pattern of evolution that has been characteristic of Schoenberg's works throughout the period covered by this book. But those two exceptions – the abrupt and simultaneous abandonment of motivic return and traditional compositional devices – create a contrast that is astonishing.

What happened? What could possibly have brought about such an abrupt tergiversation, such a complete abandonment of what had been his core artistic principles?

The record is very nearly silent. In his writings, Schoenberg barely discusses this change at all and with the exception of the quotation cited at the beginning of this chapter, never gave a reason for his sudden abandonment of motives and traditional compositional devices. His surviving letters give us no clue. It seems unlikely that there were personal reasons for this change. His marriage, however wounded, had been salvaged. There are no known disturbing professional events (such as controversial concerts with scabrous reviews) in the period between the completion of Op. 16, No. 4 and the beginning of Op. 11, No. 3 that might have prompted Schoenberg to undertake a change in direction. And Strauss had not yet written back with his rejection of the first four pieces.

Given the absence of hard evidence, the impetus for Schoenberg's sudden change in artistic direction may never be known with utter certainty. However, I believe a fairly strong circumstantial case can be built for what might have prompted this sea change in aesthetic attitudes.

It is telling that when Schoenberg looked back at this period of "intoxication" he mentions his students, Berg, Webern, and Hába, suggesting that all three played a role in the origins of this radical new concept of coherence. But Schoenberg's memory was at least partially faulty, because Hába cannot have played any role in these events, at least in 1909. In 1909 Alois Hába was only sixteen years old and was in school at the teachers' training institute of Kromeriz where he remained until 1912. Berg is also likely to have played little or no role in this aesthetic transformation. As of 1909, Berg's works were still noticeably more traditional than Schoenberg's. In 1908, Berg's most recently completed work was the Piano Sonata, Op. 1, a work that may have been considered radical in many circles, but by comparison with Schoenberg's virtually contemporaneous Pieces for Piano, Op. 11, Nos. 1 and 2, did not constitute a challenge for the leadership of the Viennese modernist movement.

Anton Webern is another story. Webern began studying with Schoenberg in 1904 and by 1908 had finished his formal studies. The last two works he wrote under Schoenberg's direct supervision were the Passacaglia, Op. 1 and *Entflieht auf leichten Kähnen*, Op. 2, both completed in 1908. Neither of these works would have threatened Schoenberg's position as the leader of the modernist movement. But Webern's works quickly became much more radical: in some of his George songs from 1908–9 (ten of which eventually appeared as Opp. 3 and 4) Webern had abandoned key signatures and referential tonics. Nevertheless, Schoenberg's own George songs (Op. 15) were at least as radical and from what we know of the chronology preceded Webern's.

That is not the case with Webern's next important work. During the spring of 1909, Webern wrote his Five Pieces for String Quartet, Op. 5. In terms of their harmonic language, dynamic range, formal freedom, and exploitation of instrumental color, these pieces were at least as radical as anything Schoenberg had done to date. If one were inclined to think in these terms (and it is crystal clear that both Webern and Schoenberg were inclined to think in precisely these terms) the stunning brevity of these works – the second piece is only thirteen measures long – could have led to the conclusion that it was Webern, and not Schoenberg, who should be regarded as the most radical of the radicals. Although Schoenberg's works had become steadily shorter ever since his abandonment of programmatic forms, his compositions to date could not compare to the shorter-than-aphoristic length of the five pieces of Webern's Op. 5.

Could Schoenberg have been concerned that Webern was about to supplant him as the leader of the avant-garde?[24] Did he worry that his position was about to be challenged by a former student?[25]

Although concerns of this sort may seem meaningless to us, it is clear that Schoenberg and Webern cared very about issues like priority and the leadership of the avant-garde. There is ample evidence that there was considerable rivalry between Schoenberg and Webern about precisely this issue. Although Webern was almost pathologically dependent on Schoenberg (to the point of failing to hold onto jobs because they took him away from his master), he continually sought to surge ahead as the leader of the avant-garde, often to Schoenberg's annoyance and anger. As a result, there are a number of places in his writings where Schoenberg sparred with Webern about who did what first. Schoenberg even revisited the events of the summer of 1909 and attempted to claim priority for the composition of small forms. In the earliest such comment, in an essay revealingly entitled "The Young and I" (1923) Schoenberg even claimed to be the inventor of the tiny musical form: "To most of them I am an architect – a drawer of bold (if old-fashioned) bows – even though it was the small form which I was the first to compose in our time."[26]

A decade later (1932), Schoenberg wrote a collection of fragmentary notes entitled "Priority". Although he was mostly concerned to establish that he and not Hauer was the inventor of twelve-tone music, he also had a bone to pick with Webern:

> Cowell told me about Webern, went into raptures about him, and said that he had seen things from the year 1907 that were supposedly already very interesting. (Why? Webern must have shown these to him specifically, for they are not among what is published; he is therefore still conducting this underground battle of falsehoods against me!) I have long since established that Webern must have simply backdated these compositions. At that time, every person in our circle knew this series of events: how Webern was breathing down my neck, and scarcely after I had written a piece he wrote a similar one; how he carried out ideas, plans, and intentions that I had

expressed in order to get ahead of me! I can hardly believe anymore that he can in good faith start up once again with this lie.[27]

Similarly, in 1951, upon hearing that Webern had claimed to be the originator of Klangfarbenmelodie, Schoenberg fumed:

> Anyone who knows me at all knows that this is not true. It is known that I should not have hesitated to name Webern, had his music stimulated me to invent this expression. One thing is certain: even had it been Webern's idea, he would not have told it to me. He kept secret everything "new" he had tried in his compositions. I, on the other hand, immediately and exhaustively explained to him each of my new ideas (with the exception of the method of composition with twelve tones – that I long kept secret, because, as I said to Erwin Stein, Webern immediately uses everything I do, plan or say, so that – I remember my words – "By now I haven't the slightest idea who I am."[28]

Schoenberg then goes on to focus in on precisely the period in question and raises the issue of who really had priority in the composition of extremely short compositions:

> On each of these occasions I then had the pleasure of finding him highly enthusiastic, but failed to realize that he would write music of this kind sooner than I would.
>
> It was like that when I had just completed the first two of the Three Piano Pieces, Op. 11. I showed him them and told him that I was planning a cycle (which I never wrote), among which would be a very short piece, consisting of only a few chords. This he found surprising, and it was obviously the cause of his extremely short compositions.[29]

From all of this the following is clear: we have a possible impetus (a radical new work by Webern), a plausible motivation (rivalry for the leadership of the avant-garde and credit for priority of innovations), and a feasible chronology (Webern's Op. 5 precedes Op. 11, No. 3). But is there any evidence that Schoenberg was aware of the radical character of Webern's Op. 5 before he began to compose his own Op. 11, No. 3? Is it possible that he could have seen this new work after he wrote Op. 16, No. 4 but before he wrote Op. 11, No. 3 and that it was Webern's work that was the impetus for his sudden change of aesthetic direction?

We do know that before he began Op. 11, No. 3 Schoenberg was aware that Webern had completed a string quartet. On 16 June 1909, Webern wrote to Schoenberg from his father's country estate, Preglhof, telling his former teacher that he had completed a string quartet. Webern even told Schoenberg that the movements were very short ("Die Saetze sind alle kurz"). He even offered to send Schoenberg a copy of the score ("Wenn ich Sie noch lange nicht sehen kann, dann moechte ich Ihnen gern mein Quartett schicken").

But did he? Did Webern send Schoenberg the score of the Five Pieces for String Quartet, Op. 5 and did Schoenberg see it before he began work on the Piece for Piano, Op. 11, No. 3 or the Piece for Orchestra, Op. 16, No. 5? Some evidence has come to light which suggests that it is very likely that Schoenberg did see Webern's quartet at just the time in question.

In July 1909, Webern was suddenly called to Innsbruck to take a job as an emergency replacement assistant conductor for a theater. Upon arriving in Innsbruck he found that he hated the work, hated the repertoire, and hated his superior. After writing a desperate letter to Schoenberg on 25 July 1909, he precipitously quit the job – an irresponsible action that would haunt him for the rest of his career – and went running home to his father's estate at Preglhof. From there he wrote Schoenberg again on 28 July 1909, telling him what he had just done.

Webern's next letter to Schoenberg is not until 20 August 1909, and it was not clear what Webern did or where he was during the intervening weeks. Did he simply remain at his father's estate? But if so, why didn't he write Schoenberg again, particularly given the emotional upheavals he was going through?

A simple postcard shows that by 31 July 1909 Webern had gone to Steinakirchen. The evidence is a postcard of that date to Alban Berg from Max Oppenheimer mailed from Steinakirchen (Österreichische Nationalbibliothek, Musiksammlung, Fonds 21 Berg) and it is co-signed by none other than Anton Webern.

This demonstrates that Webern was in Steinakirchen at exactly the right time. And it is difficult to imagine that he made the journey – or should one say pilgrimage? – to Steinakirchen without taking his new string quartet along. It should be remembered that in his letter of 16 June 1909 Webern had said that he wanted to send Schoenberg a copy of the quartet, if he would not see him for some time. Since it is now known that Webern visited Schoenberg in late July/early August 1909, he did have the opportunity to show Schoenberg the quartet.

It is clear, therefore, that Webern's arrival, undoubtedly with the string quartet in hand, happened only days before Schoenberg wrote an impassioned and poetic letter to Busoni, a letter that provides a good description, not of Schoenberg's works, but a spectacularly accurate description of many details of Webern's Op. 5. A phrase from Schoenberg's letter to Busoni captures the essence of what Schoenberg would draw from Webern: "My music must be *brief*. Concise! In two notes: not built, but 'expressed'." This is not a description of anything that Schoenberg had written (at least, not yet), but it is a very good description of Webern's Op. 5.

Given this background, can it be coincidental that only days after these events, Schoenberg began writing compositions that made a dramatic break with his own past? With no apparent warning Schoenberg abandoned motivic repetition, motivically based form, and learned compositional devices.[30]

There may have been no warning, but the chronology of events suggests that there was a powerful motivation for this sudden turn of events. If Webern had brought his new quartet with him when he went to Steinakirchen in early August, Schoenberg would immediately have realized its implications – suddenly he was facing an aggressive challenge to his leadership of the avant-garde. There can be little doubt but that it was this sudden and unexpected confrontation that was the proximate cause for Schoenberg's sudden breaking free of ties to the past and the sudden radicalization of his music. We might like to think that important decisions regarding aesthetic direction and philosophy are made with calm deliberation. The evidence suggests that Schoenberg's sudden turn to athematicism may have resulted less from careful reflection than from a sudden burst of emotion sparked by a former student's unexpected challenge to Schoenberg's leadership of the modernist movement.

In his remarks of 1949, Schoenberg stated that in 1909 he had "believed that now music could renounce motivic features and remain coherent and comprehensible nevertheless." By stating this in the past tense, he implied that in 1949 he was no longer really sure that this was possible. Small wonder; in 1949 he had been a twelve-tone composer for nearly thirty years and was scarcely going to suggest that the renunciation of motivic features was a desirable state of affairs. By contrast, in 1909 it is clear that he did believe he could write coherent compositions even in the absence of motives. But what could he possibly have meant? How can there be coherence without some form of repetition?

In Op. 11, No. 3, I believe that Schoenberg attempted to foster coherence through two types of associations. The first of these is an extension of the technique of developing variation. The second of these is the use of contrast to highlight degrees of similitude.

We have already seen how Schoenberg used these techniques to create coherent phrases and groups of phrases. Measures 1–3 hold together as a group of phrases, for example, partly because of the recurrent A D G-sharp trichord (mm. 1, 2, and 3), partly because of the recurrent rhythm in the left hand, and partly because of the similar voice-exchanges in mm. 1 and 3. Similarly, mm. 4–7 hold together as a group of phrases because of their similar contours and rhythms.

Example 16.8

On the larger scale, it is possible to make similar associations. Consider, for example, m. 21, and compare it with the opening three measures of the piece (see Ex. 16.8).

One can scarcely point to anything in m. 21 that is identical to anything in the earlier passage. No succession (pitch or interval) larger than a dyad remains the same (and precious few dyads). No chord returns in anything close to identical form.

All the same, there are similarities. The right hand in m. 21 begins in a manner similar to that of m. 1. Like the opening phrase, it divides into two layers with the lower layer moving in sixteenth notes while the upper layer moves in parallel thirds in slower values. Also, m. 21 mimics the overall rhythmic shape of mm. 1–3; like the first pair of phrases, it begins with predominantly eighth and sixteenth note motion and ends with motion in thirty-second notes. Finally, like mm. 3–4, the end of the phrase in m. 21 is followed first by a rest and then by a high, dense chord, succeeded by a precipitous drop to a lower register (beginning m. 22).

Throughout the work one is constantly struck by the feeling that a given passage sounds vaguely like things we have heard before. Never identical, mind you, but vaguely similar. Is this enough to create coherence? In 1909 Schoenberg apparently thought so.

Op. 16, No. 5

Schoenberg's next step proves that his radical new idea of musical coherence in Op. 11, No. 3 was not a flash in the pan. In its own way Op. 16, No. 5, also abjures the use of motivic recurrence. Like Op. 11, No. 3, there are no literal repetitions: the structure of both the principal melody and its accompaniment constantly mutate, never returning to a prior form. And also like Op. 11, No. 3, as one proceeds through the work one constantly has the sense that somewhere one has heard something vaguely similar.

Op. 16, No. 5 is not the last of Schoenberg's works to exploit these new ideas. Each in their own way, most of the works from 1909 to 1913 have similar notions of musical structure. It would appear, therefore, that August 1909 is a watershed moment, a point at which Schoenberg entered into a new compositional world, one whose notions of comprehensibility and coherence differ in fundamental ways from that of all of the compositions that had preceded them. Intoxication, indeed.

17 The birth (and death) of new music: August 1909 and beyond

> ... all revolutions simply bring reaction out into the open and can threaten what took years to grow. I was never *revolutionary*.[1]

On 13 July 1909, Schoenberg wrote the pianist, conductor, and composer, Ferruccio Busoni, hoping to interest him in performing some of his works.

> I have often had the pleasure of hearing of favourable comments you had made about my compositions. Therefore, in asking you if you felt inclined to perform something of mine, I hope I am not approaching you in vain. I do not know if you are still continuing your orchestral series. I do have several orchestral works, which could only rely upon a suitable public in such concerts. But I have this less in mind than something considerably easier to bring about. I have two piano pieces (several others have been started, but their completion was interrupted by another work) which could only be played by someone who, like yourself, takes the side of all those who seek.[2]

Busoni replied promptly. On 16 July 1909 he wrote: "the piano pieces interest me intensely and I would ask you to carry out your good intention and send them to me."[3]

Schoenberg wasted no time. On 20 July 1909, he sent Busoni a copy of the recently completed first two pieces of Op. 11. After receiving the pieces, Busoni wrote back, telling Schoenberg that he was greatly impressed by the music, but – as a pianist – had reservations about Schoenberg's handling of the piano. Busoni even included an example of how he would rewrite one measure to make it (in his eyes) more idiomatic for the piano. A painful exchange ensued in which Busoni tried to express his concerns without insulting Schoenberg (an impossible task) while Schoenberg tried to express his dismay and rejection of Busoni's paraphrase without so offending Busoni that it would completely rule out the possibility of his performing the works in public.[4] For our purposes, what is most important about this exchange is a letter from early August in which Schoenberg writes an impassioned (and poetic) description of his newfound credo of composition.[5] Although somewhat extended, this is important to see in its entirety:

> To close, I must add that I was overjoyed to hear that you already like the one piece. And I really hope that you will later come to like the other one. Earlier I also preferred the 12/8 one (which I composed second) to the first. But recently I looked at the first one again: I almost believe that what I had conceived in terms of freedom and variegation of expression, of unshackled

flexibility of form uninhibited by "logic," is much more evident in the first than the second.

What I had visualized has been attained in neither. Perhaps, indeed definitely also not in the third, which will soon be finished. In a few orchestral pieces which I wrote very recently, I have in certain respects come closer, but again in others have turned far from what I considered already achieved.

Perhaps this is not yet graspable. It will perhaps take a long time before I can write the music I feel urged to, of which I have had an inkling for several years, but which, for the time being, I cannot express.

I am writing in such detail because I want to declare my intentions (encouraged by your comment: my music affects you because you envisage something of the kind as the goal of our immediate developments).

I strive for: complete liberation from all forms
from all symbols
of cohesion and
of logic.
Thus:
away with "motivic working out."
Away with harmony as
cement or bricks of a building.
Harmony is *expression*
and nothing else.
Then:
Away with Pathos!
Away with protracted ten-ton scores, from erected or constructed towers, rocks and other massive claptrap.
My music must be
brief.
Concise! In two notes: not built, but '*expressed*'!!
And the results I wish for:
no stylized and sterile protracted emotion.
People are not like that:
it is *impossible* for a person to have only *one* sensation at a time.

One has *thousands* simultaneously. And these thousands can no more readily be added together than an apple and a pear. They go their own ways.

And this variegation, this multifariousness, this *illogicality* which our senses demonstrate, the illogicality presented by their interactions, set forth by some mounting rush of blood, by some reaction of the senses or the nerves, this I should like to have in my music.

It should be an expression of feeling, as our feelings, which bring us in contact with our subconscious, really are, and no false child of feelings and 'conscious logic.'

Now I have made my confession and they can burn me. You will not number amongst those who burn me: that I know.[6]

Nothing could highlight more clearly the suddenness of the transformation in Schoenberg's compositional approach than this letter. Schoenberg's rapturous description of his new compositional philosophy is a remarkably precise portrayal of his compositions, beginning with Op. 11, No. 3. Beginning in August 1909, there is "liberation from all forms" and from "symbols of cohesion and logic". There is no "motivic working out", no "harmony as cement or bricks of a building", no "ten-ton scores", no "erected or constructed towers", and Schoenberg's works have become significantly shorter than before (and in the Pieces for Chamber Orchestra of 1910 would become shorter still).[7]

At the same time, the compositional philosophy described in this letter is completely incompatible with the compositions that Schoenberg had written only days before. If one were pressed to name the single most prominent compositional feature of Op. 11, Nos. 1 and 2 or of Op. 16, Nos. 1–4, it would have to be "motivic working out", arguably some of the most careful, pervasive, comprehensive, and thorough motivic working out there ever was. "Symbols of cohesion" do not merely litter the landscape of those works, they are the landscape of those works. Harmony (a much-less-than traditional harmony, but harmony nonetheless) serves as the most binding of cements. The forms of those works may not be classical, but they are invariably simple and clear and are always based on the principle of motivic repetition. Yet, in a matter of days, Schoenberg had turned his back on all of this. This is an aesthetic transformation whose suddenness has few parallels.

In the months that followed, Schoenberg acted according to the radical principles laid out in his new manifesto. He had embarked into a period in which there would be no recurrent motives, no referential harmonies, no learned devices, and a total liberation from anything resembling purposefully constructed form. On 27 August 1909, only days after writing Busoni, Schoenberg launched into an opera (the monodrama, *Erwartung*, Op. 17) during the entire course of which (other than immediate repetitions) there was not a single recurring theme or motive.[8] The next composition was a never-completed set of pieces for a mixed chamber ensemble, the first and second of which (completed February 1910) challenge Webern for brevity: they last less than a minute each. Here too there is no motivic working out or rationalized form: in Schoenberg's words "not built, but '*expressed*'!!"

It is not only the sudden abandonment of motive, harmony, and form as organizing principles that distinguishes Schoenberg's music beginning in August 1909 so sharply from its predecessors. Throughout the decade from 1899 to 1909, Schoenberg had operated according to a basic principle: the principle of fundamental, but incremental, innovation. Almost every work had at least one new aspect, but almost everything else remained the same (or at least similar). Although the sum total of all of the changes that had taken place over the course of that decade was breathtaking, the change from piece to piece was always gradual. At any given point, most of the innovations had seemed more like a stretching of the envelope than a violent rip. Using a program in a chamber work, using a ninth chord in fourth inversion, ending a phrase with a half-augmented seventh chord, making a song-cycle a duet, avoiding referential triads for hundreds of measures, creating a chord of fourths, scoring a symphony for a chamber ensemble, adding a voice to a string quartet, constructing new chords by adding semitones to a traditional harmony, and yes, even ending a composition with something other than a triad were – none of them – revolutionary steps; they were part of a chain of evolutionary transformations. Before August 1909 there had never been a single point where one could say that there was a rupture with the past. With Op. 11, No. 3 and the compositions that followed one can make precisely such a claim.

In a celebrated essay, "'New Music' as Historical Category", Carl Dahlhaus clarified just how problematic the term "New Music" can be and thus, how cautious (or at least precise) one ought to be when using this term.[9] Mindful of Dahlhaus' critique, I would like to suggest that a strong case can be made that August 1909 marks the birth of a period which might profitably be understood as New Music.[10] Beginning in August 1909, Schoenberg stopped treating musical style as an evolutionary process and began thinking instead in plainly revolutionary terms. The quality of newness became not just one component of a larger picture, it became the central principle of the work, to all intents and purposes, its raison d'être. In that specific sense, Schoenberg's music beginning in August 1909 can be thought of as "New Music".

Consider in this regard Schoenberg's treatment of the accompanied song. From the earliest days of his career through *Das Buch der hängenden Gärten*, Op. 15, a sizeable portion of Schoenberg's output had been piano accompanied songs. Although aspects of many these songs (particularly the harmony) were, at the time, quite radical, all of them owe allegiance to the hallowed tradition of German lieder composition.

During the period I would like to designate as "New Music", however, there is a complete break from this pattern. After the completion of *Das Buch der hängenden Gärten*, Op. 15, piano accompanied songs disappear as a category in Schoenberg's works, returning only during his twelve-tone period, more than two decades later (Three Songs, Op. 48, composed in 1933).

But Schoenberg did not completely abandon the accompanied song during this period. There is one work that might be classified as a song:

"Herzgewächse", Op. 20 (1911), to a poem by Maeterlinck. However, "Herzgewächse" scarcely fits smoothly into the tradition of the German lied. To the contrary: the completely unorthodox scoring of its accompaniment (celesta, harmonium, and harp), the spectacular three-octave range of the vocal part, and the complete lack of recurrent motives or themes were plainly calculated to create an impression that does not readily bring the historical category of "lieder" to mind. Instead of mixing a few novel features with substantially more traditional features (as he had done in the period 1899–1908), Schoenberg initiated a different approach to innovation: as much as possible in as short a time as feasible.

"Herzgewächse" is in no sense unique during this period: after August 1909, Schoenberg went out of his way – sometimes far, far out of his way – to elevate the strikingly new to the central position of his musical aesthetics. In this sense, then, there is ample justification for thinking of Schoenberg's music beginning in August 1909 as "New Music".

Yet the enshrinement of innovation as the sine qua non of musical structure brought with it some unbearable burdens. A musical style that assigns primary worth to novelty places intolerable demands on itself: to repeat anything would be to be in danger of establishing that repeated feature as a new norm. And how can one possibly reconcile norms with the principle that artistic worth inheres only in that which is new?

One cannot, and Schoenberg very quickly had the good sense to see what the consequences of holding to such a philosophy would entail. He seems to have realized that exalting the idea of the "new" at the expense of everything else could not be anything other than a dead end. He seems to have realized the intolerable demands that a perpetual revolution would place on his shoulders. I believe that is why the birth of New Music was followed very quickly by its demise.

Schoenberg began writing the music for *Die glückliche Hand*, Op. 18, in 1910 and at first this work picked up where *Erwartung* left off.[11] Like its predecessor, it too began with the renunciation of motivic repetition, learned devices, and traditional formal construction. But unlike Op. 17 (which he wrote in a little more than two weeks), Schoenberg did not complete *Die glückliche Hand* in an uninterrupted frenzy of inspiration. Instead, at some point – we don't know precisely when – he stopped work on it.

The next documented compositions are the Six Little Piano Pieces, Op. 19. The first five of these appear to have been written in one day, 19 February 1911. The last (written 17 June 1911) pays homage to Mahler, whose death on 18 May 1911 left Schoenberg bereft of his most illustrious champion and protector.

By virtue of their extreme brevity and (in some of them) their avoidance of motivic repetition, these pieces might be thought to be representative examples of New Music. All of the pieces are microscopically tiny: the longest is only seventeen measures; three of the pieces last a mere nine measures each, rivaling Webern for brevity.[12]

But even here, in these, the most radical of pieces, by this, the most radical of composers, at the most radical point in his career, a crack appears in the façade. This is clearest in the fourth piece.

Something is amiss here. Only a little more than two years after the birth of New Music, Schoenberg has reintroduced traditional features into his music. The piece falls neatly into three phrases, the first ending at the downbeat of m. 5 with a fermata, the second ending in m. 9, highlighted by a rest, and the third bringing the piece to a close. For our purposes, what is important is the way in which the third phrase begins. Although there are many obvious changes (rhythm, register, dynamics, articulation, and tempo), could anyone doubt but that the opening motive has returned? Is there any question but that the third phrase begins with a varied reprise of the opening?

This is not the only restatement of the opening idea. At least two other (varied) transformations of the opening motive occur: in m. 2 and in mm. 7–8. In other words, motivic "working out" has returned. Still further, the formal structure is reinforced by the pitch language: certain tones (particularly A, F, and B) occur more often and in more stable environments than the rest.[13] In short, once again, harmony is being used as "cement".

In the works that followed, the crack widened. Schoenberg's next composition was *Pierrot Lunaire*, a work that is torn between the intuitive aesthetic as outlined in Schoenberg's letter to Busoni and more traditional notions of motivic and formal structure. On the one hand, some of the individual melodramas are as extreme in their forswearing of motivic construction as any piece Schoenberg ever wrote. On the other hand, in other melodramas there are canons, an extended retrograde, a passacaglia, and there is even an interlude that is a reprise of part of an earlier number.

When Schoenberg returned to work on the opera *Die glückliche Hand* (in 1912 or 1913), the intuitive aesthetic continued to crumble, right and left. As Joseph Auner has so carefully documented, when Schoenberg came back to this composition, he introduced ideas that had not been part of the work in its beginning stages: "intricate counterpoint, thematic recurrences, and a clear formal design".[14] Not exactly the stuff of which intuition is made. Scarcely three years old, New Music was already in its death throes.

All of this has profound implications for the periodization of Schoenberg's works. And that suggests that we need to discuss the word that has been banned since the first chapter: atonality.

As befits a post-Beethovenian composer, Schoenberg himself is partly responsible for suggesting that his music ought to be divided into three periods.[15] Subsequent scholars and writers have obliged; in histories, biographies, dictionary articles, program notes, and CD liner notes, Schoenberg's music is invariably divided into three distinct periods: a tonal period, an atonal period, and a twelve-tone period.

There are some obvious problems with this way of subdividing Schoenberg's career.[16] In the first place, the borders of the putative periods are anything but neat. Schoenberg wrote some movements that conclude with triads (e.g. the third and fourth movements of String Quartet No. 2, Op. 10) after he had already written works that do not conclude with triads (e.g. some of the songs of *Das Buch der hängenden Gärten*). He wrote some non-serial "atonal" works (e.g. several of the choral works, Op. 35) after he had already been a twelve-tone composer for quite some time. Moreover, he continued to write occasional triadic pieces even after he had become a twelve-tone composer. True, many of these were little more than exercises or trifles, not meant to stand on a par with his other compositions. His usual practice was not to give them opus numbers. But after his emigration to America in 1933, Schoenberg's output included (in addition to twelve-tone compositions) full-fledged compositions that employed profusions of triads and to which he did assign opus numbers: *Kol Nidre* and *Variations on a Recitative for Organ*. And where should we place *Ode to Napoleon*? It has some serial features but is not consistently serial. It has some triadic features, but is not really tonal – at least not in any way tonality had previously been understood. Should we make a special period just for it?

It is not just the sloppiness of the borders that bothers me. If a period joins together different works that share common features, then in general I would prefer that the features we choose to make our distinctions would be among the most important aspects of the work. By corollary, it should also follow that the works that belong to a specific period ought to resemble other members of that period more than they do works from other periods. On this count, the suggested periodization of Schoenberg's works into tonal, atonal, and serial falls short.

To illustrate this problem, let us take any song from *Das Buch der hängenden Gärten*, Op. 15, and juxtapose it opposite a work like "Herzgewächse", Op. 20. According to the three-period hypothesis, both of these works belong to Schoenberg's middle period.[17] The criterion for their common membership in this period is simple: they are both "atonal". Neither employs any obvious tonal features (triads or diatonic seventh chords). Both conclude with non-triadic sonorities.

But that is about it. As I cautioned in the first chapter, we have said virtually nothing positive about the structure of either work. We have identified what they do not have; not what they do have.

If we try to do that, however, the argument that they belong to the same period falls apart. As we discussed earlier, "Herzgewächse" purposely breaks with the tradition of the German lied. Op. 15, by contrast, not only is a part of that tradition; it is also a song-cycle, an important subgroup within that tradition. The songs from Op. 15 are representatives of a tradition of works in which motivic and thematic structure are central. Op. 20 is a representative of a trend that emphatically rejected the notion of recurrent themes and motives. The songs from Op. 15 have clear forms, ones that fit into the tradition of formal structures characteristic of German lieder. The form of "Herzgewächse" is inchoate, elusive. There is a close connection between the form and the text in Op. 15; that relationship is purposefully tenuous in Op. 20.

True, Op. 15 and Op. 20 share the characteristic that they lack prominent triads, especially in their final measure. But they share little else of importance. To join them together is to run roughshod over any useful meaning of the idea of stylistic periods.

An equally problematic situation results when we try to identify the works that belong to the "tonal" period. What criteria are necessary for membership in this class? Is it the presence of a closing triad? If so, that would mean that Op. 14, No. 1 is "tonal". Or as Schoenberg claimed, does "tonal" mean that a composition is constructed such that "in the course of a piece only those sounds (*Klänge*) and successions of sounds, and these only in a suitable arrangement, whose relations to the fundamental tone of the key, to the tonic of the piece, can be grasped without difficulty?"[18] If this is the operative definition, then many pieces that end with triads including *Pelleas und Melisande*, the String Quartet, Op. 7, the Chamber Symphony, Op. 9, and others (not to mention Op. 14, No. 1) are not tonal. Moreover, just as much as it is virtually meaningless to assign *Das Buch der hängenden Gärten* and "Herzgewächse" to the same period ("atonal"), so too, it is equally meaningless to place works as different as a string quartet by Mozart and Schoenberg's Op. 7 in the same category ("tonal").

There are a number of possible solutions to this dilemma. One would simply be to reject stylistic periods as overly and uselessly simplistic for a composer as complicated and as contradictory as Schoenberg. Although this has its attractions, I would tend to reject this solution as giving up the battle too soon. Another would be to face up to the complications and try to subdivide Schoenberg's career into more (and thus smaller) periods. Instead of three, why not nine or ten? That might work; it could not help but be an improvement over the tonal–atonal–serial subdivision. It could free us from the absurdity of putting works like "Herzgewächse" and *Das Buch der hängenden Gärten* in the same period. The problems with this are obvious: once one starts dividing into many periods, what is there to stop one from continuing on? The inevitable result: one period for each piece. Some compositions (*Gurrelieder*, String Quartet, No. 2) might require more than one period. Reductio ad absurdum, meet Schoenberg's music.

I think that there is a better way and that the narrative of this book has pointed inevitably to that way. Instead of tonal-atonal-serial, I would propose that Schoenberg's music has an initial period that begins in 1899 and lasts until July 1909. We can call this first period a period of transformation. During this first period, Schoenberg systematically, but incrementally, built on and from tradition by transforming the chordal vocabulary, harmonic syntax, role of dissonance, structure of form, and treatment of motive. Although the path was not always straight, virtually every composition during this period played a role in this transformation. True, the works at the end of this period differ greatly from the works from the beginning; nevertheless, they are all part of one, unbroken chain of musical thought. At the same time, it is possible to make some useful subdivisions within this period. A credible case could be made that it falls into two sub-periods: a predominantly word/tone period (up to the Orchestral Songs, Op. 8) and a predominantly abstract period after that, beginning with the Chamber Symphony, Op. 9. All of the works of the two sub-periods should be understood to belong to the larger period in that they share three essential features. One is that they treat it as axiomatic that musical coherence rests on recurring themes and motives, however differently that axiom is realized. The second is that music has to rely on its traditions to have meaning, that it cannot divorce itself from its past. And the third is that each composition must vary, alter, and expand that tradition by adhering to the principle of incremental change.

In August 1909, however, Schoenberg breaks with tradition and does so abruptly and precipitously. When he does so, he tries to cut himself off from the past. This new period might be called New Music. It was brief, only a few years, approximately 1909 to 1911. The compositions of this period treat it as axiomatic that aesthetic worth inheres almost entirely in the quality of newness. In this period, intuition and expression are elevated to the status of compositional techniques while traditional compositional techniques of construction are consciously avoided. The compositions of this period take pains to try to separate themselves completely from tradition (a logical impossibility, of course, but Schoenberg tried).

This second period petered out gradually, over a span of several years. That decline overlaps slightly with the next period, a period of reconstruction, in which Schoenberg started to abandon the ecstatic vision of intuitive composition captured so vividly in his letter to Busoni.

In this last period, Schoenberg sought new ways of realizing coherence. He returns to the axiomatic assumptions that musical coherence rests on recurrence of theme and motive, that the choice of pitch material cannot be arbitrary, and that musical tradition was something to be enlarged, not something to be rejected. But this did not mean a nostalgic and uncritical return to a diatonic past. Rather, Schoenberg took it as axiomatic that an essential component of tradition is the evolutionary character of musical history, something that cannot reversed. The emancipation of the dissonance was an established fact, a product of nearly a millennium in the evolution of Western music. A significant achievement of this third period was the formation and refinement of a new method of composition, the twelve-tone method. This method clearly appealed to Schoenberg because it allowed him to tie his music to the great traditions of classical music (hence the revival of classical forms and the resurfacing of the many devices of contrapuntal art). It also permitted him to re-establish himself in a position safely at the forefront of the avant-garde (which, probably not coincidentally, put Webern in the position of being Schoenberg's follower, not his leader).

The third period was mostly devoted to the twelve-tone method, but not exclusively. In the first place, the twelve-tone method was no monolith, employed in one, and only one manner. Rather, it began with a lengthy period (1914–28) in which Schoenberg formulated and then refined the idea, extending its scope to all corners of the musical fabric.[19] Although Schoenberg eventually settled upon a wide array of essential features, and thereby created a mature twelve-tone style, his was too restless a musical personality to settle into a routine. Instead, he continued looking for new solutions for the problems of musical coherence. Toward the end of his career, he experimented with using source hexachords, by reconciling tonal ideas with twelve-tone ideas, and even by trying new ways of writing triadic music.

In short, there are clearly defensible, logical, and credible ways of dividing Schoenberg's music into periods that do not rely on the demonstrably false assumption that "atonality" is a meaningful or coherent category. To assert that a work is atonal is to assert virtually nothing and certainly nothing positive. It tells us nothing about a composition other than what it does not have. It posits false and misleading connections between works that belong to different aesthetic universes.

I am realistic enough to acknowledge that it will be hard – maybe impossible – to free ourselves completely from this term. It is so deeply ingrained in our vocabulary that it scarcely seems credible that it can be expunged.

But words guide and shape thought. And this word has guided our thoughts to a misunderstanding of crucial aspects of the music of one of the most fascinating and important composers of the twentieth century. It has helped shape our view that the absence of closing triads is so important a stylistic determinant that it overrides everything else. It has prompted us to believe that the harmony and syntax of Schoenberg's "atonal" works have no meaningful connection with the harmony and syntax of his "tonal" works. These are not only absurdities; they are long-standing absurdities.

It may be difficult to free ourselves from this term and the mistaken assumptions that follow. Nevertheless, we must try.

Notes

Chapter 1 "Atonality": a revisionist thesis

1. Schoenberg, "How one Becomes Lonely," *SI*, p. 50.
2. Schoenberg, "My Evolution", *SI*, p. 86.
3. Ernest Vincent Wright, *Gadsby* (Los Angeles: Wetzel Publishing, 1939).
4. Wright, *Gadsby*, p. 5.
5. Wright, *Gadsby*, p. 6. This is called a "lipogram". There have been other attempts, including one in French (where it is probably even harder than in English): *La Disparition*, by Georges Perec (translated into English as *A Void* – also with no e's – by Gilbert Adair).
6. "Hauer's Theories", *SI*, p. 210.
7. *Ibid*, pp. 210–11.
8. *Ibid*, p. 211. Schoenberg's claim that the term "atonal" originated "as a means of overaggressive characterization" by a journalist may not be accurate. For a careful examination of this issue, see Martin Thrun, *Neue Musik im deutschen Musikleben bis 1933*, 2 vols. (Bonn: Orpheus, 1995), vol. I, pp. 205–14.
9. Schoenberg made this suggestion in a footnote written for the 1921 edition of *Harmonielehre*, *HL*, p. 432. For a discussion of what "pantonality" might mean in Schoenberg's music, see Richard Kurth, "Suspended Tonalities in Schönberg's Twelve-tone Compositions", *Journal of the Arnold Schönberg Center*, 3 (2001), pp. 243–4. Kurth suggests that *Scheintonalitätsmomente* in Schoenberg's twelve-tone music "result from temporary imbalances in the twelve-tone system's abstract counterbalancing of multiple tonal relationships." Kurth makes a similar argument in "Moments of Closure: Thoughts on the Suspension of Tonality in Schoenberg's Fourth Quartet and Trio," in *Music of My Future: The Schoenberg Quartets and Trio*, edd. Reinhold Brinkmann & Christoph Wolff (Cambridge, MA: Harvard University Press, 2000), 139–60. Kurth's explanation for tonal references in Schoenberg's twelve-tone music also works very well for the repertoire under discussion in the later chapters of this book.
10. Another way of stating this is that the presence of triads does not necessarily make for tonality and the absence (or minimal presence) of triads does not necessarily mean the absence of tonality. In an essay (originally a lecture, later published as an article), Schoenberg illustrates this paradox with two musical examples, one of which has no tonic even though its chords are traditionally classifiable, the other of which (in Schoenberg's opinion) has a tonic even though it has a succession of less-than-traditional chords. "Problems of Harmony", *SI*, pp. 281–2.

11. All three of the works cited have been described as "atonal". With reference to *The Rite of Spring* see Allen Forte, *The Harmonic Organization of The Rite of Spring* (New Haven and London: Yale University Press, 1978); with respect to Lasso's *Prophetiae Sibyllarum*, see Edward Lowinsky, *Tonality and Atonality in Sixteenth Century Music* (Berkeley: University of California Press, 1962); reprinted (New York: Da Capo Press, 1990).
12. The two articles by Richard Kurth cited above ("Suspended Tonalities" and "Moments of Closure") provide a nuanced argument for how to recognize and evaluate the presence of "suspended tonalities" and other tonal references in Schoenberg's twelve-tone compositions. Unlike some previous writers, Kurth does not overstate the case and does not claim that a work like Schoenberg's Fourth String Quartet is in a particular key. But he also does not consign all tonal references to oblivion, as was often the case in the late twentieth-century writings about Schoenberg's twelve-tone works.
13. Pitch-class set analysis is so widely accepted that it is often a central feature of many standard textbooks on twentieth-century music. See, for example, John Rahn, *Basic Atonal Theory* (New York and London: Longman, 1980); Stefan Kostka, *Materials and Techniques of Twentieth-Century Music* (Englewood Cliffs: Prentice Hall, 1990), chapter 9; Joseph Straus, *Post-Tonal Theory* (Englewood Cliffs: Prentice Hall, 1990), chapters 1–3.
14. Allen Forte, "Sets and Nonsets in Schoenberg's Atonal Music", *Perspectives of New Music*, 11/1 (1972), p. 48. The very terminology of pc set theory is designed to efface the connection with prior repertoires: a "triad" is not a triad, but a 037 trichord; a "whole step" is not a whole step, but interval class 2; a minor third is ic 3, etc.
15. In any event, many of the fundamental premises of tonality (as it was understood in the eighteenth century) were challenged during the nineteenth century. For a good summary of the evolution of tonal language during the nineteenth century, see Jim Samson, *Music in Transition: A Study of Tonal Expansion and Atonality, 1900–1920* (London: J. M. Dent, 1977; paperback edition, 1993), pp. 1–18.
16. David Lewin, "Toward the Analysis of Schoenberg's Op. 15, No. XI", *Perspectives of New Music*, 12/1–2 (1973), p. 74, fn. 10.
17. After identifying tonal aspects of the opening principal theme, Brinkmann marvels: "Für das Thema eines atonalen Werks eine merkwürdige Häufung tonaler Elemente!" *Arnold Schönberg: Drei Klavierstücke Op. 11. Studien zur frühen Atonalität bei Schönberg*. Beihefte zum Archiv für Musikwissenschaft, vol. 7 (Franz Steiner Verlag: Wiesbaden, 1969), p. 63.
18. As Michael Cherlin notes: "The relationship is circular and dialectical and cannot be reduced to tonal or not tonal, for to say that Schoenberg's post-tonal works are 'tonal' is perversely reductive in one sense (that all functions are subsumed by tonal functions), and over-inclusive in another (that tonal functions not there must be implied), while to say that Schoenberg's works are incorrectly heard when we bring our tonal memories to the work and it

reflects those back to us is to impoverish his music in more ways than the loss of its grounding in a larger tradition." Michael Cherlin, "Schoenberg and *Das Unheimliche*: Spectres of Tonality", *Journal of Musicology*, 11/3 (1993), p. 359.

19. For a preliminary version of these ideas see my "Schoenberg and the Origins of Atonality", in Juliane Brand and Christopher Hailey (edd.), *Constructive Dissonance: Arnold Schoenberg and the Transformations of Twentieth-Century Culture* (Berkeley, Los Angeles, and London: University of California Press, 1997, pp. 71–86.

Chapter 2 "Based on tradition": Four Songs, Op. 2, 1899

1. Schoenberg, "National Music (2)", *SI*, p. 174.
2. For a careful examination of Schoenberg's pre-1899 works see Walter Frisch, *The Early Works of Arnold Schoenberg: 1893–1908* (Berkeley and Los Angeles: University of California Press, 1993), pp. 20–75.
3. Walter Frisch sees the 1899 settings of poems by Richard Dehmel as the point where "Schoenberg moves definitively beyond the Brahms style to explore and gain mastery over a more progressive chromatic language and more ambitious musical forms." Frisch, *The Early Works*, p. 82. For more on Schoenberg's early Dehmel settings see his "Schoenberg and the Poetry of Richard Dehmel", *Journal of the Arnold Schoenberg Institute*, 9/2 (1986), pp. 137–79.
4. See Reinhard Gerlach, "War Schönberg von Dvořák beeinflußt?" *Neue Zeitschrift für Musik*, 133 (1972), pp. 122–7. Gerlach further elaborates on the nature of the influence of Dvořák's music on Schoenberg in *Musik und Jugendstil der Wiener Schule 1900–1908* (Laaber: Laaber-Verlag, 1985), pp. 59–66. Others question whether there was influence from this quarter. See Heinrich Helge Hattesen, *Emanzipation durch Aneignung: Untersuchungen zu den frühen Streichquartetten Arnold Schönbergs* (Kassel: Bärenreiter, 1990), pp. 37–9, and Frisch, *The Early Works*, pp. 37–9.
5. For an analysis of this song see Frisch, *The Early Works*, pp. 99–104. Edward Cone discusses (and criticizes) some aspects of the harmonic structure of this song in "Sound and Syntax: An Introduction to Schoenberg's Harmony", *Perspectives of New Music*, 13 (1974), pp. 25–6.
6. By beginning with an examination of chords, I am stressing the centrality of the concept of chords in Schoenberg's compositional thought. As Simon Harris put it in his general study of chords in early twentieth-century music: "But another reason for starting a study of twentieth-century music with the chord, rather than with the note-row, the pc set, or any other new theoretical concept is that music at the beginning of this century arguably continued to be chordally conceived after it had left behind the limits of traditional chord vocabulary, and before the note-row was invented or set theory began to apply the concept of the pc set to some of this music." *A Proposed Classification of Chords in Early Twentieth-Century Music* (New York & London: Garland Publishing, 1989), p. 24.

7. The centrality of chord in Schoenberg's compositional thought does not necessarily mean that he started with a harmonic progression when he composed. Indeed, some of the sketches of the songs show that he often started with a melody (or a melody and a bass), only completing the harmonies later. However, it is a theme in Schoenberg's writings that melody is not (or should not be) separable from its harmonization. For this reason he had objections to chorale harmonizations: "One does not harmonize, one invents with harmony." *HL*, p. 286. Later in the same discussion he implies that the harmony flows from the melody, or vice versa. As he states about the student: "He is given a melody. It is not his own; thus his harmonization of it can never be as good as that with which it was invented." *HL*, p. 287.
8. In his counterpoint manual Schoenberg states: "In the first species no dissonant interval shall be used." See *Preliminary Exercises in Counterpoint*, ed. Leonard Stein (London: Faber and Faber, 1970), p. 2.
9. For a good account of the evolution away from a purely triadic chordal vocabulary see Simon Harris, *A Proposed Classification of Chords*, pp. 36–97.
10. In the first phrase, minor seventh chords appear in mm. 2, 3, 4. Major seventh chords occur far less often. None appears in this song. There are some in "Erhebung", Op. 2, No. 3, mm. 4 and 19.
11. Within the first phrase, half-diminished seventh chords appear in mm. 1, 2 (two times), m. 3 (two times), and m. 4.
12. In the first phrase, a diminished seventh occurs on the second beat of m. 2. That diminished sevenths occur relatively rarely in Schoenberg's music may be a consequence of his feeling that the chord had become pedestrian. In *Harmonielehre* he states: "The chord had lost the appeal of novelty, hence, it had lost its sharpness, but also its luster. It had nothing more to say to a new era. Thus, it fell from the higher sphere of art music to the lower of music for entertainment. There it remains, as a sentimental expression of sentimental concerns. It became banal and effeminate. *Became* banal! It was not so originally. It was sharp and dazzling." *HL*, p. 238.
13. In Schoenberg's eyes, this was part of a historical process. He stated that other chords replaced the diminished seventh chord: "Other chords took its place, chords that were to replace its expressiveness and chords that were to replace its pivotal facility. These were the augmented triad, certain altered chords, and some sonorities that, having already been introduced in the music of Mozart or Beethoven by virtue of suspensions or passing tones, appeared in that of Wagner as independent chords." *HL*, p. 238.
14. For example, in Beethoven's Diabelli Variations, Op. 120, in m. 25 of Variation 28 there is a chord with the tones (reading from the bass up): E G-sharp C B-flat, which functions as the dominant of F.
15. In his writings Schoenberg stressed the importance of motivic structure in determining harmonic function. "Therefore the chords are presented as entities resulting from the concurrent movement of parts; but in so presenting them one should not forget that the *Motor* that drives this movement of voices,

the motive, is absent." *HL*, p. 34. For a discussion of this, see David Bernstein, "Schoenberg Contra Riemann: *Stufen*, Regions, *Verwandtschaft*, and the Theory of Tonal Function", *Theoria*, 6 (1992), pp. 51–2. Bernstein perceptively asserts that "Schoenberg viewed tonal function as an abstraction when it is considered apart from motivic processes."

16. Schoenberg's progressions typically conform to the guidelines he laid down in his *Harmonielehre*. See *HL*, pp. 119–20. For a discussion of the effect of the resultant progressions on tonal definition, see my "Schoenberg and the Origins of Atonality", in Juliane Brand and Christopher Hailey (edd.), *Constructive Dissonance: Arnold Schoenberg and the Transformations of Twentieth-Century Culture* (Berkeley, Los Angeles, and London: University of California Press, 1997), pp. 74–5.

17. "But it is evident that chords remote from the key, appearing in large numbers, will favor the establishment of a new *conceptual unit* (*Auffassungseinheit*): the chromatic scale. It is not to be ignored that through accumulation of such phenomena the solid structure of tonality could be demolished." *HL*, p. 247.

18. The total circulation of the chromatic was a feature of some of Schoenberg's earliest surviving works. For example, the complete chromatic appears in the opening four measures of Schoenberg's Piano Piece in A minor (1894). See Frisch, *The Early Works*, p. 24.

19. For a discussion of cadence in Schoenberg's writings (particularly in *Harmonielehre*), see Jonathan Dunsby, "Schoenberg on Cadence", *Journal of the Arnold Schoenberg Institute*, 4/1 (1980), pp. 41–9.

20. Schoenberg justifies progressions of this sort in a section of his *Harmonielehre* entitled "Abbreviation of Set Patterns Through Omission of Intermediate Steps". He states: "... frequently recurring usages become fixed patterns with one explicit, unmistakable meaning. So unmistakable that once we hear the very beginning we immediately and automatically expect the usual continuation: the formula is obliged to lead to a predetermined conclusion. Assuming this, we can now even omit the middle parts of the formula, set beginning and end right together, 'abbreviate', so to speak, the whole pattern, set it down merely as premise and conclusion." *HL*, p. 359. Other songs from this period in which the final tonic triad is prepared by something other than the dominant chord include "Erhebung", Op. 2, No. 3 (mm. 23–4) and "Waldsonne", Op. 2, No. 4 (mm. 40–2).

21. Arnold Whittall makes a useful distinction: "An analyst wishing to focus on the nature and function of emancipated dissonance may attempt one of two initial strategies: either the identification and interpretation of dissonant formations which are in themselves traditional in their behaviour; or the identification and interpretation of dissonant formations which are emancipated in their own actual content, to the extent of escaping plausible codification by traditional criteria." "Tonality and the Emancipated Dissonance: Schoenberg and Stravinsky", in Jonathan Dunsby (ed.), *Early Twentieth-Century Music: Models of Musical Analysis* (Oxford: Blackwell Publishers, 1993), p. 6. Schoenberg's use

of dominant seventh chords without dominant function corresponds to Whittall's first strategy and is prevalent in early works like the Op. 2 songs; his use of dissonant formations that defy codification by traditional criteria is to be a central focus of later works.

22. The asymmetric slicing (7 of 12) by the diatonic collection makes it possible to assign one tone a hierarchical standing with a unique ordering of intervals referable to the tone of reference. No such unique standing is possible when the collection is the total chromatic. See Andreas Jacob, "Das Verständnis von Tonalität in Arnold Schönbergs theoretischen Schriften", *Musiktheorie*, 15 (2000), p. 13.

23. In mm. 2–4, the bass outlines a clear circle of fifths: D, G, C, F, B-flat. No progression could be more traditional than a circle of fifths progression; however, of the five tones in the bass line, only the first (D) has diatonic function in F-sharp minor.

24. The presence of this kind of feature has encouraged some to analyze Schoenberg's early works using Schenkerian analysis. For a discussion of Schoenberg's early harmony from a Schenkerian perspective, see Harry Ballan, "Schoenberg's Expansion of Tonality, 1899–1908", Ph.D. Dissertation, Yale University (1986). Ballan stresses the importance of mediant relationships in Schoenberg's early works.

25. For analyses of this song and its chord, see Edward Cone, "Sound and Syntax", pp. 28–9 and Frisch, *The Early Works*, pp. 95–6. Frisch sees a parallel between the *Farbenspiel* in Dehmel's poem and Schoenberg's chord, hence his term "color chord". Schoenberg's interest in setting Dehmel's poetry may have been prompted by Zemlinsky. There are interesting parallels between Schoenberg's "Erwartung" and Zemlinsky's *Stimme des Abends* for piano. See Antony Beaumont, *Zemlinsky* (Ithaca, New York: Cornell University Press, 2000), p. 46.

26. Frisch, *The Early Works*, pp. 100–2.

27. Thematic transformation is more prevalent in this song than true thematic development. For a clarification of the distinction between the two types, see Walter Frisch, *Brahms and the Principle of Developing Variation* (Berkeley and Los Angeles: University of California Press, 1984), p. 36.

28. For an examination of Schoenberg's use of the techniques of developing variation in his earliest works, see Frisch, *The Early Works*, chapters 2–3 and particularly his analysis of the String Quartet in D, 1897 (pp. 34–7) and the song "Mädchenfrühling" (pp. 70–1).

29. For a discussion of the concepts of "tradition" and "new" see Beat Föllmi, *Tradition als hermeneutische Kategorie bei Arnold Schönberg* (Bern: Paul Haupt, 1996), pp. 29–43.

30. "Conservative", "radical", "progressive", "new", "modern", "traditional", and other similar expressions can be problematic in that they are often used with implicit value judgments. For a discussion of Schoenberg's use of, and reaction to, these terms see Beat Föllmi, *Tradition als hermeneutische Kategorie*, pp. 76–81. In this book I use "progressive", "avant-garde", "radical", and

similar terms to denote stylistic characteristics that seemed unfamiliar to the audiences of the time, particularly in the domains of harmony and dissonance treatment. Correspondingly, I use "conservative", "traditional", and similar terms to denote the opposite. I do not imply any value judgment, pro or con. See Janet Levy, "Covert and Casual Values in Recent Writings About Music", *Journal of Musicology*, 5/1 (1987), pp. 3–27.

Chapter 3 The principle of incremental innovation: *Verklärte Nacht*, 1899

1. Schoenberg, "How One Becomes Lonely", *SI*, p. 53.
2. Alexander Zemlinsky, in his capacity as a committee member of the Wiener Tonkünstlerverein was able to help arrange the first significant performance of one of Schoenberg's works. See Lorraine Gorrell, *Discordant Melody: Alexander Zemlinsky, His Songs and the Second Viennese School* (Westport, Connecticut: Greenwood Press, 2002), p. 23.
3. The first public performance of the Quartet in D (20 December 1898) seems to have been preceded by a semi-private performance on 17 March 1898 at the Wiener Tonkünstlerverein. See H. H. Stuckenschmidt, *Schoenberg: His Life, World and Work* (New York: Schirmer Books, 1978), trans. Humphrey Searle, p. 33. Some confusion and disagreement exists about the precise details of the early performances. See Maegaard, *Studien zur Entwicklung des dodekaphonen Satzes bei Arnold Schönberg* (Copenhagen: Wilhelm Hansen, 1972), vol. I, pp. 27–8.
4. There is an interesting fragment of a treatise on composition (probably written around 1900) that highlights the centrality of word-tone relationships in Schoenberg's early thought. For a discussion of this fragment see Charlotte Cross, "Schoenberg's Earliest Thoughts on the Theory of Composition: A Fragment from c. 1900", *Theoria*, 8 (1994), pp. 113–33. The fragment has also been reprinted in Joseph Auner, *A Schoenberg Reader: Documents of a Life* (New Haven & London: Yale University Press, 2003), p. 17.
5. For a summary of what is known about Schoenberg's beliefs and attitudes from the early stages of his career, see Charlotte Cross, "Schoenberg's 'Weltanschauung' and His Views of Music: 1874–1915" (Ph.D. Dissertation, Columbia University, 1992), pp. 2–88.
6. The theoretical work with the most potential to illuminate the early compositions is Schoenberg's *Harmonielehre* and there have been several attempts to use it for that purpose. See Christopher Wintle, "Schoenberg's Harmony: Theory and Practice", *Journal of the Arnold Schoenberg Institute*, 4/1 (1980), 50–67. See also my "Schoenberg and the Origins of Atonality", in Juliane Brand and Christopher Hailey (edd.), *Constructive Dissonance: Arnold Schoenberg and the Transformations of Twentieth-Century Culture* (Berkeley, Los Angeles, and London: University of California Press, 1997), pp. 71–86.
7. J. Peter Burkholder discusses the centrality of some version of this idea throughout Schoenberg's career and makes the intriguing observation that it is

analogous to Schoenberg's notion of developing variation. J. Peter Burkholder, "Schoenberg the Reactionary", in Walter Frisch (ed.), *Schoenberg and His World* (Princeton, New Jersey: Princeton University Press, 1999), pp. 162–91.

8. Schoenberg's belief in the importance and inevitability of progress is a common theme in his writings. "Yet, I do believe in the new; I believe it is that *Good* and that *Beauty* toward which we strive with our innermost being, just as involuntarily and persistently as we strive toward the *future*." *HL*, p. 239.

9. Although programmatic music was no longer considered novel, it was the genre of choice for progressive German composers at the turn of the century. "In writing programme music Schoenberg joined the company of Richard Strauss in becoming one of the exponents of musical 'modernism' – a 'modernism' which marked a period of transition linking the age of Wagner and the New Music of the twentieth century." Carl Dahlhaus, "Schoenberg and Programme Music", in *Schoenberg and the New Music*, trans. Derrick Puffett and Alfred Clayton (Cambridge: Cambridge University Press, 1987), p. 96.

10. Although chamber works were not normally based on programs, there were occasional examples before *Verklärte Nacht*. Bedřich Smetana's First String Quartet "Z mého života" ("From my Life"), written in 1876, depicted the course of his life, with the four instruments representing four friends who were discussing amongst themselves the troubles that had afflicted the composer.

11. Although it is commonplace to speak as if there is an ironclad distinction between programmatic and absolute music, in reality, no such clear distinction exists. See Carl Dahlhaus, "Schoenberg and Programme Music", p. 94.

12. For bibliographic information see Jan Maegaard, *Studien*, vol. I, p. 28.

13. Its instrumentation is 2222, 422, timpani, harp, strings.

14. A facsimile of the first page of the score of *Frühlings Tod* is reprinted in Walter Bailey, *Programmatic Elements in the Works of Schoenberg* (Ann Arbor: UMI Research Press, 1984), p. 54. For a detailed examination of *Frühlings Tod* see Ulrich Thieme, *Studien zum Jugendwerk Arnold Schönbergs: Einflüsse und Wandlungen* (Regensburg: Bosse, 1979), pp. 183–215.

15. *Verklärte Nacht* was preceded by an undated and relatively short (34 measures) fragment, *Toter Winkel*, also for string sextet (222). A facsimile of this fragment is printed in Bailey, *Programmatic Elements*, pp. 41–3. The opening of *Toter Winkel* is uncannily close to that of Op. 4. For an analysis and discussion of this fragment, see Thieme, *Studien*, pp. 173–83. For bibliographic information, see Maegaard, *Studien*, vol. I, p. 151.

16. Bailey, *Programmatic Elements*, pp. 8–9.

17. *Ibid*, p. 9.

18. *Ibid*, p. 10.

19. *Ibid*, p. 10.

20. It has been suggested that the rejection of *Verklärte Nacht* by the Tonkünstlerverein could have been due to reasons other than the famous fourth inversion ninth chord. "The concept of a chamber work with a programme may well have been unappealing to the jury of the Wiener Tonkünstlerverein to

whom the work was submitted; the influence of Hanslick's aesthetics, which eschewed any such tendencies, was strong in this Verein, and would have extended to orchestral music as well." Simon Trezise, "Schoenberg's Gurrelieder", Ph.D. Dissertation, Oxford University (1987), p. 24.
21. *HL*, pp. 345–6. Schoenberg gives a similar account elsewhere: "A Viennese society refused the first performance of my String Sextet, *Verklärte Nacht*, because of the 'revolutionary' use of one – that is *one* single uncatalogued dissonance." "Criteria for the Evaluation of Music", *SI*, p. 131. Zemlinsky gave another account of the rejection of *Verklärte Nacht* by the Tonkünstlerverein: "I again tried to persuade the committee of the Tonkünstlerverein to perform the work, but this time I had no luck. The piece was 'examined,' and the results were utterly negative. A member of the jury pronounced his judgment in the following words: 'It sounds as if someone had smeared the score of *Tristan* while it was still wet!' " Quoted in Willi Reich, *Schoenberg: A Critical Biography*, trans. Leo Black (New York, Washington: Praeger, 1978), p. 7.
22. At the time of his remark (1910), Schoenberg had just initiated a radical new approach to composition, one that emphasized intuition and that eschewed the traditional techniques of the compositional art. See chapter 16. Schoenberg's remark about his intuitive choice of the ninth chord may thus be an instance of his viewing his past through the prism of his then current aesthetic.
23. The search for striking new chords is characteristic of a process that Carl Dahlhaus has termed "individualization of harmony". As he states: "In Wagnerian harmony, with its reliance on chromatic alteration and its consequent tendency towards 'wandering' or 'floating' tonality (that is, a linear succession of fragmentary allusions to keys), the accent falls on harmonic details – on single chords or unusual progressions – and there is such a degree of differentiation in the compositional technique (the interrelationships of harmony and instrumentation) that it is no exaggeration to speak of an individualization of harmony, which is hardly less important than that of thematic and motivic material." See *Between Romanticism and Modernism: Four Studies in the Music of the Later Nineteenth Century*, trans. Mary Whittall (Berkeley and Los Angeles: University of California Press, 1980), p. 73.
24. For a thorough analysis of this ninth chord and its manifold nuances and compositional implications see David Lewin, "On the 'Ninth-Chord in Fourth Inversion' from *Verklärte Nacht*", *Journal of the Arnold Schoenberg Institute*, 10/1 (1987), pp. 45–64.
25. *HL*, p. 309.
26. As Schoenberg stated: "Finally, there were already some passages of unfixed tonality which may be considered premonitions of the future." "My Evolution", *SI*, p. 81 with an illustration of such a passage as his Ex. 5 on p. 82.
27. In one of the many striking passages in his *Harmonielehre*, Schoenberg described the vagrant chord as follows: "Later, the pupil will best take all these vagrant chords for what they are, without tracing them back to a key or a degree: homeless phenomena, unbelievably adaptable and unbelievably

lacking in independence; spies, who ferret out weaknesses and use them to cause confusion; turncoats, to whom abandonment of their individuality is an end in itself; agitators in every respect, but above all: most amusing fellows." *HL*, p. 258.

28. Carl Dahlhaus, "Schoenberg and Programme Music", in *Schoenberg and the New Music*, trans. Derrick Puffett and Alfred Clayton (Cambridge: Cambridge University Press, 1987), pp. 96–7. Wellesz actually never refers to the form as a rondo. He simply states: "The structure of *Verklärte Nacht*, in accordance with the poem, is made up of five sections, in which the first, third, and fifth are of more epic nature and so portray the deep feelings of the people wandering about in the cold moonlit night. The second contains the passionate plaint of the woman, the fourth the sustained answer of the man, which shows much depth and warmth of understanding." Egon Wellesz, *Arnold Schönberg*, trans. W. H. Kerridge (London: Dent, 1925). Reprint (Freeport, New York: Books for Libraries Press, 1969), p. 67.

29. Wilhelm Pfannkuch, "Zu Thematik und Form in Schönbergs Streichsextett", in Anna Amalie Abert and Wilhelm Pfannkuch (edd.), *Festschrift Friedrich Blume: Zum 70. Geburtstag* (Kassel: Bärenreiter, 1963), p. 269.

30. Richard Swift, "1-XII-99: Tonal Relations in Schoenberg's *Verklärte Nacht*", *19th Century Music*, 1/1 (1977), pp. 3–14. For a discussion and critique of the various formal models proposed for *Verklärte Nacht* see Frisch, *The Early Works*, pp. 112–16.

31. For a discussion of this issue see my "Schoenberg's Programmatic Compositions and the Ideology of Absolute Music", *Orbis Musicae*, 13 (2003), pp. 177–84.

32. For a formal analysis that relies on the poem and not on models of absolute music see Werner Breig, "Arnold Schönbergs *Verklärte Nacht* und das Problem der Programmusik" in Walter Bernhart (ed.), *Die Semantik der musiko-literarischen Gattungen: Methodik und Analyse* (Tübingen: Gunter Narr Verlag, 1994), pp. 92–7. See also Gottfried Scholz, "*Verklärte Nacht*, op. 4", in Gerold Gruber (ed.), *Schönberg: Interpretationen seiner Werke* (Laaber: Laaber-Verlag, 2002), vol. 1, p. 25. Both Breig and Scholz see the work as divided into five parts, corresponding to the five sections of Dehmel's poem, but they do not completely agree on where those formal divisions should be placed.

33. In 1950, Schoenberg himself provided just such a program. For an excerpt, see Joseph Auner, *A Schoenberg Reader: Documents of a Life* (New Haven & London: Yale University Press, 2003), pp. 38–40. The complete program (including musical examples) was printed with the booklet that accompanied a recording by Columbia Records (Columbia M2S 694), now generally unavailable. For a translation into German of the complete program, see Arnold Schönberg, *Stil und Gedanke: Aufsätze zur Musik*, ed. Ivan Vojtěch (Frankfurt am Main: S. Fischer, 1976), pp. 453–7.

34. For a table of the themes, see Frisch, *The Early Works*, p. 117. The themes in Ex. 3.7 are themes 2b, 4a, and 5a from Frisch's table.

35. "A Self-Analysis", *SI*, pp. 77–8. In another (never completed) essay (written around 1930), Schoenberg stressed how important varied repetition was in his works: "With me, variation almost completely takes the place of repetition (there is hardly a single exception to this)." "New Music: My Music", *SI*, p. 102.
36. For other instances of this procedure, see mm. 29–32 and 50–4.

Chapter 4 Conservative song-cycle, progressive cantata: *Gurrelieder*, 1900–11

1. Schoenberg, "Problems of Harmony", *SI*, p. 275.
2. For a summary discussion of the work's poetry, form, and motivic structure see Jan Maegaard, "*Gurrelieder* für Soli, Chor und Orchester", in Gerold Gruber (ed.), *Schönberg: Interpretationen seiner Werke* (Laaber: Laaber-Verlag, 2002), vol. II, pp. 232–52. See also Frisch, *The Early Works*, pp. 140–57 and Constantin Floros, "Schönbergs Gurre-Lieder", in Mogens Andersen, Niels Bo Foltmann, Claus Røllum-Larsen (edd.), *Festskrift Jan Maegaard: 14.4.1996* (Copenhagen: Engstrøm & Sødring, 1996), pp. 33–42.
3. This view of the compositional history of *Gurrelieder* is covered in detail in Simon Tresize, "Schoenberg's *Gurrelieder*", Ph.D. Dissertation, Oxford University, 1987, pp. 20–44. See also Frisch, *The Early Works*, pp. 140–4. For additional background and details, see Berthold Türcke, "Gurrelieder and Orchestra Pieces, Op. 16, for Two Pianos", *Journal of the Arnold Schoenberg Institute*, 7/2 (1983), pp. 240–2.
4. "He said that the first 9 songs of the cycle were composed for piano and voice for a song-cycle contest; he finished them half a week too late for the contest and this decided the fate of the work!" Dika Newlin, *Schoenberg Remembered: Diaries and Recollections (1938–76)*, (New York: Pendragon Press, 1980), p. 225. Zemlinsky recalled: "Wishing to compete for the prize, Schoenberg composed just a few songs, after poems by Jacobsen. I played them to him. The songs were wonderfully beautiful and really original, but we both felt they were unlikely to win the prize, for that very reason. Undeterred, Schoenberg proceeded to set the whole of Jacobsen's cycle – but not for a solo voice; he added large choirs, a melodrama, preludes, interludes, and scored the whole thing for a gigantic orchestra." Quoted in Willi Reich, *Schoenberg: A Critical Biography*, trans. Leo Black (New York, Washington: Praeger, 1971), p. 10. Interestingly enough, Zemlinsky had toyed with setting the very same poems: in the closing months of 1899, he began to write songs to some of Jacobsen's *Songs of Gurre*. "It is unclear whether he abandoned the Jacobsen setting out of deference to Schoenberg, or because he had agreed to join the jury." Beaumont, *Zemlinsky*, p. 117n.
5. Ulrich Krämer, "Oratorium oder Liederzyklus? Zur Entstehung von Schönbergs 'Gurre-Liedern'," *Journal of the Arnold Schönberg Center*, 3 (2001), pp. 86–103.
6. Measure numbers refer to the unpublished piano/vocal song-cycle. To find the comparable measure for this song in *Gurrelieder*, add 92 (the number of measures in the orchestral introduction).

7. As an applied dominant it could be vii^7/IV, but in the present instance it is not really followed by IV unless one wishes to regard the augmented triad that follows as an altered IV.
8. When Alban Berg analyzed this chord (as it appears in the orchestral introduction at m. 36) he insisted on an even more radical reading. He identified the chord "as one of the forbidden (!) inversions of a ninth-chord (root F, with missing third)." Alban Berg, "Gurrelieder Guide" (trans. Mark DeVoto), *Journal of the Arnold Schoenberg Institute*, 16 (1993), p. 71.
9. Berg cites this as an example of the "'Abbreviation of set patterns through omission of intermediate steps,' which is emphasized in Schoenberg's *Theory of Harmony*." Berg, "Gurrelieder Guide", p. 75.
10. The formal structure is A: mm. 1–17; B: mm. 18–31; A': mm. 32–46; B': mm. 47–53; C: mm. 54–68; B'': mm. 69–79. The similarities between A and A' are mildly obscured by changes Schoenberg made at some point in the compositional process (possibly when he returned to transform the work into a vocal/orchestral work). In the manuscript of the *Gurrelieder*-cycle, the first measures of A' (mm. 31–33) were originally a whole step lower than they now appear in *Gurrelieder*.
11. Given that the tempo is rather brisk, I think that this reading is the most convincing one. If one breaks the beat down into its component halves, the first half suggests an A major triad, the second half an F-sharp minor triad.
12. Enharmonic equivalence is assumed (A-sharp = B-flat). Here too, the quick tempo encourages simplifying this complicated sonority to a single chord. On the other hand it might also be regarded as an incomplete C-sharp diminished seventh chord in the first half of the last quarter and an incomplete C dominant seventh chord in the second half.
13. Berg states that "the tonality of this song almost gives the impression of hovering between C♯ minor and E major." He goes on to suggest that this was the precursor for similar procedures that were carried off "still more strongly and consciously in Schoenberg's later works (for example, in the Orchestral Song, Op. 8, No. 5)." "Gurrelieder Guide", p. 89.
14. "Volmer" is a diminutive of "Waldemar".
15. "The committee elected to judge the forty song cycles submitted consisted of R. Heuberger, E. Mandyczewski, Carl Prohaska, Anton Rückhauf, and Alexander von Zemlinsky." Trezise, "Schoenberg's *Gurrelieder*", p. 20.
16. There were no sizeable breaks after songs 7 and 8 in the *Gurrelieder*-cycle, thereby creating a continuous super-movement for songs 7–9.
17. The theme appears in augmentation for the first time in the first horn in m. 11.
18. Other themes (such as the "sunrise" leitmotif that first appears in mm. 7–8) do not originate from the first song, but rather prepare events later in the work (e.g. the sunrise motive appears in inversion as the sunset toward the end of the work).
19. Constantin Floros has pointed out the radical nature of the pitch language of some passages in *Gurrelieder*. "Schönbergs Gurre-Lieder", p. 34.

Chapter 5 Programmatic music and its implications

1. Schoenberg, "My Evolution", *SI*, p. 82.
2. For a summary of the compositional history, the relationship of Schoenberg's work to Maeterlinck's play, and an analysis, see Siglind Bruhn, "*Pelleas und Melisande*, op. 5", in Gerold Gruber (ed.), *Arnold Schönberg: Interpretationen seiner Werke* (Laaber: Laaber-Verlag, 2002), vol. I, pp. 36–60.
3. There are at least two orchestral fragments that precede *Pelleas und Melisande*: a symphonic poem (*Frühlings Tod*, 1898) and a Symphony (1900). See Maegaard, *Studien zur Entwicklung*, vol. I, pp. 28 and 31.
4. For a comprehensive examination of programmatic ideas in Schoenberg's works throughout his career, see Walter Bailey, *Programmatic Elements in the Works of Schoenberg* (Ann Arbor: UMI Research Press, 1984).
5. "His most important source of income was the orchestration of operettas, which came to him in draft, sometimes from well-known composers. He is said to have scored some thousands of pages of operetta scores about then, and a few years later he again had to devote himself to this 'creative' work." Willi Reich, *Schoenberg: A Critical Biography*, trans. Leo Black (New York, Washington: Praeger, 1978), p. 9. Relatively little is known about Schoenberg's activities as a copyist. See the discussion in the critical report, *SW*, 25–6, p. xix.
6. For background on Schoenberg's brief career as a cabaret musician, see Stuckenschmidt, *Schoenberg*, pp. 47–60.
7. Schoenberg wrote a number of cabaret songs, now known as the *Brettellieder*. The name is a misnomer: he wrote those songs before he took the position at the Bunte Theater. See Maegaard, *Studien zur Entwicklung*, vol. I, pp. 33–5. As far as is known, he never wrote cabaret music again. Regarding the artistic goals of the cabaret, see Reich, *Schoenberg*, p. 11.
8. Their first meeting seems to have been shortly after 15 April 1902. Schoenberg may have been given an introduction to Strauss by Ernst von Wolzogen, the founder of the Überbrettl café and Strauss' librettist for *Feuersnot*. Stuckenschmidt, *Schoenberg*, pp. 61–2.
9. Werner Breig suggests that Schoenberg may have alluded to Strauss' *Tod und Verklärung* in *Verklärte Nacht*. If so (and if Strauss recognized the allusion), this might have been another reason for Strauss' generous support of Schoenberg at this stage in his career. See Werner Breig, "Arnold Schönbergs *Verklärte Nacht* und das Problem der Programmusik", in Walter Bernhart (ed.), *Die Semantik der musiko-literarischen Gattungen: Methodik und Analyse* (Tübingen: Gunter Narr Verlag, 1994), pp. 91–2.
10. Schoenberg copied the parts for Strauss' *Taillefer*. Stuckenschmidt, *Schoenberg*, p. 62.
11. Stuckenschmidt, *Schoenberg*, p. 63.
12. Stuckenschmidt, *Schoenberg*, p. 63.
13. Schoenberg may have been acquainted with Maeterlinck's play before his meeting with Strauss. On the March page of Schoenberg's calendar for 1900

there is an entry: "Pelleas und Melisande/Maeterlinck". Clara Steuermann, "From the Archives: Diaries", *Journal of the Arnold Schoenberg Institute*, 2/2 (1978), p. 144. See also, *SW*, 10B, p. 205.

14. Much to Schoenberg's disappointment, *Pelleas und Melisande* would not be performed until 1905, and Schoenberg himself had to conduct the premiere.
15. Stuckenschmidt, *Schoenberg*, p. 62.
16. Schoenberg may have completed the *Erste Niederschrift* (first draft) as early as the end of July. The fair copy of the full score was not completed until 28 February 1903. *SW*, 10B, p. 205. See also Maegaard, *Studien zur Entwicklung*, vol. I, pp. 35–6.
17. Zemlinsky employed trombone glissandi in the second movement of *Die Seejungfrau*, a work that was written in 1902–3, exactly contemporaneous with *Pelleas und Melisande*. Antony Beaumont, *Zemlinsky* (Ithaca, New York: Cornell University Press, 2000), p. 60.
18. In his *Harmonielehre* Schoenberg shows how to produce many (though as he states, not all) of the triads, seventh chords, and ninth chords, that can be created by the alteration of the various degrees. His only real practical restriction is his refraining from altering the root ("I cannot readily accept the idea of an altered root; I prefer the assumption that a new root is introduced." *HL*, p. 350.) See Example 287 in *Harmonielehre*, where employing alterations in this manner yields no fewer than thirteen possible versions of the seventh chord (with "*etc.*" added at the end). *HL*, p. 355. In a similar vein, Schoenberg shows the different ninth chords that result from chromatic alterations of the third, fifth, seventh, and ninth and provides an example with eleven possible versions of the ninth chord. *HL*, p. 357 (Example 289).
19. "M" (upper case) stands for major third; "m" (lower case) stands for minor third; "d" stands for diminished third; "A" stands for augmented third.
20. Schoenberg tends toward a somewhat practical (as opposed to pedantically theoretical) approach to orthography. In *Harmonielehre* he states: "In place of a complicated notation that often results from this pedantic exactness, I prefer to write the symbol that gives a familiar chord. Such will be possible with the majority of these chords. In other cases one may concentrate on the individual voice-leading and notate *that*, at least, simply." *HL*, p. 352.
21. Chords built from segments of the whole tone collection appear with increasing frequency from this point forward. For some examples of this chord in Traumleben, Op. 6, No. 1 (1903), see Christopher Wintle, "Schoenberg's Harmony: Theory and Practice", *Journal of the Arnold Schoenberg Institute*, 4/1 (1980), pp. 58–9.
22. See *HL*, p. 393 (for the whole tone hexachord) and *HL*, pp. 399–410 (for the chord of fourths).
23. Regarding the whole tone chord Schoenberg states: "Every modern composer has undoubtedly written such; hence it is clear that neither Strauss nor Debussy, Pfitzner nor I, nor any other modern was the first, from whom 'the others got it', rather, that each discovered it for himself, independently of the

others. For example, I use the whole-tone chords in my symphonic poem *Pelleas und Melisande* – composed in 1902, at about the same time as Debussy's opera *Pelléas et Mélisande* (in which, as I have heard, he also uses the whole-tone chords and scale for the first time), but at least three or four years before I became acquainted with his music." *HL*, pp. 392–3.

24. Simon Harris identifies the historical antecedents of the chord of fourths as "quite familiar, though marginal elements of the nineteenth-century harmony." He asserts that the five-note chord of fourths (which in his identification system is type P3) makes "the commonest form of the dominant eleventh". *A Proposed Classification of Chords in Early Twentieth-Century Music* (New York & London: Garland Publishing, 1989), p. 99.

25. In most recent harmony textbooks, the triad and seventh chord are not normally described as the superposition of a succession of thirds. But that is precisely how Schoenberg described their origin. "Thus, the formation of a seventh chord by adding the seventh is of course not a necessary consequence of this initial organization, but it is a possible consequence. If it is possible, however, then ninth chords, eleventh chords, etc. are also possible; and at least one advantage could be gained from this possibility in that the system of superimposed thirds could be extended." *HL*, p. 345. At first, as here, the occurrences of the chord of fourths almost always were as a literal stack of fourths, and not with the tones appearing in any register. In Schoenberg's later works, chords of this type do appear in versions other than a literal stack of fourths. Simon Harris identifies a prominent example of this in the String Quartet No. 2, Op. 10. *A Proposed Classification*, p. 112 and the associated example (Ex. 36), Appendix, p. 37.

26. Bryan Simms shows that an important type of harmony in Schoenberg's music was what he terms the "triadic tetrachord", a sonority in which "three of the four tones almost always form a major or minor triad". *The Atonal Music of Arnold Schoenberg: 1908–1923* (New York: Oxford University Press, 2000), p. 16. Simms' "triadic tetrachord" is a specific instance of the general category of chords built using the principle of localized consonance. The concept of "chord-forms that were no longer fully consonant" is discussed by Simon Harris in *A Proposed Classification*, pp. 41ff. Harris coins the term "semiconsonance" to refer to these chordal types. My notion of "localized consonance" is based on Harris' but, as will become apparent in coming chapters, I also use the concept of localized consonance in a more general way (that is, to refer to structures other than chords) in order to show connections with Schoenberg's contrapuntal practice.

27. By traditional standards, of course, the augmented triad was not a consonant sonority. However, in Schoenberg's harmonic context, augmented and diminished triads as well as the common seventh chords all functioned as relatively consonant entities and thus were used as a localized consonance within a larger harmonic structure.

28. If we assume enharmonic equivalence, it is also possible to think of this as a seventh chord built on F with the intervallic succession minor third,

augmented third, diminished third. Schoenberg includes this chordal type in his list of seventh chords with multiple alterations. See *HL*, p. 355 (Example 287, m. 3, second chord).
29. Schoenberg may have borrowed and adapted his "fate" motive from a similar motive used by Zemlinsky. See Antony Beaumont, *Zemlinsky* (Ithaca, New York: Cornell University Press, 2000), p. 22.
30. Schoenberg's treatment of the dissonance can be readily understood as a logical continuation of historical trends. For background on this, see Carl Dahlhaus, "Emancipation of the Dissonance", in Carl Dahlhaus, *Schoenberg and the New Music*, trans. Derrick Puffett and Alfred Clayton (Cambridge: Cambridge University Press, 1987), pp. 120–27.
31. Continuing the trend we saw in the 1899 songs, Schoenberg continues to use progressions in which a referential tonic is approached by something other than its dominant. Prominent among those dominant substitutes is the German sixth. See Frisch, *The Early Works*, p. 172.
32. The bass line does end up on a B at the end of the phrase, but the B does not support a consonant triad.
33. To hear the latter half of the phrase as a D minor triad with an added sixth, one must understand the E and C-sharp of the moving voice to be non-chord tones.
34. Speaking of Schoenberg's use of the twelve-tone set Milton Babbitt wrote: "By introducing this principle as the basis of relationship, Schoenberg not only effected a fusion of the general systematic constraint with the contextually defined property – for, although the principle of formation is defined for all sets, the specific pitch-class relations defined by a set are uniquely associated with it and its transformations – but established the means of a permutational musical system, as opposed to the combinational systems of the past. Given a collection of available elements, the choice of a sub-collection of these as a referential norm provides a norm that is distinguishable by content alone; such a system, and the traditional tonal system is such, is therefore combinational. But if the referential norm is the totality of elements, there is but one such norm in terms of content, and deviations from this norm cannot exist within the system." Milton Babbitt, "Twelve-Tone Invariants as Compositional Determinants", *Musical Quarterly*, 46 (1960), pp. 247–8.
35. This is an early use of the whole-tone scale in Schoenberg's music, a collection that (in whole and in part) becomes increasingly important in his works. For his use of this scale (or segments thereof) in the String Quartet, Op. 7, see Frisch, *The Early Works*, pp. 198–201. The whole-tone scale is a specific instance of an "indeterminate scale".
36. As Frisch states: "The programmatic import of these recurrences is clear: Melisande's chromatic motive ... infiltrates the themes of the two men with whom she becomes involved." *The Early Works*, p. 161. For an extended discussion of the leitmotifs, their relationships to one another and to the drama, see Bruhn, *Pelleas*, pp. 43–60.

37. As Bailey has thoroughly documented (in *Programmatic Elements*), programmatic features (if not full-fledged programs) continue to appear in Schoenberg's works throughout his career.
38. For a discussion of Schoenberg's changing attitudes to programmatic music see my "Schoenberg's Programmatic Compositions and the Ideology of Absolute Music", *Orbis Musicae*, 13 (2003), pp. 177–84.
39. Alban Berg, "Pelleas und Melisande Guide", (trans. Mark DeVoto), *Journal of the Arnold Schoenberg Institute*, 16 (1993), pp. 270–92. Schoenberg wrote a brief analysis of *Pelleas und Melisande*. See "Analyse von *Pelleas und Melisande*", in *Stil und Gedanke: Aufsätze zur Musik*, ed. Ivan Vojtěch (Frankfurt am Main: S. Fischer, 1976), pp. 437–9.
40. For an excellent critique of Berg's analysis see Derrick Puffett, "'Music that Echoes within One' for a Lifetime: Berg's Reception of Schoenberg's *Pelleas und Melisande*", *Music and Letters*, 76/2 (1995), pp. 209–64. Reprinted in Kathryn Bailey Puffett (ed.), *Derrick Puffett on Music* (Aldershot: Ashgate, 2001), pp. 539–615.
41. Much of the correspondence between the two has been published in *The Berg-Schoenberg Correspondence: Selected Letters*, edited by Juliane Brand, Christopher Hailey, and Donald Harris (New York: W. W. Norton, 1987).
42. "Nie ist sie rein beschreibend; immer wird die symphonische Form absoluter Musik gewahrt." Berg, "Pelleas und Melisande Guide", pp. 272–3.
43. Although Frisch believes that "there is some merit to Berg's analysis of the work as a sonata-symphony *Mischform*" he notes that "this approach becomes less persuasive the more specific it gets." He cites as particularly problematic the harmonic dimension. *The Early Works*, p. 169. Bailey expresses similar reservations: *Programmatic Elements*, p. 72. See also Bruhn, *Pelleas*, pp. 41–2.
44. Bailey, *Programmatic Elements*, pp. 6–8.
45. Sandra McColl, *Music Criticism in Vienna 1896–1897: Critically Moving Forms* (Oxford: Clarendon Press, 1996).
46. For an explanation of the aesthetic arguments for and against programmatic music, see Carl Dahlhaus, "Schoenberg and Programme Music", in *Schoenberg and the New Music*, trans. Derrick Puffett and Alfred Clayton (Cambridge: Cambridge University Press, 1987), pp. 94–8.
47. Bailey, *Programmatic Elements*, pp. 8–12.
48. Schoenberg attempted similar reinterpretations of *Verklärte Nacht*. In 1932 in Barcelona, he sketched out an analysis of *Verklärte Nacht* that identified various harmonic symmetries and motivic subtleties as essential features in the work's design. This analytical fragment has been reproduced and discussed a number of times. See Ulrich Thieme, *Studien zum Jugendwerk Arnold Schönbergs: Einflüsse und Wandlungen* (Regensburg: Bosse, 1979), pp. 216–21; Bailey, *Programmatic Elements*, pp. 31–2 and 36–7; Frisch, *The Early Works*, pp. 122–7; see also my "Tonal Analogies in Arnold Schönberg's Fourth String Quartet", *Journal of the Arnold Schönberg Center*, 4 (2002), pp. 219–20. In 1950, Schoenberg made another ex post facto attempt to stress the absolute music

characteristics and to de-emphasize the programmatic aspects of this work: "It seems that due to this attitude my composition has gained qualities which can also satisfy if one does not know what it illustrates, or in other words, it offers the possibility to be appreciated as 'pure' music. Thus it can perhaps make you forget the poem which many a person today might call rather repulsive." Reprinted in Joseph Auner, *A Schoenberg Reader: Documents of a Life* (New Haven & London: Yale University Press, 2003), p. 39.

49. For a sympathetic analysis of this sort, see Bruhn, *Pelleas*.
50. For an extended discussion of the programmatic music/absolute music dichotomy and the philosophical, aesthetic, and cultural ideas that helped determine the preference for one or the other from the eighteenth to the twentieth centuries, see Carl Dahlhaus, *The Idea of Absolute Music*, trans. Roger Lustig (Chicago and London: University of Chicago Press, 1989).

Chapter 6 Consolidation: Six Songs, Op. 3, 1903–4

1. Schoenberg, "My Technique and Style", *SI*, p. 110.
2. There are some disagreements in the literature as to the precise date of publication of Schoenberg's first works. See Frisch, *The Early Works*, p. 82.
3. Stuckenschmidt, *Schoenberg*, p. 77.
4. A brief analysis of this song appears in Walter Bailey, "Sechs Lieder für eine mittlere Singstimme und Klavier, op. 3", in Gerold Gruber (ed.), *Schönberg: Interpretationen seiner Werke* (Laaber: Laaber-Verlag, 2002), vol. I, p. 18.
5. Of the six songs of Op. 3, four are tripartite and two are in modified strophic form.
6. Schoenberg's idea of developing variation may have originated, at least partially, with his friend and teacher, Zemlinsky, who in turn may have been influenced by his teacher, Robert Fuchs. See Antony Beaumont, *Zemlinsky* (Ithaca, New York: Cornell University Press, 2000), p. 19.
7. Many years later (ca. 1948), Schoenberg defined variation as "changing a number of a unit's features, while preserving others". "Connection of Musical Ideas", *SI*, p. 287.
8. For a discussion of the notion of structural gaps see Leonard Meyer, *Emotion and Meaning in Music* (Chicago and London: University of Chicago Press, 1956), pp. 130–5.
9. In the orchestral song, "Natur", Op. 8, No. 1, written at about the same time as Op. 3, No. 1, Schoenberg uses only unadorned root position triads for significant stretches of the work (e.g. mm. 5–12). Here too, there are probably text-setting motivations for his choice of triads (i.e. nature = purity and simplicity). The poetic text in mm. 5–12 reads: Nacht fließt in Tag und Tag in Nacht, der Bach zum Strom, der Strom zum Meer. (Night flows into day and day into night, the brook to the river, the river to the sea.)
10. With one exception, all other triads are dissonant (usually augmented) or in inversion (usually the dissonant second inversion). The exception is in

mm. 5–7 where several other triads (F, B-flat, and G-flat) occur in root position. However, they do so in the context of a D-flat major diatonic collection.
11. The chronology is somewhat convoluted. See Maegaard, *Studien zur Entwicklung*, vol. I, pp. 36–7.
12. At various points in his career Schoenberg devised a number of terms to describe phenomena of this sort: hovering, fluctuating, suspended, and roving. For early definitions, see *HL*, p. 383.

Chapter 7 Abstract form, secret program: String Quartet, Op. 7, 1904–5

1. Schoenberg, "How One Becomes Lonely", *SI*, p. 44.
2. Letter from Alexander Rosé to Arnold Schoenberg, dated 31 May 1902:
   Sehr geehrter Herr!
   Dass Ihr Sextett, wie es zu erwarten war, hier mit Beifall und dem Gegentheil! aufgenommen wurde, ist Ihnen ja bekannt. Mein Bruder, der Ihr Talent aufrichtig bewundert und schätzt, denkt an eine 2. Aufführung in Wien im nächsten Jahr. Auf der Tournée (Rheinprovinz [?] u. Russland) ist es aber ausgeschlossen. Wie u. wann soll er auf der Reise probiren. Mein Bruder veranlaßt mich Ihnen dies zu schreiben u. sendet Ihnen beste Grüße! Haben Sie nichts Neues, ein schönes Quartett? Was kann man auf die Reise mitnehmen!
   Freundlichste Grüße Ihr ganz ergebenster
   Alexander Rosé
3. Letter from Alexander Rosé to Arnold Schoenberg, dated 18 October 1902:
   Sehr geehrter Herr!
   Mein Bruder konnte in Folge anderer Dispositionen Ihr Sextett in sein diesjähriges Programm nicht aufnehmen. Wenn Sie ein neues Streichquartett haben, so ist er gerne bereit es noch in diesem Jahr zu spielen.
   Mit vielen Empfehlungen
   Ihr ganz ergebenster
   Alexander Rosé
4. Maegaard calls this fragment Str.qu04Fr. Maegaard, *Studien zur Entwicklung*, vol. I, p. 39. An edition of the fair copy (80 measures) has been published in *SW*, 20A, pp. 219–25, where it is identified as "Fragment eines Streichquartetts d-Moll (1901–1904)." Sketches and extended commentary are in *SW*, 20B, pp. 279–305. There is considerable disagreement and uncertainty about the date (or dates) of this fragment. Wellesz states that in the summer of 1903 Schoenberg was working on "a string quartet which may be regarded as the predecessor of the D minor, Op. 7," Egon Wellesz, *Arnold Schoenberg*, trans. W. H. Kerridge (London: Dent, 1925), p. 18. Reprinted, Freeport, New York: Books for Libraries Press, 1969. Josef Rufer places the fragment in 1903. Maegaard places it in 1904. Christian Martin Schmidt suggests that at least parts of this fragment might have originated as early as 1901 because sketches for

the fragment appear in a sketchbook interleaved with drafts of the *Brettellieder* which date from that year. *SW*, 20B, p. 279. He also argues that the portion of the fugue from m. 56 onward was written in 1904. *SW*, 20B, p. 286. Frisch sees 1903 as a more likely starting date for stylistic reasons and suggests that it was "worked on most intensively in 1903–4". Frisch, *The Early Works*, p. 184.

5. For an extended and detailed discussion of this fragment, see Heinrich Helge Hattesen, *Emanzipation durch Aneignung: Untersuchungen zu den frühen Streichquartetten Arnold Schönbergs* (Kassel: Bärenreiter, 1990), pp. 167–89.

6. The 80-measure fugal fragment appears in *SW*, 20A, pp. 219–25. The 26-measure draft/sketch of the scherzo appears in *SW*, 20B, p. 289. The sketches appear in *SW*, 20B, pp. 287–305. I will argue below that some of the sketches for Op. 7 were originally conceived of as part of the String Quartet Fragment (1903–4). That the fugue was intended to be the opening movement is clear from the first page of the fair copy where Schoenberg wrote the title "Streich Quartett" at the top of the page and entered the number "1" in the upper right hand corner. For a facsimile, see *SW*, 20A, p. xii.

7. There are two other fragments written between 1897 and 1904 that might have been intended as absolute music: Symph.00 Fr. and Klav.00–01 Fr. Maegaard, *Studien zur Entwicklung*, vol. I, pp. 31, 33.

8. In m. 9, on the last eighth of the second beat, a root position D minor triad results from the intersection of the three voices active at that point. This is followed by a hint of the dominant on the next eighth with A in the viola and C-sharp in the first violin.

9. Christian Martin Schmidt suggests a division of the first eight fugal theme statements into a group of five entries (mm. 1–23) followed by a group of three entries (mm. 24–34). *SW*, 20B, p. 290. He bases this division on the return to the original tempo and the return to the original transpositional level of the theme in m. 24. Hattesen sees two groups of four entries each. *Emanzipation durch Aneignung*, pp. 175–6.

10. "Ich arbeite nicht allzuviel. Ich habe ein neues Lied für Orchester (das 4te) angefangen. Ich glaube das wird sehr gut werden ... Mein Quartet ruht. Vielleicht komme ich aber doch noch dazu." Ernst Hilmar (ed.), *Arnold Schönberg: Gedenkausstellung 1974* (Vienna: Universal Edition, 1974), pp. 183–4.

11. Mark Benson, "Schoenberg's Private Program for the String Quartet in D Minor, Op. 7", *Journal of Musicology*, 11/3 (1993), p. 381.

12. This table is a slightly varied version of Benson's Table 1. See Benson, "Schoenberg's Private Program", p. 377.

13. Hattesen, *Emanzipation durch Aneignung*, p. 167, suggests this possibility.

14. This was not unusual for Schoenberg: there are other examples in his career where material from a fragment is not completely abandoned, but rather incorporated into a subsequent work. See Jennifer Robin Shaw, "Schoenberg's Choral Symphony, *Die Jakobsleiter*, and Other Wartime Fragments", Ph.D. Dissertation, State University of New York at Stony Brook (2002).

15. There are obvious similarities between the fugal transition of Op. 7 and the fugal structure of the fragment. See Frisch, *The Early Works*, p. 185.
16. *SW*, 20B, p. 1.
17. Although they had promised Schoenberg a performance of a new quartet, the Rosé Quartet at first declined to perform Op. 7 when it was finally completed. For a concise summary of some of the disappointments Schoenberg faced in trying to get his works performed around 1905 see Margareta Saary, "Kammersymphonie für 15 Solo-Instrumente op. 9 (und op. 9B)" in Gerold Gruber (ed.), *Schönberg: Interpretationen seiner Werke* (Laaber: Laaber-Verlag, 2002), vol. I, p. 105.
18. For extended analyses of the formal structure (with particular emphasis on the problems of the all-in-one form) see Ralf Alexander Kohler and Markus Böggemann, "I. Streichquartett op. 7", in Gerold Gruber (ed.), *Arnold Schönberg: Interpretationen seiner Werke* (Laaber: Laaber-Verlag, 2002), vol. I, pp. 73–94, and Michael Cherlin, "Motive and Memory in Schoenberg's First String Quartet", in Reinhold Brinkmann and Christoph Wolff (edd.), *Music of My Future: The Schoenberg Quartets and Trio* (Cambridge Massachusetts, London: Harvard University Press, 2000), pp. 61–80.
19. Reich, *Schoenberg*, p. 20.
20. Because of some hints that Schoenberg had dropped in the 1940s, there had been suspicions that Op. 7 was based on a program but there was no proof. Confirmation of these suspicions was provided by the discovery of the program. See Christian Schmidt, "Schönbergs 'Very Definite – But Private' Programm zum Streichquartett Opus 7", in *Bericht über den 2. Kongreß der Internationalen Schönberg-Gesellschaft*, edd. Rudolf Stephan and Sigrid Wiesmann (Vienna: Elisabeth Lafite, 1986), pp. 230–4 and Benson, "Schoenberg's Private Program".
21. Bailey, *Programmatic Elements*.
22. Mark Benson argues that Schoenberg wrote the program relatively late in the process of working on Op. 7, and that he did so to "spur his own imagination and awaken the quartet from its 'rest.'" "Schoenberg's Private Program", 382. I agree with the general outlines of Benson's argument but with some amendments. If the first sketches for Op. 7 (on pp. 4–8 and 15–17 of Sketchbook I) were originally part of the String Quartet Fragment, then a slightly different scenario emerges. This would imply that Schoenberg intended the String Quartet Fragment as an abstract work. At some point, he found himself unable to continue – perhaps because he was not yet ready to make a clean break with programmatic music. By 13 July 1903 he had put the quartet project on hold and told Oskar Posa that he "might" come back to it. Later that year Schoenberg did come back to a string quartet project, but he restructured it completely: he abandoned almost everything he had written, keeping only the material that had been intended for its D minor movement (worked out on pp. 4–8 and 15–17 of Sketchbook I). As Benson shows, the first material after the pause (on p. 31 of Sketchbook I) is the "*Neue Leben fühlend*" theme for the

scherzo section of Op. 7. This demonstrates, as Benson properly argues, that Schoenberg had decided to write a programmatic composition. In so doing, he abandoned an abstract work (the String Quartet Fragment) and began a new, programmatic work (Op. 7). But he did not abandon everything he had written for the String Quartet Fragment. Instead, he incorporated some of the material from the D minor movement of the Fragment, making it into the opening movement of the Quartet. Although he did abandon the fugue of the Fragment, he incorporated a similar fugal passage as part of Op. 7.

23. In Schoenberg's approach to programmatic music, the idea or person did not need to be explicitly referred to by the text; it could be implied as part of the composer's reading and interpretation of the text. See my "Schoenberg's Programmatic Compositions and the Ideology of Absolute Music", *Orbis Musicae*, 13 (2003), pp. 180–4.

24. Walter Frisch has shown that Schoenberg wrote the comparatively diatonic theme of the scherzo before he wrote the chromatic version of that theme for the transition. Therefore, the ordering in the composition itself (a move from a more chromatic to a more diatonic version of the theme) is in reverse order to the chronology of the compositional process. Walter Frisch, "Thematic Form and the Genesis of Schoenberg's D-Minor Quartet, Opus 7", *Journal of the American Musicological Society*, 41/2 (1988), pp. 289–314. However, if we understand the fugue of the String Quartet Fragment (1903–4), as closely related to fugal transition in Op. 7, then the chromatic fugue of the Fragment preceded the diatonic scherzo theme of Op. 7 and thus the chronology of the compositional process is not in conflict with the ordering within the composition.

25. The altered reprises also make it difficult to identify the boundaries of the components of the abstract forms. There is, for instance, a range of widely divergent views on the location of the boundary between the recapitulation of the opening movement and the beginning of the first development section. For a useful discussion of the complexities of the abstract form of this work (and a summary of the previous literature), see Claus-Steffen Mahnkopf, *Gestalt und Stil: Schönbergs Erste Kammersymphonie und ihr Umfeld* (Bärenreiter: Kassel, 1994), pp. 26–46.

26. Schoenberg seems to have cut out characters from Maeterlinck's play, precisely because they did not have enough of a role in the play to permit the integration of their thematic ideas into the whole. In an early outline of the program, Schoenberg listed King Arkel in his plan for the work. Since the King's appearances were limited in Maeterlinck's play, Schoenberg may have felt that he could not integrate the motives for King Arkel into the rest of the piece and thus cut the character entirely from his plan.

27. The thirteen reviews are reprinted in *SW*, 22B, pp. 86–91.

28. These are extracts from the reviews printed in Bailey, *Programmatic Elements*, pp. 8–11.

29. Nuria Schoenberg-Nono reports that even in the 1940s her father was so devastated by negative criticism that he would sink into despair, and that he

could extricate himself from this depression only by writing music. Personal conversation with the author.
30. Dika Newlin, *Schoenberg Remembered: Diaries and Recollections (1938–76)* (New York: Pendragon Press, 1980), p. 193.
31. When *Verklärte Nacht* was premiered, Dehmel's poem was not printed with the program, even though it appears that Schoenberg had requested that it be printed. In a letter from Alexander Rosé dated 31 October 1901 Rosé wrote Schoenberg: "Ihr Sextett ist für 18. März (letzter Abend) projectirt aber ohne Abdruck des Gedichtes. Das ist ganz unmöglich!" ("Your sextet is projected for 18 March (the last evening) but without printing of the poem. That is completely impossible!") By 1905, Schoenberg's views had changed. *Pelleas und Melisande* received its first performance on a concert of the Vereinigung schaffender Tonkünstler. Since Schoenberg was one of the co-founders of this organization and the conductor of the premiere, one presumes that if he had wanted to print a précis of the program he could have done so. But as the reviews make clear, no program was supplied, a clear indication that Schoenberg was trying to distance himself from programmatic music.
32. It is also possible that his suppression of the program of *Pelleas und Melisande* (and the use of a secret program for Op. 7) resulted at least partially from Schoenberg's desire to curry favor with his most powerful supporter, Gustav Mahler. By 1905 Mahler's views about programs had evolved to the point that he refused to print the program even when this explicitly contradicted the wishes of the composer. A prominent instance of this was Mahler's performance of the Viennese premiere of Richard Strauss' *Symphonia Domestica* (on the first orchestral concert sponsored by the Vereinigung). "In defiance of the composer's explicit instructions, he excluded his 'programmatic' allusions from the concert programme." Henry-Louis de la Grange, *Gustav Mahler, Volume 3; Vienna: Triumph and Disillusion, 1904–1907* (Oxford: Oxford University Press, 1999), p. 58.
33. For the original German text see *SW* 20B, p. 110.
34. The heading "Neues Leben Fühlend" appears in the sketches for the scherzo theme on p. 31 of Schoenberg's Sketchbook I.
35. Benson suggests that the 'c' of line 9 of the program (according to Christian Schmidt's numbering of the lines in *SW*, 20B, 110) should instead be read as an 'e.' Benson, "Schoenberg's Private Program", pp. 379–80, fn. 10. I think this emendation creates as many problems as it solves. Schoenberg has three levels in his outline: Roman numerals, Arabic numerals, and lower case letters. Making line 9 into 'e' would mean either that section I 3 (lines 6–9) would have no 'a', 'b', 'c', and 'd' or that the subheading '3' on line 6 should not exist. It is simpler to assume that Schoenberg left out 'a' and 'b', particularly since extra space was left at this spot.
36. There is, however, considerable disagreement about where the beginning of this development section should be placed. See Mahnkopf, *Gestalt und Stil*, p. 29.

37. An inconclusive reprise is also necessary for the absolute music macrostructure. A solid close at the end of the reprise of the first movement would make a continuation to the remaining movements awkward. See Kohler and Böggemann, "I. Streichquartett", pp. 85–6.
38. In the program, Schoenberg indicated that this return would be abbreviated: "Wiederholung eines Theiles von (II.1.a)".
39. Benson argues that the program plays less of a role in the final two movements: "The structure of the second half of the quartet, however, is much looser. Nor is there any explicit evidence of formal planning for the second half of the quartet in Part III of the program." "Schoenberg's Private Program", p. 388.
40. For a discussion of this passage and its intervallic relationships see Peter Schubert, "'A New Epoch of Polyphonic Style': Schoenberg on Chords and Lines", *Music Analysis*, 12/3 (1993), pp. 289–319.
41. It is probably not coincidental that the work with the highest concentration of learned devices pre-Op. 7 is the String Quartet in D (1897). See Frisch, *The Early Works*, pp. 43–4.
42. Schoenberg's manuscripts provide some useful background information regarding his interest in contrapuntal ideas. Before 1905 there is no evidence of Schoenberg having any interest in writing canons. In 1905, toward the end of his work on Op. 7, there is a sudden explosion of experimentation with canons. The fragmentary and sketchy format of these canons suggests that Schoenberg may have intended them more as compositional exercises than as works meant for public performance or publication. It also suggests that, having made the decision to begin cultivating absolute music, Schoenberg recognized the need to polish and refine his contrapuntal skills. The brief florescence of canonic writing in 1905 – immediately after his first extended use of contrapuntal devices in his compositions – suggests that this is one of the methods Schoenberg chose to hone his skills.
43. I am using a modified figured bass notation here. A = augmented; d = diminished; M = major; m = minor. The symbol 3 stands for either 3 or 10.

Chapter 8 Referential centers? Lieder and fragments, Fall 1905

1. Schoenberg, "Composition with Twelve Tones (1)", *SI*, p. 216.
2. I have ordered these songs chronologically according to their dates of completion. The actual chronology is considerably more complicated. See Maegaard, *Studien zur Entwicklung*, vol. I, pp. 42–5.
3. Allen Forte argues that the Op. 6 songs are crucial works in the transition from tonality to atonality. He suggests that these songs were the first of his works in which atonal pitch-class sets (in particular Schoenberg's "musical signature" pc-set 6-Z44) occur as significant components of the musical structure. Forte thus concludes: "What might be called 'set consciousness,' then, begins here, in the 1905 songs of Opus 6, written between September 6 and November 28 of that year, after Schoenberg had returned to Vienna from his first stay in Berlin."

Allen Forte, "Schoenberg's Creative Evolution: The Path to Atonality", *The Musical Quarterly*, 64/2 (1978), p. 138. The reasons for my disagreements with Forte's analyses of Schoenberg's works are summarized in "Atonality, Analysis, and the Intentional Fallacy", *Music Theory Spectrum*, 18/2 (1996), 167–99. Suffice it to say here that Forte's identification of segments (case in point, the Es C H B E G signature) as significant analytical objects is compromised by the arbitrary (and thus tendentious) segmentation procedures he employs. This is not to say that pitch-class set theory has no validity for the analysis of Schoenberg's works. Some set theoretical concepts are of immense value and in this book I have not hesitated to employ them when appropriate.

4. Bryan Simms points out the importance of "suspended" and "wavering" tonality in the songs from this period. See *The Atonal Music of Arnold Schoenberg: 1908–1923* (New York: Oxford University Press, 2000), pp. 24–8.
5. *HL*, p. 27. This definition was not in the original 1911 edition of *Harmonielehre*; it was inserted in 1921 for the third edition. In the original 1911 edition Schoenberg had a related definition (which he also retained in the third edition, placing it after the cited quotation), but in it, he never uses the word "tonality" ("Tonart"). It reads: "Gewiß: wenn alle Akkorde, die in einem geschlossenen Tonstück auftreten, in solchen Folgen erscheinen, daß ihre Rückbeziehung auf einen gemeinsamen Grundton möglich ist, so könnte man von einer Ausdehnung der Idee des Klanges (die man sich vertikal vorstellt) auf das horizontale Geschehen sprechen." Schoenberg, *Harmonielehre* (Vienna: Universal, 1911), p. 29. Roy Carter translates this as: "Whenever all chords of a complete piece of music appear in progressions that can be related to a common fundamental tone, one can then say that the idea of the music sound (*Klang*) (which is conceived as vertical) is extended to the horizontal plane." *HL*, p. 28.
6. Carl Dahlhaus, in a critique of the term "expanded tonality" as applied by Schoenberg to Wagner's music states: "An alternative interpretation of Wagnerian tonality is possible. As they change in quick and often 'rhapsodic' succession, the keys, or fragmentary allusions to keys, do not always relate to a constant center, around which they are to be imagined as simultaneously grouped; they should rather be seen as joined together like the links in a chain, without there necessarily being any other connection between the first and third links than the second. In the light of this theory, the characteristic function of Wagner's use of harmony is to establish not hierarchies but an order of succession." Carl Dahlhaus, *Between Romanticism and Modernism: Four Studies in the Music of the Later Nineteenth Century*, trans. Mary Whittall (Berkeley and Los Angeles: University of California Press, 1980), p. 66.
7. Schoenberg worked on an earlier version of this song around April 1905. See Maegaard, *Studien zur Entwicklung*, vol. I, p. 42.
8. *Structural Functions of Harmony*, revised edition, ed. Leonard Stein (New York: W. W. Norton, 1969), p. 110.
9. Frisch suggests that the added line is derived from the piano accompaniment in m. 1. *The Early Works*, pp. 217–18.

10. Frisch sees the whole-tone chord that prepares the emphasis on G minor as a modified dominant. *The Early Works*, p. 218.
11. For a careful and thorough discussion of this song, its text, its harmonic structure, and its relationship to Schoenberg's changing notions of organic structure, see Séverine Neff, "Reinventing the Organic Artwork: Schoenberg's Changing Images of Tonal Form," in Charlotte Cross and Russell Berman (edd.), *Schoenberg and Words: The Modernist Years* (New York and London: Garland Publishing, 2000), pp. 275–308.
12. *HL*, p. 383. The one time the E-flat major triad appears is in m. 50.
13. *Structural Functions of Tonality*, p. 111.
14. See mm. 11–15 where the dominant of E-flat is prolonged and elaborated.
15. *Structural Functions of Harmony*, p. 112.
16. See my "Redating Schoenberg's Passacaglia for Orchestra", *Journal of the American Musicological Society*, 40/3 (1987), pp. 471–94.

Chapter 9 Absolute music and its consequences: Chamber Symphony, Op. 9, 1905–6

1. Schoenberg, "Opinion or Insight?" *SI*, p. 259.
2. Maegaard has named this fragment "Orch. 05–06 Sk". *Studien zur Entwicklung*, vol. I, p. 46.
3. There is another orchestral fragment from slightly earlier which Maegaard has named Symph. 05 Sk.: *ibid*, p. 43.
4. Although its scoring is innovative, Schoenberg's work is not the first chamber symphony ever written. See Walter Frisch, "The Refractory Masterpiece: Toward an Interpretation of Schoenberg's Chamber Symphony, op. 9", in Juliane Brand and Christopher Hailey (edd.), *Constructive Dissonance: Arnold Schoenberg and the Transformations of Twentieth-Century Culture* (Berkeley, Los Angeles, and London: University of California Press, 1997), pp. 87–8.
5. Even this performance was not evidence of a wider acceptance: it was performed by Schoenberg's brother-in-law Alexander Zemlinsky with his orchestra in Prague.
6. For a listing of Schoenberg's concerts in Vienna from 1897 until 1910 see Martin Thrun, *Neue Musik im deutschen Musikleben bis 1933* (Bonn: Orpheus, 1995), vol. I, p. 105.
7. For a concise discussion of issues relating to harmony, theme, polyphony, instrumentation, form, and tone, in the Chamber Symphony, see Reinhold Brinkmann, "The Compressed Symphony: On the Historical Content of Schoenberg's Op. 9" (trans. Irene Zedlacher), in Walter Frisch (ed.), *Schoenberg and His World* (Princeton, New Jersey: Princeton University Press, 1999), pp. 141–61.
8. For a discussion of the changes in Schoenberg's orchestration and with particular emphasis on the different layers of *Gurrelieder*, see Brian Campbell, "*Gurrelieder* and the Fall of the Gods: Schoenberg's Struggle with the Legacy of Wagner", in Charlotte Cross and Russell Berman (edd.), *Schoenberg and*

Words: The Modernist Years (New York and London: Garland Publishing, 2000), pp. 44–58.

9. One cannot, of course, prove a negative, so it is theoretically possible that there is an unknown program for this work. In the case of the String Quartet, Op. 7, however, Schoenberg dropped a number of hints to his students about the existence of a program long before the program itself was discovered in the back of a sketchbook. The absence of any such hints in the case of Op. 9 suggests that there is no program, not even a hidden one. For a good survey of some of the important stages in Schoenberg's gradual move away from programmatic music see Werner Breig, "Arnold Schönbergs *Verklärte Nacht* und das Problem der Programmusik", in Walter Bernhart (ed.), *Die Semantik der musiko-literarischen Gattungen: Methodik und Analyse* (Tübingen: Gunter Narr Verlag, 1994), pp. 105–12.

10. For a thematic/formal analysis from Schoenberg's circle see Alban Berg, "Chamber Symphony Guide", (trans. Mark DeVoto), *Journal of the Arnold Schoenberg Institute*, 16 (1993), pp. 236–68. For extended analyses of Op. 9 see also Claus-Steffen Mahnkopf, *Gestalt und Stil: Schönbergs Erste Kammersymphonie und ihr Umfeld* (Bärenreiter: Kassel, 1994), pp. 47–92; Margareta Saary, "Kammersymphonie für 15 Solo-Instrumente op. 9 (und op. 9B)", in Gerold Gruber (ed.), *Schönberg: Interpretationen seiner Werke* (Laaber: Laaber-Verlag, 2002), vol. I, pp. 104–23.

11. Schoenberg, "Composition with Twelve Tones (1)", *SI*, p. 222. With respect to the "two principal themes" of the Chamber Symphony, Schoenberg claims: "After I had completed the work I worried very much about the apparent absence of any relationship between the two themes. Directed only by my sense of form and the stream of ideas, I had not asked such questions while composing; but as usual with me, doubts arose as soon as I had finished." Schoenberg goes on to claim that twenty years after he composed the work he realized that the themes are related by modified inversion. To my ear, the relationship Schoenberg proposes seems unconvincing and arbitrary; it may tell us more about Schoenberg's compositional beliefs of the late 1920s (when motivic organicism was indeed a central pillar of his aesthetic) than about his compositional practice ca. 1905–6 (when it was not).

12. There are some motivic relationships between the different themes of the work: the theme of the slow movement (mm. 382ff) is derived from a melodic pattern from the beginning of the first movement (mm. 8ff). See Frisch, *The Early Works*, pp. 226–7.

13. It is perhaps significant that this return to the single-movement structure in the Piano Concerto happens in a work with one of Schoenberg's most explicit programmatic references. In his first sketches he wrote out "Life was so easy; suddenly hate broke out." For a discussion of the programmatic aspects of this work, see Bailey, *Programmatic Elements*, pp. 136–51. Perhaps one could argue that the String Trio, Op. 46 has an all-in-one form (though not based on traditional forms); it too includes some prominent programmatic references.

14. See Frisch, *The Early Works*, pp. 221–9. The single exposition explanation does not readily account for the return of the principal theme in mm. 57ff. The double exposition explanation does, but the restatement in m. 57 is not rhythmically highlighted as a new beginning; rather, it flows smoothly out of what preceded it. Neither explanation accounts for the fact that the recapitulation (which they both agree begins in m. 136) does not restate any of the themes other than the opening one.
15. A useful definition of "dialectical opposition" is: "The process wherein progress, change, or some desired resultant is obtained through antagonisms or other types of opposition applied to matter, ideas, values, emotions, etc. against one another to result in a third force, idea, value, etc. The *opposition* is normally dyadic, pitting two forces, ideas, values, etc. against one another to result in a third force, idea, value, etc. The *opposition* can be conceived of as *necessary* in that the resultant (i.e. the "third" force, idea, value, etc.) cannot be obtained without it. Although normally dyadic, the concept of *dialectical opposition* can be enlarged to include the resultants from complex force fields of oppositions." Michael Cherlin, "Dialectical Opposition in Schoenberg's Music and Thought", *Music Theory Spectrum*, 22/2 (2000), p. 158.
16. For a slightly different reading of the form, see Frisch, *The Early Works*, p. 227.
17. Frisch sees this as part of a complex of Neapolitan relationships. For his discussion of the Neapolitan relationship in Op. 9, see *The Early Works*, pp. 236–46. For further discussion of Frisch's idea, see also Catherine Dale, *Schoenberg's Chamber Symphonies: The Crystallization and Rediscovery of a Style* (Aldershot: Ashgate, 2000), pp. 26–38.
18. Alternatively, it is a subset of the E-flat major collection.
19. Schoenberg's reluctance to approach E from a traditional dominant chord resurfaces again and again in this composition and at crucial junctures in the form. For example, at m. 497, Schoenberg arrives on E (with a restatement of the principal theme) after having given a fair amount of emphasis to a chord built above B. Beginning in m. 493, there had been four measures of an altered dominant ninth chord (B D-sharp G [= F-double sharp] A C). Yet Schoenberg could not bring himself to proceed directly to E from this (heavily) altered dominant. Instead, the dominant ninth disappears in m. 496 and is replaced first with the whole-tone collection subdivided by register into augmented triads before concluding with a very radical sonority (D A F A C D-sharp) that acts as the immediate lead-in to E. To my ear, the dominant is both compromised and fatally weakened by the intervening whole-tone collection. For a different reading, see Frisch, *The Early Works*, pp. 230–1.
20. As was discussed in the previous chapter, there are precedents for the use of the 6/4 as an apparently consonant sonority, both in Schoenberg's works as well as his predecessors (e.g. Schumann). For some examples of this use of the 6/4 in Schoenberg's "Traumleben", Op. 6, No. 1 (1903), see Christopher Wintle, "Schoenberg's Harmony: Theory and Practice", *Journal of the Arnold Schoenberg Institute*, 4/1 (1980), p. 60.

21. *Preliminary Exercises in Counterpoint*, p. 11.
22. *Ibid*, p. 93.
23. In the score, a number of instruments have the root of the dominant chord at some point during m. 31 (bass clarinet, horn 2, bassoon, contrabassoon, cello, contrabass). With the exception of the contrabassoon, all of them drop the C before the end of the measure.
24. For other aspects of Schoenberg's use of symmetry, see David Lewin, "Inversional Balance as an Organizing Force in Schoenberg's Music and Thought", *Perspectives of New Music*, 6/2 (1968), 1–21, and Tom Demske, "Registral Centers of Balance in Atonal Works by Schoenberg and Webern", *In Theory Only*, 9/2–3 (1986), pp. 60–76.

Chapter 10 Crisis: *Friede auf Erden*, Op. 13, Ballades, Op. 12

1. Schoenberg, "About Music Criticism" (1909), *SI*, p. 192.
2. At the very end of his work on *Pelleas und Melisande*, he did take time out to write a song: "Deinem Blick". Maegaard, *Studien zur Entwicklung*, vol. I, p. 36. The end date for the song is 3 January 1903. Schoenberg finished the fair copy of the score of *Pelleas und Melisande* on 28 February 1903.
3. Maegaard, *Studien zur Entwicklung*, vol. I, pp. 40–3.
4. "Sonnenuntergang", Kl.05–06 Fr., "Heilig Wesen", "Still so ist", "Nächtlicher Weg". *Ibid*, pp. 47–8.
5. Josef Rufer (and following him *SW*) refers to this as "Sketchbook III." See Josef Rufer, *The Works of Arnold Schoenberg*, trans. Dika Newlin (New York: Free Press, 1962); Maegaard calls it Sk06–16: *Studien zur Entwicklung*, vol. I, p. 21.
6. For a summary of the compositional history of Schoenberg's Second Chamber Symphony (much of which extends beyond the chronological limits covered in this book) and for analytical discussion of many details of the work in both its early and later stages, see Catherine Dale, *Schoenberg's Chamber Symphonies: The Crystallization and Rediscovery of a Style* (Aldershot: Ashgate, 2000), pp. 109–200.
7. Schoenberg may have stopped work on *Und Pippa tanzt!* for financial, not artistic, reasons. "The reason why this was not finished was the large financial demands which Hauptmann and his publisher S. Fischer demanded for the libretto of the play." Stuckenschmidt, *Schoenberg*, p. 86.
8. There appear to have been some preliminary sketches on the previous page. See *SW*, 20B, p. 112.
9. Works on the program mentioned by name by the critics include "Erwartung" (Op. 2, No.1), "Erhebung" (Op. 2, No. 3), "Wie Georg von Fundsberg von sich selber sang" (Op. 3, No. 1), "Warnung" (Op. 3, No. 3), "Hochzeitslied" (Op. 3, No. 4), "Geübtes Herz" (Op. 3, No. 5), "Mädchenlied" (Op. 6, No. 3), "Ghasel" (Op. 6, No. 5). It is clear that there were a number of other songs on the program. Since one of the reviews cites the names of some of the poets, it is possible to reconstruct what some of the other songs were, given that Schoenberg set some

poets only once. Thus, we can deduce that the program also included "Lockung" (Op. 6, No. 7), "Der Wanderer" (Op. 6, No. 8), "Waldsonne" (Op. 2, No. 4), and "Traumleben" (Op. 6, No. 1).

10. The public performance on 20 March 1898 appears to have been preceded three days earlier by a private performance under the auspices of the Tonkünstlerverein. See Martin Thrun, *Neue Musik im deutschen Musikleben bis 1933* (Bonn: Orpheus, 1995), vol. I, p. 105. There is also evidence of an even earlier performance: on 2 March 1896, Polyhymnia (an amateur group founded and conducted by Zemlinsky) performed Schoenberg's Notturno in A-flat major for solo violin, harp and strings. See Beaumont, *Zemlinsky*, p. 36. Because of contradictory statements and evidence, it is very difficult to reconstruct the history of Schoenberg's early performances with utter certainty. Schoenberg himself contributed to the confusion. For example, in his essay "Why No Great American Music" (1937), he stated that "I was twenty-five before I was performed for the first time." *SI*, p. 179. Since Schoenberg was born in 1874, it would seem that he is suggesting his first performance was not until 1899 or early 1900. This cannot be correct: we know that the String Quartet in D was performed in 1898.

11. Particularly noteworthy was a review by Eduard Hanslick where he stated "It seems to me that a new Mozart is growing up in Vienna." Quoted in Malcolm MacDonald, *Schoenberg* (London: Dent, 1976), p. 22. A mostly positive review also appeared in *Neue Freie Press*. It has been reprinted in *SW*, 20B, p. xv.

12. While there is widespread agreement that there was a concert of Schoenberg's songs in Vienna early on in Schoenberg's career and that Eduard Gärtner was the soloist, there is equally widespread disagreement about the date. Thrun, *ibid*, and Beaumont (*Zemlinsky*, 490) assert that the Two Songs, Op. 1, were performed on 19 February 1897 by Eduard Gärtner (baritone) and Alexander Zemlinsky (piano). This cannot be correct: the songs were not written until 1898. Raymond Fearn places the premiere of the Two Songs, Op. 1, in 1898 (not further specified), again with Eduard Gärtner as the soloist. See "Zwei Gesänge für eine Baritonstimme und Klavier op. 1", in Gerold Gruber (ed.), *Arnold Schönberg: Interpretationen seiner Werke* (Laaber: Laaber-Verlag, 2002), vol. I, p. 1. Willi Reich states: "Some of the songs were performed at a concert in 1898 by the Viennese singing teacher Eduard Gärtner; Zemlinsky was the accompanist." Willi Reich, *Schoenberg: A Critical Biography*, trans. Leo Black (New York, Washington: Praeger, 1978), p. 9. Egon Wellesz states that the two songs of Op. 1 (plus Op 6, No. 3) were performed by Gärtner in December, 1900. Wellesz, *Arnold Schoenberg*, trans. W. H. Kerridge (London: Dent, 1925; reprint, Freeport, New York: Books for Libraries Press, 1969), p. 13. Some of this cannot be correct: Op. 6, No. 3 was not written until 1905. Beaumont (*ibid*) dates the premiere of Op. 2 to 1 December 1901 but appears to base this claim on Wellesz (*ibid*) who had both a different date and different program for that concert. In any event, it appears that Op. 2 was not premiered until 11 February 1904. See Walter Frisch, "Vier Lieder für eine Singstimme und

Klavier, op. 2", in Gerold Gruber (ed.), *Arnold Schönberg: Interpretationen seiner Werke* (Laaber: Laaber-Verlag, 2002), vol. I, p. 5. To say the least, the history of Schoenberg's early performances is an area that needs further study.

13. There were at least thirteen published reviews. Notwithstanding their criticism of its programmatic structure, many of the critics had at least some positive things to say about *Verklärte Nacht*. For reprints of the reviews see *SW*, 22B, pp. 86–91.

14. Meyer's augmented quartet performed the work at the German Society of Musicians, 30 October 1902. The augmented Rosé Quartet gave additional performances of the work in Vienna on 19 February 1904 and again on 1 March 1904.

15. In between the premieres of Opp. 4 and 5 there are almost no documented performances in Vienna. Other than the additional performances of *Verklärte Nacht*, the only exception seems to be a lieder recital: songs from Schoenberg's Opp. 2 and 3 were performed under the auspices of the Ansorge Society on 11 February 1904 with tenor Walter Pieau accompanied by Zemlinsky. See Gorrell, *Discordant Melody*, 30 and Thrun, *Neue Musik*, vol. I, p. 105.

16. Only Zemlinsky's half of the correspondence has survived; Schoenberg's letters to Zemlinsky were destroyed. For the correspondence regarding the premiere of *Verklärte Nacht* see Alexander Zemlinsky, *Briefwechsel mit Arnold Schönberg, Anton Webern, Alban Berg und Franz Schreker*, ed. Horst Weber (Darmstadt: Wissenschaftliche Buchgesellschaft, 1995), pp. 12–15.

17. For a thorough examination of Viennese newspapers and music critics at the end of the nineteenth century, see Sandra McColl, *Music Criticism in Vienna 1896–1897: Critically Moving Forms* (Oxford: Clarendon Press, 1996). Although the period McColl discusses is slightly earlier than that covered in the present book, many of the issues, personalities, and newspapers had not changed.

18. The reviews have been collected and reprinted in: Martin Eybl (ed.), *Die Befreiung des Augenblicks: Schönbergs Skandalkonzerte 1907 und 1908, Eine Dokumentation* (Vienna, Cologne, and Weimar: Böhlau Verlag, 2004).

19. For a discussion of the evolving reception of Schoenberg's music see Leon Botstein, "Schoenberg and the Audience: Modernism, Music, and Politics in the Twentieth Century," in Walter Frisch (ed.), *Schoenberg and His World* (Princeton, New Jersey: Princeton University Press, 1999), pp. 19–54.

20. "But why then did even the works of my first period always meet resistance at the first few performances, only later to become appreciated?" "A Self Analysis", *SI*, p. 77.

21. For the complete text of this review, see Eybl, *Die Befreiung*, pp. 89–90.

22. It was a result of the merger several years earlier of two music magazines, the Musikalische Wochenblatt and the Neue Zeitschrift für Musik, the latter being the famous magazine founded by Robert Schumann in 1834.

23. Schoenberg tended to portray Viennese critics as incompetent nobodies, unqualified to judge: "But among us a musician goes to a newspaper only

when he is unfit to be even a 'professor' of singing or the piano." "About Music Crticism" (1909), *SI*, p. 193.

24. The enthusiastic reception was mentioned by other critics. "Die Anhänger des Komponisten applaudierten zwar nach Liebeskräften," *Sonn und Montags Courier*, 4 Feb. "Die Claque des Herrn Schönberg arbeitete zwar mit Dampfkraft," *Neue Musikalische Presse, Wien* (n.d., unsigned).

25. A little more than two years earlier, Helm took a similar approach in his review of the premiere of Gustav Mahler's Third Symphony (first performed, 14 December 1904). As with the Schoenberg concert, Helm felt he had to explain away the enthusiastic public success of Mahler's work. As Henry-Louis de la Grange describes it: "Theodor Helm proffered an ingenious explanation. Mahler's concerts, he thought, were attended largely by women, and his audiences were 'favourably disposed' towards him and 'looked upon him as a god' while his opponents 'normally stayed away from such events'." Henry-Louis de la Grange, *Gustav Mahler, Volume 3; Vienna: Triumph and Disillusion, 1904–1907* (Oxford: Oxford University Press, 1999), p. 68. In 1909 Schoenberg railed against the critics' unwillingness to face up to the positive reaction of audiences to his works: "One can give no credence to reporting – it sees what it wants to see and not what really happened; makes a success into a fiasco, hisses into applause; projects its own attitude on to the audience – for the critic usually lacks the courage to stand alone with his opinion. If he feels himself in accord with part of the public, even a small part, then he says the whole public was indignant or enthusiastic. If it is quite impossible to misinterpret the audience's attitude, he turns to his colleagues to protect him from public opinion. So the public is now abused along with the artists, now praised along with the critic. But true it hardly ever is; it hardly ever comes out free of distortions and insinuations ('friendship', 'clique'), even on the occasions when the truth would have the same effect as a lie." "About Music Criticism", *SI*, pp. 195–6.

26. Many years later, in his essay "My Public", Schoenberg recalled this type of criticism: "At the start of my career, when to the annoyance of my opponents a noticeable part of the audience did not hiss but applauded, and when the hissers did not succeed in carrying the day against the majority, although hisses sound more striking than applause, then these opponents of mine alleged that those bestowing their approval were my friends and had only applauded out of friendship and not because they liked the piece. My poor friends: as true as few." "My Public", *SI*, p. 96.

27. The widely accepted image of the reception of Schoenberg's works is that he and his music were subjected to unremittingly negative reactions from just about everyone, save for a few devoted members of his circle. There is evidence to suggest that the contemporaneous reception of Schoenberg's music sometimes was more positive than we normally think was the case. For example, with regard to the concert of 4 February 1912 in Berlin, Schoenberg noted in his diary "Applause strong after 'Waldsonne' (!!), the George-Lieder and at the

end." Anita Luginbühl, "*Attempt at a Diary* by Arnold Schoenberg", *Journal of the Arnold Schoenberg Institute*, 9/1 (1986), p. 22. The favorable reaction by the audience is not usually what is recalled about that and other concerts. Concerning the 4 February 1912 concert, we tend to remember Schoenberg's vitriolic exchange with Leopold Schmidt, the critic for the *Berliner Tageblatt*. See Walter Bailey, "Composer Versus Critic: The Schoenberg-Schmidt Polemic", *Journal of the Arnold Schoenberg Institute*, 4/2 (1980), pp. 119–37. Schoenberg himself was at least partially responsible for creating the impression that his works were badly received. In 1937, Schoenberg described the premiere of *Verklärte Nacht* as follows: "And so the first performance of my *Verklärte Nacht* ended in a riot and in actual fights. And not only did some persons in the audience utter their opinions with their fists, but critics also used their fists instead of their pens. So one wrote: 'This sextet seemed to me like a calf with six feet, such as one sees often at a fair.' " "How One Becomes Lonely", *SI*, p. 36. It is clear that there was no riot at the premiere. Although some of the reviews do mention opposing forces applauding or hissing, there is no description of anything that could be termed a riot. Nor in any of the thirteen surviving reviews does any critic talk about a calf with six feet. *SW*, 22B, pp. 86–91.
28. Eybl, *Die Befreiung*, pp. 99–100.
29. This is a paraphrase of "Hic Rhodus, hic saltus" ("Rhodes is here, here is the place for your jump"), a Latin translation of the punchline from one of Aesop's fables, "The Braggart". In the fable, an athlete boasted that he once had performed an astonishing jump in Rhodes, and could produce witnesses. The punchline was the somewhat cynical retort of a bystander, who suggested that there was no need of witnesses, since the athlete could simply repeat the jump then and there. The saying was used and transformed by Hegel who coined an adapted German equivalent, "Hier ist die Rose, hier tanze" ("Here is the rose, dance here"), which may also be a double pun on the Latin/Greek originals (rhodon = rose; salta = dance). In this form it implies that fulfillment should not be postponed to some Utopian future. This seems roughly to be the sense in which von Wymetal is using it.
30. The complete text appears in Eybl, *Die Befreiung*, pp. 126–9.
31. An excerpt from Bienenfeld's review appears in Walter Frisch, "The Refractory Masterpiece: Toward an Interpretation of Schoenberg's Chamber Symphony, op. 9", in Juliane Brand and Christopher Hailey (edd.), *Constructive Dissonance: Arnold Schoenberg and the Transformations of Twentieth-Century Culture* (Berkeley, Los Angeles, and London: University of California Press, 1997), p. 92 (translation) and p. 98 (transcription of the original).
32. There is evidence that Schoenberg did try to encourage colleagues and acquaintances to attend the concert and one presumes he directed most of his efforts towards those who he thought might be his supporters. The invitation he sent to Schenker has survived, but if Schoenberg thought he was courting a potential supporter, he was far off the mark. See Charlotte Erwin and Bryan Simms,

"Schoenberg's Correspondence with Heinrich Schenker", *Journal of the Arnold Schoenberg Institute*, 5/1 (1981), p. 42. It is necessary to note that the positive reviews came exclusively from members of Schoenberg's circle: Elsa Bienenfeld had been a student of Schoenberg, and Wilhelm von Wymetal was one of the founders of the Ansorge Society.

33. Several days after the performance, Schoenberg wrote to Arnold Rosé "Nachdem ich mich von den Aufregungen der vergangenen Woche, einigermaßen erholt und wieder Ruhe gewonnen habe, um den Anguß der Preßköter standhalten zu können, drängt es mich vom Neuem, Ihnen für Ihr herrliches Eintreten für meine Werke meinen tiefgefühltesten Dank auszusprechen." Eybl, *Die Befreiung*, p. 112.

34. Schoenberg's Two Ballades, Op. 12, were written for a song competition sponsored by the magazine *Die Woche*. (Zemlinsky also entered the competition, writing songs to the same texts chosen by Schoenberg. Gorrell, *Discordant Melody*, p. 77.) It is also possible that Schoenberg wrote *Friede auf Erden*, Op. 13, for a contest. See Dika Newlin, *Schoenberg Remembered: Diaries and Recollections (1938–76)* (New York: Pendragon Press, 1980), p. 273. However, there is no confirmation of that supposition.

35. Stuckenschmidt, *Schoenberg*, p. 91. To heap insult on insult, Schoenberg was also passed over when the adjudicators selected some of the remaining entries for publication; the works chosen were songs by Philip Rödelberger and Hugo Kaun. Beaumont, *Zemlinsky*, p. 267.

36. Stuckenschmidt, *Schoenberg*, p. 152. "Ihr Werk hat einen unbestrittenen Erfolg gehabt – ich wurde dreimal gerufen. Auch [k]ein Zischlaut oder Ähnliches!"

37. For an analysis of the rhythmic structure of "Jane Grey", see William Harbison, "Rhythmic Structure in Schoenberg's 'Jane Grey'," *Journal of the Arnold Schoenberg Institute*, 7/2 (1983), pp. 222–37.

38. In its final form, the first movement of the Chamber Symphony No. 2, Op. 38 is also relatively short – 165 measures and 7 minutes. However, we cannot be certain about the extent to which the final form of Op. 38 represents Schoenberg's intentions in 1906/8.

Chapter 11 Motivic economy

1. Schoenberg, "For a Treatise on Composition", *SI*, p. 226.
2. This is not meant as a criticism, simply a fact.
3. In the Serenade, Op. 24, a voice joins the ensemble for the fourth movement.
4. For a detailed accounting of the sketches and the chronology, see *SW*, 20B, pp. 111–13.
5. Unfortunately, this is one of the periods in Schoenberg's development where the chronology becomes particularly murky. Schoenberg did not use Sketchbook III when he worked on the Op. 15 songs: the sketches for that work are on separate pieces of music paper, most of which are undated. See Maegaard, *Studien zur Entwicklung*, vol. I, pp. 61–3.

6. It is likely that the final form of the Chamber Symphony No. 2, Op. 38 constitutes a significant departure from the original plan. What is now the second (and final) movement was probably originally intended to be the scherzo/trio movement of a four-movement symphony.
7. There is a sketch for what might be an instrumental slow movement. That sketch is reprinted in *SW*, 20B, p. 201. It has a key signature of six flats. The editor is correct to caution that there may be no connection at all with Op. 10, but the presence of those sketches in the same vicinity as sketches for the rest of the quartet seems strong circumstantial evidence in support of it belonging to Op. 10, possibly for the third movement.
8. There is another sketch that is also purely instrumental and which comes after Schoenberg had begun working on the vocal/instrumental fourth movement. See the sketch, *SW*, 20B, p. 202. This may simply be a draft for the instrumental introduction to a movement with voice; in the third movement, the voice only enters in m. 12.
9. An analysis of the quartet, perhaps by Heinrich Jalowetz and Alexander Zemlinsky, was published on 20 February 1909 in the Viennese periodical *Erdgeist*. See [?Heinrich] Jal[?owetz] and [?Alexander Zemlinsk]y, "Arnold Schoenberg's F♯ Minor Quartet: A Technical Analysis" (trans. Mark DeVoto), *Journal of the Arnold Schoenberg Institute*, 16 (1993), pp. 293–322.
10. E.g. mm. 18–19 and 22–3.
11. See Frisch, *The Early Works*, p. 261.
12. I have referred to these forms as "traditional", not as "neoclassic". As Martha Hyde has argued, "neoclassicism in any of the arts contains an impulse to revive or restore an earlier style that is separated from the present by some intervening period." Martha Hyde, "Neoclassic and Anachronistic Impulses in Twentieth-Century Music", *Music Theory Spectrum*, 18/1 (1996), p. 204. It seems clear that Schoenberg was expanding and revising what he regarded as still living forms (sonata form, ternary form, and rondo), not reviving dead or dormant forms from a distant period of musical history.
13. Even then, he was unable to complete the work as it had originally been planned. It remained a two-movement work, but cyclic, with themes from the first movement returning at the end of the second movement (which originally was probably intended as a scherzo and trio). For the convoluted chronology of this work see Maegaard, *Studien zur Entwicklung*, vol. I, pp. 48–51.
14. Frisch, *The Early Works*, p. 259.
15. Arnold Whittall, *Schoenberg Chamber Music* (Seattle: University of Washington Press, 1972), p. 21. For another reading of the form of this movement see Hans Keller, "Schoenberg: The Future of Symphonic Thought", *Perspectives of New Music*, 13 (1974), p. 10.
16. In their analysis, Jal[?owetz]/[?Zemlinsk]y hold to the ambiguity of the return at m. 146: "Thus is the Recapitulation thematically indicated, still in the course of the Development." "Arnold Schoenberg's F♯ Minor Quartet", p. 308.

17. Frisch, *The Early Works*, p. 260.
18. *Ibid.*
19. See *SW*, 20B, p. 112.
20. Frisch, *The Early Works*, pp. 263–4.
21. The following is drawn from my article, "The Interaction of Art and Music in Schoenberg's Career: A Reexamination", *Journal of the Arnold Schönberg Center*, 6 (2004), pp. 77–88.
22. Frisch, *The Early Works*, p. 266.
23. Whittall, *Schoenberg Chamber Music*, p. 22. Whittall is not alone in suggesting that Schoenberg was going through a psychological crisis during this period and that this is reflected in the music. "The only other thing that should be hinted at here is a 'secret programme'; this the composer would not make public, but there are various pointers to it. The texts used by Schoenberg as the basis of the last two movements (poems by Stefan George, from *Der siebente Ring*, which had appeared in 1907), and, above all, the musical expressiveness given to the soprano line, show that the composer was going through a severe psychic crisis." Willi Reich, *Schoenberg: A Critical Biography*, trans. Leo Black (New York: Praeger, 1971), p. 34.
24. Stuckenschmidt, *Schoenberg*, p. 96. Otto Breicha also sees the Augustin melody and the phrase "alles ist hin" as an allusion to the troubles in Schoenberg's marriage. See *Gerstl und Schönberg: Eine Beziehung* (Salzburg: Galerie Welz, 1993), p. 26. Following other writers I have rendered "alles ist hin" in English as "all is lost". (That is how Schoenberg himself translated it.) A more accurate translation would be "everything is gone" or "everything is destroyed." See also, Reich, *Schoenberg: A Critical Biography*, p. 35, fn. 1 where Black translates "alles ist hin" as "it's all up, or all is lost, or everything's gone".
25. So too, I believe there is no basis for the speculation that Schoenberg's use of "O du lieber Augustin" was some kind of commentary on Mahler's traumatic memories of that tune. See David Schiff, "Jewish and Musical Tradition in the Music of Mahler and Schoenberg", *Journal of the Arnold Schoenberg Institute*, 9/2 (1986), p. 228.
26. The assumption of most writers has been that Schoenberg wrote the section with the quotation from "O du lieber Augustin" during the 1907 phase of his work on this quartet. Bryan Simms has argued that this is incorrect. "Almost certainly the episode that quotes 'Alles ist hin' (mm. 165–92) was conceived as part of the movement only in July of 1908." See his " 'My Dear Hagerl': Self-Representation in Schoenberg's String Quartet No. 2," *19th-Century Music*, 26/3 (2003), pp. 272–3. Simms makes a credible case that the sketches in Sketchbook III could have stemmed from 1908. However, what is probably the very first sketch of what became the Augustin passage occurs on p. 102 of the so-called Anna Sketchbook and is undated. See *SW*, 20B, pp. 113 and 192. Thus it could have been written any time before July 1908 and this means one cannot know when it was that Schoenberg decided to incorporate the quotation into the second movement. Although Simms suggests a 1908 date for the

incorporation of "O du lieber Augustin" tune into the quartet, he rejects the idea that "Schoenberg was referring directly to himself – to his marriage and domestic situation" because those "were still intact, albeit strained, when the Quartet was reconceived" (p. 275). Instead, he suggests that Schoenberg was "pointing to triadic tonality, which was certainly on its last legs in 1908".

27. In my article "The Interaction of Art and Music in Schönberg's Career", a different version of the text of this folksong was printed. See p. 79.
28. "How One Becomes Lonely", *SI*, pp. 47–8.

Chapter 12 "Until then I lacked the strength and confidence"

1. Schoenberg, "Composition with Twelve Tones (1)", *SI*, p. 216.
2. Although the Two Songs, Op. 14 were completed in 1908, they were not published until 1920.
3. For a discussion of Opus 14 as a whole as well as analyses of its two songs (and an analysis and discussion of "Am Strande" – originally intended as a third song for the opus), see Jennifer Shaw, "Zwei Lieder für eine Singstimme und Klavier, op. 14", in Gerold Gruber (ed.), *Arnold Schönberg: Interpretationen seiner Werke* (Laaber: Laaber-Verlag, 2002), vol. I, pp. 181–95. For a discussion and Schenkerian-like analysis of both songs, see Timothy Jackson, "Schoenberg's Op. 14 Songs: Textual Sources and Analytical Perception", *Theory and Practice*, 14/15 (1989–90), 35–58.
4. For a discussion and analysis of Op. 14, No. 1 see Bryan Simms, *The Atonal Music of Arnold Schoenberg: 1908–1923* (New York: Oxford University Press, 2000), pp. 32–6.
5. For a discussion of Schoenberg's use of poems by Dehmel and George, see Robert Vilain, "Schoenberg and German Poetry", in Charlotte Cross and Russell Berman (edd.), *Schoenberg and Words: The Modernist Years* (New York and London: Garland Publishing, 2000), pp. 1–29.
6. I am not alone in feeling that this chord is problematic. See Cone, "Sound and Syntax", pp. 32–3. Cone asks: "is the 'tonic' chord necessary? Indeed, is the triad a normal for this composition?" (p. 33).
7. "Mit den Liedern nach George ist es mir zum erstenmal gelungen, einem Ausdrucks- und Formideal nahezukommen, das mir seit Jahren vorschwebt. Es zu verwirklichen, gebrach es mir bis dahin an Kraft und Sicherheit. Nun ich aber diese Bahn endgültig betreten habe, bin ich mir bewußt, alle Schranken einer vergangenen Ästhetik durchbrochen zu haben; und wenn ich auch einem mir als sicher erscheinenden Ziel zustrebe, so fühle ich dennoch schon jetzt den Widerstand, den ich zu überwinden haben werde; fühle den Hitzegrad der Auflehnung und ahne, daß selbst solche, die mir bisher geglaubt haben, die Notwendigkeit dieser Entwicklung nicht werden einsehen wollen." Auner, *A Schoenberg Reader*, p. 78. A facsimile of the program appears in Berthold Türcke, "Gurrelieder and Orchestra Pieces, Op. 16, for Two Pianos", *Journal of the Arnold Schoenberg Institute*, 7/2 (1983), p. 249.

8. Edward Cone points out that the first of these chords, a combination of a perfect and an augmented fourth, "is to become a great favorite of the composer". Cone identifies an instance as early as the song "Verlassen", Op. 6, No. 4 (1903): "Sound and Syntax", p. 29. The use of an augmented fourth should be understood as a further extension of the idea of the chord of fourths: just as Schoenberg's "tertian" chords had augmented and diminished thirds, so too, did his "quartal" chords.

9. In the two places where there are multiple statements of 'a' (mm. 24–5 and 27), Schoenberg exploits the property that the two chords of 'a' share a common interval for the top two tones – 5 semitones. This allows Schoenberg to use a transposition that holds two tones in common – down a semitone. Thus, for example, in m. 24, the C F dyad is an invariant component of two statements of 'a'. This is an early example of Schoenberg's manipulation of transpositions to produce invariants, a procedure that would become a central compositional strategy in his twelve-tone period.

10. For an extended analysis of this song, see Howard Cinnamon, "Some Elements of Tonal and Motivic Structure in 'In diesen Wintertagen,' Op. 14, no. 2 by Arnold Schoenberg: A Schoenbergian-Schenkerian Study," *In Theory Only*, 7/7–8 (1984), pp. 23–50. Cinnamon concludes that the proper perspective on Schoenberg's works from this period "can only be gained when this music is viewed as the part of the continuum of western music that Schoenberg felt it to be." Although I wholeheartedly agree with this assertion, I have doubts about the suitability of the technique (Schenkerian analysis) that Cinnamon employs to support it. For any work that ends with a triad, a reduction to a referential triad is always possible because it is a property of any triad that the nine other tones of the chromatic are stepwise removed from at least one of the tones of that triad. As a result, it is always possible to construct an analysis such that any tone can be represented as a filled-in note and connected by a slur to another tone, ultimately leading through deeper levels to the Ursatz. The question, however, is not whether a reduction can be made; the question is whether the resultant analysis provides a meaningful representation of the structure of the work. Here is where Cinnamon and I would part company. I (and if it is any comfort, Schenker) would argue that this analysis does not provide such a meaningful representation. In a subsequent article, Cinnamon has proposed a modified Schenkerian reading of a work that does not begin or end with a triad: Op. 11, No. 2. See "Tonal Elements and Unfolding Nontriadic Harmonies in the Second of Schoenberg's *Drei Klavierstücke*, Op. 11", *Theory and Practice*, 18 (1993), 127–70. Here too I strongly agree with his conclusion ("Schoenberg's post-tonal harmonic language evolved directly from, rather than as an alternative to, his tonal practices and theories of tonal harmony", p. 166), but have even more serious doubts about the suitability of the techniques used to support this conclusion. Timothy Jackson also stresses the evolutionary character of Schoenberg's language and also makes Schenkerian-like (but in his words "decidedly non-Schenkerian") analyses of both Op. 14, No. 1 and No. 2.

His analyses differ most dramatically from typically Schenkerian readings in that he does not see the work as a composing out of a single referential sonority: "Instead of the composing out of a single referential sonority, in both works the structure is realized through directed, large-scale contrapuntal motion from one sonority to another." Jackson, "Schoenberg's Op. 14 Songs", p. 47. This seems more reasonable than a reading that does claim the work to be the composing out of a single referential triadic sonority. Nevertheless, I still find it problematic to use reductive techniques that yield multiple levels for this repertoire. By claiming, for example, that the treble line in Op. 14 reduces down at the background level to a single note (F-sharp), one is effectively asserting that all of the remaining notes in that line are hierarchically subservient to that F-sharp and must be heard in terms of it. In the absence of either a consistent definition of consonance and dissonance or of codified diminution procedures, any such conclusion lacks a convincing theoretical foundation.

11. Schoenberg mistakenly gave the poet's name as George Henckel. There are also several deviations from Henckel's poem, one of which ('wilde' for 'milde') may or may not be a copying mistake. Jackson, "Schoenberg's Op. 14 Songs", pp. 43–5.

12. Cone notes that this song "does end with a dissonance derived from its opening measure, although newly redistributed as a triad with added sixth." "Sound and Syntax", p. 33.

Chapter 13 Beyond triads: the first layer of *Das Buch der hängenden Gärten*

1. This statement was included in the program notes for the first performance of Op. 15 on 14 January 1910. See Joseph Auner, *A Schoenberg Reader: Documents of a Life* (New Haven & London: Yale University Press, 2003), pp. 77–8.

2. For a general introduction to Op. 15 see Theo Hirsbrunner, "Fünfzehn Gedichte aus Das Buch der Hängenden Gärten von Stefan George op. 15", in Gerold Gruber (ed.), *Arnold Schönberg: Interpretationen seiner Werke* (Laaber: Laaber-Verlag, 2002), vol. I, pp. 196–215. For an extended pitch-class set analysis of Opus 15 see Allen Forte, "Concepts of Linearity in Schoenberg's Atonal Music: A Study of the Opus 15 Song Cycle", *Journal of Music Theory*, 36/2 (1992), pp. 285–382. Some of the individual songs of Op. 15 have been subjected to extended analyses. One of the best known (and justifiably so) is David Lewin, "Toward the Analysis of a Schoenberg Song (Op. 15, No. XI)", *Perspectives of New Music*, 12/1–2 (1973–4), pp. 43–86.

3. One of the songs (No. 6) ends with a sonority that borders on being triadic; another (No. 10) "establishes a triadic normal". See Cone, "Sound and Syntax", pp. 33–4. A less fragmentary chronology might have helped tell us when these two songs were written which, in turn, might have provided useful information about the evolution of Schoenberg's thought.

4. It has been suggested that "Schoenberg at first did not contemplate the fifteen-song cycle that he later created". Rather, the four songs contained in *Sammelhandschrift* 10 "were first intended as a separate collection". Simms, *The Atonal Music*, p. 48. The evidence for this is a title page that is now placed with *SH* 10 and that reads: "4 Lieder". However, that title page properly belongs to the Four Orchestral Songs, Op. 22 from which it has become separated: its format (landscape) and size are identical to that of the manuscript for Op. 22 and completely out of character with the format (portrait) and size of the manuscript of the four songs with which it is currently associated. This means that there is no evidence to suggest that Op. 15 was originally intended as anything other than a cycle of fifteen songs. I am indebted to David Banga for this information.

5. Simon Harris identifies this chordal type as important in early twentieth-century music. "The vast majority of new chord-forms appearing in the early years of the century, therefore, contain semitones. Many of these will contain complete traditional chord-forms, whilst others will contain chord-forms that are standard reductions of full chords in traditional harmony, to all of which one or more notes are added. The simplest of these will consist only of the notes of a traditional chord with one extra note, invariably a semitone distant from one of the notes of the traditional chord, but even with the addition of a single note two distinct traditional chord-forms may often be identified within the chord." *A Proposed Classification of Chords in Early Twentieth-Century Music* (New York & London: Garland Publishing, 1989), pp. 93–4.

6. The occasional presence of triads and other residues of prior practice have encouraged some to suggest that identifiable tonal centers remain in some of the songs of Op. 15. See, for example, Harald Krebs, "Tonalität in Schönbergs 'atonaler' Musik: Die Aussage der Skizzen," *Musiktheorie*, 4 (1989), pp. 223–34.

7. Given the emphases accorded to some tones and sonorities, it has been suggested that the Schenkerian concept of prolongation might be useful for this repertoire, even in the absence of traditional tonality. See Roy Travis, "Directed Motion in Schoenberg and Webern", *Perspectives of New Music*, 4/2 (1966), pp. 84–9. Travis' article has prompted a spirited and extended scholarly debate. See Deborah Stein, "Schoenberg's Opus 19 No 2: Voice Leading and Overall Structure," *In Theory Only*, 2/7 (1976), pp. 27–43; Robert Morgan, "Dissonant Prolongation: Theoretical and Compositional Precedents," *Journal of Music Theory*, 20/1 (1976), pp. 49–91; James Baker, "Schenkerian Analysis and Post-Tonal Music", in David Beach (ed.), *Aspects of Schenkerian Theory* (New Haven and London: Yale University Press, 1983), pp. 153–86; Joseph Straus, "The Problem of Prolongation in Post-Tonal Music", *Journal of Music Theory*, 31/1 (1987), pp. 1–21; Steve Larson, "A Tonal Model of an 'Atonal' Piece: Schönberg's Opus 15, Number 2," *Perspectives of New Music*, 25 (1987), pp. 418–33; Fred Lerdahl, "Atonal Prolongational Structure", *Contemporary Music Review*, 4 (1989), pp. 65–87; Howard Cinnamon, "Tonal Elements and Unfolding Nontriadic Harmonies in the Second of Schoenberg's *Drei Klavierstücke*, Op. 11", *Theory and Practice*, 18

(1993), pp. 127–70; Jack Boss, "Schoenberg on Ornamentation and Structural Levels", *Journal of Music Theory*, 38/2 (1994), pp. 187–215; Steve Larson, "The Problem of Prolongation in *Tonal* Music: Terminology, Perception, and Expressive Meaning," *Journal of Music Theory*, 41/1 (1997), pp. 101–36; Olli Väisälä, "Concepts of Harmony and Prolongation in Schoenberg's Op. 19/2", *Music Theory Spectrum*, 21/2 (1999), pp. 230–59; Fred Lerdahl, "Spatial and Psychoacoustic Factors in Atonal Prolongation", *Current Musicology*, 63 (1999), pp. 7–26. I tend to agree with those who argue that neither the prolongation of triads nor the prolongation of non-triadic pitch-class sets are concepts that can effectively be applied to works like Op. 15. For a useful summary of possible criteria used to establish "structurality", see Boss, "Schoenberg on Ornamentation", p. 193, table 1. If the idea of prolongation is to have any real meaning, it would probably have to be framed in terms more appropriate for the repertoire in question. Something akin to Lerdahl's approach seems to me to offer the most promise for a theory of prolongation for this music.

8. Others have pointed out similar emphases in other songs from Op. 15. However, as I argue in this and the following chapter, I believe it is claiming too much to proceed from the recognition of such emphases to the claim that specific keys are implied by those emphases. For an example of such a claim see Harald Krebs, "Three Versions of Schoenberg's Op. 15, No. 14: Obvious Differences and Hidden Similarities," *Journal of the Arnold Schoenberg Institute*, 8/2 (1984), pp. 138–40.

9. For an analysis of rhythmic and metric issues in this song see David Lewin, "Vocal Meter in Schoenberg's Atonal Music, with a Note on a Serial Hauptstimme", *In Theory Only*, 6/4 (1982), pp. 12–36.

10. Using a modified figured bass notation to identify chord types, Arnold Whittall surveyed all of the chords in the keyboard part of this song. One of his results has particular relevance to the present study: "Semitones are to be found in plenty in the higher positions of the other chords, but the emphasis is firmly on structures that, in context, often set up particular, if ambiguous associations with the traditional consonant triads and sevenths, to such a degree that there is some justification for regarding at least some of them as altered triads or sevenths." "Tonality and the Emancipated Dissonance: Schoenberg and Stravinsky", in Jonathan Dunsby (ed.), *Early Twentieth-Century Music: Models of Musical Analysis* (Oxford: Blackwell Publishers, 1993), p. 14.

11. The harmonies Schoenberg tends to use in this repertoire may result, at least in part, from the voice-leading, and in particular from two characteristics of his style: his inclination to move voices by half-steps and to avoid common tones in adjacent chords (both of which were also characteristic of his earlier practice). See John Roeder, "Harmonic Implications of Schoenberg's Observations of Atonal Voice Leading", *Journal of Music Theory*, 33/1 (1989), pp. 27–62.

12. Arnold Whittall sees a more conclusive definition of G for this song. "Many analysts today would probably prefer to describe the song as atonal, but I

would argue that, on the evidence of the harmonic goal represented by the ending, and its clear anticipation in bars 3 and 4, the possibility of an extended G tonality makes good musical sense: the most essential elements of that tonality are not excluded, but they are not allowed to function diatonically." "Tonality and the Emancipated Dissonance", pp. 13–14.
13. For an analysis of this song see George Fisher, "Text and Music in Song VIII of Das Buch der Hängenden Gärten", *In Theory Only*, 6/2 (1982), pp. 3–15.
14. Melisande's theme includes five tones from the whole tone scale on C. Since the intervals of transposition for the imitative entries are all even, the successive imitations hold four of those five tones invariant.
15. For an extended analysis of this song see David Lewin, "A Way into Schoenberg's Opus 15, Number 7", *In Theory Only*, 6/1 (1981), pp. 3–24.

Chapter 14 "On revient toujours"? Returning to Opp. 10 and 15, June 1908–February 1909

1. "My Evolution", *SI*, p. 86.
2. The Zemlinsky family name appeared in a number of variants. See Gorrell, *Discordant Melody*, pp. 18–19 and Beaumont, *Zemlinsky*, p. 9.
3. The view that the move to atonality was prompted by Schoenberg's reaction to the Gerstl/Mathilde affair is so widespread that it appears not only in the musicological literature, but also in the art historical literature. A recent example: "Under the shadow of this tragic event, the composer completed his **String Quartet, op. 10**, in which the use of dissonance and polyphonic layering bears witness to his tormented mood and explodes the boundaries of tonality in an almost painful culmination." Karin von Maur, "Arnold Schönberg, or the Convergence of Music and Painting", in Hatje Cantz, *The Visions of Arnold Schönberg: The Painting Years* (Schirn Kunsthalle: Frankfurt, 2002), p. 25.
4. "Even as he arrived in Gmunden in late June, Schoenberg was evidently experiencing such anxiety and alienation as to produce a major upheaval in his compositional work. At first this took the form of a stylistic retrenchment, a stepping back from the fully atonal George songs that he had composed earlier that spring and a return to the late tonal style of instrumental composition that he had used in his String Quartet No. 1, Op. 7 and Chamber Symphony No. 1, Op. 9." Bryan Simms, *The Atonal Music of Arnold Schoenberg* (New York: Oxford University Press, 2000), p. 40. In a more recent article, Simms elaborated on the theme that the crisis in his personal life had significant consequences for his compositional direction with Op. 10 as the centerpiece of the discussion. See his " 'My Dear Hagerl' ", pp. 258–77.
5. The complete text of the letter:
    Mein lieber, lieber Arnold,
    Du bist so lieb und gut und ich freue mich über alles, was du mir schreibst so riesig. Ich habe dich auch sehr, sehr lieb und ich könnte ohne dich nicht leben. – Nun kommst du in 3 Tagen. Mir vergeht die Zeit jetzt so

furchtbar langsam. Wenn nur schon Donnerstag wäre. Ich mach mir nämlich gar keine Hoffnung dass Du früher kommst. Sollte es aber doch sein, so schreibe mir gleich wann ich Dich erwarten kann. – Mit den Kindern spreche ich ununterbrochen von dir und sie werden gar nicht schüchtern sein. Der Bub vielleicht ein paar Minuten aber sicher nicht länger. Morgen kommen also Zemlinsky's. Ich werde nicht viel mit ihnen verkehren. Ich habe mich eigentlich über Alex sehr geärgert. Er schreibt jedes Mal an die Mutter "Ich grüsse dich und die Kinder". Ich finde dass ist doch wirklich nicht nötig! Aber schliesslich kann mir das gleichgültig sein. – Jetzt hast du viel zu thun mein Lieber. Hast du dich mit der Wäsche ausgekannt? Nimmst du die Sachen mit, oder hast du vorausgeschickt? – Wir haben hier nicht einmal so schlechtes Wetter. Am Tag ist es schön, in der Nacht regnet es. Ich finde das ist ganz angenehm. Dass du die Geldsorgen so gut los geworden bist, freut mich wie du dir denken kannst ungemein. Wie hast du's denn gemacht? Vergiß nicht Herzerl dem Hausherrn Tabak mitzubringen! – Viele, viele Küsse mein liebster, guter Herzerl von deiner
Mathilde

6. In another letter, dated 15 June 1908, Mathilde is more direct, confronting Schoenberg's suspicions head on. "I hope that this summer will go by without incident. What more do you want to know about Gerstl? I have already written to you very plainly that I long only *for you*. What still upsets you? Are you content with me now?" Simms, "'My Dear Hagerl'," p. 269 (with a transcription of the original German text in fn. 39).

7. The poem actually begins on p. 122.

8. Since the first words of the poems were written down in the sketches for the third and fourth movements in Sketchbook III, it is a reasonable assumption that this represented work done when George's poems were in his possession. Since we know he did not bring a copy of the poems to Gmunden with him from Vienna (hence his request to Horwitz to copy out the poems) we can conclude with a fair degree of certainty that the sketches were written in Vienna sometime between 17 December 1907 and 28 June 1908.

9. For background on Schoenberg's teaching during this period, see Hans Moldenhauer and Rosaleen Moldenhauer, *Webern* (New York: Alfred Knopf, 1979), p. 91; see also the Schönberg Center website (Arnold Schönberg/ Schönberg als Lehrer/Schüler in Wien und Mödling).

10. Alban Berg's exercises (frequently with his teacher's corrections) give some idea of the intensity of the pace of study and of the amount of work Schoenberg poured into his teaching. For details of Berg's studies with Schoenberg (and for a number of facsimiles of Berg's corrected exercises) see Rosemary Hilmar, "Alban Berg's Studies with Schoenberg", *Journal of the Arnold Schoenberg Institute*, 8/1 (1984), pp. 7–29.

11. Speaking of Schoenberg's situation in 1905, Wellesz wrote: "Moreover, the *Eight Songs*, Op. 6, originated at this time ... They were written in a white

heat in the small hours of the morning, which were the only times Schönberg could spare from his teaching duties." *Arnold Schönberg*, p. 22. Wellesz indicated that the situation remained difficult in the following years: "Strenuous activity as a teacher considerably limited his composing during the autumn and winter of this year. Only a chorus, *Friede auf Erden (Peace on Earth)* Op. 13 appeared; the text was the poem by C. F. Mayer and the work was finished on March 9th, 1907." *Ibid*, p. 23.

12. *SW* 20B, p. 174.
13. "Miniver Cheevy", the title character of a poem by Edwin Arlington Robinson, "loved the days of old" and "sighed for what was not".
14. Christian Martin Schmidt discusses this briefly in *SW*, 20B, p. xiv. See also, Reinhold Brinkmann, "Schoenberg's Quartets and the Viennese Tradition", in Reinhold Brinkmann and Christoph Wolff (edd.), *Music of My Future: The Schoenberg Quartets and Trio* (Cambridge, Massachusetts and London: Harvard University Press, 2000), p. 6.
15. Schoenberg was not the first to add voice to a chamber group with strings. There are several settings for voice and string quartet that preceded his. One is by Ernest Chausson but there is no evidence that Schoenberg was aware of that setting. But there is a setting from Schoenberg's own circle and it is highly likely he knew of it. It is an incomplete song for voice and string sextet by Zemlinsky dating from around 1902: "Die Astern schwankten" (to a poem of Dehmel, no less). Its manuscript is in the Library of Congress. Gorrell, *Discordant Melody*, p. 281.
16. Frisch, *The Early Works*, p. 268.
17. Based on what Gerstl's brother Alois told Otto Breicha (many years after the fact), Schoenberg became aware that something was going on when Gertud, his six-year-old daughter, told him that she had seen Gerstl kiss her mother. Bryan Simms suggests that this might have taken place around May 1908. " 'My Dear Hagerl' ", p. 267. The evidence (second hand, ex post facto testimony long after the fact about what a six-year-old claims to have seen) seems too thin to draw any conclusions whatever. But even if we accept May 1908 as the date of the kiss and thus, the beginning of Schoenberg's suspicions, we still have no way of knowing whether the sketches on pp. 104–8 of Sketchbook III preceded or antedated that event.
18. Simms claims that Schoenberg did not use Sketchbook III at all between 17 December 1907 and early July 1908: "He glued Horwitz's copy of the poems into the sketchbook, which had remained unused since the previous winter." " 'My Dear Hagerl' ", p. 271; see also p. 272. I see no basis for the claim that the sketchbook had remained unused. Page 103 of Sketchbook III is dated 17 December 1907 (the ending date for Op. 14, No. 1). On pp. 109–10 of Sketchbook III are the first 25 bars of the *Erste Niederschrift* of the third movement of Op. 10. Given the letter to Horwitz, one can assume that these pages were written on or shortly after 5 July 1908. There are no dates at all on the intervening pages (104–8) of Sketchbook III. Therefore, the sketches on

those pages could have been written anytime between 17 December 1907 and 5 July 1908. Given the character of the sketches that occur on these pages (isolated concepts and not continuity drafts) it seems likely that these pages were written during the academic year in preparation for the summer when Schoenberg knew he would have time to work on longer compositions.
19. Frisch, *The Early Works*, pp. 267–8. See also *SW*, 20B, p. 193.
20. *SW*, 20B, p. 202.
21. Included in the sketch is a single syllable "gen" in m. 20. The meaning of "gen" is not clear. It might be an indication of a vocal setting. But if so, a setting of what? There are three "gen"s in "Entrückung": "Ungründigen" (line 11) and "heiligen" (lines 23 and 24). But there seems no reasonable way to make the surrounding syllables fit with the rest of the music. In any event, it would be extremely odd to write out only this syllable; if one were interested in an aid to memory, it would make more sense to write out some of the key words, not a stray syllable.
22. Schoenberg's use of developmental procedures in this variation gave this movement the role of development section for the whole quartet. See Catherine Dale, "Schoenberg's Concept of Variation Form: A Paradigmatic Analysis of *Litanei* from the Second String Quartet, Op. 10," *Journal of the Royal Music Association*, 118/1 (1993), p. 95.
23. Stein's analysis was printed in the Philharmonic pocket score of Op. 10. It has been reprinted in Frisch, *The Early Works*, p. 269.
24. Simon Harris classifies this chord as type E1, a member of the group of "Semitonal Chords and Reduced Derivatives". *A Proposed Classification of Chords in Early Twentieth-Century Music* (New York & London: Garland Publishing, 1989), pp. 126 and 139. Given the evolution of Schoenberg's chordal vocabulary as described in this book, however, it might be better to think of this chord (like the corresponding chord in Op. 14, No. 1), as a chord of fourths with one fourth augmented. I believe this better reflects the way in which this chord originated in Schoenberg's thought because it is parallel to the evolution of "tertian" chords where thirds in the stack were also sometimes augmented or diminished (as in the French Sixth).
25. "On revient toujours" is the title of a brief essay by Schoenberg from 1948 in which he discusses his return to writing tonal compositions. *SI*, pp. 108–10.

Chapter 15 The analysis of Schoenberg's post-1908 music: Pieces for Piano, Op. 11, Nos. 1 and 2, Feb 1909

1. "My Evolution", *SI*, p. 86.
2. It is possible that Schoenberg's output was not quite this limited and that some of the undated songs of Op. 15 were completed during this period.
3. The scholarly consensus appears to be that "Am Strande" was written in 1909, not 1908. See *SW*1/2B, part 1, pp. 49–50; Reinhold Brinkmann, *Arnold Schönberg: Drei Klavierstücke Op. 11. Studien zur frühen Atonalität bei Schönberg*. Beihefte zum Archiv für Musikwissenschaft, vol. 7 (Franz Steiner Verlag: Wiesbaden,

1969), pp. 3–4; and Simms, *The Atonal Music*, p. 37. For the argument on behalf of 1908 see Jan Maegaard, "Schoenberg's Manuscripts: What Do They Tell Us?" *Journal of the Arnold Schoenberg Institute*, 1/2 (1977), pp. 69–73.

4. For analyses of this work, see Simms, *The Atonal Music*, pp. 37–9; Jennifer Shaw, "Zwei Lieder für eine Singstimme und Klavier op. 14", in Gerold Gruber (ed.), *Arnold Schönberg: Interpretationen seiner Werke* (Laaber: Laaber-Verlag, 2002), vol. I, pp. 181–4.

5. As of 1909, the only works Schoenberg had completed for piano were the Drei Klavierstücke (1894) and the Sechs Stücke für Clavier zu vier Händen (probably 1896). Fragments include Kl.00–01 Fr. and Kl.05–06. See Maegaard, *Studien zur Entwicklung*, vol. I, pp. 26, 33, and 47.

6. "Part of Schoenberg's reticence in writing for piano may have come from his own limited ability as a player and an awareness of the distance that this created between him and the idiomatic treatment of the instrument so apparent in the works of the great pianist-composers of the nineteenth century." Simms, *The Atonal Music*, p. 60.

7. Antony Beaumont (trans. and ed.), *Ferruccio Busoni: Selected Letters* (New York: Columbia University Press, 1987), p. 387.

8. There may be an element of defensiveness about Schoenberg's claim that he had "laid the foundations for a modern piano style". He made this remark in the context of answering Busoni's criticisms of what Busoni saw as unidiomatic writing for the piano in Op. 11, Nos. 1 and 2. See Daniel Raessler, "Schoenberg and Busoni: Aspects of Their Relationship", *Journal of the Arnold Schoenberg Institute*, 7/1 (1983), p. 12.

9. Allen Forte, *The Structure of Atonal Music* (New Haven and London: Yale University Press, 1973).

10. For a comprehensive pitch-class set analysis of Op. 11, No. 1, see Allen Forte, "The Magical Kaleidoscope: Schoenberg's First Atonal Masterwork, Opus 11, No. 1," *Journal of the Arnold Schoenberg Institute*, 5/2 (1981), pp. 127–68.

11. See my "Atonality, Analysis, and the Intentional Fallacy", *Music Theory Spectrum*, 18/2 (1996), pp. 167–99. For other critiques of pitch-class set analysis see William Benjamin, "Ideas of Order in Motivic Music", *Music Theory Spectrum*, 1 (1979), pp. 23–34; George Perle, "Pitch-Class Set Analysis: An Evaluation", *Journal of Musicology*, 8/2 (1990), pp. 151–72. A spirited debate between Allen Forte and Richard Taruskin was initiated by the latter's review of the former's *The Harmonic Organization of the Rite of Spring* (New Haven and London: Yale University Press, 1978). The review appeared in *Current Musicology*, 28 (1979), pp. 114–29. Forte rejected Taruskin's criticisms in "Pitch-Class Analysis Today", *Music Analysis*, 4 (1985), pp. 29–58. Taruskin responded with a letter to the editor in *Music Analysis*, 5 (1986), pp. 313–20. Forte replied in the same issue: "Letter to the Editor in Reply to Richard Taruskin from Allen Forte", pp. 321–37. Taruskin critiqued other aspects of pitch-class set analysis in "Reply to van den Toorn", *In Theory Only*, 10 (1987), pp. 47–57 and in his review of James Baker, *The Music of Alexander Scriabin*

(New Haven and London: Yale University Press, 1986) in *Music Theory Spectrum*, 10 (1988), pp. 143–68.

12. A straightforward segmentation of Op. 11, No. 1 (that is, the use only of those segmentations that mark off clear units of musical structure: phrases, chords, etc.) does not produce a coherent, limited, arsenal of set types; rather, it produces a random collection of pitch-class sets. Advocates of pitch-class set analysis typically address this problem either by ignoring the unwanted set types that result from straightforward segmentations or by actively looking "for other, less obvious, relationships". See David Beach, "Pitch Structure and the Analytic Process in Atonal Music: An Interpretation of the Theory of Sets," *Music Theory Spectrum*, 1 (1979), p. 15. For a thoughtful discussion of the problems of segmentation see Christopher Hasty, "Segmentation and Process in Post-Tonal Music", *Music Theory Spectrum*, 3 (1981), pp. 54–73. It is significant, however, that all three of the examples Hasty uses (by Wolpe, Webern, and Schoenberg) are either twelve-tone serial (Wolpe's String Quartet, Webern's Op. 24/2) or proto-serial (Schoenberg's Op. 23, No. 1) and thus have consistent intervallic patterns built into the structure. No such consistency exists in the repertoire under discussion. Inconsistent segmentation is the rock on which most pitch-class analyses founder. For example, in his analysis of Webern's Orchestral Piece (1913), Forte begins with an attempt to "delimit the structural components". He acknowledges that this is difficult: "there are a great many candidate segments". How does one choose between them? Forte suggests three general criteria: "recurrence, consistency, and parsimony". However, his analysis can meet the criterion of "recurrence" only by circling those groups of tones that yield the pitch-class sets he wants. Allen Forte, "Analysis Symposium: Webern, Orchestral pieces (1913), movement I ('Bewegt')," *Journal of Music Theory*, 18/1 (1974), pp. 13–43.

13. The "shmoo" (pl. "shmoon") was a creature of amorphous shape in the comic strip "Li'l Abner" by Al Capp.

14. Allen Forte, "Concepts of Linearity in Schoenberg's Atonal Music: A Study of the Opus 15 Song Cycle," *Journal of Music Theory*, 36/2 (1992), pp. 285–382.

15. See the analysis of Op. 11, No. 1 in George Perle, *Serial Composition and Atonality: An Introduction to the Music of Schoenberg, Berg, and Webern*, fifth edition (Berkeley, Los Angeles, London: University of California Press, 1981), pp. 10–15.

16. Allen Forte, "Sets and Nonsets in Schoenberg's Atonal Music", *Perspectives of New Music*, 11/1 (1972), p. 48.

17. "Instead of regarding the theory as a universe of possible relations and trying to determine criteria for deciding which relations are actually germane to particular contexts, analysts have sometimes assumed that any relation which holds among the simple, abstract entities named in the theory, that is, among PC sets, can be said to hold among the actual entities which represent these abstractions in those contexts. This amounts to hurling the theory at the context it is meant to transform, with the result that the latter is reduced to a densely packed but

incoherent rubble-heap of relations." William Benjamin, "Ideas of Order in Motivic Music", *Music Theory Spectrum*, 1 (1979), pp. 23–4.

18. This is particularly so in the case of sets with five or more elements. See George Perle, "Pitch-Class Set Analysis: An Evaluation", *Journal of Musicology*, 8/2 (1990), pp. 151–72.

19. A necessary assumption of pitch-class set analysis is the equivalence of inversionally related intervals. Accordingly, 1 semitone and 11 semitones are members of the same interval class and thus, equivalent. For a questioning of this assumption and for some of the consequences this has for the concept of prolongation in Schoenberg's post triadic music, see Olli Väisälä, "Concepts of Harmony and Prolongation in Schoenberg's Op. 19/2", *Music Theory Spectrum*, 21/2 (1999), pp. 230–59.

20. Op. 11, No. 1 has been one of the most extensively analyzed of all of Schoenberg's compositions. The literature is now so vast it would take inordinate space merely to list it all here. My analysis owes much to the detailed examination of Op. 11 in Brinkmann, *Arnold Schönberg: Drei Klavierstücke*.

21. For an extended examination of compositional techniques Schoenberg used to create formal structure (mostly on the small scale) in compositions from this period, see Manfred Pfisterer, *Studien zur Kompositionstechnik in den frühen atonalen Werken von Arnold Schönberg* (Neuhausen-Stuttgart: Hänssler-Verlag, 1978).

22. Forte, Ogdon, and Simms all see this movement as a kind of sonata form (Simms uses Schoenberg's term "developmental ternary"). See Forte, "The Magical Kaleidoscope", p. 131; Will Ogdon, "How Tonality Functions in Schoenberg's Opus 11, Number 1", *Journal of the Arnold Schoenberg Institute*, 5/2 (1981), p. 170; Simms, *The Atonal Music*, pp. 62–3. It is revealing, however, that although Forte, Ogdon, and Simms all see the work as a sonata form, they cannot agree on the placement of the dividing line between the exposition and development. Forte places the end of the exposition at m. 33; Ogdon places it at m. 24 with a transition in mm. 25–33; Simms sees the end of the A section at m. 11. All agree, however, that the recapitulation begins in m. 53. I think their disagreements highlight the problems in employing a sonata form model for this piece. I believe that Reinhold Brinkmann's view of the form is much closer to the mark: in his opinion Op. 11, No. 1 is characterized by the alteration of two zones, the first "thematic", the second "eruptive" (Ausbruchszone). Brinkmann, *Arnold Schönberg: Drei Klavierstücke*, p. 61.

23. For more on developing variation in Schoenberg's atonal music, see Jack Boss, "Schoenberg's Op. 22 Radio Talk and Developing Variation in Atonal Music", *Music Theory Spectrum*, 14/2 (1992), pp. 125–49.

24. Thomas Christensen has pointed out that these two trichords (B G-sharp G and A F E) are identical in pitch-class content to the trichords that initiate the first two phrases in Wagner's *Tristan* Prelude. This strikes me as a plausible connection, particularly given Schoenberg's devotion to Wagner's music. See "Schoenberg's Opus 11, No. 1: A Parody of Pitch Cells from *Tristan*," *Journal of*

the *Arnold Schoenberg Institute*, 10/1 (1987), pp. 38–44. For other claims of connection between the *Tristan* Prelude and Op. 11, No. 1, see Dieter Gostomsky, "Tonalität-Atonalität. Zur Harmonik von Schönbergs Klavierstück op. 11 Nr. 1. Analyse," *Zeitschrift für Musiktheorie*, 7/1 (1976), pp. 54–71.

25. Courtney Adams sees Op. 11, No. 1 as alternating between versions of two basic ideas: the phrase in mm. 1–3 '(a)' and the passage beginning in mm. 4–8 '(b)'. "Techniques of Rhythmic Coherence in Schoenberg's Atonal Instrumental Works", *Journal of Musicology*, 11/3 (1993), pp. 340–4.
26. Schoenberg's first piano harmonic is not in this piece, but in "Am Strande", which was probably written a few days earlier.
27. The 'e' motive is not entirely new. In m. 3 all four notes (F A C-sharp E) had occurred together in the upper voices (everything but the bass). See Exx. 15.1 and 15.2, above.
28. Perhaps also the G-sharp/G vertical relationship that involves the two notes on the registral extremes in mm. 4–5, 6, and 8.
29. Schoenberg's post World War I compositional pedagogy emphasized the importance of motivic concision and developing variation. "The study of the smallest musical unit, the motive, was the point of departure. Its logical development makes coherence in music possible, not only by exact repetition, subtle changes in melody, rhythm, or harmony, but by altering sound and character. These procedures comprise the basic compositional technique: variation. The variation should be perpetual to make the organization of a piece natural, for in spite of contrasts, a common denominator in every composition must be established." Paul Pisk, "Memories of Schoenberg", *Journal of the Arnold Schoenberg Institute*, 1/1 (1976), p. 40.
30. "THE TWO-OR-MORE-DIMENSIONAL SPACE IN WHICH MUSICAL IDEAS ARE PRESENTED IS A UNIT". "Composition with Twelve Tones", *SI*, p. 220 (emphasis in original).
31. Other analyses have shown some additional instances of vertical/horizontal equivalence. See, for example, Jerry Dean, "Schoenberg's Vertical-Linear Relationships in 1908", *Perspectives of New Music*, 12/1–2 (1973–4), pp. 173–9. Although one can find examples of this sort, such relationships are never more than isolated and exceptional.
32. It is significant that the rhythmically stable interval of the trichord is a traditional consonance. A quite different effect would have resulted had there been parallel semitones. According to pitch-class set theory, that difference would be of no account: there would still be a succession of 014 trichords. In my opinion, given the principle of localized consonance, the difference between parallel thirds and parallel semitones is highly significant.
33. See Brinkmann, *Arnold Schönberg: Drei Klavierstücke*, p. 61, for a similar listing of tones of local emphasis (he refers to them as Zentraltöne).
34. Analyses that have proposed a tonal structure for Op. 11 began as early as Edwin von der Null, see his *Moderne Harmonik* (Leipzig, 1932). For a more recent analysis of Op. 11, No. 1 as tonal see Will Ogdon, "How Tonality

Functions in Schoenberg's Opus 11, No. 1", *Journal of the Arnold Schoenberg Institute*, 5/2 (1981), pp. 169–81. Other analyses suggest that there are significant aspects of tonal structure, even if they do not see the work accountable to a single referential tonic. See, for example, Dieter Gostomsky, "Tonalität-Atonalität. Zur Harmonik von Schönbergs Klavierstück op. 11 Nr. 1. Analyse," *Zeitschrift für Musiktheorie*, 7/1 (1976), pp. 54–71.

35. Schoenberg's use of octaves to emphasize the E and the E-flat points to another significant holdover from prior music in Op. 11, No. 1: his continued use of doubling at the octave. At this stage in his development he still felt comfortable using octaves, both orchestrational doubling (e.g. mm. 14, 16, 33, 53–8, and 63–4) as well as octaves formed as a contrapuntal interval between two voices (e.g. F in m. 2 and G-sharp/A-flat in m. 10). A few years later, Schoenberg would publicly renounce the use of octaves, but in 1909, in this dimension – as in so many others – the ties to tradition are still strong. See *HL*, p. 420.

36. For analyses of Op. 11, No. 2, see Reinhold Brinkmann, *Arnold Schönberg: Drei Klavierstücke Op. 11. Studien zur frühen Atonalität bei Schönberg*. Beihefte zum Archiv für Musikwissenschaft, vol. 7 (Franz Steiner Verlag: Wiesbaden, 1969), pp. 96–108; Howard Cinnamon, "Tonal Elements and Unfolding Nontriadic Harmonies in the Second of Schoenberg's *Drei Klavierstücke*, Op. 11", *Theory and Practice*, 18 (1993), pp. 127–70; Claus Ganter, *Ordnungsprinzip oder Konstruktion? Die Entwicklung der Tonsprache Arnold Schönbergs am Beispiel seiner Klavierwerke* (Munich and Salzburg: Musikverlag Katzbichler, 1997), pp. 32–49. David Lewin analyzes a passage from Op. 11, No. 2 in the context of an explanation of "Klumpenhouwer Networks". See his "A Tutorial on Klumpenhouwer Networks, Using the Chorale in Schoenberg's Opus 11, No. 2," *Journal of Music Theory*, 38/1 (1994), pp. 79–101.

Chapter 16 "Intoxicated by the enthusiasm": Five Orchestral Pieces

1. "A Self-Analysis", *SI*, p. 79.
2. "My Evolution", *SI*, p. 88.
3. Schoenberg's correspondence with Max Marschalk reveals the lengthy and sometimes tortuous process that eventually led to the second performance of *Pelleas und Melisande* (with Oskar Fried conducting the Blüthner Orchestra, Berlin, in October 1910). A number of years before, Schoenberg had tried (but in vain) to interest Ferruccio Busoni in *Pelleas und Melisande*. See Antony Beaumont (trans. and ed.), *Ferruccio Busoni: Selected Letters* (New York: Columbia University Press, 1987), p. 381. See also Charlotte Erwin and Bryan Simms, "Schoenberg's Correspondence with Heinrich Schenker", *Journal of the Arnold Schoenberg Institute*, 5/1 (1981), pp. 27 and 31.
4. Stuckenschmidt, *Schoenberg*, p. 68.
5. Stuckenschmidt, *Schoenberg*, p. 71.
6. Letter from Richard Strauss to Arnold Schoenberg (transcribed from the copy at the Arnold Schönberg Center; original is in Library of Congress):

> Lieber Herr Schönberg!
> Es ist mir sehr schmerzlich, Ihnen Ihre Partitur ohne eine Zusage der Aufführung zurücksenden zu müssen: Sie wissen, ich helfe gern u[nd] habe auch Mut. Aber Ihre Stücke sind inhaltlich u[nd] klanglich so gewagte Experimente daß ich vorläufig es nicht wagen kann, sie einem mehr als conservativem Berliner Publikum vorzuführen. Wollen Sie einen gutgemeinten Rat von mir nehmen, so lassen sie sich die Stücke von einem befreundeten Dirigenten vielleicht Löwe oder Nedbal mal in ein paar Proben vorführen oder mieten sich zu dem Zwecke selbst mal ein gutes Orchester, um die Stücke auszuprobieren, denn ich fürchte, Sie werden keinen Dirigenten finden, der Ihnen dieselben so ohne weiteres zur Aufführung annimmt. Sollten Sie, was ich Ihnen herzlich wünsche, dafür einen Verleger finden, so will ich selbst versuchen, ein Berliner Orchester hierfür zu ein paar Proben zu bitten, mehr kann ich Ihnen heute leider nicht versprechen.
> Mit herzlichen Grüssen
> Ihr ergebener DR. Richard Strauss

7. See Michael Mäckelmann, *Schönberg: Fünf Orchesterstücke op. 16* (Wilhelm Fink: Munich, 1987), p. 16.
8. Mäckelmann, *Schönberg: Fünf Orchesterstücke*, p. 17.
9. Without other supportive features, the intervallic succession of −1 −1 might be difficult to justify as an instance of the motive. But since it occurs in note-against-note counterpoint, has the identical contour (in inversion), and the same rhythm, I believe it is a reasonable extension of the idea.
10. See Jonathan Cross, "Fünf Orchesterstücke, op. 16", in Gerold Gruber (ed.), *Arnold Schönberg: Interpretationen seiner Werke* (Laaber: Laaber-Verlag, 2002), vol. I, p. 222.
11. For a discussion and accounting of the motivic relationships throughout the piece, see Mäckelmann, *Schönberg: Fünf Orchesterstücke*, pp. 16–26.
12. The middle section is itself subdivided into two sections: mm. 23–56 and 57–76. For an analysis of this movement see Mäckelmann, *Schönberg: Fünf Orchesterstücke*, pp. 26–33.
13. For analyses of Op. 16, No. 3, see Charles Burkhart, "Schoenberg's *Farben*", *Perspectives of New Music*, 12/1–2 (1973–4), 141–72; Mäckelmann, *Schönberg: Fünf Orchesterstücke*, pp. 33–40.
14. Additional instances of the canon, "stated at other pitch levels and in shorter and shorter note values, occur at mm. 20–23 (in the upper four voices only), where the changes occur every half measure, and at the climax of the piece – mm. 26 (4th beat) to 29." Burkhart, "Schoenberg's *Farben*", p. 146.
15. Although this orchestrational idea was striking, there were some precedents. One was in the Prelude of Pfitzner's opera *Die Rose vom Liebesgarten* which Egon Wellesz and Anton Webern heard together in April 1905. See Henry-Louis de la Grange, *Gustav Mahler, Volume III; Vienna: Triumph and Disillusion, 1904–1907* (Oxford: Oxford University Press, 1999), p. 176.

16. When Schoenberg talked about *Klangfarbenmelodie* in *Harmonielehre* he did not cite the passage from Op. 16, No. 3 as an example. Mäckelmann, *Schönberg: Fünf Orchesterstücke*, p. 34. For a concise critique of the arguments against considering Op. 16, No. 3 an instance of *Klangfarbenmelodie*, see Carl Dahlhaus, "Schoenberg's Orchestral Piece Op. 16, No. 3 and the Concept of *Klangfarbenmelodie*," in Carl Dahlhaus, *Schoenberg and the New Music*, trans. by Derrick Puffett and Alfred Clayton (Cambridge: Cambridge University Press, 1987), pp. 141–3.
17. Alfred Cramer, "Schoenberg's *Klangfarbenmelodie*: A Principle of Early Atonal Harmony," *Music Theory Spectrum*, 24/1 (2002), pp. 1–34.
18. Mäckelmann (*Schönberg: Fünf Orchesterstücke*, p. 41) suggests that the final measures (mm. 59–66) constitute a coda-like section with reprise characteristics ("Codaartiger Schlußteil mit Reprisencharakter").
19. Elizabeth Keathley demonstrates that the order in which the motivic material appears in the movement is in reverse order to the order in which it was composed. What appears – analytically – to be the consequence of the developmental process was – compositionally – the original idea. See her "Schoenberg's Opus 16/IV: An Examination of the Sketches," *Theory and Practice*, 17 (1992), pp. 67–83.
20. For example, the first chord of the piece, the hexachord on the downbeat of m. 2 is a combination of two triadic sonorities: an F minor triad in the lower half, an augmented triad on G in the upper half. That Schoenberg intended the chord to be parsed this way can be confirmed from the continuation: in the brass, the three elements of the upper triad all ascend in parallel chromatic scales upward while the three elements of the lower triad all ascend in parallel chromatic scales downward, yielding another combination chord on the downbeat of m. 3: a B-flat minor triad in the lower half; a C augmented triad in the upper half.
21. Stuckenschmidt, *Schoenberg*, p. 69. Schoenberg goes on to describe the pieces already complete: "For it is these that the pieces are about – certainly not symphonic, they are the absolute opposite of this, there is no architecture and no build-up. Just a colourful, uninterrupted variation of colours, *rhythms* and mood." *Ibid*, p. 70. Schoenberg's description of his pieces does not seem to correspond with what he had written as of the date of the letter. See Mäckelmann, *Schönberg: Fünf Orchesterstücke op. 16*, p. 14.
22. "Rhythm cannot be said to be a major source of coherence in this piece, but rhythmic patterns do provide a small degree of unity by means of repeated note values within short sections." Courtney Adams, "Techniques of Rhythmic Coherence in Schoenberg's Atonal Instrumental Works", *Journal of Musicology*, 11/3 (1993), p. 349.
23. *Zusammenhang, Kontrapunkt, Instrumentation, Formenlehre [Coherence, Counterpoint, Instrumentation, Instruction in Form]*, ed. Severine Neff, trans. Charlotte Cross and Severine Neff (Lincoln: University of Nebraska Press, 1994), pp. 8, 9.

24. Throughout his career Schoenberg seemed to regard innovation as a central category of aesthetic worth and felt that his own importance stemmed, in part, from having been the innovator of important musical ideas. This frequently led him into conflicts with other composers (e.g. Hauer and Stravinsky) who he felt had improperly usurped his leadership role. Richard Hoffmann recalls that Schoenberg told him of meeting Stravinsky in 1912 and showing him a few of the pieces of *Pierrot Lunaire*. Schoenberg told Hoffmann that "a few years later, around 1914 or so, *L'Histoire du soldat* appeared. I considered that outright plagiarism." Richard Hoffmann and Leonard Stein, "Reminiscences: A Schoenberg Centennial Symposium at Oberlin College," *Journal of the Arnold Schoenberg Institute*, 8/1 (1984), 67. For more on Stravinsky's "plagiarism" of Schoenberg's ideas, see Hoffmann's remarks on pp. 67–8.
25. The 12 March 1912 entry in Schoenberg's diary reveals his feelings of competition with his students and its consequences. "In the morning was very much in the mood to compose. After a very long time! I had already considered the possibility that I may not ever compose again at all. There seemed to be many reasons for it. The persistence with which my students nip at my heels, intending to surpass what I offer, [this] puts me in danger of becoming their imitator, and keeps me from calmly building on [the stage] that I have just reached. They always bring [in?] everything raised to the tenth power. And it makes sense! It is really good. But I do not know whether it is necessary. At least not whether it is necessary to me. That is why I am now forced to distinguish even more carefully whether I must write than [I was forced to do] earlier." Luginbühl, *"Attempt at a Diary"*, p. 39.
26. "The Young and I", *SI*, p. 94.
27. See Joseph Auner, *A Schoenberg Reader*, p. 236.
28. "Anton Webern: *Klangfarbenmelodie*", *SI*, p. 484.
29. Ibid, pp. 484–5.
30. It cannot have helped matters that Webern's Op. 5, No. 3 is clearly based on the motives and themes from the Scherzo of Schoenberg's String Quartet, No. 2, Op. 10. See Heinz-Klaus Metzger, "Webern und Schönberg", in *Die Reihe. Information über serielle Musik*, vol. II: *Anton Webern* (Vienna: Universal Edition, 1955), p. 48.

Chapter 17 The birth (and death) of new music: August 1909 and beyond

1. "New Music", *SI*, p. 137.
2. Antony Beaumont (trans. and ed.), *Ferruccio Busoni: Selected Letters* (New York: Columbia University Press, 1987), pp. 381–2.
3. Beaumont, *Ferruccio Busoni*, p. 382.
4. For a discussion of the interchange between Schoenberg and Busoni see Daniel Raessler, "Schoenberg and Busoni: Aspects of Their Relationship", *Journal of the Arnold Schoenberg Institute*, 7/1 (1983), pp. 7–17.

5. The letter itself is undated. Beaumont states: "The postmark on the envelope of the letter is almost illegible, but can be construed as 13 or 18.8.1909." Beaumont, *Ferruccio Busoni*, p. 390n. The content of the letter (particularly its statement of what pieces were complete) suggests the earlier date is correct. In a postscript to his letter Schoenberg states that he had "inadvertently forgot to post this letter for a few days." He goes on to state that in the meantime, he had completed the third piano piece, *ibid*, p. 389. Since the draft of Op. 11, No. 3 was completed on 7 August 1909, I believe that this letter originated around the fourth or fifth of August, immediately after Schoenberg's receipt of Busoni's letter of 2 August. It then lay unsent until approximately 13 August 1909.
6. Beaumont, *Ferruccio Busoni*, pp. 388–9.
7. For an examination of Schoenberg's miniatures from this period see Joseph Auner, "'Warum bist du so kurz?' Schoenberg's Three Pieces for Chamber Orchestra (1910) and the Problem of Brevity", in Mogens Andersen, Niels Bo Foltmann, Claus Røllum-Larsen (edd.), *Festskrift Jan Maegaard: 14.4.1996* (Copenhagen: Engstrøm & Sødring, 1996), 43–63. Auner questions the widely held assumption that the shortness of the compositions from 1910–11 represented some kind of problem or crisis: i.e. "a temporary solution to the challenge of composing without tonality" (p. 46).
8. There are many other radical aspects to this work, the most notable being its use of but a single character. (Although that idea was probably Maria Pappenheim's, Schoenberg chose to set what she had written.) This is not to say that *Erwartung* has no connections to the past. Even if he had wanted to, Schoenberg could not sever all connections with the past, in this or in any work. This is most obvious with the harmonic language which makes no break with its immediate past. For an example of how Schoenberg himself saw harmonies in *Erwartung* as a continuation of the past, see *HL*, p. 418.
9. Carl Dahlhaus, "'New Music' as Historical Category", in Carl Dahlhaus, *Schoenberg and the New Music*, trans. Derrick Puffett and Alfred Clayton (Cambridge: Cambridge University Press, 1987), pp. 1–13. Schoenberg also questioned the usefulness of the term, arguing that it was used to describe style not artistic substance which is always "new". See his "New Music, Outmoded Music, Style and Idea", *SI*, pp. 113–24 and especially pp. 114–15.
10. For Schoenberg's skeptical reaction to slogans in general and the concept of "New Music", see Christoph von Blumröder, "Schoenberg and the Concept of 'New Music'", *Journal of the Arnold Schoenberg Institute*, 6/1 (1982), pp. 96–105. See Schoenberg's essay "New Music, Outmoded Music, Style and Idea", *SI*, 113–24. In this essay Schoenberg criticizes what he calls the slogan "NEW MUSIC" and asserts that *"Art means New Art."* I believe that the attitudes expressed in this essay reflect Schoenberg's aesthetic stance as of 1946, not as of 1909.
11. For an excellent discussion of the pivotal role of *Die glückliche Hand* in the transformation of Schoenberg's aesthetics during the years 1910–13, see Joseph Auner, "'Heart and Brain in Music'; The Genesis of Schoenberg's *Die*

glückliche Hand," in Juliane Brand and Christopher Hailey (edd.), *Constructive Dissonance: Arnold Schoenberg and the Transformations of Twentieth-Century Culture* (Berkeley, Los Angeles, and London: University of California Press, 1997), pp. 112–30.

12. Although Schoenberg claims to have been the inventor of the small form (*SI*, pp. 94), the historical record is unequivocal: Webern's Five Movements for String Quartet, Op. 5 came first.
13. See Peter Westergaard, "Toward a Twelve-tone Polyphony", in Benjamin Boretz and Edward Cone (edd.), *Perspectives on Contemporary Music Theory* (New York: W. W. Norton, 1972), p. 241.
14. Joseph Auner, "Schoenberg's Aesthetic Transformations and the Evolution of Form in *Die glückliche Hand*", *Journal of the Arnold Schoenberg Institute*, 12/2 (1989), p. 104. Auner argues persuasively that the later layer of *Die glückliche Hand* helped pave the way for key aspects of Schoenberg's twelve-tone serial music. "In Schoenberg's Workshop: Aggregates and Referential Collections in *Die glückliche Hand*", *Music Theory Spectrum*, 18/1 (1996), pp. 77–105.
15. Schoenberg sometimes contradicts himself about the division of his works into periods. In 1949, in his essay "My Evolution", he stated: "My Two Ballads, Op. 12 were the immediate predecessors of the String Quartet, Op. 10 which marks the transition to my second period." *SI*, p. 86. Since Op. 9 was completed in 1906, Op. 12 in 1907, and Op. 10 was written in 1907–8, we can infer that Schoenberg is suggesting 1907–8 as the end of his "first period". In the previous year (1948) however, Schoenberg implied a different division of his works into periods. In the essay "A Self-Analysis" he stated: "May I venture to say that, in my belief, even works of my third period as, for example, the *Three Piano Pieces*, Op. 11, or the *Five Orchestral Pieces*, Op. 16, and especially *Pierrot Lunaire*, Op. 21, are relatively easy to understand today." *SI*, p. 79. In yet another place, Schoenberg suggested that his first period only lasted until 1906: "Extended tonality is also characteristic of my first period (1896–1906)." *Structural Functions of Harmony*, revised edition, ed. Leonard Stein (New York: W. W. Norton, 1969), p. 110.
16. Similar problems are faced with other attempts at stylistic categorization. See Walter Frisch, "The Refractory Masterpiece: Toward an Interpretation of Schoenberg's Chamber Symphony, op. 9", in Juliane Brand and Christopher Hailey (edd.), *Constructive Dissonance: Arnold Schoenberg and the Transformations of Twentieth-Century Culture* (Berkeley, Los Angeles, and London: University of California Press, 1997), p. 91.
17. Revealingly, in one of his comments on this work, Schoenberg himself did not place Op. 15 in his "atonal" period. Instead, he described it as "the *first* step *towards* a style which has since been called the style of 'atonality' ". "How One Becomes Lonely", *SI*, p. 49 (emphasis added).
18. *HL*, p. 27.
19. See my *Schoenberg's Serial Odyssey: The Evolution of his Twelve-Tone Method, 1914–1928* (Oxford: Clarendon Press, 1990).

Bibliography

Adams, Courtney, "Techniques of Rhythmic Coherence in Schoenberg's Atonal Instrumental Works", *Journal of Musicology*, 11/3 (1993), 330–56.

Alden, Ashforth, "Linear and Textural Aspects of Schoenberg's Cadences", *Perspectives of New Music*, 16/2 (1978), 195–224.

Andersen, Mogens, Niels Bo Foltmann, Claus Røllum-Larsen (edd.), *Festskrift Jan Maegaard: 14.4.1996* (Copenhagen: Engstrøm & Sødring, 1996).

Auner, Joseph, "Schoenberg's Aesthetic Transformations and the Evolution of Form in *Die glückliche Hand*", *Journal of the Arnold Schoenberg Institute*, 12/2 (1989), 103–28.

"In Schoenberg's Workshop: Aggregates and Referential Collections in *Die glückliche Hand*", *Music Theory Spectrum*, 18/1 (1996), 77–105.

" 'Warum bist du so kurz?' Schoenberg's Three Pieces for Chamber Orchestra (1910) and the Problem of Brevity", in Mogens Andersen, Niels Bo Foltmann, Claus Røllum-Larsen (edd.), *Festskrift Jan Maegaard: 14.4.1996* (Copenhagen: Engstrøm & Sødring, 1996), 43–63.

" 'Heart and Brain in Music'; The Genesis of Schoenberg's *Die glückliche Hand*", in Juliane Brand and Christopher Hailey (edd.), *Constructive Dissonance: Arnold Schoenberg and the Transformations of Twentieth-Century Culture* (Berkeley, Los Angeles, and London: University of California Press, 1997), 112–30.

A Schoenberg Reader: Documents of a Life (New Haven & London: Yale University Press, 2003).

Babbitt, Milton, "Twelve-Tone Invariants as Compositional Determinants", *Musical Quarterly*, 46 (1960), 246–59. Reprinted in Paul Henry Lang (ed.), *Problems of Modern Music* (New York: W. W. Norton, 1962), 108–21.

"Past and Present Concepts of the Nature and Limits of Music", in *Perspectives on Contemporary Music Theory*, edd. Benjamin Boretz and Edward Cone (New York: W. W. Norton, 1972), 3–9.

Bailey, Walter, "Composer Versus Critic: The Schoenberg-Schmidt Polemic", *Journal of the Arnold Schoenberg Institute*, 4/2 (1980), 119–37.

Programmatic Elements in the Works of Schoenberg (Ann Arbor: UMI Research Press, 1984).

(ed.), *The Arnold Schoenberg Companion* (Westport, Connecticut and London: Greenwood Press, 1998).

"Changing Views of Schoenberg", in *The Arnold Schoenberg Companion* (Westport, Connecticut and London: Greenwood Press, 1998), 3–10.

"Sechs Lieder für eine mittlere Singstimme und Klavier, op. 3", in Gerold Gruber (ed.), *Schönberg: Interpretationen seiner Werke* (Laaber: Laaber-Verlag, 2002), vol. I, 15–21.

Baker, James, "Schenkerian Analysis and Post-Tonal Music", in David Beach (ed.), *Aspects of Schenkerian Theory* (New Haven and London: Yale University Press, 1983), 153–86.

"Voice-Leading in Post-Tonal Music: Suggestions for Extending Schenker's Theory", *Music Analysis*, 9/2 (1990), 177–200.

Ballan, Harry, "Schoenberg's Expansion of Tonality, 1899–1908", Ph.D. Dissertation, Yale University (1986).

Beach, David, "Pitch Structure and the Analytic Process in Atonal Music: An Interpretation of the Theory of Sets", *Music Theory Spectrum*, 1 (1979), 7–22.

Beaumont, Antony (trans. and ed.), *Ferruccio Busoni: Selected Letters* (New York: Columbia University Press, 1987).

Zemlinsky (Ithaca, New York: Cornell University Press, 2000).

Benjamin, William, "Ideas of Order in Motivic Music", *Music Theory Spectrum*, 1 (1979), 23–34.

Benson, Mark, "Schoenberg's Private Program for the String Quartet in D Minor, Op. 7", *Journal of Musicology*, 11/3 (1993), 374–95.

Berg, Alban, *The Berg-Schoenberg Correspondence: Selected Letters*, edited by Juliane Brand, Christopher Hailey, and Donald Harris (New York: Norton, 1987).

"Gurrelieder Guide", (trans. Mark DeVoto), *Journal of the Arnold Schoenberg Institute*, 16 (1993), 24–233.

"Chamber Symphony Guide", (trans. Mark DeVoto), *Journal of the Arnold Schoenberg Institute*, 16 (1993), 236–68.

"Pelleas und Melisande Guide", (trans. Mark DeVoto), *Journal of the Arnold Schoenberg Institute*, 16 (1993), 270–92.

Bernstein, David, "Schoenberg Contra Riemann: *Stufen*, Regions, *Verwandtschaft*, and the Theory of Tonal Function", *Theoria*, 6 (1992), 23–53.

Blumröder, Christoph von, "Schoenberg and the Concept of 'New Music' ", *Journal of the Arnold Schoenberg Institute*, 6/1 (1982), 96–105.

Boss, Jack, "Schoenberg's Op. 22 Radio Talk and Developing Variation in Atonal Music", *Music Theory Spectrum*, 14/2 (1992), 125–49.

"Schoenberg on Ornamentation and Structural Levels", *Journal of Music Theory*, 38/2 (1994), 187–215.

Botstein, Leon, "Schoenberg and the Audience: Modernism, Music, and Politics in the Twentieth Century", in Walter Frisch (ed.), *Schoenberg and His World* (Princeton, New Jersey: Princeton University Press, 1999), 19–54.

Brand, Juliane, and Christopher Hailey (edd.), *Constructive Dissonance: Arnold Schoenberg and the Transformations of Twentieth-Century Culture* (Berkeley, Los Angeles, and London: University of California Press, 1997).

Breig, Werner, "Arnold Schönbergs *Verklärte Nacht* und das Problem der Programmusik", in Walter Bernhart (ed.), *Die Semantik der musiko-literarischen Gattungen: Methodik und Analyse* (Tübingen: Gunter Narr Verlag, 1994), 87–115.

Brinkmann, Reinhold, *Arnold Schönberg: Drei Klavierstücke Op. 11. Studien zur frühen Atonalität bei Schönberg*. Beihefte zum Archiv für Musikwissenschaft, vol. 7 (Franz Steiner Verlag: Wiesbaden, 1969).
    "The Compressed Symphony: On the Historical Content of Schoenberg's Op. 9", (trans. Irene Zedlacher), in Walter Frisch (ed.), *Schoenberg and His World* (Princeton, New Jersey: Princeton University Press, 1999), 141–61.
    "Schoenberg's Quartets and the Viennese Tradition", in Reinhold Brinkmann and Christoph Wolff (edd.), *Music of My Future: The Schoenberg Quartets and Trio* (Cambridge, Massachusetts and London: Harvard University Press, 2000), 3–12.
Brinkmann Reinhold, and Christoph Wolff (edd.), *Music of My Future: The Schoenberg Quartets and Trio* (Cambridge Massachusetts, London: Harvard University Press, 2000).
Bruhn, Siglind, "*Pelleas und Melisande*, op. 5", in Gerold Gruber (ed.), *Arnold Schönberg: Interpretationen seiner Werke* (Laaber: Laaber-Verlag, 2002), vol. 1, 36–60.
Burkhart, Charles, "Schoenberg's *Farben*", *Perspectives of New Music*, 12/1–2 (1973–4), 141–72.
Burkholder, J. Peter, "Schoenberg the Reactionary", in Walter Frisch (ed.), *Schoenberg and His World* (Princeton, New Jersey: Princeton University Press, 1999), 162–91.
Campbell, Brian, "*Gurrelieder* and the Fall of the Gods: Schoenberg's Struggle with the Legacy of Wagner", in Charlotte Cross and Russell Berman (edd.), *Schoenberg and Words: The Modernist Years* (New York and London: Garland Publishing, 2000), 31–63.
Cherlin, Michael, "Schoenberg and *Das Unheimliche*: Spectres of Tonality", *Journal of Musicology*, 11/3 (1993), 357–73.
    "Dialectical Opposition in Schoenberg's Music and Thought", *Music Theory Spectrum*, 22/2 (2000), 157–76.
    "Motive and Memory in Schoenberg's First String Quartet", in Reinhold Brinkmann and Christoph Wolff (edd.), *Music of My Future: The Schoenberg Quartets and Trio* (Cambridge Massachusetts, London: Harvard University Press, 2000), 61–80.
Christensen, Thomas, "Schoenberg's Opus 11, No. 1: A Parody of Pitch Cells from *Tristan*", *Journal of the Arnold Schoenberg Institute*, 10/1 (1987), 38–44.
Cinnamon, Howard, "Some Elements of Tonal and Motivic Structure in 'In diesen Wintertagen', Op. 14, no. 2 by Arnold Schoenberg: A Schoenbergian-Schenkerian Study", *In Theory Only*, 7/7–8 (1984), 23–50.
    "Tonal Elements and Unfolding Nontriadic Harmonies in the Second of Schoenberg's *Drei Klavierstücke*, Op. 11", *Theory and Practice*, 18 (1993), 127–70.
Cone, Edward, "Sound and Syntax: An Introduction to Schoenberg's Harmony", *Perspectives of New Music*, 13 (1974), 21–40. Reprinted in Cone, *Music: A View from Delft* (Chicago: University of Chicago Press, 1989), 249–66.

Cramer, Alfred, "Schoenberg's *Klangfarbenmelodie*: A Principle of Early Atonal Harmony", *Music Theory Spectrum*, 24/1 (2002), 1–34.

Cross, Charlotte, "Schoenberg's 'Weltanschauung' and His Views of Music: 1874–1915", Ph.D. Dissertation, Columbia University, 1992.

"Schoenberg's Earliest Thoughts on the Theory of Composition: A Fragment from c. 1900", *Theoria*, 8 (1994), 113–33.

Cross, Charlotte, and Russell Berman (edd.), *Schoenberg and Words: The Modernist Years* (New York and London: Garland Publishing, 2000).

Cross, Jonathan, "Fünf Orchesterstücke, op. 16", in Gerold Gruber (ed.), *Arnold Schönberg: Interpretationen seiner Werke* (Laaber: Laaber-Verlag, 2002), vol. 1, 216–28.

Dahlhaus, Carl, *Between Romanticism and Modernism: Four Studies in the Music of the Later Nineteenth Century*, trans. Mary Whittall (Berkeley and Los Angeles: University of California Press, 1980).

Schoenberg and the New Music, trans. Derrick Puffett and Alfred Clayton (Cambridge: Cambridge University Press, 1987).

"Emancipation of the Dissonance", in Carl Dahlhaus, *Schoenberg and the New Music*, trans. Derrick Puffett and Alfred Clayton (Cambridge: Cambridge University Press, 1987), 120–27.

" 'New Music' as Historical Category", in Carl Dahlhaus, *Schoenberg and the New Music*, trans. Derrick Puffett and Alfred Clayton (Cambridge: Cambridge University Press, 1987), 1–13.

"Schoenberg and Programme Music", in Carl Dahlhaus, *Schoenberg and the New Music*, trans. Derrick Puffett and Alfred Clayton (Cambridge: Cambridge University Press, 1987), 94–104.

"Schoenberg's Orchestral Piece Op. 16, No. 3 and the Concept of *Klangfarbenmelodie*", in Carl Dahlhaus, *Schoenberg and the New Music*, trans. Derrick Puffett and Alfred Clayton (Cambridge: Cambridge University Press, 1987), 141–3.

The Idea of Absolute Music, trans. Roger Lustig (Chicago and London: University of Chicago Press, 1989).

Dale, Catherine, "Schoenberg's Concept of Variation Form: A Paradigmatic Analysis of *Litanei* from the Second String Quartet, Op. 10", *Journal of the Royal Music Association*, 118/1 (1993), 94–120.

Schoenberg's Chamber Symphonies: The Crystallization and Rediscovery of a Style (Aldershot: Ashgate, 2000).

Dean, Jerry, "Schoenberg's Vertical-Linear Relationships in 1908", *Perspectives of New Music*, 12/1–2 (1973–4), 173–9.

Delaere, Mark, *Funktionelle Atonalität: Analytische Strategien für die frei-atonale Musik der Wiener Schule* (Wilhelmshaven: Florian Noetzel, 1993).

Demske, Tom, "Registral Centers of Balance in Atonal Works by Schoenberg and Webern", *In Theory Only*, 9/2–3 (1986), 60–76.

Dunsby, Jonathan, "Schoenberg on Cadence", *Journal of the Arnold Schoenberg Institute*, 4/1 (1980), 41–9.

Erwin, Charlotte, and Bryan Simms, "Schoenberg's Correspondence with Heinrich Schenker", *Journal of the Arnold Schoenberg Institute*, 5/1 (1981), 23–43.

Eybl, Martin (ed.), *Die Befreiung des Augenblicks: Schönbergs Skandalkonzerte 1907 und 1908, Eine Dokumentation* (Vienna, Cologne, and Weimar: Böhlau Verlag, 2004).

Fearn, Raymond, "Zwei Gesänge für eine Baritonstimme und Klavier op. 1", in Gerold Gruber (ed.), *Arnold Schönberg: Interpretationen seiner Werke* (Laaber: Laaber-Verlag, 2002), vol. 1, 1–5.

Fisher, George, "Text and Music in Song VIII of Das Buch der Hängenden Gärten", *In Theory Only*, 6/2 (1982), 3–15.

Floros, Constantin, "Schönbergs Gurre-Lieder", in Mogens Andersen, Niels Bo Foltmann, Claus Røllum-Larsen (edd.), *Festskrift Jan Maegaard: 14.4.1996* (Copenhagen: Engstrøm & Sødring, 1996), 33–42.

Föllmi, Beat, *Tradition als hermeneutische Kategorie bei Arnold Schönberg* (Bern: Paul Haupt, 1996).

Forte, Allen, "Sets and Nonsets in Schoenberg's Atonal Music", *Perspectives of New Music*, 11/1 (1972), 43–64.

The Structure of Atonal Music (New Haven and London: Yale University Press, 1973).

"Analysis Symposium: Webern, Orchestral Pieces (1913), Movement I ('Bewegt')", *Journal of Music Theory*, 18/1 (1974), 13–43.

The Harmonic Organization of The Rite of Spring (New Haven and London: Yale University Press, 1978).

"Schoenberg's Creative Evolution: The Path to Atonality", *The Musical Quarterly*, 64/2 (1978), 133–76.

"The Magical Kaleidoscope: Schoenberg's First Atonal Masterwork, Opus 11, No. 1", *Journal of the Arnold Schoenberg Institute*, 5/2 (1981), 127–68.

"Pitch-Class Set Analysis Today", *Music Analysis*, 4 (1985), 29–58.

"Letter to the Editor in Reply to Richard Taruskin from Allen Forte", *Music Analysis*, 5 (1986), 321–37.

"Concepts of Linearity in Schoenberg's Atonal Music: A Study of the Opus 15 Song Cycle", *Journal of Music Theory*, 36/2 (1992), 285–382.

Frisch, Walter, *Brahms and the Principle of Developing Variation* (Berkeley and Los Angeles: University of California Press, 1984).

"Schoenberg and the Poetry of Richard Dehmel", *Journal of the Arnold Schoenberg Institute*, 9/2 (1986), 137–79.

"Thematic Form and the Genesis of Schoenberg's D-Minor Quartet, Opus 7", *Journal of the American Musicological Society*, 41/2 (1988), 289–314.

The Early Works of Arnold Schoenberg: 1893–1908 (Berkeley and Los Angeles: University of California Press, 1993).

"The Refractory Masterpiece: Toward an Interpretation of Schoenberg's Chamber Symphony, op. 9", in Juliane Brand and Christopher Hailey (edd.), *Constructive Dissonance: Arnold Schoenberg and the Transformations of Twentieth-Century Culture* (Berkeley, Los Angeles, and London: University of California Press, 1997), 87–99.

(ed.), *Schoenberg and His World* (Princeton, New Jersey: Princeton University Press, 1999).

"Vier Lieder für eine Singstimme und Klavier, op. 2", in Gerold Gruber (ed.), *Arnold Schönberg: Interpretationen seiner Werke* (Laaber: Laaber-Verlag, 2002), vol. 1, 5–14.

Ganter, Claus, *Ordnungsprinzip oder Konstruktion? Die Entwicklung der Tonsprache Arnold Schönbergs am Beispiel seiner Klavierwerke* (Munich and Salzburg: Musikverlag Katzbichler, 1997).

Gerlach, Reinhard, "War Schönberg von Dvořák beeinflußt?" *Neue Zeitschrift für Musik*, 133 (1972), 122–7.

Musik und Jugendstil der Wiener Schule 1900–1908 (Laaber: Laaber-Verlag, 1985).

Gorrell, Lorraine, *Discordant Melody: Alexander Zemlinsky, His Songs and the Second Viennese School* (Westport, Connecticut: Greenwood Press, 2002).

Gostomsky, Dieter, "Tonalität-Atonalität. Zur Harmonik von Schönbergs Klavierstück op. 11 Nr. 1. Analyse", *Zeitschrift für Musiktheorie*, 7/1 (1976), 54–71.

Grange, Henry-Louis de la, *Gustav Mahler, Volume 3; Vienna: Triumph and Disillusion, 1904–1907* (Oxford: Oxford University Press, 1999).

Gruber, Gerold (ed.), *Arnold Schönberg: Interpretationen seiner Werke* (Laaber: Laaber-Verlag, 2002); two volumes.

Haimo, Ethan, "Redating Schoenberg's Passacaglia for Orchestra", *Journal of the American Musicological Society*, 40/3 (1987), 471–94.

Schoenberg's Serial Odyssey: The Evolution of His Twelve-Tone Method, 1914–1928 (Oxford: Clarendon Press, 1990).

"Atonality, Analysis, and the Intentional Fallacy", *Music Theory Spectrum*, 18/2 (1996), 167–99.

"Schoenberg and the Origins of Atonality", in Juliane Brand and Christopher Hailey (edd.), *Constructive Dissonance: Arnold Schoenberg and the Transformations of Twentieth-Century Culture* (Berkeley, Los Angeles, and London: University of California Press, 1997), 71–86.

"Tonal Analogies in Arnold Schönberg's Fourth String Quartet", *Journal of the Arnold Schönberg Center*, 4 (2002), 219–28.

"Schoenberg's Programmatic Compositions and the Ideology of Absolute Music", *Orbis Musicae*, 13 (2003), 177–84.

"The Interaction of Art and Music in Schoenberg's Career. A Reexamination", *Journal of the Arnold Schönberg Center*, 6 (2004), 77–88.

Harbison, William, "Rhythmic Structure in Schoenberg's 'Jane Grey' ", *Journal of the Arnold Schoenberg Institute*, 7/2 (1983), 222–37.

Harris, Simon, *A Proposed Classification of Chords in Early Twentieth-Century Music* (New York & London: Garland Publishing, 1989).

Hasty, Christopher, "Segmentation and Process in Post-Tonal Music", *Music Theory Spectrum*, 3 (1981), 54–73.

Hattesen, Heinrich Helge, *Emanzipation durch Aneignung: Untersuchungen zu den frühen Streichquartetten Arnold Schönbergs* (Kassel: Bärenreiter, 1990).

Hilmar, Ernst (ed.), *Arnold Schönberg: Gedenkausstellung 1974* (Vienna: Universal Edition, 1974).

Hilmar, Rosemary, "Alban Berg's Studies with Schoenberg", *Journal of the Arnold Schoenberg Institute*, 8/1 (1984), 7–29.

Hirsbrunner, Theo, "Fünfzehn Gedichte aus Das Buch der Hängenden Gärten von Stefan George op. 15", in Gerold Gruber (ed.), *Arnold Schönberg: Interpretationen seiner Werke* (Laaber: Laaber-Verlag, 2002), vol. 1, 196–215.

Hoffmann, Richard, and Leonard Stein, "Reminiscences: A Schoenberg Centennial Symposium at Oberlin College", *Journal of the Arnold Schoenberg Institute*, 8/1 (1984), 59–77.

Hyde, Martha, "Neoclassic and Anachronistic Impulses in Twentieth-Century Music", *Music Theory Spectrum*, 18/1 (1996), 200–35.

Jackson, Timothy, "Schoenberg's Op. 14 Songs: Textual Sources and Analytical Perception", *Theory and Practice*, 14/15 (1989–90), 35–58.

Jacob, Andreas, "Das Verständnis von Tonalität in Arnold Schönbergs theoretischen Schriften", *Musiktheorie*, 15 (2000), 3–18.

Jal[?owetz], [?Heinrich], and [?Alexander Zemlinsk]y, "Arnold Schoenberg's F♯ Minor Quartet: A Technical Analysis", (trans. Mark DeVoto), *Journal of the Arnold Schoenberg Institute*, 16 (1993), 293–322.

Keathley, Elizabeth, "Schoenberg's Opus 16/IV: An Examination of the Sketches", *Theory and Practice*, 17 (1992), 67–83.

Keller, Hans, "Schoenberg: The Future of Symphonic Thought", *Perspectives of New Music*, 13 (1974), 3–20.

Kohler, Ralf Alexander, and Markus Böggemann, "I. Streichquartett op. 7", in Gerold Gruber (ed.), *Arnold Schönberg: Interpretationen seiner Werke* (Laaber: Laaber-Verlag, 2002), vol. 1, 73–94.

Kostka, Stefan, *Materials and Techniques of Twentieth-Century Music* (Englewood Cliffs: Prentice Hall, 1990).

Krämer, Ulrich, "Oratorium oder Liederzyklus? Zur Entstehung von Schönbergs 'Gurre-Liedern'", *Journal of the Arnold Schönberg Center*, 3 (2001), 86–103.

Krebs, Harald, "Three Versions of Schoenberg's Op. 15, No. 14: Obvious Differences and Hidden Similarities", *Journal of the Arnold Schoenberg Institute*, 8/2 (1984), 131–40.

"Tonalität in Schönbergs 'atonaler' Musik: Die Aussage der Skizzen", *Musiktheorie*, 4 (1989), 223–34.

Kurth, Richard, "Suspended Tonalities in Schoenberg's Twelve-tone Compositions", *Journal of the Arnold Schönberg Center*, 3 (2001), 239–65.

"Moments of Closure: Thoughts on the Suspension of Tonality in Schoenberg's Fourth Quartet and Trio", in Reinhold Brinkmann and Christoph Wolff (edd.), *Music of My Future: The Schoenberg Quartets and Trio* (Cambridge, Massachusetts: Harvard University Press, 2000), 139–60.

Larson, Steve, "A Tonal Model of an 'Atonal' Piece: Schönberg's Opus 15, Number 2", *Perspectives of New Music*, 25 (1987), 418–33.

"The Problem of Prolongation in *Tonal* Music: Terminology, Perception, and Expressive Meaning", *Journal of Music Theory*, 41/1 (1997), 101–36.

Lerdahl, Fred, "Atonal Prolongational Structure", *Contemporary Music Review*, 4 (1989), 65–87.
"Spatial and Psychoacoustic Factors in Atonal Prolongation", *Current Musicology*, 63 (1999), 7–26.
Levy, Janet, "Covert and Casual Values in Recent Writings About Music", *Journal of Musicology*, 5/1 (1987), 3–27.
Lewin, David, "Inversional Balance as an Organizing Force in Schoenberg's Music and Thought", *Perspectives of New Music*, 6/2 (1968), 1–21.
"Toward the Analysis of a Schoenberg Song (Op. 15, No. XI)", *Perspectives of New Music*, 12/1–2 (1973–4), 43–86.
"A Way into Schoenberg's Opus 15, Number 7", *In Theory Only*, 6/1 (1981), 3–24.
"Vocal Meter in Schoenberg's Atonal Music, with a Note on a Serial Hauptstimme", *In Theory Only*, 6/4 (1982), 12–36.
"On the 'Ninth-Chord in Fourth Inversion' from *Verklärte Nacht*", *Journal of the Arnold Schoenberg Institute*, 10/1 (1987), 45–64.
"A Tutorial on Klumpenhouwer Networks. Using the Chorale in Schoenberg's Opus 11, No. 2", *Journal of Music Theory*, 38/1 (1994), 79–101.
Lowinsky, Edward, *Tonality and Atonality in Sixteenth Century Music* (Berkeley: University of California Press, 1962); reprinted (New York: Da Capo Press, 1990).
Luginbühl, Anita, "*Attempt at a Diary* by Arnold Schoenberg", *Journal of the Arnold Schoenberg Institute*, 9/1 (1986), 7–51.
MacDonald, Malcolm, *Schoenberg* (London: Dent, 1976).
Mäckelmann, Michael, *Schönberg: Fünf Orchesterstücke op. 16* (Wilhelm Fink: Munich, 1987).
Maegaard, Jan, *Studien zur Entwicklung des dodekaphonen Satzes bei Arnold Schönberg* (Copenhagen: Wilhelm Hansen, 1972), 2 volumes and supplement.
"Schoenberg's Manuscripts: What Do They Tell Us?" *Journal of the Arnold Schoenberg Institute*, 1/2 (1977), 68–74.
"*Gurrelieder* für Soli, Chor und Orchester", in Gerold Gruber (ed.), *Schönberg: Interpretationen seiner Werke* (Laaber: Laaber-Verlag, 2002), vol. 2, 232–52.
Mahnkopf, Claus-Steffen, *Gestalt und Stil: Schönbergs Erste Kammersymphonie und ihr Umfeld* (Bärenreiter: Kassel, 1994).
McColl, Sandra, *Music Criticism in Vienna 1896–1897: Critically Moving Forms* (Oxford: Clarendon Press, 1996).
Metzger, Heinz-Klaus, "Webern und Schönberg", in Die Reihe. *Information über serielle Musik*, vol. II: *Anton Webern* (Vienna: Universal Edition, 1955).
Meyer, Leonard, *Emotion and Meaning in Music* (Chicago and London: University of Chicago Press, 1956).
Morgan, Robert, "Dissonant Prolongation: Theoretical and Compositional Precedents", *Journal of Music Theory*, 20/1 (1976), 49–91.
"Secret Languages: The Roots of Musical Modernism", *Critical Inquiry*, 10/3 (1984), 442–61.

Neff, Severine, "Reinventing the Organic Artwork: Schoenberg's Changing Images of Tonal Form", in Charlotte Cross and Russell Berman (edd.), *Schoenberg and Words: The Modernist Years* (New York and London: Garland Publishing, 2000), 275–308.

Newlin, Dika, *Schoenberg Remembered: Diaries and Recollections (1938–76)* (New York: Pendragon Press, 1980).

Nüll, Edwin von der, *Moderne Harmonik* (Leipzig, 1932).

Ogdon, Will, "How Tonality Functions in Schoenberg's Opus 11, No. 1", *Journal of the Arnold Schoenberg Institute*, 5/2 (1981), 169–81.

Perle, George, *Serial Composition and Atonality: An Introduction to the Music of Schoenberg, Berg, and Webern*, fifth edition (Berkeley, Los Angeles, London: University of California Press, 1981).

"Pitch-Class Set Analysis: An Evaluation", *Journal of Musicology*, 8/2 (1990), 151–72.

Pfannkuch, Wilhelm, "Zu Thematik und Form in Schönbergs Streichsextett", in Anna Amalie Abert and Wilhelm Pfannkuch (edd.), *Festschrift Friedrich Blume: Zum 70. Geburtstag* (Kassel: Bärenreiter, 1963), 258–71.

Pfisterer, Manfred, *Studien zur Kompositionstechnik in den frühen atonalen Werken von Arnold Schönberg* (Neuhausen-Stuttgart: Hänssler-Verlag, 1978).

Pisk, Paul, "Memories of Schoenberg", *Journal of the Arnold Schoenberg Institute*, 1/1 (1976), 39–44.

Puffett, Derrick, " 'Music that Echoes within One' for a Lifetime: Berg's Reception of Schoenberg's *Pelleas und Melisande*", *Music and Letters*, 76/2 (1995), 209–64. Reprinted in Kathryn Bailey Puffett (ed.), *Derrick Puffett on Music* (Aldershot: Ashgate, 2001), 539–615.

Raessler, Daniel, "Schoenberg and Busoni: Aspects of Their Relationship", *Journal of the Arnold Schoenberg Institute*, 7/1 (1983), 7–27.

Rahn, John, *Basic Atonal Theory* (New York and London: Longman, 1980).

Reich, Willi, *Schoenberg: A Critical Biography*, trans. Leo Black (New York, Washington: Praeger, 1971).

Roeder, John, "Harmonic Implications of Schoenberg's Observations of Atonal Voice Leading", *Journal of Music Theory*, 33/1 (1989), 27–62.

Rufer, Josef, *The Works of Arnold Schoenberg*, trans. Dika Newlin (New York: Free Press, 1962).

Saary, Margareta, "Kammersymphonie für 15 Solo-Instrumente op. 9 (und op. 9B)", in Gerold Gruber (ed.), *Schönberg: Interpretationen seiner Werke* (Laaber: Laaber-Verlag, 2002), vol. 1, 104–23.

Samson, Jim, *Music in Transition: A Study of Tonal Expansion and Atonality, 1900–1920* (London: J. M. Dent, 1977; reprint, 1993).

Schiff, David, "Jewish and Musical Tradition in the Music of Mahler and Schoenberg", *Journal of the Arnold Schoenberg Institute*, 9/2 (1986), 217–31.

Schoenberg, Arnold, *Structural Functions of Harmony*, revised edition, ed. Leonard Stein (New York: W. W. Norton, 1969).

Preliminary Exercises in Counterpoint, ed. Leonard Stein (London: Faber and Faber, 1970).

Style and Idea, ed. Leonard Stein, trans. Robert Black (Berkeley and Los Angeles: University of California Press, 1975).

Stil und Gedanke: Aufsätze zur Musik, ed. Ivan Vojtěch (Frankfurt am Main: S. Fischer, 1976).

Theory of Harmony, trans. Roy Carter (Berkeley and Los Angeles: University of California Press, 1978).

Zusammenhang, Kontrapunkt, Instrumentation, Formenlehre [Coherence, Counterpoint, Instrumentation, Instruction in Form], ed. Séverine Neff, trans. Charlotte Cross and Séverine Neff (Lincoln, Nebraska: University of Nebraska Press, 1994).

Scholz, Gottfried, "*Verklärte Nacht*, op. 4", in Gerold Gruber (ed.), *Schönberg: Interpretationen seiner Werke* (Laaber: Laaber-Verlag, 2002), vol. 1, 22–35.

Schmidt, Christian M., "Schönbergs 'Very Definite – But Private' Programm zum Streichquartett Opus 7", in Rudolf Stephan and Sigrid Wiesmann (edd.) *Bericht über den 2. Kongreß der Internationalen Schönberg-Gesellschaft* (Vienna: Elisabeth Lafite, 1986), 230–4.

Schubert, Peter, " 'A New Epoch of Polyphonic Style': Schoenberg on Chords and Lines", *Music Analysis*, 12/3 (1993), 289–319.

Shaw, Jennifer Robin, "Schoenberg's Choral Symphony, *Die Jakobsleiter*, and Other Wartime Fragments", Ph.D. Dissertation, State University of New York at Stony Brook (2002).

"Zwei Lieder für eine Singstimme und Klavier op. 14", in Gerold Gruber (ed.), *Arnold Schönberg: Interpretationen seiner Werke* (Laaber: Laaber-Verlag, 2002), vol. 1, 181–95.

Simms, Bryan, *The Atonal Music of Arnold Schoenberg: 1908–1923* (New York: Oxford University Press, 2000).

" 'My Dear Hagerl': Self-Representation in Schoenberg's String Quartet No. 2", *19th-Century Music*, 26/3 (2003), 258–77.

Stein, Deborah, "Schoenberg's Opus 19 No. 2: Voice Leading and Overall Structure", *In Theory Only*, 2/7 (1976), 27–43.

Steuermann, Clara, "From the Archives: Diaries", *Journal of the Arnold Schoenberg Institute*, 2/2 (1978), 143–60.

Straus, Joseph, "The Problem of Prolongation in Post-Tonal Music", *Journal of Music Theory*, 31/1 (1987), 1–21.

Post-Tonal Theory (Englewood Cliffs: Prentice Hall, 1990).

Stuckenschmidt, H. H., *Schoenberg: His Life, World and Work*, trans. Humphrey Searle (New York: Schirmer Books, 1978).

Swift, Richard, "1-XII-99: Tonal Relations in Schoenberg's *Verklärte Nacht*", *19th Century Music*, 1/1 (1977), 3–14.

Taruskin, Richard, Review of *The Harmonic Organization of The Rite of Spring* by Allen Forte, *Current Musicology*, 28 (1979), 114–29.

Letter to the Editor, *Music Analysis*, 5 (1986), 313–20.

"Reply to van den Toorn", *In Theory Only*, 10 (1987), 47–57.

Review of *The Music of Alexander Scriabin* by James Baker, *Music Theory Spectrum*, 10 (1988), 143–68.

Thieme, Ulrich, *Studien zum Jugendwerk Arnold Schönbergs: Einflüsse und Wandlungen* (Regensburg: Bosse, 1979).

Thrun, Martin, *Neue Musik im deutschen Musikleben bis 1933*, 2 vols. (Bonn: Orpheus, 1995).

Trezise, Simon, "Schoenberg's *Gurrelieder*", Ph.D. Dissertation, Oxford University, 1987.

Türcke, Berthold, "Gurrelieder and Orchestra Pieces, Op. 16, for Two Pianos", *Journal of the Arnold Schoenberg Institute*, 7/2 (1983), 239–54.

Väisälä, Olli, "Concepts of Harmony and Prolongation in Schoenberg's Op. 19/2", *Music Theory Spectrum*, 21/2 (1999), 230–59.

Vilain, Robert, "Schoenberg and German Poetry", in Charlotte Cross and Russell Berman (edd.), *Schoenberg and Words: The Modernist Years* (New York and London: Garland Publishing, 2000), 1–29.

Wellesz, Egon, *Arnold Schoenberg*, trans. W. H. Kerridge (London: Dent, 1925). Reprinted, Freeport, New York: Books for Libraries Press, 1969.

Westergaard, Peter, "Toward a Twelve-tone Polyphony", in Benjamin Boretz and Edward Cone (edd.), *Perspectives on Contemporary Music Theory* (New York: W. W. Norton, 1972), 238–60.

Whittall, Arnold, *Schoenberg Chamber Music* (Seattle: University of Washington Press, 1972).

"Tonality and the Emancipated Dissonance: Schoenberg and Stravinsky", in Jonathan Dunsby (ed.), *Early Twentieth-Century Music: Models of Musical Analysis* (Oxford: Blackwell Publishers, 1993).

Wintle, Christopher, "Schoenberg's Harmony: Theory and Practice", *Journal of the Arnold Schoenberg Institute*, 4/1 (1980), 50–67.

Index

Adams, Courtney, 405 n. 25, 408 n. 22
analysis
    pitch-class set, 4, 292–7, 309–10, 358 nn. 13, 14, 395 n. 2
    Schenkerian, 30, 362 n. 24, 393 n. 3, 394–5 n. 10, 396 n. 7
Ansorge Society, 193, 387 n. 15, 390 n. 32
Aram, Kurt, 152
Arnold, Robert Franz, 42
atonality, 1–7, 351–3, 357 n. 8, 358 nn. 11, 18
Auner, Joseph, 351, 410 n. 7, 411 nn. 11, 14

Babbitt, Milton, 372 n. 34
Bailey, Walter, 95, 118, 158, 364 nn. 14, 15, 369 n. 4, 373 nn. 37, 43, 48, 374 n. 4, 378 n. 28, 383 n. 13, 389 n. 27
Baker, James, 396 n. 7, 403 n. 11
Ballan, Harry, 362 n. 24
Banga, David, 396 n. 4
Beach, David, 403 n. 12
Beaumont, Antony, 362 n. 25, 367 n. 4, 370 n. 17, 372 n. 29, 374 n. 6, 386 nn. 10, 12, 390 n. 35, 398 n. 2, 406 n. 3, 410 n. 5
Beethoven, Ludwig van, 230, 352, 360 n. 13
    An die ferne Geliebte, 43
    Diabelli Variations, Op. 120, 360 n. 14
    String Quartet in C-sharp Minor, Op. 131, 116
Benjamin, William, 402 n. 11, 404 n. 17
Benson, Mark, 376 nn. 11, 12, 377 nn. 20, 22, 379 n. 35, 380 n. 39
Berg, Alban, 271, 318, 339, 342, 368 nn. 8, 9, 13, 399 n. 10
    analysis of *Pelleas und Melisande*, 93–5, 126, 373 nn. 40, 42, 43
    Chamber Symphony Guide, 383 n. 10
    Piano Sonata, Op. 1, 339
Berlin Court Opera, 68, 320
Bernstein, David, 361 n. 15
Bienenfeld, Elsa, 198, 199, 271, 389 n. 31, 390 n. 32
Blumröder, Christoph von, 410 n. 10
Blüthner Orchestra, 406 n. 3
Böggemann, Markus, 377 n. 18, 380 n. 37
Boss, Jack, 397 n. 7, 404 n. 23
Botstein, Leon, 387 n. 19

Brahms, Johannes, 8, 359 nn. 3, 4
Breicha, Otto, 392 n. 24, 400 n. 17
Breig, Werner, 366 n. 32, 369 n. 9, 383 n. 9
Brinkmann, Reinhold, 7, 358 n. 17, 382 n. 7, 400 n. 14, 401 n. 3, 404 nn. 20, 22, 405 n. 33, 406 n. 36
Bruhn, Siglind, 369 n. 2, 372 n. 36, 373 n. 43, 374 n. 49
Bunte Theater: *see* Überbrettl café
Burkhart, Charles, 316, 407 nn. 13, 14
Burkholder, J. Peter, 363 n. 7
Busoni, Ferruccio, 291, 342, 346, 348, 351, 355, 402 n. 8, 406 n. 3, 410 nn. 4, 5

Campbell, Brian, 382 n. 8
Chausson, Ernest, 400 n. 15
Cherlin, Michael, 358–9 n. 18, 377 n. 18, 384 n. 15
Christensen, Thomas, 404 n. 24
Cinnamon, Howard, 394 n. 10, 396 n. 7, 406 n. 36
Cone, Edward, 359 n. 5, 362 n. 25, 393 n. 6, 394 n. 8, 395 nn. 3, 12
Conradi, Hermann, 98
Cowell, Henry, 340
Cramer, Alfred, 408 n. 17
Cross, Charlotte, 363 nn. 4, 5, 409 n. 23
Cross, Jonathan, 407 n. 10

Dahlhaus, Carl, 36, 349, 364 nn. 9, 11, 365 n. 23, 366 n. 28, 372 n. 30, 373 n. 46, 374 n. 50, 381 n. 6, 408 n. 16, 410 n. 9
Dale, Catherine, 384 n. 17, 385 n. 6, 401 n. 22
Dean, Jerry, 405 n. 31
Debussy, Claude, 370 n. 23
    Pelléas et Mélisande, 68, 371 n. 23
Dehmel, Richard, 24, 36, 38, 98, 121, 143, 148, 157, 191, 231, 245, 359 n. 3, 362 n. 25, 366 n. 32, 379 n. 31, 393 n. 5, 400 n. 15
Des Knaben Wunderhorn, 98
developing variation: *see* variation, developing
Dreililienverlag, 97, 98
Dunsby, Jonathan, 361 n. 19
Dvořák, Antonin, 8, 359 n. 4

Eckl, Heinrich, 200
Erwin, Charlotte, 389 n. 32, 406 n. 3
Eybl, Martin, 387 n. 18

Fearn, Raymond, 386 n. 12
Fisher, George, 398 n. 13
Fitzner Quartet, 23, 25, 193
Floros, Constantin, 367 n. 2, 368 n. 19
Föllmi, Beat, 362 nn. 29, 30
Forte, Allen, 4, 292–4, 296, 358 n. 11, 380–1 n. 3, 395 n. 2, 402 nn. 10, 11, 403 n. 12, 404 n. 22
Fried, Oskar, 406 n. 3
Frisch, Walter, 21, 38, 221, 222–4, 359 nn. 3, 5, 361 n. 18, 362 nn. 25, 27, 28, 366 nn. 30, 34, 367 n. 2, 372 nn. 31, 35, 36, 373 nn. 43, 48, 374 n. 2, 376 n. 4, 377 n. 15, 378 n. 24, 380 n. 41, 381 n. 9, 382 nn. 4, 10, 383 n. 12, 384 nn. 14, 16, 17, 19, 386 n. 12, 389 n. 31, 411 n. 16
Fuchs, Robert, 374 n. 6

Ganter, Claus, 406 n. 36
Gärtner, Eduard, 386 n. 12
George, Stefan, 231–2, 244, 245, 270–1, 275, 278, 279, 284, 393 n. 5, 399 n. 8
  Der siebente Ring, 271, 278, 392 n. 23
Gerlach, Reinhard, 359 nn. 3, 4
Gerstl, Alois, 400 n. 17
Gerstl, Richard, 193, 268–71, 278, 290, 399 n. 6, 400 n. 17
Goethe, Johann Wolfgang von, 98
Gorrell, Lorraine, 363 n. 2, 387 n. 15, 390 n. 34, 398 n. 2, 400 n. 15
Gostomsky, Dieter, 405 n. 24, 406 n. 34
Grädener, Hermann, 24
Grange, Henry-Louis de la, 379 n. 32, 388 n. 25, 408 n. 15
Gutheil-Schoder, Marie, 290

Hába, Alois, 318, 339
Hanslick, Eduard, 95, 365 n. 20, 386 n. 11
Harbison, William, 390 n. 37
Harris, Simon, 359 n. 6, 360 n. 9, 371 nn. 24–6, 396 n. 5, 401 n. 24
Hart, Julius, 98
Hasty, Christopher, 403 n. 12
Hattesen, Heinrich Helge, 359 n. 4, 376 nn. 5, 9, 13
Hauer, Josef Matthias, 340, 409 n. 24
Hauptmann, Gerhart, 191–2, 385 n. 7
Helm, Theodor, 196–7, 388 n. 25
Henckel, Karl, 240, 395 n. 11
Hermann, Hans, 200

Heuberger, Richard, 368 n. 15
Hilmar, Rosemary, 399 n. 10
Hirsbrunner, Theo, 395 n. 2
Hoffmann, Richard, 409 n. 24
Horwitz, Karl, 270, 271, 278, 279, 399 n. 8, 400 n. 18
Hyde, Martha, 391 n. 12

Ivanov, O. de, 271

Jachimecki, Zdzislaw, 271
Jackson, Timothy, 393 n. 3, 394 n. 10, 395 n. 11
Jacob, Andreas, 362 n. 22
Jacobsen, Jens Peter, 42, 43, 54, 98, 367 n. 4
Jalowetz, Heinrich, 271, 391 nn. 9, 16

Kaun, Hugo, 390 n. 35
Keathley, Elizabeth, 408 n. 19
Keller, Gottfried, 98, 106
Keller, Hans, 391 n. 15
Kohler, Ralf Alexander, 377 n. 18, 380 n. 37
Kostka, Stefan, 358 n. 13
Kralik, Richard von, 197
Krämer, Ulrich, 42
Krebs, Harald, 396 n. 6, 397 n. 8
Krüger, Viktor, 271
Kurth, Richard, 357 n. 9, 358 n. 12

Larson, Steve, 396 n. 7, 397 n. 7
Lasso, Orlando, 3, 358 n. 11
Lazarus, Gustav, 200
leitmotif, 37
Lenau, Nikolaus, 24
Lerdahl, Fred, 396 n. 7, 397 n. 7
Levy, Janet, 363 n. 30
Lewin, David, 7, 365 n. 24, 385 n. 24, 395 n. 2, 397 n. 9, 398 n. 15, 406 n. 36
Liszt Foundation, 67
Löwe, Ferdinand, 321
Lowinsky, Edward, 358 n. 11
Luginbühl, Anita, 389 n. 27, 409 n. 25

McColl, Sandra, 95, 387 n. 17
MacDonald, Malcolm, 386 n. 11
Mackay, John Henry, 150
Mäckelmann, Michael, 407 nn. 11, 12, 13, 408 nn. 16, 18, 21
Maegaard, Jan, 159, 363 n. 3, 364 nn. 12, 15, 367 n. 2, 369 nn. 3, 7, 370 n. 16, 375 nn. 4, 11, 376 n. 7, 380 n. 2, 381 n. 7, 382 nn. 2, 3, 385 nn. 2, 5, 390 n. 5, 391 n. 13, 402 nn. 3, 5
Maeterlinck, Maurice, 350
  Pelléas et Mélisande, 67, 68, 69, 90, 93, 369 nn. 2, 13, 378 n. 26

Index

Mahler, Gustav, 194, 196, 197, 198, 350, 379 n. 32, 388 n. 25, 392 n. 25
Mahnkopf, Claus-Steffen, 378 n. 25, 379 n. 36, 383 n. 10
Mandyczewski, Eusebius, 368 n. 15
Marschalk, Max, 406 n. 3
Maur, Karin von, 398 n. 3
Mayer, C. F., 400 n. 11
Metzger, Heinz-Klaus, 409 n. 30
Meyer, Conrad, 191
Meyer, Leonard, 374 n. 8
Meyer, Waldemar, 194, 387 n. 14
Moldenhauer, Hans, 399 n. 9
Moldenhauer, Rosaleen, 399 n. 9
Morgan, Robert, 396 n. 7
Morris, Robert, 292
Mozart, Wolfgang Amadeus, 319, 353, 360 n. 13, 386 n. 11

Nedbal, Oskar, 321
Neff, Séverine, 382 n. 11, 408 n. 23
neoclassicism, 391 n. 12
Neumann, Robert, 271
Newlin, Dika, 42, 54, 367 n. 4, 379 n. 30, 390 n. 34
Nietzsche, Friedrich, 148
Null, Edwin von der, 405 n. 34

Observer, 195
Ogdon, Will, 404 n. 22, 406 n. 34
Oppenheimer, Max, 342

pantonality, 2, 357 n. 9
Pappenheim, Maria, 410 n. 8
Perle, George, 402 n. 11, 403 n. 15, 404 n. 18
Petrarch, 98
Pfannkuch, Wilhelm, 36
Pfisterer, Manfred, 404 n. 21
Pfitzner, Hans, 370 n. 23, 407 n. 15
Pieau, Walter, 387 n. 15
Pisk, Paul, 405 n. 29
pitch-class set analysis: *see* analysis, pitch-class set
Polyhymnia, 386 n. 10
polytonality, 2
Posa, Oskar, 115–16, 377 n. 22
programmatic music, 364 nn. 10, 11, 373 n. 46
Prohaska, Carl, 368 n. 15
Puffett, Derrick, 373 n. 40

Raessler, Daniel, 402 n. 8, 410 n. 4
Rahn, John, 358 n. 13
Reich, Willi, 365 n. 21, 369 nn. 5, 7, 386 n. 12, 392 n. 23
Remer, Paul, 154
Rilke, Rainer Maria, 290

Rödelberger, Philip, 390 n. 35
Roeder, John, 397 n. 11
Rosé, Alexander, 112, 375 nn. 2, 3, 379 n. 31
Rosé, Arnold, 112, 199, 390 n. 33
Rosé Quartet, 24, 68, 112, 117, 122, 159, 193, 194, 274, 290, 319, 377 n. 17, 387 n. 14
Rückhauf, Anton, 368 n. 15
Rufer, Josef, 375 n. 4, 385 n. 5

Saary, Margareta, 377 n. 17, 383 n. 10
Samson, Jim, 358 n. 15
scale, indeterminate, 372 n. 35
Schenker, Heinrich, 389 n. 32
Schenkerian analysis: *see* analysis, Schenkerian
Schiff, David, 392 n. 25
Schmidt, Christian Martin, 272, 375 n. 4, 376 n. 9, 377 n. 20, 379 n. 35, 400 n. 14
Schmidt, Leopold, 389 n. 27
Schoenberg, Arnold
 "Am Himmelsthor", 191
 "Am Strande", 290, 393 n. 3, 401 n. 3, 405 n. 26
 "Apostatenmarsch", 157
 "Aus schwerer Stunde", 191, 206–8
 "Besuch", 191
 Brettellieder, 67, 369 n. 7, 376 n. 4
 Chamber Symphony, Op. 9, 36, 157, 158, 159–89, 190–1, 192, 193, 199, 200, 201, 202, 203, 205–6, 208, 209, 230, 231, 234, 274, 291, 320, 353, 354, 411 n. 15
  compositional history, 159
  cyclic aspects, 160
  form, 160–4, 219
  harmonic vocabulary, 165–6, 176–8, 185–6, 187–9, 222
   chord of fourths, 165–6, 178
   localized consonance, 178, 189
   whole tone collection, 186–7
  instrumentation, 158, 160
  key center, 166–76, 181–5, 225, 226
  motivic organization, 160–1, 218, 383 nn. 11, 12
  symmetry, 187
  synthesizing reprise, 163–4
 Chamber Symphony No. 2, Op. 38, 156, 191, 203–5, 208, 210, 219–20, 231, 244, 272, 273, 274, 291, 297, 320, 385 n. 6, 390 n. 38, 391 nn. 6, 13
 "Darthulas Grabgesang", 97
 Das Buch der hängenden Gärten, Op. 15, 7, 210, 232, 236, 244–67, 269, 272, 273, 274, 286, 289, 293, 298, 307, 314, 320, 328, 339, 349, 352–3, 354, 390 n. 5, 401 n. 2, 411 n. 17

Schoenberg, Arnold (cont.)
　chronology, 244–5, 395 n. 3
　Op. 15, No. 3, "Als Neuling trat ich",
　　245, 260–2
　　chordal vocabulary, 261
　　　added-semitone chord, 261
　　localized consonance, 262
　　motivic organization, 262
　Op. 15, No. 4, "Da meine Lippen", 245–55
　　cadence, 252–3
　　chordal vocabulary, 253–4
　　　added-semitone chord, 253, 396 n. 5
　　closure, 251–3
　　developing variation, 246
　　form, 245–6
　　indeterminate scale, 246
　　localized consonance, 253
　　motivic organization, 246–51, 262
　　tones of reference, 254–5
　Op. 15, No. 5, "Saget mir", 245, 255–60
　　chordal vocabulary, 256–7
　　　added-semitone chord, 253, 396 n. 5
　　closure, 260
　　harmonic syntax, 257–8
　　motivic organization, 258–9, 262
　　tones of reference, 255–6
　Op. 15, No. 7, "Angst und Hoffen", 245,
　　264–7
　　developing variation, 256, 264, 266–7
　Op. 15, No. 8, "Wenn ich heut nicht
　　deinen Leib", 245, 262–4
　　harmonic structure, 262–4
　Op. 15, No. 13, "Du lehnest wider eine
　　Silberweide", 245, 289
　Op. 15, No. 15, "Wir bevölkerten", 245, 290
　"Deinem Blick", 97, 385 n. 2
　"Der Jünger", 232
　"Des Friedens Ende", 192
　Die glückliche Hand, Op. 18, 350, 351,
　　411 nn. 11, 14
　"Die Kürze", 157
　"Die Poesie", 157
　Drei Klavierstücke (1894), 361 n. 18,
　　402 n. 5
　Eight Songs, Op. 6, 97, 380 n. 3,
　　399 n. 11
　　Op. 6, No. 1, "Traumleben", 370 n. 21,
　　　384 n. 20, 386 n. 9
　　Op. 6, No. 2, "Alles", 143–7, 148
　　　developing variation, 143–4
　　　form, 143
　　　key center, 144–7, 148, 149
　　　polyphonic texture, 144
　　Op. 6, No. 3, "Mädchenlied", 143, 154–5,
　　　385 n. 9, 386 n. 12
　　　form, 154–5
　　　harmonic vocabulary, 155
　　　key center, 155
　　Op. 6, No. 4, "Verlassen", 394 n. 8
　　Op. 6, No. 5, "Ghasel", 190, 385 n. 9
　　Op. 6, No. 6, "Am Wegrand", 143, 150–2
　　　harmonic vocabulary, 151
　　　key center, 151–2
　　　whole tone scale, 151
　　Op. 6, No. 7, "Lockung", 143, 152–4, 386 n. 9
　　　harmonic vocabulary, 154
　　　schwebende Tonalität, 152
　　　tonal ambiguity, 153, 172
　　Op. 6, No. 8, "Der Wanderer", 143,
　　　148–50, 190, 252, 386 n. 9
　　　key center, 148–50
　Ein Stelldichein, 143, 152, 157–8
　　program, 157–8
　　motivic organization, 157–8
　Erwartung, Op. 17, 3, 348, 350, 410 n. 8
　Five Orchestral Pieces, Op. 16, 318, 321–33,
　　338, 348, 411 n. 15
　　Op. 16, No. 1, 318, 322–7
　　　form, 322
　　　motivic organization, 322–6
　　　pitch language, 327
　　Op. 16, No. 2, 327–9
　　　form, 327
　　　motivic organization, 328
　　　pitch language, 328–9
　　Op. 16, No. 3, 329–31
　　　canons, 329–31
　　　Klangfarbenmelodie, 331, 341,
　　　　408 n. 16
　　Op. 16, No. 4, 331–2, 333, 339, 341
　　Op. 16, No. 5, 318, 332, 333, 342, 344–5
　Four Orchestral Songs, Op. 22, 396 n. 4
　Four Songs, Op. 2, 6, 8, 31, 34, 35, 98,
　　386 n. 12, 387 n. 15
　　Op. 2, No. 1, "Erwartung", 18, 362 n. 25,
　　　385 n. 9
　　Op. 2, No. 2, "Schenk mir deinen
　　　goldenen Kamm", 9–21
　　　cadence, 14–17, 18
　　　chordal dissonance, 10, 12
　　　chordal vocabulary, 10–12
　　　chromatic circulation, 14, 17
　　　developing variation, 21
　　　figuration, 12–13
　　　harmonic progression, 13–14, 17
　　　homophony, 10
　　　indeterminate scale, 20
　　　key center, 17–19
　　　modulation, 18
　　　motivic organization, 20–1

Index

Op. 2, No. 3, "Erhebung", 18, 360 n. 10, 361 n. 20, 385 n. 9
Op. 2, No. 4, "Waldsonne", 18, 361 n. 20, 386 n. 9
Fourth String Quartet, Op. 37, 320, 358 n. 12
Friede auf Erden, Op. 13, 192, 200–1, 203, 210, 320, 390 n. 34, 400 n. 11
"Friedensabend", 232, 244
Frühlings Tod, 24, 364 n. 14, 369 n. 3
"Greif aus", 191
Gurrelieder, 42–65, 67, 68, 87, 87, 97, 131, 156, 159, 160, 190, 200, 320, 321, 354, 382 n. 8
  cadences, 58
  compositional history, 42–3, 53–5
  "Gegrüßt, o König", 60
  incremental innovation, 43, 53, 69
  introduction, tonal ambiguity of, 55–8
  key plan, 59–60
  "Mit Toves Stimme", 60–3
    tonal ambiguity, 60–3
  "Nun dämpft die Dämmrung", 55, 56
    conservative pitch language of, 43–8
  "O wunderliche Tove", 59
  "Roß, mein Roß", 48–53, 55, 63
    avoidance of tonal centers, 48–50, 51–2
    establishment of tonal centers, 50–1, 53
  "Stimme der Waldtaube", 59
Harmonielehre, 26, 71, 152, 257, 331, 360 n. 12, 361 n. 16, 363 n. 6, 365 n. 27, 370 nn. 18, 20, 408 n. 16
  definition of tonality, 147, 381 n. 5
"Heilig Wesen", 385 n. 4
"Herzgewächse", Op. 20, 4, 349–50, 352–3, 354
"Ich weiß nicht", 157
Jakobsleiter, 156
"Jeduch", 192
Klav. 00–01 Fr., 376 n. 7, 402 n. 5
Klav. 05–06 Fr., 385 n. 4, 402 n. 5
Kol Nidre, Op. 39, 352
"Lied eines Sünders", 157
"Mädchenfrühling", 362 n. 28
"Mannesbangen", 18
Moses und Aron, 156
"Nächtlicher Weg", 385 n. 4
New Music, 349–51, 354
Notturno in A-flat Major, 386 n. 10
Ode to Napoleon, Op. 41, 352
"O süße Blick", 157
"O wär mein Herz", 157
Orch. 05–06 Sk., 382 n. 2
painting career, 193

Passacaglia for Orchestra, 157
"Patrouillentritt", 192
Pelleas und Melisande, Op. 5, 36, 66–96, 97, 98, 103, 111, 112, 113, 115, 121, 131, 139, 143, 160, 190, 194, 196, 200, 208, 264, 319, 320, 353, 385 n. 2, 387 n. 15, 406 n. 3
  cadences, 83
  chordal vocabulary, 70–6
    chord of fourths, 71, 72–4, 75, 77, 166, 370 n. 22, 371 n. 24
    whole tone hexachord, 71, 74, 75, 76, 370 n. 22
  compositional history, 66–9
  incremental innovation, 69
  key centers, 83–8, 89–90, 166, 167, 172
  leitmotif, 81, 84, 90, 93, 121, 128, 131, 372 n. 36
  localized consonance, 74–5, 76, 87, 138, 371 n. 26
  motivic structure, 90–2, 218
  non-chord tones, 76–83, 86
  orchestral color, 69
  program, 66, 92–6, 157, 291, 372 n. 36
    suppression of, 124, 379 nn. 31, 32
  reference, departure, return, 88–9, 252, 307
  rhythm, 82–3
  symmetry, 89
periods in the music of, 5, 351–6, 411 n. 15
Piano Concerto, Op. 42, 161, 208, 383 n. 13
Piece for Piano, Op. 23, No. 1, 403 n. 12
Pieces for Chamber Orchestra (1910), 348, 410 n. 7
Pierrot Lunaire, Op. 21, 320, 351, 409 n. 24, 411 n. 15
pitch language (1899), 21–2
Preliminary Exercises in Counterpoint, 177
Prelude to Genesis Suite, Op. 44, 320
  program, 373 nn. 37, 38
reception of his music, 193, 196–9
rivalry with Webern, 340–3
Sechs Stücke für Clavier zu vier Händen (1896?), 402 n. 5
Serenade, Op. 24, 390 n. 3
Six Little Piano Pieces, Op. 19, 350–1
Six Pieces for Male Choir, Op. 35, 352
Six Songs, Op. 3, 6, 97, 98, 387 n. 15
  Op. 3, No. 1, "Wie Georg von Frundsberg von sich selber sang", 98–106, 107, 108, 110, 374 n. 9, 385 n. 9
    cadence, 103
    chordal vocabulary, 103
    form, 98–9
    harmonic progression, 104–5

Schoenberg, Arnold (cont.)
   indeterminate scale, 101
   key center, 99, 105–6
   motivic structure, 99–103
   Op. 3, No. 3, "Warnung", 385 n. 9
   Op. 3, No. 4, "Hochzeitslied", 385 n. 9
   Op. 3, No. 5, "Geübtes Herz", 98, 106–11, 385 n. 9
     cadence, 108–10
     chordal vocabulary, 108
     form, 106–7
     key center, 110–11
     motivic structure, 107
     non-chord tones, 107–8
   Six Songs with Orchestra, Op. 8, 97, 159, 319, 321, 354
     Op. 8, No. 1, 115, 374 n. 9
     Op. 8, No. 2, 115
     Op. 8, No. 3, 190
     Op. 8, No. 4, 115, 190
     Op. 8, No. 5, 115, 152, 190, 368 n. 13
     Op. 8, No. 6, 190
   "Sonnenuntergang", 385 n. 4
   "Still so ist", 385 n. 4
   String Quartet Fragment (1903–4), 113–17, 118, 124, 131, 157, 291, 375 n. 4, 376 nn. 5, 6, 377 nn. 15, 22, 378 n. 24
   String Quartet in D (1897), 8, 23, 112, 113, 118, 122, 193, 219, 273, 362 n. 28, 363 n. 3, 380 n. 41, 386 n. 10
   String Quartet, Op. 7, 36, 97, 98, 111, 113, 115–42, 143, 144, 157, 158, 159, 161, 162, 190, 191, 193, 198, 199, 200, 201, 209, 320, 337, 353
     absolute music, 118–30, 131, 142
     cadence, 139
     counterpoint, 131–2, 136–9, 179
       contrapuntal devices, 131–2, 281
     cyclic aspects, 119
     developing variation, 141–2
     form, 117, 118–30, 160
     harmonic rhythm, 132–5
     harmonic vocabulary, 135–6, 176
     indeterminate scale, 137
     key center, 139–40, 166, 167, 170
     leitmotif, 120, 126, 128
     localized consonance, 138–9
     motivic organization, 120–1, 141–2, 218
     non-chord tones, 134–5
     program, 93, 118–30, 142, 157, 275, 291, 383 n. 9
     reaction to premiere, 117, 198, 208
     varied reprise, 121
     whole tone scale, 372 n. 35
   String Quartet, No. 2, Op. 10, 192, 206, 208, 231, 244, 254, 268–89, 290, 291, 320–1, 352, 354, 371 n. 25, 409 n. 30, 411 n. 15
     compositional history, 210–11, 270–9
     cyclic character, 276–8
     developing variation, 285
     "Entrückung", 232, 271, 275–8, 284–9, 401 n. 21
     form, 219–21, 273, 279–83, 284, 297
     harmonic vocabulary, 222–6, 288–9
     key center, 226–7, 283, 284, 285, 286
     "Litanei", 232, 275–8, 279–83
     localized consonance, 226
     marital crisis, influence of, 268–71, 273, 276, 278–9, 398 n. 3
     motivic organization, 211–19, 298
     "O du lieber Augustin", 227–30, 392 nn. 24, 26
     overall plan, 274–9, 391 nn. 7, 8
     tones of reference, 286–7
   String Trio, Op. 46, 320, 383 n. 13
   Structural Functions of Harmony, 153, 154
   Symph. 05 Sk., 382 n. 3
   Symphony (1900), fragment, 369 n. 3, 376 n. 7
   Three Pieces for Piano, Op. 11, 290, 291, 322, 338, 339, 341, 346, 348, 411 n. 15
     Op. 11, No. 1, 7, 293–316, 318
       closure, 307
       form, 297–8, 313–14
       harmony, 308–12
       indeterminate scale, 312–13
       localized consonance, 314
       motivic organization, 297–307
       tones of reference, 314–16, 328, 405 n. 33
     Op. 11, No. 2, 316–17, 329, 394 n. 10
     Op. 11, No. 3, 318, 332, 333–8, 339, 341–2, 348, 349, 410 n. 5
       absence of motivic return, 334–8
       coherence, 343–4
       pitch language, 338
   Three Songs, Op. 48, 349
   Toter Winkel, 157, 364 n. 15
   twelve-tone music, 264, 266–7, 343, 355, 357 n. 9, 358 n. 12, 394 n. 9
   Two Ballades, Op. 12, 192, 201, 210, 272, 320, 390 n. 34, 411 n. 15
     Op. 12, No. 1, "Jane Grey", 192, 200, 202–3, 390 n. 37
     Op. 12, No. 2, "Der verlorene Haufen", 192, 200, 203
   Two Songs, Op. 1, 98, 386 n. 12

Two Songs, Op. 14, 206, 231, 244, 272, 274, 290
  Op. 14, No. 1, "Ich darf nicht dankend", 210, 231–40, 242, 353, 400 n. 18
    cadences, 233–7, 254
    chordal vocabulary, 237–8, 288, 401 n. 24
    motivic organization, 238–40
  Op. 14, No. 2, "In diesen Wintertagen", 210, 240–3, 251
    cadence, 240–1, 242–3, 252, 254
    diatonic collection, 241–2
    key center, 242
"Über unsre Liebe", 191
Und Pippa tanzt!, 191–2, 385 n. 7
Variations for Orchestra, Op. 31, 156, 157
Variations on a Recitative for Organ, Op. 40, 352
Verklärte Nacht, Op. 4, 23–41, 43, 44, 47, 48, 53, 67, 68, 83, 90, 97, 97, 98, 112, 121, 139, 157, 159, 160, 190, 194, 195, 200, 275, 319, 321, 369 n. 9, 373 n. 48, 379 n. 31, 387 n. 15, 389 n. 27
  arrangement for string orchestra, 95
  cadence, 27–8, 32–3
  chordal vocabulary, 26–31
    ninth chord in fourth inversion, 26–30, 54, 364 n. 20, 365 n. 24
  color, 25–6
  form, 36–8, 366 nn. 28, 32
  incremental innovation, 23, 41
  key center, 33–5, 166–7
  leitmotif, 37, 38, 91, 92, 118, 119, 121, 128
  motivic organization, 38–41, 214, 218
  non-chord tone, 31–2
  program, 23–5, 36, 38, 124, 125, 157, 291, 364 nn. 9, 20, 374 n. 48
  reaction to premiere of, 95, 112, 122–3, 375 n. 2, 387 n. 13
"Was thust, was denkst du", 157
"Wenn schlanke Lilien", 192
"Wie kommt es", 97
Schoenberg, Georg, 268
Schoenberg, Gertrud (Trudi), 67, 268, 400 n. 17
Schoenberg, Mathilde (née Zemlinsky), 66, 268, 289, 399 n. 5
  affair with Richard Gerstl, 193, 228, 268–71, 278, 290, 399 n. 6, 400 n. 17
Schoenberg-Nono, Nuria, 378 n. 29
Scholz, Gottfried, 366 n. 32
Schreker, Franz, 201
Schubert, Franz
  Die Schöne Müllerin, 43
  Die Winterreise, 43

Schubert, Peter, 380 n. 40
Schumann, Robert, 384 n. 20, 387 n. 22
  "Eusebius" (from *Carnaval*, Op. 9), 149–50
  Frauenliebe und Leben, 43
Secession, 25
semiconsonance, 371 n. 26
Shaw, Jennifer Robin, 376 n. 14, 393 n. 3, 402 n. 4
Simms, Bryan, 269, 371 n. 26, 381 n. 4, 389 n. 32, 392 n. 26, 393 n. 4, 396 n. 4, 398 n. 4, 399 n. 6, 400 nn. 17, 18, 402 nn. 3, 4, 6, 404 n. 22, 406 n. 3
Smetana, Bedřich, 364 n. 10
Sprechstimme, 55
Stein, Deborah, 396 n. 7
Stein, Erwin, 271, 341
Stein, Leonard, 409 n. 24
Stern Conservatory, 67
Steuermann, Clara, 370 n. 13
Straus, Joseph, 396 n. 7
Strauss, Richard, 67–8, 68–9, 97, 112, 113, 194, 198, 319–22, 331, 332–3, 339, 369 nn. 8, 9, 13, 370 n. 23, 407 n. 6
  Feuersnot, 369 n. 8
  Symphonia Domestica, 379 n. 32
  Taillefer, 369 n. 10
  Tod und Verklärung, 369 n. 9
Stravinsky, Igor, 409 n. 24
  L'Histoire du soldat, 409 n. 24
  Rite of Spring, The, 3, 358 n. 11
Stuckenschmidt, H. H., 363 n. 3, 369 nn. 6, 8, 10, 374 n. 3, 385 n. 7
Swift, Richard, 36

Taruskin, Richard, 402–3 n. 11
Thieme, Ulrich, 364 nn. 14, 15, 373 n. 48
Thrun, Martin, 357 n. 8, 382 n. 6, 386 nn. 10, 12, 387 n. 15
tonality, 5–7, 357 n. 10, 358 nn. 15, 18
  expanded, 381 n. 6
  extended, 66
  floating, 365 n. 23
  fluctuating, 152, 375 n. 12
  hovering, 375 n. 12
  roving, 375 n. 12
  suspended, 90, 153, 358 n. 12, 375 n. 12, 381 n. 4
  wandering, 365 n. 23
  wavering, 381 n. 4
Travis, Roy, 396 n. 7
Tresize, Simon, 365 n. 20, 367 n. 3, 368 n. 15
triadic tetrachord, 371 n. 26
Türcke, Berthold, 367 n. 3

Überbrettl café, 67, 369 nn. 7, 8

vagrant chord, 34, 365 n. 27
Väisälä, Olli, 397 n. 7, 404 n. 19
variation, 374 n. 7
   developing, 99, 362 n. 28, 364 n. 7, 374 n. 6
Vereinigung schaffender Tonkünstler, 379 nn. 31, 32
Vienna Philharmonic, 68, 319
Vienna Tonkünstlerverein, 26, 27, 42, 54, 363 nn. 2, 3, 364 n. 20, 365 n. 21, 386 n. 10
Vilain, Robert, 393 n. 5

Wagner, Richard, 8, 36, 90, 91–2, 360 n. 13, 364 n. 9, 365 n. 23, 381 n. 6
   leitmotif, 92
   Meistersinger, Die, 91
   Tristan und Isolde, 365 n. 21
      Prelude, 174–5, 404–5 n. 24
Wallaschek, Richard, 198
Webenau, Wilma von, 271
Webern, Anton, 268, 271, 318, 339–43, 348, 351, 355, 403 n. 12, 407 n. 15
   Entflieht auf leichten Kähnen, Op. 2, 339
   Five Pieces for String Quartet, Op. 5, 339–40, 341–2, 409 n. 30, 411 n. 12
   George Songs (Opp. 3 and 4), 339
   Passacaglia, Op. 1, 339
Weirich, Rudolf, 271
Wellesz, Egon, 36, 271, 366 n. 28, 375 n. 4, 386 n. 12, 399 n. 11, 407 n. 15
Westergaard, Peter, 411 n. 13
Whittall, Arnold, 221, 226, 227, 361–2 n. 21, 392 n. 23, 397 nn. 10, 12
Wintle, Christopher, 363 n. 6, 370 n. 21
Wolpe, Stefan, 403 n. 12
Wolzogen, Ernst von, 369 n. 8
Wright, Ernest Vincent, 1, 2
Wymetal, Wilhelm von, 198, 199, 389 n. 29, 390 n. 32

Zemlinsky, Alexander, 23, 42, 53, 54, 112, 160, 195, 268, 273, 362 n. 25, 363 n. 2, 365 n. 21, 367 n. 4, 368 n. 15, 372 n. 29, 374 n. 6, 382 n. 5, 386 nn. 10, 12, 387 nn. 15, 16, 390 n. 34, 391 nn. 9, 16, 398 n. 2
   "Die Astern schwankten", 400 n. 15
   Die Seejungfrau, 370 n. 17
   Stimme des Abends, 362 n. 25
Zemlinszky, Carla Semo von, 268